ECONOMICS

Principles and Policy **Canadian Edition**

MACROECONOMICS

William J. Baumol
New York University
and
Princeton University

Alan S. Blinder
Princeton University

William M. Scarth
McMaster University

Academic Press Canada
Toronto

To my three children,
Ellen, Daniel,
and now Sabrina
W.J.B.

For William, who loves to read
and Scott, who loves to write
A.S.B.

To Brian, David
and the memory of Michael
W.M.S.

Copyright© 1986 by Harcourt Brace Jovanovich Canada Inc.
(incorporating Academic Press Canada)
55 Barber Greene Road, Don Mills, Ontario M3C 2A1

Note: This work is derived from *Economics: Principles and Policy*, Canadian Edition by William J. Baumol, Alan S. Blinder, and William M. Scarth. Copyright© 1985 by Academic Press Canada.

Canadian Cataloguing in Publication Data

Baumol, William J.
    Economics, principles and policy, Canadian edition:
macroeconomics

Includes index.
IBSN 0-7747-3059-5

1. Macroeconomics.   I. Blinder, Alan, S.   II. Scarth,
William M., 1946-   III. Title.

HB171.5.B322 1986   339   C86-093117-X

90 89 88 87 86 BP 1 2 3 4 5 6

Printed in Canada

Cover photograph features Gold Maple Leaf bullion coins struck by the Royal Canadian Mint, Ottawa. Courtesy of Royal Canadian Mint.

Preface

For decades, the "principles of economics" book has been expected to codify the entire discipline of economics. In recent years, this has become increasingly difficult, but also more imperative. The explosion of economic knowledge has made it impossible to put all of economics between two covers. But at the same time, more and more public policy issues either are basically economic in nature or involve important economic considerations. Intelligent citizens can no longer afford to be innocent of economics.

This dilemma has guided the preparation of this book in two ways. First, we have studiously avoided the encyclopaedic approach and abandoned the fiction, so popular among textbook writers, that literally everything is of the utmost importance. Second, we have tried to highlight those important ideas that are likely to be of lasting significance—principles that you will want to remember long after the course is over because they offer insights that are far from obvious, because they are of practical importance, and because they are widely misunderstood by intelligent laymen. A dozen of the most important of these ideas have been selected as **12 Ideas for Beyond the Final Exam** and are called to your attention when they occur through the use of the book's logo. ▨

All modern economics textbooks abound with "real-world" examples, but we have tried to go beyond this, to elevate the examples to pre-eminence. For in our view, the policy issue or everyday economic problem ought to lead the student naturally to the economic principle, not the other way around. For this reason, many chapters start with a real policy issue or a practical problem that may seem puzzling or paradoxical to non-economists, and then proceed to describe the economic analysis required to remove the mystery. In doing this, we have tried to utilize technical jargon and diagrams only where there is a clear need, never for their own sake.

Still, economics is a somewhat technical subject and, except for a few rather light chapters, this is a book for the desk, not for the bed. We have, however, made strenuous efforts to simplify the technical level of the discussion as much as we could without sacrificing content. Fortunately, almost every important idea in economics can be explained in plain English, and this is how we have tried to explain them. Yet, even while reducing the technical difficulty of the book, we have incorporated some elements of economic analysis that have traditionally been left out of introductory books but that are really too important to omit.

Foremost among these is our extensive treatment of prices and inflation in Parts Two and Three. For years, textbooks devoted many chapters to unrealistic, but presumably simpler, economic models in which prices never rose. The original American edition of this book was the first introductory text to put inflation into the story from the very beginning, rather than as an afterthought—a practice we maintain and expand in this first Canadian edition.

Students are invariably interested in learning enough macroeconomics within an introductory course to enable them to make sense of (or at least evaluate) such things as major statements by the Governor of the Bank of Canada. This is simply not possible without an analysis that stresses the cost-increasing effects of a falling Canadian dollar, which requires an integrated analysis of aggregate demand *and* supply. We do not ask the student to make do with a fixed-price macroeconomic analysis; aggregate supply and demand are used from the outset.

Following the introductory material, Chapter 5 provides a brief history of macroeconomic events in Canada and an initial use of the aggregate-demand-and-supply curves. There follows a full discussion of the costs associated with unemployment and inflation (Chapter 6), and the development of multiplier theory, fiscal policy, and supply-side economics (Chapters 7 through 11). The effects of personal income-tax changes, sales tax policy, and corporate tax concessions are thoroughly examined.

Chapter 12 introduces financial considerations and explains the money supply and the chartered banking system. The study of central banking that follows (Chapter 13) stresses that pegging the exchange rate forces the Bank of Canada to conduct "open-market operations" in the foreign-exchange market, in just the same way that it does in domestic bond markets when initiating monetary policy. The nature of the foreign-exchange market is explained at this stage, and monetary and exchange-rate policy are discussed simultaneously. The chapter ends with a full discussion of a public statement issued by the Governor of the Bank of Canada concerning the viability of an independent interest-rate policy for Canada.

The following two chapters integrate the fiscal and monetary/exchange-rate policy analyses. Chapter 14 considers the Monetarist–Keynesian debate from a closed-economy viewpoint, while Chapter 15 analyses the relative effectiveness of monetary and fiscal policies under alternative exchange-rate regimes for a small open economy like Canada's. Several policy episodes (such as the Trudeau government's attempt to use monetary policy under fixed exchange rates, and the Diefenbaker government's need to rely on fiscal policy under floating exchange rates) are used to illustrate the direct importance of the economic analysis. Further issues concerning exchange rates, the balance of payments, and the history of the international monetary system are discussed in Chapter 16.

Chapters 17 through 19 represent the remaining parts of the core macroeconomic analysis in the book. Each deals with a central issue that is both highly topical, and of enduring importance. Chapter 17 discusses the question "Are large government budget deficits bad?"; Chapter 18 asks "What is the nature of the trade-off between inflation and unemployment?"; and Chapter 19 considers the question "Should the government have an active stabilization policy at all?".

Some twenty years of lag in the growth rate of Canadian productivity behind that of a substantial number of European and Far Eastern countries has elicited concern about the consequences for Canadian competitiveness. Our belief that Canadian productivity performance will continue to be a major concern of policy-makers has prompted us to include an entire chapter on this subject. Chapter 20 describes the pertinent facts, examines some of the explanations that have been offered, analyses the consequences of a protracted lag in productivity growth, and discusses some of the productivity stimulation policies that have been proposed. To make room in curricula for this chapter on productivity, we have combined economic growth and the problems of the less-developed countries into a single chapter (Chapter 22). The material on comparative advantage and tariff policy is fully integrated in the core microeconomic analysis of this book's companion volume, *Microeconomics*. In case instructors want to cover this material along with that on international finance (Chapters 15 and 16), it is included here as well (Chapter 21).

Studying Principles of Economics

Whatever the nature of your course, we would like to offer one suggestion. Unlike some of the other courses you may be taking, principles of economics is cumulative—each week's lesson builds on what you have learned before. You will save yourself a lot of frustration (and also a lot of work) if you keep up on a week-to-week basis. To help you do this, there is a chapter summary, a list of important terms and concepts, and a selection of discussion questions to help you review at the end of each chapter. In addition to these aids, many students will find the *Study Guide*, designed to accompany this text, helpful as a self-testing and diagnostic device. When you encounter difficulties in the *Study Guide*, you will know which sections of the text you need to review. (See "Note to Users of *Macroeconomics*" on page vi.)

Note to the Instructor

We have found that a few instructors are reluctant to use aggregate-supply-and-demand analysis in the introductory course. But there are several important advantages to doing so: It is the most natural vehicle for explaining stagflation; it is already very popular in intermediate macro courses, and is fast becoming the standard paradigm within which even sophisticated research issues are being discussed; and it helps integrate the macro and micro portions of the subject, so that students no longer feel that these are two different subjects. Finally, as noted above, we simply cannot make sense of newspaper reports on such topics as the cost-increasing effects of a falling Canadian dollar without this analysis.

In trying to improve the book from one edition to the next, we will rely heavily in our own experiences as teachers. But our experience using the book is small compared to that of the community of instructors who will be using it. If you encounter problems, or have suggestions for improving the book, we urge you to let us know by writing to Bill Scarth in care of Harcourt Brace Jovanovich, Canada, University and Professional Division, 55 Barber Greene Road, Don Mills, Ontario M3C 2A1. Such letters are invaluable, and we are glad to receive them, even if they are critical.

Note to Users of *Macroeconomics*

Users of Baumol, Blinder, and Scarth's *Macroeconomics* should know that chapter numbers correspond to those in *Economics: Principles and Policy*, Canadian Edition (and its Study Guide, Instructor's Manual, and Test Items) as follows:

With Thanks

Finally, and with great pleasure, we turn to the customary acknowledgments of indebtedness. Some of these have been accumulating now through two American editions of the book. The many American instructors whose comments were invaluable in planning this edition have been individually listed in the third American edition. Friends and colleagues who have made helpful suggestions directly for this Canadian edition include: John Burbidge, Martin Dooley, Jim Johnson, Wayne Lewchuk, Les Robb, and Byron Spencer of McMaster University, Doug Burgess of Burgess–Graham Securities, Michael Hare of the University of Toronto, and Brian Scarfe of the University of Alberta. We are particularly indebted to Don Dawson of McMaster University, who provided thorough and invaluable input for the chapters on industrial organization.

The book you hold in your hand was not done by us alone. The staff of Academic Press Canada, including Darlene Zeleney, Keith Thompson, Howard Davidson, and Byron Wall, worked hard and well to turn our manuscript into the book you see. Valuable services were contributed by Greg Ioannou, Ingrid Philipp Cook, Beverley Beetham Endersby, Joyce Wilson, and Jack Steiner. We appreciate all their efforts, and thank Darlene in particular for her tireless and most effective assistance.

And finally, there are our wives, Hilda Baumol, Madeline Blinder, and Kathy Scarth. They have helped in so many ways. Their patience, good judgment, and love have made everything go more smoothly than we had any right to expect. We salute them.

William J. Baumol
Alan S. Blinder
William M. Scarth

The Parts of the Book

Contents

2 The Use and Misuse of Graphs   19

Graphs Used in Economic Analysis   20

Perils in the Interpretation of Graphs   26

3 The Economic Problem   35

4 Supply and Demand: An Initial Look   51

PART II
Essentials of Macroeconomics: Aggregate Supply and Aggregate Demand   71

5   Macroeconomics and Microeconomics   73

6   Unemployment and Inflation: The Twin Evils of Macroeconomics   87

The Costs of Unemployment   88

The Costs of Inflation   96

Appendix: How Statisticians Measure Inflation   108

9 Changes on the Demand Side: Multiplier Analysis   161

10 Supply-Side Equilibrium: Unemployment *and* Inflation?   173

22 Growth in Developed and Developing Countries   421

I

What Is Economics All About?

What Is Economics?

Why does public discussion
of economic policy so often
show the abysmal ignorance
of the participants? Why do I
so often want to cry at what
public figures, the press, and
television commentators say
about economic affairs?

ROBERT M. SOLOW

E conomics is a broad-ranging discipline, both in the questions it asks and in the methods it uses to seek answers. Many definitions of economics have been proposed, but we prefer to avoid any attempt to define the discipline in a single sentence or paragraph. Instead, this chapter will introduce you to economics by letting the subject matter speak for itself.

The first part of this chapter is intended to give you some idea of the types of problems that can be approached through economic analysis and the kinds of solutions that economic principles suggest. By the time you finish this course, we can promise you a better understanding of some of the nation's and the world's most pressing problems and of some approaches to solving these problems. This is the real payoff from studying economics.

The second part briefly introduces the methods of economic inquiry and the tools that economists use. These are tools you may find useful in your life as a citizen, consumer, and worker after the course is over.

Ideas for Beyond the Final Exam

As university professors, we realize it is inevitable that you will forget much of what you learn in this course—perhaps with a sense of relief—very soon after the final exam. There is not much point bemoaning this fact; elephants may never forget, but people do. Nevertheless, there are a number of economic ideas that are important enough for you to remember well beyond the final exam. You will want to remember them because they offer insights into the workings of the economy, because their significance is enduring, and because you will have shortchanged your own education if you forget them as soon as the course is over.

To help you pick out a few of these crucial ideas, we have selected 12 of them from among the many contained in this book and its companion volume, *Microeconomics*. Some bear on important policy issues that often appear in the newspapers and that may have relevance to your own future decisions. Others point out common misunderstandings that occur among even the most thoughtful lay observers. As the quotation that opens this chapter suggests, many learned judges, politicians, business leaders, and university administrators who failed to understand or misused these economic principles could have made far wiser decisions than they did.

Each of the **12 Ideas for Beyond the Final Exam** will be discussed in depth as it occurs in the course of the book; you should not expect to understand these ideas fully after reading this first chapter. None the less, we think it useful to sketch them briefly here both to introduce you to economics and to provide a selective preview of what is to come.

We have organized our 12 Ideas into three groups. The first four are encountered in courses that specialize in *macroeconomics* (the study of the national economy). The next two concern a topic that is particularly important to Canada—international trade. The last six are covered in courses that specialize in *microeconomics* (the study of the price system). All of these topics will appear in a full-year course.

IDEA 1: The Trade-Off Between Inflation and Unemployment

At the start of this decade, Canadian policy-makers waged all-out war on inflation. The war was won: Inflation was reduced dramatically. But casualties were heavy: The national unemployment rate, which averaged 6.8 percent during the 1970s, averaged a stunning 11.5 percent in 1982 and 1983.

Economists maintain that this conjunction of events was no coincidence. Owing to features of our economy that we will study in Parts Two and Three, there is an agonizing *trade-off between inflation and unemployment,* meaning that most policies that bring down inflation also cause unemployment to rise.

Since this trade-off poses the fundamental dilemma of national economic policy, we will devote all of Chapter 18 to examining it in detail. And we shall also consider some suggestions for escaping from the trade-off, such as supply-side economics (Chapter 11) and wage–price controls (Chapter 19).

IDEA 2: The Illusion of High Interest Rates

Is it more costly to borrow money at 5 percent interest or at 13 percent interest? That would appear to be an easy question to answer, even without a course in economics. But, in fact, it is not. An example will show why.

Around 1960, banks were lending money to home buyers at annual interest rates of about 5 percent. Twenty years later, these rates had risen to 13 percent. Yet economists maintain that it was actually cheaper to borrow in 1980 than in 1960. Why? Because inflation in 1980 was running at about 10 percent per year and at only about 1 percent in 1960.

What does inflation have to do with interest rates? Consider the position of a person who lends $100 for one year at a rate of 13 percent interest when the inflation rate is at 10 percent. At the end of the year the lender gets back his $100 plus $13 interest. But over that same year, because of inflation, he loses $10 *in terms of what his money can buy.* That is, in terms of *purchasing power,* the lender gains only $3 on his $100 loan, or 3 percent.

Now consider someone who lends $100 at 5 percent interest when prices are rising only 1 percent a year. This lender gets back the original $100 plus $5 in interest and loses only $1 in purchasing power from inflation—for a net gain of $4, or a 4 percent return on his loan.

As we will learn in Chapter 6, the failure to understand this principle has caused troubles for our tax laws, and in Chapter 17 we will see that it has even led to misunderstanding of the size and nature of the government budget deficit.

IDEA 3: The Consequences of Budget Deficits

Large federal budget deficits have been much in the news in recent years, as have proposals to cut the deficit.

The conflicting claims and counterclaims that have marked the debate over budget deficits are bound to confuse the layman. Some critics claim that deficits hold dire consequences—including higher interest rates, more inflation, a stagnant economy, and an irksome burden on future generations of Canadians. Others deny these charges.

Who is right? Are deficits really malign or benign influences on our economy? The answers, economists insist, are so complicated that the only correct short answer is: It all depends. The precise factors on which the answers depend, and the reasons why, are sufficiently important that they merit an entire chapter of this book (Chapter 17). There we will learn that a budget deficit may be sound or unsound policy, depending on its size and on the reasons for its existence. However, whether or not the deficit represents sound policy, if it is generally believed to be unsound, its existence limits the government's ability to undertake new policies.

IDEA 4: Productivity Is Everything in the Long Run

In Geneva a worker in a watch factory now turns out almost exactly one hundred times as many mechanical watches per year as his ancestor did three centuries earlier. The **productivity** of labour (output per worker hour) in cotton production has probably gone up more than a thousandfold in two hundred years. It is estimated that production per hour of labour in manufacturing in the United States has gone up about seven times in the past century. This means the average American can enjoy about seven times as much clothing, housewares, and luxury goods as were available to a typical inhabitant of the United States one hundred years before. Similar data is not available for Canada, but we know that similar increases in living standards have taken place.

Economic issues such as inflation, unemployment, and monopoly are important to us all and will receive great attention in this book. But in the long run nothing has as great an effect on our material well-being and the amounts society can afford to spend on hospitals, schools, and social amenities as the rate of growth of productivity. Chapter 20 points out that, because productivity compounds like the interest on savings in a bank, what appears to be a small increase in productivity growth can have a huge effect on a country's standard of living over a long period of time. Since 1800, for example, U.S. productivity is estimated to have grown only a bit more than 1.5 percent a year on the average. But that was enough to increase the output of manufactured goods per person about twenty times—a truly incredible amount.*

IDEA 5: Mutual Gains from Voluntary Exchange

One of the most fundamental ideas of economics is that in a **voluntary exchange** both parties must gain something, or at least expect to gain something. Otherwise, why would they both agree to the exchange? This principle may seem self-evident, and it probably is. Yet it is amazing how often it is ignored in practice.

For example, it was widely believed for centuries that governments should interfere with international trade because one country's gain from a swap must be the other country's loss (see Chapter 21). Analogously, some people feel instinctively that if Mr. A profits handsomely from a deal with Mr. B, then Mr. B must have been exploited. Laws sometimes prohibit mutually beneficial exchanges between buyers and sellers—as when rental housing units are eliminated because the rent is "too high" (Chapter 4), or when a willing worker cannot be hired because the wage rate is "too low" (*Microeconomics*, Chapter 22).

*Unfortunately data are not available to make similar calculations for Canada.

In every one of these cases, and in many more, well-intentioned but misguided reasoning blocks the mutual gains that arise from voluntary exchange—and thereby interferes with one of the most basic functions of an economic system (see Chapter 3).

IDEA 6: The Surprising Principle of Comparative Advantage

The Japanese economy produces many products that Canadians buy in huge quantities—including cars, TV sets, cameras, and electronic equipment. Canadian manufacturers have complained about the competition and demanded protection against the flood of imports that, in their view, threatens Canadian standards of living. Is this view justified?

Economists think not. But what if a combination of higher productivity and lower wages were to permit Japan to produce *everything* more cheaply than we could? Would it not then be true that Canadians would have no work and that our nation would be impoverished?

A remarkable result, called the **law of comparative advantage**, shows that even in this extreme case the two nations should still trade and that each can gain as a result! We will explain this principle fully in Chapter 21, where we will also note some potentially valid arguments in favour of protecting domestic industry. But for now a simple parable will make the reason clear.

Suppose Sam grows up on a farm and is a whiz at ploughing, but he is also a successful country singer and gets paid $2000 a performance at hotels and nightclubs. Should Sam refuse some singing engagements to leave time for ploughing? Of course not. Instead he should hire Alfie, a much less efficient farmer, to plough for him. Sam is the better farmer, but he earns so much more by specializing in singing that it pays him to leave the farming to Alfie. Alfie, though a poorer farmer than Sam, is an even worse singer. Thus Alfie earns a living by specializing in the job at which he at least has a *comparative* advantage (his farming is not quite as bad as his singing), and both Alfie and Sam gain. The same is true of two countries. Even if one of them is more efficient at everything, both countries can gain by producing the things they do best *comparatively*.

IDEA 7: Attempts to Repeal the Laws of Supply and Demand: The Market Strikes Back

When a commodity is in short supply, its price naturally tends to rise. Sometimes disgruntled consumers badger politicians into "solving" the problem by imposing a legal ceiling on the price. Similarly, when supplies are abundant—say, when fine weather produces extraordinarily abundant crops—prices tend to fall. This, naturally, makes suppliers unhappy, and they often succeed in getting legislation enacted that prohibits low prices by imposing price floors. But such attempts to repeal the laws of supply and demand usually backfire and sometimes produce results virtually the opposite of those that were intended.

Where rent controls are adopted to protect tenants, housing grows scarce because the law makes it unprofitable to build and maintain apartments. When minimum-wage legislation is enacted to protect marginal workers, marginal jobs disappear. Price floors are placed under agricultural products and surpluses pile up. History provides spectacular examples of the way in which free markets strike back at attempts to interfere with the way they would otherwise work. For example, when the armies of Spain surrounded Antwerp in 1584, hoping to starve the city into submission to King Phillip's harsh rule, profiteers kept Antwerp going by smuggling food and supplies through enemy lines. However, when the city fathers adopted price controls to end these "unconscionable" profits, supplies suddenly dried up and the city soon surrendered.

As we will see in Chapter 4 and elsewhere in this book, such consequences of interference with the price mechanism are no accident. They follow inevitably from the way free markets work. Despite the many examples from history, many policy-makers still call for interference with the price mechanism. A common example in the early 1980s has been the suggestion that our government should preclude residents from buying stocks and bonds from other countries, so that our interest rates can remain lower than those in the United States.

IDEA 8: **Externalities: A Shortcoming of the Market Cured by Market Methods**

Markets are very efficient in producing the goods that consumers want in the quantities in which they are desired. They do so by offering large financial rewards to those who respond to what consumers want to buy and who make these products available economically. Similarly, the market mechanism minimizes waste and inefficiency by causing inefficient producers to lose money.

This system works out very well as long as an exchange between a seller and a buyer affects only those two parties. But often an economic transaction affects uninvolved third parties. Examples abound: The utility that supplies electricity to your home also produces soot that discolours your curtains and pollutants that despoil the air and even affect your health; after a farmer sprays his crops with toxic pesticides, the poison may seep into the ground water and affect the health of neighbouring communities.

Such social costs—called **externalities** because they affect parties *external* to the economic transaction that causes them—escape the control of the market mechanism, as we will learn in *Microeconomics*, Chapter 14. There is no financial incentive that motivates the polluter to minimize the damage he does. The electric company and the farmer do not include environmental damage in their cost calculations. As a consequence, it pays firms to make their products as cheaply as possible, disregarding externalities that may damage the quality of life.

Yet, as we will learn in *Microeconomics*, Chapters 14 and 19, there is a way for the government to use the market mechanism to control undesirable externalities. If the public utility and the farmer are charged for the harm they cause to the public, just as they are charged when they use tangible resources such as coal and fertilizer, then they will have an incentive to cut down as much as possible on the amount of pollution they generate. Thus, in this case, economists believe that market methods are often the best way to cure one of the market's most important shortcomings.

IDEA 9: **Rational Choice and True Economic Costs**

Despite dramatic improvements in our standard of living since the industrial revolution, we have not come anywhere near a state of unlimited abundance, and so we must constantly make choices. If you purchase a new house, you may not be able to afford to eat at expensive restaurants as often as you used to. If a firm decides to retool its factories, it may have to postpone plans for new executive offices. If a government expands its road networks, it may be forced to reduce its outlays on school buildings.

Economists say that the true costs of such decisions are not the number of dollars spent on the house, the new equipment, or the roads, but rather *the value of what must be given up in order to acquire the item*—the restaurant meals, the new executive offices, and the new schools. These are called **opportunity costs** because they represent the *opportunities* the individual, firm, or government must forego to make the desired expenditure. Economists maintain that opportunity costs must be considered in the decision-making process if rational choices are to be made (see Chapter 3).

The costs of a university or college education provide a vivid example that is probably close to the hearts of all students reading this book. How much do you think it *costs* to go to university? Most likely you would answer this question by adding together your expenditures on tuition, room and board, books, and the like, and then deducting any scholarship funds you may receive. Economists would not. They would first want to know how much you could be earning if you were not attending university. This may sound like an irrelevant question, but because you give up these earnings by attending university, they must be added to your tuition bill as a cost of your education. Nor would economists accept the university's bill for room and board as a measure of your living costs. They would want to know by how much this exceeds what it would have cost you to live at home, and only this extra cost would be counted as an expense. On balance, a university or college education probably costs more than you think.

IDEA 10: **The Importance of Marginal Analysis**

Many pages in this book will be spent explaining, and extolling the virtues of, a type of decision-making process called **marginal analysis** (see especially *Microeconomics*, Chapters 5–8), which can best be illustrated by an example.

Suppose that an airline is told by its accountants that the full cost of transporting one passenger from Montreal to Edmonton is $350. Can the airline profit by offering a reduced rate of $250 to students who fly on a standby basis? The surprising answer is: Probably yes. The reason is that most of the $350 cost per passenger must be paid whether the plane carries 20 passengers or 120 passengers. Marginal analysis says that full costs—which include costs of maintenance, landing rights, ground crews, and so on—are irrelevant to the decision at hand. The only costs that are relevant in deciding whether to carry standby passengers for reduced rates are the extra costs of writing and processing additional tickets, the food and beverages these passengers consume, the additional fuel required, and so on. These costs are called **marginal costs**, and they are probably quite small in this instance. Any passenger who pays the airline more than its marginal cost will add something to the company's profit, so it probably is more profitable to let the students ride for the reduced fare than to fly the plane with some empty seats.

There are many real cases in which decision-makers, not understanding marginal analysis, have rejected advantageous possibilities like the reduced fare in our hypothetical example. These people were misled by calculating in terms of *average* rather than *marginal* cost figures—an error that can be quite costly.

IDEA 11: **The Cost Disease of the Service Sector**

There is a distressing phenomenon occurring throughout the industrialized world. Many community services have apparently been growing poorer—fewer postal deliveries, larger classes in public schools, less reliable garbage pickups—while the public is paying more and more for them. Indeed, the costs have risen substantially and consistently faster than has the rate of inflation. A natural response is to attribute the problem to political corruption and government inefficiency. But this is certainly not the whole story.

As we shall see in *Microeconomics*, Chapter 14, one of the major causes of the problem is economic. And it has nothing to do with corruption or inefficiency of public employees; rather, it has to do with the dazzling growth in efficiency of private manufacturing industries! Because technological improvements make workers more productive in manufacturing, wages rise. And they rise not only for the manufacturing workers but also for postal workers, teachers, and other public employees. But here technology is not easily changed; since it still takes one person to drive a postal truck and one teacher to teach a class, the cost of these services is forced to rise.

The same sort of cost disease affects other services like medical care, university teaching, restaurant cooking, retailing, and automobile repairs. And it explains why their prices have often gone up far faster than the general inflation rate.

This is important to understand not because it excuses the financial record of our governments, but because an understanding of the problem suggests what we should expect the future to bring and, perhaps, indicates what policies should be advocated to correct it.

IDEA 12: Increasing Output May Require Sacrificing Equality

Many people favour tax cuts (which are discussed in detail in Chapter 11) to spur productivity and efficiency by providing greater incentives for working, saving, and investing.

Yet, there is at least one problem with this approach—known as supply-side economics. In order to provide stronger incentives for success in the economic game, the gaps between the "winners" and the "losers" must necessarily be widened. For it is these gaps, after all, that provide the incentives to work harder, to save more, and to invest productively.

However, some observers feel that the unequal distribution of income in our society is unjust, that it is inequitable for the super rich to sail yachts and give expensive parties while poor people live in slums and eat inadequate diets. People who hold this view are disturbed by the fact that supply-side tax cuts are quite likely to make the distribution of income even more unequal than it already is.

This example illustrates a genuine and pervasive dilemma. There is often a *trade-off* between the *size* of a nation's output and the degree of *equality* with which that output is distributed. As illustrated by the example of supply-side tax cuts, programs that increase production often breed inequality. And, as we will see in *Microeconomics*, Chapter 23, many policies designed to divide the proverbial economic pie more equally inadvertently cause the size of the pie to shrink.

Epilogue

These, then, are a dozen of the more fundamental concepts to be found in this book and in *Microeconomics*—ideas that we hope you will retain **Beyond the Final Exam**. Do not try to learn them perfectly right now, for you will hear much more about each as the book progresses. Instead, keep them in mind as you read—we will point them out to you as they occur by the use of the book's logo ▨ —and look back over this list at the end of the course. You may be amazed to see how natural, or even obvious, they will seem then.

Inside the Economist's Tool Kit

Now that you have some idea of the kinds of issues economists deal with, you should know something about how they grapple with these problems. Economics has something of a split personality. Clearly the most rigorous of the social sciences, it nevertheless looks decidedly more "social" than "scientific" when compared with physics. Economists strive to be humanists and scientists simultaneously.

What Economists Do

An economist is, by necessity, a jack of several trades and master of none. Economists borrow modes of investigation from numerous fields, adjusting each to fit the particular problems posed by economic events. Usefulness, not methodological purity, is the criterion for including a technique in the economist's tool kit.

Mathematical reasoning is used extensively in economics, but so is historical study. And neither looks quite the same as when practised by a mathematician or a historian. Statistical inference, too, plays an important role in economic inquiry, but economists have had to modify standard statistical procedures to fit the kinds of data they deal with. In 1926, John Maynard Keynes, the great British economist, summed up the many faces of economic inquiry in a statement that still rings true today:

The master-economist ... must understand symbols and speak in words. He must contemplate the particular in terms of the general, and touch abstract and concrete in the same flight of thought. He must study the present in the light of the past for the purposes of the future. No part of man's nature or his institutions must lie entirely outside his regard. He must be purposeful and disinterested in a simultaneous mood; as aloof and incorruptible as an artist, yet sometimes as near the earth as a politician.[1]

Economics is more easily distinguished by the types of *problems* it addresses than by the investigative *techniques* it employs to study them. An introductory course in economics cannot make you an economist, but it should help you approach social problems from a pragmatic and dispassionate point of view. Answers to all society's problems will not be found in this book. But you should learn how to pose questions in ways that will help produce answers that are both useful and illuminating.

The Need for Abstraction

Some students find economics unduly abstract and "unrealistic." The stylized world envisioned by economic theory seems only a distant cousin to the world they see around them. There is an old joke about three people—a chemist, a physicist, and an economist—stranded on an isolated island with an ample supply of canned food but no implements to open the cans. In debating what to do, the chemist suggested lighting a fire under the cans, thus expanding their contents and causing the cans to burst. The physicist doubted that this would work. He advocated building a catapult with which they could smash the cans against some nearby boulders. Then they turned to the economist for his suggestion. He thought for a moment and announced his solution: "Let's assume we have a can opener."

Economists *do* make unrealistic assumptions, and you will encounter many of them in the pages that follow. But this propensity to abstract from reality results from the incredible complexity of the real world, not from any fondness economists have for sounding absurd.

Compare the chemist's task of explaining the interactions of compounds in a

[1] As quoted by Robert Heilbroner in *The Worldly Philosophers*, revised edition (New York: Simon and Schuster, 1972), page 250.

chemical reaction with the economist's task of explaining the interactions of people in an economy. Are molecules ever motivated by greed or altruism, by envy or ambition? Do they ever emulate other molecules? Do forecasts about them ever influence their behaviour? People, of course, do all these things, and many, many more. It is therefore immeasurably more difficult to predict human behaviour than it is to predict chemical reactions. If economists tried to keep track of every aspect of human behaviour, they could surely never hope to understand the nature of the economy. Thus:

Abstraction from unimportant details is necessary to understand the functioning of anything as complex as the economy.

To appreciate why the economist **abstracts** from details, put yourself in the following hypothetical situation. You have just arrived, for the first time in your life, in Vancouver. You are now at the Burnaby General Hospital. This is the point marked *A* in Figures 1–1 and 1–2, which are alternative maps of part of Vancouver. You want to drive to the Vancouver General Hospital, marked *B* on each map. Which map would you find more useful? You will notice that Map 1 (Figure 1–1) has the full details of the Vancouver road system. Consequently, it requires a major effort to read it. In contrast, Map 2 (Figure 1–2) omits many minor roads so that the major arteries stand out more clearly.

Most strangers to the city would prefer Map 2. With its guidance they are likely to find the Vancouver General in a reasonable amount of time, even though a slightly shorter route might have been found by careful calculation and planning using Map 1. Map 2 seems to *abstract* successfully from a lot of confusing details while retaining the essential aspects of the city's geography. Economic theories strive to do the same thing.

Abstraction means ignoring many details in order to focus on the most important factors in a problem.

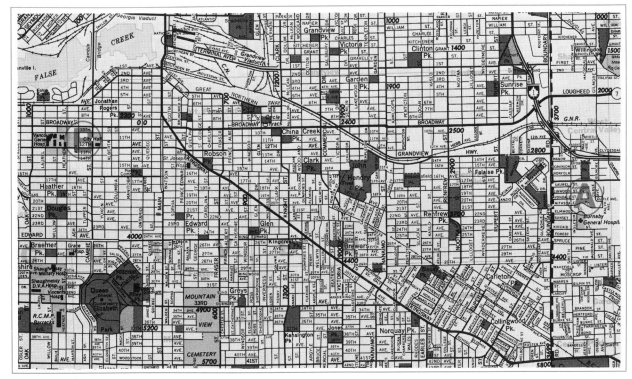

Figure 1–1: Map 1

Map 1 gives complete details of the road system of Vancouver. If you are like most people, you will find it hard to read and not very useful for figuring out how to get from the Burnaby General Hospital (point *A*) to the Vancouver General Hospital (point *B*). For this purpose, the map carries far too much detail, though for some other purposes (for example, locating some very small street in Vancouver) it may be the best map available.

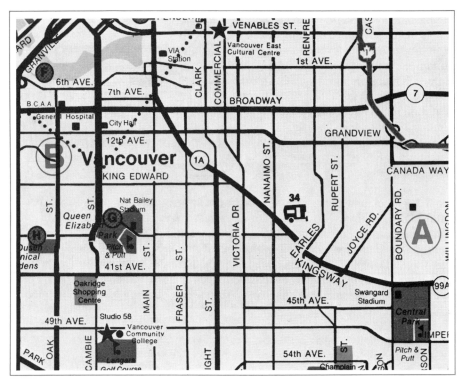

Figure 1-2: Map 2

Map 2 shows a very different perspective of Vancouver. Minor roads are eliminated—we might say, *assumed away*—in order to present a clearer picture of where the major arteries go. As a result of this simplification, several ways of getting from the Burnaby General Hospital (point *A*) to the Vancouver General (point *B*) stand out clearly. For example, we can get on Broadway or the Kingsway and drive west. While we might find a shorter route by poring over the details of Map 1, most of us will feel more comfortable with Map 2.

Figure 1-3: Map 3

Map 3 strips away still more details of the Vancouver road system. In fact, only major roads remain. This map may be useful for passing through the city or getting around it, but it will not help the tourist who wants to see the sights of Vancouver. For this purpose, too many details are missing.

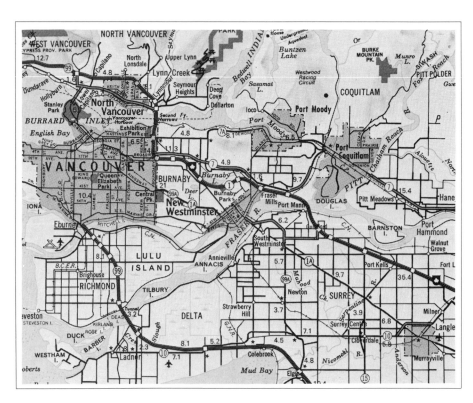

Map 3 (Figure 1–3), which shows little more than the major routes that pass through the greater Vancouver area, illustrates a danger of which all theorists must beware. Armed only with the information provided on this map, you might never find the Vancouver General. Instead of a useful idealization of the Vancouver road network, the map-makers have produced a map that is oversimplified for our purpose. Too much has been assumed away. Of course, this map was never intended to be used as a guide to the Vancouver General, which brings us to a very important point:

There is no such thing as one "right" degree of abstraction for all analytic purposes. The optimal degree of abstraction depends on the objective of the analysis. A model that is a gross oversimplification for one purpose may be needlessly complicated for another.

Economists are constantly treading the thin line between Map 2 and Map 3, between useful generalization about complex issues and gross distortions of the pertinent facts. How can they tell when they have abstracted from reality just enough? There is no objective answer to this question, which is why applied economics is as much art as science. One of the factors distinguishing good economics from bad economics is the degree to which analysts are able to find the factors that constitute the equivalent of Map 2 (rather than Maps 1 or 3) for the problem at hand. It is not always easy to do, as the following examples illustrate.

The Distribution of Income

Suppose you are interested in learning why different people have different incomes, why some are fabulously rich while others are pathetically poor. People differ in many ways, too many to enumerate, much less to study. The economist ignores most of these details in order to focus on a few important facts. The colour of a person's hair or eyes probably is not important to the problem at hand, but the colour of his skin certainly is. Height and weight may not matter, but his parents' bank balance may. Proceeding in this way, we pare Map 1 down to the manageable dimensions of Map 2. But there is a danger of going too far. To make it easy to analyze a problem we can end up stripping away some of its most crucial features.

The Determination of National Income

Suppose we want to know what factors determine the size of the output of the whole economy. Since the volume of goods and services turned out by the whole economy is affected by literally millions of decisions by investors, business managers, employees, government officials, and others, a complete enumeration of all the factors determining the nation's output clearly makes analysis unworkable (Map 1). Abstraction is necessary. We must prune the list to manageable size. Part Two of this book explains how economists do this; that is, how they draw up a Map 2 of the nation's output. Several shortcuts to this process have been proposed, but in the opinion of their critics, they have proved on inspection to be like Map 3.

The Role of Economic Theory

A person "can stare stupidly at phenomena; but in the absence of imagination they will not connect themselves together in any rational way." These words of the renowned American philosopher–scientist C. S. Peirce succinctly express the crucial role of theory in scientific inquiry and help explain why economists are so enamoured of it. To the economist or the physical scientist, the word *theory* does not mean what it does in common speech. In scientific usage, a theory is *not* an untested assertion of alleged fact. The statement that saccharine causes cancer is not a theory, it is a *hypothesis* that will either prove to be true or false after the right sorts of experiments have been completed.

Instead, a **theory** is a deliberate simplification (abstraction) of factual relationships that attempts to explain how those relationships work. In other words, it is an *explanation* of the mechanism behind observed phenomena. For example, astronomers' data describe the paths of the planets, and gravity forms the basis of theories that are intended to explain these data. Similarly, economists have data suggesting that government policies can affect the degree of a country's prosperity. Keynesian theory (which will be discussed in Parts Two and Three) seeks to describe and explain these relationships.

To economists, theorizing is not a luxury but a necessity. Economic theory provides a logical structure for organizing and analyzing economic data. It proceeds deductively from assumptions to conclusions—which can later be tested against data. Without theory, economists could only "stare stupidly" at the world. With theory, they can attempt to understand it.

People who have never studied economics often draw a false distinction between *theory* and *practical policy*. Politicians are particularly guilty of this, scoffing at abstract economic theory as something that is best ignored by "practical" policy-makers. The irony of these statements is that:

It is precisely the concern for policy that makes economic theory so necessary and important.

If there were no possibility of changing the economy through public policy, economics might be a historical and descriptive discipline, asking, for example, What happened in Canada during the Great Depression of the 1930s? or How is it that industrial pollution got to be so serious in the 1960s?

But deep concern about public policy forces economists to go beyond such historical and descriptive questions. To analyze policy options, they are forced to deal with possibilities that have not actually occurred. For example, to learn how to prevent depressions, they must investigate whether the Great Depression could have been avoided by more astute government policies. Or to determine what environmental programs will be most effective, they must examine what might happen to pollution in the 1980s if government placed taxes on industrial waste discharges and automobile emissions. As Peirce pointed out, not even a lifetime of ogling at real-world data will answer such questions.

Indeed, the facts can sometimes be highly misleading. Statistics often indicate that two variables behave very similarly: Whenever one rises so does the other, and they also both go down simultaneously. But this **correlation** between the data does not prove that either of these variables *causes* the other. For example, in rainy weather, people tend to drive their cars more slowly, and there are also more traffic accidents. But this correlation does not mean that slow driving causes accidents. Rather, both phenomena can be attributed to a common underlying factor (more rain) that leads both to more accidents and to slower driving. Thus, just looking at the degree of correlation (the degree of similarity) between the behaviour of two sets of statistics (like accidents and driving speeds) may not tell us much about cause and effect. We need to use theory as part of the analysis.

Because most economic issues hinge on some question of cause and effect, only a combination of theoretical reasoning and data analysis can hope to provide solutions. Simply observing a correlation between data is not enough. We must understand how, if at all, different government policies will lead to a lower unemployment rate or how a tax on emissions will reduce pollution.

What Is an Economic "Model"?

Economists use *models* to describe such cause-and-effect relationships. The notion of a "model" is familiar enough to children, and economists (in common with other scientists) use the term in much the same way that children do.

A child's model automobile or airplane looks and operates much like the real thing, but it is much smaller and much simpler, and so it is much easier to manipulate and understand. Engineers for General Motors and Boeing also build models of cars and planes. While their models are far bigger and much more elaborate than a child's toy, they use them for much the same purposes: to observe the workings of these vehicles "up close," to experiment with them in order to see how they might behave under different circumstances ("What happens if I do this?"). From these experiments, they make educated guesses as to how the real-life version will perform. Often these guesses prove uncannily accurate, as exemplified by the success of the Boeing 747. But sometimes they are wide of the mark: The chronic mechanical problems of General Motors' Corvair prompted Ralph Nader's acclaimed book *Unsafe at Any Speed*, which helped launch the consumer movement.

Economists use **models** for similar purposes and with similarly mixed results. A. W. Phillips, the famous engineer-turned-economist who discovered the "Phillips curve" (discussed in Chapter 18), was talented enough to construct a working model of the determination of national income in a simple economy, using coloured water flowing through pipes. For years this contraption, depicted in Figure 1–4, graced the basement of the London School of Economics. However, most economists lack Phillips's manual dexterity, so economic models are generally built with paper and pencil rather than with hammer and nails.

Because many of the models used in this book are depicted in diagrams, we explain the construction and use of various types of graphs in the next chapter. But sometimes economic models are expressed only in words. The statement "Business people produce the level of output that maximizes their profits" is the basis for a behavioural model whose consequences are explored in some detail in Part Four and in *Microeconomics*, Parts Two through Five. Don't be put off by seemingly abstract models. Think of them as useful road maps, and remember how hard it would be to find your way around Vancouver without one.

An economic **model** is a simplified, small-scale version of some aspect of the economy. Economic models are often expressed in equations, by graphs, or in words.

The Concept of "Rational" Behaviour

Many economic models rest on a fundamental assumption: namely, that the decision-maker—be it a consumer or a business firm—behaves "rationally." What do we mean by *rational* behaviour?

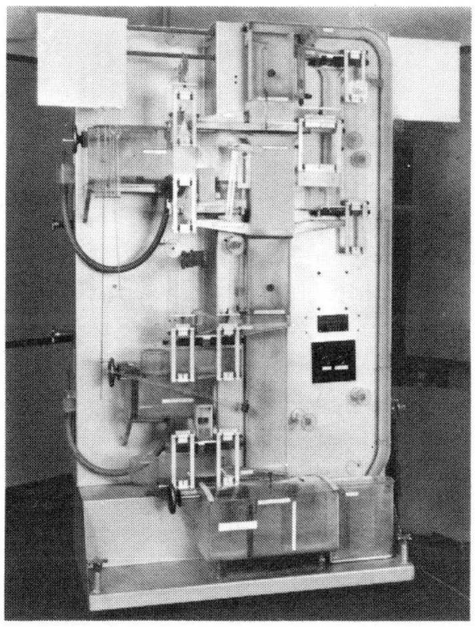

Figure 1–4
THE PHILLIPS MACHINE

The late Professor A. W. Phillips, while teaching at the London School of Economics in the early 1950s, built this machine to illustrate Keynesian theory. This is the same theory that we will explain with words and diagrams later in this book; but Phillips's background as an engineer enabled him to depict the theory with the help of tubes, valves, and pumps. Because economists are not very good plumbers, few of them try to build models of this sort; most rely on paper and pencil instead. But the two sorts of models fulfill precisely the same role. They simplify reality in order to make it understandable.

First, we do not use the phrase as a term of approval. It is not necessarily "better" to be rational than to be irrational. Some people usually behave rationally and some do not. This is simply a fact, and we are not concerned with judging the virtues of either behaviour.

Second, and perhaps more important, we use the term **rationality** to characterize *means* rather than *ends*. Rational behaviour is behaviour that is well designed to achieve the desired ends, whatever those ends may be. It is neither more nor less rational to want a pistachio ice-cream cone than to want a mushroom pizza. But once the consumer decides that he wants either the ice cream or the pizza, it is irrational for him to go to the shoe-repair shop for it.

Rationality is defined in economics as characterizing those decisions that are most effective in helping the decision-maker achieve his own objectives, whatever they may be. The objectives themselves (unless they are self-contradictory) are never considered either rational or irrational.

Reasons for Disagreements: Imperfect Information and Value Judgments

"If all the earth's economists were laid end to end, they could not reach an agreement," or so the saying goes. If economics is a scientific discipline, why do economists seem to quarrel so much? Politicians and reporters are fond of pointing out that economists can generally be found arguing both sides of every issue of public policy. Physicists, on the other hand, do not debate whether the earth revolves around the sun or vice versa.

The question reflects a misunderstanding of the nature of science. First of all, the apparently extreme disagreement is attributable in part to the greater visibility of economic discussions. As a matter of fact, physicists formerly did argue over whether the earth revolves around the sun, often with rather grim results for themselves. (Economists, fortunately, are not often burned at the stake!) Nowadays, physicists argue about "black holes," the existence of certain subatomic particles, and other esoteric phenomena. These arguments often go unnoticed by the public because most of us do not understand what they are talking about. In contrast, everyone is eager to join economic debates over inflation, unemployment, pollution, and almost everything else. Because economics is a *social* science, its disputes are aired in public, and almost everyone is personally concerned with the subject matter. Anyone who has ever bought or sold anything, it seems, fancies himself an amateur economist.

Second, there is a much greater area of agreement among economists than most people think. Virtually all economists, regardless of their politics, agree that taxing polluters is one of the best ways to protect the environment (see *Microeconomics*, Chapters 14 and 19), that a negative income tax is superior to most alternative antipoverty programs (see *Microeconomics*, Chapter 23), that free trade among nations is preferable to the erection of barriers through tariffs and quotas (see Chapter 21). The list could go on and on. It is probably true that the issues about which economists agree *far* exceed the subjects on which they disagree.

Third, many of the disputes among economists are not disputes at all. Economists, like everyone else, come in all political persuasions: conservative, middle-of-the-road, liberal, radical. Each may hold a different view of what is best for society, and so may have a different opinion on what is the "right" solution to any problem of public policy. Public policy issues can rarely be decided on purely scientific and "objective" grounds.

While economists can contribute the best theoretical and factual knowledge there is on a particular issue, the final decision on policy questions often rests either on information that is not currently available, or on tastes and ethical opinions about which people differ (the things we call "value judgments"), or on both.

To illustrate why pure scientific analysis often does not lead to a policy conclusion, consider the following problems.

Taxing Industrial Wastes

As you will learn in *Microeconomics*, Chapter 19, the proper tax to levy on industrial wastes depends on quantitative estimates both of the harm done by the pollutant and the costs of pollution abatement. For most waste products, these numbers are not yet known, although knowledge is accumulating rapidly. So a lack of complete information makes it difficult to formulate a concrete policy proposal.

Inflation and Unemployment

Government policies that succeed in shortening a recession are virtually certain to cause higher inflation for a while. Using tools that we will describe in Parts Two and Three, many economists believe they can even measure how much more inflation the economy will suffer as the price of fighting a recession. Is it worth it? An economist cannot answer this any more than a nuclear physicist could have determined whether dropping the atomic bomb on Hiroshima was a good idea. The decision rests on value judgments about the moral trade-off between inflation and unemployment, judgments that can be made only by the citizenry through its elected officials.

These examples underscore something we said earlier in this chapter: Economics cannot provide all the answers, but it can teach you how to ask the right questions. By the time you finish studying this book, you should have a good understanding of when the right course of action turns on disputed facts, when on value judgments, and when on some combination of the two.

The Economist's Odd Vocabulary

George Bernard Shaw once remarked that America and England are two nations separated by a common language. Much of the same might be said of economists and other people, for economists often assign peculiar meanings to familiar words. Here are two examples; you will find many others later on.

1. ***Cost*** We have already mentioned that when economists speak of "costs" they are normally referring to **opportunity costs**. Accountants, on the other hand, almost always measure costs as only direct monetary expenses involved in any activity. Thus, in calculating the costs of the same activity, the accountant and the economist may arrive at two very different results, as the example of the costs of going to university illustrated. Accountants and economists are indeed divided by a common language.

> The **opportunity cost** of some decision is the value of the next-best alternative which you have to give up because of that decision (for example, working instead of going to school).

2. ***Money*** Most people work for money, or so they think. Again, the economist disagrees. He will insist that people work to earn *income*, which often happens to be paid—for reasons of convenience—in the form of *money*. What is the difference? To the economist *money* refers to the amount of cash and bank-account balances you own at any particular moment. Your holdings of money change frequently, often several times in a single day. But *income* refers to the rate at which you earn money over time. A worker would answer the question "What is your income?" by saying "$10,000 a year," or "$200 a week," or something like that. Income probably changes much less frequently than holdings of money, perhaps only once a year. The distinction between money and income is important, and it will occupy our attention in Part Three.

The economist, it would appear, is much like Humpty Dumpty in *Alice in Wonderland* who said imperiously, "When I use a word it means just what I choose it to mean—neither more nor less." Why such obstinacy? Because economists need a *scientific jargon,* just as other scientists do. Any dictionary will testify to the fact that most words in any language have a multiplicity of meanings. Scientists must be more precise than that. And, rather than conjure up entirely new words, as natural scientists frequently do, economists take ordinary words and give them slightly special meanings.

One wag pointed out that Canada has two groups whose members steadfastly refuse to speak English: *separatists* and *economists*. Who, though, would prefer that we say "phlogiston" instead of "cost" or "nutches" instead of "money"?

Summary

1. To help you get the most out of your first course in economics, we have devised a list of *12 important ideas* that you will want to remember *Beyond the Final Exam*. Here we list them, very briefly, indicating where each idea occurs in the book.

   1) Most government policies that reduce inflation are likely to intensify the unemployment problem, and vice versa. (Chapter 18)

   2) Interest rates that appear very high may actually be very low if they are accompanied by rapid inflation. (Chapter 6)

   3) Budget deficits may or may not be advisable, depending on circumstances. (Chapter 17)

   4) In the long run, productivity is almost the only thing that matters for a nation's material well-being. (Chapter 20)

   5) In a voluntary exchange, both parties must expect to benefit. (Chapter 3 and 21)

   6) Two nations can gain from international trade, even if one is more efficient at making everything. (Chapter 21)

   7) Lawmakers who try to repeal the "law" of supply and demand are liable to open a Pandora's box of troubles they never expected. (Chapter 4)

   8) Externalities cause the market mechanism to misfire, but this defect of the market can be remedied by market-oriented policies. (*Microeconomics*, Chapters 14 and 19)

   9) To make a rational decision, the opportunity cost of an action must be measured, because only this calculation will tell the decision-maker what he has given up. (Chapter 3)

   10) Rational decisions often require the use of marginal analysis to isolate the costs and benefits of a particular decision. (*Microeconomics*, Chapter 8)

   11) The operation of free markets is likely to lead to rising prices for public and private services. (*Microeconomics*, Chapter 14)

   12) Most policies that equalize income exact a cost by reducing the nation's output. (*Microeconomics*, Chapter 23)

2. Economics is a discipline that uses a variety of approaches, some of them scientific and others humanistic, to address important social questions.

3. Because of the great complexity of human behaviour, the economist is forced to abstract from many details, make generalizations that he knows are not quite true, and organize what knowledge he has according to some theoretical structure.

4. Correlation need not imply causation.

5. Economists use simplified models to understand the real world and predict its behaviour, much as a child uses a model railway to learn how trains work.

6. While these models, if skillfully constructed, can illuminate important economic problems, they rarely can answer the questions that policy-makers are confronted with. For this purpose, value judgments are needed, and the economist is no better equipped to make them than is anyone else.

7. A course in economics seeks to teach the student how to formulate the right questions, questions that point to the value judgments or unknown pieces of data that must be obtained in order to make an intelligent decision. It does not try to provide all the answers.

Concepts for Review

Voluntary exchange	Correlation versus causation	Marginal analysis
Comparative advantage	Model	Marginal costs
Productivity	Rationality	Abstraction and generalization
Externalities	Opportunity cost	Theory

Questions for Discussion

1. Think about how you would construct a "model" of how your university is governed. Which officers and administrators would you include and exclude from your model if the objective were
   a. to explain how decisions on tuition payments are made?
   b. to explain the quality of the football team?
   Relate this to the map example in the chapter.

2. Relate the process of "abstraction" to the way you take notes in a lecture. Why do you not try to transcribe every word the lecturer utters? Why do you not just write down the title of the lecture and stop there? How do you decide, roughly speaking, on the correct amount of detail?

3. Explain why a government policy-maker cannot afford to ignore economic theory.

The Use and Misuse of Graphs

Everything should be made
as simple as possible, but not
more so.
ALBERT EINSTEIN

In the preceding chapter we pointed out that economic models frequently appear as diagrams. And if you flip through the pages of this book you will see that indeed they are used quite often. Because many of you may not be familiar with diagrams, this chapter explains how some of the simple graphs used by economists are constructed and how they are to be interpreted.

Most readers of this book eventually will encounter graphs quite frequently in everyday life. If you become a doctor, you will see graphs depicting trends in costs of medical care as well as graphs recording the behaviour of patients' vital functions. If you are concerned about social problems, you will have to read graphs depicting changes in ethnic composition of the population of a city or those relating frequency of conviction for a felony to family income. If you work for a large corporation, you will encounter graphs of sales, profits, and the like. Graphs appear almost daily in the financial pages of the newspaper.

Graphs are invaluable because of the large quantity of data they can display and because of the way they facilitate the interpretation and analysis of the data. They enable the eye to take in at a glance important statistical relationships that would be far less apparent from lengthy prose descriptions or long lists of numbers. It is therefore worth the effort needed to learn how data can be portrayed in graphs. At the very least, you will want to learn to avoid the serious errors into which one can easily be led by graphs that are misleading or distorted.

In this chapter we show, first, how to read a graph that depicts a relationship between two variables. Second, we define the term *slope* and describe how it is measured and interpreted. Third, we explain how the behaviour of three variables can be shown on a two-dimensional graph. Fourth, we discuss how misinterpretation is avoided by adjusting many economic graphs to accommodate changes in the purchasing power of the dollar, in the population of the nation, and in other pertinent developments. And finally, we examine several other common ways in which graphs can be misleading if not drawn and interpreted with care.

Graphs Used in Economic Analysis*

Two-Variable Diagrams

Much of the economic analysis to be found in this and other books requires that we keep track of two variables simultaneously. For example, in studying the operation of markets, we will want to keep one eye on the price of a commodity and the other on the quantity that is bought and sold.

For this reason, economists frequently find it useful to display real or imaginary figures in a *two-dimensional graph*, which simultaneously represents the behaviour of two economic variables. The numerical value of one variable is measured along the bottom of the graph (called the *horizontal axis*), starting from the **origin** (the point labelled "0"), and the numerical value of the other is measured along the side of the graph (called the *vertical axis*), also starting from the origin.

Figure 2–1 is a typical graph used in economic analysis; it depicts a *demand curve*, represented by the heavy coloured line. The diagram shows the price of natural gas on the vertical axis and the quantity of gas that people want to buy on the horizontal axis. (Demand curves will be studied in detail in Chapter 4.)

Economic diagrams are generally read as one reads latitudes and longitudes on a map. On the demand curve in Figure 2–1, the point marked *a* represents a hypothetical combination of price and quantity demanded in Halifax. By drawing a horizontal line leftward from that point to the vertical axis, we learn that the average price for gas in Halifax is $30 per thousand cubic metres. By dropping a line straight down to the horizontal axis, we find that 80 million cubic metres are wanted by consumers at this price. The other points on the graph give similar information. For example, point *b* indicates that if natural gas in Halifax costs only $20 per thousand cubic metres, quantity demanded would be higher—it would reach 120 million cubic metres.

*Students who have a nodding acquaintance with geometry and feel quite comfortable with graphs can safely skip the first sections of this chapter and proceed directly to the second part, which begins on page 26.

> The lower left-hand corner of a graph where the two axes meet is called the **origin**. Both variables are equal to zero at the origin.

Figure 2–1

A DEMAND CURVE FOR NATURAL GAS IN HALIFAX

This demand curve shows the relationship between the price of natural gas and the quantity of it that will be demanded. For example, the point labelled *a* indicates that at a price of $30 per thousand cubic metres (point *P*), the quantity demanded will be 80 million cubic metres (point *Q*).

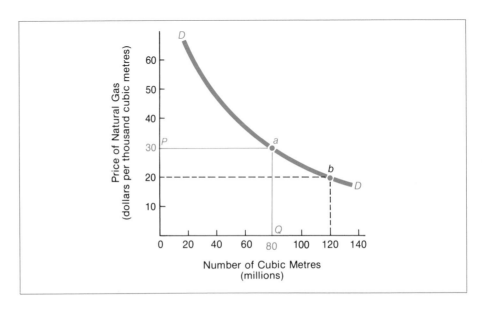

Notice that information about price and quantity is *all* we can learn from the diagram. The demand curve will not tell us about the kinds of people who live in Halifax, the size of their homes, or the condition of their furnaces. It tells us the price and the quantity demanded at that price—no more, no less.

A diagram abstracts from many details, some of which may be quite interesting, in order to focus on the two variables of primary interest—in this case, the price of natural gas and the amount of gas that is demanded at each price. All the diagrams used in this book share this basic feature. They cannot tell the reader the "whole story" any more than a map's latitude and longitude figures for a particular city can make someone an authority on that city.

The Definition and Measurement of Slope

One of the most important features of the diagrams used by economists is the rapidity with which the line, or curve, being sketched runs uphill or downhill as we move to the right. The demand curve in Figure 2–1 clearly slopes downhill (the price falls) as we follow it to the right (that is, as more gas is demanded because of the lower price). In such instances we say that *the curve has a negative slope, or is negatively sloped, because one variable falls as the other one rises.*

The **slope of a straight line** is the ratio of the vertical change to the corresponding horizontal change as we move to the right along the line, or as it is often said, the ratio of the "rise" over the "run."

The four panels of Figure 2–2 show all the possible slopes for a straight-line relationship between two unnamed variables called Y (measured along the vertical axis) and X (measured along the horizontal axis). Figure 2–2(a) shows a negative slope, much like our demand curve. Figure 2–2(b) shows a positive slope, because variable Y rises (we go uphill) as variable X rises (we move to the right). Figure 2–2(c) shows a *zero* slope, where the value of Y is the same irrespective of the value of X. Figure 2–2(d) shows an *infinite* slope, meaning that the value of X is the same, irrespective of the value of Y.

Slope is a numerical concept, not just a qualitative one. The two panels of Figure 2–3 show two positively sloped straight lines with different slopes. The line in Figure 2–3(b) is clearly steeper. But by how much? The labels should help you compute the answer. In Figure 2–3(a) a horizontal movement, *AB*, of 10 units (13 – 3) corresponds to a vertical movement, *BC*, of 1 unit (9 – 8). So the slope is

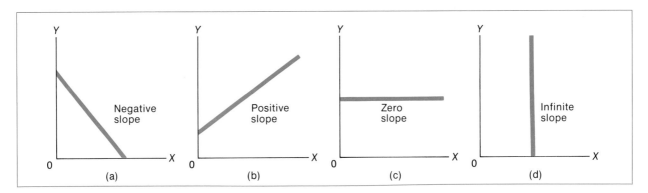

Figure 2–2
DIFFERENT TYPES OF SLOPE OF A STRAIGHT-LINE GRAPH
In Figure 2–2(a), the curve goes downward as we read from left to right, so we say it has a negative slope. The slopes in the other figures can be interpreted similarly.

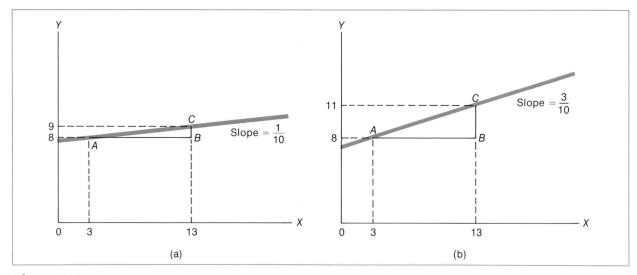

(a)   (b)

Figure 2-3
HOW TO MEASURE SLOPE
Slope indicates how much the graph rises per unit move from left to right. Thus, in Figure 2–3(b), as we go from point A to point B, we go $13 - 3 = 10$ units to the right. But in that interval, the graph rises from the height of point B to the height of point C, that is, it rises 3 units. Consequently, the slope of the line is $BC/AB = 3/10$.

$BC/AB = \frac{1}{10}$. In Figure 2–3(b), the same horizontal movement of 10 units corresponds to a vertical movement of 3 units $(11 - 8)$. So the slope is $\frac{3}{10}$, which is larger.

The slope of any particular straight line is the same no matter where on that line we choose to measure it. That is why we can pick any horizontal distance, AB, and the corresponding slope triangle, ABC, to measure slope. But this is not true of lines that are curved.

Curved lines also have slopes, but the numerical value of the slope is different at every point.

The four panels of Figure 2–4 provide some examples of **slopes of curved lines**. The curve in Figure 2–4(a) has a negative slope everywhere, while the curve in Figure 2–4(b) has a positive slope everywhere. But these are not the only possibilities. In Figure 2–4(c) we encounter a curve that has a positive slope at first but a negative slope later on. Figure 2–4(d) shows the opposite case: a negative slope followed by a positive slope.

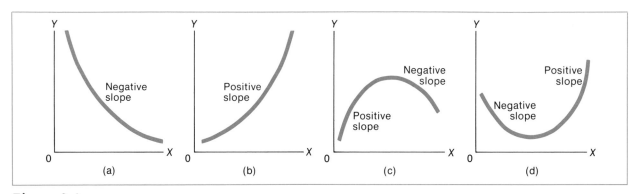

(a)   (b)   (c)   (d)

Figure 2-4
BEHAVIOUR OF SLOPES IN CURVED GRAPHS
As Figures 2-4(c) and 2-4(d) indicate, where a graph is not a straight line it may have a slope that starts off as positive but that becomes negative farther to the right, or vice versa.

It is possible to measure the slope of a smooth curved line numerically *at any particular point*. This is done by drawing a *straight* line that *touches*, but does not *cut*, the curve at the point in question. Such a line is called a **tangent to the curve**.

The slope of a curved line at a particular point is the slope of the straight line that is tangent to the curve at that point.

In Figure 2–5 we have constructed tangents to a curve at two points. Line *tt* is tangent at point *C*, and line *TT* is tangent at point *F*. We can measure the slope of the curve at these two points by applying the definition. The calculation for point *C*, then, is the following:

$$\text{Slope at point } C = \text{Slope of line } tt = \frac{\text{Distance } BC}{\text{Distance } AB}$$
$$= \frac{6-2}{10-0} = \frac{4}{10} = +0.4.$$

A similar calculation yields the slope of the curve at point *F*, which, as we can see from Figure 2–5, must be smaller:

$$\text{Slope at Point } F = \text{Slope of line } TT = \frac{14-9}{50-0} = \frac{5}{50} = +0.1.$$

EXERCISE
Show that the slope of the curve at point *D* is between + 0.1 and + 0.4.

What would happen if we tried to apply this graphical technique to the high point in Figure 2–4(c) or to the low point in Figure 2–4(d)? Take a ruler and try it. The tangents that you construct should be horizontal, meaning that they should have a slope of exactly zero. It is always true that where the slope of a smooth curve changes from positive to negative, or vice versa, there will be at least a single point with a zero slope.

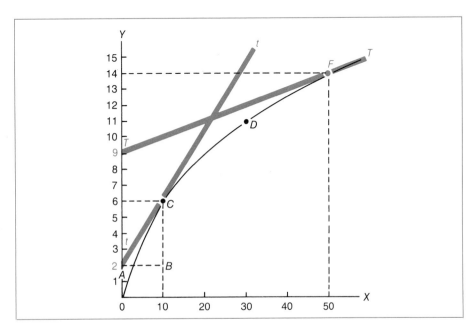

Figure 2–5
HOW TO MEASURE SLOPE AT A POINT ON A CURVED GRAPH

To find the slope at point *F*, draw the line *TT*, which is tangent to the curve at point *F*; then measure the slope of the straight-line tangent *TT* as in Figure 2–3. The slope of the tangent is the same as the slope of the curve at point *F*.

Curves that have the shape of a hill, such as Figure 2–4(c), have a zero slope at their *highest* point. Curves that have the shape of a valley, such as Figure 2–4(d), have a zero slope at their *lowest* point.

Rays Through the Origin and 45° Lines

The point at which a straight line cuts the vertical (Y) axis is called the *Y-intercept*. For example, the Y-intercept of line *tt* in Figure 2–5 is 2, while the Y-intercept of line *TT* is 9. Lines whose Y-intercept is zero have so many special uses that they have been given a special name, a **ray through the origin**, or a **ray**.

Figure 2–6 contains three rays through the origin, and the slope of each is indicated in the diagram. The ray in the centre—whose slope is 1—is particularly useful in many economic applications because it marks off points where X and Y are equal (as long as X and Y are measured in the same units). For example, at point A we have X = 3 and Y = 3, at point B, X = 4 and Y = 4, and a similar relation holds at any other point on that ray.

How do we know that this is always true for a ray whose slope is 1? If we start from the origin (where both X and Y are zero) and the slope of the ray is 1, we know from the definition of slope that:

$$\text{Slope} = \frac{\text{Vertical change}}{\text{Horizontal change}} = 1.$$

This implies that the vertical change and the horizontal change are always equal, so the two variables must always remain equal.

Rays through the origin with a slope of 1 are called **45° lines** because they form an angle of 45° with the horizontal axis. If a point representing some data is above the 45° line, we know that the value of Y exceeds the value of X. Conversely, whenever we find a point below the 45° line, we know that X is larger than Y.

A straight line emanating from the origin, or zero point on a graph, is called a **ray through the origin** or, sometimes, just a **ray**.

A **45° line** is a ray through the origin with a slope of +1. It marks off points where the variables measured on each axis have equal values.[1]

[1]The definition assumes that both variables are measured in the same units.

Figure 2-6
RAYS THROUGH THE ORIGIN

Rays are straight lines drawn through the zero point on the graph (*the origin*). Three rays with different slopes are shown. The middle ray, the one with slope = + 1, has two properties that make it particularly useful in economics: (1) it makes a 45° angle with either axis, and (2) any point on that ray (for example, point A) is exactly equal in distance from the horizontal and vertical axes (length DA = length CA). So if the items measured on the two axes are in equal units, then at any point on that ray, such as A, the number on the X-axis (the abscissa) will be the same as the number on the Y-axis (the ordinate).

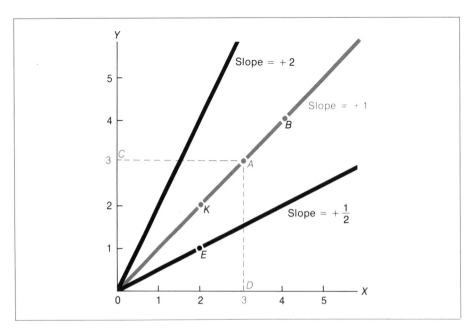

Squeezing Three Dimensions into Two: Contour Maps

Sometimes, because a problem involves more than two variables, two dimensions just are not enough, which is unfortunate since paper is only two dimensional. When we study the decision-making process of a business firm, for example, we may want to keep track simultaneously of three variables: how much labour it employs, how much machinery it uses, and how much output it creates.

Luckily, there is a well-known device for collapsing three dimensions into two, namely a *contour map*. Figure 2–7 is a contour map of Mont Tremblant, near Montreal. On several of the irregularly shaped "rings" we find a number indicating the height above sea level at that particular spot on the mountain. Thus, unlike the more usual sort of map, which gives only latitudes and longitudes, this contour map exhibits three pieces of information about each point: latitude, longitude, and altitude.

Figure 2–8 looks more like the contour maps encountered in economics. It shows how some third variable, called Z (think of it as a firm's output, for example), varies as we change either variable X (think of it as a firm's employment) or variable Y (think of it as the use of a firm's machines). Just like the map of Mont Tremblant, any point on the diagram conveys three pieces of data. At point A, we can read off the values of X and Y in the conventional way (X is 30 and Y is 40), and we can also note the value of Z by checking to see on which contour line point A falls. (It is on the $Z = 20$ contour.) So point A is able to tell us that 30 hours of labour and 40 hours of machine time produces 20 units of output.

While most of the analyses presented in this book will be based on the simpler two-variable diagrams, contour maps will find their applications, especially in the appendixes to *Microeconomics*, Chapters 5 and 7.

Figure 2–7
A GEOGRAPHIC CONTOUR MAP

All points on any particular contour line represent geographic locations that are at the same height above sea level.

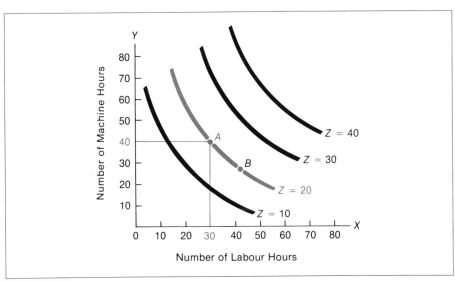

Figure 2–8
AN ECONOMIC CONTOUR MAP

In this contour map, all points on a given contour line represent different combinations of labour and capital capable of producing a given output. For example, all points on the curve $Z = 20$ represent input combinations that can produce 20 units of output. Point A on that line means that the 20 units of output can be produced using 30 labour hours and 40 machine hours. Economists call such maps *production indifference maps*.

Perils in the Interpretation of Graphs

The preceding materials contain just about all you will need in order to understand the simple graphics used in economic models. We turn now to the second objective of this chapter: to show how statistical data are portrayed on graphs and some of the pitfalls to watch out for.

The Interpretation of Growth Trends

A **time-series graph** depicts how a variable changes over time.

Probably the most common form of graph in empirical economics is a year-by-year (or perhaps a month-by-month) depiction of the behaviour of some economic variable—the profits of a particular corporation, or its annual sales, or the number of persons unemployed in the Canadian economy, or some measure of consumer prices. For example, Figure 2–9 is this sort of **time-series graph** showing the month-by-month unemployment rate in Canada from 1967 to 1984. It shows that the percentage of the labour force that was jobless was relatively low during the late 1960s and particularly high since the late 1970s. Time-series graphs are a type of two-variable diagram in which time is always the variable measured along the horizontal axis.

Such graphs can be quite illuminating, offering an instant visual grasp of the course of the relevant events. *However, if misused, such graphs are very dangerous.* They can easily mislead persons who are not experienced in dealing with them. Perhaps even more dangerous are the misinterpretations perpetuated accidentally and unintentionally by people who draw graphs without sufficient care and who may innocently mislead themselves as well as others.

A fine example of this latter occurrence is illustrated in Figure 2–10. Many people felt that there was a "cultural boom" underway in the period after World War II that led to an explosion in the demand for tickets to all sorts of artistic performances. This boom, it was thought, accounted for the rapidly rising prices of theatre tickets. Figure 2–10 shows a time-series graph that formed the basis for this allegation. The growth in spending for theatre tickets certainly looks impressive; expenditures rose about 1250 percent from 1929 to 1982.

But there is less to this graph than meets the eye—much less. Most of the spectacular growth in spending on theatre admissions was a reflection of three rather banal facts. First, there were many more North Americans alive in 1982

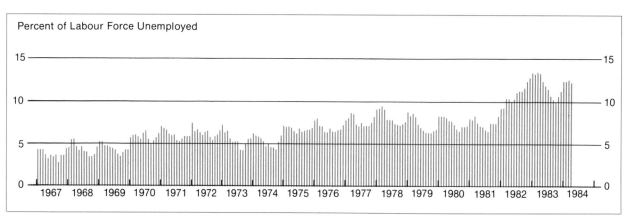

Figure 2–9
TIME-SERIES GRAPH
This graph shows the percentage of the labour force that was unemployed in each of the months indicated, from January 1967 through April 1984.

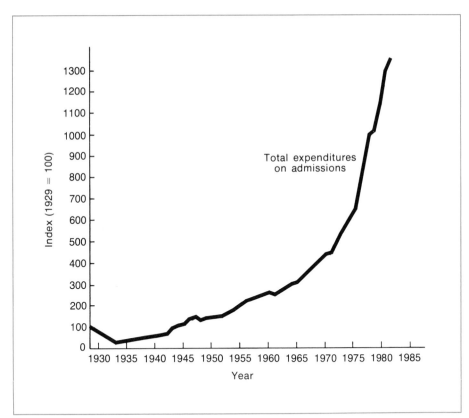

Figure 2-10
INDEX OF EXPENDITURES
ON ADMISSIONS TO
ARTISTIC PERFORMANCES
This graph, showing expenditures
on admissions to artistic
performances, seems to indicate
that since about 1932 North
Americans have become much
more interested in attending the
performing arts.
SOURCE: *Survey of Current Business*,
July issues, various years; and
Economic Report of the President,
Washington, D.C.: U.S. Government
Printing Office, various years.

than in 1929, so spending *per person* rose by much less than Figure 2-10 suggests. Second, the price of almost everything, not just theatre tickets, was higher in 1982 than in 1929. In fact, average prices were more than five times their 1929 levels. Third, the average citizen was richer in 1982 than in 1929, and consequently was more inclined to spend money on everything—not just on cultural activities.

All three of these factors can be accounted for by expressing spending on theatre admissions as a *fraction* of total consumer income. The results of this "correction" are shown in Figure 2-11. The explosive growth suggested by the uncorrected data really amounts to a decline in the share of income that the average North American spent on theatre tickets—from about 15 cents out of each $100 in 1929 to only 8 cents in 1982! How misleading it can be to simply "look at the facts." There is a general lesson to be learned from this example:

The facts, as portrayed in a time-series graph, most assuredly do not "speak for themselves." Because almost everything grows in a growing economy, one must use judgment in interpreting growth trends. Depending on what kind of data are being analyzed, it may be essential to correct for population growth, for rising prices, for rising incomes, or for all three.[2]

Distorting Trends by Choice of the Time Period

In addition to possible misinterpretations of growth trends, users of statistical data must be on guard for distortions of trends caused by unskillfully chosen first and last periods for the graph. This is best explained by an example.

[2]For a full discussion of how to use a "price index" to correct for rising prices, see the appendix to Chapter 6.

Figure 2-11

APPEARANCE AND REALITY
IN ARTS EXPENDITURE

The curve in black shows
correctly that the number of *dollars*
spent on the arts rose dramatically
since 1932. But because of
inflation, a dollar in 1982 was
worth much less than in 1929, and
there were many more North
Americans in the later year, who
were also wealthier on the
average. After correction for
inflation, population changes, and
so on, the black line is transformed
into the coloured line, showing that
in 1982 an average citizen actually
spent less of his purchasing power
on the arts than in 1929.

SOURCE: *Survey of Current Business*,
July issues, various years; and
Economic Report of the President,
Washington D.C.: U.S. Government
Printing Office, various years.

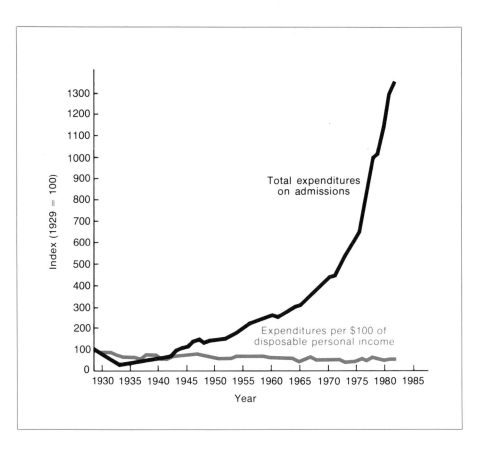

Figures 2-12 and 2-13 show the behaviour of average stock-market prices (the Dow-Jones Index in the United States) over the periods 1929–32 and 1973–75. They both display a clear downhill movement and would suggest to anyone who does not have other information that stocks are a terrible investment.

However, an unscrupulous seller of stocks could use the same set of stock-market statistics to tell exactly the opposite story by carefully selecting another group of years. Figure 2–14 shows the behaviour of average stock prices from 1940 through 1965. The persistence and size of the increase is quite dramatic. Stocks now look like a rather good investment.

An even longer and less biased period gives a less distorted picture (Figure 2–15). It indicates that investment in stocks are sometimes profitable and other times unprofitable.

The deliberate or inadvertent distortion resulting from an unfortunate or unscrupulous choice of time period for a graph must constantly be watched for.

There are no rules that can give absolute protection from this difficulty, but several precautions can be helpful.

1. Make sure the first date shown on the graph is not an exceptionally high or low point. In comparison with 1929, a year of unusually high stock-market prices, the years immediately following are bound to give the impression of a downward trend.

2. For the same reason, make sure the graph does not end in a year that is extraordinarily high or low (although this may be unavoidable if the graph simply ends with figures that are as up-to-date as possible).

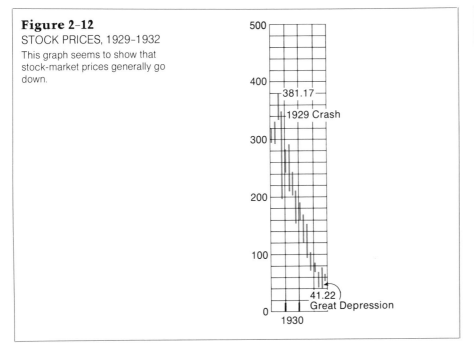

Figure 2-12
STOCK PRICES, 1929–1932
This graph seems to show that stock-market prices generally go down.

381.17
1929 Crash

41.22
Great Depression

1930

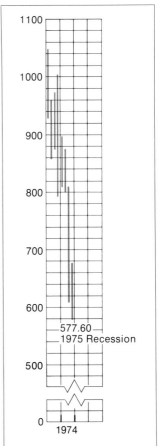

577.60
1975 Recession

1974

Figure 2-13
STOCK PRICES, 1973–1975
This figure also seems to show that stock prices generally fall.

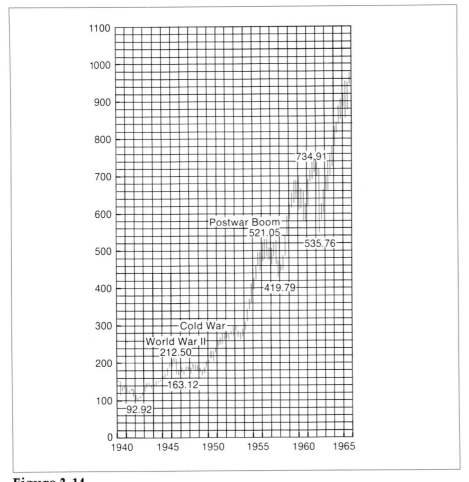

734.91

Postwar Boom
521.05
535.76

419.79

Cold War
World War II
212.50

163.12

92.92

1940   1945   1950   1955   1960   1965

Figure 2-14
STOCK PRICES, 1940–1965
This graph seems to indicate that the value of stocks is on a never-ending climb.

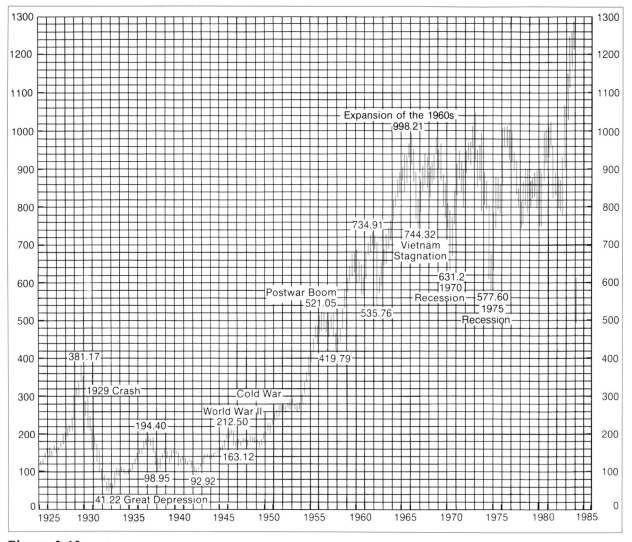

Figure 2-15
THE FULL HISTORY OF STOCK PRICES, 1925-1984
Here we see that stock prices have lots of ups and downs, though they have risen quite a bit on the average.

3. Make sure that (in the absence of some special justification) the graph does not depict only a very brief period, which can be easily atypical.

Dangers of Omitting the Origin

Frequently, the value of an economic variable described on a graph does not fall anywhere near zero during the period under consideration. For example, the prime lending rate offered by Canadian banks rose during the first half of 1984 from 11 to 13 percent. This means that a graph representing the behaviour of interest rates in 1984 would have a good deal of wasted space between the horizontal axis of the graph, where the interest rate is zero, and the level of the graph representing an 11 percent interest rate. In that area there are simply no data to plot. It is therefore tempting simply to eliminate this wasted space by beginning the graph just below the 11 percent interest-rate level. This was done by *Maclean's* in a recent issue, as reproduced in our Figure 2–16.

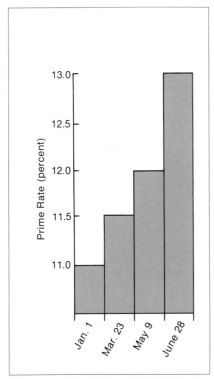

Figure 2–16
A GRAPH SHOWING
OMISSION OF THE ORIGIN
A hasty glance at this figure
seems to show that interest rates
tripled during the first half of 1984.

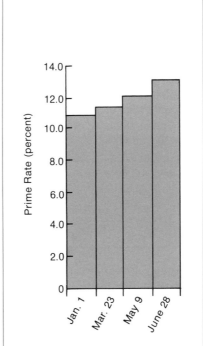

Figure 2–17
INTEREST-RATE FIGURES
INCLUDING POINT OF
ORIGIN
Adding the point of zero interest
rate to the previous graph shows
that the rise in the interest rate
was in fact not so enormous as
Figure 2-16 suggests.

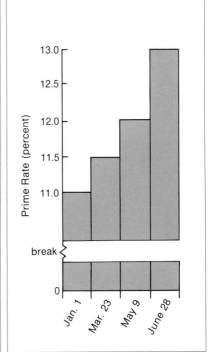

Figure 2–18
A BREAK IN A GRAPH
An alternative way of warning the
reader that the zero point has
been left out is to put a break in
the graph, as illustrated here.

What is wrong with the drawing? The answer is that it vastly exaggerates the size of the increase in the interest rate that is depicted. It makes it look like the interest rate trebled. The more informative graph, which includes the origin as well as the "wasted space" in between, is shown in Figure 2–17. Note how this alternative presentation puts matters into perspective.

Omitting the origin in a graph is dangerous because it always exaggerates the magnitudes of the changes that have taken place.

Sometimes, it is true, the inclusion of the full graph would waste so much space that it is undesirable to include it. In that case, a good practice is to put a very clear warning on the graph to remind the reader that some space has been omitted. Figure 2–18 shows one way of doing so.

Unreliability of Steepness and Choice of Units

The last problem we will consider has consequences very similar to the one we have just discussed. The problem is that we can never trust the impression we get from the steepness of an economic graph. A graph of stock-market prices that moves uphill sharply (has a large positive slope) appears to suggest that prices are rising rapidly, while another graph in which the rate of climb is much slower seems to imply that prices are going up sluggishly. Yet, depending on how one draws the graph, exactly the same statistics can produce a graph that is rising very quickly or very slowly.

The reason for this possibility is that in economics there are no fixed units of measurement. Coal production can be measured in pounds, hundredweight (hundreds of pounds), or in tons. Prices can be measured in cents, dollars, or millions of dollars. Time can be measured in days, months, or years. Any of these choices is perfectly legitimate, but it makes all the difference to the rapidity with which a graph using the resulting figures rises or falls.

An example will bring out the point. Suppose that we have the following (imaginary) figures on daily coal production from a mine, which we measure both in hundredweight and in tons (remembering that 1 ton = 20 hundredweight):

YEAR	PRODUCTION IN TONS	PRODUCTION IN HUNDREDWEIGHT
1975	5000	100,000
1980	5050	101,000
1985	5090	101,800

Look at Figures 2–19(a) and 2–19(b), one graph showing the figures in tons and the other showing the figures in hundredweight. The line looks quite flat in Figure 2–19(a) but quite steep in Figure 2–19(b).

Unfortunately, we cannot solve the problem by agreeing always to stick to the same measurement units. Pounds may be the right unit for measuring demand

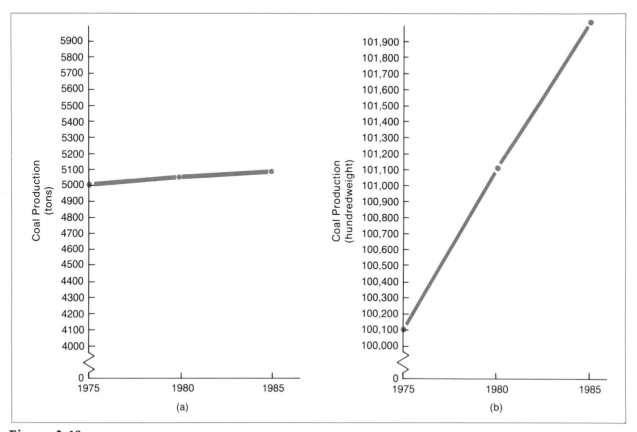

Figure 2–19

SLOPE DEPENDS ON UNITS OF MEASUREMENT

(a) Coal production is measured in tons, and production seems to be rising very slowly. (b) Production is measured in hundredweight (hundred-pound units), so the same facts now seem to say that production is rising spectacularly.

for beef, but they will not do in measuring demand for cloth or for coal. A penny may be the right monetary unit for postage stamps, but it is not a very convenient unit for the cost of airplanes or automobiles.

A change in units of measurement stretches or compresses the axis on which the information is represented, which automatically changes the slope of a graph. Therefore we must never place much faith in the apparent implications of the slope of an ordinary graph in economics.

In *Microeconomics*, Chapter 6, on demand analysis, we will encounter a useful approach economists have adopted to deal with this problem. Instead of calculating changes in "absolute" terms—like tons of coal—they use as their common unit the *percentage* increase. By using percentages rather than absolute figures the problem can be avoided. The reason is simple. If we look at our hypothetical figures on coal production again, we see that no matter whether we measure the increase in output from 1975 to 1980 in tons (from 5000 to 5050) or in hundredweight (from 100,000 to 101,000), the *percentage* increase has been the same. Fifty is 1 percent of 5000, and 1000 is 1 percent of 100,000. Since a change in units affects both the numbers *proportionately*, the result is a washout—it does not do anything to the percentage calculation.

Summary

1. Because graphs are used so often to portray economic models, it is important for students to acquire some understanding of their construction and use. Fortunately, the graphics used in economics are usually not very complex.

2. Most economic models are depicted in two-variable diagrams. We read data from these diagrams just as we read the latitude and longitude on a map: each point represents the values of two variables at the same time.

3. In a few instances, three variables must be shown at once. In these cases, economists use contour maps, which, as the name suggests, show "latitude," "longitude," and "altitude" all at the same time.

4. Often, the most important property of a line or curve drawn on a diagram will be its slope, which is defined as the ratio of the "rise" over the "run," or the vertical change divided by the horizontal change. Curves that go uphill as we move to the right have positive slopes, while curves that go downhill have negative slopes.

5. By definition, a straight line has the same slope wherever we choose to measure it. The slope of a curved line changes, but the slope at any point on the curve can be calculated by measuring the slope of a straight line tangent to the curve at that point.

6. A time-series graph is a particular type of two-variable diagram that is useful in depicting statistical data. Time is measured along the horizontal axis, and some variable of interest is measured along the vertical axis.

7. While time-series graphs are invaluable in helping us condense a great deal of information in a single picture, they can be quite misleading if they are not drawn and interpreted with care. For example, growth trends can be exaggerated by inappropriate choice of units of measurement or by failure to correct for some obvious source of growth (such as rising population). Omitting the origin can make the ups and downs in a time series appear much more extreme than they actually are. Or, by a clever choice of the starting and ending points for the graphs, the same data can be made to tell very different stories. Readers of such graphs—and this includes anyone who ever reads a newspaper—must be on guard for problems like these or they may find themselves misled by "the facts."

Concepts for Review

Two-variable diagram	Negative, positive, zero, and infinite slope	Ray through the origin, or ray
Horizontal and vertical axes		45° line
Origin (of a graph)	Tangent to the curve	Contour map
Slope of a straight (or curved) line	Y-intercept	Time-series graph

Questions for Discussion

1. Look for a graph in your local newspaper, on the financial page or elsewhere. What does the graph try to show? Is someone trying to convince you of something with this graph? Check to see if the graph is distorted in any of the ways mentioned in this chapter.

2. Portray the following hypothetical data on a two-variable diagram:

ENROLLMENT DATA:
UNIVERSITY OF NOWHERE

ACADEMIC YEAR	TOTAL ENROLLMENT	ENROLLMENT IN ECONOMICS COURSES
1980–1981	3000	300
1981–1982	3100	325
1982–1983	3200	350
1983–1984	3300	375
1984–1985	3400	400

Measure the slope of the resulting line, and explain what this number means.

3. From Figure 2–5, calculate the slope of the curve at point D.

4. From Figure 2–6, determine the values of X and Y at point K and at point E. What do you conclude?

5. From Figure 2–8, interpret the economic meaning of points A and B. What do the two points have in common? What is the difference in their economic interpretation?

6. Suppose that between 1984 and 1985 expenditures on dog food rose from $35 million to $70 million and that the price of dog food doubled. What do these facts imply about the popularity of dog food?

7. Suppose that between 1975 and 1985 the population of North America went up 10 percent and that the number of people attending professional wrestling matches rose from 3,000,000 to 3,100,000. What do these facts imply about the growth in popularity of professional wrestling?

The Economic Problem

Our necessities are few but
our wants are endless.
INSCRIPTION FOUND IN A
FORTUNE COOKIE

This chapter examines a subject that many economists consider to be *the* fundamental issue of economics: the fact that since virtually no resource is available in unlimited supply, people must consequently make decisions consistent with their limited means. A wild-eyed materialist may dream of a world in which everyone owns a yacht and five automobiles, but the earth almost certainly lacks the resources needed to make that dream come true. The scarcity of resources, both natural and man-made, makes it vital that we stretch our limited resources as far as possible.

This chapter introduces a way to describe the choices available to decision-makers, given the resources at their command. The same sort of analysis, based on the concept of *opportunity cost*, will be shown to apply to the decisions of business firms, of governments, and of society as a whole. Many of the most basic ideas of economics—such as *efficiency*, *division of labour*, *exchange*, and the *role of markets*—are introduced here for the first time. In particular, we will see that a market system can, if it is functioning properly, promote the efficient use of society's resources without intervention by government planners. Finally, this chapter introduces a broad question that constitutes the central theme of this text: What does the market do well and what does it do poorly?

The "Indispensable Necessity" Syndrome

Governments at all levels were forced to tighten their belts sharply in the early 1980s. Economic recession cut into tax revenues. Also, federal government grants to provinces and provincial grants to municipalities were reduced.

Budget cuts forced politicians and administrators to make some hard decisions over which services to cut. As they struggled with these decisions, they learned to their dismay that their constituents often were unwilling to accept *any* reductions. Mayors who proposed closing a fire station or a hospital were confronted by demonstrators decrying the proposed cutback as a "false economy" and describing the fire station or hospital as "indispensable." Groups marched to the B.C. legislative building to oppose Premier Bennett's budget cuts. University administrators found that suggestions to eliminate poorly attended courses, cut library hours, or restrict access to the Xerox machine all too frequently were met with the cry that each of these was *absolutely* essential.

Yet, regrettable as it is to have to give up any of these good things, reduced budgets mean that *something* must go. If everyone reacts by declaring *everything* to be indispensable, the decision-maker is in the dark and is likely to end up making cuts that are bad for everyone. When the budget must be reduced, it is critical to determine which cuts are likely to prove *least damaging* to the people affected.

It is nonsense to assign top priority to everything. No one can afford everything. An optimal decision is one that chooses the most desirable alternative *among the possibilities that the available resources permit.*

Scarcity, Choice, and Opportunity Cost

One of the basic themes of economics is that the resources of decision-makers, no matter how large they may be, are always limited, and that as a result everyone has some hard decisions to make. Even Philip II, of Spanish Armada fame and one of the most richly endowed kings of history, frequently had to cope with rebellion on the part of his troops, whom he was often unable to pay or to supply with even the most basic provisions.

But far more fundamental than the scarcity of funds is the scarcity of physical resources. The supply of fuel, for example, has never been limitless, and a real scarcity of fuel would force us to make some hard choices. We might have to keep our homes cooler in winter and warmer in summer, live closer to our jobs, or give up such fuel-using conveniences as dishwashers. While energy is the most widely discussed scarcity these days, the general principle of scarcity applies to all the earth's resources—iron, copper, uranium, and so on.

Even goods that can be produced are in limited supply because their production requires fuel, labour, and other scarce resources. Wheat and rice can be grown. But nations have none the less suffered famines because the land, labour, fertilizer, and water needed to grow these crops were unavailable. We can increase our output of cars, but the increased use of labour, steel, and fuel in auto production will mean that something else, perhaps the production of refrigerators, will have to be cut back. This all adds up to the following fundamental principle of economics, one we will encounter again and again in this text.

Virtually all resources are scarce, meaning that humanity has less of them than it would like. So choices must be made among a *limited* set of possibilities, in full recognition of the inescapable fact that a decision to have more of one thing means we must give up some of another thing.

In fact, one popular definition of economics is the "study of how best to use limited means in the pursuit of unlimited ends." While this definition, like any short statement, cannot possibly cover the sweep of the entire discipline, it does convey the flavour of the type of problem that is the economist's stock in trade.

The Principle of Opportunity Cost

Economics examines the options left open to households, business firms, governments, and entire societies by the limited resources at their command; and it studies the logic of how **rational decisions** can be made from among the competing alternatives. One overriding principle governs this logic—a principle we have already introduced in Chapter 1 as one of the **12 Ideas for Beyond the Final Exam**. With limited resources, a decision to have more of something is simultaneously a decision to have less of something else. Hence, the relevant *cost* of any decision is its **opportunity cost**—the value of the next best alternative that is given up. Rational decision-making, be it in industry, government, or households, must be based on opportunity-cost calculations.

To illustrate opportunity cost, we can continue the example in which production of additional cars requires the production of fewer refrigerators. While the production of a car may cost $7000 per vehicle, or some other money amount, its real cost to society is the refrigerators it must forgo to get an additional car. If the labour, steel, and fuel needed to make a car are sufficient to make eight refrigerators, we say that the opportunity cost of a car is eight refrigerators. The principle of opportunity cost is of such general applicability that we devote most of this chapter to it.

Opportunity Cost and Money Cost

Since we live in a market economy where (almost) everything "has its price," students often wonder about the connection between the opportunity cost of an item and its market price. What we just said seems to divorce the two concepts. We stressed that the true cost of a car is not its market price but the value of the other things (like refrigerators) that could have been made instead. This *opportunity cost* is the true sacrifice the economy must incur to get a car.

But isn't the opportunity cost of a car related to its money cost? The answer is that the two are often very closely tied because of the way a market economy sets the prices of the steel and electricity that go into the production of cars. Steel is valuable because it can be used to make other goods. If the items that steel can make are themselves valuable, the price of steel will be high. But if the goods that steel can make have very little value, the price of steel will be low. Thus, if a car has a high opportunity cost, then a well-functioning price system will assign high prices to the resources that are needed to produce cars, and therefore a car will also command a high price. In sum:

If the market is functioning well, goods that have high opportunity costs will tend to have high money costs, and goods whose opportunity costs are low will tend to have low money costs.

Yet it would be a mistake to treat opportunity costs and explicit monetary costs as identical. For one thing, there are times when the market does *not* function well, and hence does not assign prices that accurately reflect opportunity costs. Many such examples will be encountered, especially in *Microeconomics*, Chapters 14 and 19.

Moreover, some valuable items may not bear explicit price tags at all. We have already encountered one example of this in Chapter 1, where we contrasted the opportunity cost of going to university with the explicit money cost. We learned that one important item typically omitted from the money-cost calculation is the value of the student's time; that is, the wages he or she could have earned by working instead of attending university. These forgone wages, which are given up by students in order to acquire an education, are part of the opportunity cost of a university education just as surely as are tuition payments.

Other common examples are goods and services that are given away "free." You incur no explicit monetary cost to acquire such an item. But you may have to pay implicitly by waiting in line. If so, you incur an opportunity cost equal to the value of the next best use of your time.

Scarcity and Choice for a Single Firm

The nature of opportunity cost is perhaps clearest in the case of a single business firm that produces two outputs from a fixed supply of inputs. Given the existing technology and the limited resources at its disposal, the more of one good the firm produces the less of the other it will be able to produce. And unless management carries out an explicit comparison of the available choices, weighing the desirabil-

A **rational decision** is one that best serves the objective of the decision-maker, whatever that objective may be. The term "rational" connotes neither approval nor disapproval of the objective itself.

The **opportunity cost** of any decision is the forgone value of the next best alternative that is not chosen.

ity of each against the others, it is unlikely that it will make rational production decisions.

Consider the example of a farmer whose available supplies of land, machinery, labour, and fertilizer are capable of producing the various combinations of soybeans and wheat listed in Table 3-1. Obviously, the more land and other resources he devotes to production of soybeans, the less wheat he will be able to produce. Table 3-1 indicates, for example, that if he produces only soybeans, he can harvest 40,000 bushels. But, when soybean production is reduced to only 30,000 bushels, the farmer can also grow 38,000 bushels of wheat. Thus the opportunity cost of obtaining 38,000 bushels of wheat is 10,000 fewer bushels of soybeans. Or put the other way around, the opportunity cost of 10,000 bushels of soybeans is 38,000 bushels of wheat. The other numbers in Table 3-1 have similar interpretations.

Table 3-1
PRODUCTION POSSIBILITIES OPEN TO A FARMER

BUSHELS OF SOYBEANS	BUSHELS OF WHEAT	LABEL IN FIGURE 3-1
40,000	0	A
30,000	38,000	B
20,000	52,000	C
10,000	60,000	D
0	65,000	E

Figure 3-1 is a graphical representation of this same information. Point *A* corresponds to the first line of Table 3-1, point *B* to the second line, and so on. Curves like *AE* will appear frequently in this book; they are called **production possibilities frontiers**. Any point *on or below* the production possibilities frontier is attainable. Points above the frontier cannot be achieved with the available resources and technology.

The production possibilities frontier always slopes downward to the right. Why? Because resources are limited. The farmer can *increase* his wheat production (move to the right in Figure 3-1) only by devoting more of his land and labour to growing wheat, meaning that he must simultaneously *reduce* his soybean produc-

A **production possibilities frontier** shows the different combinations of various goods that a producer can turn out, given the available resources and existing technology.

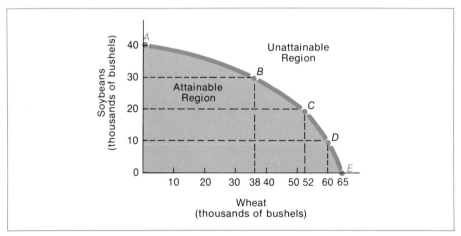

Figure 3-1
PRODUCTION POSSIBILITIES FRONTIER FOR PRODUCTION BY A SINGLE FIRM
With a given set of inputs, the firm can produce only those output combinations given by points in the shaded area. The production possibilities frontier, *AE*, is not a straight line but one that curves more and more as it nears the axes. That is, when the firm specializes in only one product, those inputs that are especially adapted to the production of the other good lose at least part of their productivity.

tion (move downward) because less of his land and labour remains available for growing soybeans.

Notice that in addition to having a negative slope, our production possibilities frontier, curve AE, has another characteristic—it is "bowed outward." Let us consider a little more carefully what this curvature means.

Suppose our farmer is initially producing only soybeans, so that he uses for this purpose even land that is much more suitable for wheat cultivation (point A). Now suppose he decides to switch some of his land from soybean production into wheat production. Which part of his land will he switch? Obviously, if he is sensible, he will use the part best suited to wheat growing. If he shifts to point B, soybean production falls from 40,000 bushels to 30,000 bushels as wheat production rises from zero to 38,000. A sacrifice of only 10,000 bushels of soybeans "buys" 38,000 bushels of wheat.

Imagine now that the farmer wants to produce still more wheat. Figure 3–1 tells us that the sacrifice of an additional 10,000 bushels of soybeans (from 30,000 down to 20,000) will yield only 14,000 more bushels of wheat (see Point C). Why? The main reason is that inputs tend to be specialized. As we noted, at point A the farmer was using resources for soybean production that were much more suitable for growing wheat. Consequently, their productivity in soybeans was relatively low, and when they were switched into wheat production the yield was very high. But this cannot continue forever. As more wheat is produced, the farmer must utilize land and machinery that are better suited to producing soybeans and less well-suited to producing wheat. This is why the first 10,000 bushels of soybeans forgone "buys" the farmer 38,000 bushels of wheat while the second 10,000 bushels of soybeans "buys" him only 14,000 bushels of wheat. Figure 3–1 and Table 3–1 show that these returns continue to decline as wheat production expands: the next 10,000-bushel reduction in soybean production yields only 8000 bushels of additional wheat, and so on.

We can now see that the *slope* of the production possibilities frontier represents graphically the concept of *opportunity cost*. Between points C and B, for example, the opportunity cost of acquiring 10,000 additional bushels of soybeans is 14,000 bushels of forgone wheat, and between points B and A, the opportunity cost of 10,000 bushels of soybeans is 38,000 bushels of forgone wheat. In general, as we move upward to the left along the production possibilities frontier (toward more soybeans and less wheat), the opportunity cost of soybeans in terms of wheat increases. Or, putting the same thing differently, as we move downward to the right, the opportunity cost of acquiring wheat by giving up soybeans increases.

The Principle of Increasing Costs

We have just described a very general phenomenon, which is applicable well beyond farming. The **principle of increasing costs** states that as the production of one good expands, the opportunity cost of producing another unit of this good generally increases.

This principle is not a universal fact; there can be exceptions to it. But it does seem to be a technological regularity that applies to a wide range of economic activities. As our example of the farmer suggests, the principle of increasing costs is based on the fact that resources tend to be specialized, at least in part, so that some of their productivity is lost when they are transferred from doing what they are relatively good at doing to what they are relatively bad at doing. In terms of diagrams like Figure 3–1, the principle simply asserts that the production possibilities frontier is bowed outward.

Perhaps the best way to understand this idea is to contrast it with a case in which there are no specialized resources. Figure 3–2 depicts a production possibilities frontier for producing black shoes and brown shoes. Because the labour and capital used to produce black shoes are just as good at producing brown shoes, the

The **principle of increasing costs** states that as the production of one good expands, the opportunity cost of producing another unit generally increases.

Resources that produce black
shoes are just as good at
producing brown shoes. So there
is no loss of productivity when
black-shoe production is
decreased in order to increase
brown-shoe production. For
example, if the firm moves from
point *A* to point *B*, black-shoe
output falls by 10,000 pairs and
brown-shoe output rises by 10,000
pairs. The same would be true if it
moved from point *B* to point *C* or
from point *C* to point *D*. The
production possibilities frontier is
therefore a straight line.

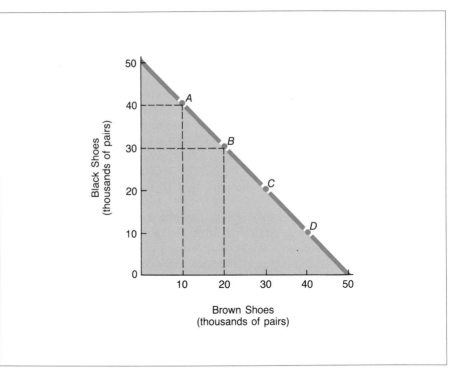

frontier is a straight line. If the firm cuts back its production of black shoes by
10,000 pairs, it always gets 10,000 additional pairs of brown shoes. No productivity
is lost in the switch because resources are not specialized.

Scarcity and Choice for the Entire Society

Like an individual firm, the entire economy is also constrained by its limited
resources and technology. If society wants more aircraft and tanks, it will have to
give up some boats and automobiles. If it wants to build more factories and stores,
it will have to build fewer homes and sports arenas. In general:

The position and shape of the production possibilities frontier that constrains the
choices of the economy are determined by the economy's physical resources, its
skills and technology, its willingness to work, and its investments in factories,
research, and innovation.

Since the debate over acid rain has been so active in recent years, let us
illustrate the nature of society's choices by the example of choosing between clean
air and manufactured goods. Just like a single firm, the economy as a whole has a
production possibilities frontier for these items determined by its technology and
the available resources of land, labour, capital, and raw materials. This production
possibilities frontier may look like curve *BC* in Figure 3-3.

If most workers are employed at factories, coal mines, and refineries, the
production of manufactured goods will be large but the availability of clean air
will be small. If resources are transferred from the mines and factories to emission
treatment operations, the mix of output can be shifted toward cleaner air at some
sacrifice of manufactured goods (the move from *D* to *E*). However, something is
likely to be lost in the transfer process—some of the machines and chemicals that
helped produce the manufactured goods will not help in the emission treatment
operations. As summarized in the principle of increasing costs, physical resources
tend to be specialized, so the production possibilities frontier probably curves
downward and toward the axes.

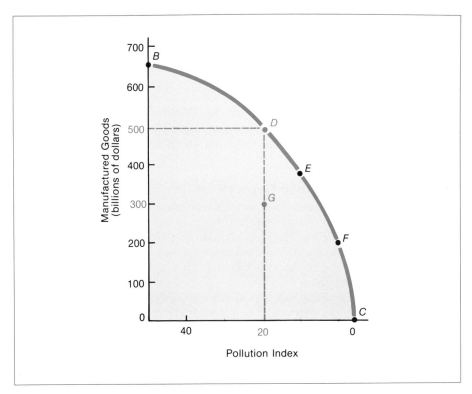

Figure 3-3
THE PRODUCTION
POSSIBILITIES FRONTIER
FOR THE ENTIRE ECONOMY
This production possibilities
frontier is curved because
resources are not perfectly
transferable from goods
production to emission treatment
operations. The limits on available
resources place a ceiling, C, on
the availability of clean air (a
reading of zero on the pollution
index), and a ceiling, B, on the
output of manufactured goods.

We may even reach a point where the only resources left are items that are not very useful outside of factories. In that case, even a very large additional sacrifice of goods yields very little cleaner air. That is the meaning of the steep segment, FC, on the frontier. At point C the air is only slightly cleaner than at F, even though at C goods production has been given up entirely.

The downward slope of society's production possibilities frontier implies that hard choices must be made. Our nation's pollution problems can be solved only by decreasing material consumption, not by rhetoric nor by wishing it so. The curvature of the production possibilities frontier implies that, as emission treatment increases, it becomes progressively more expensive to "buy" cleaner air by sacrificing manufactured goods.

Scarcity and Choice Elsewhere in the Economy

We have stressed that limited resources force hard choices upon business managers and society as a whole. But the same type of choices arise elsewhere—in households, in universities, in nonprofit organizations, and in the government.

The nature of opportunity cost is perhaps most obvious for a household that must decide how to divide its income among the goods and services that compete for the family's trade. If the Higgins family buys an expensive new car, they may be forced to cut back sharply on their other purchases. This does not make it unwise to buy the car. But it does make it unwise to buy the car until the full implications of the purchase for the family's overall budget are considered. If the Higgins family are to use their limited resources most effectively, they must explicitly acknowledge that the opportunity costs of the car are, say, a shorter vacation and making do with the old TV set.

Even a rich and powerful government like that of the United States or the

Soviet Union must cope with the limitations implied by scarce resources. The necessity for choice imposed on the government by its limited budget is similar in character to the problems faced by business firms and households. For the goods and services it buys from others, a government has to prepare a budget similar to that of a very large household. For the items it produces itself—education, police protection, libraries, and so on—it faces a production possibilities frontier much like that of a business firm. Even though the Canadian government spent over $100 billion in 1984, some of the most acrimonious parliamentary debates were over how to allocate the government's limited resources among competing programs.

Application: Economic Growth in Canada and Japan

Among the economic choices that any society must make, there is one very important choice that illustrates well the concept of opportunity cost. This choice is embodied in the question "How fast should the economy grow?"[1] At first, the question may seem ridiculous. Since economic growth means, roughly, that the average citizen has more and more goods and services, is it not self-evident that faster growth is always better?

Again, the fundamental problem of scarcity intervenes. Economies do not grow by magic. Scarce resources must be devoted to the process of growth. Cement and steel that could be used to make swimming pools and stadiums must be diverted to build more machinery and factories. Wood that could be made into furniture and skis must be used for hammers and ladders instead. Grain that could be eaten must be ploughed back into the soil to increase future yields. By deciding how large a quantity of resources to devote to future needs rather than to current consumption, society in effect *chooses* (within limits) how fast it will grow.

Figure 3-4 illustrates the nature of the choice by depicting production possibilities frontiers for goods that are consumed today (like food and electricity) versus **investment goods** that provide for future consumption (like grocery stores and generating plants) for two different societies.

Figure 3-4(a) depicts a society like Canada's that devotes a relatively small quantity of resources to growth, preferring current consumption instead. It chooses a point like *A* on this year's production possibilities frontier, *FF*. At *A*, consumption is relatively high and investment is relatively low, so the production possibilities frontier shifts only to *GG* next year. Figure 3-4(b) depicts a society much more enamoured of growth, like Japan's. It selects a point like *B*, on its production possibilities frontier, *ff*. At *B*, consumption is much lower and investment is much higher; so its production possibilities frontier moves all the way to *gg* by next year. Japan grows faster than Canada, but the more rapid growth has a price—an *opportunity cost*. The Japanese must give up some of the current consumption that Canadians enjoy.

An economy grows by giving up some current consumption and investing instead for the future. The more it invests, the faster will its production possibilities frontier shift outward over time.

An **investment good** is an item that is used to produce other goods and services in the future, rather than being consumed today.

The Concept of Efficiency

So far in our discussion of scarcity and choice, we have assumed that either the single firm or the whole economy always operates *on* its production possibilities frontier rather than *below it*. In other words, we have tacitly assumed that, whatever it decides to do, the firm or economy does so *efficiently*. An efficient economy utilizes all of its available resources, and produces the maximum amount

[1]Economic growth will be studied in detail in Chapter 22.

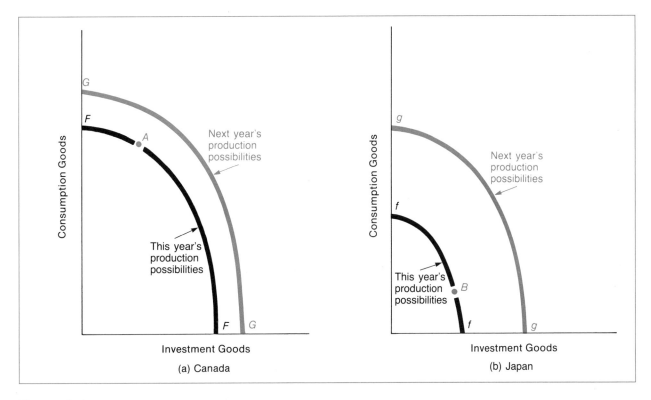

Figure 3-4

GROWTH IN TWO ECONOMIES

Growth shifts the production possibilities frontiers *FF* and *ff* (black) outward to the frontiers *GG* and *gg* (blue), meaning that each economy can produce more of both goods than it could before. If the shift in both economies occurs in the same period of time, then the Japanese economy (b) is growing faster than the Canadian economy (a) because the outward shift in (b) is much greater than the one in (a).

of output that its technology permits.[2] Economists define *efficiency* as the absence of waste.

To see why any point on the economy's production possibilities frontier in Figure 3-3 represents an efficient decision, suppose for a moment that society has decided to settle for air with a purity level of 20. According to the production possibilities frontier, if this level of clean air is to be attained, then the maximum amount of manufactured goods that can be made is $500 billion (point *D* in Figure 3-3). The economy is, therefore, operating efficiently if it actually produces $500 billion worth of goods rather than some smaller amount, such as $300 billion (as at point *G*). Point *D* is efficient while point *G* is not.

Note that the concept of efficiency does not tell us which point on the production possibilities frontier is *best*; it only tells us that no point that is *not* on the frontier can be best, because any such point represents wasted resources. For example, should society ever find itself at point *G*, the necessity of making hard choices would (temporarily) disappear. It would be possible to increase both the production of goods *and* air purity by moving to a point such as *E*.

Why, then, would an economy ever find itself at a point below its production possibilities frontier? There are a number of ways in which resources are wasted in real life. The most important of them, unemployment, is an issue that will take up a substantial part of this book (especially in Parts Two and Three). When many workers are unemployed, the economy finds itself at a point like *G*, below the frontier, because by putting the unemployed to work in both manufacturing and emission treatment jobs the economy could produce more goods and have cleaner air. The economy would then move from point *G* to the right (cleaner air) and

[2]A more formal definition of *efficiency* is offered in *Microeconomics*, Chapter 11, page 209.

upward (more goods) toward a point like *E* on the production possibilities frontier. Only when no resources are wasted by unemployment or misuse is the economy *on* the frontier.

Analogous problems occur in the firm. For example, if a firm uses fertilizer wastefully, it will end up at a point *inside* its production possibilities frontier. It will not be operating efficiently.

The Three Co-ordination Tasks of Any Economy

In deciding how to use its scarce resources, society must somehow make three sorts of decisions. First, as we have just emphasized, it must figure out **how to utilize its resources efficiently**; that is, it must find a way to get *on* its production possibilities frontier. Second, it must decide **what combination of goods to produce**—how many goods versus cleaner air and so on; that is, it must select one specific point on the production possibilities frontier. Finally, it must decide **how much of each good to distribute to each person**, doing it in a sensible way so that meat does not go to vegetarians and wine to teetotallers.

Certainly, each of these decisions could be made by a central planner who told people how to produce, what to produce, and what to consume.[3] But many of the decisions can also be made without central direction, through a system of prices and markets. Let us consider each task in turn.

Specialization, Division of Labour, and Exchange

Efficiency in production is one of the three basic tasks. Many features of society contribute to efficiency; others interfere with it. While different societies pursue the goal of economic efficiency in different ways, one source of efficiency is so fundamental that we must single it out for special attention: the tremendous gains in productivity that stem from **specialization** and the consequent **division of labour**.

Division of labour means breaking up a task into a number of smaller, more specialized tasks so that each worker can become more adept at his or her particular job.

Adam Smith, the founder of modern economics, first marvelled at this mainspring of efficiency and productivity on a visit to a pin factory. In a famous passage near the beginning of his monumental book *The Wealth of Nations* [1776], he described what he saw:

One man draws out the wire, another straightens it, a third cuts it, a fourth points it, a fifth grinds it at the top for receiving the head; to make the head requires two or three distinct operations; to put it on is a peculiar business, to whiten the pins is another; it is even a trade by itself to put them into the paper. . . .[4]

Smith observed that by dividing the work to be done in this way, each worker became quite skilled in his particular specialty, and the productivity of the group of workers as a whole was enhanced enormously. As Smith related it:

I have seen a small manufactory of this kind where ten men only were employed. . . . Those ten persons . . . could make among them upwards of forty-eight thousand pins in a day. . . . But if they had all wrought separately and independently, . . . they

---

[3]Central planning will be considered in some detail in *Microeconomics*, Chapter 24.

[4]Adam Smith, *The Wealth of Nations* (New York: Random House, Modern Library Edition, 1937), page 4.

certainly could not each of them have made twenty, perhaps not one pin in a day. . . .[5]

In other words, through the miracle of division of labour and specialization, ten workers accomplished what would otherwise have required thousands. This was the secret of the Industrial Revolution, which helped lift humanity out of the abject poverty that had for so long been its lot.

But specialization created a problem. With division of labour, people no longer produced only what they wanted to consume themselves. The workers in the pin factory had no use for the thousands of pins they produced each day; they wanted to trade them for things like food, clothing, and shelter. Specialization thus made it necessary to have some mechanism by which workers producing pins could **exchange** their wares with workers producing such things as cloth and potatoes.

Without a system of exchange, the productivity miracle achieved by the division of labour would have done society little good. With it, standards of living rose enormously. As we observed in Chapter 1:

Mutual Gains from Voluntary Exchange

Unless there is deception or misunderstanding of the facts, a voluntary exchange between two parties must make both parties better off. Even though no additional goods are produced by the act of trading, the welfare of society is increased because each individual acquires goods that are more suited to his needs and tastes. This simple but fundamental precept of economics is one of our **12 Ideas for Beyond the Final Exam**.

While goods can be traded for other goods, a system of exchange works better when everyone agrees to use some common item (such as pieces of paper) for buying and selling goods and services. Enter *money*. Then workers in pin factories, for example, can be paid in money rather than in pins, and they can use this money to purchase cloth and potatoes. Textile workers and farmers can do the same.

These two principles—specialization and exchange (assisted by money)—working in tandem led to a vast improvement in the well-being of mankind. This process of specialization and exchange is extended when a country's citizens trade with those living in other countries. Indeed it can be shown that even if the citizens in one country are more efficient at producing *everything* than are the citizens in the other country, *both* countries benefit from specializing and trading. We explain this *principle of comparative advantage* fully in Chapter 21. We show there that a country can obtain points *beyond* its own production possibilities curve by engaging in foreign trade.

Markets, Prices, and the Three Co-ordination Tasks

We have emphasized above that the two important principles—specialization and exchange—have led to a vast improvement in material welfare. But what forces induce workers to join together so that the fruits of the division of labour can be enjoyed? And what forces establish a smoothly functioning system of exchange so that each person can acquire what he or she wants to consume? One alternative is to have a central authority telling people what to do. But Adam Smith explained and extolled another way of organizing and co-ordinating economic activity—the use of markets and prices.

Smith noted that people were very good at pursuing their own self-interest,

[5]Ibid., page 5.

Biographical Note: Adam Smith (1723-1790)

Adam Smith, who was to become the leading advocate of freedom of international trade, was born the son of a customs official in 1723 and ended his career in the well-paid post of collector of customs for Scotland. He received an excellent education at Glasgow College, where, for the first time, some lectures were being given in English rather than Latin. A fellowship to Oxford University followed, and for six years he studied there mostly by himself, since, at that time, teaching at Oxford was virtually nonexistent.

After completing his studies, Smith was appointed professor of logic at Glasgow College and, later, professor of moral philosophy, a field which then included economics as one of its branches. Fortunately, he was a popular lecturer because, in those days, a professor's pay in Glasgow depended on the number of students who chose to attend his lectures. At Glasgow, Smith was responsible for helping young James Watt find a job as an instrument maker. Watt later invented the steam engine, so in this and many other respects, Smith was present virtually at the birth of the Industrial Revolution, whose prophet he was destined to become.

After thirteen years at Glasgow, Smith accepted a highly paid post as a tutor to a young Scottish nobleman with whom he spent several years in France, a customary way of educating nobles in the eighteenth century. Primarily because he was bored during these years in France, Smith began working on *The Wealth of Nations*. Several years after his return to England, in 1776, the book was published and rapidly achieved popularity.

The Wealth of Nations contains many brilliantly written passages. It was one of the first systematic treatises in economics, contributing to both theoretical and factual knowledge about the subject. Among the main points made in the book are the importance for a nation's prosperity of freedom of trade and the division of labour permitted by more widespread markets; the dangers of governmental protection of monopolies and imposition of tariffs; and the superiority of self-interest—the instrument of the "invisible hand"—over altruism as a means of improving the economy's service to the general public.

The British government was grateful for the ideas for new tax legislation Smith proposed, and to show its appreciation appointed him to the lucrative sinecure of collector of customs, which, together with the lifetime pension awarded him by his former pupil, left him very well off financially, although he eventually gave away most of his money to charitable causes.

In the eighteenth century, the intellectual world was small, and among the many people with whom Smith was acquainted were David Hume, Samuel Johnson, James Boswell, Benjamin Franklin, and Jean Jacques Rousseau. Smith got along well with everyone except Samuel Johnson, who was noted for his dislike of Scots. Smith was absent-minded and apparently timid with women, being visibly embarrassed by the public attention of the eminent ladies of Paris during his visits there. He never married, and lived with his mother most of his life. When he died, the Edinburgh newspapers recalled only that when Smith was four years old he was kidnapped by gypsies. But thanks to his writings, he is remembered for a good deal more than that.

and that a *market system* was a very good way to harness this self-interest. As he put it, with pretty clear religious overtones, in doing what is best for themselves, people are "led by an invisible hand" to promote the economic well-being of society.

Since we live in a market economy, the outlines of the process by which the invisible hand works are familiar to all of us.[6] Firms are encouraged by the profit motive to use inputs efficiently. Valuable resources (like energy) will command high prices, thus causing producers to economize on their use. The price system also guides firms' output decisions, and hence those of society. A rise in the price

[6]This topic is studied in detail in *Microeconomics*, Chapter 11.

of wheat, for example, will persuade farmers to produce more wheat and fewer soybeans. Finally, a price system determines who gets what goods through a series of voluntary exchanges. Workers with valuable skills and owners of scarce resources will be able to sell what they have at attractive prices. With the incomes they earn, they can then purchase the goods and services they want most, within the limits of their budgets.

This, in broad terms, is how a market economy solves the three basic problems facing any society: how to produce any given combination of goods efficiently, how to select an appropriate combination of goods, and how to distribute these goods sensibly among the people. As we proceed through the following chapters, you will learn much more about these issues. You will see that they constitute the central theme that permeates not only this text, but the work of economists in general. As you progress through the book, keep in mind the following two questions: **What does the market do well and what does it do poorly?** There are plenty of answers to both questions. As you will learn in coming chapters:

1. Society has many important goals. Some of them, such as producing goods and services with maximum efficiency (minimum waste), can in certain circumstances be achieved extraordinarily well by letting markets operate more or less freely.

2. Free markets will not, however, achieve all of society's goals. For example, as we will see in Part Two, they often have trouble keeping unemployment and inflation low. And there are even some goals—such as protection of the environment—for which the unfettered operation of markets may be positively harmful.

3. But even in cases where the market does not perform at all well, there may be ways of harnessing the power of the market mechanism to remedy its own deficiencies, as you will learn particularly in Part Three and in *Microeconomics*, Part Four.

Radicalism, Conservatism, and the Market Mechanism

Since economic debates often have political and ideological overtones, we think it important to close this chapter by stressing that the central theme that we have just outlined is neither a defence of nor an attack upon the capitalist system. Nor is it a "right-wing" position. One does not have to be a conservative to recognize that the market mechanism can be a helpful instrument for the pursuit of economic goals. A number of socialist countries, including Yugoslavia and Hungary, have openly and deliberately organized parts of their economies along market lines, and the People's Republic of China is now moving in that direction.

The point is not to confuse means and ends in deciding on how much to rely on market forces. Radicals and conservatives surely have different goals, and they may also differ in the means they advocate to pursue these goals. But means should be chosen on the basis of how effective they are in achieving the adopted goals, not on some ideological prejudgments.

For example, radicals may assign a much higher priority to pollution control than conservatives do. Consequently, radicals may favour very strict controls even if such controls cut into business profits; conservatives may prefer things the other way around. Nevertheless, each side may want to use the market mechanism to achieve its goals. Indeed, each side may conclude that, should it lose the political struggle and the other side's position be adopted, less damage will be done to its own goals if market methods are used.

Certainly, there are economic problems with which the market cannot deal. Indeed, we have just noted that the market is the *source* of a number of significant problems. But the evidence leads economists to believe that many economic problems are best handled by market techniques. The analysis in this book is intended to help you identify the strengths and weaknesses of the market mechanism. Forget the slogans you have heard—whether from the Left or from the Right—and make up your own mind after you have read this book.

Summary

1. Supplies of all resources are limited. Because resources are scarce, a rational decision is one that chooses the best alternative among the options that are possible with the available resources.

2. It is irrational to assign highest priority to everything. No one can afford everything, and so hard choices must be made.

3. With limited resources, if we decide to obtain more of one item, we must give up some of another item. What we give up is called the *opportunity cost* of what we get; this is the true cost of any decision. The concept of opportunity cost is one of the **12 Ideas for Beyond the Final Exam**.

4. When the market is functioning effectively, firms are led to use resources efficiently and to produce the things that consumers want most. In such cases, opportunity costs and money costs (prices) correspond closely. When the market performs poorly, or when important items of cost do not get price tags, opportunity costs and money costs can be quite different.

5. A firm's production possibilities frontier shows the combinations of goods the firm can produce with a given quantity of resources, given the state of technology. The frontier usually is not a straight line but is bowed outward because resources tend to be specialized.

6. The principle of increasing costs states that as the production of one good expands, the opportunity cost of producing another unit of this good generally increases.

7. The economy as a whole has a production possibilities frontier whose position is determined by its technology and by the available resources of land, labour, capital, and raw materials.

8. If a firm or an economy ends up at a point below its production possibilities frontier, it is using its resources inefficiently or wastefully. This is what happens, for example, when there is unemployment.

9. Economic growth means there is an outward shift in the economy's production possibilities frontier. The faster the growth, the faster this shift will occur. But growth requires a sacrifice of current consumption and this is its opportunity cost.

10. Efficiency is defined by economists as the absence of waste. It is achieved primarily by gains in productivity brought about through specialization, division of labour, and a system of exchange.

11. If an exchange is voluntary, both parties must benefit even though no new goods are produced. This is another of the **12 Ideas for Beyond the Final Exam**.

12. Every economic system must find a way to answer three basic questions: How can goods be produced most efficiently? How much of each good should be produced? How should goods be distributed?

13. The market system works very well in solving some of society's basic problems, but it fails to remedy others and may, indeed, create some of its own. Where and how it succeeds and fails constitute the theme of this book and characterize the work of economists in general.

Concepts for Review

Scarcity	Principle of increasing costs	Division of labour
Choice	Investment goods	Exchange
Opportunity cost	Efficiency	Market system
Production possibilities frontier	Specialization	Three co-ordination tasks

Questions for Discussion

1. Discuss the resource limitations that affect:
   a. the poorest person on earth
   b. the richest person on earth
   c. a firm in Switzerland
   d. a government agency in China
   e. the population of the world

2. If you were president of your university, what would you change if your budget were cut by 5 percent? By 20 percent? By 50 percent?

3. If you were to drop out of university, what things would change in your life? What, then, is the opportunity cost of your education?

4. A person rents a house for which he pays the landlord $5000 a year and keeps money in a bank account that pays 9 percent interest a year. The house is offered for sale at $70,000. Is this a good deal for the potential buyer? Where does opportunity cost enter the picture?

5. Construct graphically the production possibilities frontier for Lower Atlantis given in the table at the top of the next column.

   Does the principle of increasing cost hold in Lower Atlantis?

PRODUCTION POSSIBILITIES FOR LOWER ATLANTIS, 1986

SOUFFLÉS (millions)	COMPUTERS (thousands)
75	0
60	12
45	22
30	30
15	36
0	40

6. Consider two alternatives for Lower Atlantis in the year 1986. In case (a) its inhabitants eat 60 million soufflés and build only 12,000 computers. In case (b) the population eats only 15 million soufflés but builds 36,000 computers. Which case will lead to a more generous production possibilities frontier for Atlantis in 1987? (*Note*: In Atlantis, computers are used for cooking soufflés.)

7. Mel's Sports Shop sells two brands of tennis balls. Brand X costs Mel $1.50 per can, and Brand Y costs Mel $2 per can. Draw Mel's production possibilities frontier if he has $60 to spend on tennis balls. Why is it not "bowed out"?

Supply and Demand: An Initial Look

Reformers have the idea that
change can be achieved by
brute sanity.
GEORGE BERNARD SHAW

If the issues of scarcity, choice, and co-ordination constitute the basic *problem* of economics, then the mechanism of supply and demand is its basic investigative tool. Whether your course concentrates on macroeconomics or microeconomics, you will find that the so-called law of supply and demand is the fundamental tool of economic analysis. Supply and demand analysis is used in this book to study issues seemingly as diverse as inflation and unemployment, the international value of the dollar, government regulation of business, and protection of the environment. So careful study of this chapter will pay rich dividends.

The chapter describes the rudiments of supply and demand analysis in steps. We begin with demand, then add supply, and finally put the two sides together. *Supply and demand curves*—graphs that relate price to quantity supplied and quantity demanded, respectively—are explained and used to show how prices and quantities are determined in a free market. Influences that shift either the demand curve or the supply curve are catalogued briefly. And the analysis is used to explain why housing prices in Calgary and Edmonton rose so dramatically following the "energy crisis" in the 1970s, and why the home-computer industry has grown so fast.

One major theme of this chapter is that governments around the globe and throughout recorded history have attempted to tamper with the price mechanism. We will see that these bouts with Adam Smith's invisible hand often have produced undesired side effects that surprised and dismayed the authorities. And we will show that many of these unfortunate effects were no accidents but were inherent consequences of interfering with the operation of free markets. The invisible hand fights back!

Finally, a word of caution. This chapter makes heavy use of graphs such as those described in Chapter 2. If you encounter difficulties with these graphs, we suggest you review pages 19–34.

Fighting the Invisible Hand

Adam Smith was a great admirer of the price system. He marvelled at its intricacies and extolled its accomplishments. Many people since Smith's time have shared his enthusiasm; but many others have not. His contemporaries in the American colonies, for example, were often unhappy with the prices produced by free markets and thought they could do better by legislative decree. And there have been countless other instances in which the public's sense of justice was outraged by the prices charged on the open market, particularly when the sellers of the expensive items did not enjoy great popularity—landlords, moneylenders, and oil companies are good examples.

Attempts to control interest rates (which may be thought of as the price of borrowing money) go back hundreds of years before the birth of Christ, at least to the code of laws compiled under Hammurabi in Babylonia about 1800 B.C. Our historical legacy also includes a rather long list of price ceilings on foods and other products imposed in the reign of Diocletian, emperor of the declining Roman Empire. More recently, Canadians have been offered the "protection" of a variety of price controls. Ceilings have been placed on prices of some items (such as energy) to protect buyers, while floors have been placed under prices of other items (such as farm products) to protect sellers. Many if not most of these measures were adopted in response to popular opinion, and there is a great outcry whenever it is proposed that any one of them be weakened or eliminated.

Yet, somehow, everything such regulation touches seems to end up in even greater disarray than it was before. Despite rent controls, rents in Vancouver and Toronto have considerably more than doubled in the last ten years. Despite laws against ticket "scalping," tickets for popular shows and sports events sell at tremendous premiums. Surplus agricultural products have had to be destroyed or stored indefinitely. The list could go on.

Still, legislators continue to turn to controls whenever the economy does not work to their satisfaction. The 1970s and 1980s have seen a return to rent controls in many Canadian cities, the Anti-Inflation Board and the "6 and 5" program for wage restraint in the public sector, a web of controls over energy prices, and the continued use of agricultural price support schemes.

Interferences with the "Law" of Supply and Demand
Public opinion frequently encourages legislative attempts to "repeal the law of supply and demand" by controlling prices. The consequences usually are quite unfortunate, exacting heavy costs from the general public and often aggravating the problem the legislation was intended to cure. This is another of the **12 Ideas for Beyond the Final Exam**, and it will occupy our attention throughout this chapter.

To understand what goes wrong when markets are tampered with, we must first learn how they operate when they are unfettered. This chapter takes a first step in that direction by studying the machinery of supply and demand. Then, at the end of the chapter, we return to the issue of price controls, illustrating the problems that can arise by case studies of rent controls and price supports for milk.

We begin our analysis on the demand side of the market.

Demand and Quantity Demanded

Non-economists are apt to think of consumer demands as fixed amounts. For example, when the production of a new type of machine tool is proposed, management asks "What is its market potential? How many will we be able to sell?" Similarly, government bureaus conduct studies to determine how many engineers will be "required" in succeeding years.

Economists respond that such questions are not well posed—that there is no *single* number that describes the information required. Rather, they say, the "market potential" for machine tools or the number of engineers that will be "required" depends on a great number of things, *including the price that will be charged for each.*

Price Controls
in the Eighteenth Century

The following excerpts illustrate the unfortunate results that have followed from two of the many attempts to override market forces with legislation that have occurred over the years. In these examples, price ceilings made it unprofitable for suppliers to operate, so that scarcities and lost jobs were the unintended by-products.

The French Revolution

During the twenty months between May 1793 and December 1794, the Revolutionary Government of the new French Republic tried almost every experiment in wage and price controls which has been attempted before or since....

...[The] first Law of the Maximum, as it was called, provided that the price of grain and flour in each district of France should be the average of local market prices which were in effect from January to May 1793....

...By the summer of 1794, demands were coming from all over the country for the immediate repeal of the Law. In some towns in the South the people were so badly fed that they were collapsing in the streets from lack of nourishment. The department of the Nord complained bitterly that their shortages all began just after the passage of the by now hated Law of the Maximum. "Before that time," they wrote to the Convention in Paris, "our markets were supplied, but as soon as we fixed the price of wheat and rye we saw no more of those grains. The other kinds not subject to the maximum were the only ones brought in. The deputies of the Convention ordered us to fix a maximum for all grains. We obeyed and henceforth grain of every sort disappeared from the markets. What is the inference? This, that the establish-ment of a maximum brings famine in the midst of abundance. What is the remedy? Abolish the maximum."

...When Robespierre and his colleagues were being carried through the streets of Paris on their way to their executions, the mob jeered their last insult: "There goes the dirty Maximum."

Early Canada—Louisbourg

During 1750 rules were made as to the price that must be charged for fresh cod fish. It was, by this order, explicitly forbidden for fishermen to refuse to sell their fish at the posted price provided only that the buyer was solvent. To appreciate the serious nature of this law, it is necessary to remember that the bulk of New France's wealth was derived from the cod fishery. Of course, from time to time this regulation led to desperate circumstances for the fishermen and there is some reason to believe that it was responsible for the decline in the fishery in that area of New France.

SOURCE: Robert L. Schuettinger, "The Historical Record: A Survey of Wage and Price Controls over Fifty Centuries," in *Tax-Based Incomes Policies—A Cure for Inflation?* edited by M. Walker (Vancouver: The Fraser Institute, 1982), pages 67, 73–76.

The **quantity demanded** of any product normally depends on its price. Quantity demanded also has a number of other determinants, including population size, consumer incomes, tastes, and the prices of other products.

Because of the central role of prices in a market economy, we begin our study of demand by focusing on the relationship between quantity demanded and price. Shortly, we will bring the other determinants of quantity demanded back into the picture.

Consider, as an example, the quantity of milk demanded. Almost everyone purchases at least some milk. However, if the price of milk is very high, its "market potential" may be very small. People will find ways to get along with less milk, perhaps by switching to tea or coffee. If the price declines, people will be encouraged to drink more milk. They may give their children larger portions or switch away from juices and sodas. Thus:

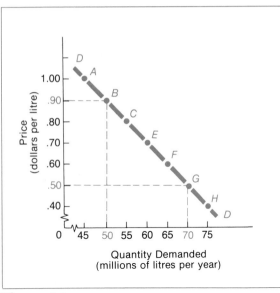

Figure 4-1

DEMAND CURVE FOR MILK

This curve shows the relation between price and quantity demanded. To sell 70 million litres per year, the price must be only 50¢ (point *G*). If, instead, price is 90¢ only 50 million litres will be demanded (point *B*). To sell more milk, the price must be reduced. That is what the negative slope of the demand curve means.

Table 4-1

DEMAND SCHEDULE FOR MILK

PRICE (dollars per litre)	QUANTITY DEMANDED (millions of litres per year)	LABEL IN FIGURE 4-1
1.00	45	A
0.90	50	B
0.80	55	C
0.70	60	E
0.60	65	F
0.50	70	G
0.40	75	H

There is no *one* demand figure for milk, for machine tools, or for engineers. Rather there is a series of alternative quantities demanded, each corresponding to a different price.

The Demand Schedule

*A **demand schedule** is a table showing how the quantity demanded of some product during a specified period of time changes as the price of that product changes, holding all other determinants of quantity demanded constant.*

Table 4-1 displays this information for milk in what we call a **demand schedule**. It shows the quantity of milk that will be demanded in a year at each possible price ranging from $1 to 40¢ per litre. We see, for example, that at a relatively low price, like 50¢ per litre, customers wish to purchase 70 million litres per year. But if the price were to rise to, say, 90¢ per litre, quantity demanded would fall to 50 million litres.

Common sense tells us why this should be so.[1] First, as prices rise, some customers will reduce their consumption of milk. Second, higher prices will induce some customers to drop out of the market entirely—for example, by switching to soda or juice. On both counts, quantity demanded will decline as the price rises.

As the price of an item rises, the quantity demanded normally falls. As the price falls, the quantity demanded normally rises.

The Demand Curve

*A **demand curve** is a graph showing how the quantity demanded of some product during a specified period of time will change as the price of that product changes, holding all other determinants of quantity demanded constant.*

The information contained in Table 4-1 can be summarized in a graph, which we call a **demand curve**, displayed in Figure 4-1. Each point in the graph corresponds to a line in the table. For example, point *B* corresponds to the second line in the table, indicating that at a price of 90¢ per litre, 50 million litres per year will be demanded. Since the quantity demanded declines as the price increases, the demand curve has a negative slope.[2]

Notice the last phrase in the definitions of the demand schedule and the demand curve: "holding all other determinants of quantity demanded constant." These "other things" include consumer incomes and preferences, the prices of

---

[1]This common-sense answer is examined more fully in *Microeconomics*, Chapter 5.

[2]If you need to review the concept of *slope*, refer back to Chapter 2, especially pages 21–24.

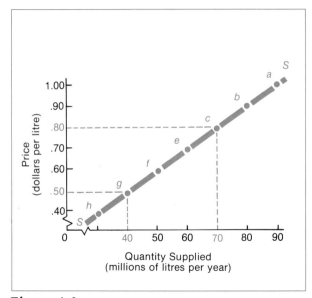

Figure 4-2
SUPPLY CURVE FOR MILK
This curve shows the relation between the price of milk and the quantity supplied. To stimulate a greater quantity supplied, price must be increased. That is the meaning of the positive slope of the supply curve.

Table 4-2
SUPPLY SCHEDULE FOR MILK

PRICE (dollars per litre)	QUANTITY SUPPLIED (millions of litres per year)	LABEL IN FIGURE 4-2
1.00	90	a
0.90	80	b
0.80	70	c
0.70	60	e
0.60	50	f
0.50	40	g
0.40	30	h

soda and orange juice, and perhaps even advertising by the dairy association. We will examine the influences of these factors later in the chapter. First, however, let's look at the supply side of the market.

Supply and Quantity Supplied

Like quantity demanded, the quantity of milk that is supplied by dairy farmers is not a fixed number but also depends on many things. Obviously, if there are more dairy farms, or larger ones, we expect more milk to be supplied. Or if bad weather deprives the cows of their feed, they may give less milk. As before, however, let's turn our attention first to the relationship between *quantity supplied* and one of its major determinants—the price of milk.

Economists generally suppose that a higher price calls forth a greater quantity supplied. Why? Remember our analysis of the principle of increasing cost in Chapter 3 (page 39). According to that principle, as more of any farmer's (or the nation's) resources are devoted to milk production, the cost of obtaining another litre of milk increases. Farmers will therefore find it profitable to raise milk production only if they can sell the milk at a higher price—high enough to cover the higher costs involved.

Looked at the other way around, we have just concluded that higher prices normally will be required to persuade farmers to raise milk production. This idea is quite general and applies to the supply of most goods and services.[3] As long as suppliers want to make profits, and the principle of increasing costs holds:

As the price of an item rises, the quantity supplied normally rises. As the price falls, the quantity supplied normally falls.

The Supply Schedule and the Supply Curve
The relationship between the price of milk and its quantity supplied is recorded in Table 4-2, which we call a **supply schedule**. The table shows that a low price

A **supply schedule** is a table showing how the quantity supplied of some product during a specified period of time changes as the price of that product changes, holding all other determinants of quantity supplied constant.

[3]This analysis is carried out in much greater detail in *Microeconomics*, Chapters 7 and 8.

like 50¢ per litre will induce suppliers to provide only 40 million litres, while a higher price, like 80¢ will induce them to provide much more—70 million litres.

As you might have guessed, when information like this is plotted on a graph, it is called a **supply curve**. Figure 4-2 is the supply curve corresponding to the supply schedule in Table 4-2. It slopes upward because quantity supplied is higher when price is higher.

Notice again the same phrase in the definition: "holding all other determinants of quantity supplied constant." We will return to these "other determinants" a bit later. But first we are ready to put demand and supply together.

Equilibrium of Supply and Demand

To analyse how price is determined in a free market, we must compare the desires of consumers (demand) with the desires of producers (supply) and see whether the two sets of plans are consistent. Table 4-3 and Figure 4-3 are designed to help us do this.

Table 4-3 brings together the demand schedule from Table 4-1 and the supply schedule from Table 4-2. Similarly, Figure 4-3 puts together the demand curve from Figure 4-1 and the supply curve from Figure 4-2 on a single graph. Such a graphic device is called a **supply-demand diagram**, and we will encounter many of them in this book. Notice that, for reasons already discussed, the demand curve has a negative slope and the supply curve has a positive slope. Most supply-demand diagrams are drawn with slopes like these.

There is only one point in Figure 4-3, point *E*, at which the supply curve and the demand curve intersect. At the price corresponding to point *E*, which is 70¢ per litre, the quantity supplied is equal to the quantity demanded. At a lower price, such as 50¢, only 40 million litres of milk will be supplied (point *g*) whereas 70 million litres will be demanded (point *G*). Thus, quantity demanded will exceed quantity supplied. There will be a **shortage** equal to 70 – 40 = 30 million litres.

Alternatively, at a higher price, such as $1, quantity supplied will be 90 million litres (point *a*) while quantity demanded will be only 45 million (point *A*). Quantity supplied will exceed quantity demanded, so there will be a **surplus** equal to 90 – 45 = 45 million litres.

Since 70¢ is the price at which quantity supplied and quantity demanded are equal, we say that 70¢ per litre is the **equilibrium price** in this market. Similarly, 60 million litres per year is the **equilibrium quantity** of milk.

The term "equilibrium" merits a little explanation, since it arises so frequently in economic analysis. An **equilibrium** is a situation in which there are no inherent forces that produce change; that is, a situation that does not contain the seeds of its own destruction. Think, for example, of a pendulum at rest at its centre point. If no outside force (such as a person's hand) comes to push it, the pendulum will remain where it is; it is in *equilibrium*.

But, if someone gives the pendulum a shove, its equilibrium will be disturbed and it will start to move upward. When it reaches the top of its arc, the pendulum will, for an instant, be at rest again. But this is not an equilibrium position. A force known as gravity will pull the pendulum downward, and thereafter its motion from side to side will be governed by gravity and friction. Eventually, we know, the pendulum must return to the point at which it started, which is its only equilibrium position. At any other point inherent forces will cause the pendulum to move.

The concept of equilibrium in economics is similar and can be illustrated by our supply and demand example. Why is no price other than 70¢ an equilibrium price in Table 4-3 or Figure 4-3? What forces will change any other price?

Consider first a low price like 50¢, at which quantity demanded (70 million) exceeds quantity supplied (40 million). If the price were this low, there would be many frustrated customers unable to purchase the quantities they desire. They

A **supply curve** is a graph showing how the quantity supplied of some product during a specified period of time will change as the price of that product changes, holding all other determinants of quantity supplied constant.

A **shortage** is an excess of quantity demanded over quantity supplied. When there is a shortage, buyers cannot purchase the quantities they desire.

A **surplus** is an excess of quantity supplied over quantity demanded. When there is a surplus, sellers cannot sell the quantities they desire to supply.

An **equilibrium** is a situation in which there are no inherent forces that produce change. Changes away from an equilibrium position will occur only as a result of "outside events" that disturb the status quo.

Table 4-3

DETERMINATION OF THE EQUILIBRIUM PRICE AND QUANTITY OF MILK

PRICE (dollars per litre)	QUANTITY DEMANDED	QUANTITY SUPPLIED	SURPLUS OR SHORTAGE?	PRICE WILL:
	(millions of litres per year)			
1.00	45	90	Surplus	Fall
0.90	50	80	Surplus	Fall
0.80	55	70	Surplus	Fall
0.70	60	60	Neither	Remain the same
0.60	65	50	Shortage	Rise
0.50	70	40	Shortage	Rise
0.40	75	30	Shortage	Rise

would compete with one another for the available milk. Some would offer more than the prevailing price and, as customers tried to outbid one another, the market price would be forced up. In other words, a price below the equilibrium price cannot persist in a free market because a shortage sets in motion powerful economic forces that push price upward.

Similar forces operate if the market price is *above* the equilibrium price. If, for example, the price should settle at $1, Table 4–3 tells us that quantity supplied (90 million) would far exceed quantity demanded (45 million). Sellers would be unable to sell their desired quantities of milk at the prevailing price, and some would find it in their interest to undercut their competitors by reducing price. This process of competitive price-cutting would continue as long as the surplus persisted, that is, as long as quantity supplied exceeded quantity demanded. Thus, a price above the equilibrium price cannot persist indefinitely.

We are left with only one conclusion. The price 70¢ per litre and the quantity 60 million litres is the only price-quantity combination that does not sow the seeds of its own destruction. It is the only *equilibrium*. Any lower price must rise, and any higher price must fall. It is as if natural economic forces place a magnet at point E that attracts the market just like gravity attracts the pendulum.

The analogy to a pendulum is worth pursuing further. Most pendulums are more frequently in motion than at rest. However, unless they are repeatedly buffeted by outside forces (which, of course, is exactly what happens to pendulums used in clocks), pendulums gradually return to their resting points. The same is

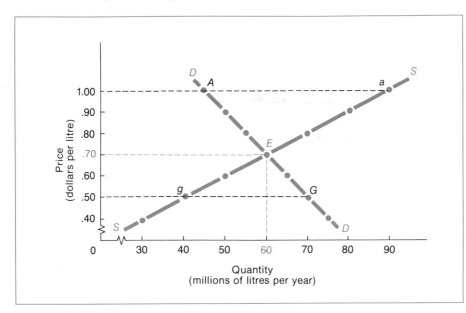

Figure 4-3

SUPPLY–DEMAND EQUILIBRIUM

In a free market, price and quantity are determined by the intersection of the supply curve and the demand curve. In this example, the equilibrium price is 70¢ and the equilibrium quantity is 60 million litres of milk per year. Any other price is inconsistent with equilibrium. For example, at a price of 50¢, quantity demanded is 70 million litres (point *C*), while quantity supplied is only 40 million litres (point *g*), so that price will be driven up by the unsatisfied demand.

true of price and quantity in a free market. Markets are not always in equilibrium, but, if they are not interfered with, we have good reason to believe that they normally are *moving toward equilibrium.*

In principle, in a free market the forces of supply and demand are capable of selecting an equilibrium price and an equilibrium quantity toward which, in practice, we may expect actual price and actual quantity to gravitate.

The last interesting aspect of the analogy concerns the "outside forces" of which we have spoken. A pendulum that is being blown by the wind or pushed by a hand does not remain in equilibrium. Similarly, many outside forces can disturb a market equilibrium. A frost in Florida will disturb equilibrium in the market for oranges. A strike by miners will disturb equilibrium in the market for coal.

Many of these outside influences actually *change the equilibrium price and quantity* by shifting either the supply curve or the demand curve. If you look again at Figure 4–3, you can see clearly that any event that causes *either* the demand curve *or* the supply curve to shift will also cause the equilibrium price and quantity to change. Such events constitute the "other things" that we held constant in our definitions of supply and demand curves. We are now ready to analyse how these outside forces affect the equilibrium of supply and demand, beginning on the demand side.

Shifts of the Demand Curve

Returning to our example of milk, we noted earlier that the quantity of milk demanded is probably influenced by a variety of things other than the price of milk. Changes in population, consumer income, and the prices of alternative beverages such as soda and orange juice presumably cause changes in the quantity of milk demanded, even if the price of milk is unchanged.

Since the demand curve for milk depicts only the relationship between the quantity of milk demanded and the price of milk, holding all other factors constant, a change in any of these other factors produces a *shift of the entire demand curve.* That is:

A change in the price of a good produces a **movement along a fixed demand curve**. By contrast, a change in any other variable that influences quantity demanded produces a **shift of the demand curve**. If consumers want to buy *more* at any given price than they wanted previously, the demand curve shifts to the right (or outward). If they desire less at any given price, the demand curve shifts to the left (or inward).

To make this general principle more concrete and to show some of its many applications, let us consider some specific examples.

1. ***Consumer incomes.*** If incomes increase, consumers may purchase more of many foods, including milk, even if the price of milk remains the same. That is, *increases in income normally shift demand curves outward to the right*, as depicted in Figure 4-4(a). In this example, the quantity demanded at the old equilibrium price of 70¢ increases from 60 million litres per year (point E on demand curve D_0D_0) to 75 million (point R on demand curve D_1D_1). We know that 70¢ is no longer the equilibrium price, since at this price quantity demanded (75 million) exceeds quantity supplied (60 million). To restore equilibrium, price will have to rise. The diagram shows the new equilibrium at point T, where the price is 80¢ per litre and the quantity (demanded and supplied) is 70 million litres per year. This illustrates a general result.

Any factor that causes the demand curve to shift outward to the right, and does not affect the supply curve, will raise the equilibrium price and the equilibrium quantity.[4]

Everything works in reverse if consumer incomes fall. Figure 4–4(b) depicts a leftward (inward) shift of the demand curve that results from a decline in consumer incomes. For example, the quantity demanded at the previous equilibrium price (70¢) falls from 60 million litres (point E) to 45 million (point L on demand curve D_2D_2). At the initial price, quantity supplied must begin to fall. The new equilibrium will eventually be established at point M, where the price is 60¢ and both quantity demanded and quantity supplied are 50 million. In general:

Any factor that shifts the demand curve inward to the left and does not affect the supply curve will lower both the equilibrium price and the equilibrium quantity.

2. **Population.**   Population growth should affect quantity demanded in more or less the same way as increases in consumer incomes. A larger population will presumably wish to consume more milk, even if the price of milk is unchanged, thus shifting the entire demand curve to the right as in Figure 4–4(a). The equilibrium price and quantity both rise. Similarly, a decrease in population should shift the demand curve for milk to the left, as in Figure 4–4(b), causing equilibrium price and quantity to fall.

3. **Consumer preferences.**   If the dairy industry mounts a successful advertising campaign extolling the benefits of drinking milk, families may decide to raise their quantities demanded. This would shift the entire demand curve for

[4]This statement, like many others in the text, assumes that the demand curve is downward-sloping and the supply curve is upward-sloping.

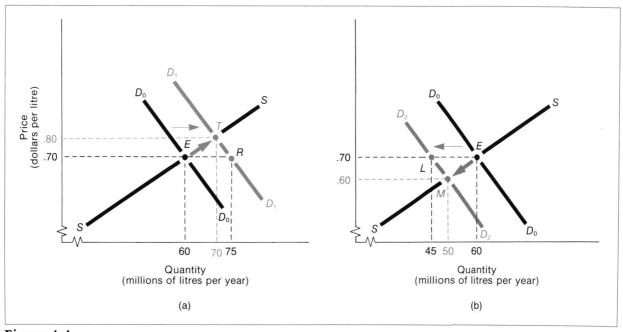

Figure 4-4
THE EFFECTS OF SHIFTS OF THE DEMAND CURVE
A shift of the demand curve will change the equilibrium price and quantity in a free market. In part (a), the demand curve shifts outward from D_0D_0 to D_1D_1. As a result, equilibrium moves from point E to point T; both price and quantity rise. In part (b), the demand curve shifts inward from D_0D_0 to D_2D_2, and equilibrium moves from point E to point M; both price and quantity fall.

milk to the right, as in Figure 4–4(a). Alternatively, a medical report on the dangers of high cholesterol may persuade consumers to drink less milk, thereby shifting the demand curve inward, as in Figure 4–4(b).

Again, these are quite general phenomena. *If consumer preferences shift in favour of a particular item, that item's demand curve will shift outward to the right, causing both price and quantity to rise* [Figure 4–4(a)]. *Conversely, if consumer preferences shift against a particular item, that item's demand curve will shift inward to the left, causing price and quantity to fall* [Figure 4–4(b)].

4. **Prices and availability of related goods.** Because soda, orange juice, and coffee are popular drinks that compete with milk, a change in the price of any of these beverages can be expected to shift the demand curve for milk. If any of these alternative drinks become cheaper, some consumers will switch away from milk. Thus the demand curve for milk will shift to the left, as in Figure 4–4(b). The introduction of an entirely new beverage—like coconut milk—can be expected to have a similar effect.

But other price changes shift the demand curve for milk in the opposite direction. For example, suppose that cookies, a commodity that goes well with milk, become less expensive. This may induce some consumers to drink more milk and thus shift the demand curve for milk to the right as in Figure 4–4(a).

Common sense normally will tell us in which direction a price change for a related good will shift the demand curve for a good in question. *Increases in the prices of goods that are substitutes for the good in question (as soda is for milk) move the demand curve to the right, thus raising both the equilibrium price and quantity. Increases in the prices of goods that are normally used together with the good in question (such as cookies and milk) shift the demand curve to the left, thus lowering both the equilibrium price and the quantity.*

Application: Housing Prices in Calgary and Edmonton During the Energy Crisis

While the preceding list does not exhaust the possible influences on quantity demanded, enough has been said to indicate the principles involved. Let us therefore turn to a concrete example.

In 1973, the Organization of Petroleum Exporting Countries (OPEC) quadrupled its selling price of oil. This led to a dramatic increase in the demand for oil from other sources, such as Western Canada. The resulting boom in the energy-related industries in Alberta meant that the demand for homes in Calgary and Edmonton in particular soared, as did housing prices and rents. Average housing prices in these cities rose from $30,000 in 1973 to about $90,000 in 1980, and there was a construction boom in both cities.

Our supply and demand diagram makes it easy to interpret these events. The boom in the energy industries caused a sharp rightward shift of the demand curve for houses in Calgary and Edmonton. As Figure 4–5 shows, we expect such a shift to raise housing prices and to increase the number of homes. This is precisely what happened. After 1980, however, the world recession and certain aspects of the National Energy Program led to a decline in the energy industries in Alberta. This means that the demand curve in Figure 4–5 shifted back to the left, and it is therefore no surprise that housing prices declined in Calgary and Edmonton during the 1980s, and that housing construction halted.

Shifts of the Supply Curve

Like quantity demanded, the quantity supplied on a market typically responds to a great number of influences other than price. The weather, the cost of feed, the number and size of dairy farms, and a variety of other factors all influence how much milk will be brought to market. Since the supply curve depicts only the relationship between the price of milk and the quantity of milk demanded, holding

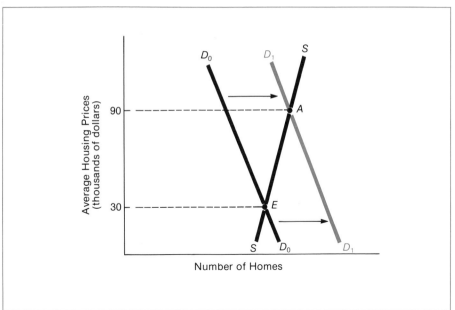

Figure 4-5
THE EFFECT OF THE
ENERGY CRISIS ON
HOUSING PRICES IN
CALGARY AND EDMONTON
The energy crisis of the 1970s
caused a rightward shift of the
demand curve for houses in
Calgary and Edmonton, from D_0D_0
to D_1D_1. As a consequence, the
market equilibrium point shifted
from E to A. Price and quantity
both increased.

all other factors constant, a change in any of these other factors will cause the entire supply curve to shift. That is:

A change in the price of the good causes a **movement along a fixed supply curve**. But price is not the only influence on quantity supplied. And, if any of these other influences changes, **the entire supply curve shifts**.

Let us consider what some of these other factors are, and how they shift the supply curve.

1. **Size of the industry.** We begin with the most obvious factor. If more farmers enter the milk industry, the quantity supplied at any given price probably will increase. For example, if each farm provides 60,000 litres of milk per year when the price is 70¢ per litre, then 1000 farmers provide 60 million litres and 1300 farmers provide 78 million. Thus, the more firms that are attracted to the industry, the greater will be the quantity of milk supplied at any given price and, hence, the farther to the right will be the supply curve.

Figure 4-6(a) illustrates the effect of an expansion of the industry from 1000 farms to 1300 farms—a rightward shift of the supply curve from S_0S_0 to S_1S_1. Notice that at the initial price of 70¢, the quantity supplied after the shift is 78 million litres (point I on supply curve S_1S_1), which exceeds the quantity demanded of 60 million (point E on supply curve S_0S_0). We can see in the graph that the price of 70¢ is too high to be the equilibrium price; so price must fall. The diagram shows the new equilibrium at point J, where the price is 60¢ per litre and the quantity is 65 million litres. The general point is that:

Any factor that shifts the supply curve outward to the right, and does not affect the demand curve, will lower the equilibrium price and raise the equilibrium quantity.

This must *always* be true if the industry's demand curve has a negative slope because the greater quantity supplied can be sold only if price is decreased to induce customers to buy more.[5]

[5]Graphically, whenever a positively sloped curve shifts to the right, its intersection point with a negatively sloping curve must always move lower (just try drawing it yourself).

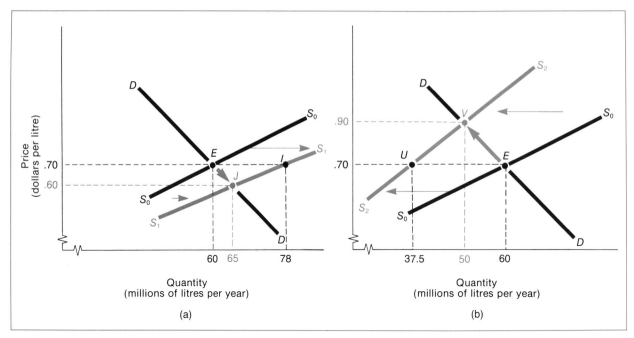

Figure 4-6

EFFECTS OF SHIFTS OF THE SUPPLY CURVE

A shift of the supply curve will change the equilibrium price and quantity in a market. In part (a), the supply curve shifts outward to the right, from S_0S_0 to S_1S_1. As a result, equilibrium moves from point E to point J; price falls as quantity increases. Part (b) illustrates the opposite case—an inward shift of the supply curve from S_0S_0 to S_2S_2. Equilibrium moves from point E to point V, which means that price rises as quantity falls.

Figure 4-6(b) illustrates the opposite case: a contraction of the industry from 1000 farms to 625 farms. The supply curve shifts inward to the left and equilibrium moves from point E to point V, where price is 90¢ and quantity is 50 million litres. In general:

Any factor that shifts the supply curve inward to the left, and does not affect the demand curve, will raise the equilibrium price and reduce the equilibrium quantity.

Even if no farmers enter or leave the industry, results like those depicted in Figure 4-6 can be produced by expansion or contraction of the existing farms. If farms get larger by adding more land, expanding the herds, and so on, the supply curve shifts to the right as in Figure 4-6(a). If farms get smaller, the supply curve shifts to the left, as in Figure 4-6(b).

2. **Technological progress.** Another influence that shifts supply curves is technological change. Suppose someone discovers that cows give more milk if Mozart is played during milking. Then, at any given price of milk, farmers will be able to provide a larger quantity of output; that is, the supply curve will shift outward to the right, as in Figure 4-6(a). This, again, illustrates a quite general influence that applies to most industries: *cost-reducing technological progress shifts the supply curve outward to the right.* Thus, as Figure 4-6(a) shows, the usual consequences of technological progress are lower prices and greater output.

3. **Prices of inputs.** Input price changes also shift supply curves. Suppose that farm workers become unionized and win a raise. Farmers will have to pay higher wages and consequently will no longer be able to provide 60 million litres of milk profitably at a price of 70¢ per litre [point E in Figure 4-6(b)].

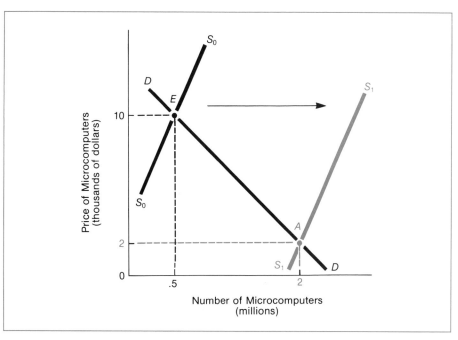

Figure 4-7
TECHNOLOGICAL CHANGE
AND THE COMPUTER
MARKET
The invention of the microchip,
and subsequent improvements in
microchip technology, caused the
supply curve of minicomputers to
shift outward to the right—moving
from $S_0 S_0$ to $S_1 S_1$. Consequently,
equilibrium shifted from point E to
point A. The price of
microcomputers fell from $10,000
to $2000, and the quantity
increased from 0.5 million to 2
million per year.

Perhaps they will provide only 37.5 million (point U on supply curve $S_2 S_2$). This example illustrates that *increases in the prices of inputs that suppliers must buy will shift the supply curve inward to the left.*

4. Prices of related outputs. Dairy farms produce more than milk. If cheese prices rise sharply, farmers may decide to use some raw milk to make cheese, thereby reducing the quantity of milk supplied. On a supply–demand diagram, the supply curve would shift inward, as in Figure 4-6(b).

Similar phenomena occur in other industries, and sometimes the effect goes in the opposite direction. For example, suppose the price of beef goes up, which increases the quantity of meat supplied. That, in turn, will cause a rise in the number of cowhides supplied at any given price of leather. Thus, a rise in the price of beef will lead to a rightward shift in the supply curve of leather. In general: *A change in the price of one good produced by a multiproduct industry may be expected to shift the supply curves of all the other goods produced by that industry.*

Application: A Computer in Every Home?

Only about a decade ago, no one owned a home computer. Now there are millions in North America, and enthusiasts look toward the day when computers will be as commonplace as television sets. What happened to bring the computer from the laboratory into the home? Did people suddenly develop a craving for computers?

Hardly. What actually happened is that scientists in the early 1970s invented the microchip—a major breakthrough that drastically reduced both the size of computers and, more important, the cost of manufacturing them. Within a few years, microcomputers were in commercial production. And microchip technology continued to improve throughout the 1970s and 1980s, leading to ever smaller, better, and cheaper computers. Today, for a few hundred dollars you can buy a desktop machine whose computing powers rival those of the giant computers of the early 1960s.

In terms of our supply and demand diagrams, the rapid technological progress in computer manufacturing shifted the supply curve dramatically to the right. As Figure 4-7 shows, a large outward shift of the supply curve should bring down the equilibrium price and increase the equilibrium quantity—which is just what happened in the computer industry. The figure calls attention to the fact that consumers naturally buy more computers as the price of computers falls (*a movement along* demand curve *DD* from *E* to *A*), even if the demand curve does not *shift*.

Restraining the Market Mechanism: Price Ceilings

As we have noted already, lawmakers and rulers have often been dissatisfied with the outcomes of the operation of the market system. All through the ages, legislators have done battle with the invisible hand. Sometimes, rather than trying to make adjustments in the workings of the market, governments have sought to raise or to lower the prices of specific commodities by decree. In many of these cases, the feeling of those in authority was that the prices set by the market mechanism were, in some sense, immorally low or immorally high. Penalties were therefore imposed on anyone offering the commodities in question at prices lower or higher than those determined by the authorities.

But the market has proven itself a formidable foe that strongly resists attempts to circumvent its workings. In case after case where legal ceilings on prices are imposed, virtually the same set of consequences ensues:

1. A persistent shortage develops of the items whose prices are controlled. Queuing, direct rationing, or any of a variety of other devices, usually inefficient and unpleasant, have to be substituted for the distribution process provided by the price mechanism. *Example*: U.S. price controls on gasoline led to long lines at service stations in 1979.

2. An illegal or "black" market often arises to supply the commodity. There are usually some individuals who are willing to take the risks involved in meeting unsatisfied demands illegally, if legal means will not do the job. *Example*: Although it is illegal in most places, ticket "scalping" occurs at most popular sporting events.

3. The prices charged on the black market are almost certainly higher than those that would prevail in a free market. After all, black marketeers expect compensation for the risk of being caught and punished. *Example*: Goods that are illegally smuggled into a country are normally quite expensive.

4. In each case, a substantial portion of the price falls into the hands of the black-market supplier instead of going to those who produce the good or who perform the service. *Example*: A constant complaint in the series of hearings that have marked the history of theatre-ticket price controls in New York City has been that the "ice" (the illegal excess charge) falls into the hands of ticket scalpers rather than going to those who invested in, produced, or acted in the play.

These points and others are best illustrated by considering a concrete example of price ceilings.

Case Studies:
(1) Rent Controls in New York City

New York is the only major city in North America that has had rent controls continuously since World War II. The objective of rent control is, of course, to protect the consumer from high rents. But most economists believe that rent control does not help the cities or their inhabitants and that, in the long run, it makes almost everyone worse off. Let's use supply–demand analysis to see what actually happens.

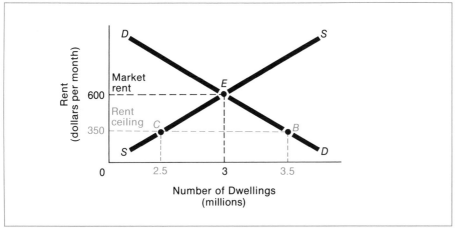

Figure 4-8
SUPPLY-DEMAND
DIAGRAM FOR HOUSING
When market forces are permitted
to set rents, the quantity of
dwellings supplied will equal the
quantity demanded. But when a
rent ceiling forces rent below the
market level, the number of
dwellings supplied (point C) will be
less than the number demanded
(point B). Thus, rent ceilings
induce housing shortages.

Figure 4-8 is a supply-demand diagram for rental units in New York. Curve *DD* is the demand curve and curve *SS* is the supply curve. Without controls, equilibrium would be at point *E*, where rents average $600 per month and 3 million units are occupied. Effective rent controls must set a ceiling price below the equilibrium price of $600, because otherwise the rent level would simply settle at the point determined by market forces. But with a low rent ceiling, such as, say, $350, the quantity of housing demanded will be 3.5 million (point *B*) while the quantity supplied will be only 2.5 million (point *C*).

The diagram shows a shortage of 1 million apartments. This theoretical concept of a "shortage" shows up in New York City as an abnormally low vacancy rate—typically about half the national urban average.

As we expect, rent controls have spawned a lively black market in New York. The black market works to raise the effective price of rent-controlled apartments in many ways, including bribes, "key money" paid to move up on the waiting list and requiring prospective tenants to purchase worthless furniture at inflated prices.

According to the diagram, rent controls reduce the quantity supplied from 3 million to 2.5 million apartments. What do we see in New York? First, some property owners, discouraged by the low rents, have converted apartment buildings into office space or other uses. Second, some apartments have not been maintained adequately. After all, rent controls create a shortage which makes even dilapidated apartments easy to rent. Third, some landlords have actually abandoned their buildings rather than pay rising tax and fuel bills. These abandoned buildings rapidly become eyesores and eventually pose threats to public health and safety.

With all these problems, why do rent controls persist in New York City? And why are some other cities moving in the same direction? Part of the explanation is that many people simply do not understand the problems that rent controls cause. Another part is that landlords are unpopular politically. But a third, and important, part of the explanation is that not everyone is hurt by rent controls, and those who benefit from controls fight hard to preserve them. In New York, for example, many tenants pay rents that are only a fraction of what their apartments would fetch on the open market.

This last point illustrates another very general phenomenon:

Virtually every price ceiling or floor creates a class of people with a vested interest in preserving the regulations because they benefit from them. These people naturally use their political influence to protect their gains, which is one reason why it is so hard to eliminate price ceilings or floors.

(2) Rent Controls in Ontario

The effects of rent control in New York and in several European cities have prompted Swedish economist Assar Lindbeck to quip: "In fact, next to bombing, rent control seems in many cases to be the most efficient technique so far known for destroying cities. . ." [6]

Despite this evidence, rent control was introduced in Ontario in 1975. Again, the evidence on the impact of the controls illustrates the power of basic supply and demand analysis. Both apartment vacancy rates and the rate of apartment construction starts declined. Cities were not "destroyed" however, and one reason is that provincial-government subsidies for apartment construction were increased dramatically. In a study of rent controls in Toronto, it is reported that the proportion of apartment starts which depended on government support increased from 13 percent in 1974 to 91 percent in 1977.[7]

Restraining the Market Mechanism: Price Floors

Interferences with the market mechanism are not always designed to keep prices low. Agricultural price supports and minimum wages are two notable examples in which the law keeps prices *above* free-market levels. Price floors are typically accompanied by a standard set of symptoms:

1. A surplus develops as some sellers cannot find buyers. *Example*: The minimum-wage law helps create high unemployment among teenagers.[8]

2. Where goods, rather than services, are involved, the surplus creates a problem of disposal. Something must be done about the excess of quantity supplied over quantity demanded. *Example*: The government has often been forced to purchase, and then store, large amounts of surplus agricultural commodities.

3. To get around the regulations, sellers may offer discounts in disguised—and often unwanted—forms. *Example*: When transatlantic air fares were more heavily regulated, airlines offered bargains on the land portions of package holidays to the U.K. that were often not fully used.

Once again, a specific example is useful.

A Case Study: Milk-Price Supports

Perhaps you have seen news items about farmers having to throw away surplus eggs, milk, or other agricultural products. The surpluses are by-products of various government programs designed to raise the incomes of farmers. For many products, a price higher than the equilibrium price is maintained through the provincial marketing boards, which stipulate production limits for each farmer. For other products, a high price is maintained because the government buys up any output that the market does not absorb at the higher price.

One example is the Canadian Dairy Commission, established in 1966. One of its purposes is to stabilize the price of dairy products at a high enough level to permit reasonable incomes to be earned by all existing dairy farmers. Generally, this involves a support price well above the free-market level, so a surplus develops, as indicated in Figure 4–9. To maintain the price above the free-market level, the government must buy the surplus milk and other dairy products. But this creates a problem. Milk is so highly perishable that it must be turned into cheese or butter or dried milk before it can be stored. Buying and storing these products is costly,

[6]Assar Lindbeck, *The Political Economy of the New Left: An Outsider's View*, Second Edition (New York: Harper & Row, 1977), page 39.

[7]Basil A. Kalymon, "Apartment Shortages and Rent Control", in *Rent Control: Myths and Realities*, edited by W. Block and E. Olsen (Vancouver: The Fraser Institute, 1981), page 241.

[8]This subject is dealt with more fully in *Microeconomics*, Chapter 22.

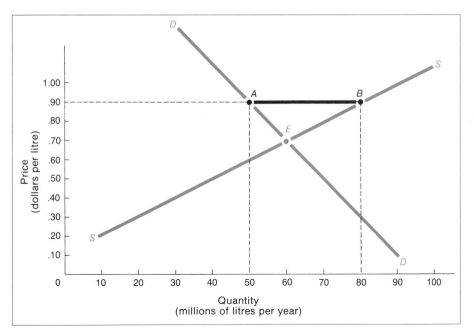

Figure 4-9
PRICE SUPPORTS FOR MILK
In this diagram, which repeats the supply and demand curves from Figure 4-3, the support price for milk (90¢ per litre) is above the equilibrium price (70¢). Quantity supplied is 80 million litres per year (point B), while quantity demanded is only 50 million (point A). To keep the price at 90¢, the government must buy 30 million litres of milk per year and store it as cheese or milk powder, or dispose of it.

so often the products are simply disposed of. Similar problems have developed in the United States and in Europe. One solution to the surplus wine that has resulted from price-support programs in Europe has been to convert it to automobile fuel (gasohol), at much expense to the taxpayer.

This analysis does not imply that individual farm incomes should be lower than they are. It simply shows how the basic forces of supply and demand lead to inefficiencies under the current methods for maintaining farm incomes.

Fixed Exchange Rates

One of the most common prices to be set by government policy is the international value of the Canadian dollar, known as the **exchange rate**. The federal government often stands ready to buy or sell quantities of foreign currencies in whatever amounts that are required to stabilize the price of the Canadian dollar. For example, for a period during 1984, the government tried to keep the value of the Canadian dollar from falling below a price of 75 cents (U.S.). They tried to maintain this price floor by trading currencies in the foreign exchange market. Whenever private traders who desired U.S. dollars or other foreign currencies could not find a trader who would give up Canadian dollars at this price (exchange rate), the Canadian authorities would buy up the otherwise unwanted Canadian currency. The authorities did this by selling off part of their foreign currency reserves. Thus the foreign exchange rate can be fixed in precisely the same manner as in the milk-price supports discussed above. The only difference is that there are no direct storage costs for holding inventories of foreign currencies. Because of this, and because a fluctuating value of the Canadian dollar is often thought to deter foreign trade, this price is heavily managed and sometimes absolutely fixed.

The **exchange rate** states the price at which one currency can be bought in terms of another currency.

Unfortunately, we must wait until Chapters 15 and 16 to assess the costs and benefits of this form of market intervention. It turns out that it very much determines which government policies the Minister of Finance can or cannot use to fight unemployment and inflation.

A Can of Worms

Our two major case studies—rent controls and milk-price supports—illustrate some of the major side effects of price floors and ceilings but barely hint at others.

And there are yet more difficulties that we have not even mentioned. For the market mechanism is a tough bird that imposes suitable retribution on those who seek to circumvent it by legislative decree. Here is a partial list of other problems that may arise when prices are controlled.

Favouritism and Corruption

When price ceilings create a shortage, someone must decide who gets the limited quantity that is available. This can lead to political favouritism, to corruption in government, or even to discrimination along racial or religious lines.

Unenforceability

Attempts to control prices are almost certain to fail in industries with numerous suppliers, simply because the regulating agency must monitor the behaviour of so many sellers. Some ways will be found to evade or to violate the law, and something akin to the free-market price will generally re-emerge. But there is a difference: since the evasion mechanism, whatever its form, will have some operating costs, those costs must be borne by someone. That someone will be the consumer.

Auxiliary Restrictions

Fears that a system of price controls will break down invariably lead to regulations designed to shore up the shaky edifice. Consumers may be told when and from whom they are permitted to buy. The powers of the police and the courts may be used to prevent the entry of new suppliers. Occasionally, an intricate system of market subdivision is imposed, giving each class of firms its protected category of operations in which others are not permitted to compete. Milk-marketing orders are one good example. Laws banning conversion of rent-controlled apartments to condominiums are another.

Limitation of Volume of Transactions

To the extent that controls succeed in affecting prices, they can be expected to reduce the volume of transactions. Curiously, this is true whether the regulated price is above or below the free market's equilibrium price. If it is set above the equilibrium price, quantity demanded will be below the equilibrium quantity. On the other hand, if the imposed price is set below the free-market level, quantity supplied will be cut down. Since sales volume cannot exceed either the quantity supplied or the quantity demanded, a reduction in the volume of transactions (and hence employment) is likely to result.

Encouragement of Inefficiency

A price that is above the equilibrium level permits the survival of less-efficient firms whose high operating costs would doom them in an unrestricted market. This invitation to continued inefficiency becomes even more serious if entry of new suppliers is prevented as part of the program of enforcement of price regulations. (This is why deregulation of the airline industry in the United States led to a painful "shake out" of the weaker companies in the early 1980s.) Moreover, with the penalties for inefficiency severely restricted, the motivation for continued economy of operation by any firm is reduced.

Misallocation of Resources

Departures from free-market prices are likely to produce misuse of the economy's resources because the connection between production costs and prices is broken. For example, shippers use trucks or barges over routes where the resource cost of rail transportation is lower because artificial restrictions impose floors on railway rates. In addition, just as more complex locks lead to more sophisticated burglary tools, more complex regulations lead to the use of yet more resources for their avoidance. New jobs are created for executives, lawyers, and economists. It may well be conjectured that at least some of the expensive services of these professionals could have been used more productively elsewhere.

Economists put it this way. Free markets are capable of dealing with the three basic co-ordination tasks outlined in Chapter 3: deciding *what* to produce, *how* to produce it, and *to whom* the goods should be distributed. Price controls throw a monkey wrench into the market mechanism. Though the market is surely not flawless, and government interferences often have praiseworthy goals, good intentions are not enough. Any government that sets out to repair what it sees as a defect in the market mechanism must take care lest it cause serious damage elsewhere. As a prominent economist once quipped, societies that are too willing to interfere with the operation of free markets soon find that the invisible hand is nowhere to be seen.

Summary

1. The quantity of a product that is demanded is not a fixed number. Rather, quantity demanded depends on such factors as the price of the product, consumer incomes, and the prices of other products.

2. The relationship between quantity demanded and price, holding all other things constant, can be displayed graphically on a demand curve.

3. For most products, the higher price, the lower the quantity demanded. So the demand curve usually has a negative slope.

4. The quantity of a product that is supplied also depends on its price and many other influences. A supply curve is a graphical representation of the relationship between quantity supplied and price, holding all other influences constant.

5. For most products, the supply curve has a positive slope, meaning that higher prices call forth greater quantities supplied.

6. A market is said to be in equilibrium when quantity supplied is equal to quantity demanded. The equilibrium price and quantity are shown by the point on a graph where the supply and demand curves intersect. In a free market, price and quantity will tend to gravitate to this point.

7. A change in quantity demanded that is caused by a change in the price of the good is represented by a movement along a fixed demand curve. A change in quantity demanded that is caused by a change in any other determinant of quantity demanded is represented by a shift of the demand curve.

8. This same distinction applies to the supply curve: Changes in price lead to movements along a fixed supply curve; changes in other determinants of quantity supplied lead to shifts of the whole supply curve.

9. Changes in consumer incomes, tastes, technology, prices of competing products, and many other influences cause shifts in either the demand curve or the supply curve and produce changes in price and quantity that can be determined from supply-demand diagrams.

10. An attempt by government regulations to force prices below or above their equilibrium levels is likely to lead to shortages or surpluses, black markets in which goods are sold at illegal prices, and to a variety of other problems. This is one of the **12 Ideas for Beyond the Final Exam**.

Concepts for Review

Demand schedule	Shortage	Shifts in vs. movements along
Demand curve	Surplus	supply and demand curves
Supply schedule	Equilibrium price and quantity	Price ceiling
Supply curve	Equilibrium	Price floor
Supply-demand diagram		Exchange rate

Questions for Discussion

1. How often do you go to the movies? Would you go less often if a ticket cost twice as much? Distinguish between your demand curve for movie tickets and your "quantity demanded" at the current price.

2. What would you expect to be the shape of a demand curve:

a. for a type of medicine that means life or death for a patient?

b. for the gasoline sold by Sam's gas station, which is surrounded by many other gas stations?

3. The following are the assumed supply and demand schedules for transistor radios:

DEMAND SCHEDULE		SUPPLY SCHEDULE	
PRICE (dollars)	QUANTITY DEMANDED	PRICE (dollars)	QUANTITY SUPPLIED
30	70,000	30	120,000
25	80,000	25	110,000
20	90,000	20	90,000
15	100,000	15	60,000
10	110,000	10	0

  a. Plot the supply and demand curves and indicate the equilibrium price and quantity.
  b. What effect will an increase in the price of copper wire (a production input) have on the equilibrium price and quantity of transistor radios, assuming all other things remain constant? Explain your answer with the help of a diagram.
  c. What effect will a decrease in the price of television sets (a substitute commodity) have on the equilibrium price and quantity of transistor radios, assuming again that all other things are held constant? Use a diagram in your answer.

4. Assume that the supply and demand schedules for wheat are the following:

PRICE (dollars)	QUANTITY DEMANDED (millions of bushels)	QUANTITY SUPPLIED (millions of bushels)
6	13	20
4	17	17
2	21	16

  a. Suppose that the government sets a floor under the price of wheat at $6. What is greater, the quantity demanded or the quantity supplied? What will be the effect on the wheat market?
  b. Now assume that the government abolishes the minimum price for wheat. What will happen to the price and the quantity of wheat consumed?
  c. Now assume that the government sets a ceiling on the price of wheat at $2. What would be the effect on the wheat market?

5. Show how the following demand curves are likely to shift in response to the indicated changes:
  a. The effect on the demand curve for boots when snowfall increases.
  b. The effect on the demand curve for tea when coffee prices fall.
  c. The effect on the demand curve for tea when sugar prices fall.

6. Discuss the likely effects of:
  a. rent ceilings on the supply of apartments.
  b. minimum wages on the demand for teenage workers.
  Use supply–demand diagrams to show what may happen in each case.

7. Drinking water is costly to supply. Draw a supply–demand diagram showing how much water would be bought if water were supplied by a private industry controlled by supply and demand. In the same diagram show how much will be consumed if water is supplied by a city government at zero charge. What do you conclude from these results about areas of the country in which water is in short supply?

8. On page 68 it is claimed that either price floors or price ceilings reduce the actual quantity exchanged in a market. Use a diagram, or diagrams, to support this conclusion, and explain the common sense behind it.

9. The same rightward shift of the demand curve may produce a very small or a very large increase in quantity, depending on the slope of the supply curve. Explain with diagrams.

10. (More difficult.) Consider the market for milk discussed in this chapter (Tables 4–1 through 4–3 and Figures 4–1 through 4–3). Suppose the government decides to fight kidney stones by levying a tax of 30¢ per litre on sales of milk. Follow these steps to analyse the effects of the tax:
  a. Construct the new supply curve (to replace Table 4–2) that relates quantity supplied to the price consumers pay. (*Hint:* Before the tax, when consumers paid 70¢, farmers supplied 60 million litres. With a 30¢ tax, when consumers pay 70¢ farmers will receive only 40¢. Table 4–2 tells us they will provide only 30 million litres at this price. This is one point on the new supply curve. The rest of the curve can be constructed in the same way.)
  b. Graph the new supply curve constructed in part (a) on the supply–demand diagram depicted in Figure 4–3. What are the new equilibrium price and quantity?
  c. Does the tax succeed in its goal of reducing the consumption of milk?
  d. How much does the equilibrium price increase? Is the price rise greater than, equal to, or less than the 30¢ tax?
  e. Who actually pays the tax, consumers or producers? (This may be a good question to discuss in class.)

II

Essentials of Macroeconomics: Aggregate Supply and Aggregate Demand

Macroeconomics and Microeconomics

Where the telescope ends,
the microscope begins.
Which of the two has the
grander view?

VICTOR HUGO

Economics traditionally has been divided into two fields: microeconomics and macroeconomics. These rather inelegant words are derived from the Greek—"micro" means something small and "macro" means something large. Although they were not specifically described as such, the basic notions and subject matter of **microeconomics** were introduced in Chapters 3 and 4. This chapter does the same for **macroeconomics**.

We begin the chapter by investigating the dividing line between microeconomics and macroeconomics: How do the two parts of the discipline differ and why? Next, we stress that while the *questions* studied by macroeconomists differ from those addressed by microeconomists, the underlying *tools* each group uses are almost the same. Supply and demand provide the basic organizing framework for constructing macroeconomic models, just as they do for microeconomic models. Third, we define some important macroeconomic concepts, like recession, inflation, and gross national product. Fourth, we look briefly at the broad sweep of Canadian economic history to obtain some evaluation of the prevalence and seriousness of the macroeconomic problems of recession and inflation. And, finally, we preview what is to come in subsequent chapters by introducing the notion of government management of the economy.

Drawing a Line Between Macroeconomics and Microeconomics

In microeconomics *we study the behaviour of individual decision-making units.* The dairy farmers and consumers of Chapter 4 are individual decision-making units. How do they decide what courses of action are in their own best interests? How are these millions of decisions co-ordinated by the market mechanism, and with what consequences? Questions like these are the substance of microeconomics and are taken up in *Microeconomics,* Parts Two through Five.

Although Plato and Aristotle might wince at the abuse of their language, microeconomics applies to the decisions of some astonishingly large units. Exxon and the American Telephone and Telegraph Company, for instance, have annual sales that exceed the total production of many nations. Yet an American economist who studies the pricing policies of AT&T is a microeconomist, whereas someone who studies inflation in Trinidad and Tobago is a macroeconomist. So the micro versus macro distinction in economics is certainly not predicated solely on size.

What, then, is the basis for this time-honoured distinction? Whereas microeconomics focuses on the decisions of individual units (no matter how large), *macroeconomics concentrates on the behaviour of entire economies* (no matter how small). Rather than looking at the price and output decisions of a single company, macroeconomists study the overall price level, unemployment rate, and other things that we call *economic aggregates*.

Aggregation and Macroeconomics

What is an "economic aggregate"? Nothing but an *abstraction* that people find convenient in describing some salient feature of economic life. For example, while we observe the prices of butter, telephone calls, and movie tickets every day, we never observe "the price level." Yet many people (not only economists) find it both meaningful and natural to speak of "the cost of living"—so natural, in fact that Statistics Canada's monthly attempts at measuring it are widely publicized by the news media.

Among the most important of these abstract notions is the concept of *national product*, which represents the total production of a nation's economy. The process by which real objects like hairpins, baseballs, cigarettes, and theatre tickets get combined into an abstraction called national product is called **aggregation**, and it is one of the foundations of macroeconomics. We can illustrate it by a simple example.

Imagine a nation called Agraria, whose economy is far simpler than the Canadian economy: Business firms in Agraria produce nothing but foodstuffs to sell to consumers. Rather than deal separately with all the markets for pizzas, candy bars, hamburgers, and so on, macroeconomists group them all into a single abstract "market for output." Thus, when macroeconomists in Agraria announce that output in Agraria rose 10 percent this year, are they referring to more potatoes or hot dogs, more soybeans or green peppers? The answer is: They do not care! In the aggregate measures of macroeconomics, output is output, no matter what form it takes.

Amalgamating many markets into one means that distinctions among different products are ignored. Can we really believe that no one cares whether the national output of Agraria consists of $800,000 worth of pickles and $200,000 worth of ravioli rather than $500,000 each of lettuce and tomatoes? Surely this is too much to swallow. Macroeconomists clearly do not believe that no one cares; instead, they rest the case for aggregation on two foundations.

1. While the *composition* of demand and supply in the various markets may be terribly interesting and important for *some* purposes (such as how income is distributed and what kinds of diets the citizens enjoy or endure), it may be of little consequence for the economy-wide issues of inflation and unemployment—the issues that concern macroeconomists.

2. During economic fluctuations, markets tend to move in unison. When demand in the economy rises, there is more demand for potatoes *and* tomatoes, more demand for artichokes *and* pickles, more demand for ravioli *and* hot dogs.

Though there are exceptions to these two principles, both seem serviceable enough as approximations. In fact, if they were not, there would be no discipline called macroeconomics, and this book would not exist. (Lest this cause you a twinge of regret, bear in mind that unemployment and inflation would be far more difficult to control without macroeconomics, and that would be even more regrettable.)

Aggregation means combining many individual markets into one overall market.

The Line of Demarcation Revisited

These two principles—that markets normally move together and that the composition of demand and supply may be unimportant for some purposes—enable us to draw a different kind of dividing line between the territories of microeconomics and macroeconomics.

In macroeconomics, we typically assume that most details of resource allocation and income distribution are of secondary importance to the study of the overall rates of inflation and unemployment.

In microeconomics, we typically ignore inflation and unemployment and focus instead on how individual markets allocate resources and distribute income.

To use a well-worn metaphor, the macroeconomist analyses the determination of the size of the economic "pie," paying scant attention to what is inside it or to how it gets divided among the dinner guests. A microeconomist, on the other hand, assumes that the pie is of the right size and shape and frets over its ingredients and its division. If you have ever baked or eaten a pie, you will realize that either approach alone is a trifle myopic.

In the majority of chapters in this book (especially in Parts Two and Three), macroeconomic issues are discussed as if they could be divorced from questions of resource allocation and income distribution. In many of the chapters in *Microeconomics* (especially in Parts Two through Five), microeconomic problems are investigated with scarcely a word about overall inflation and unemployment. This is done solely for the sake of pedagogical clarity. In reality, the crucial interconnection between macroeconomics and microeconomics is always with us. There is, after all, only one economy.

Supply and Demand in Macroeconomics

Some students reading this book will be taking a course that concentrates on macroeconomics while others will be studying microeconomics. The discussion of supply and demand in Chapter 4 serves as an invaluable introduction to both fields because the basic apparatus of supply and demand is just as important in macroeconomics as it is in microeconomics.

Figure 5–1 shows two diagrams that should look familiar from Chapter 4. In Figure 5–1(a), there is a downward-sloping demand curve, labelled DD, and an upward-sloping supply curve, labelled SS. The axes labelled "Price" and "Quantity" do not specify what commodity they refer to because this is a multipurpose diagram. To start on familiar terrain, first imagine that this is a picture of the market for milk, so the price axis measures the price of milk while the quantity axis measures the quantity of milk demanded and supplied. As we know, if there are no interferences with the operation of a free market, equilibrium will be at point E with a price P_0 and a quantity of output Q_0.

Next, suppose something happens to shift the demand curve outward. For example, we learned in Chapter 4 that an increase in consumer incomes might do this. Figure 5–1(b) shows this shift as a rightward movement of the demand curve from D_0D_0 to D_1D_1. Equilibrium has shifted from E to A, so both price and output have risen.

Now let us reinterpret Figure 5–1 as representing an abstract market for "national product." This is one of those abstractions—an economic aggregate—that we described earlier. No one has ever seen, touched, smelled, or eaten a "unit of national product," but these are the kinds of abstractions upon which macroeconomic analysis is built. Consistent with this reinterpretation, think of the price measured on the vertical axis as being another abstraction—the overall price index, or "cost of living."[1] Then curve DD in Figure 5–1(a) is called an **aggregate-demand curve**, and curve SS is called an **aggregate-supply curve**.

The **aggregate-demand curve** shows the quantity of national product that is demanded at each possible value of the price level.

The **aggregate-supply curve** shows the quantity of national product that is supplied at each possible value of the price level.

[1] The appendix to Chapter 6 explains how such price indexes are calculated.

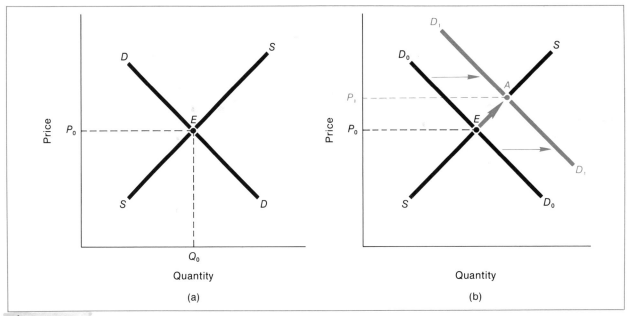

Figure 5-1
TWO INTERPRETATIONS OF A SHIFT IN THE DEMAND CURVE
Part (a) shows an equilibrium at point *E*, where demand curve *DD* intersects supply curve *SS*. Part (b) shows how this equilibrium moves from point *E* to point *A* if the demand curve moves outward. If this graph represents the market for milk as it did in the previous chapter, then it shows an increase in the price of milk. But if the graph represents the aggregate market for "national product," then it shows inflation—a rise in the general price level.

Inflation refers to a sustained *increase* in the general price level.

With this reinterpretation, Figure 5-1(b) can depict the macroeconomic problem of **inflation**. We see from the figure that the outward shift of the aggregate-demand curve, whatever its cause, pushes the price level up from P_0 to P_1. If aggregate demand keeps shifting out month after month, the economy will suffer from inflation, that is, a sustained increase in the general price level.

The other principal problems of macroeconomics, recession and unemployment, also can be illustrated on a supply–demand diagram, this time by shifting the demand curve in the opposite direction. Figure 5-2 repeats the supply and demand curves of Figure 5-1(a) and in addition depicts a leftward shift of the aggregate-demand curve from D_0D_0 to D_2D_2. Equilibrium now moves from point *E* to point *B* so that national product (total output) declines from Q_0 to Q_2. This is what we normally mean by a **recession**.

A **recession** is a period of time during which the total output of the economy declines.

Gross National Product

Gross national product (GNP) is the sum of the money values of all final goods and services produced by the economy during a specified period of time, usually one year.

The economy's total output, we have just seen, is one of the major variables of concern to macroeconomists. While there are several ways to measure it, the most popular choice undoubtedly is the **gross national product**, a term you have probably encountered in the news media. The gross national product, or "GNP" for short, is the most comprehensive measure of the output of all the factories, offices, and shops in the Canadian economy. Specifically, it is the sum of the money values of all final goods and services produced within the year.

Several features of this definition need to be underscored.[2] First, you will notice that:

We add up the *money values* of things.

[2]Certain exceptions to the definition, which are not important here, are noted in the appendix to Chapter 7, especially on pages 133–34.

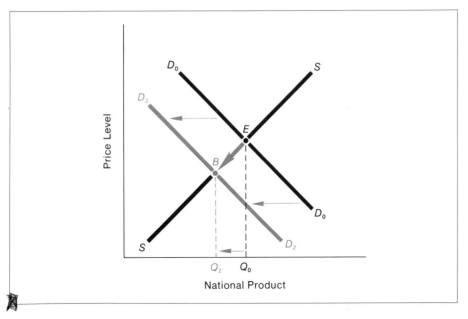

Figure 5-2
AN ECONOMY SLIPPING
INTO A RECESSION
In this aggregate supply-demand
diagram, there is an initial
equilibrium at point E, where
demand curve D_0D_0 intersects
supply curve SS. When the
demand curve falls from D_0D_0 to
D_2D_2, equilibrium moves to point B,
and output falls from Q_0 to Q_2.

The GNP consists of a bewildering variety of goods and services: mousetraps and computers, bologna and caviar, ballet performances and rock concerts, cars and textbooks. How are we to combine all of these into a single number? To an economist, the natural way to do this is first to convert every good and service into *money* terms. If we want to add 10 apples and 20 oranges, we first ask: How much *money* does each cost? If apples cost 20¢ and oranges cost 25¢, then the apples count for $2 and the oranges for $5, so the sum is $7 worth of "output." The market *price* of each good or service is used as an indicator of its *value* to society simply because *someone* is willing to pay that much money for it.

This decision raises the question of what prices to use in valuing the different outputs. The official data offer two choices. First, we can value each good and service at the price at which it was actually sold during the year. If we do this, the resulting measure is called **nominal GNP**, or *money GNP*, or *GNP in current dollars*. This seems like a perfectly sensible choice. But as a measure of output, it has one serious drawback: nominal GNP rises when prices rise, even if there is no increase in actual production. For example, if hamburgers cost $1 this year but cost only 75¢ last year, then 100 hamburgers will contribute $100 to this year's nominal GNP but only $75 to last year's. But 100 hamburgers are still 100 hamburgers—output has not grown.

For this reason, government statisticians have devised an alternative measure that corrects for inflation by valuing all goods and services at some fixed set of prices. (Currently, the prices of 1971 are used.) For example, if the hamburgers were valued at 75¢ each in both years, $75 worth of hamburger output would be included in GNP in each year. When we treat every output in this way, we obtain the **real GNP** or *GNP in constant dollars*. The news media often refer to it as "GNP corrected for inflation." Throughout most of this book, and certainly when we are discussing the nation's output, it is the real GNP that we shall be concerned with. The distinction between nominal and real GNP leads us to a working definition of a *recession* as a period in which *real* GNP declines. For example, between 1981 and 1982, nominal GNP rose from $339 billion to $357 billion; but real GNP *fell* from $136 billion to $130 billion.

The next important aspect of the definition of GNP is that:

Current
Nominal GNP is calculated by valuing all outputs at current prices.

Real GNP is calculated by valuing all outputs at the prices that prevailed in some agreed-upon year (currently 1971). Therefore, real GNP is a far better measure of changes in national production.

The GNP for a particular year includes only goods and services produced during that year. Sales of items produced in previous years are explicitly excluded.

For example, suppose you buy a perfectly beautiful 1974 Plymouth next week and are overjoyed by your purchase. The national-income statistician will not share your glee because she already counted your car in the GNP in 1974 when it was first produced and sold; the car will never be counted again. The same holds true of houses. An old house (unlike an old car) often will sell for more than its purchasers originally paid, yet the resale value of the house does not count in the GNP since it was already counted in the year it was built. For the same reason, transactions on the stock market and other exchanges of existing assets are not included in the GNP.

Third, you will note the use of the phrase **final goods and services** in the definition. The adjective "final" is the key word here. For example, when a supermarket buys milk from a farmer, the transaction is not included in the GNP because the supermarket does not want the milk for itself. It buys milk only for resale to consumers. Only when the milk is sold to consumers is it considered a final product. When the supermarket buys it, economists consider it an **intermediate good**. The GNP does not include sales of intermediate goods or services.

Finally, although the definition does not state this explicitly:

For the most part, only goods and services that pass through organized markets count in the GNP.

This, of course, excludes many economic activities. For example, illegal activities are not included in the GNP. Thus, illegal gambling services are not in the GNP, but the costs of running the many official lotteries are. The definition reflects the statisticians' confession that they could not hope to measure the value of many of

Final goods and services are those that are purchased by their ultimate users.

An **intermediate good** is a good purchased for resale or for use in producing another good.

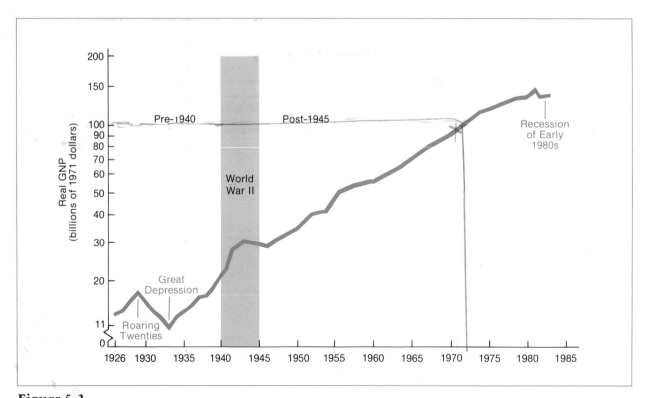

Figure 5-3

REAL GROSS NATIONAL PRODUCT OF CANADA, 1926–1983

This time-series chart displays the behaviour of real gross national production in Canada from 1926 to 1983. (Here real GNP is measured in 1971 prices.) The Great Depression (1929–33) stands out vividly. The years during World War II are shaded. Does the line look smoother to the right of this shaded area? Notice that the vertical axis is calibrated by what is called a "ratio scale." This means, for example, that the distance between 1000 and 100 is the same as the distance between 100 and 10.

SOURCE: Historical Statistics of Canada, and Statistics Canada.

the economy's most important activities, such as housework, do-it-yourself repairs, and leisure time. While these are certainly economic activities that result in currently produced goods or services, they all lack that important measuring rod—a price.

This omission results in certain oddities. For example, suppose that each of two neighbouring families hires the other to clean house, generously paying $1000 a week for the services. Each family can easily afford such generosity since it collects an identical salary from its neighbour. Nothing real changes, but GNP goes up by about $100,000 a year. If this example seems foolish, consider the potential effect of the women's movement on the GNP. Presumably, more and more housework is being done by hired men and women (and thus channelled through the market) and less and less is being done by unpaid housewives. Thus more housework is being included in the GNP. Billions of dollars may be added to the GNP in this way.

The Economy on a Roller Coaster

Having defined several of the basic concepts of macroeconomics, let us breathe some life into them by perusing the economic history of Canada. Figures 5–3 and 5–4 provide a capsule summary of this history since 1926. Figure 5–3 charts the behaviour of real GNP over a period of almost sixty years. The pronounced upward slope of the line indicates that the main feature has been economic growth. But the figure also shows that recessions—periods during which the real GNP decreased—have occurred. The ups and downs that are evident in Figure 5–3 are often referred to as *business cycles*.

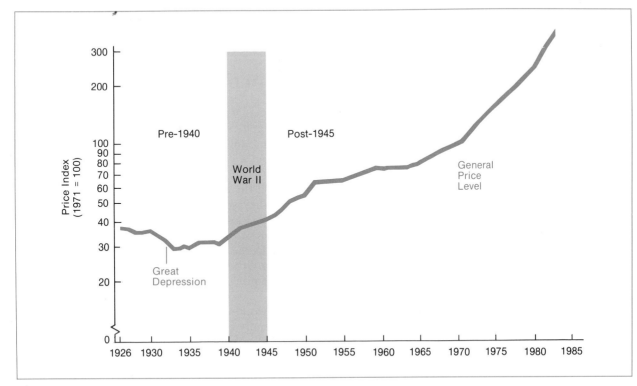

Figure 5–4
THE PRICE LEVEL IN CANADA, 1926–1983
This time-series chart portrays the behaviour of the Canadian price level from 1926 to 1983. (The specific price index used is called the *GNP deflator* and it is defined as the ratio of nominal GNP divided by real GNP.) Once again, the vertical axis has a ratio scale, and the World War II years are shaded. The difference between the 1926–40 period and the 1946–83 period is quite pronounced.
SOURCE: Historical Statistics of Canada, and Statistics Canada.

The history of the price level (Figure 5-4) displays a broadly similar pattern, but one that differs in some important respects. Prices also have been generally rising—that is, inflation has been much more common than deflation—but there have been two exceptions: stable prices during the 1920s and later 1930s, and the falling prices of the early 1930s (the Great Depression).

The following exercise may be enlightening. Cover the portions of Figures 5-3 and 5-4 that deal with the period beginning in 1940, the portions to the right of the shaded area in each figure. The picture that emerges is of an economy on a roller coaster. In Figure 5-3, the ups and downs around the underlying growth trend are quite pronounced. In Figure 5-4 we see periods of both inflation and **deflation**, with hardly any upward trend at all. Indeed, prices at the eve of World War II were lower than they were in the mid-1920s.

Now do the reverse. Cover the data prior to 1946 and look only at the postwar period. There is, indeed, a difference. The upward trend in real GNP predominates more, and business cycles are much less severe. While perfection has not been achieved, things do look much better. When we turn to the price level, however, things look rather worse. Gone is any period of falling prices that occurred before World War II, even periods of reasonable price stability are rather rare.

This quick inspection of the data suggests that something has happened. The Canadian economy behaved differently in 1946-83 than it did before World War II. Many economists attribute this shift in the economy's behaviour to lessons the government has learned about managing the economy—lessons that we will be learning in Part Three. When you look at the pre-1940 data, you are looking at an unmanaged economy that went through booms and recessions for "natural" economic reasons. The government did little about either. When you examine the post-1945 data, on the other hand, you are looking at an economy that has been increasingly managed by government policy—sometimes successfully and sometimes unsuccessfully. While the recessions are less severe, a cost seems to have been exacted: The economy appears to be more inflation-prone than it was in the more distant past.

The Great Depression of the 1930s

As you look at these graphs, the Great Depression of the 1930s is bound to catch your eye. The decline in economic activity from 1929 to 1933 (see Figure 5-3) was the most severe in our nation's history, and the rapid deflation (see Figure 5-4) was most unusual. The Depression is but a dim memory now, but those who lived through it will never forget it.

While statistics usually conceal the true drama of economic events, this is not so of the Great Depression—they stand here as a bitter testimony to its severity. From its 1929 high to its 1933 low, the production of goods and services dropped 30 percent and the price level fell 18.5 percent. Business investment almost ceased entirely. The unemployment rate rose ominously to 20 percent in 1933. From the data alone, one can virtually conjure up pictures of soup lines, beggars on street corners, closed factories, and homeless families. (See the boxed insert on the next page.)

The Great Depression was a worldwide event; no country was spared its ravages. This traumatic episode literally changed the history of many nations. In Germany, it facilitated the ascendancy of the Nazi party. In the United States, it enabled Franklin Roosevelt's Democratic party to engineer one of the most dramatic political realignments in history and to push through a host of political and economic reforms.

The worldwide depression also caused a much-needed revolution in the thinking of economists. Up until the 1930s, the prevailing economic theory held that a capitalist economy, while it occasionally misbehaved, had a "natural"

Deflation refers to a sustained *decrease* in the general price level.

Ten Lost Years

During the worst years of the Great Depression, about 25 percent of Canadian families were forced onto "relief." The loss of work for city dwellers was compounded by the loss of work for farmers due to dust, drought, and grasshoppers. The Canadian government provided rent for cheap, overcrowded accommodation and money for food (about $10 to $15 per month for a family). These desperate times have been described by Canadian author Barry Broadfoot in his *Ten Lost Years*. The quotation and picture below are from his moving descriptions.

For the men who had been taught that their main goal was to be a good family provider, the depression was a degrading time. Sometimes relief officers added to the humiliation by withdrawing liquor permits. Some families were too proud to go on relief, and the starving children stayed home from school so people would not know they had no shoes.

With so much hunger in the family, older sons and depressed fathers became transients, so those remaining at home would have more food and room to sleep. They would pick fruit, harvest crops, and hop a train, hoping to find work elsewhere. Thousands of men were riding back and forth across the country on top of trains or in boxcars. The men lived in "hobo jungles" on the edge of large cities, where they built small shacks and tents from old boards, cardboard, and blankets.

The government worried that the unemployed might start a revolution, so they started relief camps far from the cities, and ran them in a military fashion. The government felt this was a practical solution to the problem, and the men were clothed and fed. However, many men felt they had been forced to the camps and that they worked under slave conditions.

You've got to realize this, in the relief camps of the Thirties we weren't treated as humans. We weren't treated as animals, either, and I've always thought we

A relief camp scene near Ottawa.

(Public Archives of Canada)

were just statistics written into some big ledger in Ottawa. I was 18 and had come out west from Brantford because there was no work for a young fellow in that part of Ontario....

I headed for Vancouver where at least I wouldn't freeze to death, but we were harassed there and kicked around and so I joined up for a relief camp.

It was one of several up the old Hope-Princeton Trail, made up of board and canvas tents, and buildings they called cabooses where we slept. There was about 150 of us in this one, guys as young as 16 and up to 35 or 45, I should guess, and the thing was, we were all single and no jobs, stony broke and no future and the politicians considered us as dangerous. Their thinking was that if we were isolated then we wouldn't be hanging around vacant lots and jungles listening to Communist troublemakers.

SOURCE: Excerpts from *Ten Lost Years, 1929-1939* by Barry Broadfoot. Copyright © 1973 by Barry Broadfoot. Reprinted by permission of Doubleday & Company, Inc.

---

tendency to cure recessions or inflations by itself. The roller coaster bounced around but did not normally run off the tracks.

This optimistic view was not confined to academia. It characterized the views of most politicians (certainly including Prime Minister William Lyon McKenzie King) and business leaders as well.

The stubbornness of the Great Depression shook almost everyone's faith in the ability of the economy to right itself. In Cambridge, England, this questioning attitude led John Maynard Keynes, one of the world's most respected economists to write *The General Theory of Employment, Interest, and Money* (1936). Probably the most important book in economics of the twentieth century, it carried a rather revolutionary message. Keynes discarded the notion that the economy always gravitated toward high levels of employment, replacing it with the assertion that—if a pessimistic outlook led business firms and consumers to curtail their spending plans—the economy might be condemned to stagnation for years.

While this doleful prognosis sounded all too realistic at the time, Keynes closed his book on a hopeful note, for he showed how government actions might prod the economy out of its depressed state. The lessons he taught the world then are the lessons we shall be learning in Part Two. They show how governments can manage their economies so that recessions will not turn into depressions and depressions will not last as long as the Great Depression. While Keynes was working on *The General Theory*, he wrote his friend George Bernard Shaw that, "I believe myself to be writing a book on economic theory which will largely revolutionize ... the way the world thinks about economic problems." In many ways, he was right.

From World War II to the 1970s

The Great Depression finally ended when the country engaged in war at the end of the 1930s. With total spending at extraordinarily high levels during the war, mostly because of government expenditures, the economy boomed and the unemployment rate fell to less than 2 percent.

Wartime spending of this magnitude usually leads to inflation, but much of the potential inflation during World War II was contained by price controls. With prices held below the levels at which quantity supplied equalled quantity demanded, many goods had to be rationed, and shortages of consumer goods were quite common. All of this ended with a burst of inflation when controls were lifted after the war.

The period from the end of the war until the early 1960s resembled an earlier period of growth with recessions before 1929. The main difference was that the recessions between 1945 and 1965 were noticeably shorter and less severe than their prewar counterparts. Moderate but persistent inflation also became a fact of life. This period of sustained growth, reasonably low unemployment, and non-accelerating inflation was thought by many to be the result of "The New Economics," a term the media created for the policy of economic management prescribed by Keynes in the 1930s. For a while it looked as if we could avoid both unemployment and inflation. But the optimistic verdicts were premature in both cases.

Inflation was the first problem to crop up, beginning in about 1965. Its major cause, as it had been so many times in the past, was high levels of wartime spending—this time for the Vietnam War by the United States. Demand for Canadian goods was very high during this period partly because of record-level exports to the United States, and partly because we followed a fixed exchange-rate policy. By not letting the international value of the Canadian dollar rise, our government blocked a major route by which demands for our exports could have been held in check.

The Great Stagflation, 1973–1980

In October 1973, things began to get much worse for the oil-importing nations of the world. The war between Israel and the Arab nations led to an embargo on oil shipments to several Western countries and then to a quadrupling of the price of oil by the Organization of Petroleum Exporting Countries (OPEC).

While staggering price increases for oil and other energy resources were principal components of the inflation of this period, they were not the only ones. Continued poor harvests in 1974 in many parts of the globe kept world food prices rising rapidly. Prices of other raw materials also skyrocketed. Naturally, these higher costs of fuel and other materials soon were reflected in the prices of manufactured goods.

For these reasons, the inflation rate in the United States soared to above 12 percent during 1974. Meanwhile, the U.S. economy was slipping into its longest and most severe recession since the 1930s. Real GNP fell by about 5 percent between late 1973 and early 1975, and the unemployment rate almost doubled. Thus, both the twin evils of macroeconomics—inflation and unemployment—were unusually virulent in 1974 and 1975. Indeed, a new term—**stagflation**—was coined to refer to the simultaneous occurrence of economic *stag*nation and rapid in*flation* in the United States.

Stagflation is inflation that occurs while the economy is growing slowly ("stagnating") or having a recession.

Canada suffered less unemployment and more inflation than the United States during the mid-1970s for two reasons. The Canadian government cushioned the recession that would have followed from the large drop in export sales to the United States by policies that stimulated demand. Second, the government did not allow the Canadian consumer price of oil to increase to world levels. Nevertheless, the stimulation of the general demand for goods was sufficient to cause inflation to rise dramatically in Canada.

The price of oil began to "misbehave" again in 1979 when the revolution that deposed the Shah of Iran caused a disruption in the flow of Iranian oil, thus sparking chaos in the world oil market. In a series of price increases, OPEC more than doubled the price of its oil during 1979. The consequences of OPEC's actions were similar to those of 1973–75: stagflation returned. By 1980, the Canadian unemployment rate was 7.5 percent, and the inflation rate was over 10 percent.

Disinflation in the Early 1980s

Disinflation is the process of reducing inflation.

During the early 1980s, Canada followed Margaret Thatcher's and Ronald Reagan's contractionary high interest-rate policies to curb inflation. The policy worked but at a tremendous cost. Inflation fell to 5.8 percent in 1983 (the lowest value since 1972), but unemployment soared to 11.9 percent in 1983 (over twice what it was in 1973).

The Problem of Macroeconomic Stabilization

This brief look at the historical record shows that our economy has not generally produced a steady pattern of growth without inflation. Rather, it has been buffeted by periodic bouts of unemployment or inflation, and sometimes has been plagued by both. Also, the discussion involved numerous references to the fact that government policies contributed to our macroeconomic performance (both good and bad). Let us now commence a more formal discussion of this connection.

We can provide a preliminary analysis of **stabilization policy**, the name given to government programs designed to prevent or shorten recessions and to counteract inflation, by using the basic tools of aggregate-supply and aggregate-demand analysis. To facilitate this, we have reproduced as Figures 5–5 and 5–6 two of the diagrams found earlier in this chapter [Figures 5–1(b) and 5–2], but we now give them slightly different interpretations.

Stabilization policy is the name given to government programs designed to prevent or shorten recessions and to counteract inflation (that is, to *stabilize* prices).

Figure 5–5 gives a simplified view of government policy to fight unemployment. We suppose that, in the absence of government intervention, the economy would reach an equilibrium at point E, where demand curve D_0D_0 crosses supply curve SS. Now, if the output corresponding to point E is so low that many workers are unemployed, *the government can reduce unemployment by increasing aggregate demand*. In the diagram, this action shifts the demand curve to D_1D_1, causing equilibrium to move to point A. In general:

Recessions and unemployment are often caused by insufficient aggregate demand. When this is so, government policies that augment demand—such as increases in government spending—can be an effective way to increase output and reduce unemployment.

Figure 5-5

Figure 5-5

STABILIZATION POLICY TO FIGHT UNEMPLOYMENT

This diagram duplicates Figure 5-1(b), but here we assume that point E—the intersection of demand curve D_0D_0 and supply curve SS—corresponds to high unemployment. With the kind of policy tools that we will study in later chapters, the government can shift the aggregate-demand curve outward to D_1D_1. This would raise output and lower unemployment.

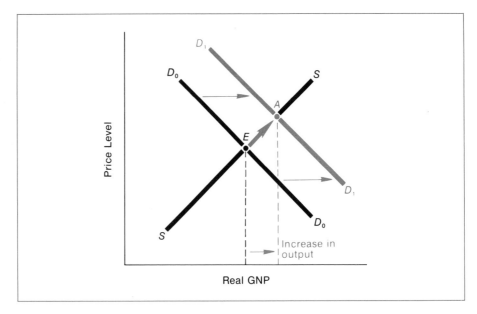

The opposite type of demand management is often called for when inflation is the main macroeconomic problem. Figure 5-6 illustrates this case. Here again, point E, the intersection of demand curve D_0D_0 and supply curve SS, is the equilibrium that would be reached in the absence of government policy. But now we suppose that the price level corresponding to point E is considered "too high," meaning that the *change* in the price level from the previous period to this one would be too rapid if the economy moved to point E. A government program that reduces demand from D_0D_0 to D_2D_2 (for example, a reduction in government spending) can keep prices down and thereby reduce inflation. Thus:

Inflation is frequently caused by aggregate demand racing ahead too fast. When this is the case, government policies that reduce aggregate demand can be effective anti-inflationary devices.

This, in brief, summarizes the job of stabilization policy. When demand behaviour is the source of economic instability, the government can limit both recession and inflation by managing aggregate demand, pushing it ahead when it

Figure 5-6

STABILIZATION POLICY TO FIGHT INFLATION

This diagram duplicates Figure 5-2, but here we assume that point E—the equilibrium the economy would attain without government intervention—represents high inflation (that is, the price level corresponding to point E is far above last year's price level). By using its policy instruments to shift the aggregate-demand curve inward to D_2D_2, the government can keep this year's price level lower than it would otherwise have been; in other words, the government can reduce inflation.

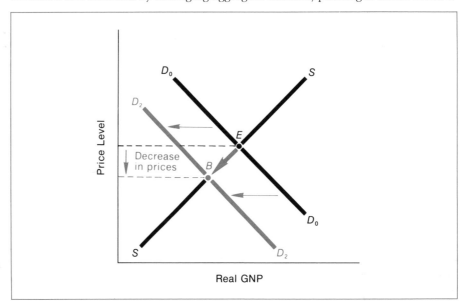

would otherwise lag, and restraining it when it would otherwise grow too quickly.

Sound simple? It's not. In reality, managing aggregate demand is a lot more complicated than shifting around lines on graphs with pencil and paper. We will spend several chapters examining the methods of demand management and learning why these methods do not always lead to the results that policy-makers hope for.

One problem is that the economy is sometimes plagued by both unemployment and inflation *at the same time*. In this case, the tools of demand management, even if wielded with great precision, are simply not up to the task. In Part Three we will see why demand management is not enough and study some suggestions for dealing with unemployment and inflation at the same time.

Summary

1. Microeconomics studies the decisions of individuals and firms, how these decisions interact, and how they influence the allocation of society's resources and the distribution of income. Macroeconomics looks at the behaviour of entire economies and studies the pressing social problems of inflation and unemployment.

2. While their respective subject matters differ greatly, the basic tools of microeconomics and macroeconomics are virtually identical. Both rely on the supply and demand analysis introduced in Chapter 4.

3. Macroeconomic models use abstract concepts like "the price level" and "national product" that are derived by amalgamating many different markets into one. This process is known as aggregation; it should not be taken literally but should be viewed as a useful approximation.

4. The best specific measure of the abstract concept "national product" is the gross national product (GNP), which is obtained by adding up the money values of all final goods and services produced in a given year. These outputs can be evaluated at current market prices (to get nominal GNP), or the prices of some previous year (to get real GNP). Neither intermediate goods nor transactions that take place outside organized markets are included in GNP.

5. Canada's economic history is one of growth punctuated by periodic recessions; that is, periods in which real GNP declined. While the distant past included some periods of falling prices (deflation), more recent history shows only rising prices (inflation).

6. The Great Depression of the 1930s was the worst in our country's history. It had profound effects both on our nation and on other countries throughout the world and led also to a revolution in economic thinking, thanks to the work of John Maynard Keynes.

7. From World War II to the early 1970s, the Canadian economy exhibited much steadier growth than it had in the past. Many observers attribute this to the implementation of the economic policies that Keynes suggested. At the same time, however, the price level seems only to rise, never to fall, in the modern economy. The economy seems to have become more "inflation prone."

8. Since the mid-1970s, the Canadian economy has suffered through several serious recessions. At the same time, inflation has been unusually virulent. This unhappy combination of economic stagnation with rapid inflation was nicknamed "stagflation."

9. One major cause of inflation is that aggregate demand may grow more quickly than aggregate supply. In such a case, a government policy that reduces aggregate demand may be able to check the inflation.

10. Similarly, recessions often occur because aggregate demand grows too slowly. In this case, a government policy that stimulates demand may be an effective way to fight the recession.

Concepts for Review

Microeconomics
Macroeconomics
National product
Aggregation
Aggregate-demand and aggregate-
    supply curves

Inflation
Deflation
Recession
Gross national product (GNP)
Nominal versus real GNP
Final goods and services

Intermediate goods
Stagflation
Disinflation
Stabilization policy

Questions for Discussion

1. Which of the following problems are likely to be studied by a microeconomist and which by a macroeconomist?
   a. The allocation of a university's limited budget.
   b. Why the Great Depression lasted so long.
   c. Why Japan's economy grows faster than the United States' economy, while Britain's grows slower.
   d. Why General Motors sells more cars than Ford Motor Company.

2. You probably use "aggregates" quite frequently in everyday discussions. Try to think of some examples. (Here is one: Have you ever said, "The student body at this school generally ..."? What, precisely, did you mean?)

3. Use an aggregate supply–demand diagram to study what would happen to an economy in which the aggregate-supply curve never moved while the aggregate-demand curve shifted outward year after year.

4. Try asking a friend who has not studied economics in which year he or she thinks prices were higher: 1928 or 1940? (You can find the correct answer by referring to Figure 5–4.) Most people your age think that prices have always risen. Why do you think they have this opinion?

5. When were the two worst recessions of the past 60 years?

6. Which of the following transactions are included in the gross national product, and by how much does each raise GNP?
   a. Smith pays a carpenter $4000 to build a garage.
   b. Smith purchases $1000 worth of lumber and materials and builds himself a garage, which is worth $4000.
   c. Smith goes to the woods, cuts down a tree, and uses the wood to build himself a garage that is worth $4000.
   d. The Jones family sells its old house to the Reynolds family for $80,000. The Joneses then buy a newly constructed house from a builder for $130,000.
   e. Your university purchases a used computer from another university, paying $500,000.
   f. Your university purchases a new computer from IBM, paying $1 million.
   g. You lose $100 in a Las Vegas casino.
   h. You lose $100 in the stock market.

Unemployment and Inflation: The Twin Evils of Macroeconomics

6

Nothing so weakens
governments as inflation.
J. K. GALBRAITH

When men are employed they
are best contented.
BENJAMIN FRANKLIN

Among the many trials faced by Odysseus, the hero of Homer's *Odyssey*, one of the most difficult was to steer his fragile boat through a narrow strait. On one side lay the rock of the monster Scylla, which threatened to break his craft into pieces, and on the other was the menacing whirlpool of Charybdis. The makers of national economic policy face a similarly difficult task in trying to chart a middle course between the Scylla of unemployment and the Charybdis of inflation. If they steer the economy far from the rocks of unemployment, they run the risk of being swept up in the swift currents of inflation. But if they maintain a safe distance from inflation, they may smash against the rocks of unemployment.

In Part Three we will explain how economic planners attempt to strike a balance between high employment and low inflation, why these goals cannot be attained with machinelike precision, and why improvement on one front generally spells deterioration on the other. A great deal of attention will be paid to the *causes* of inflation and unemployment.

But before getting involved in such important issues of theory and policy, we pause in this chapter to take a rather close look at the twin evils themselves: Why is it that a rise in unemployment is generally considered bad news? Why is inflation so loudly deplored? Can we measure the costs of unemployment and inflation? The answers to some of these questions may at first seem obvious, but we will see that there is more to them than meets the eye.

The chapter is divided into two parts. In the first part we deal with unemployment. After a few words on the human costs of high unemployment, we explain how government statisticians measure unemployment and consider how the concept of "full employment" can be defined. We turn next to our country's system of unemployment insurance, and we conclude by investigating—and quantifying—the economic losses associated with unemployment.

In the second part of the chapter we turn to inflation. We begin by exploding some persistent myths about inflation, myths that help explain why inflation is so universally deplored. But the costs of inflation are not all mythical. The first real cost we consider is how and why inflation redistributes income and wealth from one group of people to another. Next, we learn how certain laws cause inflation to have heavy economic costs that could be avoided if the laws were written differently. This leads us to one of our **12 Ideas for Beyond the Final Exam** mentioned in Chapter 1. We shall see that it is the failure to understand the effect of inflation on interest rates that explains the existence of some of these laws and accounts for these costs of inflation. Finally, we define and analyse the difference between creeping and galloping inflation and explode another myth about inflation: the myth that creeping inflation always leads to galloping inflation. In an appendix, we explain how inflation is measured.

The Costs of Unemployment

The human costs of unemployment are probably sufficiently obvious. Years ago, loss of a job meant not only enforced idleness and a catastrophic drop in income, it often led to hunger, cold, ill health, and even death. This is the way one unemployed worker during the Great Depression described his family's plight in a mournful letter to his political representative:

I have six little children to take care of. I have been out of work for over a year and a half. Am back almost thirteen months and the landlord says if I don't pay up before the 1 of 1932 out I must go, and where am I to go in the cold winter with my children. If you can help me please for God's sake and the children's sakes and like please do what you can and send me some help, will you, I cannot find any work. I am willing to take any kind of work if I could get it now. Thanksgiving dinner was black coffee and bread and was very glad to get it. My wife is in the hospital now. We have no shoes to were [sic]; no clothes hardly. Oh what will I do I sure will thank you.[1]

Nowadays, unemployment does not have such dire consequences for most families, although it still holds these terrors for some. Part of the sting has been taken out of temporary unemployment by our system of unemployment insurance (discussed below), and there are other social-welfare programs to support the incomes of the poor (see *Microeconomics*, Chapter 23). Yet most families still do suffer a painful loss of income when their breadwinner becomes unemployed.

Even families that are well protected by unemployment compensation suffer when joblessness strikes. Ours is a work-oriented society. A man's "place" has always been in the office or factory or shop, and lately this has become increasingly true for women as well. A worker forced into idleness by a recession endures a psychological cost that is no less real for our inability to measure it. Enforced joblessness is a demoralizing mental burden on the unemployed worker. High unemployment leads to a higher incidence of psychological disorders, divorces, suicides, and the like. (See the boxed insert on the next page.)

Nor are the costs only psychological. Accumulated work experience is a valuable asset. When forced into idleness, workers not only cease accumulating experience, but lengthy periods of unemployment may make them "rusty," and thus less productive when they are reemployed. Short periods of unemployment exact different kinds of costs. A record of steady employment is important in applying for a new job, and a worker who has frequently been laid off will lack this record of reliability.

It is important to realize that these costs, whether large or small in total, are distributed most unevenly across the population. At the bottom of the severe recession of 1981–84, the **unemployment rate** among all workers was 12.5 percent. This is a shockingly big increase from the 7.5 percent figure for 1981. It is also important to note that the 1983 situation was even worse for certain groups. For example, the unemployment rate in Newfoundland was 19 percent, and the unemployment rate among those 15 to 24 years old was 23 percent.

The **unemployment rate** is the number of unemployed people, expressed as a percentage of the **labour force**.

The **labour force** is the number of people employed or seeking employment.

[1]From *Brother, Can You Spare a Dime? The Great Depression 1929–1933*, by Milton Meltzer, page 103. Copyright© 1969 by Milton Meltzer. Reprinted by permission of Alfred A. Knopf, Inc.

Health, Crime, and Unemployment: Evidence from a U.S. Study

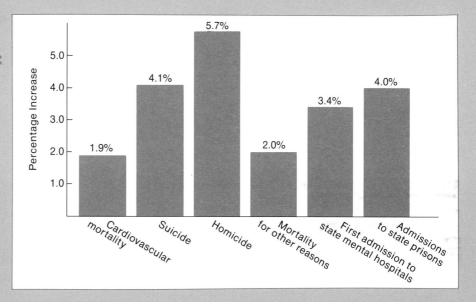

The social costs of unemployment are by no means limited to narrow economic losses such as reduced incomes and output. It is widely believed, for example, that high unemployment breeds crime, mental anxiety, and ill health. A study by a researcher at Johns Hopkins University documented the strong statistical association between unemployment and various measures of mental and physical health and criminal aggression.

Using these statistical relationships, it has been estimated how many more cases of various maladies the United States would have if the unemployment rate over a six-year period were one percentage point higher than it actually was. The results are summarized in the accompanying bar chart. For example, such a rise in unemployment would be expected to lead to about 2 percent more deaths from heart disease. The other figures in the chart have similar interpretations.

In looking at these numbers, it should be kept in mind that while the study found a high correlation between unemployment and the various maladies, it does not necessarily imply that unemployment was the *cause* of these ills. Still, the figures are dramatic enough to suggest that there is a real link between unemployment and ill health.

SOURCE: M. Harvey Brenner, "Influence of the Social Environment on Psychopathology: The Historical Perspectives" in James E. Barrett *et al* eds., *Stress and Mental Disorder* (New York: Raven Press, 1979).

Counting the Unemployed: The Official Statistics

Statistics Canada is responsible for measuring unemployment. How do they do it? How accurate are their measurements?

Statistics Canada's basic method for counting the unemployed is quite direct: it asks people. Specifically, a survey of 56,000 households is conducted each month. The sample is designed to represent all persons 15 years of age and over residing in Canada, with the exception of the following: full-time members of the armed forces, inmates of institutions, residents of the Yukon and Northwest Territories, and those living on Indian reserves. The census-taker asks several questions about the employment status of each member of the household. On the basis of these answers, each person is categorized as being *employed*, *unemployed*, or *not in the labour force.*

The first category is simplest to define. It includes everybody currently working at a job, including part-time workers. Although some part-time workers work less than a full week because they choose to, others do so only because they cannot find a suitable full-time job. Nevertheless, these workers are not considered "unemployed," though many would consider them "underemployed."

The second category is a bit trickier. For those not currently working, Statistics Canada first determines whether they are temporarily laid off from a job to which they expect to return. If so, they are counted as unemployed. The remaining workers are asked whether they actively sought work during the previous week. If they did, they are also counted as unemployed. But if they did not, they are classified as not in the labour force; that is, since they failed to look for a job they are not considered unemployed.

This seems a reasonable way to draw the distinction—after all, we would not want to count all university students who work during the summer months as unemployed between September and May. Yet, there is a problem: Research has shown that many unemployed workers give up looking for jobs after a time. These so-called **discouraged workers** are victims of poor job prospects, just like the officially unemployed. Ironically, when they give up hope, the official unemployment statistics decline! Some critics have therefore argued that an estimate should be made of the number of discouraged workers and that these people should be added to the roles of the unemployed.

Statistics Canada has made an effort to estimate the number of discouraged workers by periodically conducting a much more detailed survey. The results of the recent survey are discussed in the accompanying newspaper article on the opposite page.

Involuntary part-time work, loss of overtime or shortened work hours, and discouraged workers are all examples of "hidden" or "disguised" unemployment. And those who are concerned about these phenomena argue that we should include them in the official unemployment rate because, if we do not, the magnitude of the problem will be *underestimated*.

There is, however, an opposing school of thought that argues that the official unemployment rate really *overestimates* the unemployment problem. First, they argue, the unemployment rate of 1985 is not directly comparable to the unemployment rate of, say, 1955 because the composition of the labour force has changed dramatically over these years. Specifically, a larger fraction of all workers are young and female today than was the case 30 years ago. These groups have always had higher rates of unemployment than adult males. Therefore, even if adult men, adult women, and teenagers each had the *same* unemployment rates in 1985 that they had in 1955, the unemployment rate for the entire population would have been higher in 1985 than in 1955.[2] Second, they argue, to count as unemployed, a person need only *say* that he is looking for work, even if he is not really interested in finding a job. No one knows to what extent the unemployment problem is overstated on account of this, but some think that it may be considerable.

Types of Unemployment

Providing jobs for those willing to work is one principal goal of macroeconomic policy. How are we to define this goal? One clearly *incorrect* answer would be "a zero measured unemployment rate." Ours is a dynamic and highly mobile economy. Households move from one province to another. Individuals quit jobs to look for better positions or to "retool" for more attractive occupations. These phenomena, and many more, produce some minimal amount of unemployment—people who literally are *between* jobs. Economists call this the level of **frictional unemployment**.

[2]If you do not understand why, consider the following analogy. Suppose your university class contains a mixture of "A" students and "C" students. If, between your first year and your final year, more "C" students enter the class as transfers from other universities, your class's overall average grade will decline even if every student earns the same grades in the final year that he or she did in first year.

Many Jobless Missed in Statscan's Survey of the Unemployed

When Statistics Canada reported that more than a million people were unemployed in December, the official announcement sent shockwaves through the country.

But the one million mark was probably surpassed some months ago, because the labour force survey fails to count a significant number of the jobless as unemployed.

Statscan conducts a monthly survey ... and ... based on this sampling ... defines the employed as all people who worked one hour or more during the reference week of the survey.

There were 1,599,000 people in December who were working part-time (defined as less than 30 hours a week). The part-time labour force represented 15 percent of the total employment figure....

Statscan reported in its December survey that 266,000 part-time workers wanted full-time work, and social planners thus consider these people underemployed.

The part-time labour force worked an average of less than 20 hours a week in December, compared with about 40 hours for full-time employees. Critics of the survey method argue, therefore, that half of the 266,000 underemployed should be added to the unemployment figure to more accurately reflect the lack of full employment opportunities.

In addition, Statscan defines the unemployed as all those who were without jobs but were actively seeking work in the reference week. But the agency also acknowledges that substantial numbers of people were not counted as unemployed because they failed to satisfy the job-search criterion.

A special survey conducted by Statscan in March last year revealed that 339,000 people wanted work even though they were not officially counted as unemployed because they had not been actively looking for work.

Slightly more than 100,000 of these people said they were not looking for work because they believed no work was available. Other reasons given included illness and waiting for a job recall. Depending on various interpretations of the data, the inclusion of the hidden unemployed in the official jobless figures would significantly raise the unemployment levels.

The labour force survey also fails to reflect the high unemployment levels in the Northwest Territories and the Yukon and on Indian reserves. Statscan officials say it would be too costly and difficult to extend the survey's coverage to these areas....

SOURCE: Abridged article from *The Globe and Mail*, Toronto, February 1, 1982, page 4.

The critical distinguishing feature of frictional unemployment is that it is short-lived. A frictionally unemployed person has every reason to expect to find a new job soon. People tend to think of frictional unemployment as irreducible, but that is not the case. During World War II, for example, unemployment in this country fell below 2 percent—substantially below the frictional level. Frictional unemployment is "irreducible" only in the sense that—under normal circumstances—it is socially undesirable to reduce it.

Geographical and occupational mobility play important roles in our market economy—enabling people to search for better jobs. Similarly, waste is avoided by allowing inefficient firms, or firms producing items no longer desired by consumers, to be replaced by new firms. Inhibition of either of these phenomena must hamper the workings of the market economy. But, if these adjustment mechanisms are allowed to operate, there will always be some temporarily unemployed workers looking for jobs just as there will always be some firms with unfilled positions looking for workers. This is the genesis of frictional unemployment.

Structural unemployment refers to workers who have lost their jobs because they have been displaced by automation, because their skills are no longer in demand, or for similar reasons.

Cyclical unemployment is the portion of unemployment that is attributable to a decline in the economy's total production. Cyclical unemployment rises during recessions and falls as prosperity is restored.

A second type of unemployment is often difficult to distinguish from frictional unemployment, but it has very different implications. **Structural unemployment** arises when jobs are eliminated by changes in the structure of the economy, such as automation or permanent changes in demand. The crucial difference between frictional and structural unemployment is that, unlike a frictionally unemployed worker, a structurally unemployed worker cannot realistically be considered "between jobs." Instead, he may find his skills and experience unwanted in the changing economy in which he lives. He is thus faced with either a prolonged period of unemployment or the necessity of making a major change in his occupation. For older workers in particular, this may be difficult.

The remaining type of unemployment, **cyclical unemployment**, will occupy our attention most in this book. Cyclical unemployment arises when the overall level of economic activity declines. Whenever the unemployment rate rises ominously or falls precipitously, the data are almost certainly reflecting changes in cyclical unemployment.

What Is "Full Employment"?

After World War II, the Canadian federal government committed itself to pursue a policy of full employment. In the White Paper of April 1945 it was stated that "the government will be prepared, in periods when unemployment threatens, to incur deficits and increases in the national debt resulting from its employment and income policy." The government has consistently followed this part of their plan, but follow through has been less obvious on the other part of their plan: "In periods of buoyant employment and income, budget plans will call for surpluses." Part of the reason for this excess of budget deficits over surpluses over the years is that the government seems to be constantly optimistic about what "full employment" is.

During the prosperous years of the late 1940s and early 1950s, unemployment rates were consistently below 4 percent, dropping as low as 2.2 percent in 1947. This led the Economic Council of Canada (formed in the early 1960s) to select 3 percent as a definition of full employment. By this it was meant that 3 percent was the normal level of frictional unemployment in Canada. However, as Figure 6–1 shows, the unemployment rate has never fallen below 3.5 percent since 1956. As a result, economists now feel that the 3 percent target is unrealistic, and most now define full employment as involving a 6.5 or 7 percent unemployment rate.

There are several reasons for this upward adjustment. First, there is the changed composition of the labour force that we discussed above. The big growth in those wanting work has been among females and the young, while the rapid growth in job vacancies since the mid-1970s has been in the processing, fabricating, and extractive fields (occupations that traditionally have employed males in the 25–54 age bracket). Estimates show that about one-half of the increase in the "floor" unemployment rate shown in Figure 6–1 is due to this mismatching difficulty and other related structural factors. Another reason for this rise is the increased generosity of the unemployment-insurance legislation that took effect in 1971. These changes have reduced an individual's incentive to get himself off the unemployment rolls. Why work if unemployment benefits and other programs provide an income nearly as large as the salary one could earn on the job? This lack of work incentives made low unemployment harder to achieve. Finally, many economists have claimed that substantial increases in the minimum-wage levels during the 1970s have made it harder to employ teenagers and other workers whose productivity was low. If, for example, their productivity was exceeded by the legal minimum wage, who would hire them?[3]

[3]For a full discussion of minimum-wage laws, including their effect on unemployment, see *Microeconomics*, Chapter 22.

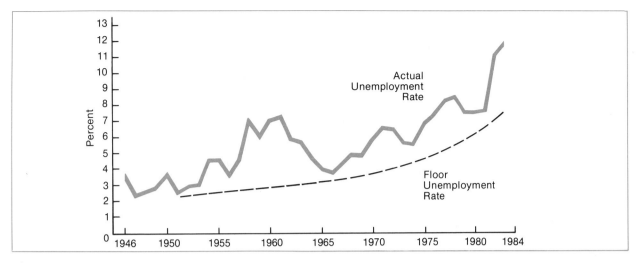

Figure 6-1

UNEMPLOYMENT RATE IN CANADA SINCE WORLD WAR II

The unemployment rate has risen dramatically since the war, but not all of this increase is cyclical unemployment. Cyclical unemployment was high in the recessions of 1958-62, 1970-71, 1977-78, and the early 1980s. The increase in the floor unemployment rate is due to structural factors such as demographic changes (the baby boom and increased labour-force participation of females) and certain institutional changes (the unemployment-insurance provisions).

SOURCE: Statistics Canada

While there is disagreement about whether "full" employment should be defined as slightly more or less than the 6.5 to 7 percent range, there is no argument about whether a significant amount of cyclical unemployment exists in the 1980s.

Unemployment Insurance: The Invaluable Cushion

A surprising feature of the recession of the early 1980s was the equanimity with which the electorate tolerated high unemployment rates. One major reason for this was our system of **unemployment insurance**.

One of the most valuable pieces of legislation to emerge from the trauma of the Great Depression was the Unemployment Insurance Act of 1941. It established a system whereby employers, employees, and the federal government would share the burden of financing the unemployment benefits. The federal government required the consent of all provinces to amend the BNA Act to permit the introduction of this legislation, which formerly came under provincial jurisdiction. Thanks to this system, many—but, as we shall see, not all—Canadian workers need never experience the complete loss of income that so many suffered during the 1930s.

The benefits paid to an unemployed worker are set at 60 percent of his or her average weekly insurable earnings. These payments are taxable, but the individual can earn up to 25 percent of his benefits through part-time or temporary work, without having his benefits reduced. There is a two-week waiting period following unemployment before benefits are paid. Though a 40 percent drop in earnings poses problems, especially if there are no other earners in the family, families covered by unemployment insurance simply do not go hungry when they lose their jobs, and they are only rarely dispossessed from their homes.

Who is eligible to receive these benefits? Precise qualifications vary from region to region, but some stipulations apply quite generally.

1. *Only experienced workers qualify.* The amount of experience necessary to establish eligibility varies between 10 and 14 weeks of work (depending on the unemployment rate in the region). This means that persons just joining the labour force (for instance, new graduates of high schools, universities, or community colleges) or reentering after a protracted absence (such as women resuming work after many years of child rearing) are not eligible.

2. **Job quitters must wait longer.** With certain exceptions, people who quit their last jobs must wait several extra weeks to collect benefits.

3. **You must be looking for work to qualify.** People unwilling or unable to work cannot receive unemployment benefits, and a recipient of benefits must conduct an active search for employment.

4. **Benefits can run up to 50 weeks.** This time limit depends on one's employment history, and the unemployment rate of both the country and region.

Over the years, the government has extended the unemployment-insurance program. In 1971 several new groups were included, such as: seasonally unemployed fishermen, pregnant women (with sufficient work experience), those on extended sickness, and those attending retraining programs. Since 1977, the insurance fund has been administered in tandem with Canada Employment Centres, so that claimants have more convenient access to job and retraining information and to counselling. Also since 1977, some unemployment-insurance funds have been used to keep people working rather than to compensate them for not working. There have been a series of job-sharing plans. For example, if all employees work four days a week instead of five, the company pays the wages for four days and the insurance fund pays wages for the fifth day.

The importance of unemployment insurance to the unemployed is obvious. But there are also significant benefits to citizens who never become unemployed. During recession years many billions of dollars are paid out in unemployment benefits, and since recipients probably spend most of their benefits, unemployment insurance limits the severity of recessions by providing additional purchasing power when and where it is most needed.

The unemployment-insurance system is one of several "cushions" that have been built into our economy since the 1930s to prevent the possibility of another Great Depression. By giving the money to those who become unemployed, the system helps prop up aggregate demand during recessions.

While the Canadian economy is now probably "depression proof," this should not be a cause for too much rejoicing, for the recession of the early 1980s has demonstrated that we are very far from being "recession proof."

The Economic Costs of High Unemployment

The fact that unemployment insurance and other social-welfare programs replace a significant fraction of lost income has led some skeptics to claim that unemployment is no longer a serious problem. But the fact is that:

Unemployment insurance is just what the name says—an *insurance* program. And insurance can never prevent a catastrophe from occurring; it can only *spread the costs* of a catastrophe among many people instead of letting them all fall on the shoulders of those few unfortunate souls whom it affects directly.

Fire insurance is an example. If you are covered by fire insurance and your house burns down, you will probably suffer only a small financial loss because the insurance company will pay most of the expenses. Where does it get the money? It cannot create it out of thin air. Rather, it must have collected the funds from the many other families who purchased insurance but did not suffer any fire damages. Thus, one family's loss of perhaps $75,000 is covered by the insurance payments of 300 families each paying $250 a year. In this way, the costs of the catastrophe are spread among hundreds of families, and in the process, made much more bearable.

But despite the insurance, the family whose house is destroyed by fire suffers anguish and inconvenience. No insurance policy can eliminate this. Furthermore, society loses a valuable resource—a house. It will take a great deal of wood, cement, nails, paint, and labour to replace the burnt-out home. *An insurance policy cannot insure society against losses of real resources.*

The case is precisely the same with insurance against unemployment. All workers and employers pay for the insurance policy by a tax that the government levies on wages and salaries. With the funds so collected, the government compensates the victims of unemployment. Thus, instead of letting the costs of unemployment fall entirely on the minority of workers who are out of work, the system of payroll taxes and unemployment benefits *spreads* the costs over the entire population. But it does not eliminate the basic economic cost.

When the economy does not generate enough jobs to employ all those who are willing to work, a valuable resource is lost. Potential goods and services that might have been enjoyed by consumers are lost forever. This is the real economic cost of high unemployment, and no insurance plan can eliminate it.

And these costs are by no means negligible. Table 6–1 summarizes the idleness of workers and machines, and the resulting loss of national output, for some of the years of lowest economic activity in recent decades. The first column lists the unemployment rate, and thus measures unused labour resources. The second lists the percentage of industrial capacity that Canadian manufacturers were actually using, and thus indicates the extent of unused plant and equipment. And the third column shows how much more output (real GNP) could have been produced if these labour and capital resources had been fully employed.

Table 6–1
THE ECONOMIC COSTS OF HIGH UNEMPLOYMENT

YEAR	UNEMPLOYMENT RATE (percent)	CAPACITY UTILIZATION RATE (percent)	PERCENTAGE OF REAL GNP LOST DUE TO IDLE RESOURCES
1961	7.1	72	6.3
1971	6.4	80	2.6
1977	8.1	80	2.8
1983	11.9	67	6.4

SOURCES: Statistics Canada, and Figure 6-1.

While these years are extreme examples, the inability to utilize all of the nation's available resources has been a recurrent problem for our economy. The blue line in Figure 6–2 shows the actual real GNP in Canada from 1960 to 1983, while the black line shows the real GNP we *could have* produced if "full employment" had been maintained. This last statement defines a concept called **potential GNP**. As our previous discussion of full employment pointed out, it *is* possible to push employment beyond its normal full-employment level. This occurs whenever the unemployment rate dips below the "full-employment unemployment rate"—a rate now thought to be 6.5 or 7 percent. Consequently, it *is* possible for actual GNP to exceed potential GNP. Figure 6–2 shows several instances where this happened. But it also shows that, more typically, actual GNP falls short of potential GNP. The total shortfall of actual GNP below potential GNP since 1960 provides some startling information.

Potential gross national product is the real GNP the economy would produce if its labour and other resources were fully employed.

Figure 6-2

ACTUAL AND POTENTIAL
GNP IN CANADA, 1960–1983
This chart compares the growth of
actual GNP (blue line) with that of
potential GNP (black line). There
have been three lengthy periods
during which real GNP remained
below its potential (1960-64,
1969-72, and 1975 to the present),
but only two brief periods during
which GNP was above potential
(1965-66 and 1973-74).
SOURCE: Economic Council of
Canada, *Annual Review* (1979),
updated by the authors.

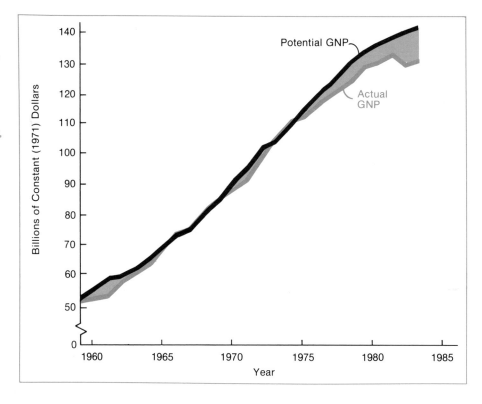

The cumulative gap between actual and potential GNP over the years 1960-83 (all
evaluated in 1971 prices), which is shown by the shaded area in Figure 6-2, is an
astounding $48 billion. At 1983 levels of output, this loss in output as a result of
unemployment would be just over four months' worth of production. And there is
no way to redeem these losses. The labour wasted in 1982 cannot be utilized in
1986.

Those who argue that unemployment is nothing to worry about today because
of unemployment insurance, or because unemployment is concentrated among
certain kinds of workers (such as teenagers), or because many unemployed workers
become reemployed within a few weeks, should ponder Figure 6-2. Is the loss of
this much output really no cause for worry? Would these optimists react the same
way if the government collected a fraction of the output of every factory in Canada
and dumped it into the sea? Waste is waste no matter who ultimately pays the
cost.

The Costs of Inflation

Both the human and the economic costs of inflation are less obvious than the
costs of unemployment. But this does not necessarily make them any less real, for
if one thing is crystal clear about inflation, it is that people do not like it.

Public-opinion polls consistently show that inflation ranks high on people's
list of major national problems, sometimes ahead of unemployment. Surveys also
find that inflation, like unemployment, causes a deterioration in consumers' sense
of well-being—it makes people unhappy. Why?

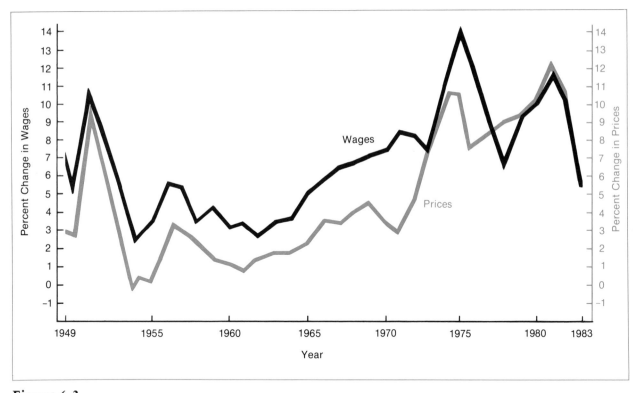

Figure 6-3

RATES OF CHANGE OF WAGES AND PRICES IN CANADA, 1949-1983

This chart compares the rate of price inflation (blue line) with the rate of growth of nominal wages in the postwar period. The patterns are clearly quite similar, with wages and prices normally accelerating or decelerating together. Notice that the traditional gap between wage increases and price increases has not prevailed in recent years.

SOURCE: Statistics Canada. The price index is the Consumer Price Index, and the wage series is average weekly wages and salaries (industrial composite).

Inflation: The Myth and the Reality

At first, the question may seem ridiculous. During times of inflation, people must keep paying higher prices for the same quantities of goods and services they had before. So more and more income is needed just to maintain the same standard of living. Is it not obvious that this erosion of **purchasing power**—that is, the decline in what money will buy—makes everyone worse off?

This would indeed be the case were it not for one very significant fact. The wages people earn are also prices—prices for labour services. During a period of inflation, wages also rise and, in fact, the average wage typically rises more or less in step with prices. Thus, contrary to popular myth, workers as a group are not usually victimized by inflation.

The purchasing power of wages is not systematically eroded by inflation. Sometimes wages rise faster than prices, and sometimes prices rise faster than wages. The fact is that in the long run wages tend to outstrip prices as new capital equipment and innovation increase output per worker.

Figure 6-3 illustrates this simple fact. The blue line shows the annual rate of increase of consumer prices in Canada for each year since 1949 while the black line shows the annual rate of wage increases. Generally, wages rise faster than prices, reflecting the steady advance of technology and of labour productivity. So the black line is usually above the blue line. The years from 1973 to 1983 stand out as an unusual period in which wages often did not rise faster than prices. This

The **purchasing power** of a given sum of money is the volume of goods and services it will buy.

single fact goes a long way toward explaining why people have been so dissatisfied with economic performance since the mid-1970s.

The feature of Figure 6–3 that virtually jumps off the page is the way the two lines dance together. Wages normally rise rapidly when prices rise rapidly, and rise slowly when prices rise slowly. But you should not draw any hasty conclusions from this association. We cannot, for example, learn from this figure whether rising prices cause rising wages or whether rising wages cause rising prices. Remember the warnings given in Chapter 1 about trying to infer causation just by looking at data. But analysing cause and effect is not our purpose right now. We merely want to explode the myth that inflation inevitably robs workers of their wages.

Why is this myth so widespread? Imagine a world without inflation in which wages are rising 2 percent a year because of the increasing productivity of labour. Now imagine that, all of a sudden, inflation sets in and prices start rising 5 percent a year but that nothing else changes. Figure 6–3 suggests that, with perhaps a small delay, wage increases will accelerate to 2 percent plus 5 percent, or 7 percent a year.

Will workers view this change with equanimity? Probably not. To each worker, the 7 percent wage increase will be seen as something he earned by the sweat of his brow. In his view, he *deserves* every penny of his 7 percent raise. And, in a sense, he is right because "the sweat of his brow" earned him a 2 percent increment in purchasing power that, when the inflation rate is 5 percent, can only be achieved by increasing his wages by a total of 7 percent. An economist would divide the wage increase in the following way:

REASON FOR WAGE INCREASE	AMOUNT
Higher productivity	2%
Compensation for higher prices	5%
Total	7%

"Sure, you're raising my allowance. But am I actually gaining any purchasing power?"

An item's **relative price** is its price in terms of some other item, rather than in terms of dollars.

But the worker will probably keep score differently. Feeling that he earned the entire 7 percent by his own merits, he will view inflation as having "robbed" him of 5 percent of his just deserts. The higher the rate of inflation, the more of his raise the worker will feel robbed of.

Of course, nothing could be farther from the truth. Basically, the economic system is rewarding the worker with *the same 2 percent increment for higher productivity regardless of the rate of inflation.* The "evils of inflation" are often exaggerated because of a failure to understand this mechanism.

A second reason for misunderstanding the effects of inflation is that people are in the habit of thinking in terms of the number of dollars it takes to buy something rather than in the terms of the *purchasing power* of these dollars. For example, if inflation doubles both prices and wages, workers will have to labour exactly the same amount of time as before to earn the price of a loaf of bread. But because they now pay $1 a loaf instead of 50¢, they feel that the price of bread is scandalously high. In fact, nothing has really changed; but people remain stuck with an outmoded idea of what bread *should* cost.

A third misperception results from failure to distinguish between a *rise in the general price level* and a change in **relative prices**, that is, a rise in the price of one commodity relative to that of another. To see the distinction most clearly, imagine first a *pure inflation* in which *every* price rises by 10 percent during the year, so that relative prices do not change. Table 6–2 gives an example in which movie tickets go up from $4 to $4.40, candy bars from 50¢ to 55¢, and automobiles from $8000 to $8800. After the inflation, just as before, it will still take 8 candy bars to buy a movie ticket, 2000 movie tickets to buy a car, and so on. A person

Table 6-2			
ITEM	LAST YEAR'S PRICE	THIS YEAR'S PRICE	PERCENT INCREASE
Candy bar	$ 0.50	$ 0.55	10
Movie ticket	4.00	4.40	10
Automobile	8000.00	8800.00	10

Table 6-3			
ITEM	LAST YEAR'S PRICE	THIS YEAR'S PRICE	PERCENT INCREASE
Candy bar	$ 0.50	$ 0.50	0
Movie ticket	4.00	5.00	25
Automobile	8000.00	8400.00	5

who manufactures candy bars in order to purchase movie tickets is neither helped nor harmed by the inflation. Neither is a car dealer with a sweet tooth.

But real inflation is not like this. When there is 10 percent general inflation—meaning that the "average price" rises by 10 percent[4]—some prices may jump 20 percent or more while others actually fall. Suppose that, instead of the price increases shown in Table 6-2, prices rise as shown in Table 6-3. Movie prices go up by 25 percent, but candy prices do not change. Surely, candy manufacturers who love movies will be disgruntled because it now costs 10 candy bars instead of 8 to get into the theatre. They will blame inflation for raising the price of movie tickets, even though their real problem stems from the *increase in the price of movies relative to candy*. (They would have been hurt just as much if movie tickets had remained at $4 while the price of candy fell to 40¢.)

Since car prices have risen by only 5 percent, theatre owners in need of new cars will be delighted by the fact that an auto now costs only 1680 movie admissions (just as they would have cheered if car prices had fallen to $6720 while movie tickets remained at $4). However, they are unlikely to attribute their good fortune to inflation—as indeed they should not. What has actually happened is that *cars became cheaper relative to movies*.

Because real-world inflation proceeds at *uneven* rates, relative prices are constantly changing. There are gainers and losers, just as some would gain and others lose if relative prices changed without any general inflation. Inflation, however, gets a bad name because losers often blame inflation for their misfortune while gainers rarely credit inflation for their good luck. Alas, nobody loves inflation.

These three kinds of misconceptions may go a long way toward explaining why respondents to public-opinion polls consistently list inflation as a major national issue, and why higher inflation rates depress consumers.

Inflation does not systematically erode the purchasing power of wages. Nor does it lead to "unfair" prices. Nor is it usually to blame when some goods become more expensive relative to others.

But not all the costs of inflation are mythical. Let us now turn to some of the real costs.

Inflation as a Redistributor of Income and Wealth

We have just seen that the *average* person is neither helped nor harmed by inflation. But almost no one is exactly average! Some persons gain from inflation and others lose. It is hard to say anything more systematic than this about the effects of inflation on particular prices and wages.

But inflation does have systematic effects on the distribution of income and wealth. Senior citizens trying to scrape by on pensions or other fixed incomes

[4]The way statisticians figure out "average" price increases is discussed in the appendix to this chapter.

suffer badly from inflation. Since they earn no wages, it is little solace to them that wages are keeping pace with prices. Their private pension incomes tend not to.[5]

This example actually illustrates a much more general problem. We can think of pensioners as people who "lend" money to an organization (the pension fund) when they are young in order to be "paid back" with interest when they are old. Because of the rise in the price level during the intervening years, the unfortunate pensioners get paid back in less valuable dollars than those they originally loaned. In general:

Those who lend money are usually victimized by inflation.

While lenders lose heavily, borrowers do quite well. For example, homeowners who borrowed money from banks in the form of mortgages back in the 1950s, when interest rates were 3 or 4 percent, gained enormously from the surprisingly virulent inflation of the late 1960s and 1970s. They paid back dollars of much lower value than those that they borrowed. And the same is true of other borrowers.

Borrowers usually gain from inflation.

Since the redistribution caused by inflation generally benefits borrowers at the expense of lenders, and since both lenders and borrowers can be found at every income level, we must conclude that:

Inflation does not always steal from the rich to aid the poor, nor does it always do the reverse.

Why, then, is the redistribution caused by inflation so widely condemned? Because its victims are selected capriciously. Nobody legislates this redistribution. Nobody enters into it voluntarily. The gainers do not earn their spoils, and the losers do not deserve their fate. Moreover, there have been particular classes of people whom inflation has systematically robbed of purchasing power year after year—old-age pensioners, people who have saved money and "loaned" it to banks, and workers on long-term contracts or those whose wages and salaries do not adjust easily for some other reason. Even if people "on the average" suffer no damage from inflation, that offers little consolation to those who are hurt by it persistently and systematically. This is the fundamental indictment of inflation.

Inflation redistributes income in an arbitrary way that distorts society's distribution of income. The actual income distribution should reflect the interplay of the operation of free markets and the deliberate efforts of government to alter the distribution. Inflation interferes with and distorts this process.

Real Versus Nominal Interest Rates

But wait. Must inflation always rob lenders to bestow gifts upon borrowers? If both parties see inflation coming, won't lenders demand that borrowers pay a higher interest rate as compensation for the coming inflation? Indeed they will. For this reason, economists draw a conceptual distinction between inflation that is *expected* and inflation that comes as a surprise.

What happens when inflation is fully expected by both parties? Suppose Diamond Jim wants to borrow $1000 from Scrooge, and both agree that, in the absence of inflation, which erodes the value of money, a fair rate of interest would

---

[5]This is not true, for example, for Canada's Old Age Security plan. These benefits are financed out of tax revenues rather than directly through accumulated savings, and benefit levels are generally increased to compensate recipients for changes in the price level. For further discussion of Canada's pension provisions, see *Microeconomics*, Chapter 18.

---

be 4 percent on a one-year loan. This means that Diamond Jim would pay back $1040 at the end of the year for the privilege of having $1000 now.

If both expect prices to increase by 6 percent, Scrooge may reason as follows: "If Diamond Jim pays me back $1040 a year from today, that money will buy less than what $1000 buys today. Thus I'll really be *paying him* to borrow from me! I'm no philanthropist. Why don't I charge him 10 percent instead? Then he'll pay back $1100 at the end of the year. With prices 6 percent higher, this will buy roughly what $1040 is worth today. So I'll get the same 4 percent increase in purchasing power that we would have agreed on in the absence of inflation, and won't be any worse off. That's the least I'll accept."

Diamond Jim may follow a similar chain of logic. "With no inflation, I was willing to pay $1040 a year from now for the privilege of having $1000 today, and Scrooge was willing to lend it. He'd be crazy to do the same with a 6 percent inflation. He'll want to charge me more. How much should I pay? If I offer to him $1100 a year from now, that will have roughly the same purchasing power as $1040 today, so I won't be any worse off. That's the most I'll pay."

This kind of thinking will lead Scrooge and Diamond Jim to write a contract with a 10 percent interest rate—4 percent as the increase in purchasing power that Diamond Jim pays to Scrooge and 6 percent as compensation for the expected inflation. Then, if the expected 6 percent inflation actually materializes, neither party will have been made better or worse off than was expected at the time the contract was signed.[6]

This example illustrates a very general principle. The 4 percent increase in purchasing power that Diamond Jim agrees to hand over to Scrooge is called the **real rate of interest**. And the 10 percent contractual interest charge that Diamond Jim and Scrooge write into the loan agreement is called the **nominal rate of interest**. The nominal rate of interest is arrived at by adding the **expected rate of inflation** to the real rate of interest. Expected inflation is added to compensate the lender for the loss in purchasing power that he is expected to suffer as a result of inflation. Because of this:

Inflation that is accurately predicted need not redistribute income between borrowers and lenders. If the *expected* rate of inflation that is embodied in the nominal interest rate closely approximates the *actual* rate of inflation, no one gains and no one loses. However, to the extent that expectations prove incorrect, inflation will still redistribute income.

It need hardly be pointed out that errors in predicting the rate of inflation are the norm, not the exception. Published forecasts bear witness to the fact that economists have great difficulty in predicting the rate of inflation. The task is no easier for businesses, consumers, and banks. This is one reason why inflation is so widely condemned as unfair and undesirable. It sets up a guessing game that no one likes.

Inflation and the Tax System

So inflation imposes costs on society because it is hard to predict. But there are other costs of inflation, perhaps even more serious, that arise from high inflation, even when inflation is predicted accurately. These costs stem from the fact that our taxation system was designed for an inflation-free economy; and these laws may malfunction when inflation is high.

Our tax law does not recognize the distinction between nominal and real interest rates. The law simply taxes nominal interest regardless of how much real

The **real rate of interest** is the percentage increase in purchasing power that the borrower pays to the lender for the privilege of borrowing. It indicates the increased ability to purchase goods and services that the lender earns.

The **nominal rate of interest** is the percentage by which the money the borrower pays back exceeds the money that he borrowed, making no adjustment for any fall in the purchasing power of this money that results from inflation.

---

[6]EXERCISE: Who gains and who loses if the inflation turns out to be only 4 percent instead of the 6 percent that Scrooge and Diamond Jim expected? What if the inflation rate is 8 percent?

Table 6-4

INFLATION AND THE TAXATION OF INTEREST INCOME

(1)	(2)	(3)	(4)	(5)	(6)	(7)	(8)	(9)
INFLATION RATE (percent)	NOMINAL INTEREST RATE (percent)	INTEREST INCOME (dollars)	LOSS OF PURCHASING POWER DUE TO INFLATION (dollars)	REAL INTEREST INCOME (dollars)	TAXES PAID (dollars)	REAL INCOME AFTER TAX	(as a percentage of $1000 loan)	EFFECTIVE RATE OF TAXATION (percent)
						(dollars)		
0	4	40	0	40	20	20	2	50
6	10	100	60	40	50	−10	−1	125

interest it represents. As a result, strange things happen when there is high inflation. Our example of Scrooge's loan to Diamond Jim will illustrate the problem.

The top line of Table 6–4 shows how taxation affects the loan agreement where there is no inflation and the nominal and real interest rates are both at 4 percent. Scrooge earns $40 in nominal interest income (column 3). Since there is no inflation, this also represents $40 in real interest income (column 5). If Scrooge pays 50 percent of his income in taxes, his tax bill rises by $20 (column 6), leaving him with $20 after tax (column 7). This $20 amounts to 2 percent of the $1000 originally loaned (column 8). Because his $20 tax payment is half of his $40 in real interest income, Scrooge's effective tax rate is 50 percent (column 9), just as Parliament intended.

Now let's consider the same transaction when the inflation rate is 6 percent and Scrooge and Diamond Jim settle on a 10 percent nominal interest rate. Scrooge collects $100 in interest (column 3). But, with 6 percent inflation, the purchasing power of the $1000 he lends declines by $60 (column 4). Thus his real interest income is again $40 (column 5). However, assuming that Scrooge has already used up his $1000 interest income-tax exemption, the tax collector taxes the $100 nominal interest income, not the $40 real interest income, so Scrooge must pay $50 (50 percent of $100) in taxes (column 6). As we can see in column 7, his after-tax real income on the loan is –$10. Or, putting the same point a different way, the effective real after-tax interest rate he earns is –1 percent! As column 9 shows, the effective tax rate on Scrooge's real interest income is 125 percent, far larger than the 50 percent rate intended by Parliament.

So a tax system that works well at zero inflation misfires at 6 percent inflation because it taxes nominal, rather than real, interest. This little example illustrates a general, and very serious, problem:

Because it fails to recognize the distinction between nominal and real interest rate, our tax system levies high, and presumably unintended, tax rates on interest income when there is high inflation. And similar problems arise in the taxation of dividends, corporate profits, and other items.[7] Many economists feel that these high tax rates discourage saving, lending, and investing, and that high inflation therefore retards economic growth. Thus, there are major costs of inflation that are not purely redistributive.

[7]A particularly serious problem arises in the taxation of capital gains. Capital gains are the difference between the price at which one sells an asset and the price at which one bought it. In Canada, capital gains are taxed at one-half of their actual values, without any adjustment for changes in their purchasing power resulting from inflation. An example will bring out the point. Between 1971 and 1980 the price level doubled, approximately. Consider a piece of land that was purchased for $50,000 in 1971 and sold for $75,000 in 1980. The owner would have lost purchasing power in the transaction because 75,000 1980 dollars purchased less than 50,000 1971 dollars. Yet, since the tax authorities do not correct for inflation, the owner will be forced to pay tax on $12,500 as though there had been a profit rather than a loss.

Why do inappropriate tax laws stay on the books so long? One reason is a general lack of understanding of the difference between real and nominal interest rates. People seem not to understand that it is normally the *real* rate of interest that matters in an economic transaction because only that rate reveals how much borrowers pay (and lenders receive) *in terms of the goods and services which that money can buy.* They think about the high nominal rates caused by inflation, even if these rates correspond to very low real interest rates. Here are some other examples that may help you appreciate how widespread and important this interest-rate illusion is.

Regulation of Public Utilities

During the early 1960s, when the rate of inflation averaged about 1.5 percent a year, interest rates on high-grade corporate bonds hovered around 5 percent, yielding a real rate of interest about 3.5 percent. Regulated public utilities were permitted to earn profits at rates that exceeded 3.5 percent, since the utilities were able to afford borrowing funds at this rate. There were few public complaints suggesting that there was anything scandalous about such earning rates.

Yet during 1980 when the rate of inflation rose above 10 percent and corporate interest rates rose to 13 percent (implying a slightly lower real interest rate than earlier), there were many complaints. Regulated utilities, which asked the regulatory agencies to permit them a nominal rate of return closer to 13 percent so that they could afford to borrow the money needed to serve expanding public demand, found that their requests were considered exorbitant by the commissions and by the general public.

Record Profit Rates

Amazingly, even business managers were subject to the same form of illusion. Often they were taken aback by the notion that their investors actually lost out (earned a negative *real* rate of return) when the company was earning a 10 percent nominal profit. The managers noted that 10 percent was the company's highest earnings rate in recent history; but with inflation at 12 percent, it turned out that in real terms it was in fact the firm's lowest.

Monetary Policy

Throughout the first half of the 1970s, Western governments increased their countries' money supplies at record rates, because they thought credit must be made more available to lower the apparent high borrowing costs. But it was only nominal, not real, interest rates that were high. Real interest rates had never been lower. The extra money simply worsened the inflation and widened the gap between the real and nominal interest rates.

Thus, failure to understand that high *nominal* interest rates can signify very low *real* interest rates has been known to impoverish savers during a period of inflation. It has made profits appear high when they were really low, and it has led to major mistakes in the formation of monetary policy.

The Illusion of High Interest Rates

The difference between real and nominal interest (and profit) rates, and the fact that the real rate matters most in terms of economic effects while the nominal rate is politically significant, are matters that are of the utmost importance and yet are understood by very few people, including many persons who make public-policy decisions in these areas.

This concept is one of the **12 Ideas for Beyond the Final Exam**, and if you remember it ten years from now, you will truly have gotten a great deal out of studying economics.

Indexation of the Personal Income-Tax System

Some reforms have occurred. Since 1975, the authorities have properly separated the real and nominal interest rates in all discussions of their monetary policies. Also, in 1973, the federal government indexed the major provisions in the personal income-tax system.

Without indexing, inflation generates increasingly larger amounts of government revenue without any change in tax rates. One reason for the increase in revenue is that the deductions allowed on the tax form decline as a proportion of income in an inflationary situation, so that a larger proportion of income is subject to tax. The other reason for the unintended increase in revenues is that individuals are pushed into successively higher income-tax brackets as nominal incomes rise due to inflation. Thus, even if wages rise as rapidly as prices, people's real *after-tax* incomes fall.

The case for indexing rests generally on two arguments. One argument is that, in the absence of indexing, a greater share of national income flows automatically to the government with inflation, and it is felt by many that decisions about the division of resources between the public and private sectors should be made explicitly by legislation rather than by the amount of inflation in the economy. The second argument is that indexing will improve the equity or fairness of the personal income tax. Without indexing, inflation erodes the value of the allowed income-tax deductions, so that many low-income individuals are brought on to the tax rolls as inflation raises their incomes in nominal terms above the cut-off level provided by exemptions and deductions. Indexing the personal income tax for inflation reduces this as well as other inequities.

The Canadian indexing system works as follows: The limits on each income bracket and the value of the exemptions are multiplied annually by a factor that represents the amount of inflation during the past year. An illustration may make this more clear. The exemption for a taxpayer was $1600 and the tax rate was 19 percent for taxable income between $1000 and $2000 in Canada in 1973. If prices had risen 10 percent in 1973, the value of the exemption would have increased to $1760, and taxable income between $1100 and $2200 would have been taxed at a rate of 19 percent in 1974. (The actual inflation adjustment factor for 1974 was 6.6 percent.) Since indexing has been in operation, the basic exemption for a single taxpayer has risen from $1600 in 1973 to $3770 for the 1983 tax year.

Indexing, along with the government's refusal to explicitly raise tax rates or cut expenditures, has been a major factor contributing toward the large budget deficits. Partly because of this, and partly to advertise its restraint program in the early 1980s, the government limited the indexing factor to a maximum of 6 percent and 5 percent for the 1983 and 1984 tax years.

Other Costs of Inflation

Another cost of inflation is that rapidly changing prices make it risky to enter into long-term contracts. In an extremely severe inflation, the "long term" may be only a few days. But even moderate inflation can have remarkable effects on long-term loans. Suppose a corporation wants to borrow $1 million to finance the purchase of some new equipment and needs the loan for 20 years. If the inflation rate averages 8 percent over this period, the $1 million it repays at the end of 20 years will be worth only $214,548 in today's purchasing power. If inflation averages 4 percent instead, it will be worth $456,387. Lending or borrowing for this long a period is obviously a big gamble. With the stakes this high, the outcome may be that neither lenders nor borrowers want to get involved in long-term contracts. But without long-term loans, business investment becomes impossible. The economy stagnates.

Inflation also makes life difficult for the shopper. You probably have a group of stores that you habitually patronize because you know they generally carry the items you want to buy at (roughly) the prices you want to pay. This knowledge saves you a great deal of time and energy. But when prices are changing rapidly, your list becomes obsolete very quickly. You return to your favourite clothing store only to find that the price of jeans has risen drastically. Should you buy? Should you shop around at other stores? Will they have also raised their prices? And business firms have precisely the same problem with their suppliers. Rising prices force them to shop around more than they are accustomed to, which imposes costs on the firms and, more generally, reduces the efficiency of the whole economy.

Shopping costs may sound frivolous and unimportant, but they are not. The late Arthur Okun, who chaired the Council of Economic Advisers under U.S. President Johnson, suggested an ingenious mental exercise that illustrates the importance of shopping costs. Ask yourself the following question: How much would you have to be paid to promise never again to buy anything from any of the stores you have patronized in the past? When you ponder this for a while, you realize the great value of having normal places to shop. Inflation takes some of this value away.

Creeping Versus Galloping Inflation

The preceding litany of costs of inflation alerts us to one very important fact: *predictable inflation is far less burdensome than is unpredictable inflation.* When will inflation be most predictable? When it proceeds year after year at more or less the same rate. Thus the *variability of the inflation rate* is a crucial factor. Inflation of 6 percent a year for three consecutive years will exact far lower social costs than inflation that is 8 percent in the first year, zero in the second, and 10 percent in the third. In general:

Steady inflation is much more predictable than variable inflation and therefore has much smaller social and economic costs.

But the *average level of the inflation rate* is also important. Partly because of the incomplete indexing provisions in taxes and the interest rate illusions mentioned above, and partly because of the more rapid breakdown in normal customer relationships that we have just mentioned, a steady inflation of 8 percent a year is more damaging than a steady inflation of 3 percent a year.

Economists distinguish between **creeping inflation** and **galloping inflation** partly on their average level and partly on their variability. Under creeping inflation, prices rise for a long time at a moderate and fairly steady rate. Postwar Sweden provides a good example. During the 13-year period from 1954 to 1967, prices climbed a total of 64 percent (compared with only 33 percent in Canada), for an average annual inflation rate of 3.9 percent. And the pace of inflation was remarkably steady, rarely dropping below 2.5 percent or rising above 5 percent.

Galloping inflation refers to inflation that proceeds at an exceptionally high rate, perhaps for only a relatively brief period. Galloping inflation is generally characterized by accelerating rates of inflation so that the rate of inflation is higher this month than it was last month.

Germany after World War I suffered through one of the more severe inflations in history. Wholesale prices increased over 140 percent in 1921 and a colossal 4100 percent during 1922. At this point, what had been very serious galloping inflation simply got out of control. Between December 1922 and November 1923, when a hard-nosed reform finally broke the inflationary spiral, wholesale prices in Germany increased by almost 100 million percent! But even this experience was dwarfed by the great Hungarian inflation of 1945–46, the greatest inflation of them all. For a period of one year, the rate of inflation averaged about 20,000

Creeping inflation refers to inflation that proceeds for a long time at a moderate and fairly steady pace.

Galloping inflation refers to inflation that proceeds at an exceptionally high rate, perhaps for only a relatively brief period.

These children in Germany during the hyperinflation of the 1920s are building a pyramid with cash, worth no more than the sand or sticks used by children elsewhere.

percent *per month*. And in the final month, the price level skyrocketed 42 quadrillion percent!

While the distinction between creeping and galloping inflation is a quantitative one, we refrained from putting any specific numbers into the definitions. This is because different societies at different points in time have very different conceptions about what rate constitutes creeping inflation and what rate constitutes galloping inflation. For example, in Canada today, annual rates of inflation in the 3 to 7 percent range are generally considered to be "creeping," while rates in the 25 to 30 percent range would surely be construed as "galloping." In most Latin American countries, however, inflation consistently in the 25 to 30 percent range is viewed as "creeping." And in the Canada of the 1950s a 7 percent annual inflation might have been branded "galloping."

The Costs of Creeping Versus Galloping Inflation

If you review the costs of inflation that have been discussed in this chapter, you will see why the distinction between creeping and galloping inflation is so fundamental. Many economists feel we can live reasonably well, indeed can prosper, in an environment of creeping inflation. No one feels we can survive very well under galloping inflation.

Under creeping inflation, the rate at which prices rise is relatively easy to predict and to take into account in setting interest rates. Under galloping inflation, where prices are rising at ever-increasing rates, this is very difficult, and perhaps impossible, to accomplish. The potential redistributions become monumental, and as a result, lending and borrowing may cease entirely.

Any inflation makes it difficult to write long-term contracts. With creeping inflation, the "long term" may be 20 years, or 10 years, or 5. But with galloping inflation, the "long term" may be measured in weeks or even hours. Restaurant prices may change before you finish your dessert. Railway fares may go up while you are in the middle of your journey. When it is impossible to enter into contracts of any duration longer than a few minutes, economic activity becomes paralysed. We conclude that:

The horrors of galloping inflation either are absent in creeping inflation or are present in such muted forms that they can scarcely be considered horrors.

Creeping Inflation Does Not Necessarily Lead to Galloping Inflation

We noted earlier that inflation is surrounded by a mythology that bears precious little relation to reality. It seems appropriate to conclude this chapter by disposing of one particularly persistent myth: that creeping inflation invariably leads to galloping inflation.

There is neither statistical evidence nor theoretical support for the myth that creeping inflation leads to galloping inflation. To be sure, creeping inflation sometimes accelerates. But at other times it slows down.

Galloping inflation has only occurred when the government has printed incredible amounts of money, usually to finance wartime expenditures.

In the German inflation of 1923, the government finally found that its printing presses could not produce enough paper money to keep pace with the exploding prices. Not that it did not try. By the end of the inflation, the *daily* output of currency was over 400 quadrillion marks! The Hungarian authorities in 1945–46 tried even harder. The average growth rate of the money supply was more than 12,000 percent *per month*. Needless to say, these are not the kinds of inflation problems that are likely to face Canada in the foreseeable future.

But this should not be interpreted to imply there is nothing wrong with creeping inflation. Much of this chapter has been spent analysing the very real costs of inflation, no matter how slow. A case against even moderate inflation can indeed be built, but it does not help this case to shout foolish slogans like "Creeping inflation always leads to galloping inflation." Fortunately, it is simply not true.

Summary

1. Unemployment exacts heavy financial and psychological costs from those who are its victims, costs that are borne quite unevenly by different groups in the population.
2. Unemployment is measured by a government survey. Some critics claim that the survey methods understate the unemployment problem, while others contend that the methods overstate the problem.
3. Frictional unemployment arises when people are between jobs for normal reasons. Thus, most frictional unemployment is acceptable.
4. Structural unemployment is due to shifts in the pattern of demand or to technological change that results in certain skills becoming obsolete.
5. Cyclical unemployment is the portion of unemployment that rises in recessions and falls when the economy booms.
6. In 1945, the federal government committed itself to limiting unemployment to the frictional variety. However, it set no numerical goals.
7. During the 1950s and 1960s, most economists regarded cyclical unemployment as anything above 3.5 percent. Now, with increased structural problems, most economists regard cyclical unemployment as about 6.5 percent.
8. Unemployment insurance replaces about sixty percent of the lost income of unemployed persons who are insured. But not all the unemployed are covered by insurance, and no insurance program can bring back the lost output that could have been produced had these people been working.
9. In recent decades, the Canadian economy typically has produced less output than it could have were it operating at full employment. This shortfall has been particularly large since the mid-1970s.
10. People have many misconceptions about inflation. For example, many people believe that inflation systematically erodes the purchasing power of wages, are appalled by rising prices even when wages are rising just as fast, and blame inflation for any unfavourable changes in relative prices. All of these are myths.
11. Other costs of inflation are very real indeed. For example, inflation often redistributes income from lenders to borrowers.
12. This redistribution can be eliminated by adding the expected rate of inflation to the interest rate, but expectations often prove to be quite inaccurate.
13. The real rate of interest is the nominal rate of interest minus the expected rate of inflation.
14. Since the real rate of interest indicates the command over real resources that the borrower surrenders to the lender, it is of primary economic importance.
15. Yet public attention often is riveted on nominal rates of interest, and this confusion can lead to costly policy mistakes when high inflation converts high nominal interest rates into very low real interest rates. This is one of the **12 Ideas for Beyond the Final Exam**.
16. Despite indexing of the basic personal income-tax system in 1973, our tax system levies very heavy taxes on interest income when inflation is high, since nominal, not real, interest income is taxed.
17. Creeping inflation, which proceeds at moderate and fairly predictable rates year after year, carries far lower social costs than galloping inflation, which proceeds at high and variable rates.
18. The notion that creeping inflation inevitably leads to galloping inflation is a myth with no foundation in economic theory and no basis in historical fact.

Concepts for Review

Unemployment rate
Labour force
Discouraged workers
Frictional unemployment
Structural unemployment
Cyclical unemployment

Full employment
Unemployment insurance
Potential GNP
Purchasing power
Relative prices
Redistribution by inflation

Real rate of interest
Nominal rate of interest
Expected rate of inflation
Indexed taxes
Creeping inflation
Galloping inflation

Questions for Discussion

1. Why is it not as terrible to become unemployed nowadays as it was during the Great Depression?

2. "Since unemployed workers receive unemployment benefits and other benefits that make up for most of their lost wages, unemployment is no longer a social problem." Comment.

3. Using what you learned about aggregate demand and aggregate supply in Chapter 5, try to explain why the Canadian economy has failed so frequently to produce up to its potential. (You will learn more about this question in later chapters, so don't worry if you find the question difficult now.)

4. Do you think that Statistics Canada overestimates or underestimates the number of people that are unemployed? Why?

5. Why is it so difficult to define "full employment"? What unemployment rate should the government be shooting for today?

6. Show why each of the following complaints is based on a misunderstanding about inflation:
   a. "Inflation must be stopped because it robs workers of their purchasing power."
   b. "Inflation is a terrible social disease. It leads to unconscionably high prices for basic necessities."
   c. "Inflation makes it impossible for working people to afford many of the things they were hoping to buy."

   d. "Inflation must be stopped today, for if we do not stop it, it will surely accelerate to ruinously high rates and lead to disaster."

7. What is the *real interest rate* paid on a loan bearing 18 percent nominal interest per year, if the rate of inflation is:
   a. zero
   b. 2 percent
   c. 7 percent
   d. 12 percent
   e. 19 percent

8. Suppose you agree to lend money to your friend on the day you both enter university, at what you both expect to be a zero *real* rate of interest. Payment is to be made at graduation, with interest at a fixed *nominal* rate. If inflation proves to be *lower* during your four years in university than what you both had expected, who will gain and who will lose?

9. You have lived with inflation all your life. Think about the costs that inflation has imposed on you personally. How do these costs relate to the material in this chapter?

10. Add a third line to Table 6-4 showing what would happen if the inflation rate went to 12 percent and the real interest rate remained 4 percent.

Appendix

How Statisticians Measure Inflation

Index Numbers for Inflation

Inflation is generally measured by the change in some index of the general price level. For example, between 1973 and 1983, the Consumer Price Index (CPI), which stood at 100 in 1981, rose from 47.6 to 117.2, an increase of 146 percent. The meaning of the *change* is clear enough. But what is the meaning of the 47.6 figure for 1973 and the 117.2 figure for 1983?

These numbers are **index numbers**; each expresses the cost of a market basket of goods *relative to its cost in some "base" period*. Since the CPI uses 1981 as its base period, the CPI of 117.2 for 1983 means that it cost $117.20 in 1983 to purchase the same basket of goods and services that cost $100 in 1981.

Now, the particular basket of consumer goods and services under scrutiny really did not cost $100 in 1981. When constructing index numbers, it is conventional to set the index at 100 in the base year. How is this conventional figure used in obtaining index numbers for other years? Very simply. Suppose the budget needed to buy the roughly 400 items included in the CPI was $500 per month in 1981 and $586 per month in 1983. Then the index is defined by the following rule:

$$\frac{\text{CPI in 1983}}{\text{CPI in 1981}} =$$

$$\frac{\text{Cost of the 400-item market basket in 1983}}{\text{Cost of the 400-item market basket in 1981}}$$

Since the CPI in 1981 is set at 100:

$$\frac{\text{CPI in 1983}}{100} = \frac{\$586}{\$500} = 1.172$$

or

$$\text{CPI in 1983} = 117.2.$$

Exactly the same sort of equation enables us to calculate the CPI in any other year. We have the rule:

$$\text{CPI in given year} = \frac{\text{Cost of market basket in given year}}{\text{Cost of market basket in base year}} \times 100.$$

Of course, not every combination of consumer goods that cost $500 in 1981 rose to $586 by 1983. For example, a colour TV set that cost $500 in 1981 might have sold for $450 in 1983, but a $500 insurance bill in 1981 might have ballooned to $700. Since no two families buy precisely the same bundle of goods and services, no two families suffer precisely the same increase in their cost of living unless all prices rise at the same rate. Economists refer to this phenomenon as the **index number problem**.

When relative prices are changing, there is no such thing as a "perfect price index" that is correct for every consumer. Any statistical index will understate the increase in the cost of living for some families and overstate it for others. At best, the index can represent the situation of an "average" family.

The Consumer Price Index

The most closely watched price index is surely the **Consumer Price Index**, which is calculated and announced each month by Statistics Canada. When you read in the newspaper or see on television that the "cost of living" rose by 0.8 percent last month, chances are the reporter is referring to the CPI.

The CPI is measured by pricing the items on a list representative of a typical urban household budget. To know what items to include and in what amounts, Statistics Canada conducts an extensive survey of spending habits roughly twice every decade (the last one was in 1978). This means that the *same* bundle of goods and services is used as a standard for several years, whether or not spending habits change.[8]

---

[8]Economists call this a *base-period weight index* because the relative importance it attaches to each price depends on how much money consumers actually chose to spend on it during the base period.

The 1978 family expenditure survey examined the spending patterns of Canadians living in the 64 urban communities of 30,000 people or more. In addition to the overall CPI, a separate one is published for each of the 15 major cities within this group.

A simple example will help us understand how the CPI is constructed. Imagine that university students purchase only three items—hamburgers, jeans, and movie tickets—and that we want to devise a cost-of-living index (call it SPI, for "student price index") for them. First we would conduct a survey of spending habits in the base year (suppose it is 1973). Table 6-5 represents the hypothetical results. You will note that the frugal students of that day spent only $50 per month: $28 on hamburgers, $12 on jeans, and $10 on movies.

Table 6-5
RESULTS OF STUDENT EXPENDITURE SURVEY, 1973

ITEM	AVERAGE PRICE	AVERAGE QUANTITY PURCHASED PER MONTH	AVERAGE EXPENDITURE PER MONTH
Hamburger	$ 0.40	70	$28
Jeans	12.00	1	12
Movie ticket	2.50	4	10
			Total $50

Table 6-6
PRICES IN 1985

ITEM	PRICE	PERCENTAGE INCREASE OVER 1973
Hamburger	$ 1	150
Jeans	15	25
Movie ticket	4	60

Table 6-6 presents hypothetical prices of these same three items in 1985. Each price has risen by a different amount, ranging from only 25 percent for jeans to 150 percent for hamburgers. By how much has the SPI risen? Pricing the 1973 student budget at 1985 prices, we find that what once cost $50 now costs $101, as the following calculation shows:

COST OF 1973 STUDENT BUDGET IN 1985 PRICES	
70 hamburgers at $1	$70
1 pair of jeans at $15	15
4 movie tickets at $4	16
	Total $101

Thus the SPI, based on 1973 = 100, is

$$SPI = \frac{\text{Cost of budget in 1985}}{\text{Cost of budget in 1973}} = \frac{\$101}{\$50} \times 100 = 202.$$

So the SPI in 1985 stands at 202, meaning that a student's cost of living has increased 102 percent over the 12 years.

How to Use a Price Index to "Deflate" Monetary Figures

One of the most common uses of price indexes is in the comparison of monetary figures relating to two different points in time. The problem is that, if there has been inflation, the dollar is not a good measuring rod because it is worth less now that it was in the past.

Here is a simple example. Suppose that the average student spent $50 per month in 1973, and that this monthly spending figure had grown to $90 per month in 1985. If there was an outcry that students had become spendthrifts, how would you answer the charge?

The obvious answer is that a dollar in 1985 does not buy what it did in 1973. Specifically, our SPI shows us that it takes $2.02 in 1985 to purchase what $1 would purchase in 1973. To compare the spending habits of students in the two years, we must divide the 1985 spending figure by 2.02. Specifically, *real* spending per student in 1985 (where "real" is defined by 1973 dollars) is:

$$\text{Real spending in 1985} = \frac{\text{Nominal spending in 1985}}{\text{Price index of 1985}}.$$

Thus,

$$\text{Real spending in 1985} = \frac{\$90}{2.02} = \$44.55.$$

In sum, this calculation shows that, despite appear-ances to the contrary, the change in nominal spending from $50 to $90 actually represented a *decrease* in real spending.

This calculation procedure is called **deflating by a price index**, and it serves to translate non-comparable monetary figures into more directly com-parable real figures.

Deflating is the process of finding the real value of some monetary magnitude by dividing by some ap-propriate price index.

The GNP Deflator

In macroeconomics, one of the most important of the monetary magnitudes that we have to deflate is the nominal gross national product (GNP). The price index used to do this is called the **GNP deflator**. Our general principle for deflating a nominal magnitude tells us just how to go from nominal GNP to real GNP:

$$\text{Real GNP} = \frac{\text{Nominal GNP}}{\text{GNP deflator}} \times 100.$$

As with the CPI, the 100 simply serves to establish the base of the index as 100, rather than 1.00.

Economists often consider the GNP deflator to be a better measure of overall inflation in the economy than the Consumer Price Index. The main reason for this is that the two price indexes are based on different market baskets. As already mentioned, the CPI is based on the budget of a typical urban family. By contrast, the GNP deflator is constructed from a market basket that includes *every* item in the GNP—that is, every final good and service produced by the economy. Thus, in addition to prices of consumer goods, the GNP deflator includes the prices of air-planes, lathes, and other goods purchased by business. It also includes government services. For this reason, the measures of inflation that these two indexes give are rarely the same. Usually their disagreements are minor, but sometimes they can be quite substantial.

Summary

1. Inflation is measured by the percentage increase in an index number of prices, which shows how the cost of some basket of goods has changed over a period of time.
2. Since relative prices are changing all the time, and since all families purchase different items, no price index can represent precisely the change in the cost of living for every family.
3. The Consumer Price Index (CPI) tries to measure the cost of living for an "average" urban household by pricing a "typical" market basket every month.
4. Price indexes like the CPI can be used to *deflate* monetary figures to make them more comparable. This amounts to dividing the monetary magnitude by the appropriate price index.
5. The GNP deflator is a better measure of economy-wide inflation than is the CPI because it includes the price of every good and service in the economy.

Concepts for Review

Index number
Index number problem
Consumer Price Index

Deflating by a price index
GNP deflator

Questions for Discussion

1. Just below you will find nominal GNP and the GNP deflator for 1963, 1973, and 1983.
   a. Compute real GNP for each year.
   b. Compute the percentage change in nominal and real GNP from 1963 to 1973, and from 1973 to 1983.
   c. Compute the percentage change in the GNP deflator over these two periods.

GNP STATISTICS			
	1963	1973	1983
Nominal GNP (billions of dollars)	45.9	123.5	388.6
GNP deflator	74.6	114.6	290.0

2. Fill in the blanks in the following table of GNP statistics.

YEAR	1981	1982	1983
Nominal GNP	339.0	356.7	388.6
Real GNP	136.1	130.1	134
GNP deflator	249.09	274.2	290.0

3. Use the following data to compute the University Price Index for 1984, using the base 1972=100.

ITEM	PRICE IN 1972	QUANTITY PER MONTH IN 1972	PRICE IN 1984
Button-down shirts	$10	1	$20
Loafers	25	1	45
Sneakers	10	3	15
Textbooks	12	12	22
Jeans	12	3	36
Restaurant meals	5	11	10

4. (More difficult.) The example in the appendix showed that the Student Price Index (SPI) rose by 102 percent from 1973 to 1985. You can understand the meaning of this better if you:
   a. Use Table 6-5 to compute the fraction of total spending accounted for by each of the three items in 1973. Call these the "expenditure weights."
   b. Compute the weighted average of the percentage increases of the three prices shown in Table 6-6, using the expenditure weights you have just computed.
   c. You should get 102 percent as your answer. This shows that "inflation," as measured by the SPI, is a weighted average of the percentage price increases of all the items that are included in the index.

Income and Spending: The Powerful Consumer

Men are disposed, as a rule
and on the average, to
increase their consumption
as their income increases,
but not by as much as the
increase in their income.
JOHN MAYNARD KEYNES

In Chapter 5 we saw how the strength of aggregate demand influences the performance of the economy. When aggregate demand is growing briskly, the economy is likely to be booming, though it may also be having trouble with inflation. Similarly, when aggregate demand stagnates, a recession is likely to follow.

This chapter begins our detailed study of the *determination* of aggregate demand. In this and the next few chapters, we will learn why the *aggregate-demand curve* of Chapter 5 has a negative slope and how the government can *manage* aggregate demand. Since consumer spending accounts for over 60 percent of total demand, it is natural to begin with the consumer. The following chapters will bring investment spending, government spending, foreign spending, and the supply side of the economy into the picture.

We start the chapter with some definitions of alternative concepts of economic activity—distinguishing carefully among total *spending* (aggregate demand), total *output*, and total *income*. Next, we turn to the interactions among these three concepts, using a convenient pictorial device that shows how they are all interrelated. Then we note that government attempts to influence consumer spending have sometimes succeeded and sometimes failed, and we pose the question: Why?

The bulk of this chapter is devoted to this question. To answer it, we first describe the important relationship between consumer income and consumer spending, and we use this relationship to show how government policies have worked when they have been successful. Then we discuss some complications that arise from the fact that consumer income, though crucial, is not the only factor governing consumer spending. One of these complications gives us the first of several reasons why the aggregate-demand curve slopes downward. Another holds the clue to why the government's income-tax policies have sometimes failed to influence consumer spending as expected. Also, the analysis explains why the Canadian federal government has tried to arrange sales-tax changes to avoid the problems associated with income-tax policy.

Aggregate Demand, National Product, and National Income

We begin with some definitions. We have already introduced the concept of **gross national product** as the standard measure of the total output of the economy.[1]

For the most part, goods are produced in a market economy only if they can be sold. **Aggregate demand**, another concept encountered in Chapter 5, is the total amount that all consumers, business firms, government agencies, and foreigners wish to spend on all final goods and services. Many factors enter into the determination of aggregate quantity demanded, including price level, consumer incomes, various government policies, and the level of foreign incomes. We can understand the nature of aggregate demand best if we break it up into its major components.

Consumer expenditure ("**consumption**" for short) is simply the total demand for all consumer goods and services. This is the focus of the current chapter, and we shall represent it by the letter **C**.

Investment spending, which we represent by the letter **I**, is the amount that firms spend on factories, machinery, and the like, plus the amount that families spend on new homes. Notice that this is a very different usage of the word "investment" from that which is found in common parlance. Most people speak of "investing" in the stock market or in a bank account. This kind of "investment" merely swaps one form of financial asset (such as money) for another form (such as a share of stock). When economists speak of "investment," they mean instead the purchase of some new physical asset, like a drill press or an oil rig or a home. It is only this kind of investment that leads directly to additional demand for newly produced goods in the economy.

Another major component of aggregate demand is **government purchases** of goods and services; that is, things like paper, typewriters, airplanes, ships, and labour that are bought by all levels of government—federal, provincial, and municipal. We use the letter **G** to denote this variable.

Finally, the last major component of aggregate demand is **net exports**. This consists of exports, which we represent by the letter **X**, and imports, which we denote by **IM**. Exports are the sum of all expenditures by foreigners on Canadian-produced final goods (such as wheat, fish, and snowmobiles) and services (such as transportation, hotel, and restaurant services purchased by foreigners while vacationing in Canada). Canadian expenditures on imports from other countries must be subtracted when calculating total demand for domestic production, since the spending by households, firms, and governments include their expenditures on the products from other countries.

Given all these abbreviations, we have the following shorthand definition of aggregate demand.

Aggregate demand is the sum $C + I + G + X - IM$.

The last concept we need is a measure of the total *income* of all the individuals in the economy. There are two versions of this: one for before-tax incomes, called **national income**, and one for after-tax incomes, called **disposable income**.[2] The term "disposable income" is meant to be descriptive: it tells us how many dollars consumers actually have available to spend or to save. Because it plays such a prominent role in this chapter, we shall need an abbreviation for it as well; we call it **DI**.

[1] See Chapter 5, pages 76–79.

[2] More detailed information on these and other concepts is provided in an appendix to this chapter.

Aggregate demand is the total amount that all consumers, business firms, government agencies, and foreigners are willing to spend on final goods and services.

Consumer expenditure, symbolized by the letter *C*, is the total amount spent by consumers on newly produced goods and services (excluding purchases of new homes, which are considered investment goods).

Investment spending, symbolized by the letter *I*, is the sum of the expenditures of business firms on new plant, equipment, and inventories, plus the expenditures of households on new homes. Financial "investments" are not included, nor are resales of existing physical assets.

Government purchases, symbolized by the letter *G*, refers to all the goods (such as airplanes and paper clips) and services (such as school teaching and police protection) purchased by all levels of government. It does not include government **transfer payments** to individuals (such as welfare benefits), nor transfer payments from one level of government to another.

Net exports, symbolized by *X – IM*, is the excess of foreign expenditures on our products over our purchases of their goods (Canadian exports minus Canadian imports).

The Circular Flow of Spending, Production, and Income

National income is the sum of the incomes of all the individuals in the economy earned in the forms of wages, interest, rents, and profits. It is calculated before any deductions are taken for income taxes.

Disposable income is the sum of the incomes of all the individuals in the economy after all taxes have been deducted.

Enough definitions. How do these three concepts—national product, aggregate demand, and national income—interact in a market economy? We can answer this best with a rather elaborate diagram (Figure 7–1). For obvious reasons, Figure 7–1 is called a **circular flow diagram**. It depicts a large circular tube in which a fluid is circulating in a clockwise direction. There are several breaks in the tube where either some of the fluid leaks out or additional fluid is injected in.

Let us examine this system beginning on the far left. Here, at point 1 on the circle, we find consumers. Disposable income (*DI*) is flowing into them, and two things are flowing out: consumption (*C*), which stays in the circular flow, and saving (*S*), which "leaks out." This just says that consumers normally spend less than they earn and save the balance. The "leakage" to savings, of course, does not disappear, but flows into the financial system. We postpone a consideration of what happens there until Chapter 12.

The upper loop of the circular flow represents expenditures, and as we move clockwise to point 2, we encounter the first "injection" into the flow: investment spending (*I*). The diagram shows this as coming from "investors"—a group that includes both business firms and consumers who buy new homes.[3] As the circular flow moves beyond point 2, it is bigger than it was before. Total spending has increased from *C* to *C* + *I*.

---

[3] You are reminded of the specific definition of investment on the preceding page.

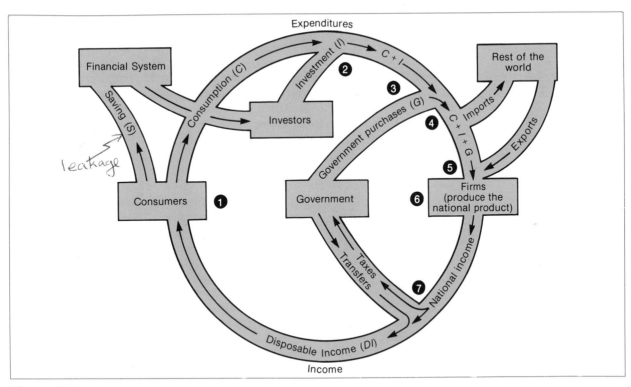

Figure 7-1

THE CIRCULAR FLOW OF EXPENDITURE AND INCOME

The upper half of this circular flow diagram depicts the flow of expenditures on goods and services that comes from consumers (point 1), investors (point 2), government (point 3), and foreigners (point 5), and goes to the firms that produce the output (point 6). Some of the expenditures are spent on imports (point 4), and so never reach domestically operating firms. The lower half of the diagram indicates how the income paid out by firms (point 6) flows to consumers (point 1), after some is siphoned off by the government in the form of taxes and part of this is replaced by transfer payments (point 7).

At point 3 there is yet another injection. The government adds its demand for goods and services (*G*) to those of consumers and investors (*C* + *I*). At point 4 there is another leakage, which allows some of the demands for goods and services to flow out to foreign producers. Demand for Canadian products is less than the total expenditures of households, firms, and governments by the amount of these imports. At point 5 there is the final injection—exports. Thus, by the time we have passed point 5 and have added in the foreign purchases, we have accumulated the full amount of aggregate demand, *C* + *I* + *G* + *X* – *IM*.

The circular flow diagram shows this aggregate demand for goods and services arriving at the business firms, located at point 6 on the extreme right of the diagram. Responding to this demand, firms produce the national product. As the circular flow emerges from the firms, however, we have renamed it *national income*. Why? Because, except for some complications explained in the appendix:

National income and national product must be equal.

Why is this the case? When a firm produces and sells $100 worth of output, it pays most of the proceeds to its workers, to people who have lent it money, and to the landlord who owns the property on which it is located. All of these payments are *income* to some individuals. But what about the rest? Suppose, for example, that the wages, interest, and rent that the firm pays add up to $90, while its output is $100. What happens to the remaining $10? The answer is that the owners of the firm receive it as *profits*. But these owners are also citizens of the country, so their incomes count in national income, too. Thus, when we add up all the wages, interest, rents, *and profits* in the economy to obtain the national income, we must arrive at the value of the national output.

A slight complication occurs when some of the firms are foreign-owned, as is the case in Canada. In this case, some of the profits earned in Canada add to another country's national income, not ours. This is partly compensated for by the fact that some Canadians earn profits by being part owners of firms that operate outside Canada. To allow for these activities, we could complicate our circular flow diagram with an additional leakage and injection between points 6 and 7. The leakage is incomes paid to foreigners operating within Canada, and the injection is incomes received by Canadians operating elsewhere. These flows do not exactly cancel off, so national product and national income are not exactly equal. National product is called *gross domestic product* (GDP), and national income is called GNP. We have followed the convention of ignoring the difference between these two aggregates for two reasons. First, we wish to keep the circular flow diagram simplified; second, the cyclical swings in GNP and GDP are virtually identical, as can be seen in Figure 7–2. Employment variations depend on these cyclical swings, not on the absolute level of either GNP or GDP.

The lower loop of the circular flow diagram traces the flow of income by showing national income leaving the firms and heading for consumers. But there is a detour along the way. At point 7, the government does two things. First, it siphons off a portion of the national income in the form of taxes. Second, it adds back government **transfer payments** to individuals, like disability compensation and government pension benefits, which are sums of money that certain individuals receive as *grants* from the government rather than as payments for services rendered to employers.

Transfer payments are sums of money that certain individuals receive as *grants* from the government rather than as payments for services rendered to employers.

When taxes are subtracted from GNP, and transfer payments are added, we obtain disposable income.[4]

DI = GNP – Taxes + Transfer payments.

Disposable income flows unimpeded to consumers at point 1, and the cycle repeats.

[4] This equation omits a few minor details, which are explained in an appendix to this chapter.

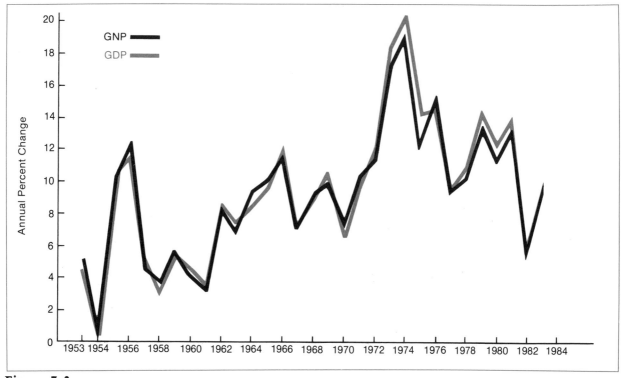

Figure 7-2

THE CLOSE RELATIONSHIP BETWEEN GDP AND GNP

GNP is the total income of Canadian factors of production, wherever they are employed. GDP is the total amount of employment-creating economic activity that actually takes place within Canada. For stabilization policy, we are concerned only with the cyclical swings in national income and production. The figure shows that the swings in nominal GNP and GDP are virtually identical.
SOURCE: Statistics Canada.

Figure 7-1 raises several complicated questions. Although we pose them here, we will not try to answer them at this early stage. The answers will be made clear in subsequent chapters.

1. Is the output that the firms produce at point 6 (the GNP) equal to aggregate demand? If so, what makes these two quantities equal? If not, what happens?

2. Is the flow of spending and income growing larger or smaller as we move clockwise around the circle, and why?

Chapter 8 provides the answers to questions 1 and 2.

3. Are the government's accounts in balance, so that what flows in at point 7 (taxes minus transfers) is equal to what flows out at point 3 (government purchases)? What happens if they are not?

This important question is first addressed in Chapter 11 and then recurs many times, especially in Chapter 17, which discusses budget deficits.

We cannot discuss these issues profitably now because first we must understand what goes on at point 1 (where consumers make decisions) and point 2 (where investors make decisions). We turn next, therefore, to the determinants of consumer spending.

Demand Management and the Powerful Consumer

As we suggested in Chapter 5, the government sometimes wants to shift the aggregate-demand curve. There are a number of ways in which it can try to do so.

One direct approach is to alter its own spending (G), becoming extravagant when private demand is weak and miserly when private demand is strong. But the government can also take a more indirect route by using taxes and other policy tools to influence *private* spending decisions.

A government desiring to change private spending can concentrate its energies on consumer spending (C), on investment spending (I), or on net exports (X – IM). At various times in our history, the Canadian government has elected to pursue one of these courses of action. Their favourite target has been firms' investment spending, which they try to manipulate with variations in the corporate tax system. We discuss these in Chapter 11. For the present, we discuss attempts to alter household consumption and consider some illuminating policy experiments that were tried in the United States. Also, we describe the Canadian government's attempt to benefit from this U.S. experience.

While there are many things it can do to alter consumer spending, the government's principal weapon is the personal income tax. Any reduction in personal taxes leaves consumers with more disposable income to spend. Any increase in taxes leaves them with less. The linkage from taxes to disposable income to consumer spending seems direct and unmistakable, and, in a certain sense, it is. But a look at the history of some major U.S. tax changes aimed at altering C is sobering. The varying degrees of success both of the measures themselves and of the predictions of their effects explain why economic research into the relationship between taxes and consumption continues.

Case 1: The U.S. Income-Tax Reduction of 1964

The year 1964 was a good one for economists. For years economists had been proclaiming that a cut in personal taxes would be an excellent way to stimulate a stagnating economy. But the plea fell on deaf ears until President John F. Kennedy was persuaded of the basic logic of the argument. Under his successor, Lyndon B. Johnson, the U.S. Congress reduced personal taxes by about 18 percent. The legislation was designed to spur consumer spending, and it succeeded admirably. Consumers reacted just about as the textbooks of the day predicted, the economic situation improved rapidly and markedly, and economists smiled knowingly.

Case 2: The U.S. Income-Tax Increase of 1968

The euphoria of 1964 was both unwarranted and short-lived. In 1968–69, the United States learned—the hard way—that economists did not have all the answers. Largely because of the massive defense spending associated with the Vietnam War, the macroeconomic problem confronting the United States in 1966–68 was precisely the opposite of that in 1964: too much demand rather than too little. It appeared logical, then, to prescribe the opposite medicine, and economists were quick to suggest an increase in personal income taxes to force consumers to spend less.

After a considerable delay, President Johnson recommended a temporary tax increase and Congress enacted a 10 percent rise in personal tax payments (calling it a "surcharge"). However, this attempt to cut aggregate demand by reducing C enjoyed only modest success. While consumer spending probably was below what it would have been in the absence of the surcharge, it was substantially above what the 1964 experience had led economists to predict.

Case 3: The U.S. Income-Tax Reduction of 1975

The next major change in U.S. tax laws for stabilization purposes also met with partial success at best. In the spring of 1975, as the American economy neared the bottom of what was then its worst postwar recession, President Gerald R. Ford and the Congress agreed on a double-edged tax cut to spur consumer spending. First, they returned to each taxpayer part of the taxes paid in 1974. Second, they reduced income-tax rates for the balance of 1975. However, consumers confounded the wishes of the president and Congress by saving a good deal of their rebates rather than spending them.

What went wrong in 1968 and 1975 that had not gone wrong in 1964? This chapter will attempt to provide some answers. We begin by exploring the important relationship between consumer income and consumer spending, more or less retracing the chain of logic that led American economists to the right conclusion in 1964. Once this is accomplished, we turn to some of the complications that made things go awry in 1968 and 1975.

Case 4: The Canadian Sales-Tax Reduction of 1978

At the end of this chapter, we describe how the Canadian federal government tried to avoid the problems encountered by the Americans, by relying on *sales-tax* changes rather than *personal income-tax* policies, in their 1978 budget.

Consumer Spending and Income: The Important Relationship

An economist interested in predicting how consumer spending will respond to a change in personal income-tax payments must first ask how C is related to disposable income; for an increase in taxes is a decrease in after-tax income, and a reduction in taxes is an increase in after-tax income. This section, therefore, will examine what we know about the response of consumer spending to a change in disposable income.

Figure 7–3 depicts the historical paths of C and DI for Canada since 1926. The association is obviously rather close and certainly suggests that consumption will rise whenever disposable income does and fall whenever income falls. The difference between the two lines is personal saving. Notice how little saving consumers did during the Great Depression of the 1930s, where the two lines are very close together, and how much more they did during World War II, when many consumer goods were either unavailable or rationed so there was little on which to spend money. The only puzzling feature of Figure 7–3 is the apparent bulge in savings that has occurred in the last ten years. The main reason for this is the inflation in this period. When there is no sustained inflation, real and nominal interest rates coincide, so that households do not need to save any of their interest earnings to keep the real value of their bonds and shares constant. With a sustained inflation, however, much of the received nominal interest rate is the inflation premium, and *all* of this part of interest must be saved just to keep real asset holdings constant. (Real asset holdings can be constant only if nominal holdings of bonds and stocks increase as rapidly as the inflation rate.) To be comparable with the earlier (non-inflationary) periods, then, the consumption expenditure series for the last ten years should be adjusted for the gap that has emerged between the real and nominal interest rates.

There is a mirror image of this overstatement of household savings in inflationary times. The *dissaving* by the other sectors (firms and governments) is overstated in the standard data by the same amount and for the same reason. We return to this point when discussing the size of the government budget deficit in Chapter 17. This discussion represents another application of the important **12 Ideas for Beyond the Final Exam**: the difference between nominal and real interest.

Of course, knowing that consumer expenditures, C, will move in the same direction as disposable income, *DI*, is not enough for policy planners. They need to know *how much* one will go up when the other rises a given amount. Figure 7–4 presents the same data that we saw in Figure 7–3 but in a way designed to help answer the "how much" question.

Economists call such pictures **scatter diagrams**, and they are very useful in predicting how one economic variable (in this case, consumer spending) will change in response to a change in another economic variable (in this case, disposable income). Each dot in the diagram represents the data on *C* and *DI* corresponding to a particular year. For example, the point labelled "1970" shows that real consumer expenditures in 1970 were $51.5 billion (which we read off the vertical axis), while real disposable incomes amounted to $55.3 billion (which we read off the horizontal axis). Similarly, each year from 1926 to 1983 is represented by its own dot in Figure 7–4.

How can such a diagram assist the fiscal policy planner? Imagine that you are an American economist in 1963 and you must decide whether to recommend to the government a tax cut of $5 billion, $10 billion, or $15 billion. (It has already

A **scatter diagram** is a graph showing the relationship between two variables (such as consumption and disposable income). Each year is represented by a point in the diagram. The co-ordinates of each year's point show the values of the two variables in that year.

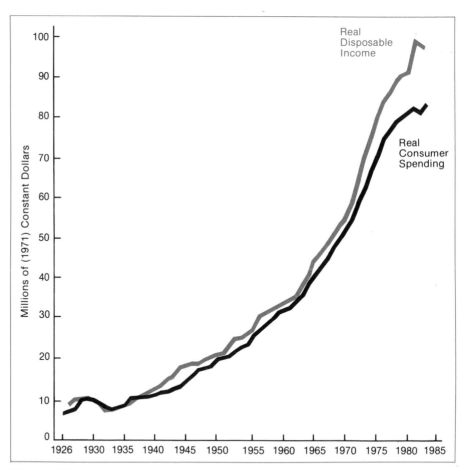

Figure 7–3
CONSUMER SPENDING AND DISPOSABLE INCOME IN CANADA SINCE 1926
This time-series chart shows the behaviour of consumer spending and disposable income in Canada since 1926. The correspondence between the two variables is remarkably close. The distance between the two lines represents measured consumer saving, which was quite small during the Great Depression of the 1930s, quite large during World War II, and quite large in the last ten years. This recent bulge in savings is largely due to a measurement problem that is based on the large inflation premium that has become incorporated within nominal interest rates.
SOURCE: Statistics Canada.

been decided that a cut smaller than $5 billion is not worth the legislative effort and that a cut of more than $15 billion is politically not feasible.) You have forecasts of what consumer expenditures are expected to be if taxes are not reduced. This, plus other forecasts of investment, government spending, and net exports has led you to conclude that aggregate demand in 1964 will be insufficient if taxes are not reduced. To assist you, the pre-1964 scatter diagram for the United States is given in Figure 7–5. With no more training in economics than you have right now, what would you do?

One rough-and-ready approach is to get a ruler, set it down on Figure 7–5, and sketch a straight line that comes as close as possible to hitting all the points. Try that now. You will not be able to hit each point exactly, but you will find that you can come remarkably close. The line you have just drawn summarizes, in a very rough way, the consumption–income relationship that is the focus of this chapter. We see at once that it confirms something we might have guessed—that a rise in income is associated with a rise in consumer spending. The slope of the line is certainly positive.

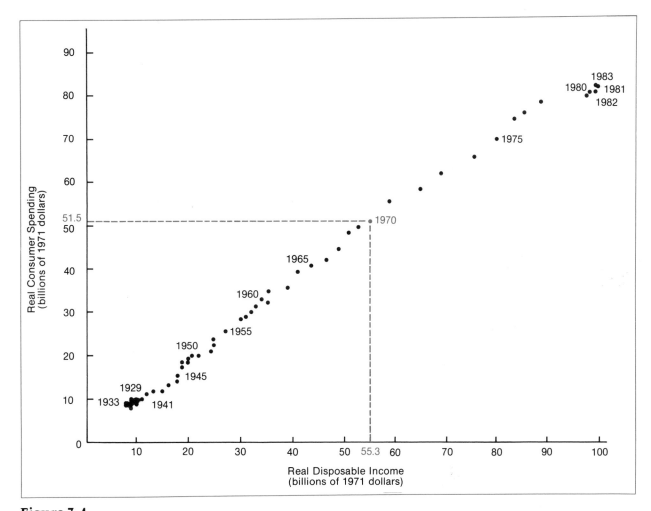

Figure 7–4

SCATTER DIAGRAM OF CONSUMER SPENDING AND DISPOSABLE INCOME IN CANADA, 1926–1983
This diagram shows the same data as depicted in Figure 7-3 but in a different manner. Each point on the diagram represents the data for both consumer spending and disposable income during a particular year. For example, the point labelled "1970" indicates that in that year consumer spending was $51.5 billion while disposable income was $55.3 billion. Diagrams like this one are called "scatter diagrams."

Figure 7-5

SCATTER DIAGRAM OF
CONSUMER SPENDING AND
DISPOSABLE INCOME IN THE
UNITED STATES, 1947-1963
This scatter diagram indicates the
information that policy planners
might have used in deciding upon
the size of the 1964 income-tax
cut in the United States.

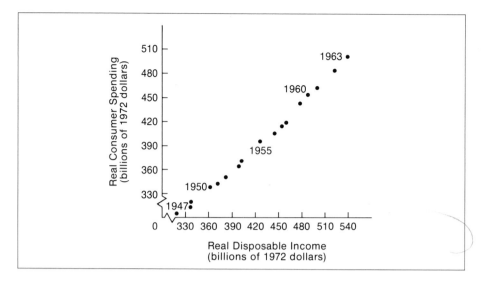

The slope of your line is very important.[5] That line has been drawn into Figure 7-6, and we note that its slope is:

$$\text{Slope} = \frac{\text{Vertical change}}{\text{Horizontal change}} = \frac{\$90 \text{ billion}}{\$100 \text{ billion}} = 0.90.$$

Since the horizontal change involved in the move from *A* to *B* represents a rise in disposable income of $100 billion (from $420 billion to $520 billion), and the corresponding vertical change represents the associated $90 billion rise in consumer spending (from $390 billion to $480 billion), the slope of the line indicates how spending responds to changes in disposable income. In this case, we see that each additional $1 of income leads to 90¢ of additional spending.

In terms of the policy issue of 1964, this line can therefore help provide an answer to the question: How much more consumer spending will be induced by tax cuts of $5 billion, $10 billion, or $15 billion if the effects are similar to those observed in the past? First, we need to keep in mind that each dollar of tax cut increases disposable income by $1. Then we apply Figure 7-6's finding that each additional dollar of disposable income increases consumer spending by 90¢, and

[5] To review the concept of *slope*, turn back to pages 21-24.

Figure 7-6

SCATTER DIAGRAM OF
CONSUMER SPENDING AND
DISPOSABLE INCOME IN THE
UNITED STATES, 1947-1963
This diagram is the same as
Figure 7-5 except for the addition
of a straight line that comes about
as close as possible to fitting all
the data points.

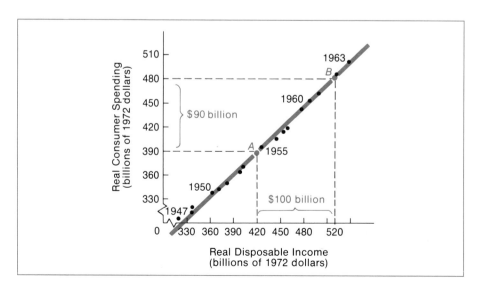

Table 7-1

CONSUMPTION AND INCOME IN MACROLAND

YEAR	(1) CONSUMPTION, C (billions of dollars)	(2) DISPOSABLE INCOME, DI (billions of dollars)	(3) MARGINAL PROPENSITY TO CONSUME, MPC
1980	170	200	
1981	210	250	0.8
1982	250	300	0.8
1983	290	350	0.8
1984	330	400	0.8
1985	370	450	0.8

conclude that proposed tax cuts of $5 billion, $10 billion, or $15 billion would be expected to increase consumer spending by $4.5 billion, $9 billion, and $13.5 billion, respectively. Similar questions addressed by U.S. economists in 1964 led to a decision to cut taxes by about $9 billion.

Later in this and other chapters, we will encounter several reasons why this procedure, while basically valid, must be used with great caution.

The Consumption Function and the Marginal Propensity to Consume

It has been said that economics is just systematized common sense. Let us, then, try to organize and generalize what has been a completely intuitive discussion thus far. One thing we have learned is that there is a close and apparently reliable relationship between consumer spending, C, and disposable income, DI. Economists call this relationship the **consumption function**.

A second fact we have picked up from these figures is that the slope of the consumption function is fairly constant. We infer this from the fact that the straight line in Figure 7-6 comes close to touching every point. If the slope of the consumption function had changed a lot, it would not be possible to do so well with a single straight line. Because of its importance in such applications as the tax-cut example, economists have given a special name to this slope—the **marginal propensity to consume**, or MPC for short. The MPC tells us how many more dollars consumers will spend if disposable income rises by $1 billion.

The MPC is best illustrated by an example, and for this purpose we turn away from both Canadian and U.S. data for a moment and look at the consumption and income data of a hypothetical country called Macroland (see Table 7-1). The data for Macroland resemble those for Canada and the United States, except that in Macroland, C and DI figures happen to be nice round numbers, which facilitates computation.

Columns 1 and 2 of Table 7-1 show annual consumer expenditure and disposable income from 1980 to 1985. These two columns constitute Macroland's consumption function and are plotted in Figure 7-7. Column 3 in the table shows the marginal propensity to consume (MPC), which is the slope of the line in Figure 7-7; it is derived from the first two columns. We can see that between 1982 and 1983, DI rose by $50 billion (from $300 billion to $350 billion) while C rose by $40 billion (from $250 billion to $290 billion). Thus the MPC was:

$$\frac{\text{Change in consumption}}{\text{Change in disposable income}} = \frac{\$40 \text{ billion}}{\$50 \text{ billion}} = 0.80.$$

As you can easily verify, the MPC between any other pair of years in Macroland was also 0.80.

The **consumption function** is the relationship between total consumer expenditure and total disposable income in the economy holding all other determinants of consumer spending constant.

The **marginal propensity to consume** (or MPC for short) is the ratio of the change in consumption to the change in disposable income that produces the change in consumption. On a graph, it appears as the slope of the consumption function.

MPC =

Change in consumption

Change in disposable income that produces the change in consumption

Figure 7-7

THE CONSUMPTION FUNCTION OF MACROLAND

This diagram is similar to Figure 7-6, except that it applies to a hypothetical (and blissfully simple!) economy called Macroland. As can be seen, a straight-line consumption function passes through every point exactly. The slope of this line is 0.8, which is the marginal propensity to consume in Macroland.

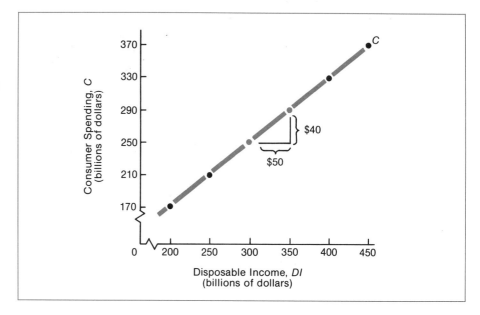

This explains why the slope of the line in Figure 7-6 was so crucial in estimating the effect of a tax cut. Since the slope is the MPC, it tells us how much *additional* spending will be induced by each dollar *change* in disposable income. For each $1 of tax cut, economists expect consumption to rise by $1 times the marginal propensity to consume. Thus:

To estimate the *initial* effect of a tax cut on consumer spending, economists must first estimate the MPC and then multiply the amount of the tax cut by the estimated MPC. But since they never know the true MPC with certainty, this prediction is always subject to some margin of error.[6]

In 1963, for example, economists multiplied the anticipated $9 billion tax cut by the estimated MPC of 0.90 and concluded that consumer spending would initially rise by about $8 billion. Their estimate seems to have been remarkably accurate.

Movements Along Versus Shifts of the Consumption Function

Unfortunately, this sort of calculation does not always yield such precise results. Among the most important reasons for this is that the consumption function does not always stand still; sometimes it shifts.

You will recall from Chapter 4 the important distinction between a *movement along* a demand curve and a *shift* of the curve.

A demand curve depicts the relationship between quantity demanded and only *one* of its many determinants—price. Thus, a change in price causes a movement *along* the demand curve, but a change in any other factor that influences quantity demanded causes a *shift of the entire demand curve*.

Because consumer spending is influenced by factors other than disposable income, a similar distinction is vital to understanding real-world consumption functions. A change in disposable income leads to a **movement along the consumption function**, because the consumption function depicts the relationship between C and DI. This is what we have been considering in the last

---

[6] The word "initial" in the first sentence is an important one. Later chapters explain why the effects discussed in this chapter are only the beginning of the story.

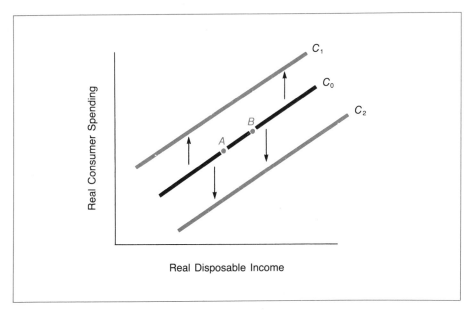

Figure 7-8
SHIFTS OF THE
CONSUMPTION FUNCTION
An increase in disposable income
causes a movement along a fixed
consumption function, such as the
movement from point A to point B
on consumption function C_0. But a
change in any other determinant
of consumer spending will cause
the whole consumption function to
shift upward (consumption
function C_1) or downward
(consumption function C_2).

two sections. But consumption also has other determinants. And a change in any of these "other determinants" of consumer spending will **shift the entire consumption function**, as indicated in Figure 7-8. These unexpected shifts account for many of the errors in forecasting consumption. To summarize:

Any change in disposable income moves us *along* a given consumption function. But a change in any of the other variables that influence consumption results in a *shift* of the entire consumption schedule (see Figure 7-8).

Let us now list some of these "other variables" that can shift the consumption function.

Other Determinants of Consumer Spending

Recent Past Incomes

One factor is simple *inertia*, the fact that households normally take some time to adjust to changes in their economic circumstances. If income rises at an extraordinary pace—as in an economic boom—consumer spending does not surge ahead as fast as income. You can understand why by considering a close-to-home example. Unless you continue on to graduate study, your income will register a very sharp increase when you graduate from university and get a job. See how long it takes until your spending habits have caught up. The same process works in reverse. At the onset of a recession, consumers normally try to maintain their customary spending levels despite losses of income.

Wealth

A second factor affecting consumption is consumers' *wealth*, which is a source of demand in addition to income. Wealth and income are different things. A wealthy person may currently have very little *income*. Similarly, a high-income individual who spends all he earns will not accumulate wealth. To appreciate the importance of the distinction, consider two consumers, both earning $25,000 this year. One of them has $50,000 in the bank, while the other has no assets at all. Who do you think will spend more this year? Presumably the one with the big bank account.

The general point is that current income is not the only source of funds that households have; they can also finance spending by withdrawals from their bank accounts or by cashing in other forms of wealth. A stock-market boom may therefore raise the consumption function (see the shift from C_0 to C_1 in Figure 7–8), while a collapse of stock prices may lower it (see the shift from C_0 to C_2).

The Price Level

A good deal of consumer wealth is held in forms whose values are fixed in money terms. Money itself is the most obvious example of this, but government bonds, savings accounts, and corporate bonds are all assets with fixed face values in money terms. The purchasing power of any **money fixed asset** obviously declines whenever the price level rises, which means that the asset can buy less. For example, if the price level rises by 10 percent, a $1000 government bond will buy about 10 percent less than it could when prices were lower. Consequently:

Higher overall prices, by eroding the purchasing power of consumer wealth, decrease the demand for goods and services.

This is no trivial matter. It has been estimated that the total volume of money fixed assets in Canada is around $100 billion, so that each 1 percent rise in the price level reduces the purchasing power of consumer wealth by about $1 billion, a tidy sum. The process, of course, operates equally well in reverse. A decline in the price level increases the purchasing power of money fixed assets. So:

Lower overall prices, by enhancing the purchasing power of consumer wealth, increase the demand for goods and services. For these reasons a change in the price level will shift the entire consumption function. Specifically:

A higher price level leads to lower real wealth and therefore to less spending *at any given level of real income.* Thus, a higher price level leads to a lower consumption function (such as C_2 in Figure 7–8). Conversely, a lower price level leads to a higher consumption function (such as C_1 in Figure 7–8).

Students are often confused on this point, so it is worth repeating that the depressing effect of the price level on consumer spending works through real *wealth,* not real *income.* The consumption function is a relationship between *real* consumer income and *real* consumer spending. Thus any decline in real income, regardless of its cause, moves the economy *leftward along a fixed consumption function;* it does not shift the consumption function.[7] By contrast, any decline in *real wealth* will *shift the whole consumption function downward,* meaning that there is less spending at any given level of real income.

The Inflation Rate

Prices may be high and rising slowly, or they may be low but rising rapidly. Therefore, the depressing effect of a high *price level* on real consumer spending must be distinguished from any effect on spending of the *rate of inflation* (that is, the rate at which prices are rising).

Conclusions about the effect of the inflation rate on spending are more complicated. In the past, economists believed that high rates of inflation caused consumers to spend more to "beat" the inflation. That is, people were thought to purchase goods ahead of their needs in order to avoid the higher prices that loomed on the horizon. But behaviour during the inflationary period since 1974 shows that consumer spending was actually unusually low. We explained this on page 119 in terms of the inflation premium that gets embedded in nominal interest rates during inflationary times.

---

[7] This is true even if a rise in the price level lies behind the decline in real income. However, wages and prices normally move together, so there is no reason to expect real wages to fall when the price level rises.

Margin note:

A **money fixed asset** is an asset with a face value fixed in terms of dollars, such as money itself, government bonds, and corporate bonds.

To keep our model economy simplified, we ignore these complications and assume that the position of the consumption function is influenced by the *price level*, but not by the *inflation rate*.

Expectations of Future Incomes

It will hardly be considered earth shattering to suggest that consumers' expectations about future income may affect their spending in important ways. This final determinant of consumer spending turns out to hold the key to answering the question we posed earlier. Why did the U.S. tax policy that succeeded so well in 1964 fail to alter consumer spending as much in 1968 and 1975?

Why U.S. Income-Tax Policy Failed in 1968 and 1975

To understand how expectations of future incomes affect current consumer expenditures, consider the abbreviated life histories of three consumers given in Table 7-2. The reason for giving our three imaginary individuals such odd names will be apparent shortly.

The consumer named "No Change" earned $100 in each of the four years considered in the table. The consumer named "Temporary Rise" earned $100 in three of the four years but had a good year in 1975. The consumer named "Permanent Rise" enjoyed a permanent rise in income in 1975 and was clearly the richest.

Table 7-2

INCOMES OF THREE CONSUMERS

| CONSUMER | INCOMES IN EACH YEAR | | | | TOTAL INCOME |
	1974	1975	1976	1977	
No Change	100	100	100	100	400
Temporary Rise	100	120	100	100	420
Permanent Rise	100	120	120	120	460

Now let us use our common sense to figure out how much each of these consumers might have spent in 1975. Temporary Rise and Permanent Rise had the same income that year. Do you think they spent the same amount? Not if they had some ability to foresee their future incomes, because Permanent Rise was richer in the long run.

Now compare No Change and Temporary Rise. Temporary Rise had 20 percent higher income in 1975 ($120 versus $100) but only 5 percent more over the entire four-year period ($420 versus $400). Do you think her spending was closer to 20 percent above No Change's or closer to 5 percent above it? Most people guess the latter.

The point of this example is that it is reasonable for consumers to decide on their *current* consumption spending by looking at their *long-run* income prospects. This should not be a shocking idea to most university students. How many of you are spending only what you earn this year? Probably not very many. And this is not because you are all foolish spendthrifts. On the contrary, you are rational planners. Knowing that your university education gives you a reasonable expectation of future income prospects much greater than those you now have, you are no doubt spending with that in mind.

Now what does all this have to do with the failure of the 1975 income-tax rebate in the United States? Imagine that the three rows in Table 7-2 now represent the entire economy under three different government policies. Recall that 1975 was the year of the rebate. The first row (No Change) shows the unchanged path of disposable income if no tax cut was enacted. The second (Temporary Rise) shows an increase in disposable income attributable to a tax cut *for one year only*. The bottom row (Permanent Rise) shows a policy that increases *DI* in *every future year* by cutting taxes permanently in 1975. Which of the two lower rows do you imagine would have generated more consumer spending in 1975? The bottom row (Permanent Rise), of course. What we have concluded, then, is this:

Permanent cuts in income taxes cause greater increases in consumer spending than do temporary cuts of equal magnitude.

The application of this analysis to the case of the 1975 tax cut is immediate. About half the cut was a refund of some of the 1974 taxes that had already been paid. These rebates were clearly one-time increases in income like that experienced by Temporary Rise in Table 7–2. No future income was affected. The remaining cuts came in the form of special reduced tax rates announced to apply in 1975 *only*, and thus might reasonably have been expected to be temporary as well. Since the 1975 tax-cut package had little effect on expected future incomes, it is not surprising that its impact on consumer spending was rather mild.

Much the same situation prevailed in 1968, when the U.S. Congress enacted a temporary 10 percent increase in income taxes to help finance the Vietnam War. Consumers considered the resulting decrease in their disposable income as only a *temporary* loss and did not curtail their spending as much as government officials had hoped. The general lesson is:

A permanent increase in income taxes provides a greater deterrent to consumer spending than does a temporary increase of equal magnitude.

We have, then, what appears to be a general principle, backed up both by historical evidence and common sense. Permanent changes in income taxes have a more significant impact on consumer spending than do temporary changes.

Though it may now seem obvious, this is not a lesson you would have learned from the introductory textbooks of 1968; it is one that was learned the hard way, through bitter experience. The tax surcharge of 1968 was meant to slow down inflation. Yet consumer prices rose faster in 1968 than they had in 1967, and faster in 1969 than in 1968. The tax reductions of 1975 were meant to halt a precipitous downswing in economic activity. It was subsequently learned that the recession had bottomed out, of its own accord, before the cuts became effective, and the recovery in consumer spending was far from spectacular.

The Canadian Sales-Tax Reduction of 1978

A sales-tax change does not affect consumption by changing household incomes. Instead, alterations in sales taxes change the relative price of buying a good now versus in the future. Indeed, the more *temporary* a sales-tax change is, the more *effective* it is.

For example, if a sales tax is cut for a six-month period, and households know that this is temporary, they probably will accelerate some purchases to fit within the six-month period. However, if they expect that the lower price will apply indefinitely, they may respond more sluggishly, so less spending is transferred to the recession period. This suggests that temporary sales-tax changes should be far more effective measures for managing aggregate demand than temporary income-tax changes.

Unfortunately, there is an important implementation problem that stems from our constitution. The retail sales tax is a provincial government instrument in Canada, while aggregate demand management is a federal government responsibility. The federal government does control the manufacturers' sales tax, which is levied at the wholesale level, but this tax raises relatively little revenue.

The federal government's Budget of 1978 represented an attempt to overcome this implementation problem (and it therefore illustrates the government's appreciation of the lessons we have learned from the U.S. experience with temporary income-tax changes). The federal government transferred some of its personal income-tax revenue to the provinces in return for a specified temporary sales-tax cut by the provinces. A full agreement was reached with all provinces except Alberta and Quebec. Alberta was excluded because there is no sales tax there. The Quebec government decided that political points could be scored by refusing to agree to the deal and by publicly decrying the meddling in provincial matters by the federal government. After two months of intense political wrangling, the federal government just paid all Quebec taxpayers directly an income-tax rebate of either $85 or the person's federal tax payable (whichever was less). This episode has made federal–provincial co-operation on sales-tax policy unlikely in the near future—which is unfortunate, in light of the lessons of this chapter.

The Predictability of Consumer Behaviour

We have now learned enough to see why the economist's problem in predicting how consumers will react to an increase or decrease in taxes is not quite as simple as suggested earlier in this chapter.

The principal problem seems to be anticipating how taxpayers will view any changes in the income-tax law. If the government *says* that an income-tax cut is permanent, will consumers *believe* it and increase their spending accordingly? Perhaps not, if the government has a history of raising taxes after promising to keep them low. Similarly, when (as in 1968 in the United States) the government explicitly announces that an income-tax increase is temporary, will consumers always believe this? Or might they greet such an announcement with a hefty dose of skepticism? This is quite possible if there is a long history of "temporary" tax increases that stayed on the books indefinitely.

Thus the effectiveness of any *future* tax-policy move may well depend on the government's *past* track record. A government that repeatedly uses a succession of so-called "permanent" income-tax cuts and income-tax increases for short-run stabilization purposes may find consumers beginning to ignore the tax changes entirely. The story of the boy who cried wolf is not yet required reading for fiscal policy planners, but it probably should be recommended.

Nor is this the only problem. Economists may underestimate or overestimate the degree of inertia in consumer behaviour. Their predictions may fail to take adequate account of large and rapid accumulations of wealth (as happened immediately after World War II, when consumption forecasts were notoriously low) or of sizable losses of wealth (such as the drastic decline in the stock market in 1973–75, when consumption forecasts were too high). Poor forecasts of future prices may lead consumption forecasts astray. And there are further hazards that we have not even mentioned here. Economic predictions are inexact, and predictions of consumption illustrate this well.

There is much more that can be said about the determinants of consumption, but it is best to leave the rest to more advanced courses. For we are now ready to apply our knowledge of the consumption function to the construction of the first model of the whole economy. While it is true that income determines consumption, the consumption function in turn helps to determine the level of income. If that sounds like circular reasoning, read the next chapter!

Summary

1. Aggregate demand is the total amount of goods and services that consumers, businesses, government units, and foreigners are willing to purchase. It can be expressed as the sum $C + I + G + X - IM$ where C is consumer spending, I is investment spending, G is government purchases, and $X - IM$ is exports minus imports.

2. Economists reserve the term "investment" to refer to purchases of newly produced factories, machinery, and homes.

3. National product is the total output of final goods and services of the economy. It is most commonly measured by the gross national product (GNP).

4. National income is the sum of the before-tax wages, interest, rents, and profits earned by all individuals in the economy. If we ignore incomes earned in other countries, and foreign-owned factors of production operating here, national income must by necessity be equal to national product.

5. Disposable income is the sum of the incomes of all individuals in the economy, after taxes and transfers, and is the chief determinant of consumer expenditure.

6. All of these concepts, and others, can be depicted in a circular flow diagram that shows expenditures from all four sources flowing into business firms and national income flowing out.

7. The government often has tried to manipulate aggregate demand by influencing private expenditure decisions.

8. The close relationship between consumer spending (C) and disposable income (DI) is called the consumption function. Its slope, which is used to predict the change in consumption that will be caused by a change in income taxes, is called the marginal propensity to consume (MPC).

9. Changes in disposable income move us along a given consumption function. Changes in any of the other variables that affect C will shift the entire consumption function. Among the most important of these other variables are total consumer wealth, the price level, and expected future incomes.

10. Because consumers hold so many money fixed assets, they lose out when prices rise, which leads them to reduce their spending. This decline in consumer demand when prices rise helps explain why the aggregate-demand curve slopes downward.

11. Future income prospects help explain why U.S. tax policy did not affect consumption as much as was hoped in 1968 and 1975. This is because the 1968 tax increase and the 1975 tax cut were both temporary, and therefore left future incomes unaffected. By contrast, the U.S. tax cut of 1964 was "permanent," and affected future as well as current incomes. It is no surprise, then, that the 1964 actions had stronger effects on spending than did the 1968 or 1975 actions.

12. Temporary sales-tax changes affect consumption by changing the ratio of current to future prices, and therefore their impact does not depend on any change in people's permanent income position. However, the retail sales tax is a provincial matter in Canada, while aggregate-demand management is a federal responsibility.

Concepts for Review

Aggregate demand
Consumer expenditure (C)
Investment spending (I)
Government purchases (G)
Exports (X)
Imports (IM)
$C + I + G + X - IM$

National income (GNP)
Gross domestic product (GDP)
Disposable income (DI)
Circular flow diagram
Transfer payments
Scatter diagram
Consumption function

Marginal propensity to consume (MPC)
Movements along versus shifts of the consumption function
Money fixed assets
Temporary versus permanent tax changes

Questions for Discussion

1. What are the four components of aggregate demand? Which of these is the largest?

2. What is the difference between "investment" as the term is used by most people and "investment" as defined by an economist? Which of the following acts constitute "investment" according to the economist's definition?
   a. General Motors constructs a new assembly line.
   b. You buy 100 shares of General Motors stock.
   c. A small steel company goes bankrupt, and Stelco purchases its factory and equipment.
   d. Your family buys a newly constructed home from a developer.
   e. Your family buys an older home from another family. (Hint: Are any new products demanded by this action?)

3. What would the circular flow diagram (Figure 7-1, page 115) look like in an economy with no government? Draw one for yourself.

4. The marginal propensity to consume (MPC) for the nation as a whole is roughly 0.90. Explain in words what this means. What is your personal MPC?

5. Look at the scatter diagram in Figure 7-4 (page 121). What does it tell you about what was going on in this country in the years 1942–45?

6. What is a "consumption function," and why is it a useful device for government economists planning a tax cut?

7. On a piece of graph paper, construct the consumption function for Simpleland from the following data:

YEAR	CONSUMER SPENDING	DISPOSABLE INCOME
1981	110	100
1982	155	150
1983	200	200
1984	245	250
1985	290	300

What is the MPC?

8. In which direction will the consumption function for Simpleland shift if the price level rises? Show this on your graph.

9. Explain why permanent income-tax cuts are likely to lead to bigger increases in consumer spending than are temporary income-tax cuts.

Appendix A
The Saving Function and the Marginal Propensity to Save

There is an alternative way of looking at the relationships we have discussed in this chapter. Disposable income that is not spent must be saved. Therefore we can examine the effect of income on *saving* as well as its effect on consumer *spending*.

To see how saving appears on the consumption function diagram, we have repeated the consumption function of Macroland (see Figure 7-7) in Figure 7-9 and added a 45° line. You will recall that a 45° line marks those points where the distances along the horizontal and vertical axes are equal. (If you wish to review, see page 24.) Since the consumption schedule is below the 45° line, the figure shows that consumer spending is less than income, so some is being *saved*.

To find the amount of saving at each level of income, we need only read the vertical distance from the consumption function up to the 45° line. For example, when income is $400 billion, saving is the distance *AB*, or $70 billion.

There is also a more direct way to find saving. Table 7-3 repeats the consumption and disposable income data for Macroland from Table 7-1 (page 123). Then, in column 3, we compute the difference between disposable income and consumption, which gives us **aggregate saving**.

Aggregate saving is the difference between disposable income and consumer expenditure. In symbols, $S = DI - C$.

The subtraction is exactly what we showed graphically in Figure 7-9. Columns 2 and 3 of Table

7-3 constitute what economists call the **saving function**.

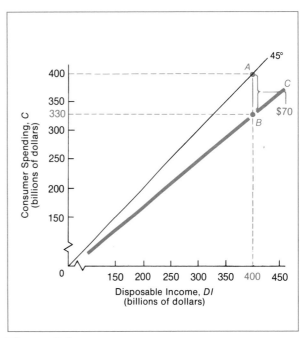

Figure 7-9

THE CONSUMPTION FUNCTION OF MACROLAND

The consumption function of Macroland, which we encountered in Figure 7-7 (page 124), is repeated here, and a 45° line is added for convenience. Since consumption and saving must always add up to disposable income, the vertical distance between the two lines represents saving. For example, points *A* and *B* indicate that when disposable income is $400 billion, saving is $70 billion.

Table 7-3

SAVING IN MACROLAND

YEAR	(1) CONSUMPTION, C	(2) DISPOSABLE INCOME, DI	(3) SAVING, S	(4) MARGINAL PROPENSITY TO SAVE, MPS
1980	170	200	30	0.2
1981	210	250	40	0.2
1982	250	300	50	0.2
1983	290	350	60	0.2
1984	330	400	70	0.2
1985	370	450	80	0.2

The **saving function** is the schedule relating total consumer saving to total disposable income in the economy, holding other determinants of saving constant.

These data are portrayed in Figure 7-10, which is constructed from the numbers in Table 7-3. It could equally well have been constructed as the difference between the 45° line and the C line in Figure 7-9. (Because saving is so much less than consumption, we have stretched the scale of the vertical axis considerably.) Points A and B correspond to the same points in Figure 7-9. When the consumption function is a straight line, and thus has a constant slope, the same will be true of the saving function. In Figure 7-10, we show this slope as the ratio of distance EB to distance DE or $40 billion/$200 billion = 0.2. Economists call this slope the **marginal propensity to save**.

The **marginal propensity to save** (or MPS) is the slope of the saving function. It tells us how much more consumers will save if disposable income rises by one unit.

You may have noticed that the MPS is 0.2 while the MPC for Macroland is 0.8. They add up to 1, and not by accident. Since the portion of each additional dollar of disposable income that is not spent must be saved, the MPC and the MPS always add up to 1. It is a simple fact of accounting.

The MPC and the MPS always add up to 1, meaning that an additional dollar of income must be divided between consumption and saving. In symbols:

$$MPC + MPS = 1.$$

This enables us to compute either one of them from the other.

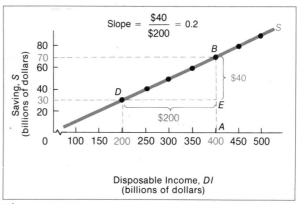

Figure 7-10

THE SAVING FUNCTION OF MACROLAND

The saving function of Macroland, depicted here, can be constructed either from the data in Table 7-3 or from Figure 7-9. This is because when we plot saving against disposable income (as we do here), we are also plotting the difference between consumption and disposable income (the vertical distance between line C and the 45° line in Figure 7-9) against disposable income.

Summary

1. Instead of studying the consumption function, it is possible to study the same data by looking at the saving function, which is defined as the relationship between disposable income and consumer saving.

2. Since consumer saving is merely the difference between disposable income and consumer expenditure, everything we have learned about the consumption function applies to the saving function.

3. The amount of additional saving caused by a growth of $1 in disposable income is called the marginal propensity to save, or MPS.

4. Since each additional $1 of disposable income is either spent or saved, the MPC and the MPS must always add up to 1. Thus, knowledge of one implies knowledge of the other.

Concepts for Review

Aggregate saving
Saving function
Marginal propensity to save (MPS)

Questions for Discussion

1. Look at the circular flow diagram in Figure 7–1 (page 115). Where does the saving function enter the picture?

2. Take the data from Simpleland in Question 7 on page 131 and use them to construct a saving function for Simpleland on a piece of graph paper.

3. (More difficult.) If taxes are cut *temporarily* and consumer spending does not increase much, what must happen to consumer saving?

Appendix B
National Income Accounting

The type of macroeconomic analysis presented in this book dates from the publication of John Maynard Keynes's *The General Theory of Employment, Interest, and Money* in 1936. But at that time there was really no way to test Keynes's theories because the necessary data did not exist. It took some years for the theoretical notions used by Keynes to find concrete expression in real-world data. The system of measurement devised for this purpose is called **national income accounting**.

The development of this system of accounts ranks as a great achievement in applied economics, perhaps as important in its own right as Keynes's theoretical work. For without it the practical value of Keynesian analysis would be severely limited. Many men and women spent long hours wrestling with the numerous difficult conceptual questions that arose in translating the theory into numbers, but they had one acknowledged leader: Professor Simon Kuznets of Harvard University, who, in 1971, was awarded the Nobel Prize in Economics for his contributions to economic measurement techniques. Along the way some more-or-less arbitrary decisions and conventions had to be made. You may not agree with all of them, but the accounting framework that was devised is eminently serviceable, though, inevitably, it has some limitations that must be understood.

Defining GNP: Exceptions to the Rules

We first encountered the concept of **gross national product** (GNP) in Chapter 5.

Gross national product (GNP) is the sum of the money values of all final goods and services produced by domestically owned factors of production during a specified period of time, usually one year.

However, the definition of GNP given there, and repeated above for your convenience, has certain exceptions we have not yet noted. Three major exceptions are discussed here.

First, the treatment of government output involves a minor departure from the principle of using market prices. Outputs of private industries are sold on markets, so their prices are observed. But "outputs" of government offices are not sold; indeed, it is sometimes even difficult to define what those outputs are. Lacking prices for outputs, national income accountants fall back on the only prices they have: prices for the inputs from which the outputs are produced. Thus:

Government outputs are valued at the cost of the inputs needed to produce them.

This means, for example, that if a clerk at the Department of Transportation and Communications earns $8 an hour and spends one-half hour torturing you with explanations of why you cannot get a driver's licence, that particular government "service" is considered as being worth $4, and will increase GNP by that amount.

Second, some goods that are not actually sold on markets during the year are none the less counted in that year's GNP. These are the goods that are produced during the year but not sold; that is, goods that firms stockpile as *inventories*. Goods that are added to inventories are part of the GNP even though they do not pass through markets.

National income statisticians treat inventories as if they were "bought" by the firms that produced them, even though this "purchase" never takes place.

Finally, the treatment of investment goods runs slightly counter to the rule that only final goods are to be counted. In a broad sense, factories, generators, machine tools, and the like might be considered as intermediate goods. After all, their owners want them only for use in producing other goods, not for any innate value that they possess. But this would present a real problem, for factories and machines normally are never sold to consumers. So when would we count them in GNP? National income statisticians avoid this problem by defining investment goods as final products demanded by the firms that buy them.

Now that we have a complete definition of just what the GNP is, let us turn to the problem of actually measuring it. National income accountants have devised three ways to perform this task, and we consider each of them in turn.

GNP as the Sum of Final Goods and Services

The first way to measure GNP seems to be the most natural, since it follows so directly from the circular flow diagram in this chapter. It also turns out to be the most useful definition from the point of view of macroeconomics. We simply add up the final demands of all consumers, business firms, the government and foreigners. Using the symbols $C, I, G, X,$ and IM as we did in the text, we have:

$$GNP = C + I + G + X - IM.$$

The I that appears in the actual Canadian national accounts is called **gross private domestic investment**. The word "gross" will be explained presently. "Private" indicates that government investment is considered part of G, and "domestic" just means that machinery sold by Canadian firms to foreign companies is included in exports. Gross private domestic investment in Canada has three components: business investment in plant and equipment, residential construction (home building),[8] and inventory investment. We repeat again that *only* these three things

---

[8] Thus purchases of new homes are considered part of *I* rather than part of *C*.

are **investment** in national income accounting terminology.

As defined in the national income accounts, **investment** includes only newly produced goods, such as machinery, factories, and new homes. It does not include exchanges of existing assets.

In common parlance, all sorts of activities that are not part of the GNP are often called "investment." People are said to "invest" in the stock market when they purchase shares. Or wealthy individuals "invest" in works of art. But since transactions like these merely exchange one type of asset (money) for another (stock or art works), they are not included in the GNP.

The symbol G, for government purchases, represents the *volume of current goods and services purchased by all levels of government*. Thus, anything the government pays to its employees is counted in G, as are its purchases of paper, pencils, airplanes, bombs, typewriters, and so forth.

Very few citizens realize that *most of what the federal government spends its money on is not for purchases of goods and services*. Instead, it is on **transfer payments**—literally, giving away money—either to individuals or to other levels of government.

The importance of the conceptual distinction lies in the fact that G represents the part of the national product that government uses up for its own purposes—to pay for armies, bureaucrats, paper, and ink—whereas transfer payments merely represent shuffling of purchasing power from one group of citizens to another group. Except for the administrators needed to run the programs, real economic resources are not used up in this process. In adding up the nation's total output as the sum of $C + I + G + X - IM$, we are summing the shares of GNP that are used up by consumers, investors, governments, and foreigners, respectively. Since transfer payments merely give someone the capability to spend on C, it is logical to exclude them from our definition of G, including in C only the portion of these transfer payments that is spent. If we included them in G, the same spending would get counted twice: once in G and then again in C.

Table 7–4 shows the GNP for 1983 computed as the sum of $C + I + G + X - IM$.

GNP as the Sum of All Factor Payments

There is another way to count up the GNP—*by adding up all the incomes in the economy*. Let's see how this method handles some typical transactions. Suppose Canadian General Electric sells a generator to Ontario

Table 7-4

GROSS NATIONAL PRODUCT IN 1983 AS THE SUM OF FINAL DEMANDS

ITEM		AMOUNT (billions of dollars)
Personal consumption expenditures (C)		229.0
Gross private domestic investment (I)		64.5
Government purchase of goods and services (G)		94.5
Net exports (X–IM)		0.7
exports (X)	108.2	
imports (IM)	107.5	
Gross national product (Y)		388.7

SOURCE: Statistics Canada

Hydro for a price of $1 million. The first method of calculating GNP simply counts the $1 million as part of *I*. The second method asks: What incomes resulted from the production of this generator? The answer might be something like this:

Wages of C.G.E. employees	$400,000
Interest to bondholders	$50,000
Rentals of buildings	$50,000
Profits of C.G.E. stockholders	$100,000.

The total is $600,000. The remaining $400,000 is accounted for by inputs that C.G.E. purchased from other companies: steel, circuitry, tubing, rubber, and so on.

But if we traced this $400,000 back further, we would find that it is accounted for by the wages, interest, and rentals paid by these other companies, *plus* their profits, *plus* their purchases from other firms. In fact, for *every* firm in the economy, there is an accounting identity that says:

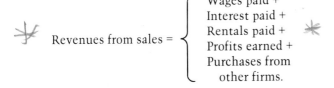

$$\text{Revenues from sales} = \left\{ \begin{array}{l} \text{Wages paid +} \\ \text{Interest paid +} \\ \text{Rentals paid +} \\ \text{Profits earned +} \\ \text{Purchases from} \\ \text{other firms.} \end{array} \right.$$

Why must this always be true? Because profits are the balancing item; they are what is *left over* after the firm has made all its other payments. In fact, this accounting identity is really just the definition of profits: sales revenue less all costs of production.

Now apply this accounting identity to *all the firms in the economy*. Total purchases from other firms are precisely what we call *intermediate goods*. What, then, do we get if we subtract these intermediate transactions from both sides of the equation?

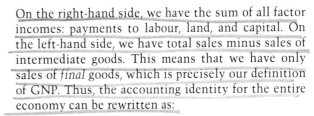

$$\left. \begin{array}{c} \text{Revenues from sales} \\ \text{minus} \\ \text{Purchases from} \\ \text{other firms} \end{array} \right\} = \left\{ \begin{array}{l} \text{Wages paid +} \\ \text{Interest paid +} \\ \text{Rentals paid +} \\ \text{Profits earned.} \end{array} \right.$$

On the right-hand side, we have the sum of all factor incomes: payments to labour, land, and capital. On the left-hand side, we have total sales minus sales of intermediate goods. This means that we have only sales of *final* goods, which is precisely our definition of GNP. Thus, the accounting identity for the entire economy can be rewritten as:

$$GNP = \text{Wages} + \text{Interest} + \text{Rents} + \text{Profits},$$

and this gives national income accountants another way to measure the GNP.

Table 7-5 shows 1983's GNP measured by the sum of all incomes. Once again, a few details have been omitted in our discussion. The sum of wages, interest, rents, and profits actually adds up to only $299 billion (whereas GNP was $388.7 billion). We call this sum the **national income** because it is the sum of all factor payments. But the actual selling prices of goods include another category of income

Table 7-5

GROSS NATIONAL PRODUCT IN 1983 AS THE SUM OF INCOMES

ITEM	AMOUNT (billions of dollars)
Wages, salaries, and supplementary labour income	219.8
plus	
Interest and miscellaneous investment income	30.4
plus	
Rents and net income of farmers and unincorporated business	16.5
plus	
Corporation profits before profits taxes	32.3
equals	
National income	299.0
plus	
Indirect business taxes (less subsidies) and miscellaneous items	42.7
equals	
Net national product	341.7
plus	
Depreciation	47.0
equals	
Gross national product	388.7

SOURCE: Statistics Canada

that we have ignored so far: sales taxes, excise taxes, and the like. National income statisticians call these *indirect business taxes*, and when we add these to national income we obtain the **net national product (NNP)**.

Now we are almost at the GNP. The only difference between GNP and NNP is **depreciation** of the nation's capital stock.

Depreciation is the value of the portion of the nation's capital equipment that is used up within the year. It tells us how much output is needed just to keep the economy's capital stock intact.

The difference between "gross" and "net" simply refers to whether depreciation is included or excluded. We add depreciation to NNP to get GNP. Thus, GNP is a measure of all final output taking no account of the capital used up in the process (and therefore in need of replacement). NNP deducts the required replacements to arrive at a *net* production figure.

From a conceptual point of view, most economists feel that NNP is a more meaningful indicator of the economy's output than GNP. After all, the depreciation component of GNP represents the output that is needed just to repair and replace worn out factories and machines; it is not available for anybody to consume.[9] So NNP seems to be a better measure of well-being than GNP. But, alas, GNP is much easier to measure because depreciation is a particularly tricky item. (What fraction of his tractor did Farmer Jones "use up" last year? How much did Montreal's Olympic Stadium depreciate during 1984?) Since the sum of expenditure method of calculation can be used for it, most economists feel that GNP is measured more accurately than is NNP. For this reason, most economic models are based on GNP.

In Table 7-5 you can hardly help noticing the preponderant share of employee compensation in total national income—75 percent. Labour is by far the most important factor of production. Corporate profits before tax account for 11 percent of national income (8 percent of GNP), perhaps less than the public thinks. If, by some magic stroke, we could eliminate all corporate profits without upsetting the performance of the economy, the average worker would get a raise of about 14 percent!

GNP as the Sum of Values Added

We come now to the third, and final, way to measure the GNP. But before we explain this method, we must introduce a new concept, called **value added**.

[9] If it is used for consumption, the capital stock will decline, and the nation will wind up poorer than before.

The **value added** by a firm is its revenue from selling a product minus the amounts paid for goods and services purchased from other firms.

The intuitive sense of the concept is clear: If a firm buys some inputs from other firms, does something to them, and sells the resulting product for a price higher than it paid for the inputs, we say that the firm has "added value" to the product. If we sum up the values added in this way by all the firms in the economy, we must get the total value of all final products. Thus:

GNP can be measured as the sum of the values added by all firms.

To verify that this is so, look back at the first accounting identity on page 135. The left-hand side of this equation, sales revenue minus purchases from other firms, is just what we mean by the firm's value added. Thus:

Value added = Wages + Interest + Rents + Profits.

Since the second method we gave for measuring GNP is to add up wages, interest, rents, and profits, we see that the value-added approach must also yield the same answer.

The value-added concept is particularly useful in avoiding double counting. Often it is hard to distinguish intermediate goods from final goods. Paint bought by a painter, for example, is an intermediate good. But paint bought by a do-it-yourselfer is a final good. What happens, then, if the professional painter has some paint left over and uses it to refurbish his own garage? The intermediate good becomes a final good. You can see that the line between intermediate goods and final goods is a fuzzy one in practice.

If we measure GNP by the sum of values added, however, it is not necessary to make such subtle distinctions. In this method, *every* purchase of a new good or service counts, but we do not count the entire selling price, only the part that represents value added.

To illustrate this idea, consider the data in Table 7-6 and how they would affect GNP as the sum of final products. Our example begins when a farmer who grows soybeans sells them to a mill for $3 a bushel. This transaction does *not* count in the GNP, because the miller does not purchase the soybeans for his own use. The miller then grinds up the soybeans and sells the resulting bag of soy meal to a factory that produces soy sauce. The miller receives $4, but GNP still has not increased because the ground beans are also an intermediate product. Next, the factory turns the beans into soy sauce, which it sells to your favorite Chinese restaurant for $8. Still no effect on

Table 7-6

AN ILLUSTRATION OF FINAL AND INTERMEDIATE GOODS

ITEM	SELLER	BUYER	PRICE
Bushel of soybeans	Farmer	Miller	$ 3
Bag of soy meal	Miller	Factory	4
Bottle of soy sauce	Factory	Restaurant	8
Bottle of soy sauce used as seasoning	Restaurant	Consumers	10
		Total:	$25
		Addendum: Contribution to GNP:	$10

GNP. But then the big moment arrives: The restaurant sells the sauce to you and other customers as a part of your meals, and you eat it. At this point, the $10 worth of soy sauce becomes a final product and is included in the GNP.

What is the logic of this procedure? Transactions in intermediate goods also have value. So why do we not count these along with transactions in final goods? The reason is that we are interested in measuring the economy's new output, and if we counted all the intermediate goods, we would be double or triple counting by including an item each time it changed hands. We would get an exaggerated impression of the amount of job-creating economic activity that is actually going on.

Look again at Table 7-6, which summarizes the four transactions in the life of the soybeans. As we have just noted, only the last transaction counts in the GNP. So all of this activity raises GNP by $10. If we had also counted the three intermediate transactions (farmer to miller, miller to factory, factory to restaurant), we would have come up with $25—two and one-half times too much.

Why is it too much? The reason is straightforward. Neither the miller nor the factory owner nor the restauranteur value the product we have been considering *for its own sake*. Only the customers who eat the final product (the soy sauce) have had an increase in their material well-being. So only this last transaction counts in the GNP. However, as we shall now see, value-added calculations enable us to come up

with the right answer ($10) by counting only part of each transaction. The basic idea is to count at each step only the contribution to the value of the ultimate final product that is made at that step, excluding the values of items produced at earlier steps.

Ignoring the minor items (such as fertilizer) that the farmer purchases from others, the entire $3 selling price of the bushel of soybeans is new output produced by the farmer; that is, the whole $3 is value added. The miller then grinds the beans and sells them for $4. He has added $4 - $3 = $1 to the value of the beans. When the factory turns this soy meal into soy sauce and sells it for $8, it has added $8 - $4 = $4 more in value. And finally, when the restaurant sells it to hungry customers for $10, a further $2 of value is added.

Table 7-7 shows this chain of creation of value added by appending another column to Table 7-6. We see that the total value added by all four firms is $10, exactly the same as the restaurant's selling price. This is as it must be, for only the restaurant sells the soybeans as a final product.

Alternative Measures of the Income of the Nation

Economists use the term *national income* in two different ways. The most common usage is as a general term indicating the size of the income of the nation as a whole, without being very specific as to exactly how this income is to be measured. This is the sense in

Table 7-7

AN ILLUSTRATION OF VALUE ADDED

ITEM	SELLER	BUYER	PRICE	VALUE ADDED
Bushel of soybeans	Farmer	Miller	$ 3	$ 3
Bag of soy meal	Miller	Factory	4	1
Bottle of soy sauce	Factory	Restaurant	8	4
Bottle of soy sauce used as seasoning	Restaurant	Consumers	10	2
		Totals:	$25	$10

Addendum: Contribution to GNP
Final products $10
Sum of values added $10

which the term "national income" is used in this book. The second, and much more precise, use of the term refers to a very specific concept in national income accounting, which we encountered in Table 7–5 on page 135.

Aside from this formal definition of national income, what other accounting concept might be used to measure the total income of the nation? The first and most obvious candidate is the GNP itself. We noted earlier that GNP correlates very well with GDP, and so is a good measure of employment-creating production activity in the nation. However, the GNP has several drawbacks as a measure of income. First, it includes some output that represents income to no one—output that simply replaces worn out machinery and buildings (depreciation). When we deduct this depreciation, we obtain the net national product (NNP), as shown in Figure 7–11. Second, because of sales taxes and related items (indirect business taxes), part of the price paid for each good and service does not represent the income of any individual. When we deduct these indirect business taxes from NNP, we arrive at the formal definition of national income (refer again to Figure 7–11). Both of these accounting concepts have already been described.

There are, however, two other measures of income. **Personal income** is meant to be a better measure of the income that actually accrues to indi-viduals. It is obtained from national income by *sub-tracting* corporate profits taxes, retained earnings, and payroll taxes (because these items are never received by individuals) and then *adding in* transfer payments to individuals (because these sources of income are not part of the wages, interest, rents, or profits that constitute the national income). As Figure 7–11 suggests, this adding and subtracting normally results in a number that is rather close to national income. Finally, if we subtract personal income taxes from personal income, we obtain **disposable income**.

Among all the concepts of the nation's income depicted in Figure 7–11, only two are used frequently in the construction of models of the economy: gross national product (GNP) and disposable income (*DI*). Since the models presented in this book ignore depreciation and indirect business taxes, GNP is basically identical to national income (see Figure 7–11). Similarly, if we ignore retained earnings, GNP and *DI* differ only by the amounts of taxes and transfers (again, see Figure 7–11).

Limitations of the GNP: What GNP Is Not

Having seen in some detail what the GNP *is*, it is worth pausing to expand upon what it *is not*. In particular:

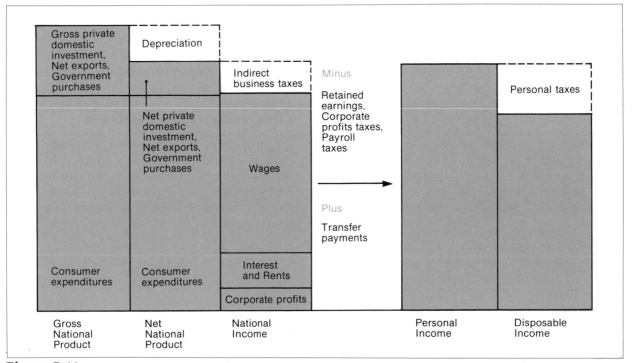

Figure 7–11
ALTERNATIVE MEASURES OF THE INCOME OF THE NATION
This bar chart indicates the relationships among the five alternative measures of the total income of the nation, starting with the largest and most comprehensive measure (GNP) and ranging down to the measure that most closely approximates the spendable income of consumers (disposable income).

Gross national product is not a measure of the nation's economic well-being.

Here are several reasons why:

1. *Only market activity is included in GNP.*

Work done by housewives and do-it-your-selfers certainly contributes to the nation's well-being, but it is not measured in the GNP because it has no price tag.

An important implication of this exclusion is seen when we try to compare the GNPs of developed and less developed countries. Canadian students are always incredulous to learn that the per-capita GNP of the poorest African countries is less than $200 a year. Surely, no one could survive in Canada on $4 a week. How can Africans do it? One part of the answer, of course, is that these people are incredibly poor. We shall study their plight in Chapter 40. But another part of the answer is that:

International GNP comparisons are vastly misleading when the two countries differ greatly in the fraction of economic activity that each conducts in organized markets.

This fraction is relatively large in Canada and relatively small in the less developed countries, so when we compare their respective measured GNPs we are not comparing the same economic activities at all. Many things that get counted in the Canadian GNP are not counted in the GNPs of less developed nations. So it is ludicrous to think that these people, poor as they are, survive on what to Canadians would amount to $4 a week.

2. *GNP places no value on leisure.*

As a country gets richer, one of the things that happens is that its citizens take more and more leisure time. The steady decrease in the length of the typical workweek in Canada is sufficient evidence for this. This means that the gap is steadily widening between official GNP and some truer measure of national well-being that would include the value of leisure time. For this reason, growth in GNP systematically *understates* the growth in national well-being. But there are also reasons why the GNP *overstates* how well off we are; we consider these next.

3. *"Bads" as well as "goods" get counted in GNP.*

Suppose there is a natural disaster—as when the Ocean Ranger oil-drilling rig sank off the coast of Newfoundland in 1982. Surely the well-being of the nation was diminished by this catastrophe. Much expensive equipment was lost, and of course, many people were killed. Yet the disaster may well have caused GNP to rise. Replacing the machinery added to *I*; extra government spending for relief, searches, and legal investigations all added to *G*. Yet no one would think that the nation was better off for its higher GNP.

Wars represent an extreme example of this. Mobilization for outright war always causes a country's GNP to rise rapidly. But men called into the army could be producing civilian output. Factories needed to produce armaments could instead be making cars, washing machines, and televisions. A country at war is surely worse off than a country at peace, but this fact will not be reflected in its GNP accounts.

4. *Ecological costs are not netted out of the GNP.*

Many of the activities in a modern industrial economy that produce goods and services also have undesirable side effects on the environment. Automobiles provide enjoyment and a means of transportation, but they also despoil the atmosphere. Factories pollute rivers and lakes while manufacturing valuable commodities. Almost everything seems to produce garbage, which creates the problem of what to do with it. None of these ecological costs are deducted from the GNP in an effort to give us a truer measure of the *net* increase in economic welfare that our economy produces. Is this foolishness? Not if we remember the job that national income statisticians are trying to do: They are measuring the economic activity conducted through organized markets not national welfare. Our main interest in the GNP stems from its being a measure of the amount of job-creating economic activity that is taking place. Thus, the fact that it is not intended to measure well-being is not a serious limitation.

Summary

1. Gross national product (GNP) is the sum of the money values of all final goods and services produced during a year and sold on organized markets. There are, however, certain exceptions to this definition.
2. One way to measure the GNP is to add up the final demands of consumers, investors, governments, and foreigners: GNP = $C + I + G + X - IM$.
3. A second way to measure the GNP is to start with all the factor payments—wages, interest, rents, and profits—that constitute the national income, and then add indirect business taxes and depreciation.
4. A third way to measure the GNP is to sum up the values added by every firm in the economy (and then once again add indirect business taxes and depreciation).
5. Except for possible bookkeeping and statistical errors,

all three methods must give the same answer.

6. The GNP is meant to be a measure of the *production* of the economy, not of the increase in its *well-being*. For example, the GNP places no value on housework and other do-it-yourself activities, nor on leisure time.

On the other hand, even commodities that might be considered as "bads" rather than "goods" are counted in the GNP (for example, activities that harm the environment).

Concepts for Review

National income accounting
Gross national product (GNP)
Inventories
Gross private domestic investment
Government purchases

Transfer payments
Net exports
National income
Net national product (NNP)

Depreciation
Value added
Personal income
Disposable income

Questions for Discussion

1. Which of the following transactions are included in the gross national product, and by how much does each raise GNP?
   a. You buy a new car, paying $6000.
   b. You buy a used car, paying $2000.
   c. IBM builds a $40 million factory to make computers.
   d. An unemployed worker receives a government check for $300 in unemployment compensation.
   e. General Motors builds 1000 Cadillacs at a cost of $14,000 each. Unable to sell them, it holds them as inventories.
   f. Mr. Black and Mr. Blue, each out for a Sunday drive, have a collision in which their cars are destroyed. Black and Blue each hire a lawyer to sue the other, paying the lawyers $2000 each for services rendered. The judge throws the case out of court.
   g. You sell a $200 painting to your roommate.

2. Explain the difference between final goods and intermediate goods. Why is it sometimes difficult to apply this distinction in practice? In this regard, why is the concept of value added useful?

3. Explain the difference between government spending and government purchases of goods and services (G). Which is larger?

4. Explain why national income and gross national product would be exactly equal if there were no depreciation and no indirect business taxes.

5. Give some reasons why the gross national product is not a suitable measure of the well-being of the nation. (Have you noticed newspaper accounts in which journalists seem to use GNP for this purpose?)

6. The following is a complete description of all economic activity in Trivialand for the year 1984. Draw up versions of Tables 7–4 and 7–5 for Trivialand showing GNP computed in two different ways.
   a. There are thousands of farmers but only two big business firms in Trivialand: Specific Motors (an auto company) and Super Duper (a chain of food markets). There is no government and no depreciation.

   b. Specific Motors produced 1000 small cars, which they sold at $6000 each, and 100 trucks, which they sold at $8000 each. Consumers bought 800 of the cars, and the remaining 200 cars were exported to the United States. Super Duper bought all the trucks.
   c. Sales at Super Duper markets amounted to $14 million, all of it sold to consumers.
   d. All the farmers in Trivialand are self-employed and sell all their wares to Super Duper.
   e. The costs incurred by all the businesses were as follows:

	SPECIFIC MOTORS	SUPER DUPER	FARMERS
Wages	$3,800,000	$4,500,000	0
Interest	100,000	200,000	700,000
Rent	200,000	1,000,000	2,000,000
Purchases of food	0	7,000,000	0

7. (More difficult.) Now complicate Trivialand in the following ways and answer the same questions. In addition, calculate national income, personal income, and disposable income.
   a. The government bought 50 cars, leaving only 150 cars for export. In addition, the government spent $800,000 on wages for soldiers and made $1,200,000 in transfer payments.
   b. Depreciation for the year amounted to $600,000 for Specific Motors and $200,000 for Super Duper. (The farmers had no depreciation.)
   c. The government levied sales taxes amounting to $500,000 on Specific Motors and $200,000 on Super Duper (none on farmers). In addition, the government levied a 10 percent income tax on all wages, interest, and rental income.
   d. In addition to the food and cars mentioned in Question 6, consumers in Trivialand imported 500 computers from Canada at $2000 each.

Demand-Side Equilibrium: Unemployment or Inflation?

Investment ... is a flighty bird, which needs to be controlled.

J.R. HICKS

s we learned in Chapter 5, the interaction of aggregate demand and aggregate supply determines whether the economy will stagnate or prosper, and whether our resources of labour and capital will be fully employed or unemployed. This is the first of eight chapters devoted to studying this important process.

A simplified model of aggregate demand is constructed in Chapters 8 and 9, and the supply side is added in Chapter 10. This first model of the economy teaches us much about the causes of unemployment and inflation, but it is too simple to deal with policy issues because the government and the financial system are largely ignored. Chapters 11–14 remedy these omissions, thereby making it possible to study how government policies affect unemployment and inflation. By Chapter 15 we will have provided a model that is capable of dealing with a wide variety of policy issues.

In Chapter 7 we examined the largest component of aggregate demand, which is consumer expenditure (C); here, we turn our attention first to the most volatile component, investment (I), and discuss its determinants and the reasons why investment spending is so variable and so difficult to predict.[1] Then, rather than waiting for a full discussion of the other components of aggregate demand, government purchases (G), and net exports $(X - IM)$, we construct an abbreviated model of the determination of national income based only on the C and I components. We use this model to provide a preliminary description of how the state of aggregate demand influences the level of the gross national product and to consider a question of great importance to policy-makers: Can the economy be expected to achieve full employment of its resources if the government does not intervene?

[1] We repeat the warning given in the previous chapter about the meaning of the word *investment*. It *includes* spending by businesses and individuals on *newly produced* factories, machinery, and houses. But it *excludes* sales of *used* industrial plants, equipment, and homes, and it *also excludes* purely financial transactions, such as the purchase of stocks and bonds.

The Extreme Variability of Investment

The first thing to be said about investment spending is that it is extraordinarily variable.

Unlike consumer spending, which follows movements in disposable income with great (though not perfect) reliability, investment spending swings from high to low levels with annoying rapidity. During recessions, for example, the decline in investment generally constitutes the greatest part of the total drop in real GNP, despite the fact that investment is a much smaller portion of GNP than is consumption. What accounts for these movements of investment demand?

Business Confidence and Expectations About the Future

While many factors influence business people's desires to invest, Keynes himself laid great stress on the *state of business confidence*, which in turn depends on *expectations about the future*.

While it is tricky to measure, it does seem obvious that businesses will build more factories and purchase more new machines when their expectations are optimistic. Conversely, their investment plans will be very cautious if the economic outlook appears bleak. Keynes pointed out that psychological perceptions like these are subject to abrupt shifts, so that fluctuations in investment can be a major cause of instability in aggregate demand. Thus, we see the logic in Hicks's analogy to a "flighty bird."

Unfortunately, neither economists nor, for that matter, psychologists have any very good ideas about how to *measure*—much less how to *control*—business confidence. Therefore, economists usually focus on several more objective determinants of investment—determinants that are easy to quantify and more easily influenced by government policy.

The Rate of Interest

The interest rate is the determinant of investment that is perhaps most extensively discussed by economists. A good deal of business investment is financed by borrowing, and the interest rate indicates how much firms must pay for that privilege. The higher the interest rate, the more costly it is to borrow. Some investment projects that look profitable at an interest rate of 7 percent will look disastrous if the firm has to pay 12 percent. Thus:

The amount that businesses will want to invest depends on the real interest rate they have to pay on their borrowings. The lower the real rate of interest, the more investment spending there will be.

In Chapter 13 we will study in some detail how the government can influence the rate of interest. Since interest rates affect investment, policy-makers have a handle on aggregate demand—a handle they do not hesitate to use. The point is that, unlike business confidence, interest rates are visible and manipulable, at least for short periods. Therefore, even if investment responds much more dramatically to changes in confidence than to changes in interest rates, interest rates attract more attention as a potential instrument of government policy.

The State of Demand and Capacity Utilization

There will be a strong incentive to invest when firms find that demand is pressing against their capacity. Under these circumstances, firms are very likely to feel that new factories and machinery can be employed profitably. By contrast, if there is a great deal of spare capacity (unused machinery, empty factories, and so on), business managers will not find investment attractive even if interest rates are very low.

The Growth of Demand

Since it takes a substantial amount of time to order machinery or to build a factory, investment plans are made with an eye on the future. Even when pressures on current capacity are not particularly severe, a firm experiencing rapid growth in sales is likely to start investing *now* so that it will have adequate capacity when it is needed in the future. In addition, briskly growing sales are likely to make business people more optimistic. Conversely, slow growth of output will discourage investment.

We can summarize these last two points by saying that:

High levels of sales in relation to available capacity and rapid economic growth create an atmosphere favourable to investment. On the other hand, low levels of sales and slow growth are likely to discourage investment.

Government stabilization policy thus has another handle on investment spending, for by stimulating aggregate demand it can induce business firms to invest more, though the precise amount may be hard to predict.

Tax Provisions

The government has still another important way to influence investment spending—by altering various provisions of the tax law. For example, the tax law sets maximum **depreciation allowances**, which govern how firms may deduct the costs of investment from their taxable income. In many of the federal government budgets in the last 20 years, the government has made these allowances more generous in a variety of ways. The idea was simple. More generous depreciation allowances lead to bigger tax deductions, and hence smaller tax bills, for firms that invest. This enhances the profitability of investment, and so should encourage more investment. We examine the effectiveness of these tax breaks, and their implications for the distribution of income, in Chapter 11. For now, we simply summarize:

> **Depreciation allowances** are tax deductions that businesses may claim when they spend money on investment goods.

The tax law gives the government several ways to influence business spending on investment goods. But its control is imperfect. Investment remains a "flighty bird."

A Simplified Circular Flow

Let us now put consumption and investment together and see how they interact, using as our organizing framework the circular flow diagram introduced in the last chapter. For this purpose, we simplify the circular flow somewhat by leaving out the government and the foreign sector.

There are two reasons for doing this. The first is pedagogical: The workings of the model are much clearer if we strip away some of its complications. But there is a much more important reason. One of the crucial questions surrounding government attempts to stabilize the economy is whether the economy would *automatically* gravitate toward full employment if the government simply left it alone. We can study this issue best by imagining an economy that has no government, so that all the aggregate demand comes from the private sector. This is just what we do in this chapter.

Look now at Figure 8–1, which is the same as Figure 7–1 of the last chapter except that the government and foreign sectors have been omitted. The first thing you may notice is that, with the government and foreigners out of the picture, there is no longer any leakage out of the national income for taxes (nor are there transfer payments) and imports, so there is no important difference between national income and disposable income. Second, there is no government or foreign component of total spending; instead, spending is represented by the sum $C + I$.

The Meaning of Equilibrium GNP

We can use Figure 8-1 to begin the construction of a simple model of the determination of national income. A first step is to understand what we mean by "equilibrium income."

As was explained in the last chapter, national *product* and national *income* must, of necessity, be equal. But the same cannot automatically be said of total *spending*. Look again at Figure 8-1 and imagine that, for some reason, the total expenditures $(C + I)$ that are being made at point 3 are greater than the output that is being produced by the business firms at point 4.

Two things may happen in such a situation. Since consumers and firms together are buying (in the forms of C and I) more than firms are producing, business firms are being forced to take goods out of their warehouses to meet customer demands. Thus, inventory stocks must be falling. These inventory reductions are a signal to retailers of a need to increase their orders, and to manufacturers of a need to step up their production. Consequently, production is likely to rise. At some later date, if there is evidence that the high level of aggregate demand is not just a temporary aberration, either manufacturers or retailers (or both) may also respond to the buoyant sales performances by raising their prices. Economists therefore say that neither output nor the price level is in **equilibrium** when aggregate demand exceeds the current rate of production.

It is clear from the definition of equilibrium that the economy cannot be in equilibrium when aggregate demand exceeds production, for the falling inventories demonstrate to firms that their production and pricing decisions were not quite

Equilibrium refers to a situation in which consumers and firms have no incentive to change their behaviour. They are content to continue with things as they are.

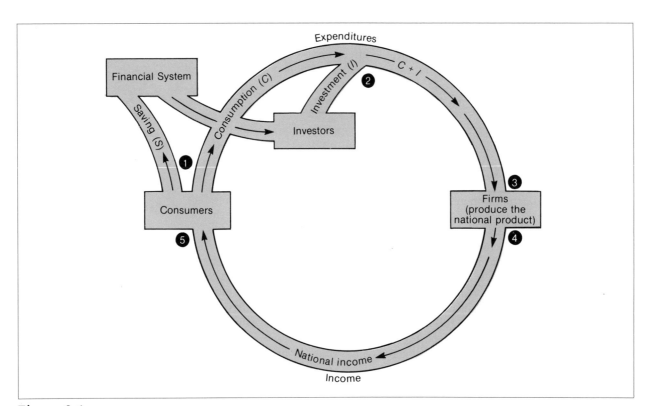

Figure 8-1
A SIMPLIFIED CIRCULAR FLOW

Here we show a simplified version of the circular flow of income and expenditures that we introduced in Chapter 7. The simplification amounts to shutting off the pipes leading into and out of the government and the rest of the world. Thus, this circular flow represents an economy with no government or foreign sector. Notice that aggregate demand now has only two components (consumer spending and investment spending) and that the entire national income flows to consumers without taxation.

appropriate. Thus, since we normally use GNP to measure output:

The equilibrium level of GNP cannot be one at which aggregate demand exceeds output because firms will notice that inventory stocks are being depleted. They may first decide to increase production sufficiently to meet the higher demand. Later they may decide to raise prices as well.

Now imagine the other case, in which the flow of aggregate demand reaching firms falls short of current production. Some output cannot be sold and winds up as additions to inventories. The inventory pile-up acts as a signal to firms that at least one of their decisions was wrong. Once again, they will probably react first by cutting back on production, causing the GNP to fall. If the imbalance persists, they may also lower prices in order to stimulate sales. But they certainly will not be happy with things as they are. Thus:

The equilibrium level of GNP cannot be one at which aggregate demand is less than output because firms will not allow inventories to continue to pile up. They may decide to decrease production, or they may decide to cut prices in order to stimulate a demand. Normally, firms are reluctant to cut prices until they are quite certain that the low level of demand is not a temporary phenomenon. So, they rely more heavily on reductions in output.

Equilibrium on the Demand Side of the Economy

You may have noticed that we have now determined, through a process of elimination, the level of national income and product that is consistent with peoples' desires to spend. We have reasoned that whenever GNP is below total spending $(C + I)$, the GNP will rise; and that whenever GNP is above $C + I$, the GNP will fall. Equilibrium can only occur, then, when there is just enough spending to absorb the current level of production. Under such circumstances, producers conclude that their price and output decisions are correct, and they have no incentive to change them. We conclude that:

The **equilibrium level of GNP on the demand side** is the one at which total spending equals production. In such a situation, firms find their inventories remaining at desired levels; so there is no incentive to change output or prices.

The simple circular flow diagram, then, has helped us to understand the concept of the equilibrium level of GNP and also how the economy is driven toward it. It leaves unanswered, however, three important questions.

1. How large is the equilibrium level of GNP?
2. Will the economy suffer from unemployment, inflation, or both?
3. Is the equilibrium level of GNP on the demand side also consistent with firms' desires to produce? That is, is it also an equilibrium on the *supply* side?

The first two questions will occupy our attention in this chapter; the third question is reserved for Chapter 10.

Constructing the Expenditure Schedule

Our first objective is to determine precisely the equilibrium level of GNP and to see what factors it depends upon. To make the analysis more concrete, we turn to

Table 8-1

TOTAL EXPENDITURE IN MACROLAND (billions of dollars)

(1) INCOME (Y)	(2) CONSUMPTION (C)	(3) INVESTMENT (I)	(4) A E TOTAL EXPENDITURE (C + I)
200	170	70	240
250	210	70	280
300	250	70	320
350	290	70	360
400	330	70	400
450	370	70	440
500	410	70	480
550	450	70	520
600	490	70	560

This table illustrates the derivation of the expenditure schedule, which is shaded in blue. It is derived from the consumption schedule, columns 1 and 2, and from the investment schedule, columns 1 and 3, by simple addition. This is because total spending is the sum $C + I$.

a numerical example. Specifically, we examine the relationship between aggregate demand and GNP in Macroland, the hypothetical economy that was introduced in the last chapter.

Columns 1 and 2 of Table 8-1 incorporate the consumption function of Macroland that we first encountered in Table 7-1. They show how consumer spending, C, depends on national income, which we now begin to symbolize by the letter Y. However, one thing has changed here. The consumption function in Chapter 7 related C to *disposable* income (DI), whereas the consumption function in Table 8-1 relates C to *national* income (Y).This change is legitimate because, in this chapter, we have eliminated the government and the foreign sector from the picture. With no taxes and no transfer payments, there is no difference between DI and Y. Because (as we showed in Chapter 7) national income must equal national product, Y can be used to represent either income or output.

Column 3 provides the other component of aggregate demand, I, through the simplifying assumption that investment spending is $70 billion in Macroland, regardless of the level of GNP. By adding together the second and third columns, we calculate $C + I$, or total expenditure, which is displayed in column 4. Columns 1 and 4, shaded in blue, show how total expenditure depends on income in Macroland. We call this the **expenditure schedule**.

Figure 8-2 shows the construction of the expenditure schedule graphically. The line labelled C is the consumption function of Macroland and simply duplicates Figure 7-7 of the last chapter, except that Y, not DI, appears on the horizontal axis. It plots on a graph the numbers given in columns 1 and 2 of Table 8-1. The line labelled $C + I$ in the diagram depicts the total expenditure schedule that we have just derived by plotting the data in columns 1 and 4 of the table. That is, at each level of GNP measured along the horizontal axis, the height of the $C + I$ line indicates the sum of consumption plus investment.

The difference between the two lines, therefore, is investment. In the diagram, the lines are parallel; that is, the distance between them is always the same. This distance is $70 billion—the volume of investment assumed in the example. If investment were not always $70 billion, the two lines would either move closer together (at income levels at which investment was below $70 billion) or grow farther apart (at income levels at which investment was above $70 billion). For example, our list of determinants of investment spending suggested that I might be larger at higher levels of GNP. Because of this added investment—which is called **induced investment**—the resulting $C + I$ schedule would have a steeper slope than the C schedule.

An **expenditure schedule** shows how total spending varies with the level of national income (GNP).

Induced investment is investment that rises when GNP rises and falls when GNP falls.

Table 8-2

THE DETERMINATION OF EQUILIBRIUM OUTPUT

(1) OUTPUT (Y) (billions of dollars)	(2) TOTAL SPENDING (C + I) (billions of dollars)	(3) BALANCE OF SPENDING AND OUTPUT	(4) INVENTORIES ARE:	(5) PRODUCERS WILL RESPOND BY:
200	240	Spending exceeds output	Falling	Producing more
250	280	Spending exceeds output	Falling	Producing more
300	320	Spending exceeds output	Falling	Producing more
350	360	Spending exceeds output	Falling	Producing more
400	400	Spending equals output	Constant	Not changing production
450	440	Output exceeds spending	Rising	Producing less
500	480	Output exceeds spending	Rising	Producing less
550	520	Output exceeds spending	Rising	Producing less
600	560	Output exceeds spending	Rising	Producing less

Columns 1 and 2 are the expenditure schedule derived in the previous table. The remaining columns explain how the equilibrium level of national income can be derived from these data. For example, reading across the first row we see that when GNP is $200 billion, total spending is $240 billion. Thus spending exceeds production (by $40 billion), so that inventories must be falling. Producers are likely to respond to this drop in inventory stocks by raising their rate of production. The other rows are read similarly, and together they show that only $400 billion can be the equilibrium level of GNP. This is the only output level that firms will not want to change.

The Mechanics of Income Determination

We are now ready to determine the equilibrium level of GNP in Macroland. Look first at Table 8-2, which presents the logic of our circular flow argument in tabular form. The first two columns of this table reproduce the expenditure schedule that was constructed in Table 8-1. The other columns explain the process by which equilibrium is approached. Let us see why a GNP of $400 billion must be the equilibrium level.

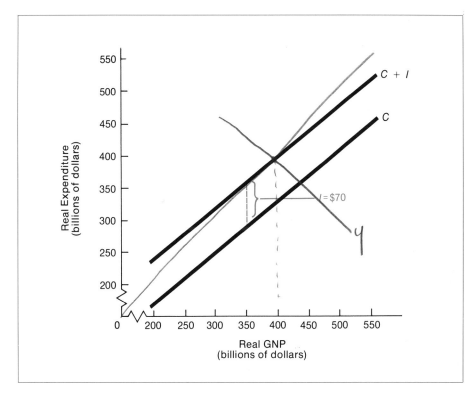

Figure 8-2

CONSTRUCTION OF THE EXPENDITURE SCHEDULE
This figure shows in a diagram what Table 8-1 showed numerically—the construction of a total expenditure schedule from its components. Line C is the consumption function that we first encountered in Figure 7-7, except that GNP, not disposable income, is measured along the horizontal axis. Line C + I is the expenditure schedule and is obtained by adding investment (assumed always to be $70 billion in this example) to the consumption function.

Consider first any output level below $400 billion. For example, at output level $Y = \$350$ billion, total expenditure is $360 billion (column 2), which is $10 billion more than production. With spending greater than output (column 3), inventories will be falling (column 4). As the table suggests, this will be a signal to producers to raise their output (column 5). Clearly, then, no output level below $Y = \$400$ billion can be an equilibrium. Output is too low.

A similar line of reasoning can eliminate any output level above $400 billion. Consider, for example, $Y = \$450$ billion. The table shows that total spending would be $440 billion if national income were $450 billion. So $10 billion of the GNP would go unsold. This would raise producers' inventory stocks and signal them that their rate of production is too high.

Just as we concluded from our circular flow diagram, then, equilibrium will be achieved only when total spending $(C + I)$ is equal to GNP (Y). In symbols, our condition for equilibrium GNP is:

$$C + I = Y.$$

The table shows that this occurs only at a GNP of $400 billion. This, then, must be the equilibrium level of GNP.

Figure 8–3 shows this same conclusion graphically, by adding a 45° line to Figure 8–2. Why a 45° line? Recall that a 45° line marks all points on a graph at which the value of the variable measured on the horizontal axis is equal to the value of the variable measured on the vertical axis. In this convenient graph of the expenditure schedule, gross national product (Y) is measured on the horizontal axis and total expenditure $(C + I)$ is measured on the vertical axis. So the 45° line shows all the points at which output and spending are equal: that is, where $Y = C + I$. The 45° line therefore displays all the points at which the economy *can possibly* be at equilibrium.

Figure 8–3

INCOME-EXPENDITURE DIAGRAM

This figure adds a 45° line—which marks off points where expenditure and output are equal—to Figure 8-2. Since the condition for equilibrium GNP is that expenditure and output must be equal, this line can be used to determine the equilibrium level of GNP. In this example, equilibrium is at point E, where GNP is $400 billion—precisely as we found in Table 8-2.

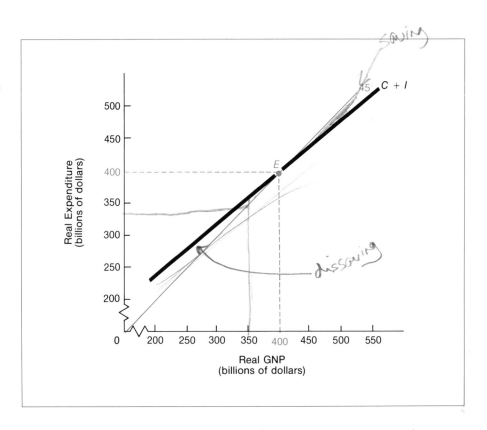

Now we must compare these potential equilibrium points with the actual combinations of spending and output that the economy can attain, given the behaviour of consumers and investors. That behaviour, as we have seen, is described by the $C + I$ line in Figure 8-3, which shows how total expenditure varies as income changes. Thus, the economy will *always* be on the $C + I$ line; only points on the $C + I$ line are consistent with the spending plans of consumers and investors. Similarly, *if* the economy is in equilibrium, it *must* be on the 45° line. As Figure 8-3 shows, these two requirements together imply that the only viable equilibrium is at point E, where the $C + I$ line intersects the 45° line. Only this point is consistent both with equilibrium and with the actual desires to consume and invest.

Notice that to the left of the equilibrium point, E, the $C + I$ line lies above the 45° line. This means that total spending exceeds total output, as we have already noted in words and with numbers. The opposite is true to the right of equilibrium point E; here, spending falls short of output.

Diagrams like this one will recur so frequently in this and the next several chapters that it will be convenient to have a name for them. Let us, therefore, call them **income-expenditure diagrams** since they show how expenditures vary with income. Sometimes we shall also refer to them simply as **45° line diagrams.**

The Aggregate-Demand Curve

Chapter 5 sketched a framework for macroeconomic analysis by introducing aggregate-demand and aggregate-supply curves that relate aggregate quantities demanded and supplied to the price level. Yet the price level has not even been mentioned so far in our discussion of equilibrium. It is now time to remedy this omission, for only by explicit analysis of the determination of the price level will we be able to deal with important issues relating to inflation.

Fortunately, no further mechanical apparatus is required. The price level can be brought into our income–expenditure analysis by recalling something we learned in the last chapter: At any given level of real income, higher prices lead to lower real consumer spending. The reason, you will recall, is that consumers own many assets whose values are fixed in money terms, and which therefore lose purchasing power when prices rise.[2] With real wealth lower, consumers spend less and therefore total spending in the economy falls.

In terms of our 45° line diagram, then, a rise in the price level will lower the consumption function depicted in Figure 8-2 and, hence, will lower the total expenditure schedule as well. Conversely, a fall in the price level will raise both the C and $C + I$ schedules in the diagram. Figure 8-4 illustrates both these sorts of shifts.

What, then, do changes in the price level do to the equilibrium level of real GNP on the demand side? Common sense says that, with lower spending, equilibrium GNP should fall. And Figure 8-5 shows that this conclusion is correct. Part (a) shows that a rise in the price level, by shifting the expenditure schedule downward from $C_0 + I$ to $C_1 + I$, leads to a reduction in the equilibrium quantity of real GNP demanded from Y_0 to Y_1. Part (b) shows that a fall in the price level, by shifting the expenditure schedule upward from $C_0 + I$ to $C_2 + I$, leads to a rise in the equilibrium quantity of real GNP demanded from Y_0 to Y_2. In summary:

A rise in the price level leads to a lower equilibrium level of real aggregate quantity demanded. This relationship between the price level and the equilibrium quantity

An **income-expenditure diagram**, also called a **45° line diagram**, plots total real expenditure (on the vertical axis) against real income (on the horizontal axis). The 45° line marks off points where income and expenditure are equal.

[2]Two warnings issued in Chapter 7 (page 126) are worth repeating: First, the effect referred to here comes from changes in the *price level*, not from changes in the *inflation rate*. Second, a higher price level does not reduce spending by reducing real income. Quite to the contrary, real income is held constant when we compare consumer expenditures at different price levels.

Figure 8-4

THE EFFECT OF THE PRICE LEVEL ON THE EXPENDITURE SCHEDULE

A higher price level will cause the $C + I$ schedule to shift downward, as shown by the black arrows. A lower price level will cause the $C + I$ schedule to shift upward, as shown by the blue arrows.

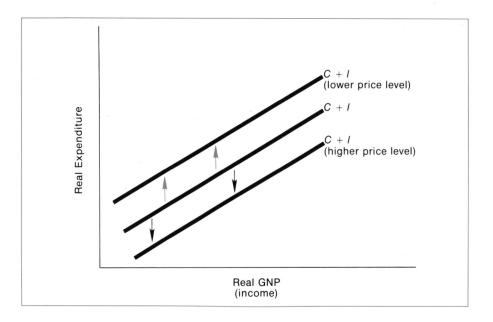

of real GNP demanded is depicted in Figure 8-6 and is precisely what we called the **aggregate-demand curve** in earlier chapters. It comes directly from the 45° line diagrams in Figure 8-5. Thus, points E_0, E_1, and E_2 in Figure 8-6 correspond to the points bearing the same labels in Figure 8-5.

Thus we have now learned the first reason why the aggregate-demand curve relating the price level to real GNP demanded slopes downward. (More reasons will come later in the book.) We have also been warned that:

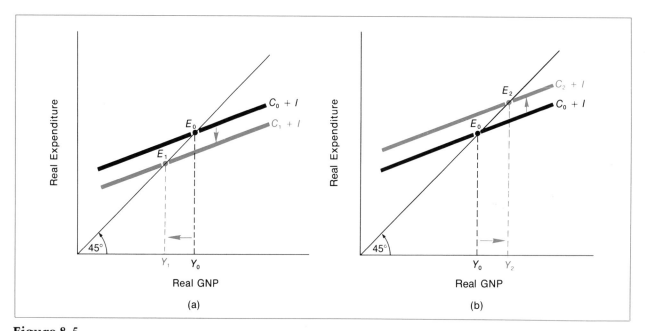

Figure 8-5

THE EFFECT OF THE PRICE LEVEL ON EQUILIBRIUM AGGREGATE QUANTITY DEMANDED

Because a change in the price level causes the expenditure schedule to shift, it changes the equilibrium quantity of real GNP demanded. Part (a) shows what happens when the price level rises, causing the expenditure schedule to shift downward from $C_0 + I$ to $C_1 + I$. Equilibrium quantity demanded falls from Y_0 to Y_1. Part (b) shows what happens when the price level falls, causing the expenditure schedule to shift upward from $C_0 + I$ to $C_2 + I$. Equilibrium quantity demanded rises from Y_0 to Y_2.

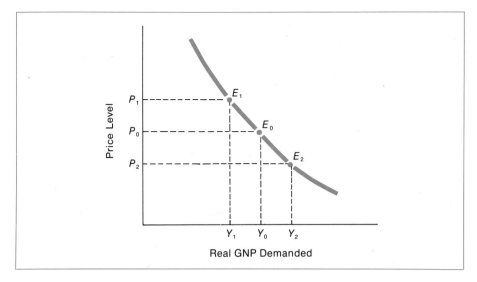

Figure 8-6
THE AGGREGATE-DEMAND CURVE
The graphical analysis in Figure 8-5 showed that higher prices lead to lower aggregate quantity demanded. This relationship is called the aggregate-demand curve and is shown in this figure.

An income–expenditure diagram like Figure 8-3 can only be drawn up for a *specific* price level. At different price levels, the $C + I$ schedule will be different and, hence, the equilibrium quantity of GNP demanded will be different.

As we shall now see, this finding is critical to understanding the genesis of unemployment and inflation.

Demand-Side Equilibrium and Full Employment

We now turn to the second major question of this chapter: Will the economy achieve an equilibrium at full employment without inflation, or will there be unemployment, inflation, or both?

In the income–expenditure diagrams used so far, the equilibrium level of GNP demanded has been shown as the intersection of the expenditure schedule and the 45° line, regardless of whatever level of GNP might correspond to full employment of the nation's available resources. However, as we will see now, when equilibrium GNP exceeds the full-employment level of output, the result is inflation. And when equilibrium falls below full employment, there will be unemployment and recession.

This fact was one of the principal messages of Keynes's *General Theory of Employment, Interest, and Money*. Writing during the Great Depression, it was natural for him to stress the case in which equilibrium falls short of full employment so that there are unemployed resources. Figure 8-7 illustrates this possibility. A vertical line has been erected at the full-employment level of GNP (called "potential GNP"), which is assumed to be $500 billion in the example. We see that the $C + I$ curve cuts the 45° line at point E, which corresponds to a GNP (Y = $400 billion) below potential GNP. In this case, the $C + I$ curve is too low to lead to full employment. Such a situation might arise because either consumers or investors are unwilling to spend at normal rates, or because the price level is "too high," thereby depressing the $C + I$ curve. Unemployment must occur because not enough output will be demanded to keep the entire labour force busy.

The distance between the equilibrium level of output demanded and the full-employment level of output (that is, potential GNP) is called the **recessionary gap**—and is shown by the horizontal distance from E to B.

The **recessionary gap** is the amount by which the equilibrium level of real GNP falls short of potential GNP.

Biographical Note: John Maynard Keynes (1883–1946)

It may be one of history's great ironies that the death of Karl Marx, the prophet of capitalism's doom, and the birth of John Maynard Keynes, who many consider capitalism's saviour, both occurred in the same year—1883. The son of a prominent upper-class British economist, Keynes was something of a child prodigy. After an outstanding scholastic career at Eton and Cambridge, Keynes took the civil service examination. His second-place score was not good enough to land him the position he wanted and should have had (in the Treasury), so in 1907 he found himself in the India Office. Some years later, reflecting on the fact that his lowest score on the exam was in the economics section, he suggested with characteristic immodesty that, "The examiners presumably knew less than I did."* He was probably right.

While Keynes disliked his work at the India Office, his time there was not wasted. It was during that period that he wrote his *Treatise on Probability* (1909), which drew the admiration of Bertrand Russell and won Keynes election as a lifetime Fellow of Cambridge's King's College.

During World War I, Keynes was called to the Treasury to assist in planning various financial aspects of the war. There his "unique combination of the guts of a burglar and the intellect of a first-class economist"‡ established him as a dominant figure. At the war's end, though only 36, Keynes represented the British Treasury at the peace conference in Versailles.

The conference was a turning point in Keynes's life, though it was one of his few failures. He sought unsuccessfully to persuade the Allies to take a less punitive attitude toward the vanquished Germans, and then left the conference in protest in June 1919, telling David Lloyd George, the English Prime Minister, "I am slipping away from this scene of nightmare."§ Keynes immediately went to work on his *Economic Consequences of the Peace*, which created a furor when it was published in 1919. In addition to stinging personal portraits of Lloyd George, Georges Clemenceau, and Woodrow Wilson ("the blind and deaf Don Quixote"), Keynes demonstrated with exquisite logic that the Germans could never meet the

Figure 8-7

A RECESSIONARY GAP
Sometimes equilibrium GNP may fall below potential GNP, so that some workers are unemployed. This diagram illustrates such a case. The horizontal distance *EB* between equilibrium GNP and potential GNP is called the recessionary gap.

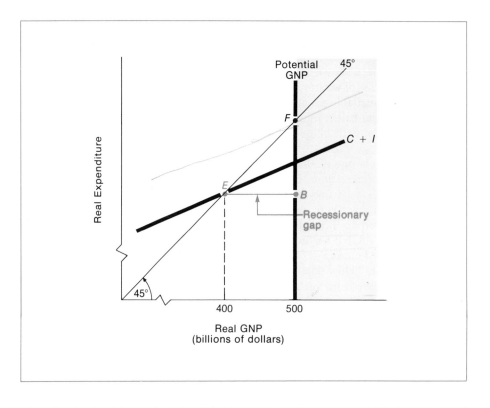

harsh economic terms of the treaty and that its very viciousness posed the threat of continued instability and perhaps another war in Europe. Sadly, his visions were remarkably accurate.

No longer welcome in government, Keynes returned to Cambridge and to his distinguished circle of literary and artistic friends in London's Bloomsbury district—a group that included Virginia Woolf, Lytton Strachey, and E. M. Forster. In 1925 he married the beautiful ballerina Lydia Lopokova, who gave up her stage career for him (though she later acted in a theatre that Keynes himself established).

Between the wars, Keynes devoted himself to making money (both for himself and for King's College), to economic theory, and to political economy. Spending about one-half hour each morning with newspapers and financial reports (apparently while still in bed!), Keynes managed to make himself a rich man and increase his college's unrestricted fund from £30,000 to £380,000 by speculating in international currencies and commodities. As a scholar, he wrote the *Tract on Monetary Reform* (1923), a stunning denunciation of the gold standard, which was published two years before Churchill once again tied the pound to gold and, in the view of modern observers, sealed Britain's economic doom. In 1936, he published his masterpiece, *The General Theory of Employment, Interest, and Money*, upon which modern macroeconomics is based. Finally, as a tireless political activist and polemicist, he used newspaper and magazine articles, and visits to Whitehall and Washington, to urge governments to lift their economies out of the Depression (which began for Britain in the 1920s) through policies that we would now call "Keynesian."

A heart attack in 1937 reduced Keynes's activities somewhat, though he maintained careers as both an academic economist and a businessman. He returned to the Treasury during World War II and conducted several delicate financial negotiations with the Americans. Then, as the capstone to a truly remarkable career, he represented the United Kingdom—and by all accounts dominated the proceedings—at the conference in Bretton Woods, New Hampshire, in 1944 that established an international financial system that served the Western world for 27 years. (See Chapter 16.)

He died of a heart attack at his home on Easter Sunday of 1946 as Lord Keynes, Baron of Tilton, a man who had achieved almost everything that he sought, and who had only one regret: He wished he had drunk more champagne.

*Quoted in E. A. G. Robinson, "John Maynard Keynes," in R. Lekachman, ed., *Keynes' General Theory: Reports of Three Decades* (New York: St. Martin's Press, Inc., 1964), page 25.

‡Robert Lekachman, *The Age of Keynes* (New York: Random House, 1966), page 27. This book contains a marvelous biography of Keynes, as does Robert Heilbroner's *The Worldly Philosophers*, 4th edition (New York: Simon and Schuster, 1972).

§Quoted in R. F. Harrod, *The Life of John Maynard Keynes* (New York: Macmillan, 1951), page 253.

It is clear from Figure 8–7 that full employment can be reached only by raising the total spending schedule to eliminate the recessionary gap. Specifically, the $C + I$ schedule must move upward until it cuts the 45° line at point F. Can this happen without government intervention? We shall return to this question after we have brought the supply side into the picture. But first let us consider the other case, in which equilibrium GNP exceeds full employment.

Figure 8–8 illustrates this possibility. The expenditure schedule intersects the 45° line at point E, where GNP is $600 billion. But this exceeds the full-employment level, $Y = $500 billion. A case like this can arise when consumer or investment spending is unusually buoyant or when a "low" price level pushes the $C + I$ curve upward.

To reach an equilibrium at full employment, the price level would have to rise enough to drive the $C + I$ schedule *down* until it passed through point F. The horizontal distance BE—which indicates the amount by which the quantity of GNP demanded exceeds potential GNP—is called the **inflationary gap**. If there is an inflationary gap, a higher price level or some other means of reducing total expenditure is necessary to reach an equilibrium at full employment.

In sum, only if the price level and the spending plans of consumers and investors are "just right" will the $C + I$ curve intersect the 45° line precisely at full employment, so that neither a recessionary gap nor an inflationary gap occurs. Are there reasons to expect this outcome? Does the economy have a self-correcting mechanism that automatically eliminates recessionary or inflationary gaps and propels it toward full employment? And how is it that inflation and unemployment sometimes occur together? These are questions we are not quite ready to address

The **inflationary gap** is the amount by which equilibrium real GNP exceeds the full-employment level of GNP.

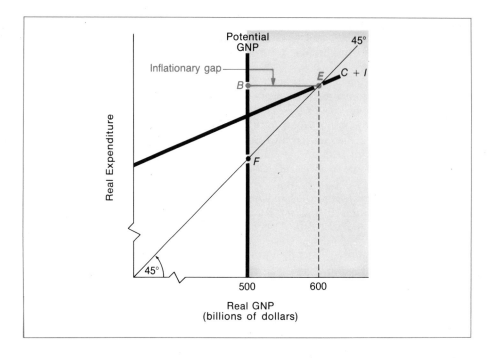

Figure 8-8

AN INFLATIONARY GAP
Sometimes equilibrium GNP may lie above potential GNP, meaning that there are more jobs than required for full employment. This diagram illustrates such a case. The horizontal distance *BE* between potential GNP and equilibrium GNP is called the inflationary gap. It is gradually eliminated by rising prices, which pull the *C + I* schedule down until it passes through point *F*.

because we have yet to bring *aggregate supply* into the picture. And, as we learned in Chapter 4, the price level is determined by the interaction of *both* aggregate demand *and* aggregate supply. However, it is not too early to get an idea about why things can go wrong, why the economy can find itself far away from full employment.

The Co-ordination of Saving and Investment

To understand what goes wrong with the economy in a recession, it is useful to pose the following question: How can the full-employment level of GNP fail to be an equilibrium?

To find an answer look back at the simplified circular flow diagram (Figure 8-1 on page 144). Suppose that firms produce the full-employment level of GNP, and this becomes the national income that emerges at point 4 in the diagram. This full-employment level of income then flows to consumers at point 5, who save some of it and spend the rest. The saving, you will note, "leaks out" of the circular flow at point 1. So, once we pass this point, consumption is less than full-employment GNP. But then at point 2, an additional source of spending enters: investment. Recalling that the condition for equilibrium is that the sum *C + I* equals the GNP, we have the following conclusion:

The economy will reach an equilibrium at full employment only if the amount that consumers wish to save out of full-employment incomes is precisely equal to the amount that investors want to invest. If these two magnitudes happen to be unequal, then full employment will not be an equilibrium for the economy.

Specifically, we can see from the circular flow diagram that if saving exceeds investment at full employment, then the total demand arriving at the firms (point 3) will fall short of total output because the added investment spending is not enough to replace the leakage to saving. With demand inadequate to support production at full employment, we know that the GNP must fall below potential. There will be a recessionary gap. Conversely, if investment exceeds saving when the economy is at full employment, then total demand (*C + I*) will exceed potential

GNP and production will rise above the full-employment level. There will be an inflationary gap.

Now this discussion does nothing but restate what we already know in different words.[3] But these words hold the key to understanding why the economy can find itself stuck below full employment (or above it, for that matter), for *the people who do the investing are not the same people who do the saving.* In a modern capitalist economy, investing is done by one group of individuals (corporate executives and home buyers) while saving is done by another group.[4] It is easy to imagine that their plans may not be well co-ordinated. If they are not, we have just seen how either unemployment or inflation can arise.

Notice that these problems would never arise if the acts of saving and investing were not separated. Imagine a primitive economy of farmers, each of whom invests only in his own farm. There is no borrowing or lending, and no financial system. In this world, any farmer wanting to buy a new plough or tractor (that is, wanting to *invest*) would have to refrain from consuming part of his income (that is, would have to *save*). Therefore, the amount that all farmers together planned to save out of full-employment income would of necessity be equal to the amount of planned investment. Total spending and production would always have to be equal at full employment.

Almost the same sequence holds true in a centrally planned economy like that of the Soviet Union. There, the state decides how much will be invested and has a great deal of leverage over how much saving people do. If the planners do their calculations correctly, they can force saving to be equal to investment at full employment. Consequently, business fluctuations are not a major problem in the Soviet Union. (They have plenty of others!)

Keynes observed that modern market economies differ from either primitive societies or centrally planned societies in this fundamental way and that this separation of decisions within the market system is what leaves them vulnerable to recessions. However, one should not conclude that in order to avoid unemployment and recession the Canadian economy should revert either to a primitive form of capitalism or to rigid central planning. These "remedies" may be far worse than the disease. Fortunately, there are policies the government can follow in an advanced capitalist economy to ease the pain of unemployment and recession—policies that we shall be studying in the following chapters.

---

[3]In symbols, our previous equilibrium condition was $C + I = Y$. If we note that Y is also the sum of consumption plus saving, $Y = C + S$, it follows that $C + I = C + S$, or $I = S$, is a restatement of the equilibrium condition. The saving = investment approach is described in an appendix to this chapter.

[4]In a modern economy, it is not only households that save. Businesses save also, in the form of retained earnings. None the less, households are the ultimate source of the saving needed to finance investment.

Summary

1. Investment is the most volatile component of aggregate demand, largely because it is tied so closely to the state of business confidence and to expectations about the future performance of the economy.

2. Government policy cannot influence business confidence in any reliable way, so policies designed to alter investment spending are aimed at more objective, though possibly less important, determinants of investment. Among these are interest rates, the overall state of aggregate demand, and corporate tax incentives.

3. The equilibrium level of national income on the demand side is the level at which total spending just equals production (GNP). In this chapter we ignore government and foreign demand, so total spending is the sum of consumption plus investment. Thus, in symbols, the condition for equilibrium is $Y = C + I$.

4. Income levels below equilibrium are bound to rise because, when spending exceeds output, firms will see their inventory stocks being depleted and will react by stepping up production.

5. Income levels above equilibrium are bound to fall because, when total spending is insufficient to absorb total output, inventories will pile up and firms will react by curtailing production.

6. The determination of the equilibrium level of GNP on the demand side can be portrayed on a convenient "income–expenditure diagram" as the point at which the expenditure schedule—defined as the sum of the consumption and investment schedules—crosses the 45° line. The 45° line is significant because it marks off points at which spending and output are equal (that is, at which $C + I = Y$), and this is the basic condition for equilibrium.

7. An income–expenditure diagram can only be drawn up for a specific price level, however. Thus the equilibrium GNP so determined depends on the price level.

8. Because higher prices reduce the purchasing power of consumers' wealth, and hence reduce their spending, equilibrium real GNP demanded is lower when prices are higher. This downward-sloping relationship is known as the aggregate–demand curve.

9. Equilibrium GNP can be above or below potential GNP, which is defined as the GNP that would be produced if the labour force were fully employed.

10. If equilibrium GNP exceeds potential GNP, the difference is called an inflationary gap. If equilibrium GNP falls short of potential GNP, the resulting difference is called a recessionary gap.

11. Such gaps can occur in a decentralized economy because the saving that consumers want to do at full-employment income levels may differ from the investing that investors want to do. This problem is not likely to arise in a planned economy or in a primitive economy.

Concepts for Review

Depreciation allowances	Income–expenditure (or 45° line) diagram	Recessionary gap
Equilibrium level of GNP		Inflationary gap
Expenditure schedule	Aggregate–demand curve	Co-ordination of saving and investment
Induced investment	Full-employment level of GNP (or potential GNP)	
$C + I = Y$		

Questions for Discussion

1. Why would someone interested in stabilization policy want to study a model of an economy in which there is no government?

2. Analysts of the economy often argue that the rate of business investment in Canada is too low. Does this chapter give you any ideas about what is meant by the phrase "too low"? What factors do you think accounted for the low level of investment spending in the early 1980s? (You may want to discuss this last issue with your instructor.)

3. Why is not any arbitrary level of GNP an equilibrium for the economy? (Do not give a mechanical answer to this question but explain the economic mechanism involved.)

4. From the following data, construct an expenditure schedule on a piece of graph paper. Then use the income–expenditure (45° line) diagram to determine the equilibrium level of GNP.

$$Y = C + I$$

INCOME	CONSUMPTION	INVESTMENT
1100	980	130
1150	1025	130
1200	1070	130
1250	1115	130
1300	1160	130

PRICE LEVEL	CONSUMER SPENDING
80	740
90	720
100	700
110	680
120	660

5. From the following data, construct an expenditure schedule on a piece of graph paper. Then use the income–expenditure (45° line) diagram to determine the equilibrium level of GNP.

INCOME	CONSUMPTION	INVESTMENT
1100	1010	100
1150	1040	115
1200	1070	130
1250	1100	145
1300	1130	160

Compare your answer with your answer to Question 4.

6. Suppose investment spending were always $200, and consumer spending depended on the price level in the following way:

On a piece of graph paper, use these data to construct an aggregate-demand curve. Why do you think this example supposes that consumption declines as the price level rises?

7. Does the economy this year seem to have an inflationary gap or a recessionary gap? (If you do not know the answer from reading the newspaper, ask your instructor.)

8. Why are there no recessions in the Soviet Union?

9. (More difficult.)* Consider an economy in which the consumption function takes the following simple algebraic form:

$$C = 100 + 0.8Y$$

and in which investment (I) is always 700. Find the equilibrium level of GNP from the requirement that $C + I = Y$. Compare your answer to Table 8-2 and Figure 8-3.

*The answer to this question is provided in Appendix B.

Appendix A
The Saving and Investment Approach

As we mentioned in the chapter, there is another way of looking at the determination of the equilibrium level of GNP on the demand side. Instead of studying the condition that total expenditure $(C + I)$ is equal to production (Y), we can study the condition that saving (S) is equal to investment (I). This is what we will do in this appendix.

It must be emphasized at the outset that this is not a *new* approach. It is merely another way of looking at precisely the same phenomenon. The reason is that income (Y) must be either spent on consumer goods (C) or saved (S). Since $Y = C + S$ *always*, and since $Y = C + I$ *when Y is at its equilibrium value*, we can describe equilibrium by the condition that $C + S = C + I$, or simply:

$$S = I.$$

Graphical Analysis

This way of looking at equilibrium has a different graphical representation: It does not use the 45° line

diagram, but it contains precisely the same information. Recall that in an appendix to Chapter 7 we constructed the saving schedule, which we repeat here as Figure 8-9. Since the equilibrium condition now under scrutiny is $S = I$, we can complete the story by providing an investment schedule. In the example used in the text, investment was taken to be a fixed number irrespective of income. We again do this here, so the investment schedule is as shown in Figure 8-10.

To find the point at which saving and investment are equal, we need only put both curves on the same diagram, which we have done in Figure 8-11. Point E shows the equilibrium level of GNP, which is at an income level of $400 billion. As must be the case, this is the same answer we obtained with the 45° line diagram.

You will notice that at income levels below $400 billion, investment exceeds saving, just as $C + I$ exceeded output in the 45° line diagram. Similarly, at income levels above $400 billion, S exceeds I. (In the

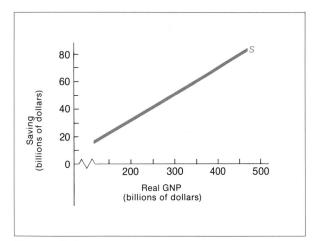

Figure 8-9
THE SAVING SCHEDULE
This diagram shows the relationship between saving and income in Macroland and duplicates Figure 7-10 (page 132).

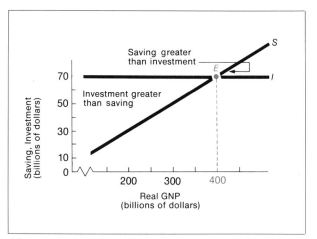

Figure 8-11
DETERMINATION OF EQUILIBRIUM GNP BY SAVING-INVESTMENT
This diagram, which combines Figures 8-9 and 8-10, depicts the equilibrium of the economy at point *E*, where the saving and investment schedules intersect. The equilibrium is at a real GNP of $400 billion, which, as must be the case, is the same conclusion that we reached with the aid of the 45° line diagram (Figure 8-3 on page 148).

45° line diagram, *Y* exceeded *C* + *I* in this range.) This must be the case since the two graphs are alternative depictions of the same phenomena. The economic analyses behind them are precisely the same.

Induced Investment

In the chapter we mentioned the possibility of *induced investment*, that is, of an investment schedule that rises as GNP rises, but we did not examine this possibility in our graphs. (However, this case did arise in Discussion Question 5.) The reason is that what matters in the 45° line diagram is the slope of the *combined C + I* schedule, not the *individual* slopes of the *C* and *I* schedules. So an upward-sloping invest-

ment schedule does not make much difference to the analysis.

When using the saving and investment approach, however, the slope of the investment schedule becomes more apparent, if not more important. So Figure 8-12 illustrates the case of induced investment. In

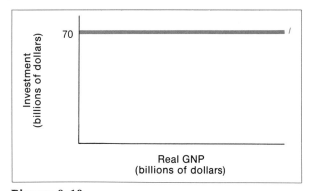

Figure 8-10
THE INVESTMENT SCHEDULE
In this simple example, investment spending is a fixed number—$70 billion—regardless of the level of GNP. Therefore, the investment schedule is a horizontal line at $70 billion.

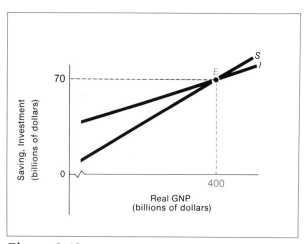

Figure 8-12
INCOME DETERMINATION WITH INDUCED INVESTMENT
When investment rises with GNP ("induced investment"), the investment schedule acquires a positive slope. Apart from this, the determination of equilibrium output is precisely as it was before. Point *E*, where the *S* and *I* schedules cross, is the equilibrium.

this diagram, the investment schedule is upward sloping. Equilibrium, however, is still at point E—where the S and I schedules cross. Thus, allowance for induced investment does not change our analysis in any significant way.[5]

[5]Some students may wonder what happens if the slope of the investment schedule exceeds that of the saving schedule. This is a difficult question and one that is best reserved for more advanced courses. Suffice it to say here that the simple model of income determination constructed in this chapter will not work in such a case.

Summary

1. The condition for equilibrium GNP—which we gave in the chapter as the equation of total spending with output $(C + I = Y)$—can be restated as the requirement that saving and investment be equal $(S = I)$. This does not change anything, but simply says the same thing in different words.

2. These different words lead to a different graphical presentation, in which we look for equilibrium at the point where the saving schedule crosses the investment schedule.

3. Induced investment—that is, investment that rises as the GNP rises—leads to an upward-sloping investment schedule, but requires no other change in the analysis.

Concepts for Review

$S = I$
Saving schedule

Investment schedule
Induced investment

Questions for Discussion

1. From the data in Discussion Question 4 at the end of the chapter, construct the saving schedule and the investment schedule on a piece of graph paper. (In doing so, remember that any income that is not consumed must have been saved.) Use these constructions to find the equilibrium level of GNP.

2. Do the same thing with the data in Discussion Question 5. (*Hint*: You will find *negative* saving at income level 100. There is nothing wrong with this. You do negative saving any time you draw down your bank account balance.)

Appendix B
The Simple Algebra of Income Determination

The model of demand-side equilibrium that the chapter presented graphically and in tabular form can also be handled with some simple algebra.

Written as an equation, the consumption function in our example is:

$$C = 10 + 0.8Y.$$

This is simply the equation of a straight line with intercept 10 and slope 0.8. Investment in the example was assumed to be 70, regardless of the level of income. So the sum $C + I$ is:

$$C + I = 10 + 0.8Y + 70 = 80 + 0.8Y.$$

This is the equation of the $C + I$ curve found in Figure 8–3.

Since the equilibrium quantity of GNP demanded is defined by:

$$Y = C + I,$$

we can solve for the equilibrium value of Y algebraically by substituting $80 + 0.8Y$ for $C + I$. Thus, we have:

$$Y = C + I = 80 + 0.8Y.$$

To solve this equation for Y, first subtract $0.8Y$ from both sides to get:

$$0.2Y = 80.$$

Then divide both sides by 0.2 to obtain the answer:

$$Y = 400.$$

This, of course, is precisely the solution we found by graphical and tabular methods in the chapter.

The method of solution is easily generalized to deal with any set of numbers in our equations. Suppose the consumption function is:

$$C = a + bY.$$

(In the example, $a = 10$ and $b = 0.8$.) Then the equilibrium condition that $Y = C + I$ implies:

$$Y = a + bY + I.$$

Subtracting bY from both sides leads to:

$$(1 - b)Y = a + I,$$

and dividing through by $1 - b$ gives:

$$Y = \frac{a + I}{1 - b}.$$

This formula, which is certainly not to be memorized, is valid for any numerical values of a, b, and I (so long as b is between zero and one).

Questions for Discussion

1. Find the equilibrium level of GNP demanded in an economy in which investment is always $200 and the consumption function is described by the following algebraic equation:

$$C = 120 + 0.8Y.$$

2. Do the same for an economy in which investment is fixed at $150 and the consumption function is:

$$C = 250 + 0.5Y.$$

3. In each of the above cases, how much saving is there in equilibrium? (*Hint*: Income not consumed must be saved.) Is saving equal to investment?

4. Imagine an economy in which consumer expenditure is represented by the following equation:

$$C = 100 + 0.75Y.$$

Imagine also that investors want to spend $500 at every level of income: $I = 500$.

a. What is the equilibrium level of income?
b. If the full employment level of income is $2000, is there a recessionary or inflationary gap? If so, how much?
c. What will happen to the equilibrium level of income if investors become pessimistic about the country's future and reduce their investment to $250?
d. Is there a recessionary or inflationary gap now? How much?

5. Ivyland has the following consumption function:

$$C = 200 + 0.75Y.$$

Firms in Ivyland always invest $200.
a. Find the equilibrium level of GNP.
b. How much is saved? Is saving equal to investment?
c. Suppose consumers are given an inducement to save, so that the consumption function falls to $C = 150 + 0.75Y$, but at the same time firms boost investment spending to $240. Answer questions (a) and (b) under these new circumstances.

(handwritten:)

$Y = C + I = 120 + .8Y + 200$

$Y = 320 + .8Y$

$-2Y = 320$ *(struck through)*

$Y = 1600$

$Y = 390 + .75Y$

$.25Y = 390$

$1560 = Y$

$Y = C + S$

$1560 = (150 + .75Y) + S$

$1560 = 150 + .75$

$210 = S$ / $I = S$

$C + I = 400 + .75Y$

$Y = 400 + .75Y$

$.25Y = 400$

$Y = 1600$

$I = 200$

$Y = C + S$

$1600 = (200 + .75Y) + S$

$200 = S$

LW

$I = 200$

$S = I$

Changes on the Demand Side: Multiplier Analysis

9

A definite ratio, to be called the Multiplier, can be established between income and investment.
JOHN MAYNARD KEYNES

In the last chapter we derived the economy's aggregate-demand curve, which shows how the equilibrium quantity of real GNP demanded depends on the price level—holding all other factors constant. But often these "other factors" do not remain constant and, as a consequence, the entire aggregate-demand curve shifts. This chapter is the first of several that are devoted to enumerating these "other factors" and explaining how and why they make the aggregate-demand curve shift.

The central concept of this short chapter is the *multiplier*—the idea that an increase in spending will bring about an *even larger* increase in overall demand. We approach this idea from three different perspectives, each of which provides the reader with different and significant insights into the multiplier process. First, the multiplier is illustrated graphically using the income–expenditure diagram from Chapter 8. Next, we reach the same conclusion through the use of a numerical example, and finally, we offer an algebraic statement.

At the end of the chapter, we use multiplier analysis to explain why a drive to increase national saving might not succeed.

The Magic of the Multiplier

Because it is subject to such abrupt swings, investment spending is often the cause of business fluctuations in Canada and elsewhere. Let us, therefore, ask what would happen to equilibrium income in our fictitious country, Macroland, if firms there suddenly decided to spend more on investment goods. As we shall see, such a decision would have a *multiplied* effect on GNP in Macroland. The same would be true in the Canadian economy.

For simplicity, we begin by assuming that the price level is fixed—an assumption we maintain *only* for this short chapter. Refer first to Table 9-1, which looks very much like Table 8-1 (page 146). The only difference is that we assume here that, for some reason, firms in Macroland now want to invest $20 billion more than they previously did—for a total of $90 billion. The multiplier principle says that Macroland's GNP will rise by more than the $20 billion increase in investment. Specifically, **the multiplier** is defined as the ratio of the change in equilibrium GNP (Y) divided by the original change in spending that causes the

The multiplier is the ratio of the change in equilibrium GNP (Y) divided by the original change in spending that causes the change in GNP.

Table 9-1
TOTAL EXPENDITURE AFTER THE RISE IN INVESTMENT SPENDING (billions of dollars)

(1) INCOME (Y)	(2) CONSUMPTION (C)	(3) INVESTMENT (I)	(4) TOTAL EXPENDITURE (C + I)
200	170	90	260
250	210	90	300
300	250	90	340
350	290	90	380
400	330	90	420
450	370	90	460
500	410	90	500
550	450	90	540
600	490	90	580

(handwritten annotation: $Y = C + I$ *equilibrium GNP)*

This table shows the construction of a total expenditure schedule for Macroland after investment has risen to $90 billion. As indicated by the numbers shaded in blue, only income level Y = $500 billion is equilibrium on the demand side of the economy because only at this level is total spending (C + I) equal to production (Y).

change in GNP. In shorthand, when we deal with the multiplier for investment (I), the formula is:

$$\text{Multiplier} = \frac{\text{Change in Y}}{\text{Change in } I}.$$

Let us verify that the multiplier is indeed greater than 1. Table 9–1 shows how to derive a new expenditure schedule by adding up C and I at each level of Y, just as we did in Chapter 8. If you compare the last column of Table 9–1 to that of Table 8–1, you will see that the new expenditure schedule lies uniformly above the old one by $20 billion. Figure 9–1 illustrates this diagrammatically. The schedule marked $C + I_0$ is derived from the last column of Table 8–1, while the higher schedule marked $C + I_1$ is derived from the last column of Table 9–1. The two C + I lines are parallel and $20 billion apart.

So far no act of magic has occurred—things look just as you might expect. But one more step will bring the multiplier rabbit out of the hat. Let us see what the upward shift of the C + I line does to equilibrium income. We see in Figure 9–1 that equilibrium moves outward from point E_0 to point E_1, that is, from $400 billion to $500 billion. The difference is an increase in national income of $100 billion. All this from a $20 billion stimulus to investment? That is the magic of the multiplier.

Because the change in I is $20 billion and the change in equilibrium Y is $100 billion, by applying our definition, the multiplier is:

$$\text{Multiplier} = \frac{\text{Change in Y}}{\text{Change in } I} = \frac{\$100 \text{ billion}}{\$20 \text{ billion}} = 5.$$

This tells us that, in our example, every additional dollar of investment demand will add $5 to the equilibrium GNP!

This does indeed seem mysterious. Can something be created from nothing? Let us, therefore, check to be sure that the graph has not deceived us. The first and last columns of Table 9–1 show in numbers what Figure 9–1 shows in a picture. Notice that, at any income level below $500, spending (C + I) exceeds output (Y). As we know, this cannot be an equilibrium situation because inventories would be disappearing. On the other hand, at any income level above $500, inventories would be piling up, since C + I is less than Y.

Only at Y = $500 billion are spending and production in balance, as Table 9–1 shows. This is $100 billion higher than the $400 billion equilibrium GNP obtained

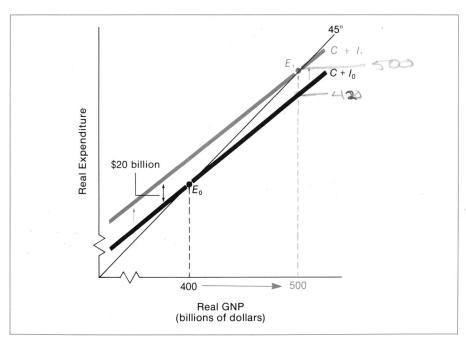

Figure 9-1
ILLUSTRATION OF THE
MULTIPLIER
This figure depicts the multiplier
effect of a rise in investment
spending of $20 billion. The
expenditure schedule shifts
upward from $C + I_0$ to $C + I_1$, thus
moving equilibrium from point E_0 to
point E_1. The rise in income is
$100 billion, so the multiplier is
$100/$20 = 5.

in the discussion of Table 8–1, where investment was only $70 billion. Thus a $20 billion rise in investment leads to a $100 billion rise in equilibrium GNP, which goes up from an initial value of $400 billion to $500 billion. The multiplier really is 5.

Demystifying the Multiplier: How It Works

The multiplier result seems peculiar at first, but it loses its mystery once we remember the circular flow of income and expenditure, and the simple fact that one person's spending is another person's income. To illustrate the logic of the multiplier, and see why it is exactly 5 in our model economy, let us look more closely at what actually happens if businesses decide to spend an additional $1 million on investment goods.

For the sake of concreteness, suppose that Generous Motors—a major corporation in Macroland—decides to spend $1 million to retool a factory to manufacture pollution-free electronically powered automobiles. Its $1 million expenditure goes to construction workers and owners of construction companies as wages and profits. That is, it becomes their *income*.

But the owners and workers of the construction firms will not simply keep their $1 million in the bank. They will spend some of it. If they are "typical" consumers, their spending will, by definition, be $1 million times the marginal propensity to consume (MPC). In our example, the MPC is 0.8. So let us assume that they spend $800,000 and save the rest. *This $800,000 expenditure is a net addition to the nation's demand for goods and services exactly as GM's original $1 million expenditure was.* So, at this stage, the $1 million investment has already pushed GNP up some $1.8 million.

But the process by no means stops here. Shopkeepers receive the $800,000 spent by construction workers, and these shopkeepers in turn also spend 80 percent of their new income. This accounts for $640,000 (80 percent of $800,000) in additional consumer spending in the "third round." Next follows a fourth round in which the recipients of the $640,000, in their turn, spend 80 percent of this amount, or $512,000, and so on. At each stage in the spending chain, people spend 80 percent of the additional income they receive, and the process continues.

Where does it all end? Does it all end? The answer is that it does, indeed, eventually end—with GNP a total of $5 million higher than it was before Generous Motors spent the original $1 million. The multiplier, as stated, is 5.

Table 9-2 displays the basis for this conclusion. In the table, "round 1" represents GM's initial investment, which creates $1 million in income for construction workers; "round 2" represents the construction workers' spending, which creates $800,000 in income for shopkeepers. The rest of the table proceeds accordingly. Each entry in column 2 is 80 percent of the previous entry, and column 3 tabulates the running sum of column 2.

We see that after 10 rounds of spending the initial $1 million investment has mushroomed to nearly $4.5 million, and the sum is still growing. After 20 rounds, the total increase in GNP is over $4.9 million—quite near its eventual value of $5 million. While it takes quite a few rounds of spending before the multiplier chain is near 5, we see from the table that it approaches 4 within seven periods.

Figure 9-2 provides a graphical presentation of the numbers in the last column of Table 9-2. Notice how the multiplier builds up rapidly at first, and then tapers off to approach its ultimate value (5 in this example) gradually.

Algebraic Statement of the Multiplier

Figure 9-2 and Table 9-2 probably make a persuasive case for the fact that the multiplier eventually reaches 5. But for the remaining skeptics we offer a simple algebraic proof.[1] Most of you learned about an "infinite geometric progression" in high school. This is simply an infinite series of numbers, each one of which is a fixed fraction of the previous one. This fraction is called the "common ratio." A geometric progression beginning with 1 and having a common ratio equal to 0.8 would look like this:

$$1 + 0.8 + (0.8)^2 + (0.8)^3 + \ldots .$$

More generally, a geometric progression beginning with 1 and having a common ratio R would be:

$$1 + R + R^2 + R^3 \ldots .$$

A simple formula enables us to sum such a progression as long as R is less than 1.[2]

The formula is:[3]

$$\text{Sum of infinite geometric progression} = \frac{1}{1 - R} .$$

Now we can recognize that the multiplier chain in Table 9-2 is just an infinite geometric progression with 0.8 as its common ratio. That is, each $1 spent by GM

[1]Students who blanch at the sight of algebra should not be put off. Anyone who can balance a chequebook (even many who cannot!) will be able to follow the argument.

[2]If R exceeds 1, nobody can possibly sum it—not even with the aid of a modern computer!

[3]The proof is simple. Let the symbol S stand for the (unknown) sum of the series:

$$S = 1 + R + R^2 + R^3 + \ldots .$$

Then, multiplying by R,

$$RS = R + R^2 + R^3 + \ldots .$$

By subtracting RS from S, we obtain:

$$S - RS = 1$$

or

$$S = \frac{1}{1 - R} .$$

leads to a $(0.8) \times \$1$ expenditure by construction workers, which in turn leads to a $(0.8) \times (0.8 \times \$1) = (0.8)^2 \times \$1$ expenditure by the shopkeepers, and so on. Thus, for each initial dollar of investment spending, the progression is:

$$1 + 0.8 + (0.8)^2 + (0.8)^3 + (0.8)^4 + \ldots.$$

Table 9-2
THE MULTIPLIER SPENDING CHAIN

(1) ROUND NUMBER	(2) SPENDING IN THIS ROUND	(3) CUMULATIVE TOTAL
1	$1,000,000	$1,000,000
2	800,000	1,800,000
3	640,000	2,440,000
4	512,000	2,952,000
5	409,600	3,361,600
6	327,680	3,689,280
7	262,144	3,951,424
8	209,715	4,161,139
9	167,772	4,328,911
10	134,218	4,463,129
. . .	. . .	. . .
20	14,412	4,942,354
. . .	. . .	. . .
50	18	4,999,929
. . .		. . .
"Infinity"	0	5,000,000

This table shows how the multiplier unfolds through time. Round 1 is GM's initial spending, which leads to $1 million in additional income to construction workers. Round 2 shows the construction workers spending 80 percent of this amount, since the marginal propensity to consume is 0.8. The other rounds proceed accordingly, with spending in each successive round equal to 80 percent of that in the previous round. Technically, the full multiplier of 5 is reached only after an "infinite" number of rounds. But, as can be seen, we are quite close to the full amount after 20 rounds.

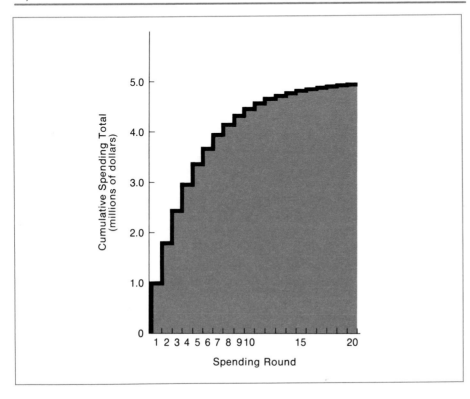

Figure 9-2
HOW THE MULTIPLIER BUILDS
This diagram portrays the numbers from Table 9-2 and shows how the multiplier builds through time. Notice how the effect grows quickly at first and how the full effect is almost reached after 15 rounds.

Applying the formula for the sum of such a series, we find that:

$$\text{Multiplier} = \frac{1}{1 - 0.8} = \frac{1}{0.2} = 5.$$

Notice how this result can be generalized. If we did not have a specific numerical value for the marginal propensity to consume, but simply called it "MPC," the geometric progression would have been:

$$1 + MPC + (MPC)^2 + (MPC)^3 + \dots,$$

which has the MPC as its common ratio. Applying the same formula for summing a geometric progression to this more general case gives us the following general result:

Oversimplified Formula for the Multiplier

$$\text{Multiplier} = \frac{1}{1 - MPC}. \quad = \frac{1}{MPS}$$

We call this formula "oversimplified" because it ignores many factors that are important in the real world. One of them is *inflation*, a complication to which we will turn in the next chapter. A second is *income taxation*, and a third is *imports*; both of these points will be elaborated on in Chapter 11. Two further factors, interest rates and exchange rates, arise from the financial system. We explain these complications in Chapters 14 and 15, after money and banking is explained. As it turns out, *all* of these factors *reduce* the size of the multiplier.

The *simplified multiplier formula* ignores the effects of inflation, taxation, imports, interest rates, and exchange rates. Later chapters show how all these factors lower the multiplier.

We can begin to appreciate just how unrealistic the "oversimplified" formula is by considering some real numbers for the Canadian economy. The marginal propensity to consume (MPC) has been estimated many times, and is about 0.9. From our oversimplified formula, then, it would seem that the multiplier should be:

$$\text{Multiplier} = \frac{1}{1 - 0.9} = \frac{1}{0.1} = 10 \, .$$

In fact, the actual multiplier for the Canadian economy is believed to be no more than 2. This is quite a discrepancy! But it does not mean that anything we have said about the multiplier so far is incorrect. Our story is simply incomplete. As we progress through the following chapters, you will learn why the multiplier is close to 2 even though the MPC is close to 0.9. For now we simply point out that:

While the multiplier is larger than 1 in the real world, it cannot be calculated with any degree of accuracy from the oversimplified formula. The actual multiplier is lower than the formula suggests.

The Multiplier Effect of Consumer Spending

Business firms that invest are not the only ones that can work the magic of the multiplier; so can consumers. Let us see how the multiplier works when the process is initiated by an upsurge in consumer spending.

First, we need to distinguish between two types of change in consumer

Table 9-3

TOTAL EXPENDITURE AFTER CONSUMERS DECIDE TO SPEND $20 BILLION MORE (billions of dollars)

(1) INCOME (Y)	(2) CONSUMPTION (C)	(3) INVESTMENT (I)	(4) TOTAL EXPENDITURE (C + I)
200	190	70	260
250	230	70	300
300	270	70	340
350	310	70	380
400	350	70	420
450	390	70	460
500	430	70	500
550	470	70	540
600	510	70	580

This table shows the construction of the total expenditure schedule for Macroland following an autonomous increase of $20 billion in consumption rather than in investment. Notice that columns 2 and 3 differ from the corresponding columns in Table 9-1, but column 4 is the same in both tables. Thus the expenditure schedule in the 45° line diagram is the same as in the earlier example.

spending. When C rises because income rises—that is, when consumers move outward *along a fixed consumption function*—we call the increase in C an **induced increase in consumption**. However, if instead C rises because the entire consumption function *shifts* up, we call this an **autonomous increase in consumption**. The name indicates that consumption changes independently of income, and Chapter 7's discussion pointed out that a number of events, such as a change in the price level or in the value of the stock market, can initiate such a shift.

Let us suppose that, for some reason, consumer spending rises autonomously by $20 billion. In this case, our table of aggregate demand would have to be revised to look like Table 9-3. Comparing this to Table 9-1 on page 162, we note that each entry in column 2 is $20 billion *higher* than the corresponding entry in Table 9-1 (because consumption is higher) and each entry in column 3 is $20 billion *lower* (because investment is lower).

The equilibrium level of income is clearly Y = $500 billion once again. Indeed, the entire expenditure schedule is the same as it was in Table 9-1. The initial rise of $20 billion in spending leads to an ultimate rise of $100 billion in GNP, just as occurred in the case of higher investment spending. In fact, Figure 9-1 applies to this case without any changes. The multiplier for autonomous changes in consumer spending, then, is also 5 ($100/$20).

The reason is straightforward. It does not matter who injects an additional dollar of spending into the economy, whether it is business investors or consumers. Wherever it comes from, 80 percent of it will be respent if the MPC is 0.8, and the recipients of this second round will in turn spend 80 percent of their additional income, and so on and on. And that is what constitutes the multiplier process. In the next chapter we will learn, not surprisingly, that this same multiplier applies equally well to the third component of aggregate demand—government purchases of goods and services.

An **induced increase in consumption** is an increase in consumer spending that stems from an increase in consumer incomes. It appears on a graph as a movement along a fixed consumption function.

An **autonomous increase in consumption** is an increase in consumer spending without any increase in incomes. It appears on a graph as a shift of the entire consumption function.

The Multiplier in Reverse

A good way to check your understanding of the multiplier process is to run it in reverse: What happens if, for example, consumers autonomously decide to spend less? For example, suppose a wave of thriftiness comes over the people of Macroland so that, no matter what their total income, they now want to spend $20 billion *less* than they did previously.

A decision to spend $20 billion less out of any given level of income is, by definition, a *downward* shift of the total expenditure schedule by $20 billion. This is shown in Figure 9–3, where the $C + I$ schedule falls from $C_0 + I$ to $C_1 + I$. The horizontal distance between these two parallel lines is the $20 billion drop in spending.

There are two ways of calculating the multiplier. First, our oversimplified multiplier formula tells us that the multiplier is

$$\frac{1}{1 - \text{MPC}} = \frac{1}{1 - 0.8} = \frac{1}{0.2} = 5.$$

So a $20 billion drop in spending will lead to a multiplier effect of $100 billion. Alternatively, we can read this conclusion from Figure 9–3. Here the economy's equilibrium point moves down the 45° line from point E_0 to E_1; income drops from $400 billion to $300 billion—a decline of $100 billion.

Now compare the analysis of a decline in spending that is summarized in Figure 9–3 with our previous analysis of an increase in spending, as shown in Figure 9–1 on page 163. You will see that everything is simply turned in the opposite direction. The multiplier works in either direction.

The Paradox of Thrift

This last example of multiplier analysis teaches us an important lesson: It shows that an increase in the desire to save will lead to a cumulative fall in GNP. And, because saving depends on income, the resulting decline in national income will pull saving down.

Let us be a bit more specific about this. Before the upsurge in saving, consumers were spending $330 billion out of a total national income of $400 billion, as we can see in Table 8–1 on page 146. Hence $70 billion was being saved. In Figure 9–3, income falls to $300 billion. Since investment is still $70 billion, and $C + I$ must add up to Y, we know that consumption at point E must be $230 billion. So total saving is still $70 (= $300 – $230) billion. The effort to save more has been totally frustrated by the decline in GNP.[4]

[4]It is even possible for total saving to go down when people attempt to save more. This occurs in this model economy if there is induced investment (that is, if the investment line is positively sloped).

Figure 9–3
THE MULTIPLIER IN REVERSE
This diagram shows the multiplier effect of an autonomous decline in consumer spending of $20 billion. The decline appears as a downward shift of $20 billion in the expenditure schedule, which falls from $C_0 + I$ to $C_1 + I$. Equilibrium, which is always at the intersection of the expenditure schedule and the 45° line, moves from point E_0 to point E_1, and income falls from $400 billion to $300 billion.

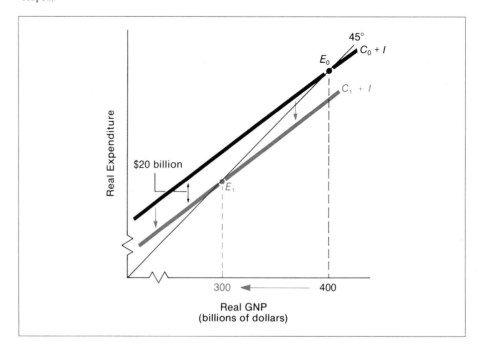

This remarkable result is called the **paradox of thrift**, because it shows that, while saving may pave the road to riches for an individual, if the nation as a whole decides to save more, the result may be a recession and lower incomes for all. The paradox of thrift is important because it is contrary to most people's thinking, and it means that greater saving may be a mixed blessing if it is not accompanied by equally greater investment. The paradox of thrift reminds us that it is not always accurate to think of the nation's economic problems as simply a big version of an individual family's economic problems.

The **paradox of thrift** is the fact that an effort by a nation to save more may simply reduce national income and fail to raise total saving.

The Multiplier and the Aggregate-Demand Curve

At this point we must recall something that was mentioned at the start of this chapter: Income–expenditure diagrams such as Figures 9–1 or 9–3 can be drawn up only for a given price level. A different price level leads to a different total-

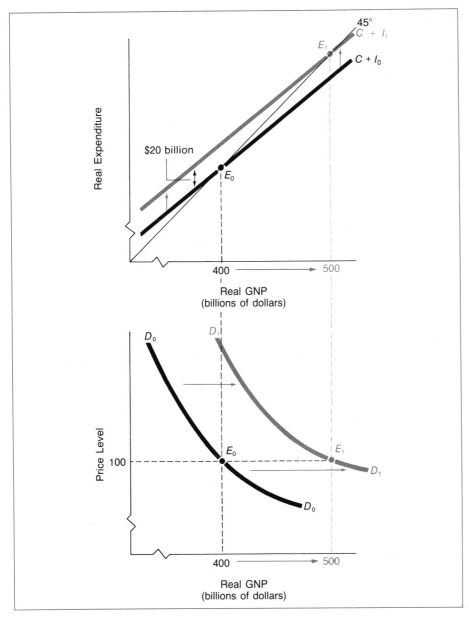

Figure 9-4

TWO VIEWS OF THE MULTIPLIER

The top panel repeats Figure 9–1. The bottom panel shows two aggregate-demand curves. Curve D_0D_0, which applies when investment is $70 billion, shows that equilibrium GNP on the demand side comes at $Y=\$400$ billion when $P=100$ (point E_0). Curve D_1D_1, which applies when investment is $90 billion, shows that equilibrium GNP on the demand side comes at $Y=\$500$ billion when $P=100$ (point E_1). The horizontal distance between points E_0 and E_1 in the bottom panel indicates the oversimplified multiplier effect.

expenditure curve. This means that our oversimplified multiplier formula measures *the increase in real GNP demanded, that is, the increase in the level of GNP that would occur if the price level were fixed.* In other words, it measures the horizontal shift of the economy's aggregate-demand curve.

Figure 9–4 illustrates this conclusion by supposing that the price level that underlies Figure 9–1 is $P=100$. The top panel simply repeats Figure 9–1 and shows how an increase in investment spending from $70 billion to $90 billion leads to an increase in GNP from $400 billion to $500 billion.

The bottom panel shows two downward-sloping aggregate-demand curves. The first, labelled D_0D_0, depicts the situation when investment is $70 billion. Point E_0 on this curve indicates that, at the given price level ($P=100$), the equilibrium quantity of GNP demanded is $400 billion. It corresponds exactly to point E_0 in the top panel. The second aggregate-demand curve, D_1D_1, depicts the situation after investment has risen to $90 billion. Point E_1 on this curve indicates that the equilibrium quantity of GNP demanded when $P=100$ has risen to $500 billion, which corresponds exactly to point E_1 in the top panel.

As Figure 9–4 shows, the horizontal distance between the two aggregate-demand curves is exactly equal to the increase in real GNP shown in the income-expenditure diagram—in this case, $100 billion. Thus:

An autonomous increase in spending leads to a horizontal shift of the aggregate-demand curve by an amount given by the oversimplified multiplier formula.

In the next chapter, after we bring the aggregate-supply curve into the picture, we will use this finding to explain one reason why GNP actually rises by *less* than the oversimplified multiplier formula suggests.

Summary

1. Any autonomous increase in expenditure has a multiplier effect on GNP, that is, it increases GNP by more than the original increase in spending.
2. The reason for this multiplier effect is that one person's additional expenditure constitutes a new source of income for another person, and this additional income leads to still more spending, and so on.
3. The multiplier also works in reverse: an autonomous decrease in any component of aggregate demand leads to a multiplied decrease in national income.
4. A simple formula for the multiplier says that its numerical value is $1/(1-\text{MPC})$. This formula, which is

too simple to give accurate results, measures the horizontal shift of the aggregate-demand curve.
5. The simplified multiplier formula ignores the effects of inflation, taxation, imports, interest rates, and exchange rates. Later chapters show how all these factors lower the multiplier.
6. If the nation as a whole decides to save more, that is, to consume less, the resulting decline in national income may serve to make everyone poorer. This possibility that thriftiness, while helpful for the individual, may be disastrous for an entire nation, is called the paradox of thrift.

Concepts for Review

The multiplier
Induced increase in consumption

Autonomous increase in
consumption

Paradox of thrift

Questions for Discussion

1. Try to remember where you last spent a dollar. Explain how this dollar will lead to a multiplier chain of increased income and spending. (Who received the dollar? What will he or she do with it?)

 2. Use both numerical and graphical methods to find the multiplier effect of the following shift in the consumption function in an economy in which investment is always $110.

INCOME	CONSUMPTION BEFORE SHIFT	CONSUMPTION AFTER SHIFT
$510	$440	$470
540	460	490
570	480	510
600	500	530
630	520	550
660	540	570
690	560	590
720	580	610

(*Hint*: What is the marginal propensity to consume?)

3. Turn back to Discussion Question 4 in Chapter 8 (page 156). Suppose investment spending rises to $140 and the price level is fixed. By how much will the equilibrium GNP increase? Derive the answer both numerically and graphically.

4. Explain the paradox of thrift. Why do you think it is called a paradox?

5. (More difficult.) Suppose the consumption function is as given in Discussion Question 9 of Chapter 8 (page 157)

$$C = 100 + 0.8Y$$

and investment (*I*) rises to $900. Use the equilibrium condition $Y = C + I$ to find the equilibrium level of GNP. (In working out the answer, assume the price level is fixed.) Compare your answer to Table 9-1 and Figure 9-1. Now compare your answer to the answer to Discussion Question 9 of Chapter 8. What do you learn about the multiplier?

Appendix
The Simple Algebra of the Multiplier

In Appendix B to Chapter 8, we worked out a general expression for the equilibrium level of GNP when the price level is fixed, investment is some fixed number, *I*, and the consumption function is:

$$C = a + bY.$$

The answer obtained there (which can be found on page 160) was:

$$Y = \frac{a + I}{1 - b}.$$

From this formula it is easy to derive the over-simplified multiplier formula algebraically and to show that it applies equally well to a change in investment or to a change in autonomous consumer spending. To do this, suppose that *either I or a* increased by 1 unit. In either case, the sum $C + I$ would rise from:

$$C + I = a + bY + I,$$

to:

$$C + I = a + bY + I + 1.$$

Using the equilibrium condition that *Y* must be equal to $C + I$, we can solve for *Y* just as we did in Appendix B of Chapter 8:

$$Y = C + I$$

so that:

$$Y = a + bY + I + 1$$

and therefore:

$$(1 - b)Y = a + I + 1,$$

or:

$$Y = \frac{a + I + 1}{1 - b}.$$

By comparing this with our previous expression for *Y*, we see that a 1 unit change in *either a or I* changes equilibrium GNP by:

$$\text{change in } Y = \frac{a + I + 1}{1 - b} - \frac{a + I}{1 - b}$$

$$\text{change in } Y = \frac{a + I + 1 - (a + I)}{1 - b}$$

or:

$$\text{change in } Y = \frac{1}{1 - b}.$$

Recalling that *b* is the marginal propensity to consume, we see that this is precisely the over-simplified multiplier formula.

Supply-Side Equilibrium: Unemployment *and* Inflation?

We might as well reasonably dispute whether it is the upper or the under blade of a pair of scissors that cuts a piece of paper, as whether value is governed by [demand] or [supply].

ALFRED MARSHALL

In Chapter 8 we learned that the level of prices, in conjunction with the economy's consumption and investment schedules, governs whether the economy will experience a recessionary or an inflationary gap. If the $C + I$ schedule is "too low," a *recessionary gap* will arise, while a $C + I$ schedule that is "too high" leads to an *inflationary gap*. Which sort of gap actually occurs is of some importance because, as we shall see in this chapter, a recessionary gap normally spells unemployment while an inflationary gap means inflation.

The tools provided in Chapter 8, however, are not sufficient to determine which sort of gap will arise, because the position of the $C + I$ schedule depends on the price level—and the price level is determined by *both* aggregate demand *and* aggregate supply. Thus, the task of the present chapter is to bring the supply side of the economy into the picture.

After reviewing some puzzling aspects of recent economic history, we explain how the *aggregate-supply curve* is derived from business costs. Next we consider the interaction of aggregate supply and aggregate demand, and the joint determination of output and the price level. With this apparatus in hand, we return to the phenomena of recessionary and inflationary gaps and study how the economy adjusts to each type. Doing this puts us in a position to deal with the crucial question raised in earlier chapters: Does the economy have an efficient self-correcting mechanism? As we shall learn, the economy is better at curing inflationary gaps than recessionary gaps. Finally, we use aggregate-supply–aggregate-demand analysis to explain the vexing problem of *stagflation*—the simultaneous occurrence of high unemployment *and* high inflation—which has plagued the economy so often since the mid-1970s. The chapter ends by explaining how inflation affects the multiplier.

The Mystery of Stagflation

The analysis of demand-side equilibrium presented in Chapter 8 seems to suggest that while we can have *either* unemployment (from a recessionary gap) *or* inflation (from an inflationary gap), we should not have both at the same time. And, for many decades, this seemed to be the way things worked out. The Great Depression witnessed severe unemployment and falling prices; World War II led to an inflationary boom; there was very little inflation during the 1958–62 recession.

But things started to change in the 1970s, the decade of stagflation. The inflation rate fell only slightly during the 1971 recession, and it rose dramatically during the 1971–76 period, when unemployment also rose. Inflation also increased during the 1980 recession. Thus, recent events have made clear that inflation and unemployment can coexist in unhappy wedlock.

Throughout the 1970s, and right up to the present time, journalists, politicians, and even some economists have proclaimed frequently that the phenomenon of stagflation is a mystery to economists, that somehow it "defies the laws of economics." A *New York Times* article in 1970 was entitled "Impossible! Recession *and* Rising Prices?" Even today the coexistence of high unemployment and inflation leads many to view macroeconomics as a bankrupt discipline.

Despite the many times such claims have been made, the plain fact is that they are false. Standard economic theory *does* provide an explanation of stagflation; and by the end of this chapter, you will be able to explain it yourself. But, unfortunately, *understanding* why stagflation occurs and being able to *cure* it are two very different things. We might as well admit right now that, while some suggestions have been made, no economist has a costless cure for stagflation.

The Aggregate-Supply Curve

In earlier chapters we noted that *aggregate demand* is a schedule, not a fixed number. The quantity of real GNP that will be demanded depends on the price level, as summarized in the economy's *aggregate-demand curve*.

Analogously, the concept of *aggregate supply* does not refer to a fixed number but, rather, to a schedule (to a supply *curve*). The volume of goods and services that will be provided by profit-seeking enterprises depends on the prices they obtain for their outputs, wages and other production costs, the state of technology, and other things. The relationship between the price level and the quantity of real GNP supplied, *holding all other determinants of quantity supplied constant*, is called the economy's **aggregate-supply curve**.

The **aggregate-supply curve** shows, for each possible price level, the quantity of goods and services that all the nation's businesses are willing to produce, holding all other determinants of aggregate quantity supplied constant.

A typical aggregate-supply curve is drawn in Figure 10–1. It slopes upward, meaning that as prices rise more output is produced, *other things held constant*. It is not difficult to understand why this curve slopes upward. Producers in the Canadian economy are motivated mainly by profit. Since the profit made by producing a unit of output is simply the difference between the price at which it is sold and the unit cost of production,

Profit per unit = Price – Cost per unit,

it is clear that the response of production to a rising price level (henceforth, P) depends on the response of costs.[1]

One critical fact affecting this response is that labour and other inputs used by firms normally are available at *relatively fixed prices* for some period of time—though certainly not forever. There are many reasons for this. Some workers and firms enter into long-term labour contracts that set money wages up to three years in advance. Even where there are no explicit contracts, employees typically have their wages increased only about once per year. During the interim period, money wages are fixed. Much the same is true of other factors of production. Many firms get deliveries of raw materials under long-term contracts according to which suppliers have agreed to provide the materials at prearranged prices. None of these contracts lasts forever, of course, but many of them last long enough to be of importance.

Why is it significant that firms often purchase inputs like labour and raw materials at prices that stay fixed for considerable periods? Because firms decide

[1]For a full discussion of business output decisions and how they respond to costs, see *Microeconomics*, Chapter 8.

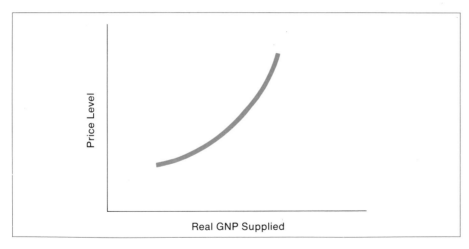

Figure 10-1

AN AGGREGATE-SUPPLY CURVE

This graph shows a typical aggregate-supply curve. It has a positive slope (that is, it rises as we move to the right), meaning that the quantity of output supplied rises as the price level rises.

how much to produce by comparing selling prices with costs of production; and production costs obviously depend on input prices. If the selling prices of the firm's products rise while wages and other factor costs are relatively fixed, production becomes more profitable, and so firms are persuaded to increase output.

A simple example will illustrate the idea. Suppose a firm uses one hour of labour time to manufacture a gadget that sells for $9. If workers earn $8 per hour, and the firm has no other production costs, its profit per unit is:

$$\text{Profit per unit} = \text{Price} - \text{Cost per unit}$$
$$= \$9 \quad - \$8$$
$$= \$1 \ .$$

Let us assume that this level of profit is just enough to compensate firms for the risks involved, and so make the current production level worthwhile. Now what happens if the price of a gadget rises to $10, but wage rates remain constant? The firm's profit per unit becomes:

$$\text{Profit per unit} = \text{Price} - \text{Cost per unit}$$
$$= \$10 \quad - \$8$$
$$= \$2 \ .$$

With production more profitable, it is likely that the firm will supply more gadgets.

The same process operates in reverse. Suppose selling prices fall while input costs are relatively fixed. Since this squeezes their profit margins, firms may react by cutting back on production. For example, if the price of a gadget fell from $9 to $8.50, profit per unit would fall from $1 to 50¢, and firms would probably produce less.

The behaviour we have just described is summarized by the upward slope of the aggregate supply curve: Production rises when the price level (*P*) rises, and falls when *P* falls. In other words:

The aggregate-supply curve slopes upward because firms normally can purchase labour and other inputs at fixed costs for some period of time. Thus, higher selling prices make production more attractive.

The phrase "for some period of time" alerts us to the possibility that the aggregate-supply curve may not stand still for long. If wages or prices of other inputs change, as they surely will during inflationary times, then the aggregate-supply curve will shift.

Shifts of the Aggregate-Supply Curve

We have concluded so far that, for any given levels of wages and other input prices, there will be an upward-sloping aggregate-supply curve relating aggregate quantity supplied to the price level. But what factors determine the *position* of this curve? What things can make it shift?

The Wage Rate

Our previous discussion suggests that the most obvious determinant of the position of the aggregate-supply curve is the wage rate. Wages are the major element of cost for most firms, typically accounting for something like 70 percent of all expenses. Higher wages spell higher costs, thereby lowering profits at any given price.

Let us return to our example and consider what would happen to a gadget producer if the wage rate rose to $8.75 per hour while the price of a gadget remained $9. Profit per unit would decline from $9 – $8 = $1 to $9 – $8.75 = $0.25. With profits squeezed, the firm would probably cut back on production, since this lower level of profits would be less than that which had previously just made it worthwhile for the firm to bear the associated risks.

This is the typical reaction of firms in our economy to a rise in wages. Therefore, a wage increase leads to a decrease in aggregate quantity supplied at current prices. Graphically, the aggregate-supply curve shifts to the left (or inward), as shown in Figure 10–2. In this diagram, when wages are low, firms are willing to supply $400 billion in goods and services at a price level of 100 (point A). After wages increase, however, these same firms are willing to supply only $350 billion at this price level (point B). By similar reasoning, the aggregate-supply curve will shift to the right (or outward) if wages fall. Thus:

A rise in the money wage rate causes the aggregate-supply curve to shift inward, meaning that the quantity supplied at any price level declines. A fall in the money

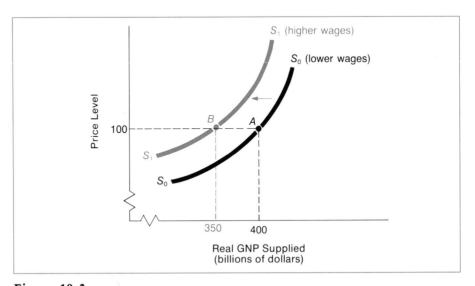

Figure 10–2
A SHIFT OF THE AGGREGATE-SUPPLY CURVE

This diagram shows what happens to the economy's aggregate-supply curve when money wages rise. Higher wages shift the supply curve inward from S_0S_0 to S_1S_1, leading, for example, to an output level of $350 billion (point B), rather than $400 billion (point A), when the price level is 100. The aggregate-supply curve will shift inward in the same manner if the price of any other input (such as energy) increases. Since some inputs are imported, a fall in the foreign value of the Canadian dollar also shifts the supply curve inward.

wage rate causes the aggregate-supply curve to shift outward, meaning that the quantity supplied at any price level increases.

Prices of Other Inputs

In this regard, there is nothing special about wages. An increase in the price of *any* input that firms buy will shift the aggregate-supply curve in the same way. That is:

The aggregate-supply curve is shifted inward by an increase in the price of any input to the production process, and is shifted outward by a decrease.

While there are many inputs other than labour, the one that has attracted the most attention in recent years is energy. We shall have much to say about energy, including further discussion in this chapter and in an entire chapter on the energy problem (*Microeconomics*, Chapter 20). But for present purposes the important thing to realize is that increases in the price of energy, such as those that took place in the 1970s, push the aggregate-supply curve inward more or less as shown in Figure 10–2.

The Exchange Rate

Since some production inputs are imported intermediate goods, a fall in the foreign value of the Canadian dollar raises business costs. Thus, the **exchange rate** is an important shift variable for the aggregate-supply curve as well.

The aggregate-supply curve is shifted inward by depreciation in the foreign value of the Canadian dollar and is shifted outward by an appreciation of the Canadian dollar.

The **exchange rate** states the price at which one currency can be bought in terms of another currency.

Technology and Productivity

Another factor that determines the position of the aggregate-supply curve is the state of technology. Suppose, for example, that a technological breakthrough increases the **productivity** of labour. Such an improvement in productivity will *decrease* business costs and thus improve profitability and encourage more production.

Productivity is the amount of output produced by a unit of input.

Once again, our gadget company will help us understand how this works. Suppose the price of a gadget stays at $9 and the hourly wage rate stays at $8, but gadget workers become much more productive. Specifically, suppose the labour input required to manufacture a gadget falls from one hour (which costs $8) to three-quarters of an hour (which costs $6). Then profit per unit rises from $9 – $8 = $1 to $9 – $6 = $3. The lure of higher profits should induce gadget manufacturers to increase production. In brief, we have concluded that:

Improvements in productivity shift the aggregate-supply curve outward.

Figure 10–2 can be viewed as applying to a *decline* in productivity. As we shall learn in later chapters, especially in Chapter 20, slow growth of productivity is one factor that contributed to the stagflation of the 1970s, and it remains a source of great concern for the 1980s.

Available Supplies of Labour and Capital

The last determinant of the position of the aggregate-supply curve is quite obvious, but we list it anyway for the sake of completeness. The bigger the economy—as measured by its available supplies of labour and capital—the more it is capable of producing. So:

As the labour force grows, and as the capital stock is increased by investment, the aggregate-supply curve will shift outward (to the right), meaning that more output will be produced at any given price level.

These, then, are the "other things" that we hold constant when drawing up an aggregate-supply curve: wage rates, prices of other inputs (like energy), the exchange rate, technology, labour force, and capital stock. While a change in the price level moves the economy *along a given supply curve*, a change in any of these other determinants of aggregate quantity supplied *shifts the entire supply schedule*.

The Shape of the Aggregate-Supply Curve

One other feature of the aggregate-supply curve depicted in Figure 10–1 merits comment. We have drawn our supply curve with a characteristic curvature: It is relatively flat at low levels of output and gets steeper at high levels of output (as we move to the right). There is a reason for this.

When economic activity is weak, product demand slack, and capacity utilization low, firms are likely to respond to an upsurge in demand by bringing their unused capital and labour resources back into production. They will find it neither necessary nor advisable to raise prices very much. The aggregate-supply curve, in a word, will be relatively flat.

By contrast, if the economy is booming, demand is buoyant, and production is straining capacity, firms will be unable to increase output without incurring higher costs. Price increases will thus become necessary because of cost developments and, incidentally, they will not be resisted very forcefully on the demand side. In this case, the aggregate-supply curve will be rather steep. Thus:

The slope of the aggregate-supply curve, which tells us the price increase that is associated with a unit increase in quantity supplied, generally rises as the degree of resource utilization rises.

Equilibrium of Aggregate Demand and Supply

In Chapter 8 we learned that the level of prices is a crucial determinant of whether equilibrium GNP is below full employment (a recessionary gap), precisely at full employment, or above full employment (an inflationary gap). We are now in a position to analyse which type of gap, if any, will actually occur in any particular case by combining the analysis of aggregate supply just completed with the analysis of aggregate demand from the last two chapters to determine *simultaneously* the equilibrium level of real GNP (Y) and the equilibrium price level (P).

Figure 10–3 shows the mechanics graphically. The aggregate-demand curve DD and the aggregate-supply curve SS intersect at point E, where real GNP is $400 billion and the price level is 100. As can be seen in the graph, at any higher price level, such as 120, aggregate quantity supplied would exceed aggregate quantity demanded. There would be a glut on the market as firms found themselves unable to sell all their output. As inventories piled up, firms would compete more vigorously for the available customers, thereby forcing prices down. The price level would fall.

At any price level lower than 100, such as 80, quantity demanded would exceed quantity supplied. There would be a shortage of goods on the market. With inventories disappearing and customers knocking on their doors, firms would be encouraged to raise prices. The price level would rise.

Only when the price level is 100 are the quantities of real GNP demanded and supplied equal. Hence, only the combination $P = 100$, $Y = $400 billion is an equilibrium.

Table 10–1 illustrates this same conclusion in another way, using a tabular analysis similar to that of Chapter 8 (refer back to Table 8–2 on page 147). Columns 1 and 2 constitute an aggregate-demand schedule corresponding to the aggregate-demand curve DD in Figure 10–3. Columns 1 and 3 constitute an aggregate-supply

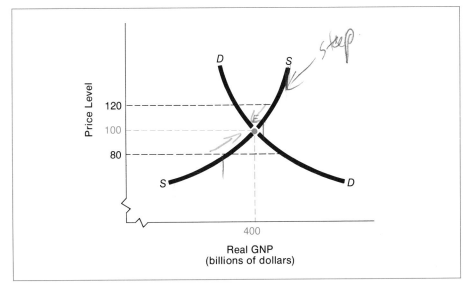

Figure 10-3

EQUILIBRIUM OF REAL GNP
AND THE PRICE LEVEL
This diagram shows how the
equilibrium levels of real GNP and
the price level are simultaneously
determined by the intersection of
the aggregate-demand curve (DD)
and the aggregate-supply curve
(SS). In this example, equilibrium
occurs at point E, with a real GNP
of $400 billion and a price level of
100.

schedule with the general shape discussed in this chapter. It corresponds exactly
to aggregate-supply curve SS in the figure.

It is clear from the table that equilibrium occurs only at P = 100 and Y = $400
billion. At any other price level, aggregate quantities supplied and demanded
would be unequal, with consequent upward or downward pressure on prices. For
example, at a price level of 80, customers demand $430 billion worth of goods and
services, but firms wish to provide only $370 billion. The price level is too low and
will be forced upward. Conversely, at a price level of, say, 120, quantity supplied
($420 billion) exceeds quantity demanded ($380 billion), implying that the price
level must fall.

Recessionary and Inflationary Gaps Revisited

Let us now reconsider a question we posed, but could not answer, in Chapter 8:
Will equilibrium occur at, below, or above full employment?

We could not give a complete answer to this question in Chapter 8 because
we had no way to determine the equilibrium price level, and therefore no way to
tell which type of gap, if any, would arise. The aggregate supply and demand
analysis summarized in Figure 10-3 gives us the information we need to determine

Table 10-1
THE DETERMINATION OF THE EQUILIBRIUM PRICE LEVEL

(1)	(2)	(3)	(4)	(5)
PRICE LEVEL (P)	AGGREGATE QUANTITY DEMANDED (billions of dollars)	AGGREGATE QUANTITY SUPPLIED (billions of dollars)	BALANCE OF SUPPLY AND DEMAND	PRICES WILL:
75	440	360	Quantity demanded exceeds quantity supplied	Rise
80	430	370	Quantity demanded exceeds quantity supplied	Rise
100	400	400	Quantity demanded equals quantity supplied	Remain the same
120	380	420	Quantity supplied exceeds quantity demanded	Fall
150	360	440	Quantity supplied exceeds quantity demanded	Fall

the price level. But we find that our answer is none the less the same as it was in Chapter 8: Anything can happen.

The reason is that nothing in Figure 10-3 tells us where full employment is; it could be above the $400 billion equilibrium level or below it. Depending on the locations of the aggregate-demand and aggregate-supply curves, then, we can reach equilibrium above full employment (an inflationary gap), at full employment, or below full employment (a recessionary gap).

All three possibilities are illustrated in Figure 10-4. The three upper panels are familiar from Chapter 8. As we move from left to right, the $C + I$ schedule rises from $C + I_0$ to $C + I_1$ to $C + I_2$, leading respectively to a recessionary gap, an equilibrium at full employment, and an inflationary gap. In fact, the upper left-hand diagram is a repeat of Figure 8-7 (page 152), and the upper right-hand diagram repeats Figure 8-8 (page 154). We stressed in Chapter 8 that any one of the three cases is possible, depending on the price level and on the consumption and investment schedules.

In the three lower panels, the equilibrium price level is determined at point E by the intersection of the aggregate-supply curve (SS) and the aggregate-demand curve (DD). But the same three possibilities emerge none the less.

In the lower left-hand panel, aggregate demand is too small to provide jobs for the entire labour force, so there is a recessionary gap equal to distance EB, or $100 billion. This corresponds precisely to the situation depicted on the income-expenditure diagram immediately above it.

In the lower right-hand panel, aggregate demand is so high that the economy reaches an equilibrium well beyond full employment. There is an inflationary gap equal to BE, or $100 billion, just as in the diagram immediately above it.

In the lower middle panel, the aggregate-demand curve D_1D_1 is at just the right level to produce an equilibrium at full employment. There is neither an inflationary nor a recessionary gap, as in the diagram just above it.

Thus, it may seem that we have done nothing but restate our previous conclusions. But, in fact, we have done much more, because now that we have studied the determination of the equilibrium price level, we are in a position to examine how the economy adjusts to either a recessionary gap or an inflationary gap.

Adjusting to an Inflationary Gap: Inflation

We have already suggested that an inflationary gap sets the stage for inflation. As we shall see now, this happens because the economy, if left to its own devices, produces an inflation that eventually eliminates an inflationary gap. In other words, the gap self-destructs, although the process may be slow and painful. Let us see how this works.

When equilibrium GNP is above potential, jobs are plentiful and labour is in great demand. Although some workers are unemployed, this minimal unemployment is less than the frictional (and structural) level—that is, less than the number we expect to be jobless because they are moving, changing occupations, and so on; or because the existing job vacancies do not match the skills and aspirations of the unemployed (labour force composition problems). Because of the low level of unemployment, many firms have trouble finding workers. They may even be having trouble hanging on to their current employees, as other firms try to lure them away with higher wages.

Such a situation is bound to lead to rising wages, and rising wages add to business costs, thus shifting the aggregate-supply curve inward. But as the aggregate-supply curve shifts inward—eventually moving from S_0S_0 to S_1S_1 in Figure 10-5, for example—the size of the inflationary gap steadily declines. Thus, inflation erodes the inflationary gap, eventually leading the economy to an equilibrium at full employment (point F in Figure 10-5).

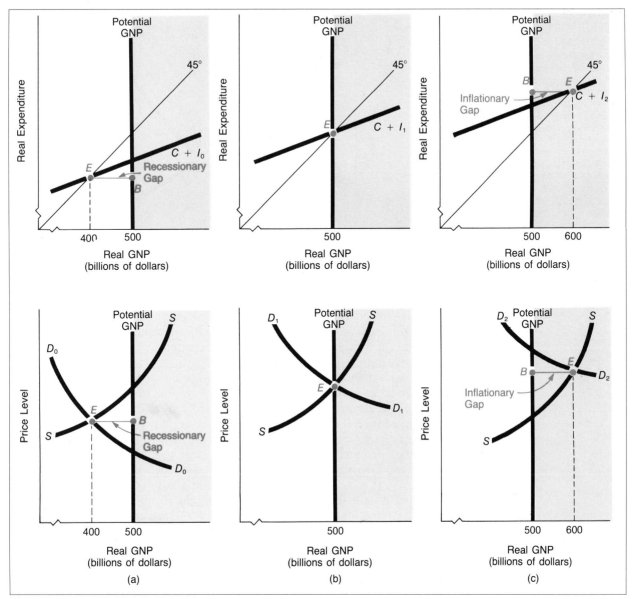

Figure 10-4

RECESSIONARY AND INFLATIONARY GAPS REVISITED

This figure shows three possible types of equilibrium on two different diagrams. In the top row, income–expenditure diagrams from Chapter 8 are used to depict a recessionary gap, an equilibrium at full employment, and an inflationary gap. In the bottom row, these same three situations are shown on aggregate supply and demand diagrams. In each case, the aggregate-supply curve is the same (SS), equilibrium occurs at point E, and full employment GNP is $500 billion. In part (a), the aggregate-demand curve D_0D_0 is relatively low, so that equilibrium falls below full employment. There is a recessionary gap measured by the distance EB, or $100 billion. In part (b), the aggregate demand-curve D_1D_1 is higher, and equilibrium occurs precisely at full employment. There is no gap of either kind. In part (c), the aggregate-demand curve D_2D_2 is so high that equilibrium occurs beyond full employment. There is an inflationary gap measured by the distance BE, or $100 billion.

There is a straightforward way of looking at how this self-correcting process works. The trouble arises in the first place because consumers and investors are demanding more output than the economy is capable of producing at normal operating rates. To paraphrase an old cliché, there is too much demand chasing too little supply. Naturally, prices will be rising in such an environment. And the rising prices will eat away at the purchasing power of consumers' wealth, forcing them to cut back on consumption, as explained in Chapter 7. Eventually,

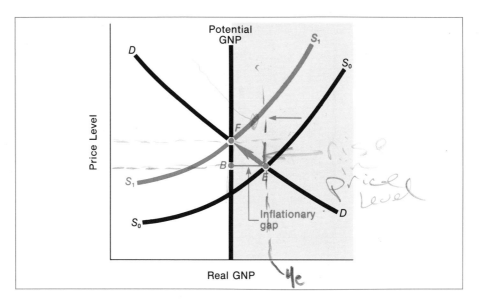

Figure 10-5

THE ELIMINATION OF AN INFLATIONARY GAP

When the aggregate-supply curve is S_0S_0 and the aggregate-demand curve is DD, the economy will initially reach equilibrium (point E) with an inflationary gap. The resulting inflation of wages will push the supply curve inward until it has shifted to the position indicated by curve S_1S_1. Here, with equilibrium at point F, the economy is at normal full employment. But, during the adjustment period from E to F, there will have been inflation.

consumers' appetites for goods will be scaled down to the economy's capacity to provide those goods; and at this point, the self-correcting process stops. That, in essence, is the unhappy process by which the economy cures itself of the problem of excessive aggregate demand.

One caveat should be entered. The conclusion that an inflationary gap sows the seeds of its own destruction holds *only in the absence of further forces propelling the aggregate demand curve outward.* But in Chapter 9 we have already encountered several forces that might shift the aggregate-demand curve outward. As you can see by manipulating the aggregate-demand–aggregate-supply diagram, if aggregate demand is shifting out at the same time that aggregate supply is shifting in, there will certainly be inflation, but the inflationary gap may not shrink. (Try this as an exercise, to make sure you understand how to use the apparatus.) As a historical proposition, then, not all inflationary episodes have come to a smooth and gradual end. At times, the self-correcting mechanism is overridden by rapid expansion of aggregate demand—which is sometimes even due to government policy!

Demand Inflation and Stagflation

Simple as it is, this adjustment model teaches us a number of important lessons about inflation in the real world. First of all, Figure 10-5 reminds us that the real culprit in this particular inflation is the excessive level of aggregate demand. The aggregate-demand curve is initially so high that it intersects the aggregate-supply curve at an output level higher than full employment. The resulting intense demand for workers pushes wages higher; and higher wages spell higher prices. While excessive demand is not the only possible cause of inflation in the real world, it certainly is the cause in our example.

However, business managers and journalists are very likely to blame inflation on rising wages. In a superficial sense, of course, they are right, because higher wages do indeed lead firms to raise their prices. But in a deeper sense they are wrong. Both rising wages and rising prices are only symptoms of an underlying malady: too much aggregate demand. Blaming labour for inflation in such a case is a bit like blaming high doctor bills for making you ill.

Second, we see that output falls while prices rise as the economy adjusts from point E to point F in Figure 10-5. This process thus provides our first (but not our last!) explanation of the phenomenon of stagflation. We see that:

A period of stagflation is part of the normal aftermath of a period of excessive aggregate demand.

It is easy enough to understand why stagflation occurs. When aggregate demand is excessive, the economy will (temporarily) produce beyond its normal capacity. Labour markets become very tight and wages rise. Machinery and raw materials may also become scarce and so start rising in price. Faced by higher costs, the natural reaction of business firms is both to produce less and to charge a higher price. This is stagflation.

It may be useful to review what we have learned about inflationary gaps thus far.

If aggregate demand is exceptionally high, the economy may reach an equilibrium above full employment (an inflationary gap). When this occurs, the tight situation in the labour market soon forces wages to rise. Since wages are business costs, prices rise and there is inflation. With cuts in consumer purchasing power, the inflationary gap begins to close. As the inflationary gap is closing, output falls while prices continue to rise, so the economy experiences stagflation until the inflationary gap is eliminated. At this point, a long-run equilibrium is established with a higher price level and with GNP equal to potential GNP.

Examples from Canadian History

Because inflationary gaps have been rare birds in recent years, we have to go back to the late 1960s, and to the 1973–75 period, to find a "textbook" example of an inflationary gap that extinguished itself in this way. During the 1966–69 period, the Canadian economy was booming, unemployment got down to 4 percent, and jobs were plentiful. According to official estimates of potential GNP, there was an inflationary gap.

Our analysis suggests that wages should have been accelerating, and indeed they were. The bright blue bars in Figure 10-6 illustrate this acceleration. The dark blue bars show that the rate of price inflation followed the rate of increase of

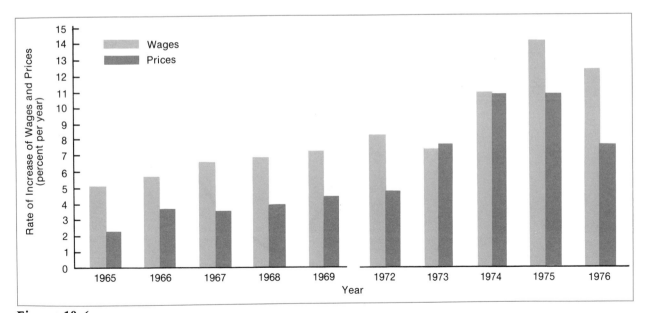

Figure 10-6
GROWTH RATES OF WAGES AND PRICES IN CANADA, 1965-1969 and 1972-1976
These data illustrate what happened when an inflationary gap arose in the late 1960s. Notice the acceleration of both wages and prices. By 1969, the gap was eliminated and wage increases levelled off. Price increases subsequently fell back to 2.9 percent in 1971. The second inflationary gap appeared in 1973-74. Again the wage increases first accelerated and then levelled off after the inflationary gap was eliminated.
SOURCE: Statistics Canada.

wages—rising from 2.4 percent a year to over 4.6 percent. This is, again, in line with what our model predicts.

The upsurge in inflation naturally ate away at the inflationary gap, which was gone by 1969. Price inflation subsequently fell back to 2.9 percent by 1971. Despite outcries of "excessive" wage demands that "caused" inflation, it is clear that the ultimate cause of the acceleration in both wages and prices was the excessive aggregate demand caused by large increases in government expenditure and exports (due to the boom in the United States that resulted from the Vietnam War).

The second example of an inflationary gap occurred in 1973–75, as the Canadian government over-stimulated aggregate demand in an attempt to avoid a recession following the OPEC oil price increases in 1973. Again, Figure 10-6 shows the acceleration in wages and prices that occurred. However, as the inflation eliminated the inflationary gap (as the higher wages shifted the aggregate-supply curve to the left), the unemployment rate rose (from 5.4 percent in 1974 to 7.1 percent in 1976). Once again, the economy behaved just as our simple model suggests.

Adjusting to a Recessionary Gap: Deflation or Unemployment?

Let us now consider what can happen when the economy finds itself in equilibrium *below* full employment—that is, when there is a recessionary gap. This might be caused, for example, by inadequate consumer spending or by anemic investment spending.

Figure 10-7 illustrates such a case and gives an impression of the economic situation of the early 1980s.

You might expect that we could just run our previous analysis in reverse: High unemployment leads to falling wages; falling wages reduce business costs and shift the aggregate-supply curve outward, so firms cut prices; falling wages and prices eliminate the recessionary gap by propping up consumer spending; and full employment is restored. The economy moves smoothly from point E to point F in Figure 10-7. Very simple. And very misleading in our modern economy!

Why is it misleading? While the economy may have operated like this long ago, it certainly does not work this way now. The history of Canada and other similar Western economies shows *many examples* of falling wages and prices before World War II but *none* since then. Not even the severe recession of 1981–84,

Figure 10-7

THE ELIMINATION OF A RECESSIONARY GAP?

At point *E*, there is a recessionary gap because the aggregate-demand curve *DD* crosses the aggregate-supply curve S_0S_0 below the level of potential GNP. If wages fall, the aggregate-supply curve gradually shifts outward until it reaches the position indicated by supply curve S_1S_1. Here the economy has attained a full-employment equilibrium at point *F*. But if wages refuse to fall, the economy gets stuck with a recessionary gap and a long period of unemployment.

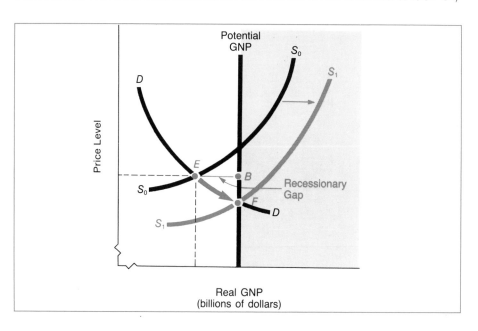

Real GNP
(billions of dollars)

during which unemployment climbed above 12 percent, was able to force average prices and wages down.

Exactly *why* wages and prices are rigid in the downward direction in our modern economy has been a subject of intense controversy among economists for years. And the controversy continues.

Some economists emphasize institutional features like minimum-wage laws, union contracts, and a variety of government regulations that place legal floors under particular wages and prices. Because most of these institutions are of relatively recent vintage, this theory successfully explains why wages and prices are more rigid now than they were before World War II. However, most of the Canadian economy is not subject to legal restraints on cutting wages and prices. So it seems doubtful that legal restrictions can provide a complete explanation.

Other observers subscribe to the theory that holds that workers have a profound psychological resistance to accepting a wage reduction. This theory certainly has the ring of truth. Think how you would react if your boss announced that she was cutting your hourly wage rate. You might quit, or you might devote less care and attention to your job. Genuine wage "concessions" are rare enough to be news headlines. For example, Chrysler workers accepted paycuts in the early 1980s, but only when it appeared that the company was in grave danger of going bankrupt. And they demanded that their wages be restored as soon as the company was back on its feet.

While no one doubts that wage cuts are bad for morale, the psychological theory has one major drawback. It fails to explain why the psychological resistance to wage cuts apparently started only after World War II. Until a satisfactory answer to this question is provided, many economists will remain skeptical.

A third explanation is based on a fact we emphasized in Chapter 5—that business cycles have been far less severe in the postwar period than they were in the prewar period. Because of the government commitment to "full" employment, firms and workers know that recessions will not turn into depressions. Thus, workers and firms may decide to wait out the bad times rather than accept wage or price reductions that they will later regret. It is this explanation that was favoured by the Reagan and Thatcher administrations. They rejected the previous approaches, which involved an "inflationary bias." They observed that previous governments had always stimulated aggregate demand sufficiently to keep unemployment from rising too much. Taking employment for granted, labour leaders pushed for large wage increases. Either some wage- and price-control scheme seemed to be necessary to preclude labour's quite natural reaction to the inflationary gap, or they must not be allowed to take employment for granted. By essentially dropping any commitment to full employment, and by bluntly announcing that they would not permit an inflationary gap, these governments attempted to reduce the downward inflexibility of wages.

There are other theories as well, none of which commands anything like universal acceptance. But, regardless of the cause, we might as well accept the fact that, in the modern Canadian economy, prices and wages will rise when demand is strong but generally will not fall significantly when demand is weak.

The implications of this rigidity are quite serious, for a recessionary gap cannot cure itself without some deflation. And if wages and prices will not fall, *the economy gets stuck at a point like E in Figure 10–7, that is, at an equilibrium below full employment.* Keynes was the first economist to point out the possibility of a long-lasting equilibrium below full employment and to distinguish it from the full-employment equilibrium that we have just been considering.

When aggregate demand is low, the economy may get stuck in an *unemployment equilibrium.* There is a recessionary gap, but wages and prices refuse to fall; so the gap persists. The economy endures a prolonged period of production below potential GNP.

Does the Economy Have a Self-Correcting Mechanism?

Now a situation like this would, presumably, not last forever. As the recession lengthened, and perhaps deepened, more and more workers would be unable to obtain jobs at the prevailing high wages. Eventually their resistance to wage cuts, whatever its cause, would be worn down by their need to be employed.

Firms, too, would become increasingly willing to cut prices as the period of weak demand lasted longer and longer, and managers became convinced that the slump was not merely a temporary aberration. Prices and wages did, in fact, fall during the Great Depression of the 1930s. And they might fall again if a sufficiently drastic depression were allowed to occur.

Nowadays, political leaders of all three major parties believe it is folly to wait for falling wages and prices to eliminate a recessionary gap. But while they agree that *some* government action is both necessary and appropriate under recessionary conditions, there is still vocal—and highly partisan!—debate over how much and what kind of intervention is warranted.

One reason for this disagreement is that the **self-correcting mechanism** does operate—if only weakly—to cure recessionary gaps. Recent history provides a vivid illustration.

The Economy in the 1980s: A Case Study

As the current decade opened, the Canadian economy was operating not too far below full employment, but the inflation rate was very high. A policy-induced recession (to fight inflation) drove the unemployment rate up from only 7.5 percent in 1980 to 12.0 percent in 1983. Throughout this period, the recessionary gap was growing larger, not smaller. Does this mean that the self-correcting mechanism failed to work? Not quite. It just worked weakly, and with some delay.

Between 1980 and 1981, as the recessionary gap increased, wage and price inflation accelerated slightly, as Figure 10–8 shows. According to our model of the self-correcting mechanism, this is not supposed to happen. But then, with unemployment and the recessionary gap setting postwar records, things began to change. While wages and prices did not actually decline, their rates of increase did slow down markedly in 1982–83. By 1983, as you can see in Figure 10–8, the rate of inflation had fallen to just over half its 1980 level.

Figure 10–8
GROWTH RATES OF WAGES AND PRICES IN CANADA, 1980–1983
These data illustrate what happened when the Canadian economy developed a large recessionary gap in 1980–83. Notice that wage and price inflation did not slow down in 1980–81 but then did drop markedly in 1982 and 1983. SOURCE: Statistics Canada.

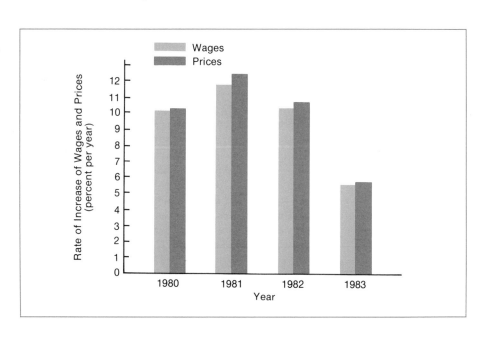

Inflation was significantly lowered, but at substantial cost. More than a million unemployed workers and hundreds of bankrupted businesses were the casualties of the war against inflation. The self-correcting mechanism is a rocky road to full employment.

Our overall conclusion about the economy's ability to right itself, then, seems to run something like this:

The economy does indeed have a self-correcting mechanism that tends to eliminate either unemployment or inflation. However, this mechanism is much more efficient at curing inflationary gaps through inflation than at curing recessionary gaps through deflation. In addition, its ability to curb inflation is sometimes overridden by increases in aggregate demand. Thus the self-correcting mechanism cannot always be relied upon.

Stagflation from Supply Shifts

We have so far encountered one type of stagflation in this chapter—the stagflation that often follows in the aftermath of an inflationary boom. As we saw, the "mystery" of the Canadian stagflations of the late 1960s and 1970s is solved in this way. However, the same model does not fit the facts of the more serious stagflationary episodes of 1973–75 and 1978–80 in the United States. What happened during these "mysteries"?

The economic boom of 1972–73 left the U.S. economy with an inflationary gap. In 1973, the U.S. unemployment rate stood at 4.9 percent—a rate considered to be below the full-employment level. By 1975, however, it had skyrocketed to 8.5 percent—well above even the most pessimistic estimates of the full-employment rate. This hardly looks like the workings of a smoothly functioning self-correcting mechanism. On the inflation front, the Consumer Price Index, which had risen only 3.4 percent during 1972, rose 8.8 percent in 1973 and 12.2 percent in 1974.

What was going on during 1973–75 that caused so much more unemployment and inflation than was expected? What were the causes of this more virulent type of stagflation? Several things, but the principal villain was the rising price of energy.

In 1973, the Organization of Petroleum Exporting Countries (OPEC) reached a collusive agreement to limit production that succeeded in quadrupling the price of crude oil in only a few months. American consumers found the prices of gasoline and home-heating fuels increasing sharply. American businesses found that one of the most important inputs into the production process—energy—rose drastically in price, thus increasing the cost of doing business. Other raw materials prices also skyrocketed in 1974.

Higher energy prices, we observed earlier, shift the economy's aggregate-supply curve inward in the manner shown in Figure 10–2 (page 176). If the aggregate-supply curve shifts inward, as it surely did for the United States in 1973–74, production will be reduced. And in order to reduce demand to the available supply, prices will have to rise. The result is the worst of both worlds: falling production and rising prices.

This conclusion is shown in Figure 10–9, which superimposes an aggregate-demand curve, DD, on the two aggregate-supply curves of Figure 10–2. The economy's equilibrium shifts upward to the left, from point E to point A. Thus, output falls while prices rise.

Stagflation is the typical result of adverse supply shifts.

The numbers used in Figure 10–9 are roughly indicative of what happened in the United States between 1973 (represented by supply curve S_0S_0 and point E) and 1975 (represented by supply curve S_1S_1 and point A). Real GNP, in 1972 prices, fell by about $22 billion, while the price level rose almost 20 percent.

Figure 10-9

STAGFLATION FROM A
SHIFT IN AGGREGATE
SUPPLY

This diagram illustrates how
stagflation arises if the aggregate-
supply curve shifts inward to the
left (from S_0S_0 to S_1S_1). If the
aggregate-demand curve does not
change, equilibrium moves from
point E to point A. Output falls as
prices rise, which is what we mean
by stagflation. The diagram
indicates roughly what happened
in the United States during
1973-75, when higher energy
prices caused stagflation.

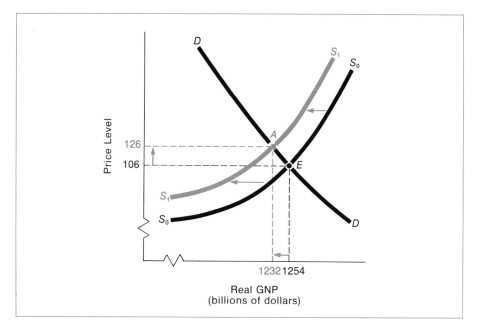

By 1978 the U.S. economy had just about recovered from the severe disloca-
tions of 1973 and 1974, only to be clobbered by OPEC again. The ousting of the
Shah of Iran in early 1979 led to a cutoff of Iranian oil supplies and virtual panic in
the world oil market. Oil prices escalated as consumers scrambled to secure sources
of supply and to build inventories. OPEC was only too happy to follow suit by
raising prices.

The results of this second "energy shock" were much the same as those of the
first. The inflation rate, which had been 9 percent in 1978, rose to 13.3 percent in
1979, and to 16 percent in the first half of 1980. Americans were almost panic-
stricken over these unprecedented inflation rates, which dwarfed even the worst
months of 1974.

As was the case in 1973–75, recession followed inflation. The economy, which
had operated near the full-employment range (approximately 6 percent unemployment) throughout 1978, began to weaken slightly in 1979 and slipped into
recession in early 1980. The unemployment rate rose to nearly 8 percent.

The general lesson to be learned from the experience of the United States
during the 1970s is as important as it is clear:

The typical results of an adverse supply shock are a fall in output and an
acceleration in inflation. This is one reason why the world economy was plagued
by stagflation in the mid-1970s and early 1980s. And it can happen again if another
series of supply-reducing events takes place.

Why didn't Canada suffer the adverse supply shocks to the same extent as the
United States during the 1970s? The answer is that our government followed a
rather different policy. Much to the chagrin of the oil-producing provinces, the
federal government prevented domestic oil prices from rising as much as world
prices did. For oil consumers in the eastern provinces who relied on imported oil,
the government paid the difference between the high world price and the much
lower domestic price. To a large extent, therefore, the Canadian policy precluded
any big leftward shift of the aggregate-supply schedule from occurring.

Another aspect of Canadian policy was also important. The authorities
correctly predicted the recession that followed OPEC in the United States and
elsewhere, and they knew that this would decrease the demand for Canadian-
produced goods. In an attempt to override this expected leftward shift of our

aggregate-demand curve, the government stimulated aggregate demand rather dramatically. (The specific policies involved are discussed in the next few chapters.) As a result, Canada had an inflationary gap in 1973–74, not a deflationary gap as did the United States.

Was Canada's reaction to the world oil-price shocks a good policy? By comparing our experience with that of the United States, we see that Canadians suffered less unemployment. However, Canada's inflation performance has been somewhat worse. Also, citizens of the oil-producing provinces are very bitter about the big loss in their income caused by the ceiling imposed on domestic oil prices. Finally, to some extent the Canadian policy has only delayed, not eliminated, the adverse supply shifts. The Canadian oil price was gradually increased each year following 1974. Also, to cover part of the mushrooming budget deficit (partly caused by the government's oil-price subsidy to eastern consumers during the 1970s), the federal government raised the manufacturers' sales tax in 1984. This increased business costs and shifted the aggregate-supply curve inward, thereby worsening the recession of the 1980s instead of the one in the 1970s.

Inflation and the Multiplier

When we introduced the concept of the multiplier in Chapter 9, we said that there were several reasons why its actual value is smaller than that suggested by the oversimplified multiplier formula. We are now in a position to understand one of these reasons: *Inflation reduces the size of the multiplier.*

The basic idea is quite simple. In Chapter 9, we described a multiplier process in which one person's spending became another person's income, which led to further spending by the second person, and so on. But this story is confined to the demand side of the economy.

Let us therefore consider what is likely to happen on the supply side as the multiplier process unfolds. Will the additional demand be taken care of by firms without raising prices?

If the aggregate-supply curve is upward sloping, the answer is no; more goods will only be provided at higher prices. Thus, as the multiplier chain progresses, pulling income and employment up, prices will also rise. And this, as we know from Chapter 7, will dampen consumer spending because rising prices reduce the purchasing power of consumers' wealth. So the multiplier chain will not proceed as far as it would have in the absence of inflation. How much inflation results from the rise in demand? How much of the multiplier chain is cut off by inflation? The answers depend on the slope of the economy's aggregate-supply curve.

For a concrete example of the analysis, let us return to the $20 billion increase in investment spending used in Chapter 9. As we learned there (see especially page 169) $20 billion in additional investment spending eventually leads—through the multiplier process—to *a horizontal shift of $100 billion in the aggregate-demand curve.* But to know the actual quantity that will ultimately be produced, and the actual price level, we must bring the aggregate-supply curve into the picture.

Figure 10–10 does this. Here we show the $100 billion horizontal shift of the aggregate-demand curve, from D_0D_0 to D_1D_1, that is derived from the oversimplified multiplier formula (which ignored rising prices). The aggregate-supply curve, SS, then tells us how this expansion of demand is apportioned between higher output and higher prices. We see that as the economy's equilibrium moves from point E_0 to point E_1, real GNP does not rise by $100 billion. Instead, prices rise, which, as we know, tends to cancel out part of the rise in quantity demanded. So output increases only from $400 billion to $480 billion—an increase of $80 billion. Thus, in our example, inflation has reduced the multiplier from $100/$20 = 5 to $80/$20 = 4. In general:

As long as the aggregate-supply curve is upward sloping, any increase in aggregate

Figure 10-10

INFLATION AND THE MULTIPLIER

This figure illustrates the complete analysis of the multiplier, including the effect of inflation. The simple multiplier of Chapter 9, which ignored changes in the price level, appears here as a *horizontal* shift of $100 billion in the aggregate-demand curve, meaning that the multiplier would be $100/$20 = 5 if prices did not rise. However, when aggregate demand shifts from $D_0 D_0$ to $D_1 D_1$, prices rise. In the diagram, the price level increases from 100 to 120 or by 20 percent. Consequently, equilibrium real income increases from $400 billion to only $480 billion—for a rise of $80 billion, or a multiplier of $80/$20 = 4.

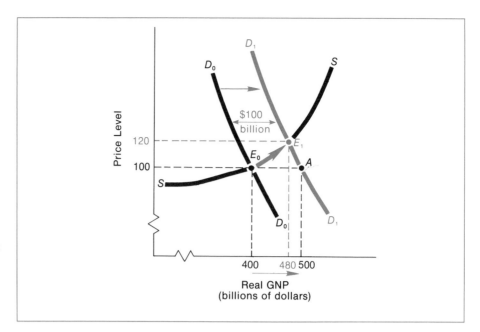

demand will push up the price level. This will, in turn, drain off some of the higher real demand by eroding the purchasing power of consumer wealth. Thus, inflation reduces the multiplier below that suggested by the oversimplified formula.

Notice also that the price level in this example has been pushed up (from 100 to 120, or 20 percent) by the rise in investment demand. This, too, is a general result:

As long as the aggregate-supply curve is upward sloping, any upward shift in the aggregate demand curve will cause some rise in prices in the economy.

The economic behaviour behind these results certainly cannot be considered surprising. Firms faced with a large increase in aggregate quantity demanded at their original prices respond to the changed circumstances in two natural ways: They raise production (so GNP rises) and they raise prices (so the price level rises). But this rise in the price level reduces the purchasing power of the bank accounts and bonds held by consumers, and they also react in the natural way: They cut down on their spending. Such a reaction amounts to a movement *along* aggregate-demand curve $D_1 D_1$ in Figure 10-10 from point A to point E_1.

Higher prices thus play their usual dual role in a market economy: They encourage suppliers to produce more and, at the same time, encourage demanders to consume less. In this way, equilibrium is re-established at higher levels of output and higher prices through the process of inflation.

Figure 10-10 also shows us exactly where the oversimplified multiplier formula goes wrong. By ignoring the effects of the higher price level, the oversimplified formula supposes the economy moves horizontally from point E_0 to point A. As the diagram clearly shows, output does not actually rise this much. Output *would* rise this much *only* if the aggregate-supply curve were horizontal. (Verify this for yourself by pencilling in an imaginary horizontal aggregate-supply curve through points E_0 and A in Figure 10-10.) That is, the oversimplified multiplier formula tacitly assumes that the aggregate-supply curve is horizontal. Normally, this is an unrealistic assumption, and that is one reason why the oversimplified formula exaggerates the size of the multiplier.

As a summary, it may be useful to put together what we have learned about multiplier analysis in Chapters 9 and 10.

STEPS IN CALCULATING THE MULTIPLIER

1. Shift the expenditure schedule in the 45° line diagram vertically by the amount of the autonomous shift in spending (as, for example, in Figure 9–1 on page 163).

2. Use the 45° line diagram, or the oversimplified multiplier formula, to calculate the multiplier effect on the GNP that *would* occur *if* the price level, wage rates, interest rate, exchange rate, and level of imports stayed constant (see again Figure 9–1).

3. Now move from the 45° line diagram to an aggregate supply and demand diagram like Figure 10–10 to see how the price level will react. Enter the multiplier effect calculated in Step 2 as a horizontal shift of the aggregate-demand curve in the supply–demand diagram.

4. The supply–demand diagram shows what *would* happen to real output and the price level *if* wages, the interest and exchange rates, and imports were constant.

We consider these remaining provisos in following chapters. It turns out that the exchange rate and interest rates will remain roughly constant in the face of a shift in autonomous expenditure, *if* the central bank follows a fixed exchange-rate policy (as explained in Chapter 15). However, the assumptions that imports and wages are constant are not plausible. The analysis in Chapter 14 indicates that making more plausible assumptions about the response of wages raises the effect of aggregate demand increases on the price level and lowers its effect on real output.

Summary

1. The economy's aggregate-supply curve relates the quantity of goods and services that will be supplied to the price level. It normally slopes upward to the right because the costs of labour and other inputs are relatively fixed in the short run, meaning that higher selling prices make input costs relatively "cheaper" and therefore encourage greater production.

2. The position of the aggregate-supply curve can be shifted by changes in wage rates, prices of other inputs, the exchange rate, technology, or the quantities of labour and capital available for employment.

3. The aggregate-supply curve normally gets steeper as output increases. This means that, as output and capacity utilization rise, any given increase in aggregate demand leads to more inflation and less growth of real output.

4. The equilibrium price level and the equilibrium level of real GNP are jointly determined by the intersection of the economy's aggregate-supply and aggregate-demand schedules. This intersection may come at full employment, below full employment (a recessionary gap), or above full employment (an inflationary gap).

5. If there is an inflationary gap, the economy has a self-correcting mechanism that erodes the gap through a process of inflation. Specifically, unusually strong job prospects push wages up, which shifts the aggregate-supply curve to the left and reduces the inflationary gap.

6. One consequence of this self-correcting mechanism is that, if a surge in aggregate demand opens up an inflationary gap, part of the economy's natural adjustment to this event will be a period of stagflation; that is, a period in which prices are rising while output is falling.

7. The economy also has a self-correcting mechanism that erodes a recessionary gap. However, this mechanism works much more slowly and less reliably than the inflationary-gap mechanism because it relies on falling wages to shift the aggregate-supply curve outward, and wages do not fall easily.

8. An inward shift of the aggregate-supply curve will cause output to fall while prices rise; that is, it will cause stagflation. Among the events that have caused such a shift are the abrupt increases in the price of foreign oil and the falling foreign currency value of the Canadian dollar.

9. Adverse supply shifts like this have occurred: foreign oil-price increases in the 1970s, and a falling value of the Canadian dollar in the 1980s. Thus the stagflation of the 1970s and 1980s is no mystery at all.

10. Among the reasons why the oversimplified multiplier formula is wrong is the fact that it ignores any inflation that may be caused by an increase in aggregate demand. Such inflation decreases the multiplier by reducing consumer spending, because consumers as a group suffer a loss of purchasing power when prices rise.

Concepts for Review

Aggregate-supply curve
Productivity
Equilibrium of real GNP and the
    price level

Inflationary gap
Self-correcting mechanism
Stagflation

Recessionary gap
Inflation and the multiplier

Questions for Discussion

1. In an economy with the following aggregate-demand and aggregate-supply schedules, find the equilibrium levels of real output and the price level. Graph your solution. If full employment comes at $1800 billion, is there an inflationary or a recessionary gap?

AGGREGATE QUANTITY DEMANDED (in billions)	PRICE LEVEL	AGGREGATE QUANTITY SUPPLIED (in billions)
2000	75	1400
1950	80	1450
1800	100	1600
1700	120	1700
1600	150	1800

2. Suppose a worker receives a wage of $9.50 per hour. Compute the *real* wage (money wage deflated by the price index) corresponding to each of the following possible price levels: 85, 95, 100, 110, 120. What do you notice about the relationship between the real wage and the price level? Relate this to the slope of the aggregate-supply curve.

3. In 1980, capacity utilization averaged 80 percent in Canada. In 1982 it averaged 70 percent. In which year do you think the economy found itself on a steeper portion of its aggregate-supply curve? Explain why.

4. Explain why an increase in the price of foreign oil shifts the aggregate-supply curve inward to the left. What are the consequences of such a shift?

5. Comment on the following statement: "Inflationary and recessionary gaps are nothing to worry about because the economy has a built-in mechanism that cures either type of gap automatically."

6. Give *two* different explanations of how the economy can suffer from stagflation.

7. Why do you think wages tend to be rigid in the downward direction?

8. Add the following aggregate-supply and aggregate-demand schedules to the data in Question 3 of Chapter 9 (page 171) to see how inflation affects the multiplier.

(1) PRICE LEVEL	(2) AGGREGATE DEMAND (when investment is $130)	(3) AGGREGATE DEMAND (when investment is $140)	(4) AGGREGATE SUPPLY
90	$1210	$1310	$1110
95	1205	1305	1155
100	1200	1300	1200
105	1195	1295	1245
110	1190	1290	1290
115	1185	1285	1335

Draw these schedules on a piece of graph paper. Then:
  a. Notice that the difference between columns 2 and 3 (the aggregate-demand schedule at two different levels of investment) is always $100. Discuss how this relates to your answer in the previous chapter.
  b. Find the equilibrium GNP and the equilibrium price level both before and after the increase in investment. What is the value of the multiplier?

9. Explain in words why rising prices reduce the multiplier effect of an autonomous increase in aggregate demand.

10. Use an aggregate supply and demand diagram to show that multiplier effects are smaller when the aggregate-supply curve is steeper. Which case gives rise to more inflation—the steep aggregate-supply curve or the flat one?

III

Fiscal, Monetary, and Exchange-Rate Policy

Fiscal Policy and Supply-Side Economics

11

Facts do not cease to exist
because they are ignored.
ALDOUS HUXLEY

In the last several chapters, we have constructed and analysed a model of an economy in which there is no government spending, taxes, exports, or imports. We have seen how equilibrium is determined and how changes in the consumption and investment components of aggregate demand can change that equilibrium.

But in the Canadian economy, the government's budgetary decisions exercise a profound influence over aggregate demand, and we export and import more than one-quarter of our national product. Furthermore, net exports is almost as volatile a component of aggregate demand as is investment. Thus, to make our model fit the Canadian economy, our task in this chapter is to put the government and the foreign sector back into the picture. More than a desire for realism dictates that we bring the government into the model. Without including the government we cannot study what national economic policy can do about inflation and unemployment, and this is perhaps the main purpose of macroeconomic analysis.

Traditionally, the government has used its taxing and spending powers to manage aggregate demand. So this chapter begins there. Specifically, we expand the basic model to allow, first, for government purchases of goods and services as a component of aggregate demand, and, second, for an income tax that makes disposable income less than national income. As we shall see, neither of these complications requires any fundamental change in the way we analyse the determination of GNP and the price level, although taxes do reduce the multiplier. But, while the *model* does not change much when the government is introduced, the *policy implications* of the analysis are drastically altered. In fact, the main topic of this chapter is how the government can use its spending and taxes to influence economic activity.

When Ronald Reagan became the U.S. president in 1981, he rejected the conventional emphasis on aggregate-demand management and argued that the government could and should use tax policy to influence aggregate supply. The terms "Reaganomics" and "supply-side economics" became the popular labels for this approach, which we analyse in the final part of this chapter.

Government Purchases and Equilibrium Income

The government's **fiscal policy** is its plan for spending and taxation. It is designed to steer aggregate demand in some desired direction.

The federal Minister of Finance normally presents a budget to Parliament each year. This economic report outlines the government's proposed **fiscal policy**, a highly volatile issue. In these statements, the finance minister outlines taxing and spending proposals, explains the effects that government economists expect these proposals to have on aggregate demand, and offers an explanation indicating why this is the right policy at that time.

This chapter is concerned with how these important budget decisions are, or should be, made. If you were a member of parliament, how would you evaluate the budget? How much spending is the right amount? How much taxation is appropriate? Perhaps more to the point, how can you as a voter decide whether your elected representatives have made sound decisions?

Before attempting to answer questions like these, we must integrate the government into our model of the determination of national income and the price level. We do this in stages, starting first with **government purchases of goods and services** (G), and then adding taxes. Thus, in considering once again the circular flow of income and expenditure (see Figure 11-1), we ignore for the moment the flows of tax revenues and transfer payments at point 5. How would the equilibrium level of GNP be determined in an economy in which the government bought goods but did not levy taxes or make transfers?

The circular flow diagram shows us the answer, just as it did in an economy with no government (Chapter 8). If the size of the circular flow of income and expenditure is to be maintained, then the total amount of new goods and services that firms produce at point 4 (Y) must be equal to the sum of the demands of consumers at point 1 (C), investors at point 2 (I), and government at point 3 (G). We

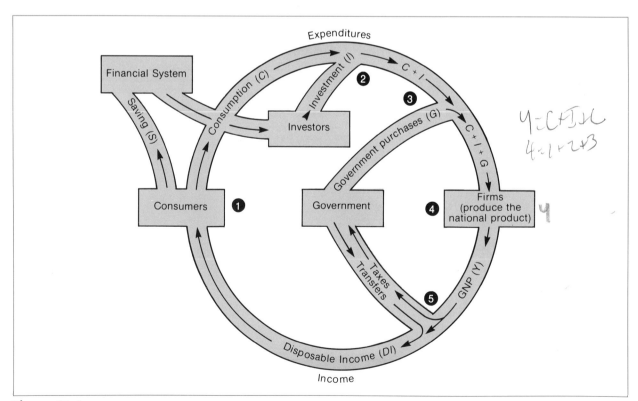

Figure 11-1
THE CIRCULAR FLOW OF EXPENDITURE AND INCOME

thus obtain the following restatement of the condition for equilibrium on the demand side of the economy:

For any given price level, equilibrium GNP on the demand side of the economy occurs when the sum of consumption demand, investment demand, and government demand for goods and services just equals the GNP. In symbols:

$$Y = C + I + G.$$

The reasoning behind this equilibrium condition is precisely the same as it was in Chapter 8. At income levels below equilibrium, the sum $C + I + G$ would exceed Y; and so inventories would be disappearing, signaling firms that they should raise their production. Conversely, at income levels above equilibrium, $C + I + G$ would be less than Y, so that unwanted inventories would be accumulating and firms would have incentives to cut back production.

Table 11-1, which may usefully be compared to Table 8-1 in Chapter 8 (page 146, illustrates this process. The first three columns give the same consumption and investment schedules that we worked with there. The fourth column reflects the assumption that government purchases will be $80 billion, irrespective of the level of GNP. Summing these three components gives us our new total expenditure schedule in columns 1 and 5.

What, then, is the equilibrium level of GNP? As the table indicates, only a GNP of $800 billion can be an equilibrium, for only at this level is total spending in balance with production.

Figure 11-2 shows the same conclusion graphically. The line labelled C is the same consumption function we used in previous chapters. The line labelled $C + I$ adds the fixed $70 billion in investment to this; again, this amount is taken from previous chapters. Finally, the line labelled $C + I + G$ adds an additional $80 billion in government spending to the $C + I$ line, which gives us our new total expenditure schedule.

Just as in previous chapters, the equilibrium of the economy is at point E, where the total expenditure schedule crosses the 45° line. This is because the 45° line includes all the points at which $C + I + G$ add up to Y. The diagram shows that equilibrium is at a GNP of $800 billion, which consists of $650 billion in consumption, $70 billion in investment, and $80 billion in government purchases. This agrees precisely with Table 11-1, as must be the case. If all this seems

Table 11-1
DERIVATION OF A TOTAL EXPENDITURE SCHEDULE WITH GOVERNMENT PURCHASES

(1) NATIONAL INCOME (Y) (billions of dollars)	(2) CONSUMPTION (C) (billions of dollars)	(3) INVESTMENT (I) (billions of dollars)	(4) GOVERNMENT PURCHASES (G) (billions of dollars)	(5) TOTAL EXPENDITURE (C + I + G) (billions of dollars)
400	330	70	80	480
450	370	70	80	520
500	410	70	80	560
550	450	70	80	600
600	490	70	80	640
650	530	70	80	680
700	570	70	80	720
750	610	70	80	760
800	650	70	80	800
850	690	70	80	840

This table adds government purchases of $80 billion to our model economy. Notice that the equilibrium level of GNP grows to $800 billion, for this is the level at which output is equal to total spending (the sum of $C + I + G$).

Figure 11-2

INCOME DETERMINATION
WITH GOVERNMENT
SPENDING

This diagram adds government purchases of goods and services (G) to the income-expenditure diagrams that we have been using. The C + I + G curve is the total expenditure schedule, and the point where it crosses the 45° line (point E) marks the equilibrium level of GNP. The C + I + G line is parallel to the C + I line because of the assumption that whatever the level of GNP, government spending remains at $80 billion.

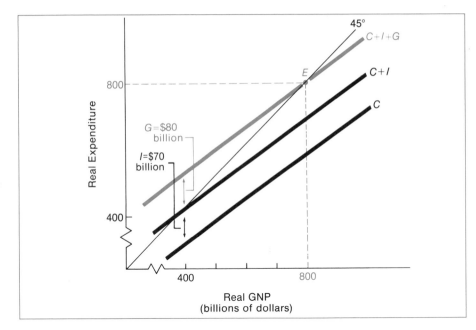

familiar from previous chapters, it should; for the analysis is precisely the same.[1]

In Chapter 9 we stated that when government spending was introduced, the multiplier for G would be the same as the multiplier for autonomous changes in C and I. We can now demonstrate this conclusion.

If you flip back to page 147, you will see that the equilibrium reached there was at a level of output Y = $400 billion. Now, in an economy that is identical with the one in Chapter 8 except for the $80 billion in government spending, we see that the equilibrium is at Y = $800 billion. Thus an $80 billion increment in G (from zero to $80 billion) has pushed up GNP by $400 billion. In this example, then, the multiplier for government spending is $400/$80 = 5, which, you will recall, was also the value of the multiplier for autonomous increases in investment or consumption.

The two multipliers are identical because the logic behind them is identical. In Chapter 9 we studied an example of a multiplier spending chain set in motion when Generous Motors spent $1 million to build a factory. This process could equally well have been kicked off by the federal government buying $1 million worth of new cars from GM. Thereafter, each recipient of additional income would spend 80 percent of it (the assumed marginal propensity to consume), until $5 million in new income had eventually been created.

And the qualification that we placed on the oversimplified multiplier formula in Chapter 10 also applies here. Government spending normally leads to some inflation, which pulls down consumer spending and thus reduces the value of the multiplier below our illustrative figure of 5.

Income Taxes and the Consumption Schedule

You can see, then, that it takes little effort to bring government purchases into our model of income determination. Let us turn our attention next to taxes and, in particular to the personal income tax.

For present purposes, the most important aspect of taxes is that they create a discrepancy between gross national product (GNP) and disposable income (DI), as

[1]An algebraic version of this and other topics discussed here can be found in the appendix to this chapter.

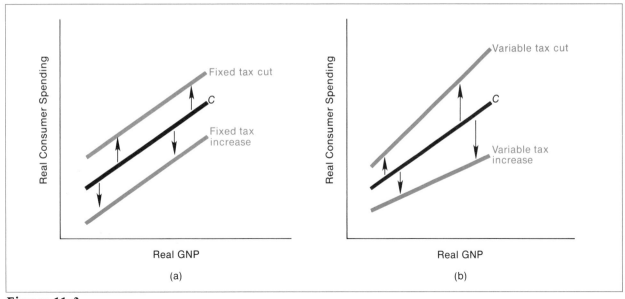

Figure 11-3

HOW TAX POLICY SHIFTS THE CONSUMPTION SCHEDULE

Because consumption depends on disposable income, not GNP, any change in taxes will shift the consumption schedule relating consumption to GNP. Part (a) shows how the curve shifts for changes in taxes of fixed amounts. Part (b) shows how the C curve shifts if the tax cut (or tax increase) is larger at high incomes than at low incomes.

can be seen in the circular flow diagram (Figure 11-1). Tax revenues flow out of the circular flow and into the hands of the government. (The effects of the transfer payments, which enter the circular flow at point 5, will be considered presently.)

We learned in Chapter 7 that there is a close and reliable relationship between consumer spending and *disposable* income. Therefore, if we want to construct a relationship between consumer spending and GNP, we first have to allow for the fact that taxes are deducted from GNP before *DI* is arrived at. The importance of this piece of accounting is that when taxes are increased, disposable income falls—and hence so does consumption—*even if GNP is unchanged.* As a result:

An increase in personal income taxes shifts the consumption schedule in our 45° line diagram downward. Similarly, a reduction in taxes shifts the consumption schedule upward.

The specific manner in which the consumption schedule shifts depends on the nature of the tax change. One way to reduce taxes is to introduce a flat, per person tax credit. The increase in disposable income from this legislation is the *same* regardless of the level of GNP; hence the increase in consumer spending is the same. In a word, the C schedule shifts upward in a parallel manner, as shown in Figure 11-3(a).

But often tax policy is designed to make the change in disposable income depend on the level of income, normally being larger at high income levels than at low ones. This is true, for example, when the government changes tax *rates*. Since this sort of tax policy changes disposable income more when GNP is higher, the upward or downward shift in the C schedule is sharper at high income levels than at low ones. Figure 11-3(b) illustrates how this type of tax policy shifts the consumption schedule.

Tax Policy and Equilibrium Income

We are now in a position to put taxes into our model of income determination. To do this, we must first adjust the consumption schedule we have been using to allow for an income tax.

Table 11-2
DERIVATION OF A CONSUMPTION SCHEDULE WITH INCOME TAXATION

(1) GROSS NATIONAL PRODUCT (billions of dollars)	(2) TAXES (billions of dollars)	(3) DISPOSABLE INCOME (GNP minus taxes) (billions of dollars)	(4) CONSUMPTION (billions of dollars)
250	62.5	187.5	160
300	75.0	225.0	190
350	87.5	262.5	220
400	100.0	300.0	250
450	112.5	337.5	280
500	125.0	375.0	310
550	137.5	412.5	340

Because taxes (column 2) must be subtracted from gross national product (column 1) to get disposable income (column 3), this table shows how an income tax lowers the consumption schedule (column 4) in a concrete example. (Compare column 4 with the consumption schedule in Table 11-1 to see that the C schedule has indeed fallen.)

Table 11-2 does this on the assumption that taxes are 25 percent of GNP. Column 1 shows alternative values of GNP ranging from $250 billion to $550 billion, and column 2 indicates that taxes are always one-quarter of this amount. Column 3 subtracts column 2 from column 1 to arrive at disposable income (DI). Column 4 then shows the amount of consumer spending corresponding to each level of DI. Note that columns 3 and 4 just repeat the consumption function that we studied in Chapter 7. But the consumption schedule that we need for our 45° line diagram relates C to Y, not to DI—that is, it relates spending to total consumer income, not to income net of taxes—and the schedule is therefore found in columns 1 and 4.

To derive the new expenditure schedule for an economy with taxes, we need only replace the old consumption schedule with this new one—that is, we must replace column 2 of Table 11-1 with column 4 of Table 11-2. This is done numerically in Table 11-3, and the results are shown diagrammatically in Figure 11-4. In particular, the expenditure schedule contained in columns 1 and 5 of Table 11-3 is shown as the C + I + G line in Figure 11-4. Naturally, the inclusion of taxes has lowered the expenditure schedule.

Since the 45° line is given in the diagram, we can immediately locate the equilibrium level of GNP at point E. Here, gross national product is $400 billion, consumption is $250 billion, investment is $70 billion, and government purchases

Table 11-3
THE TOTAL EXPENDITURE SCHEDULE WITH TAXES AND GOVERNMENT PURCHASES

(1) GROSS NATIONAL PRODUCT (Y) (billions of dollars)	(2) CONSUMPTION (C) (billions of dollars)	(3) INVESTMENT (I) (billions of dollars)	(4) GOVERNMENT PURCHASES (G) (billions of dollars)	(5) TOTAL EXPENDITURE (C + I + G) (billions of dollars)
250	160	70	80	310
300	190	70	80	340
350	220	70	80	370
400	250	70	80	400
450	280	70	80	430
500	310	70	80	460
550	340	70	80	490

This table replaces the previous consumption schedule with a new one that adjusts for the income tax (as shown in Table 11-2) and shows that the equilibrium level of income is $400 billion.

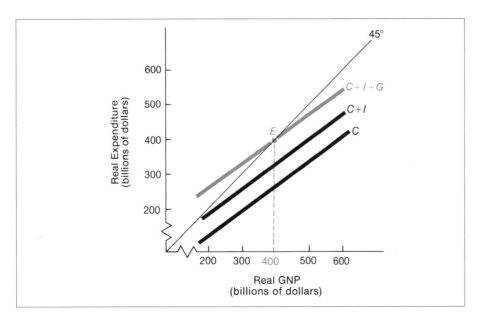

Figure 11-4

INCOME DETERMINATION WITH GOVERNMENT SPENDING AND TAXATION

This diagram adds a 25 percent income tax to the model economy portrayed in Figure 11-2. Because of this, the C schedule is shifted down (and hence the C + I and C + I + G schedules are also shifted down). Equilibrium is at point E, where the C + I + G schedule crosses the 45° line. Thus equilibrium GNP is $400 billion, the same as it was in the economy with no government. This, however, is certainly not a general result; government actions can either raise or lower GNP.

are $80 billion. As we know, full employment may occur above or below Y = $400 billion. If below, there is an inflationary gap. Prices probably will start to rise, pulling the expenditure schedule down and reducing equilibrium GNP. If above, there is a recessionary gap, and history suggests that prices will fall only slowly. In the interim, there will be a period of high unemployment.

In a word, once we adjust the expenditure schedule to include the effects of taxes, the determination of national income proceeds exactly as before. The effects of government spending and taxation, therefore, are fairly straightforward, and can be summarized as follows:

Government purchases of goods and services add to total spending directly through the G component of C + I + G. Taxes indirectly *reduce* total spending by lowering disposable income, and thus reduce the C component of C + I + G. On balance, then, the government's actions may raise or lower the equilibrium level of GNP, depending on how much spending and taxing it does.

Multipliers for Tax Policy

We saw earlier that government purchases (G) have a multiplier effect on GNP. So do changes in tax policy. But because they work indirectly via consumption, the multipliers for tax changes must be worked out in two steps.

Step 1. Before turning to the 45° line diagram, we must figure out what any proposed change in the tax law is likely to do to the consumption schedule.

Step 2. We can then enter this effect as a shift of the C + I + G schedule in the 45° line diagram, and work out the multiplier.

A reduction in income taxes provides a convenient example of this two-step analysis, because we have already done Step 1 in an earlier chapter. Specifically, in Chapter 7 we studied how consumer spending would respond to a cut in income taxes. We concluded that if the tax reduction were viewed as permanent, consumers would increase their spending by an amount equal to the tax cut times the marginal propensity to consume. (If you need review, turn back to pages 119–124.)

Figure 11-5
THE MULTIPLIER FOR A
REDUCTION IN INCOME
TAXES

In this example, the $C + I + G$ schedule is shifted upward, from $C_0 + I + G$ to $C_1 + I + G$, by a tax cut. Equilibrium GNP therefore increases from Y_0 to Y_1.

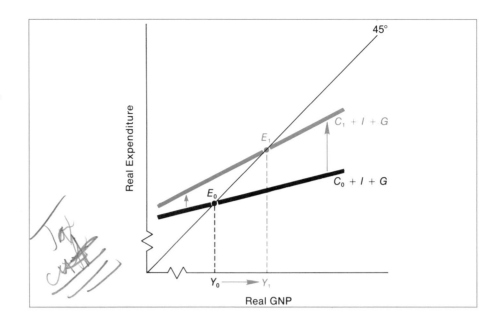

This is the shift that must be entered in the 45° line diagram to complete Step 2, and Figure 11–5 displays such a shift. The tax cut raises the expenditure schedule from $C_0 + I + G$ to $C_1 + I + G$ by raising its C component. The diagram then shows the multiplier effect on GNP, which rises from Y_0 to Y_1.

Government Transfer Payments

Finally, we should mention the last major tool of fiscal policy: **government transfer payments**. How are transfers treated in our models of income determination—like purchases of goods and services (G) or like taxes?

The answer follows readily from the circular flow diagram on page 196 or the accounting identity back on page 116. The important thing to understand about transfer payments is that they intervene between gross national product (Y) and disposable income (DI) in precisely the *opposite* way from income taxes. Specifically, starting with the wages, interest, rents, and profits that constitute the national income, we *subtract* income taxes to calculate disposable income. We do so because these taxes represent the portion of incomes that are *earned* but never *received* by consumers. But then we must *add* transfer payments because they represent sources of income that are *received* though they were not *earned* in the process of production. Thus, transfer payments are basically *negative taxes*, and giving a consumer $1 in the form of a transfer payment is equivalent to reducing her taxes by $1.

So to answer our question, in terms of the 45° line diagram, *increases in transfer payments can be treated simply as decreases in taxes.* And we see that Figure 11–5, which we devised to illustrate a tax cut, can also be used to illustrate a rise in unemployment benefits, or in social security benefits, or in any other such transfer payment. Similarly, the analysis of a decrease in transfer payments would proceed exactly like the analysis of an increase in taxes.

The Multiplier Revisited

We now have acquired most of the tools we need to understand how fiscal policy decisions are made. But, before members of parliament vote on the budget, they should have an idea of the magnitude of the multiplier. Our figure of 5 is too high, and we can now understand how the income tax works to lower its value. But before getting involved in the mechanics, let us understand the basic reason.

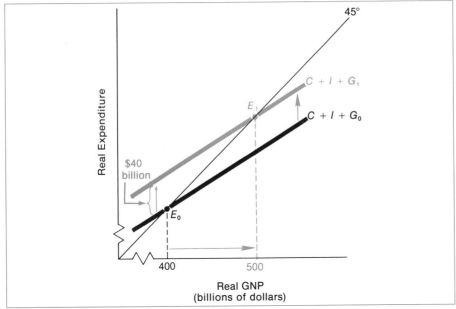

Figure 11-6

THE MULTIPLIER IN THE PRESENCE OF AN INCOME TAX

This diagram illustrates that an economy with an income tax (in this case a 25 percent income tax) has a lower multiplier than an economy without one. Specifically, the $C + I + G$ curve is shifted upward by a $40 billion increase in G, and the diagram shows that equilibrium GNP rises by $100 billion—from $400 billion to $500 billion. The multiplier is, therefore, $100/$40 = $2\frac{1}{2}$, whereas without an income tax it was 5.

As we learned in Chapter 9, the multiplier works through a chain of spending and respending, as one person's expenditure becomes another's income. But through taxation some of the additional income leaks out of the circular flow at each stage. Specifically, if the income tax rate is 25 percent, when Generous Motors spends $1 million on salaries, workers actually receive only $750,000 in *after-tax* (or disposable) income. If workers spend 80 percent of this amount (based on a marginal propensity to consume of 0.8), spending in the next round will be only $600,000. Notice that this is only *60 percent* of the original expenditure, not *80 percent* as in our earlier example. Thus the multiplier chain for each original dollar of spending shrinks from:

$$1 + 0.8 + (0.8)^2 + (0.8)^3 + \ldots = \frac{1}{1 - 0.8} = \frac{1}{0.2} = 5$$

to:

$$1 + 0.6 + (0.6)^2 + (0.6)^3 + \ldots = \frac{1}{1 - 0.6} = \frac{1}{0.4} = 2\frac{1}{2}.$$

This is clearly a very large reduction in the multiplier. We thus have a second reason why our oversimplified multiplier formula of Chapter 9 gives an exaggerated impression of the size of the multiplier:

REASONS WHY THE OVERSIMPLIFIED MULTIPLIER FORMULA IS WRONG

1. It ignores price-level changes, which serve to reduce the size of the multiplier.

2. It ignores income taxes, which serve to reduce the size of the multiplier.

Later in this chapter, and in later chapters, we shall encounter still more reasons.

This conclusion about the multiplier is shown graphically in Figure 11-6, where we have drawn our $C + I + G$ schedules with a slope of 0.6 to reflect an MPC of 0.8, and a tax rate of 25 percent rather than the 0.8 slope that we used previously. The figure depicts the effect of an increase in government purchases of goods and services of $40 billion, which shifts the $C + I + G$ schedule from $C + I + G_0$ to $C + I + G_1$. Equilibrium moves from point E_0 to point E_1—a growth in GNP from $Y = $400 billion to $Y = $500 billion. Thus, if we ignore for the moment any increases in the price level (which would reduce the multiplier shown in Figure 11-6), a $40 billion increment in government spending leads to a $100 billion increment in GNP. So when taxes are included in our model, the multiplier is only $100/$40 = 2½, just as we concluded before.

To test your understanding of the multiplier, consider how the multiplier would work if the government decided to cut taxes by a fixed amount, such as $50 billion. According to our previous analysis, we should multiply $50 billion by the MPC to arrive at the implied shift in the C schedule (Step 1). Since the MPC in our example is 0.8, we obtain a figure of $40 billion. Next, we should enter this shift on a 45° line diagram to see how GNP changes (Step 2). But Figure 11–6 has already done this for us. In showing the effect of an *increase* in government spending of $40 billion, it also shows the effect of a *decrease* in fixed taxes of $50 billion because both policies shift the $C + I + G$ schedule upward by $40 billion. This example illustrates a very general point:

The multiplier for changes in fixed taxes is smaller than the multiplier for changes in government purchases.

The reason is quite straightforward. While G is a direct component of $C + I + G$, taxes are not. Taxes work indirectly, first by changing disposable income and then by changing C. But some of the higher disposable income caused by a tax cut will be saved, not spent, and hence a dollar of tax cut does not have as much effect on spending as does a dollar of G.

✗ Equilibrium Income with Exports and Imports

The complete circular flow diagram that we studied in Chapter 7 (Figure 7–1, page 115) involved one additional injection and leakage of funds which we have so far ignored. The additional sector is the rest of the world. *Exports* (X) represent foreign purchases of our goods and thus constitute the final injection. *Imports* (IM) represent purchases by Canadians that do *not* involve sales by firms producing in Canada, and so they represent an important leakage of funds. Using the same reasoning as before, we now obtain the final restatement of the condition for equilibrium on the demand side of the economy:

For any given price level, equilibrium GNP on the demand side occurs when the sum of consumption, investment, government, and net exports just equals GNP. In symbols:

$$Y = C + I + G + (X - IM.)$$

Let us now see how exports and imports can be brought into our model of income determination and the multiplier.

While both exports and imports depend on many factors, the predominant one is national income. Some of the additional consumption and investment goods that Canadian consumers and firms buy as income rises are foreign goods. So to construct a simple model of an economy with international trade:

We assume that our imports rise as our GNP rises and fall as our GNP falls.

Similarly, our exports are the imports of other countries, so it is natural to assume that our exports depend on *their* GNPs, not on *ours*. Thus:

We assume that our exports are insensitive to our own GNP.

These two assumptions enable us to bring international trade into our income determination model.

Table 11-4
INCOME DETERMINATION WITH INTERNATIONAL TRADE

(1) GROSS NATIONAL PRODUCT (Y) (billions of dollars)	(2) DOMESTIC EXPENDITURE (C + I + G) (billions of dollars)	(3) EXPORTS (X) (billions of dollars)	(4) IMPORTS (IM) (billions of dollars)	(5) NET EXPORTS (X – IM) (billions of dollars)	(6) TOTAL EXPENDITURE (C + I + G + X – IM) (billions of dollars)
250	310	40	25	15	325
300	340	40	30	10	350
350	370	40	35	5	375
400	400	40	40	0	400
450	430	40	45	–5	425
500	460	40	50	–10	450
550	490	40	55	–15	475

Table 11-4 displays the mechanics in a concrete example. The first two columns are an abbreviated version of Table 11-3 on page 200; they show the sum of $C + I + G$—now labelled "Domestic Expenditure"—at alternative levels of GNP.

Columns 3 and 4 provide specific numerical versions of the assumptions we have just listed: Exports are assumed to be $40 billion regardless of (our) GNP, and imports are assumed to rise by $5 billion for every $50 billion rise in GNP. Column 5 simply subtracts imports from exports to get net exports, $X – IM$, and column 6 adds net exports to domestic expenditure to get total expenditures, $C + I + G + X – IM$.

The equilibrium, you can see, comes at $Y = \$400$ billion. At any lower level of GNP, Y is less than $C + I + G + X – IM$, so output will rise. At any higher level of GNP, Y is greater than $C + I + G + X – IM$, so output will fall.

Figure 11-7 shows the same conclusion graphically. The line labelled $C + I + G$ shows how domestic expenditures vary with GNP, and duplicates the $C + I + G$ line in Figure 11-4 (page 201). The line labelled $C + I + G + X – IM$ adds net exports to get total expenditures. (Net exports are therefore shown on the diagram by the vertical distance between the $C + I + G + X – IM$ line and the $C + I + G$ line.) Equilibrium occurs where $Y = C + I + G + X – IM$, that is, where the $C + I + G + X – IM$ line crosses the 45° line—at point E in the diagram.

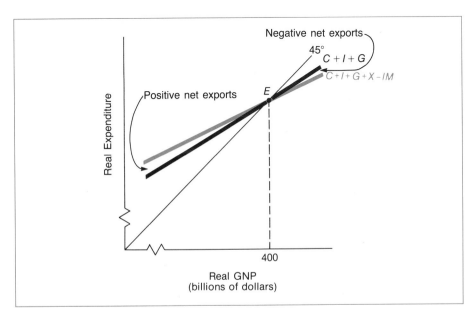

Figure 11-7
EQUILIBRIUM GNP WITH FOREIGN TRADE

In the presence of foreign trade, equilibrium GNP occurs where the $C + I + G + X – IM$ line crosses the 45° line, for here $Y = C + I + G + X – IM$. In the graph, equilibrium is at point E, where GNP is $400 billion. This matches the equilibrium we found in Figure 11-4 (on page 201) without international trade because our example assumes that net exports are zero when $Y = \$400$ billion. In the diagram, net exports are shown by the vertical distance—positive or negative—between the $C + I + G + X – IM$ line and the $C + I + G$ line. The $C + I + G + X – IM$ line is *flatter* than the $C + I + G$ line because net exports decline as GNP rises.

If you turn back to Figure 11-4 on page 201, you will see that $Y = \$400$ billion is the same equilibrium we found in an economy with no international trade. (Figure 11-7 shows this quite clearly, since the $C + I + G$ and $C + I + G + X - IM$ lines both cross the 45° line at $Y = \$400$ billion.) Does international trade therefore not affect domestic income?

Hardly. Notice in the table or the figure that we have constructed our example so that exports exactly balance imports (net exports are zero) when GNP is $400 billion. This is just a coincidence. And because of this coincidence, net exports have no effect on equilibrium GNP.

The Foreign Trade Multiplier

But this is not the normal state of affairs. Let us consider what happens if exports rise to $65 billion while imports remain as in Table 11-4. Table 11-5 shows us that equilibrium now occurs at a GNP of $Y = \$450$ billion. So world trade has raised domestic GNP. In general:

When net exports are positive, world trade raises equilibrium GNP. When net exports are negative, world trade lowers equilibrium GNP.

More specifically, in this example a rise of $25 billion in exports (from $40 billion to $65 billion) leads to a rise of $50 billion in GNP (from $400 billion to $450 billion). So the **foreign trade multiplier** is 2 (= $50/$25).[2] This same conclusion is shown graphically in Figure 11-8, where the line $C + I + G + X_0 - IM$ represents the original expenditure schedule and the line $C + I + G + X_1 - IM$ represents the expenditure schedule after the rise in exports. Equilibrium shifts from point E to point A, and GNP rises by $50 billion.

Notice that the multiplier in this example is 2, whereas in the absence of international trade it was $2\frac{1}{2}$. There is nothing special that makes the multiplier for exports different from any other multiplier. The same multiplier of 2 would apply to an autonomous change in any component of total expenditure.[3] What we have discovered is that:

International trade lowers the value of the multiplier.

[2]EXERCISE: Construct a version of Table 11-4 to show what would happen if imports rose by $25 billion at every level of GNP. You should be able to show that the new equilibrium would be $Y = \$350$ billion.

[3]EXERCISE: Construct a version of Table 11-4 that shows the effects of a rise in domestic expenditure by $25 billion at every level of GNP. Show that the new equilibrium occurs at $Y = \$450$.

Table 11-5
EQUILIBRIUM GNP AFTER A RISE IN EXPORTS

(1) GROSS NATIONAL PRODUCT (Y) (billions of dollars)	(2) DOMESTIC EXPENDITURE ($C + I + G$) (billions of dollars)	(3) EXPORTS (X) (billions of dollars)	(4) IMPORTS (IM) (billions of dollars)	(5) NET EXPORTS ($X - IM$) (billions of dollars)	(6) TOTAL EXPENDITURE ($C + I + G + X - IM$) (billions of dollars)
250	310	65	25	40	350
300	340	65	30	35	375
350	370	65	35	30	400
400	400	65	40	25	425
450	430	65	45	20	450
500	460	65	50	15	475
550	490	65	55	10	500

Figure 11-7 shows us graphically why this is true. Because net exports decline as GNP rises, the total expenditure line is *flatter* in the presence of international trade $(C + I + G + X - IM)$ than in its absence $(C + I + G)$. As we know already, the size of the multiplier depends on the *slope* of the expenditure schedule—steeper expenditure schedules lead to larger multipliers. Since international trade flattens the expenditure schedule, it lowers the multiplier.

Thus international trade gives us yet another reason why the oversimplified multiplier formula first given in Chapter 9 (page 166) overstates the true value of the multiplier.

The Canadian and World Economies

In Canada we export more than one-quarter of our national product, and as a result we are tremendously exposed to business conditions in the rest of the world. Since the lion's share of our exports is to the United States, whenever they have a recession, our spending schedule shifts down by a significant amount (exports decrease), and we have a recession too.

But our heavy reliance on foreign trade is not all bad. Our high tendency to import means that Canada's total expenditure line is quite flat so that our multiplier is quite small. Thus, the openness of our economy is a mixed blessing. It exposes us to additional shocks to aggregate demand, especially from the United States. But it also means that domestically generated shocks have a smaller multiplier effect than they would in an economy less involved in foreign trade.

One final point concerning exports and imports should be stressed. Since both are affected by the exchange rate and tariffs, these variables become important influences on aggregate demand. If foreigners put a tax on their imports (that is, a **tariff**), our exports fall. This shifts our $C + I + G + X - IM$ line down, moving our aggregate-demand curve to the left. Similarly, if we put a tariff on our imports, less domestic spending leaks out of the circular flow, so aggregate demand is increased.

A **tariff** is a tax on imports

When recessions occur, countries are often tempted to raise tariffs to "export" their unemployment problem. However, all countries cannot do this, and an attempt to do this can involve a series of retaliations, which very much restricts world trade. As a result, most Western countries have agreed to avoid using tariffs to stimulate domestic demand.

The exchange rate is also an important influence on exports and imports. The lower the foreign value of the Canadian dollar, the less it costs foreigners to buy

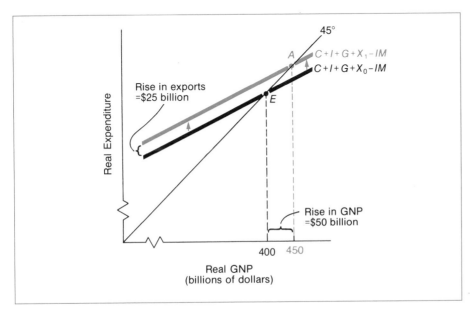

Figure 11-8
THE FOREIGN TRADE MULTIPLIER

This diagram shows a $25 billion increase in exports as a vertical shift of the total expenditure schedule from $C + I + G + X_0 - IM$, to $C + I + G + X_1 - IM$. As a result, equilibrium shifts from point E to point A, and GNP rises from $400 billion to $450 billion. The multiplier is therefore 2 (= $50/$25).

our exports and the more it costs Canadians to buy foreign imports. Thus:

A depreciation of the Canadian dollar raises net exports $(X - IM)$, shifts the $C + I + G + X - IM$ line up, and so moves the aggregate-demand curve to the right. For the same reason, an appreciation of the Canadian dollar lowers net exports and shifts the aggregate-demand curve to the left. Our general summary is:

Government expenditures, tax rates, transfer payments, exports, tariffs, and the exchange rate are all important variables that shift the aggregate-demand curve.

Planning Expansive Fiscal Policy

Now, at last, you are ready to pretend that you are a member of parliament deciding how to respond to the finance minister's proposed budget. Suppose that the economy would have a GNP of $400 billion if last year's budget were simply repeated. Suppose further that your goal is to achieve a fully employed labour force and that staff economists tell you that your goal can be achieved with a GNP of approximately $500 billion. Further, just to keep the calculations manageable, suppose that the price level is fixed. (We will drop this unrealistic assumption in just a few pages.) What budget should you support?

First we must consider what options are available if we want to raise GNP by $100 billion. This chapter has taught us that the government can raise government purchases, reduce taxes, or increase transfer payments by enough to close the recessionary gap between actual and potential GNP.

Figure 11-9 illustrates the problem, and its cure through higher government spending, on our 45° line diagram. Figure 11-9 (a) shows the equilibrium of the economy if no changes are made in the budget. Except for the full-employment line at $Y = \$500$ billion, the corresponding recessionary gap, and the extended label for the total spending line, it looks like Figure 11-4. With an expenditure multiplier of 2, you can figure out that an additional $50 billion of government spending will be needed to push the GNP up $100 billion and eliminate this gap ($100 billion/2 = $50 billion).

So you might vote to raise G from $G_0 = \$80$ billion to $G_1 = \$130$ billion, hoping to move the $C + I + G + X - IM$ line in Figure 11-9 (a) out to the position indicated in Figure 11-9 (b), thereby achieving full employment. Of course you might prefer to achieve this fiscal stimulus by lowering income taxes rather than increasing expenditures. Or you might prefer to rely on more generous transfer payments. The point is that there are a variety of budgets capable of pushing the economy up to full employment by increasing GNP by $100 billion. Figure 11-9 applies equally well to any of them.

Planning Restrictive Fiscal Policy

The preceding example assumed that the basic problem of fiscal policy is to overcome a deficiency of aggregate demand, as is often the case. But at other times the problem is that demand is excessive relative to the economy's capacity to produce. In this case, fiscal policy should assume a restrictive stance in order to reduce inflation.

It does not take much imagination to run our previous analysis in reverse. If, under a continuation of current budget policies, there would be an inflationary gap, there are fiscal policy tools that can eliminate it. Either by cutting spending programs out of the budget, or by raising taxes, or by some combination of these policies, the government can pull the $C + I + G + X - IM$ schedule down to a noninflationary position and achieve an equilibrium at full employment.

Notice the difference between this way of eliminating an inflationary gap and the natural self-correcting mechanism of the economy that we discussed in Chapter

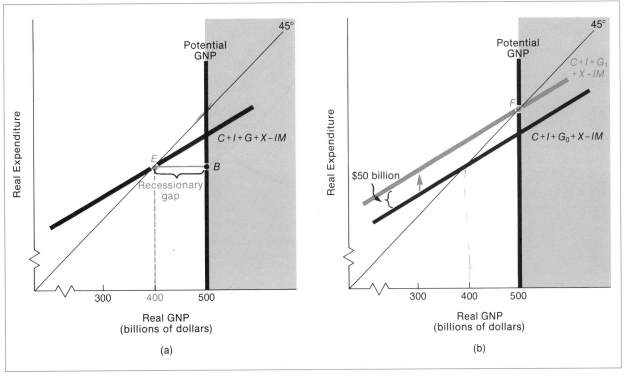

Figure 11-9

FISCAL POLICY TO ELIMINATE A RECESSIONARY GAP

This diagram shows, with more precision than can actually be achieved in practice, how fiscal policy can eliminate a recessionary gap. Part (a) shows the gap: Equilibrium GNP ($400 billion) falls short of potential GNP ($500 billion). Part (b) shows how fiscal policy—by moving the $C + I + G + X - IM$ line up just enough—can wipe out this gap and restore full employment. With a multiplier of 2, a rise in G of $50 billion or a cut in taxes large enough to shift C up by $50 billion would do the trick.

10. There we observed that if the economy were left to its own devices, a cumulative but self-limiting process of inflation eventually would eliminate the inflationary gap and return the economy to full employment. Here we see that it is not necessary to put the economy through the inflationary wringer. Instead, a restrictive fiscal policy can limit aggregate demand to the level that the economy can produce at full employment.

The Choice Between Spending Policy and Tax Policy

In principle, fiscal policy can nudge the economy in the desired direction equally well by changing government spending or by changing taxes. For example, if the government wants to expand the economy, it can raise G or lower taxes. Either policy shifts the total expenditure schedule upward, as depicted in Figure 11-9, thereby raising the equilibrium GNP on the demand side.

In terms of our aggregate demand and supply diagram, either policy shifts the aggregate-demand curve outward from D_0D_0 to D_1D_1 in Figure 11-10. As a result, the economy's equilibrium moves from point E to point A. Both real GNP and the price level rise. As this diagram points out, any combination of higher spending and lower taxes that produces the same aggregate-demand curve leads to the same increases in real GNP and prices.

How, then, do we decide whether it is better to raise spending or to cut taxes? The answer depends mainly on how large a public sector we want, and this is a contentious issue.

One point of view, expressed most eloquently in the writings of Canadian-born

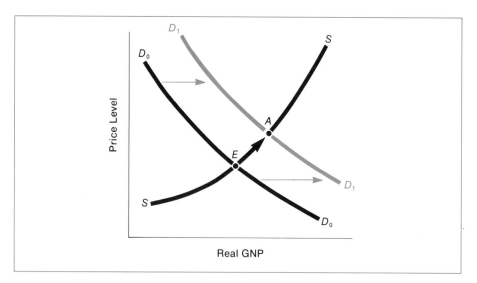

Figure 11-10

EXPANSIONARY FISCAL POLICY

Any of a variety of expansionary fiscal policies will push the aggregate-demand curve outward to the right, as depicted by the shift from D_0D_0 to D_1D_1, in this aggregate-supply and demand diagram. The economy's equilibrium moves upward to the right along aggregate-supply curve SS, from point E to point A. Comparing A with E, we note that output is higher but prices are also higher. The expansionary policy has caused some inflation.

economist John Kenneth Galbraith, is that there is something amiss when a country as wealthy as the United States has such an impoverished public sector. In Galbraith's view, America's most pressing needs are not for more designer jeans, sports cars, and video games, but rather for better schools, more efficient public-transportation systems, and cleaner city streets and lakes. Those who agree with him believe that we should *increase G* when the economy needs stimulus and pay for these improved public services by *increasing taxes* when the economy needs to be reined in.

An opposing opinion, advocated by conservative politicians in all the Western countries, is that the government sector is already too large; that we are foolish to rely on government to do things that private individuals and businesses could do better on their own; and that the growth of government interferes too much in our everyday lives and in so doing circumscribes our freedom. Those who hold this view argue for *tax cuts* when macroeconomic considerations call for expansionary fiscal policy, and for *reductions in public spending* when restrictive policy is required.

This is an important point, and one on which so many people are confused. Too often the use of fiscal policy for economic stabilization is erroneously associated with a large and growing public sector—that is, with "big government." This need not be the case. Individuals favouring a smaller public sector can advocate an active fiscal policy just as well as those who favour a larger public sector. Advocates of big government budgets should seek to expand demand (when appropriate) through higher government spending and contract demand (when appropriate) through tax increases. By contrast, advocates of small public budgets should seek to expand demand by cutting taxes and reduce demand by cutting expenditures.

There are potentially legitimate arguments against an active stabilization policy, as we noted in Chapter 10. For example, the downward rigidity of wages may be strengthened if workers can count on the government's active commitment to full employment. But this issue is entirely separate from questions concerning the relative worth of big or small government.

Some Harsh Realities

The mechanics outlined so far in this chapter make the fiscal policy planner's job look rather simple. The elementary diagrams suggest, rather misleadingly, that the authorities can drive GNP to any level they please simply by manipulating their spending and tax programs. It seems as though they should be able to hit the full-employment bull's-eye every time.

But, in fact, a better analogy is shooting through dense fog at an erratically moving target with a gun of uncertain accuracy. The target is moving because, in the real world, the investment schedule (and, to a lesser extent, the consumption schedule) is constantly shifting on account of changes in expectations, new technological breakthroughs, changes in consumers' tastes, and the like. Furthermore, the export and import schedules often shift due to unforeseen events in other countries. This means that the policies decided upon today, which are to take effect at some future date, may no longer be appropriate by the time that future date rolls around. Policy must be based, to some extent, on *forecasting*, and no one has yet discovered a foolproof method of economic forecasting. Since our forecasting ability is so modest, and because fiscal policy decisions sometimes take a long time to be carried out, the government may occasionally find itself fighting the last inflation just when the new recession gets under way.

A second misleading feature of our diagrams is that multipliers are not known with as much precision as our examples may suggest. Thus, while the "best guess" may be that a $10 billion cut in government purchases will reduce GNP by $20 billion, the actual outcome may be as little as $12 billion or as much as $28 billion. It is therefore impossible to "fine tune" every wobble out of the economy's growth path through fiscal policy; economics is simply not that precise a science. The point is even more cogent with respect to tax policy. For example, we get involved in trying to guess whether consumers will view tax changes as permanent or temporary.

A third complication is that our target—full-employment GNP—may be only dimly visible, as if through a fog. Especially when the economy's last experience with full employment is very far in the past, economists may have difficulty estimating the GNP level that represents full employment. In fact, as was mentioned in Chapter 6, there is a great deal of controversy over how much unemployment constitutes "full employment" right now.

Finally, in trying to decide whether to push the economy out of a position of unemployment, legislators would like to know what the inflationary costs will be. As Figure 11-10 reminds us, any expansionary fiscal policy that closes a recessionary gap by increasing aggregate demand also pushes prices higher, that is, causes more inflation. This undesired side-effect may make the government hesitant to use fiscal policy to end a recession.

Is there a way out of this dilemma? Can we stimulate the economy by fiscal policy without worsening inflation? During the late 1970s and early 1980s, a small but influential minority of economists and politicians argued that we could. They called their approach "supply-side economics."

The Idea Behind Supply-Side Tax Cuts

The central idea of supply-side economics is that certain types of tax cuts increase aggregate supply at the same time as they increase aggregate demand. What kinds of measures are these? The basic principle is simple to state but not quite so simple to carry out.

If taxes can be cut in such a way that people's incentives to work are increased, *and if people actually respond to these incentives*, then the tax system can be used to increase the total amount of labour that is available for employment. Similarly, if the tax system is changed in ways that encourage households to save more and businesses to invest more, *and if people respond to these changes in the way that policy-makers hope*, then the total amount of capital that is available for use will begin to rise. Both sorts of tax policies, if successful, increase aggregate supply.

Figure 11-11 illustrates this conclusion on an aggregate supply and demand

Figure 11-11

THE IDEA BEHIND SUPPLY-SIDE TAX CUTS

The basic idea of supply-side cuts is that if they achieve their desired objective, they will cause the economy's aggregate-supply curve to shift outward to the right. For example, the aggregate-supply curve might be S_1S_1 under a program of supply-side tax cuts, whereas it would only be S_0S_0 without such tax cuts. In this case, if aggregate demand is the same in either case, the tax cuts would lead to the equilibrium point B instead of the equilibrium point A. Comparing B with A, we see that the program leads to lower prices and higher output.

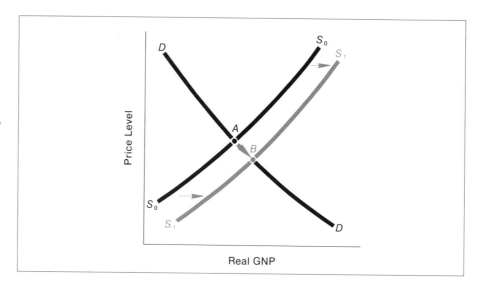

diagram. If policy measures can shift the economy's aggregate supply to position S_1S_1, then prices will be lower and output higher than if the aggregate-supply curve were S_0S_0. Policy-makers will have succeeded in reducing inflation and raising real output (lowering unemployment) at the same time. The trade-off between inflation and unemployment will have been defeated. This is the goal of supply-side economics.

What sorts of policies do supply-siders advocate? There is a long list, but most supply-side tax cuts are aimed at stimulating capital formation. For example:

1. **Accelerated Depreciation.** As mentioned in Chapter 8, a company investing in a machine or factory is not permitted to take the entire cost of that asset as a tax write-off in the year it is purchased. Instead, it must spread the cost over the lifetime of the asset in a series of **depreciation allowances**, which are annual tax deductions that in total add up to the value of the asset. Naturally, firms prefer to take their depreciation allowances sooner rather than later, because higher depreciation allowances in the early years of an investment mean lower immediate tax burdens.

    Many supply-siders argue that an effective way to provide greater incentives for investment is to speed up ("accelerate") depreciation allowances. There are many ways to do this, and the details are best left to courses on accounting. However, one very straightforward way is simple enough to explain right here. If the government reduces the "lifetime" of a machine for tax purposes from, say, seven years to five, then obviously firms will get the tax savings from depreciation faster. This is precisely the course of action taken in Canada. Since 1972, the official lifetime (for tax purposes) of a machine in the manufacturing and processing sector has been two years.

2. **Reducing the Corporation Income Tax.** Another type of tax cut that supply-siders often favour is reducing the statutory rates of taxation on corporate income. By letting companies retain more of their pre-tax income, it is argued, government will provide both greater investment incentives (by raising the profitability of investments) and more investable funds (by letting companies keep more of their earnings). This policy has also been implemented in Canada. In 1972 the main corporate tax rate in the manufacturing and processing sectors was cut from 50 percent to 40 percent.

A **capital gain** is an increase in the market value of a piece of property, such as a common stock or a parcel of land, that occurs during the period between when it is bought and when it is sold. A **capital loss** is a decrease in that property's value.

3. **Reducing Taxes on Capital Gains.** Many investments, particularly financial investments such as stocks and bonds, often lead to **capital gains and losses.** For example, if Mr. Cabot purchases Canadian Pacific shares in 1960

for $10,000 and sells them in 1985 for $100,000, the law says he has reaped a $90,000 *capital gain*, and must pay tax. Supply-siders argue that lower taxes on capital gains would provide greater incentives for individuals and firms to invest more. Partly for these reasons, the Canadian government taxes capital gains at only half the normal rates.[4]

Not all supply-side tax cuts are aimed at spurring investment. If there is to be more investment, someone must be providing the saving to finance it. Thus, supply-siders typically favour:

4. ***Reducing Taxes on Income from Savings.*** One extreme form of this proposal would simply exempt from taxation all income from interest and dividends. Since income must be either consumed or saved, this would, in effect, change our present personal income tax into a tax on consumer spending. While this has not been adopted explicitly in Canada, our income-tax system allows a substantial part of interest income to be exempt. Registered Retirement Savings Plans (RRSPs), Registered Home Ownership Savings Plans (RHOSPs), and the $1,000 exemption for interest earnings are the three most common provisions used to shield the earnings on savings from tax.

Supply-siders recognize that capital is not the only factor of production. Aggregate supply can be expanded by increasing the supply of labour services as well. For this reason, they generally advocate:

5. ***Lowering Personal Income-Tax Rates.*** Such cuts, they argue, encourage people to work harder and for longer hours, and induce them to spend more time at productive activities and less time worrying about how to avoid taxes. In fact, sharp cuts in personal taxes have been the cornerstone of the economic strategies of both Thatcher in England and Reagan in the United States.

Aggregate supply depends on the state of technology and the availability of raw materials. So supply-siders are interested in using the tax system to encourage technological progress and resource exploration by offering:

6. ***Tax Credits for Research and Exploration.*** Canadian corporate tax law has consistently allowed companies that spend money on research and development (R & D) and resource exploration to have dramatic reductions in their tax bills. The hope is obvious: Tax incentives should increase spending on R & D, and more R & D should lead to improvements in technology. Similarly, tax incentives should increase spending on drilling for oil (etc.), and more energy resources and other raw materials should lead to lower business costs.

Finally, business costs can be decreased by:

7. ***Reducing Sales and Payroll Taxes.*** If firms are allowed to pay less to the government in the form of sales taxes or Canada pension and unemployment insurance contributions, they can afford to lower their selling prices (so the aggregate-supply curve should shift down). Given the government's goals at the time, it is unfortunate that the large government budget deficit forced increases in all these levies in 1983 and 1984. Since these tax increases shift the aggregate supply curve to the left, they result in stagflation.

Let us suppose, for the moment, that a successful supply-side tax cut is enacted to help close a recessionary gap. Since *both* aggregate demand *and* aggregate supply increase simultaneously, the economy may be able to avoid the painful inflationary consequences of an expansionary fiscal policy that were shown in Figure 11–10.

Figure 11–12 illustrates this conclusion. The two aggregate-demand curves and the initial aggregate-supply curve S_0S_0 are carried over directly from Figure 11–10. But we have introduced an additional supply curve, S_1S_1, to reflect the

---

[4]More will be said about capital gains taxation, which is viewed by many as a major tax shelter, in *Microeconomics*, Chapter 18.

Figure 11-12

A SUCCESSFUL SUPPLY-
SIDE TAX REDUCTION

A tax cut specifically aimed at the supply side, if successful, will shift *both* aggregate demand and aggregate supply to the right. In this diagram, equilibrium is initially at point E, where demand curve D_0D_0 intersects supply curve S_0S_0. After the supply-side tax cut, the aggregate-demand curve is D_1D_1 and the aggregate-supply curve is S_1S_1, so equilibrium is at point C. As compared with the results of a tax cut that works only on the demand side (point A), the supply-side tax cut raises output more and prices less.

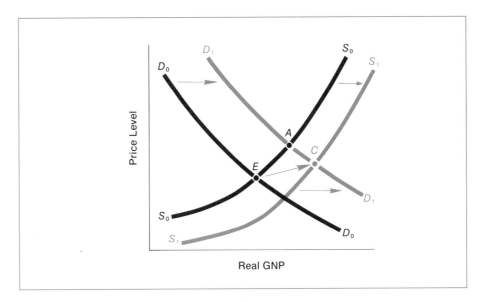

successful supply-side tax cut depicted in Figure 11–11. The equilibrium of the economy moves from E to C, whereas with a conventional demand-side tax cut it would have moved from E to A. As compared with point A, output is higher and prices are lower at point C.

A good deal, you say! Indeed it is. The supply-side argument is extremely attractive. It certainly was appealing to Ronald Reagan in 1980 and, as a consequence, it has had a profound influence on U.S. economic policy. Also, as just noted, the Canadian government has applied supply-side reasoning for years. But does the supply-side approach work in practice? Can we actually do what is depicted in Figure 11–12? Let us consider some difficulties.

Some Flies in the Ointment

Supply-side economics has been controversial. Supporters have touted it as a painless remedy for all our economic ills. Detractors have derided it as wishful thinking. But the critics of supply-side economics rarely question the goals of the program. Nor do they question the basic idea that the tax system can be used to improve incentives. They argue, instead, that supply-siders exaggerate the beneficial effects of supply-side tax cuts and ignore some undesirable side effects. Here is a list of the main objections to supply-side tax cuts that have fuelled the debate.

1. ***The Uncertainty of Supply-Side Effects***. The first objection is that supply-siders are simply too optimistic: We really do not know how to do what Figure 11–9 shows. It is easy to design tax cuts that, for example, make working more *attractive* financially; that is, which raise take-home pay. All you have to do is cut tax rates. Doing this, however, does not guarantee that people will actually work more. Instead, they may find themselves able to afford the goods and services they want with fewer hours of labour and react by working less. Similarly, if tax cuts raise the return on savings, people may find their savings goals easier to achieve and react by saving less.

   Most of the statistical evidence suggests that it is unrealistic to expect tax reductions to lead to very substantial increases in either labour supply or household savings.

2. ***Demand-Side Effects***. The second objection is that supply-siders underestimate the effects of tax cuts on aggregate demand. If you cut personal taxes, individuals *may possibly* work more, but they *will certainly* spend more. If you reduce business taxes and successfully encourage expansion of industrial

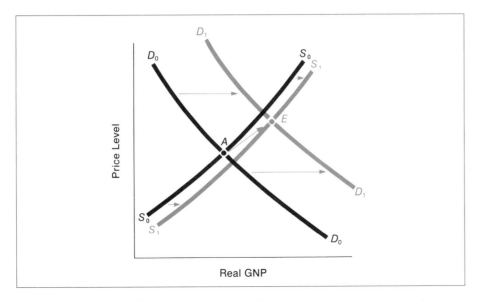

Figure 11-13
A MORE PESSIMISTIC VIEW
OF SUPPLY-SIDE TAX CUTS
If the effect of supply-side tax
initiatives on the aggregate-supply
curve is actually much smaller
than suggested by Figure 11-11,
the anti-inflationary impact will be
correspondingly smaller. As you
can see in this diagram, it is
possible that a large shift in the
aggregate-demand curve could
overwhelm the favourable effects
of the tax cuts on the price level.

capacity, business firms will necessarily demand more investment goods.

Reagan's response to this criticism was to link the tax cuts to reductions in government spending that would cancel out the demand-side effects. Let us review the reasoning briefly. We learned in earlier chapters that tax cuts raise aggregate demand while reductions in government spending reduce it. Thus, whatever demand stimulus is caused by the tax cuts, there is some expenditure reduction big enough to cancel its demand-side effects. By combining these two programs into a fiscal package, it may be possible to obtain the situation depicted in Figure 11-11: a rise in aggregate supply with no accompanying rise in aggregate demand.

The problem with this strategy is that if *large* tax cuts are made, then *large* spending cuts must accompany them. Many observers in 1981 worried that the expenditure cuts proposed by President Reagan, while substantial, were not nearly as large as the tax cuts. They turned out to be right.

If we put these two objections together, we are led to Figure 11-13. Here we depict a small outward shift in the aggregate-supply curve (which reflects the first objection) and a large outward shift of the aggregate-demand curve (which reflects the second). The result is that the economy's equilibrium moves from point A (the intersection of S_0S_0 and D_0D_0) to point E (the intersection of S_1S_1 and D_1D_1). Prices rise as output expands. The outcome differs only a little from the straight "demand side" fiscal stimulus depicted in Figure 11-10 (page 210).

3. **Problems in Timing**. The most popular types of supply-side tax cuts in Canada seek to encourage greater business investment by, for example, making depreciation allowances more generous. But investment does not create new industrial capacity overnight. It takes time to plan new investment projects, arrange the financing, get delivery on machinery, build factories, and then actually put these things into operation. The crucial point is that the *expenditures* on investment goods come before the *expansion of capacity*. Thus, even if supply-side policies are successful, aggregate *demand* expands first and aggregate *supply* follows later.

4. **Limited Effect on Inflation**. Supply-side policies were offered as a cure for inflation. Unfortunately, even a very successful supply-side program can be expected to make only a small dent in the inflation rate.

Inflation depends on the *difference* between the rates at which the *aggregate-demand* and *aggregate-supply* curves are shifting outward over time. Aggregate supply is, as a matter of definition, the product of the amount of labour available times the amount of output produced by each hour of labour—

The **productivity of labour** is the amount of output produced per hour of labour input.

the **productivity of labour**. There is little that can be done to affect the long-run growth rate of labour supply, which depends fundamentally on population growth. Thus, if supply-side policies are to increase the growth rate of aggregate supply, they must focus on productivity.

But the historical growth rate of productivity in Canada is only about 2 percent per year.[5] A 50 percent improvement in productivity growth (from 2 percent to 3 percent) would constitute a truly remarkable achievement. No serious economist thinks we really known how to achieve such a feat. But even a supply-side miracle of this magnitude would add only one percentage point to the growth rate of aggregate supply, and therefore would lower the inflation rate by only about one percentage point, a very small effect.

5. *Effect on the Distribution of Income*. The preceding objections all pertained to the likely effects of supply-side policies on aggregate supply and demand. But there is a very different problem that bears mention: Most supply-side initiatives would increase income inequality. Why? Because, while raising the incomes of the wealthiest members of our society may not be their primary aim, most supply-side cuts cannot help but concentrate benefits on the rich simply because it is the rich who earn most of the capital gains, interest, and dividends, and who own most of the corporations.

Indeed, this tilt toward the rich is almost an inescapable corollary of supply-side logic. The basic aim of supply-side economics is to increase the incentive for working and investing; that is, to increase the gap between the rewards of those who succeed in the economic game (by working hard, investing well, and so on) and those who fail. It can hardly be surprising therefore, that supply-side policies tend to increase economic inequality.

6. *Losses of Tax Revenue*. You can hardly help noticing that most of the policies suggested by supply-siders involve reductions in one tax or another. Thus, unless some other tax is raised or spending is cut, supply-side tax cuts are bound to raise the government budget deficit. Critics of President Reagan's program, for example, argued that such large tax cuts would leave monstrous budget deficits for years to come.

Once again, extreme supply-siders answered this objection by denying the obvious. Lower tax rates, they argued, need not lead to lower tax revenues if the tax base grows quickly enough. For example, suppose the GNP starts at $400 billion when the tax rate is 25 percent; so the government collects $100 billion in tax revenues. Then, if the tax rate is cut to 20 percent, but GNP grows to $500 billion as a result, tax receipts will remain at $100 billion. Reasoning like this led extreme supply-siders like Professor Arthur Laffer of the University of California at Los Angeles to predict that the Reagan tax cuts would actually lead to more tax revenue and smaller budget deficits![6]

To the vast majority of economists, this claim was implausible. In the preceding example, if the GNP starts at $400 billion, a cut in the tax rate from 25 percent to 20 percent lowers tax revenues initially by $20 billion (from $100 billion to $80 billion). For this to cause a $100 billion increase in the GNP (from $400 billion to $500 billion), the tax multiplier would have to be $100/$20 = 5. This is about three times as large as the actual multiplier. Turning from hypothetical examples to reality, U.S. federal tax revenues did not rise, but rather fell sharply after the 1981–83 tax cuts—just as the critics had predicted. And the large budget deficits that ensued have been a major economic issue ever since.[7]

[5] See Chapter 20 for a full discussion of productivity growth in Canada and why it has slowed in recent years.

[6] The famous, or infamous, Laffer Curve is a graph showing how tax revenues first rise, but then fall, as the tax rate rises from zero, to 10 percent, then 20 percent, and so on, up to 100 percent. Therefore, if tax rates are high enough, we can actually raise more revenue by cutting rates.

[7] Chapter 17 is devoted to the causes and consequences of budget deficits.

Corporate Tax Concessions in Canada

Canadians have been actively involved with supply-side economics, both at the academic and policy levels. The acknowledged intellectual leader of this school of thought is Robert Mundell, a Canadian economist who currently teaches at Columbia University. (Mundell has also taught at the universities of British Columbia, Waterloo, McGill, Stanford, Chicago, and Bologna.) Mundell had worked out the principles underlying the supply-side approach a full decade before the terms "supply-side" and "Reaganomics" were invented.

At the policy level, the Canadian federal government has been using corporate tax concessions as its favourite instrument of fiscal policy for more than 30 years. Its intention has been to stimulate investment spending. While this policy is an attempt to raise aggregate demand, and therefore create jobs while the new equipment is constructed and installed, the government has consistently stressed the supply-side motivation of their policies. The idea is to get new and better equipment in place so that Canadian labour is more productive and our level of potential GNP is increased.

One indication of the extent to which these policies were used is the fact that in 1969 Statistics Canada began publishing two separate volumes entitled *Corporation Taxation Statistics* and *Corporation Financial Statistics*. Mr. Duffett, the Chief Statistician at the time, gave the following explanation for the two volumes:

During the early part of the twenty-year period that the Department of National Revenue compiled financial statistics on corporations, corporation profit was essentially the same as taxable income and therefore it was possible to satisfy both needs with one set of statistics. However, during this period (1944–64) and particularly during the last decade, taxation legislation, through special provisions, has been used to an increasing extent as an instrument of government policy.... As a result, it was becoming increasingly difficult to use the same information to satisfy the needs for data of both corporation finance generally and corporation income taxation.*

Perhaps the most dramatic use of corporate tax concessions came in the 1972 Budget, when the corporate profits tax rate was cut from 50 percent to 40 percent, and firms in the manufacturing and processing sector were allowed to claim for tax purposes that machines and equipment were fully worn out within two years of purchase. An election occurred before the budget was passed, and the Liberals just stayed in office with a minority government. Most analysts credit the NDP's criticism of the tax concessions as an important reason for the decline in the government's support (although others criticized, too, as the cartoon from the *Toronto Star* indicates). The political problem facing the Con-

Tit for tat

Reprinted by permission of the *Toronto Star*.

servatives was that they wanted to support the tax concessions, but they had to express concern about their unpopularity. They decided to support the government, provided the government conducted a study of the effectiveness of the tax cuts.

In the study, the Department of Finance surveyed companies and simply asked them whether the tax cuts had *any* effect on their investment spending. When the answers were published in 1975, we learned that only 47 percent of the firms said "yes"! This is a surprising answer, since the tax concessions definitely increase a firm's profits. However, the fact that many firms in Canada are foreign-owned may explain this surprise. When foreign-owned firms file for corporation profits taxes in their home country (say, the United States) they are allowed a tax credit equal to the amount of taxes already paid in other countries (like Canada). Thus, if the Canadian government collects less revenue as a result of our tax concessions, the foreign-owned firm qualifies for precisely that much less of a tax credit when filing in the United States. The end result is that the Canadian government has given revenue to the American government, and the firm (and its investment decision) is unaffected.

Despite these and other problems, corporate tax concessions formed a major part of the 1977 and 1983 federal government Budgets. In 1983, the motivation was simply to avoid bankruptcies that were threatening Canadian-owned firms because of the severity of the recession.

*Corporation Taxation Statistics (Ottawa: Revenue Canada, 1965), Introduction.

Toward Assessment of Supply-Side Economics

On balance, most economists have reached the following conclusions about supply-side tax initiatives:

1. The likely effectiveness of supply-side tax cuts depends very much on what kinds of taxes are cut. Tax reductions aimed at stimulating business investment can pack more punch than tax reductions aimed at getting people to work longer hours or to save more.

2. Such tax cuts probably *will* increase aggregate supply, but the increase in aggregate supply will come much more slowly than the increase in aggregate demand.

3. The demand-side effects are very likely to be larger than the supply-side effects.

4. Supply-side policies can be expected to make, at most, only a small dent in the inflation rate.

5. Supply-side income-tax cuts are likely to benefit the rich more than the poor. However, this defect does not hold for sales-tax cuts.

6. Supply-side tax cuts are almost certain to lead to bigger, not smaller, budget deficits.

But this list does not close the books on the issue. It does not even tell us whether supply-side tax cuts are a good idea or a bad one. Some people will look over this list and decide that they favour supply-side tax cuts; indeed, the Canadian government budgets have included an almost endless series of corporate tax concessions over the last 20 years. Also, many economists and most of the U.S. Congress supported President Reagan's program in 1981. Others, perusing the same facts, will reach the opposite conclusion. We cannot say that either group is "wrong" because, like almost every economic policy, supply-side economics has its pros and cons. While the claims made by the most ardent supply-siders in the United States were clearly excessive, there is definitely some truth in supply-side economics. Reductions in marginal tax rates do improve economic incentives. Sales-tax reductions definitely lower prices. Hence, any specific supply-side tax cut must be judged on its individual merits.

How did things work out in the United States after the Reagan tax cuts of 1981? Although supply-siders had predicted an exuberant boom, the U.S. economy in 1981–82 suffered through its worst recession since the Great Depression. But, when recovery finally came, the economy grew rapidly in 1983—confounding many pessimistic forecasters. There has been very little evidence to date that supply-side incentives have increased saving, investment, or labour supply to any noticeable degree. But inflation did fall rapidly in the early 1980s. Finally, income inequality did grow larger and, as already mentioned, the budget deficit grew ominously.

In a nutshell, then, the specific supply-side tax cuts enacted in the United States in 1981 appear to have had some beneficial effects and some harmful ones—as was to be expected.

Summary

1. The government's fiscal policy is its plan for managing aggregate demand through its spending and taxing programs. It is announced and described in the federal budget.

2. Government purchases of goods and services (G) and net exports (X – IM) are direct components of the total spending. Therefore, they have the same multiplier as do autonomous changes in consumption or investment.

3. When income taxes are introduced, there is a dif-

ference between GNP and disposable income. Since consumer spending (C) depends on disposable income, any change in taxes will shift the consumption schedule on a 45° line diagram.

4. Shifts in the consumption function caused by tax policy are subject to the same multiplier as autonomous shifts in the consumption schedule. However, the income tax reduces the size of this common multiplier just as it reduces the size of the multiplier for G, I, or X. High tendencies to import also reduce the size of the multiplier.

5. Government transfer payments are treated like negative taxes, not like government purchases of goods and services, because they influence total spending only indirectly through their effect on consumption.

6. The net effect of the government on aggregate demand—and hence on equilibrium output and prices—depends on whether the expansionary effects of its spending are greater or smaller than the contractionary effects of its taxes.

7. If the multipliers were known precisely, it would be possible to plan fiscal policies to eliminate either a recessionary or an inflationary gap. Recessionary gaps can be cured by raising G, cutting taxes, or increasing transfers. Inflationary gaps can be cured by cutting G, raising taxes, or reducing transfers.

8. Active stabilization policy can be carried out either by means that tend to expand the size of government (by raising either G or taxes when appropriate) or by means that hold back the size of government (by reducing either G or taxes when appropriate).

9. Expansionary fiscal policy can lessen recessions, but it normally exacts a cost in terms of higher inflation. This dilemma has led to interest in "supply-side" tax cuts designed to stimulate aggregate supply.

10. Supply-side tax cuts aim to push the economy's aggregate-supply curve outward to the right. If successful, they can expand the economy and reduce inflation at the same time—a desirable outcome.

11. But critics point out five problems of supply-side tax cuts: They also stimulate aggregate demand; the beneficial effects on aggregate supply may be quite small; the demand-side effects occur before the supply-side effects; they make the income distribution more unequal; and large tax cuts lead to large budget deficits.

12. Supply-side policies can be expected to make only a small contribution to the long-term battle against inflation.

Concepts for Review

Fiscal policy
Government purchases of goods and
    services (G)
Net exports (X – IM)

Tariffs
Government transfer payments
Effect of income taxes and imports
    on the multiplier

Supply-side tax cuts
Depreciation allowances
Capital gains and losses
Productivity of labour

Questions for Discussion

1. Consider an economy involved in no foreign trade, in which tax collections are always $200 and in which the three components of aggregate demand are as follows:

GNP	TAXES	DI	C	I	G
$480	$200	$280	$210	$100	$215
540	200	340	255	100	215
600	200	400	300	100	215
660	200	460	345	100	215
720	200	520	390	100	215

Find the equilibrium of this economy graphically. What is the marginal propensity to consume? What is the multiplier? What would happen to equilibrium GNP if government purchases were raised by $15 and the price level were unchanged?

2. Now consider a related economy in which investment is also $100, government purchases are also $215, and the price level is also fixed. But taxes now vary with income, and as a result the consumption schedule looks like the following:

GNP	TAXES	DI	C
$480	$160	$320	$255
540	180	360	285
600	200	400	315
660	220	440	345
720	240	480	375

Find the equilibrium graphically. What is the marginal propensity to consume? What is the tax rate? Use your diagram to show the effect of an increase of $15 in government purchases. What is the multiplier? Compare this answer with your answer to Question 1 above. What do you conclude?

3. Explain why G has the same multiplier as autonomous shifts in C or I, while taxes have a different multiplier.

4. Return to the hypothetical economy in Question 1 and suppose that both taxes and government purchases are increased by $60. Find the new equilib-

rium under the assumption that consumer spending continues to be exactly three-quarters of disposable income (as it is in Question 1).

5. If the government today decides that aggregate demand is excessive and is causing inflation, what options are open to it? What if it decides that aggregate demand is too weak instead?

6. Discuss the difference between a government purchase of a good or service and a government transfer payment.

7. Suppose that you are in charge of the fiscal policy of the economy in Question 1. There is an inflationary gap with income at $660, and you want to reduce income to $600. What specific actions can you take to achieve this goal?

8. Now put yourself in charge of the economy in Question 2, and suppose that full employment comes at a GNP of $720. How can you push income up to that level?

9. Which of the proposed supply-side tax cuts appeals to you most? Draw up a list of arguments for and against enacting such a cut right now.

10. (More difficult.) Consider an economy with a horizontal aggregate-supply curve. Investment is fixed at $700, government purchases are $800, the consumption function is:

$$C = 100 + 0.8DI,$$

and taxes are one-quarter of GNP—making disposable income (DI) equal to three-quarters of GNP. Find the equilibrium level of GNP. How would this equilibrium change if taxes were abolished? Compare your answer with the examples in this chapter.

11. Consider the following fictitious economy.

GNP	SAVINGS	IMPORTS
$500	$50	$10
600	70	20
700	90	30
800	110	40
900	130	50
1000	150	60
1100	170	70
1200	190	80

Investment and exports are $100 and $110, respectively. What is the equilibrium value of GNP? What is the multiplier? What is equilibrium GNP if exports drop to $80?

Appendix
Algebraic Treatment of Fiscal Policy and Aggregate Demand

In this appendix we explain the simple algebra behind the fiscal policy multipliers discussed in the chapter. In so doing, we deal only with a simplified case in which prices do not change. While it is possible to work out the corresponding algebra for the more realistic aggregate demand–aggregate supply analysis with variable prices, the analysis is rather complicated and is best left to more advanced courses.

We start with the example used in the chapter (especially on pages 199–202 and 204–206). The government spends $80 billion on goods and services ($G = 80$), and levies an income tax equal to 25 percent of GNP. So, if the symbol T denotes tax receipts:

$$T = 0.25\ Y.$$

Since the consumption function we have been working with is

$$C = 10 + 0.8\ DI,$$

where DI is disposable income, and since disposable income and GNP are related by the accounting identity

$$DI = Y - T,$$

it follows that the C schedule used in the 45° line diagram is described by the algebraic equation:

$$C = 10 + 0.8\ (Y - T)$$
$$= 10 + 0.8\ (Y - 0.25\ Y)$$
$$= 10 + 0.8\ (0.75\ Y)$$
$$= 10 + 0.6\ Y.$$

We can now apply the equilibrium condition for an economy with a government, which is:

$$Y = C + I + G.$$

Since investment in this example is $I = 70$, substituting for C, I, and G into this equation gives:

$$Y = 10 + 0.6\ Y + 70 + 80$$
$$0.4\ Y = 160$$
$$Y = 400.$$

This is all there is to finding equilibrium GNP in an economy with a government, but no foreign sector.

To find the multiplier for government spending, increase G by 1 and resolve the problem:

$$Y = C + I + G$$
$$Y = 10 + 0.6\ Y + 70 + 81$$
$$0.4\ Y = 161$$
$$Y = 402.5.$$

So the multiplier is $402.5 - 400 = 2.5$, as stated in the text.

To find the multiplier for an increase in fixed taxes, change the tax schedule to:

$$T = 0.25\ Y + 1.$$

Disposable income is then

$$DI = Y - T = Y - (0.25\ Y + 1) = 0.75\ Y - 1,$$

so the consumption function is

$$C = 10 + 0.8\ DI$$
$$= 10 + 0.8\ (0.75\ Y - 1)$$
$$= 9.2 + 0.6\ Y.$$

Solving for equilibrium GNP as usual gives

$$Y = C + I + G$$
$$Y = 9.2 + 0.6\ Y + 70 + 80$$
$$0.4\ Y = 159.2$$
$$Y = 398.$$

So a \$1 increase in fixed taxes lowers Y by \$2. The tax multiplier is -2.

Now let us proceed to a more general solution, using symbols rather than specific numbers. The equations of the model that involves no foreign sector are as follows:

$$(1)\quad Y = C + I + G$$

is the equilibrium condition, as usual;

$$(2)\quad C = a + b\ DI$$

is the same consumption function we have used in the appendixes of Chapters 8 and 9;

$$(3)\quad DI = Y - T$$

is the accounting identity relating disposable income to GNP;

$$(4)\quad T = T_0 + tY$$

is the tax function, where T_0 represents fixed taxes

(which were zero in our numerical example) and t represents the tax rate (which was 0.25 in the example). Finally, I and G are just fixed numbers.

We begin the solution by substituting (3) and (4) into (2) to derive the consumption schedule relating C to Y:

$$C = a + b\ DI$$
$$C = a + b(Y - T)$$
$$C = a + b(Y - T_0 - tY)$$
$$(5)\quad C = a - bT_0 + b(1 - t)Y.$$

You will notice that a change in fixed taxes (T_0) shifts the intercept of the C schedule while a change in the tax rate (t) changes its slope, as explained in the text (pages 198–99).

Next substitute (5) into (1) to find equilibrium GNP:

$$Y = C + I + G$$
$$Y = a - bT_0 + b(1 - t)Y + I + G$$
$$[1 - b(1 - t)]\ Y = a - bT_0 + I + G$$

or

$$(6)\quad Y = \frac{a - bT_0 + I + G}{1 - b(1 - t)}.$$

Equation (6) shows us that G has the same multiplier as I or a, and that this multiplier is:

$$\text{Multiplier} = \frac{1}{1 - b(1 - t)}.$$

To see that this is in fact the multiplier, raise G or I or a by 1 unit. In each case, equation (6) would be changed to read:

$$Y = \frac{a - bT_0 + I + G + 1}{1 - b(1 - t)}.$$

Subtracting equation (6) from this expression gives the change in Y stemming from a one-unit change in G or I or a:

$$\text{Change in } Y = \frac{1}{1 - b(1 - t)}.$$

We noted in Chapter 9 (page 166) that if there were no income tax $(t = 0)$, a realistic value for b (the marginal propensity to consume) would yield a multiplier of 10, which is much bigger than the true multiplier. Now that we have added taxes to the model, our multiplier formula produces much more realistic numbers, but only for an economy with a relatively insignificant foreign sector like the United

States. Reasonable values for the parameters for the U.S. economy are $b = 9/10$ and $t = 1/3$. The multiplier formula then gives:

$$\text{Multiplier} = \cfrac{1}{1 - \cfrac{9}{10}\left(1 - \cfrac{1}{3}\right)} = \cfrac{1}{1 - \cfrac{9}{10} \times \cfrac{2}{3}}$$

$$= \cfrac{1}{1 - \cfrac{6}{10}} = \cfrac{1}{\cfrac{4}{10}} = 2.5,$$

which is not far from its true value, approximately 2.

Finally, we can see from equation (6) that the multiplier for a change in fixed taxes (T_0) is:

$$\text{Tax multiplier} = \frac{-b}{1 - b(1 - t)}$$

For the example considered in the text and earlier in this appendix, $b = 0.8$ and $t = 0.25$, so the formula gives:

$$\frac{-0.8}{1 - 0.8(1 - 0.25)} = \frac{-0.8}{1 - 0.8(0.75)}$$

$$= \frac{-0.8}{1 - 0.6} = \frac{-0.8}{0.4} = -2.$$

According to these figures, each $1 *increase* in T_0 *reduces* Y by $2.

For an economy *with* foreign trade, the equilibrium condition is:

$$(1a) \quad Y = C + I + G + X - IM,$$

and we add an import function:

$$(7) \quad IM = i_0 + iY,$$

where i is the marginal propensity to import. Similar substitution of (5) and (7) into (1a) yields the revised expression for equilibrium output:

$$(6a) \quad Y = \frac{a - bT_0 + I + G + X - i_0}{1 - b(1 - t) + i}.$$

The expenditure multiplier for the open economy is therefore:

$$\frac{1}{1 - b(1 - t) + i}$$

For the plausible parameter values ($b = 0.9$, $t = 0.33$, and $i = 0.2$) the multiplier formula gives a most realistic answer for Canada, 1.67.

Questions for Discussion

1. In an economy described by the following set of equations:

$$C = 10 + 0.9 \, DI$$
$$I = 180$$
$$G = 255$$
$$T = 50 + (1/3) \, Y,$$

find the equilibrium level of GNP. Then find the multipliers for government purchases and for fixed taxes. If it is desired to lower GNP by $100, what are some policies that would do the trick?

2. This is a variant of the previous problem that approaches things the way a fiscal policy planner might. In an economy whose consumption function and tax function are as given in Question 1, and with investment fixed at $180, find the value of G that would make GNP equal to $1200.

3. You are given the following information about an economy.

$$C = 50 + 0.8 \, (Y - T)$$
$$I = 120$$
$$G = 550$$
$$T = 0.25 \, Y$$

a. Find equilibrium GNP and the budget deficit.
b. Suppose the government, unhappy with the budget deficit, decides to cut government spending by precisely the amount of the deficit in (a). What actually happens to the budget deficit and why?

4. (More difficult.) In the economy considered in Question 3, suppose the government, seeing that it has not wiped out the deficit, keeps cutting G until it succeeds in balancing the budget. What level of GNP will then prevail?

5. You are given the following information about an economy.

$$C = 40 + 0.75 \, (Y - T)$$
$$I = 100$$
$$G = 80$$
$$X = 80$$
$$T = 0.2 \, Y$$
$$IM = 0.2 \, Y$$

Find the equilibrium values for GNP, budget surplus, and trade surplus.

Banking and the Creation of Money

12

[Money] is a machine for doing quickly and commodiously what would be done, though less quickly and commodiously, without it.

JOHN STUART MILL

The circular flow diagrams that were used in earlier chapters to explain equilibrium GNP (see, for example, Figure 11–1 on page 196) had a "financial system" in their upper left-hand corners. Savings flowed into this system and investment flowed out. Something obviously goes on inside the financial system to channel the saving into investment, and it is time we learned just what this something is.

There is another, equally important, reason for studying the financial system. *Fiscal policy* is not the only lever the government has on the economy's aggregate-demand curve: It also exercises significant control over aggregate demand by manipulating *monetary and exchange-rate policy*. If we are to understand monetary and exchange-rate policy (the subjects of Chapters 13–15), we must first acquire some understanding of the financial system.

The present chapter has three major objectives. It first seeks to explain the nature of money: What it is, what purposes it serves, and how it is measured. Once this is done, we turn our attention to the banking system, explaining its historical origins, the nature of banking as a business, and why this industry is so heavily regulated. Finally, we learn how banks create money—a subject that is of great importance because it is simply impossible to understand monetary policy without knowing how money is created.

At the end of the chapter, we will see why government authorities must exercise control over the supply of money in a modern economy, and this leads naturally into the discussion in Chapter 13 of *central banking*, that is, the techniques used to implement monetary and exchange-rate policy. In Chapters 14 and 15, we integrate what we will by then have learned about money and monetary policy into our model of income determination, as the culmination of our study of macroeconomic theory.

Policy Issue: Competition Among Banks

Excluding a class of special banks that deal mostly with the financial markets, there are only thirteen regular chartered banks in Canada, and the "big five" account for over 90 percent of all bank deposits across the country. Each of these five companies has more than 1000 branches. This situation is in stark contrast to the

U.S. banking system, where branching across state lines is not permitted. As a result, there are 15,000 separate banks in the United States. In 1980 significant legal changes were made in the United States to deregulate the operations of their many banks. One of the purposes of deregulation is to provide benefits to households through increased industry competition.

With Canada's highly concentrated banking industry, it would seem that increased competition would be desirable here too. This was the opinion of a Royal Commission in the 1960s and a study by the Economic Council of Canada in the 1970s. Some small steps in this direction were taken in 1980. But to form a judgment on deregulation, we must first address an even more basic question: Why were banks so heavily regulated in the first place?

One reason is that governments often feel compelled to regulate any monopolized industry. The intention is that government regulation can insure that "the public interest" gets some weight in the decision-making process of these private firms. The Canadian banking industry has certainly become more concentrated through time. The largest number of banks in Canada was 51, in 1874. By 1914, that number was down to 22. During that period, there were 17 new banks established; however, there were also 25 failures and 21 mergers. But industry concentration cannot be the only reason for regulation, since the U.S. banks have historically been subject to even more regulation than banks in Canada.

A major reason for regulation is simply that the major "output" of the banking industry—the nation's supply of money—is of vital importance to the health of the economy. Bank managers presumably do what is best for their shareholders. That, at any rate, is their job. But, as we shall see, what is best for bank shareholders may not be best for the whole economy. For this reason, the government does not allow bankers to determine the level of the nation's money supply by profit considerations alone.

Another reason for the extensive regulation of banks is concern for the safety of depositors. In a free-enterprise system, new businesses are born and die every day; and no one save those people immediately involved takes much notice of these goings-on. When a firm goes bankrupt, shareholders lose money and employees may lose their jobs. (The latter may not even happen if new management takes over the assets of the bankrupt firm.) But, except for the case of very large firms, that is about it.

But banking is different. If banks were treated like other firms, depositors would lose money whenever one went bankrupt. That is bad enough by itself, but the real danger comes in the case of a **run on a bank**. When depositors get jittery about the security of their money, they may all rush in at once to cash in their accounts. For reasons we will learn in this chapter, most banks could not survive a "run" like this and would be forced into insolvency. Worse yet, this disease is highly contagious. If Mrs. Smith hears that her neighbour has just lost her life savings because the Victoria Street National Bank went broke, she is quite likely to rush to her own bank to make a hefty withdrawal.

Without modern forms of bank regulation, therefore, one bank failure might lead to another; and indeed, as noted above, bank failures certainly did occur in the past. They were much more common in the United States. For instance, failures were not an important feature of the Great Depression in Canada, while 2200 banks failed in 1932 alone in the United States. Failures of banks in the United States are relatively rare nowadays, although there were 42 of them in 1982. Failures are very infrequent in Canada, because "head office" can always bail out any local branch that may get into difficulties. Nevertheless, the governments in both Canada and the United States have taken steps to ensure that the infectious disease of bank failure, if it occurs, will not spread. It has done this in several ways that will be mentioned later in this chapter.

A **run on a bank** occurs when many depositors withdraw cash from their accounts simultaneously.

Barter Versus Monetary Exchange

Money is so much a part of our day-to-day existence that we are likely to take it for granted, failing to appreciate all that it accomplishes. But it is important to realize that money is very much a social contrivance. Like the wheel, it had to be invented. The most obvious way to trade commodities is not by using money, but by **barter**—a system in which people exchange one good directly for another. And the best way to appreciate what monetary exchange accomplishes is to imagine a world without it.

Under a system of direct barter, if Farmer Jones grows corn and has a craving for spinach, he has to find a spinach farmer with a taste for corn. If he finds such a person (this was called the *double coincidence of wants* by the classical economists), they make the trade. If this sounds easy, try to imagine how busy Farmer Jones would be if he had to repeat the sequence for every commodity he consumed in a week. For the most part, the desired double coincidences of wants are more likely to turn out to be double wants of coincidence, where Jones gets no spinach and the spinach farmer gets no corn. Worse yet, with so much time spent looking for trading partners, Jones would have far less time to grow corn.

Money greases the wheels of exchange, and thus makes the whole economy more productive.

Under a monetary system, the corn farmer gives up his corn for money. He does so not because he wants the money per se, but because of what that money can buy. Money makes Farmer Jones's shopping tasks much easier, for it allows him simply to locate a spinach farmer who wants money. And what spinach farmer does not?

For these reasons, monetary exchange replaced barter at a very early stage of human civilization, and only extreme circumstances, like massive wars and runaway inflations, have been able to bring barter (temporarily) back.

Barter is a system of exchange in which people directly trade one good for another, without using money as an intermediate step.

The Conceptual Definition of Money

Monetary exchange is the alternative to direct barter. In a system of monetary exchange, people trade **money** for goods when they purchase something and trade goods for money when they sell something, but they do not trade goods directly for other goods. This defines money's principal role as the **medium of exchange**. But once it has come into use as the medium of exchange, whatever object is serving as money is bound to take on other functions as well. For one, it

Money is the standard object used in exchanging goods and services. In short, money is the **medium of exchange**.

The **unit of account** is the standard unit for quoting prices.

A **store of value** is an item used to store wealth from one point in time to another.

A **commodity money** is an object in use as a medium of exchange that also has a substantial value in alternative (non-monetary) uses.

Fiat money is money that is decreed as such by the government. It is of little value as a commodity, but it maintains its value as a medium of exchange because people have faith that the issuer will stand behind the pieces of printed paper and limit their production.

will inevitably become the **unit of account**, that is, the standard unit for quoting prices. Thus, if inhabitants of an idyllic tropical island used coconuts as money, they would be foolish to quote prices in terms of sea shells.

Money may also come to be used as a **store of value**. If Farmer Jones temporarily produces and sells corn of more value than he wants to consume right away, he may find it convenient to store the difference in the form of money until he wants to use it. This is because he knows that money can be "sold" easily for goods and services at a later date, whereas land, gold, and other stores of value might not be. Of course, if money pays no interest and inflation is substantial, he may decide to forgo the convenience of money and store his wealth in some other form rather than see its purchasing power rapidly eroded. So this role of money is far from inevitable.

Since money may not always serve as a store of value, and since there are many stores of value other than money, it is best not to include the store-of-value function as part of our conceptual definition of money. Instead, we simply label as "money" whatever serves as the medium of exchange.

What Serves as Money?

Anthropologists and historians will testify that a bewildering variety of things have served as money in different times and places. Cattle, stones, candy bars, cigarettes, woodpecker scalps, porpoise teeth, and giraffe tails are a few of the more colourful examples. In the early settlements in Quebec, playing cards were used as money.

In primitive or less organized societies, the commodities that served as money generally had value in themselves. If not used as money, cattle could be slaughtered for food, cigarettes could be smoked, and so on. But such **commodity money** generally runs into several severe difficulties. To be useful as a medium of exchange the commodity must be divisible. This makes cattle a very poor choice. It must also be of uniform, or at least readily identifiable, quality so that inferior substitutes are easy to recognize. This may be why woodpecker scalps never achieved great popularity. The medium of exchange must also be storable and durable, which presents a serious problem for candy-bar money. Finally, because commodity moneys need to be carried and stored, it is helpful if the item is compact, that is, has high value per unit of volume and weight. (See the boxed insert on page 227.)

All of these traits make it sensible that gold and silver have circulated as money since the first coins were struck about 2500 years ago. Since they have high value in non-monetary uses, a lot of purchasing power can be carried without too much weight. Pieces of gold are also storable, divisible (with a little trouble), and of identifiable quality (with a little more trouble).

The same characteristics suggest that paper would make an ideal money. Since we can print any number on it that we want, we can make paper money as divisible as we please and also make it possible to carry a large value in a lightweight and compact form. Paper is easy to store and, with a little cleverness, we can make counterfeiting very hard (though never impossible). The Chinese apparently originated paper money in the 12th century.

Paper cannot, however, serve as a commodity money because its value per square inch in alternative uses is so small. A paper currency that is repudiated by its issuer can, perhaps, be used as wallpaper or to wrap fish, but these uses will surely represent only a small fraction of the paper's value as money. Contrary to the popular expression, such a currency literally *is* worth the paper it is printed on, which is to say that it is not worth very much. Thus paper money is always **fiat money**.

Contemporary Canadian money is fiat money. Look at a dollar bill. Between the Coat of Arms and the Queen's picture it states: "This note is legal tender."

Dealing by Wheeling on Yap

As this extract from a recent newspaper article shows, primitive forms of money still exist in some remote places.

YAP, Micronesia—On this tiny South Pacific Island... the currency is as solid as a rock. In fact, it is rock. Limestone to be precise.

For nearly 2,000 years the Yapese have used large stone wheels to pay for major purchases, such as land, canoes and permission to marry. Yap is a U.S. trust territory, and the dollar is used in grocery stores and gas stations. But reliance on stone money ... continues.

Buying property with stones is "much easier than buying it with U.S. dollars," says John Chodad, who recently purchased a building lot with a 30-inch stone wheel. "We don't know the value of the U.S. dollar."

Stone wheels don't make good pocket money, so for small transactions, Yapese use other forms of currency, such as beer....

Besides stone wheels and beer, the Yapese sometimes spend *gaw*, consisting of necklaces of stone beads strung together around a whale's tooth. They also can buy things with *yar*, a currency made from large sea shells. But these are small change.

The people of Yap have been using stone money ever since a Yapese warrior named Anagumang first brought the huge stones over from limestone caverns on neighboring Palau, some 1,500 to 2,000 years ago. Inspired by the moon, he fashioned the stone into large circles. The rest is history....

By custom, the stones are worthless when broken. You never hear people on Yap musing about wanting a piece of the rock....

SOURCE: Adapted from Art Pine, "Hard Assets, or Why a Loan in Yap is Hard to Roll Over," *The Wall Street Journal*, March 29, 1984, page 1.

Nowhere on the certificate is there a promise, stated or implied, that the Canadian government will exchange it for anything else. A dollar bill is convertible into 4 quarters, or 10 dimes, or 20 nickels, or any other similar combination, but not into gold, chocolate, or any other commodity.

Why do people hold these pieces of paper? Only because they know that others are willing to accept them for things of intrinsic value—food, rent, shoes, and so on. If this confidence ever evaporated, these dollar bills would cease serving as a medium of exchange and, given that they make ugly wallpaper, would become virtually worthless.

But don't panic. This is not likely to occur. Our current monetary system has evolved over hundreds of years during which *commodity money* was first replaced by *"full-bodied" paper money*—paper certificates that were backed by gold or silver of equal value held in the issuer's vaults. Then the full-bodied paper money was replaced by certificates that were only partially backed by gold and silver. Finally, we arrived at our present system, in which paper money has no "backing" whatsoever. Like a hesitant swimmer who first dips her toes, then her legs, then her whole body into a cold swimming pool, we have "tested the water" at each step of the way—and found it to our liking. It is unlikely that we will ever take a step back in the other direction.

How the Quantity of Money Is Measured

As we will learn in coming chapters, the amount of money circulating in the economy is of profound importance for the determination of national income and the price level. Thus it becomes important for the government to know how much money there is at any given time.

Our conceptual definition of money describes it as the medium of exchange.

But this raises questions about just what items should be included and what items excluded when we count up the money supply. Some items are easy. All of our coins, the small change of our economic system, clearly should count as money. So should paper money, which accounts for a far greater volume of transactions. But we cannot stop here if we want to include the main vehicle for making payments in our society, because the lion's share of our nation's payments are made neither in metal nor in paper money, but by cheque.

Chequing deposits are actually no more than bookkeeping entries in bank ledgers. Many people think of cheques simply as a convenient way to give coins or dollar bills to someone else. But, in fact, cheques are something quite different, which is why the country can have more money in the form of chequing deposits than it has in the form of currency. For example, if you pay the grocer $50 by cheque, no dollar bills or coins normally will change hands. Instead, that cheque will travel back to your bank, where $50 will be deducted from the bookkeeping entry that records your account and added to the bookkeeping entry for your grocer's account. (If you and the grocer hold accounts at different banks, more books get involved; but still no coins or bills are likely to be moved.) Since so many transactions are made by cheque, it seems imperative that chequing deposits be included in any specific definition of the money supply.

One popular definition of the money supply stops here and includes only currency held outside chartered bank vaults, plus chequing deposits at chartered banks. In the official statistics, this narrowly defined concept of money is called **M1**. The left-hand side of Figure 12–1 shows the composition of M1 as of January 1984.

But there are other types of accounts that allow withdrawals by cheque, and which therefore are candidates for inclusion in the money supply. Strictly speaking, withdrawals from the savings account at your bank can require up to seven days prior notice. However, in practice this procedure is not followed, and everyone

The narrowly defined money supply, usually abbreviated **M1**, is the sum of all coins and paper money in circulation, plus pure chequing deposits at chartered banks.

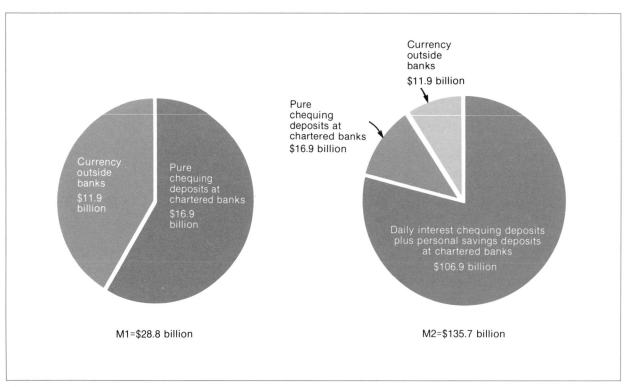

Figure 12–1
DEFINITIONS OF THE MONEY SUPPLY (JANUARY 1984)
SOURCE: Bank of Canada *Review*.

regards their savings-account holdings as equivalent to money. Furthermore, since many banks offer convenient electronic transfers of funds from one account to another, either by telephone or by pushing a button on an automated teller, savings balances can serve the same purposes as chequing balances. For this reason, savings accounts are included in the broader statistical definition of the money supply known as **M2**.

The composition of M2 as of January 1984 is shown on the right-hand side of Figure 12–1. You can see that the savings accounts predominate, dwarfing everything that is included in M1.

Some economists do not want to stop counting at M2; they prefer still broader definitions of money that include other closely related assets. For example, many people do their "banking" at trust companies or credit unions; this is especially true in Quebec, with the Caisses Populaires. The problem with extending the definition of the money supply by including the deposits at these institutions is that there is no clear-cut place to stop. There is no obvious line of demarcation between those assets that *are* money and those that are merely *close substitutes* for money—so-called **near moneys**.

If we define an asset's **liquidity** as the ease with which it can be converted into cash, then there is a range of assets of varying degrees of liquidity. Everything in M1 is completely "liquid"; savings accounts included in M2 are a bit less so; and so on, until we encounter such things as short-term government bonds, which, while still quite liquid, would not normally be included in the money supply. Any number of different "M's" can be defined—and have been—by drawing the line in different places.

And there are still more complexities. For example, credit cards clearly serve as a medium of exchange. So should they be included in the money supply? Yes, you say. But how would we do this? How much money does your credit card represent? If you think about questions like this for a while, you will realize that there are no good answers—which is one reason why research on the definition of money continues. But, in a first course in economics, we do not want to get bogged down in complex definitional issues. So we will simply adhere to the convention that *"money" consists only of coins, paper money, and chequing deposits at chartered banks*.

Now that we have defined money and seen how it can be measured, we turn our attention to the principal creators of money—the banks.

How Banking Began

When Adam and Eve left the Garden of Eden, they did not encounter a bank. Banking had to be invented, and some time passed before it came to be practised as it is today. With a little imagination, we can see how the first banks must have begun.

When money was made of gold it was most inconvenient for consumers and merchants to carry it around and to have to weigh and assay it for purity every time a transaction was made. So it is not surprising that the practice developed of leaving one's gold in the care of a goldsmith, who had safe storage facilities, and carrying in its place a receipt from the goldsmith stating that John Doe did indeed own five ounces of gold of a certain purity. The goldsmiths, of course, charged a fee for this service. When people began trading goods and services for the goldsmiths' receipts, rather than for the gold itself, the receipts became an early form of paper money.

At this stage, paper money was fully backed by gold. But gradually the goldsmiths began to notice that the amount of gold they were actually required to pay out in a day was but a small fraction of the total gold they had stored in their warehouses. Then one day some enterprising goldsmith hit upon a momentous idea that must have made him fabulously wealthy.

The broadly defined money supply, usually abbreviated **M2,** is the sum of currency in public hands, plus chequing and all savings deposits at chartered banks.

Near moneys are liquid assets that are close substitutes for money.

An asset's **liquidity** refers to the ease with which it can be converted into cash.

His thinking probably ran something like this. "I have 2000 ounces of gold stored away in my vault, for which I collect storage fees from my customers. If I get much more, I'll need an expensive new vault. But in the last year, I was never called upon to pay out more than 100 ounces on a single day. What harm could it do if I lent out, say, half the gold I now have? I'll still have more than enough to pay off any depositors that come in for a withdrawal, so no one will ever know the difference. And I could earn 30 additional ounces of gold each year in interest on the loans I make (at 3 percent interest on 1000 ounces). With this profit, I could lower my service charges to depositors and so attract still more deposits. I think I'll do it."

With this resolution, the modern system of **fractional reserve banking** was born. This system has three important features—features that are crucially important to this chapter.

1. *Bank profitability*. By getting deposits at zero interest and lending some of them out at positive interest rates, goldsmiths made a profit. The history of banking as a profit-making industry was begun and has continued to this date. *Banks, like other enterprises, are in business to earn profits.*

2. *Bank discretion over the money supply*. When goldsmiths decided that they could get along by keeping only a fraction of their total deposits on reserve in their vaults and lending out the balance, they acquired the ability to *create money*. As long as they kept 100 percent reserves, each gold certificate represented exactly one ounce of gold. So whether people decided to carry their gold or leave it with their goldsmith did not affect the money supply, which was set by the volume of gold.

   With the advent of fractional reserve banking, however, new paper certificates were added whenever goldsmiths lent out some of the gold they held on deposit. The loans, in effect, created new money. In this way, the total amount of money came to depend on the amount of gold that each goldsmith felt compelled to maintain as reserves in his vault. For any given volume of gold on deposit, the lower the reserves the goldsmiths kept, the more loans would be made, and therefore the more money there would be. While we no longer use gold to back our money, this principle remains true today. *Bankers' business decisions influence the supply of money.*

3. *Exposure to runs*. A goldsmith who kept 100 percent reserves never had to worry about a run on his vault. Even if all his depositors showed up at the door at once, he always had enough gold to return their deposits. But as soon as the first goldsmith decided to get by with only fractional reserves, the possibility of a run on the vault became a real concern. If that first goldsmith who lent out half his gold had found 51 percent of his customers at his door one unlucky day, he would have had a lot of explaining to do. Similar problems have worried bankers for centuries. *The danger of a run on the bank has induced bankers to keep prudent reserves and to lend out money carefully.*

Principles of Bank Management: Profits Versus Safety

Bankers have a reputation, probably deserved, for conservatism in politics, dress, and business affairs. From what has been said so far, the economic rationale for this conservatism should be clear. Today's chequing deposits are pure fiat money. For years now these deposits have been "backed" by nothing more than the bank's promise to convert them into currency on demand. Thus, banks depend entirely on people's trust, and so must acquire a reputation for prudence. This they did (and continue to do) in two principal ways. First, they had to maintain a sufficiently generous level of reserves to minimize their vulnerability to runs. Second, they had to be somewhat cautious in making loans and investments, since any large losses on their loans could undermine the confidence of depositors.

It is important to realize that banking under a system of fractional reserves is an inherently risky business that is rendered relatively safe only by cautious and prudent management. The history of bank failures in the United States before World War II bears sober testimony to the fact that many bankers were neither cautious nor prudent. Why? Because this is not a recipe for high profits. Bank profits are maximized by keeping reserves as low as possible, by making at least some risky investments, and by giving loans to borrowers of questionable credit standing (because these borrowers will pay the highest interest rates). The art of bank management is to strike the appropriate balance between the lure of profits and the need for safety. When a banker errs by being too stodgy, his bank will earn inadequate profits. When he errs by taking unwarranted risks, his bank may not survive at all.

Bank Regulation

The public authorities apparently have decided that the balance struck by profit-minded bankers often would not be at the place where society would like it struck. So government has thrown up a web of regulations designed to insure the safety of depositors and to control the supply of money.

The principal innovation guaranteeing the safety of bank deposits is **deposit insurance**. Today most bank deposits are insured against loss by the federal government, up to an amount of $60,000 per account regardless of what happens to the bank. Thus, while bank failures may spell disaster for the bank's shareholders, they do not give many depositors cause for concern. Deposit insurance eliminates the motive for customers to rush to their bank just because they hear some bad news about the bank's finances. Many observers give this innovation much of the credit for the pronounced decline in bank failures in the United States since 1933 (the year in which deposit insurance was started there). They had 2200 bank failures in 1932, and 60 in 1934.

In addition to insuring depositors against loss, the government takes steps to see that banks do not get into financial trouble. For one thing, various regulatory authorities conduct periodic *bank examinations and audits* in order to keep tabs on the financial condition and business practices of the banks under their purview. For another, laws and regulations *limit the kinds and quantities of assets in which banks may invest*. For example, banks are limited in the amount of common stock they may purchase, and it wasn't until 1954 that banks were allowed to make household mortgages. Both these forms of regulation are clearly aimed at maintaining bank safety.

A final type of regulation also has some bearing on safety but it is motivated primarily by the government's desire to control the money supply. We have seen that the amount of money any bank will issue depends on the amount of reserves it elects to keep. For this reason, most banks are subject by law to minimum **required reserves**. While banks may (and sometimes do) keep reserves in excess of these legal minimums, they may not keep less. It is this regulation that places an upper limit on the money supply. The rest of this chapter is concerned with the details of this mechanism.

How Bankers Keep Books

Before we can fully understand the mechanics of modern banking and the process by which money is "created," we must acquire at least a nodding acquaintance with the way in which bankers keep their books. The first thing to know is how to distinguish assets from liabilities.

Deposit insurance is a system that guarantees that depositors will not lose money even if their bank goes bankrupt.

Required reserves are the minimum amount of reserves (in cash or the equivalent) that is mandated by law. Normally, required reserves are proportional to the volume of deposits.

An **asset** of an individual or business firm is an item that the individual or firm owns.

A **liability** of an individual or business firm is an item that the individual or firm owes. Many liabilities are known as "debts."

An **asset** of a bank is something that the bank *owns*. This "thing" may be a physical object, such as the bank building, a typewriter, or a vault, or it may be just a piece of paper, such as an IOU of a customer to whom the bank has made a loan. A **liability** of a bank is something that the bank *owes*. Most bank liabilities take the form of bookkeeping entries. For example, if you have a chequing account in the Victoria Street Bank, your bank balance there is a liability of the bank. (It is, of course, an asset for you.)

There is an easy test to see whether some piece of paper or bookkeeping entry is a bank's asset or a liability. Ask yourself whether, if this paper were converted into cash, the bank would receive the cash (if so, it is an asset) or pay it out (if so, it is a liability). This test makes it clear that loans to customers are bank assets (when the loans are repaid, the bank collects), while customers' deposits are bank liabilities (when deposits are cashed in, the bank must pay up).

A **balance sheet** is an accounting statement listing the values of all the assets on the left-hand side and the values of all the liabilities and **net worth** on the right-hand side.

When accountants draw up a complete list of all the bank's assets and liabilities, the resulting document is called the bank's **balance sheet**. Typically, the value of all the bank's assets exceeds the value of all its liabilities. (On the rare occasions when this is not the case, the bank is in serious trouble.) In what sense, then, do balance sheets "balance"?

They balance because accountants have invented the concept of **net worth** to balance the books. Specifically, they have defined the net worth of a bank to be the difference between the value of all its assets and the value of all its liabilities. Thus, by definition, when accountants add net worth to liabilities, the sum they get must be the same as the value of the bank's assets. In short:

Net worth is the value of all assets minus the value of all liabilities.

$$\text{Assets} = \text{Liabilities} + \text{Net worth.}$$

Table 12–1 illustrates this with the balance sheet of a fictitious bank, Bank-a-mythica, whose finances are extremely simple. On December 31, 1984, it had only two kinds of assets (listed on the left-hand side of the balance sheet)—$1 million in cash, which it held as reserves in its vault, and $4.5 million in outstanding loans to its customers, that is, in customers' IOUs. And it had only one type of liability (listed on the right-hand side)—$5 million in chequing deposits. The difference between total assets ($5.5 million) and total liabilities ($5 million) was the bank's net worth ($500,000), shown on the right-hand side of the balance sheet.

The Limits to Money Creation by a Single Bank

Let us now turn to the process of deposit creation. Many bankers will deny that they have any ability to "create" money. (The very phrase has a suspiciously

Table 12–1
BALANCE SHEET OF BANK-A-MYTHICA, DECEMBER 31, 1984

ASSETS		LIABILITIES AND NET WORTH	
Assets		**Liabilities**	
Cash in vault	$1,000,000	Chequing deposits	$5,000,000
Loans oustanding	4,500,000		
Total	$5,500,000		
Addendum: Bank Reserves		**Net Worth**	
Actual reserves	$1,000,000	Shareholders' equity	500,000
Required reserves	1,000,000		
Excess reserves	0	Total	$5,500,000

hocus-pocus sound to it.) But they are not quite right. For although any individual bank's ability to create money is severely limited in a system with many banks, the banking system as a whole can achieve much more than the sum of its parts. Through the modern alchemy of **deposit creation**, it can turn one dollar into many dollars. But to understand this important process, we had better proceed in steps, beginning with the case of a single bank, our hypothetical Bank-a-mythica.

According to the balance sheet in Table 12–1, Bank-a-mythica is holding cash reserves in its vault that are equal to 20 percent of its deposits ($1 million in cash is equal to 20 percent of the $5 million in deposits). Let us assume that this is the minimum reserve ratio prescribed by law and that the bank strives to keep its reserves down to the legal minimum; that is, it strives to keep its **excess reserves** down to zero.

Now let us suppose that on January 2, 1985, an eccentric widower comes into Bank-a-mythica and deposits $100,000 in cash in his chequing account. The bank now has acquired $100,000 more in cash reserves, and $100,000 more in chequing deposits. But since deposits are up by $100,000, *required* reserves are up by only 20 percent of this amount, or $20,000, leaving $80,000 in *excess* reserves. Table 12–2 illustrates the effects of this transaction on Bank-a-mythica's balance sheet. It is tables such as this, which show *changes* in balance sheets rather than the balance sheets themselves, that will help us follow the money-creation process.

If Bank-a-mythica does not want to hold excess reserves, it will be unhappy with the situation illustrated in Table 12–2, for it is holding $80,000 in excess reserves on which it earns no interest. So as soon as possible it will lend out the extra $80,000—let us say to Hard-Pressed Construction Company. This loan leads to the balance sheet changes shown in Table 12–3: Bank-a-mythica's loans rise by $80,000 while its holdings of cash reserves fall by $80,000.

Excess reserves are any reserves held in excess of the legal minimum.

Table 12–2
CHANGES IN BANK-A-MYTHICA'S BALANCE SHEET, JANUARY 2, 1985

ASSETS		LIABILITIES	
Cash in vault	+ $100,000	Chequing deposits	+ $100,000
Addendum: Bank Reserves			
Actual reserves	+ $100,000		
Required reserves	+ 20,000		
Excess reserves	+ $ 80,000		

Bank-a-mythica receives a $100,000 cash deposit. It now holds excess reserves of $80,000, since required reserves rise by only $20,000 (20 percent of $100,000).

Table 12–3
CHANGES IN BANK-A-MYTHICA'S BALANCE SHEET, JANUARY 3–6, 1985

ASSETS		LIABILITIES	
Loans outstanding	+ $80,000	No change	
Cash in vault	– $80,000		
Addendum: Changes in Reserves			
Actual reserves	– $80,000		
Required reserves	No change		
Excess reserves	– $80,000		

Bank-a-mythica gets rid of its excess reserves by making a loan of $80,000 to Hard-Pressed Construction Company.

Table 12-4

CHANGES IN BANK-A-MYTHICA'S BALANCE SHEET, JANUARY 2-6, 1985

ASSETS		LIABILITIES	
Cash in vault	+ $20,000	Chequing deposits	+ $100,000
Loans outstanding	+ 80,000		
Addendum: Changes in Reserves			
Actual reserves	+ $20,000		
Required reserves	+ 20,000		
Excess reserves	No change		

When it receives $100,000 in cash deposits, Bank-a-mythica keeps only the required $20,000 in reserves and lends out the remaining $80,000 to Hard-Pressed Construction Company. Its excess reserves return to zero.

By combining Tables 12-2 and 12-3, we arrive at Table 12-4, which summarizes all the bank's transactions for the week. Cash reserves are up $20,000, loans are up $80,000, and now that the bank has had a chance to adjust to the inflow of deposits, it no longer holds excess reserves.

Looking at Table 12-4 and keeping in mind our specific definition of money, it appears at first that the chairman of Bank-a-mythica is right when he claims not to have engaged in the nefarious practice of "money creation." All that happened was that, in exchange for the $100,000 in cash it received, the bank issued the widower a chequing balance of $100,000. This does not change M1, it merely converts one form of money into another.

But wait. What happened to the $100,000 in cash that the eccentric man brought to the bank? The table shows that $20,000 was retained by Bank-a-mythica in its vault. Since this currency is no longer in circulation, it no longer counts in the official money supply. (Notice that Figure 12-1 included only "currency outside banks.") But the other $80,000, which the bank lent out, is still in circulation. It is held by Hard-Pressed Construction, which probably will redeposit it in some other bank. But even before this happens, the original $100,000 in cash has supported a rise in the money supply: There is now $100,000 in chequing deposits of the widower and $80,000 of cash in circulation, making a total of $180,000. The money-creation process has begun.

Multiple Money Creation by a Series of Banks

Let us now trace the $80,000 in cash and see how the process of money creation gathers momentum. Suppose that Hard-Pressed Construction Company, which banks across town at the First National Bank, deposits the $80,000 into its bank account. First National's reserves increase by $80,000. But because deposits are up by $80,000, *required* reserves rise by only 20 percent of this amount or $16,000. If the management of First National Bank behaves like that of Bank-a-mythica, the $64,000 of excess reserves will be lent out.

Table 12-5 shows the effects of these events on First National Bank's balance sheet. (The preliminary steps corresponding to Tables 12-2 and 12-3 are not shown separately.) At this stage in the chain, the original $100,000 in cash has led to $180,000 in deposits—$100,000 at Bank-a-mythica and $80,000 at First National Bank—and $64,000 in cash, which is still in circulation (in the hands of the recipient of First National's loan—Al's Auto Shop). Thus, from the original $100,000, a total of $244,000 has been added to the money supply ($180,000 in chequing deposits plus $64,000 in cash).

Table 12-5

CHANGES IN FIRST NATIONAL BANK'S BALANCE SHEET

ASSETS		LIABILITIES	
Cash in vault	+ $16,000	Chequing deposits	+ $80,000
Loans outstanding	+ 64,000		
Addendum: Changes in Reserves			
Actual reserves	+ $16,000		
Required reserves	+ 16,000		
Excess reserves	No change		

Hard-Pressed deposits its $80,000 in First National Bank, which sets aside the required $16,000 in reserves (20 percent of $80,000) and lends $64,000 to Al's Auto Shop.

Table 12-6

CHANGES IN SECOND NATIONAL BANK'S BALANCE SHEET

ASSETS		LIABILITIES	
Cash in vault	+ $12,800	Chequing deposits	+ $64,000
Loans outstanding	+ 51,200		
Addendum: Changes in Reserves			
Actual reserves	+ $12,800		
Required reserves	+ 12,800		
Excess reserves	No change		

When Al deposits his $64,000 in Second National Bank, that bank retains $12,800 as required reserves (20 percent of $64,000) and lends out the remaining $51,200.

But, to coin a phrase, the bucks do not stop here. Al's Auto Shop will presumably deposit the proceeds from its loan into its own account at Second National Bank, leading eventually to the balance sheet adjustments shown in Table 12–6 when Second National makes an additional loan rather than hold on to excess reserves. You can see how the money-creation process continues.

Table 12–7 adds up the balance-sheet changes of the first five banks in the chain (from Bank-a-mythica through the Fourth National Bank) on the assumptions that each bank holds exactly the 20 percent required reserves (no excess reserves), and that each loan recipient redeposits the proceeds in his own bank. At this stage, $336,160 in bank deposits have been created, and there is still $32,768 in cash circulating (the original $100,000 less $67,232 in bank vaults), for a total increase in the money supply of $268,928 ($368,928 less the original $100,000).

But the chain does not end there. For the Main Street Movie Theatre, which received the $32,768 loan from the Fourth National Bank, then deposits these funds into the Fifth National Bank. Fifth National has to keep only 20 percent of this deposit, or $6,553.60, on reserve and will lend out the balance. And so the chain continues.

What are the final effects on the money supply? If you look carefully at the three sections of Table 12–7, you will see that each column of numbers forms a *geometric progression*; specifically, each entry is equal to exactly 80 percent of the entry that preceded it. Recall that in the discussion of the multiplier in Chapter 9 we learned how to sum an infinite geometric progression, which is just what each

Table 12-7

CHANGES IN THE COMBINED BALANCE SHEETS OF THE FIRST FIVE BANKS

ASSETS		LIABILITIES	
Cash in Vault		**Chequing Deposits**	
Bank-a-mythica	+ $20,000	Bank-a-mythica	+ $100,000
First National Bank	+ 16,000	First National Bank	+ 80,000
Second National Bank	+ 12,800	Second National Bank	+ 64,000
Third National Bank	+ 10,240	Third National Bank	+ 51,200
Fourth National Bank	+ 8,192	Fourth National Bank	+ 40,960
Total	+ $67,232	Total	+ $336,160
Loans Outstanding			
Bank-a-mythica	+ $80,000		
First National Bank	+ 64,000		
Second National Bank	+ 51,200		
Third National Bank	+ 40,960		
Fourth National Bank	+ 32,768		
Total	+ $268,928		
Total change in assets	+ $336,160		

After five banks have participated, the chain of deposit creation looks like this. But there are still excess reserves in the system (held by Fifth National Bank), so the chain continues.

of these chains eventually will be. In particular, if the common ratio is R, the sum of an infinite geometric progression is

$$1 + R + R^2 + R^3 + \ldots = \frac{1}{1 - R}.$$

By applying this formula to the chain of chequing deposits on the right-hand side of Table 12–7, we get:

$$\$100,000 + \$80,000 + \$64,000 + \$51,200 + \ldots$$
$$= \$100,000 \times (1 + 0.8 + 0.64 + 0.512 + \ldots)$$
$$= \$100,000 \times (1 + 0.8 + 0.8^2 + 0.8^3 + \ldots)$$
$$= \$100,000 \times \frac{1}{1 - 0.8} = \frac{\$100,000}{0.2} = \$500,000.$$

So eventually the original $100,000 in cash will support $500,000 in new chequing deposits—a multiple expansion of $5 for every one original dollar. Table 12–8 shows the ultimate effect of the entire chain of deposit creation on the balance sheet of the banking system as a whole. The banks have converted $100,000 in cash into $500,000 in chequing deposits.

Notice that 5 is the reciprocal of 20 percent (that is, $5 = 1/0.2$). This suggests the general formula for multiple deposit creation when the required reserve ratio is some number other than 20 percent:

OVERSIMPLIFIED MONEY-MULTIPLIER FORMULA
If the required reserve ratio is some fraction, m, an injection of $1 of reserves into the banking system can lead to the creation of $\$1/m$ in new deposits. That is, the so-called "money multiplier" is given by:

Change in deposits = $(1/m)$ × Change in reserves.

Table 12–8

CHANGES IN COMBINED BALANCE SHEET OF THE ENTIRE BANKING SYSTEM

ASSETS		LIABILITIES	
Cash in vault	+ $100,000	Chequing deposits	+ $500,000
Loans outstanding	+ 400,000		
Addendum: Changes in Reserves		**Addendum: Changes in Money Supply**	
Actual reserves	+ $100,000	Demand deposits	+ $500,000
Required reserves	+ 100,000	Currency outside banks	– 100,000
Excess reserves	No change	Net change	+ $400,000

By the end of the chain of deposit creation, the entire $100,000 of cash has found its way into bank vaults, where it can support $500,000 in deposits. No excess reserves remain; and the money supply has expanded by $400,000.

While we have derived this formula in a rather mechanical fashion, there is a simple piece of logic behind it. If banks want to hold only the legal minimum in cash reserves, then an injection of $1 in new reserves into the banking system must induce them to expand their loans until *required* reserves have risen by $1. For only then will all *excess* reserves have been eliminated.

But if each dollar of deposits requires only a fraction m (one-fifth in our example) of a dollar in reserves, then deposits must expand by $1/m$ for each dollar of new reserves. This is the common sense behind the money-multiplier formula.

Since later chapters will be concerned with changes in the *money supply*, not just with changes in *bank deposits*, it is worth pointing out that the money supply grew by only $400,000, not $500,000, in Table 12–8. The reason is that the original $100,000 cash deposit was part of the money supply before it was deposited in Bank-a-mythica. While the *chequing-deposit* component of the money supply rose by $500,000 (as our formula suggests), the *cash* component of the money supply fell by $100,000, leaving a net increase of $400,000. You will avoid confusion if you keep in mind the fact that the money supply has *two* components: cash (outside banks) and deposits.

The Process in Reverse: Multiple Contractions of the Money Supply

Let us now briefly consider how this deposit-creation mechanism operates in reverse—as a system of deposit *destruction*. In particular, suppose that our eccentric widower came back to Bank-a-mythica to withdraw $100,000 from his checking account and return it to his mattress, where it rightfully belongs. Bank-a-mythica's *required* reserves would fall by $20,000 as a result of this transaction (20 percent of $100,000), but its *actual* reserves would fall by $100,000. The bank would be $80,000 short, as indicated in Table 12–9(a).

How does it react to this discrepancy? As some of its outstanding loans are routinely paid off, the bank will cease granting new ones until it has accumulated the necessary $80,000 in required reserves. The data for Bank-a-mythica's contraction are shown in Table 12–9(b), assuming that borrowers pay off their loans in cash.[1]

But where did the borrowers get this money? Probably by making withdrawals from other banks. In this case, let us assume it all came from First National Bank, which loses an $80,000 deposit and $80,000 in reserves. It finds itself short some

---

[1]In reality, they would probably pay with cheques drawn on other banks. Bank-a-mythica would then cash these cheques to acquire the reserves.

Table 12-9
CHANGES IN THE BALANCE SHEET OF BANK-A-MYTHICA

(a)				(b)	
ASSETS		LIABILITIES		ASSETS	LIABILITIES
Cash in vault	– $100,000	Chequing deposits – $100,000		Cash in vault + $80,000	
				Loans outstanding – 80,000	
Addendum: Changes in Reserves				**Addendum: Changes in Reserves**	
Actual reserves	– $100,000			Actual reserves + $80,000	
Required reserves	– 20,000			Required reserves No change	
Excess reserves	– $ 80,000			Excess reserves + $80,000	

When Bank-a-mythica loses a $100,000 deposit, it must reduce its loans by $80,000 to replenish its reserves.

$64,000 in reserves [see Table 12–10(a)] and therefore must reduce its loan commitments by $64,000 [see Table 12–10(b)]. This, of course, causes some other bank to suffer a loss of reserves and deposits of $64,000, and the whole process repeats just as it did in the case of deposit expansion.

After five banks had become involved, the picture would be just as shown in Table 12–7, except that all the *plus* signs would be *minus* signs. And the final results are just the mirror image of Table 12–8. Deposits shrink by $500,000, loans fall by $400,000, bank reserves are reduced by $100,000, and the money supply falls by $400,000. As suggested by our money-multiplier formula with $m = 0.2$, the decline in deposits is $1/0.2 = 5$ times as large as the decline in reserves.

During the height of the radical student movements of the late 1960s, a circular appeared in Cambridge, Massachusetts, urging citizens to withdraw all funds from their chequing accounts on a prescribed date, hold them in cash for one week, and then redeposit them. This act, the circular argued, would surely wreak havoc upon the capitalist system. Obviously, some of these radicals were well-schooled in modern money mechanics, for the argument was basically correct. The tremendous multiple contraction of the banking system and consequent multiple expansion that a successful campaign of this sort could have caused might have disrupted the local financial system quite seriously. But history records that the appeal met with little success.

Table 12-10
CHANGES IN THE BALANCE SHEET OF FIRST NATIONAL BANK

(a)				(b)	
ASSETS		LIABILITIES		ASSETS	LIABILITIES
Cash in vault	– $80,000	Chequing deposits – $80,000		Cash in vault + $64,000	
				Loans outstanding – 64,000	
Addendum: Changes in Reserves				**Addendum: Changes in Reserves**	
Actual reserves	– $80,000			Actual reserves + $64,000	
Required reserves	– 16,000			Required reserves No change	
Excess reserves	– $64,000			Excess reserves + $64,000	

First National Bank's loss of an $80,000 deposit forces it to cut back its loans by $64,000.

Why the Money-Creation Formula Is Oversimplified

So far, our discussion of the process of money creation has made it all seem rather mechanical. If all proceeds according to formula, each $1 in new reserves will lead to a $1/m increase in deposits. But in reality things are not this simple. Just as we did in the case of the expenditure multiplier, we must stress that the oversimplified formula for money creation is accurate only under very particular circumstances. These circumstances require that:

1. Every recipient of a bank loan must redeposit the proceeds of that loan into another bank rather than hold it in cash.

2. Every bank must hold reserves no larger than the legal minimum.

Let us see what happens to the chain of deposit creation when either of these assumptions is violated.

Suppose first that the business firms and individuals who receive bank loans decide not to redeposit all of the proceeds into their bank accounts. For example, Hard-Pressed Construction Company and all the other borrowers might decide to hold half of their loan proceeds in cash and deposit only the remaining half. Then First National Bank would receive only a $40,000 deposit, and could, therefore, make only a $32,000 loan. Second National Bank would then receive only $16,000 (half of $32,000), and so on. The whole chain of deposit creation would be reduced drastically. Thus:

If individuals and business firms decide to hold more cash, the multiple expansion of the money supply will be curtailed because fewer dollars of cash will be available in bank vaults to be used as reserves to support new chequing deposits. Consequently, the money supply will be smaller.

The basic idea here is simple. Each $1 of cash held by a bank can support several dollars (specifically, $1/m) of money. But each $1 held by an individual is exactly one dollar of money. Hence, any time cash leaves the banking system, the money supply will decline. And any time cash enters the banking system, the money supply will rise.

Next, suppose that Bank-a-mythica's management becomes very conservative, or that the outlook for loan repayments worsens because of a recession. The bank might then decide to keep more reserves than the legal requirement (say, 30 percent) and lend out less than the $80,000 assumed in Table 12–4 (say, $70,000). If this happens, then First National Bank will receive a smaller injection of cash reserves than that shown in Table 12–5. And if First National's management is as jittery as Bank-a-mythica's, it too will hold more in reserves and lend out less. Thus:

If banks wish to keep excess reserves, the multiple expansion of the money supply will be restricted. A given amount of cash will support a smaller supply of money than would be the case if banks held no excess reserves.

The Need for Monetary Control

If we pursue this point a bit further, we will see why government regulation of the money supply is so important for economic stability. We have just suggested that banks will wish to keep excess reserves when they do not foresee profitable and secure opportunities to make loans. This is likely to happen during the downswing and around the bottom of a business contraction. If it occurs, the propensity of banks to hold excess reserves will turn the money-creation process into one of money destruction.

During a recession, profit-oriented banks would be prone to reduce the money supply by increasing their excess reserves—if the monetary authorities did not intervene. As we will learn in subsequent chapters, the money supply is an important influence on aggregate demand, so such a contraction of the money supply would exacerbate the severity of the recession.

On the other hand, banks will want to squeeze the maximum possible money supply out of any given amount of cash reserves by keeping their reserves at the bare minimum when the demand for bank loans is buoyant, profits are high, and many investments suddenly start to look profitable. This reduced incentive to hold excess reserves in prosperous times means that:

During an economic boom, the behaviour of profit-oriented banks is likely to make the money supply expand, adding undesirable momentum to the booming economy and paving the way for a burst of inflation. The authorities must intervene to prevent this.

Regulation of the money supply, then, is necessary because bankers, in the pursuit of profit, might otherwise provide the economy with a widely fluctuating money supply that dances to the tune of the business cycle. Precisely how the authorities can keep the money supply under control is the subject of the next chapter.

Summary

1. It is much more efficient to exchange goods and services by using money as a medium of exchange than by bartering them directly.

2. In addition to being the medium of exchange, whatever serves as money is likely to become the standard unit of account and a popular store of value.

3. Throughout history, all sorts of things have served as money. Commodity moneys gave way to full-bodied paper money (certificates backed 100 percent by some commodity, like gold), which in turn gave way to partially backed paper money. Nowadays our paper money has no commodity backing whatsoever: that is, it is pure fiat money.

4. The most widely used definition of the Canadian money supply is M1, which includes coins and paper money held outside banks, and chequing deposits. However, many economists prefer the M2 definition, which adds to M1 savings and most notice deposits held at chartered banks.

5. Under our modern system of fractional reserve banking, banks keep cash reserves equal to only a fraction of their total deposit liabilities. This is the key to their profitability, since their remaining funds can be loaned out at interest. But it also leaves them potentially vulnerable to runs.

6. Because of this vulnerability, bank managers are generally very conservative in their investment strategy, and they also like to keep a prudent level of reserves. Even so, the government keeps a watchful eye over banking practices.

7. Before bank mergers and deposit insurance, bank failures were fairly common. Some still occur in the United States, where branching across state lines is not permitted.

8. Because it holds only fractional reserves, even a single bank can create money. But its ability to do so is severely limited because the funds it lends out probably will be deposited in another bank.

9. As a whole, the banking system can create several dollars of deposits for each dollar of cash reserves it receives. Under certain assumptions, the ratio of new deposits to new reserves will be $1/m$, where m is the required reserve ratio.

10. The same process works in reverse, as a system of money destruction, when cash is withdrawn from the banking system.

11. Because banks and individuals may want to hold more cash when the economy is shaky, the money supply would probably contract under such circumstances if the monetary authorities did not intervene. Similarly, the money supply would probably expand rapidly in boom times if it were unregulated.

Concepts for Review

Run on a bank	Fiat money	Asset
Barter	M1 versus M2	Liability
Unit of account	Near moneys	Balance sheet
Money	Liquidity	Net worth
Medium of exchange	Fractional reserve banking	Deposit creation
Store of value	Deposit insurance	Excess reserves
Commodity money	Required reserves	

Questions for Discussion

1. If ours were a barter economy, how would you pay your tuition bill? What if your university did not want the goods or services you offered in payment?

2. How is "money" defined, both conceptually and in practice? Does the Canadian money supply consist of commodity money, full-bodied paper money, or fiat money?

3. What is fractional reserve banking, and why is it the key to bank profits? (*Hint:* What opportunities to make profits would banks have if reserve requirements were 100 percent?) Why does fractional reserve banking give bankers discretion over how large the money supply will be? Why does it make banks potentially vulnerable to runs?

4. Do you hold an account in a bank? If so, what will happen to your account if the bank goes bankrupt?

5. Suppose that no banks keep excess reserves and no individuals or firms hold on to cash. If someone suddenly discovers $1 million in buried treasure, explain what will happen to the money supply if the required reserve ratio is one-sixth (16.67 percent).

6. How would your answer to Question 5 differ if the reserve ratio were 25 percent? If the reserve ratio were 100 percent?

7. Each year during the Christmas shopping season, consumers and stores wish to increase their holdings of cash. Explain how this could lead to a multiple contraction of the money supply. (As a matter of fact, the authorities prevent this contraction from occurring by methods explained in the next chapter.)

8. Excess reserves make a bank less vulnerable to runs. Why, then, don't bankers like to hold excess reserves? What circumstances might persuade them that it would be advisable to hold excess reserves?

9. Use tables such as Tables 12–2 and 12–3 to illustrate what happens to bank balance sheets when each of the following transactions occurs:
   a. You withdraw $200 from your chequing account to purchase textbooks at the university book store.
   b. Paul steals $100 in cash from Peter and deposits it into his chequing account.
   c. Mary Q. Contrary withdraws $500 in cash from her account at Hometown Bank, carries it to the city, and deposits it into her account at Big City Bank.

10. For each of the transactions listed in Question 9, what will be the ultimate effect on the money supply if the required reserve ratio is 10 percent? (Assume that the oversimplified money-multiplier formula applies.)

Central Banking and Monetary Policy

Victorians heard with grave attention that the Bank Rate had been raised. They did not know what it meant. But they knew that it was an act of extreme wisdom.

J.K. GALBRAITH

From what we learned in Chapter 12 about the normal practices of profit-oriented banks we might expect the money supply to expand rapidly during prosperous times and to grow sluggishly, or even to shrink, during recessions. Fortunately, the historical record for *postwar* Canada does not exhibit this pattern. Why not? One reason is that Canada's *central bank*, the Bank of Canada, has prevented it from happening.

The Bank of Canada is a very special kind of bank. Its customers are banks rather than individuals, and it performs some of the same services for them that your bank performs for you. Though it turns out to be quite an effective profit-maker, its actions are not guided by the profit motive. Instead, the Bank of Canada acts in what it perceives to be the national interest. While its actions are certainly not free from error, and while many people do not share its view of what constitutes the national interest, the Bank of Canada's actions have by and large caused the money supply to be a stabilizing influence on the Canadian economy. Just how the Bank of Canada regulates the money supply and the international value of the Canadian dollar, and why its performance has fallen short of perfection, are the main subjects of this chapter.

The Bank of Canada

The Bank of Canada was officially created by the Bank of Canada Act of 1935. It was originally a privately owned bank with approximately 12,000 individual shareholders. In 1938, complete nationalization took place when the federal government bought all the shares. The Bank of Canada is now a crown corporation, and all its profits accrue to the government.

Before the creation of the Bank of Canada, much of our currency was dollar bills, or notes, issued by the various chartered banks. In 1934, 53 percent of the currency was Dominion of Canada notes, while 47 percent was private bank liabilities. In 1950, all chartered bank notes were withdrawn from circulation.

One of the reasons for the creation of the Bank of Canada was to provide more stability for the economy. During the first four years of the Great Depression, the Canadian money supply fell by 12.5 percent. While no chartered banks failed, this contraction in the money supply accentuated the fall in aggregate demand that took place. Now the Bank of Canada tries to control Canada's money supply in an attempt to have the "appropriate" level of aggregate demand.

The Independence of the Bank of Canada

Canadians have had four governors of its central bank. According to the original act, the governor was appointed for seven years, and once appointed, he could not be removed by the government. This institutional independence of the governor was looked upon as a source of pride by some and as an anti-democratic embarrassment by others. The proponents of central bank independence argue that it enables monetary-policy decisions to be made on objective, technical criteria and keeps monetary control out of the "political thicket." Without this independence, it is argued, there would be a tendency for politicians to force the Bank of Canada to expand the money supply too rapidly, thereby contributing to chronic inflation and undermining faith in the financial system.

Opponents of this view counter that there is something profoundly undemocratic about having an unelected banker and his advisors make decisions that affect the well-being of all Canadians. Monetary policy, they argue, ought to be formulated by the elected representatives of the people, just like fiscal policy. Those who argue for government control over the Bank can point to historical instances in which monetary and fiscal policy have been at loggerheads—with the Bank of Canada undoing or even overwhelming the effects of fiscal-policy decisions.

This conflict did not occur under our first governor, Graham Towers, who headed the central bank from 1935 to 1954. However, the second governor, James Coyne (1955–61), was the centre of a dramatic conflict with the Diefenbaker government. During the severe recession of the late 1950s, Diefenbaker's government used expansionary fiscal policy in an attempt to create jobs. Coyne was more concerned with avoiding inflation and a possible depreciation of the Canadian dollar. Thus, he put a tight limit on the growth of the money supply and operated a contractionary monetary policy. This counteracted the government's fiscal policy. After much wrangling, the government's constitutional advisors suggested that an act be passed declaring the governor's seat to be vacant. The government could not fire Mr. Coyne, but they could define his position out of existence. Although the Senate refused to pass this bill, Mr. Coyne felt that he had had his chance to have his reasoning officially recorded during the Senate hearings, and he resigned.

When our third governor, Louis Rasminsky (1961–73), took office, he formally acknowledged that the government had the final power "to direct the Bank as to the policy which the Bank is to carry out." This principle was officially included in the 1967 revision of the Bank of Canada Act. As a result, our fourth and current governor, Gerald Bouey, must take his basic instructions from the government. However, should he consider the government's dictates to be irresponsible monetary policy, he can resign and explain his reasons. Since this would be extremely embarrassing for the government, from a political point of view, the governor still has a significant degree of power. For example, since 1975, the governor has consistently warned the government that the Bank of Canada is not printing up new money to buy up very many of the government bonds being issued to cover the record budget deficits. Several recent annual reports of the Bank stress that the government must get better control of its deficit. Hence, the governor of the Bank is not a pawn of the government.

Controlling the Money Supply: Reserve Requirements

Chapter 12 taught us one important way in which the monetary authorities can control the money supply: by varying the minimum required reserve ratio. The lower is the reserve ratio, the more the chartered banks can loan out, and therefore the more deposit money they can create. However, since the 1967 revision of the Bank Act, the main reserve ratio has been fixed by law, and so the reserve requirement is no longer an instrument of monetary control.

The reserve requirements that rule today are those that were set in the 1980 revision of the Bank Act. Chartered banks must hold at least the following amounts in their vaults, or in their deposits at the Bank of Canada: 10 percent of their chequing deposit obligations; 2 percent of the first $500 million of savings and notice deposit obligations; 3 percent of the remaining savings and notice deposits; 3 percent of their foreign currency deposit obligations.

The fact that there are several different reserve requirements means that the actual money-creation formula is more complicated than the one we derived in Chapter 12. The fact that the reserve requirement is less stringent on deposit accounts that formally require prior notice of withdrawals is an anachronism. The reserves are not required for public confidence, given the existing deposit insurance. Unfortunately, this anachronism has a cost, since it makes monetary control more difficult. Chartered banks can vary deposit interest rates and service charges for cheques to induce the public to change the proportion of the deposits it holds in chequing accounts. By doing so, the chartered banks (not the central bank) can control the overall reserve requirement ratio.

Controlling the Money Supply: Open-Market Operations

The Bank of Canada buys and sells in the nation's bond markets, and this is its main method of affecting chartered bank reserves. Since these operations involve the Bank of Canada as simply one (sometimes large) participant in the bond markets that are open to anyone, they are called **open-market operations**. To appreciate the mechanics of this policy, we must consider the balance sheet of the central bank; this is presented in Table 13–1.

We see from Table 13–1 that the Bank of Canada limits most of its purchases to one class of assets: Government of Canada bonds. Either the Bank purchases newly printed bonds that have been issued by the government to cover some of its current budget deficit, or it purchases existing government bonds previously held by members of the private sector. The latter operation, which is called an open-market purchase, allows the Bank to increase the money supply even if there is no current budget deficit, as we shall presently see. Unlike the chartered banks, the Bank of Canada returns all bond-interest earnings to the government.

The other major asset purchased by the Bank is foreign exchange. Some of these holdings are gold (since gold was the original international medium of

Open-market operations refer to the Bank of Canada's purchase or sale of government securities through transactions in the open bond market.

Table 13-1

THE CONSOLIDATED BALANCE SHEET OF THE BANK OF CANADA AND THE EXCHANGE FUND ACCOUNT, 1983

ASSETS (billions of dollars)		LIABILITIES (billions of dollars)	
Government of Canada bonds	17.03	Notes in circulation (currency)	14.16
Gold and foreign currency reserves	5.45	Deposits: of chartered banks of federal government	3.45 0.09
Advances	0.03	Miscellaneous accounts and net worth	4.81

SOURCE: Bank of Canada *Review*.

exchange) and the rest are stocks of various major foreign currencies. Our discussion of the reasons for, and the implications of, the Bank's purchasing or selling foreign exchange is postponed until later in this chapter. What we emphasize now is simply the fact that exchange-rate policy is carried out by the Bank of Canada.[1]

Table 13-1 also shows that the bulk of the Bank of Canada "liabilities" is the stock of currency that is used by chartered banks and the general public. We also see that the Bank of Canada serves as a bank for the chartered banks. A large part of the reserves held by the chartered banks to satisfy the reserve requirement laws are held in the form of chequing deposits at the Bank of Canada. The cheque-clearing process between chartered banks is accomplished by the banks writing cheques (to each other) drawn against their own accounts at the Bank of Canada. The federal government also holds an account with the Bank of Canada; and, of course, the government has deposit accounts at the various chartered banks as well. The government uses all of these accounts to store tax revenue as it comes in and to write cheques to make payments.

An open-market purchase of federal government bonds (previously held by the general public) by the Bank of Canada on January 2, 1985, is illustrated in Table 13-2.

The +$100,000 entry on the asset side of the Bank of Canada's balance sheet indicates its purchase of bonds from some member of the general public on the open market. The Bank of Canada pays for the bond by cheque, and the bond dealer gives the cheque to the member of the public for whom he sold the bond. The member of the public then deposits the cheque for $100,000 in his chartered bank, and this is recorded as the +$100,000 entry on the liability side of the

[1]The third asset, advances, is explained on pages 247–48.

Table 13-2
CHANGES IN THE BALANCE SHEETS OF THE BANK OF CANADA AND THE CHARTERED BANKS FOLLOWING AN OPEN MARKET PURCHASE OF BONDS

CHANGES IN BALANCE SHEET OF BANK OF CANADA, JANUARY 2, 1985

ASSETS		LIABILITIES	
Government bonds	+$100,000	Currency outstanding	
Foreign exchange		Deposits:	
		of federal government	
Advances to chartered banks		of chartered banks	+$100,000

CHANGES IN BALANCE SHEET OF CHARTERED BANKS, JANUARY 2, 1985

ASSETS		LIABILITIES	
Reserves:		Deposits:	
vault cash		of general public	+$100,000
deposits at the Bank of Canada	+$100,000	of federal government	
Loans		Advances from Bank of Canada	

Addendum: Changes in Reserves			
Actual reserves	+$100,000		
Required reserves	+ $20,000		
Excess reserves	+ $80,000		

A multiple expansion of loans and deposits begins as the chartered banks get rid of their excess reserves by making new loans totalling $80,000.

chartered bank's balance sheet. The other entries on the balance sheets indicate the cheque-clearing process. The chartered bank sends the cheque back to the Bank of Canada, and the central bank pays the chartered bank by simply granting it an increase of $100,000 in its deposits at the Bank of Canada. This cheque-clearing operation requires two entries on the balance sheet, since the chartered bank's deposit is both its own asset *and* the Bank of Canada's liability.

The net result of this transaction is that the chartered bank has its reserves increase by the same amount as its deposits. Given the low reserve requirements, most of this increase is excess reserves; so the chartered banking system is now in a position to commence the process of multiple expansion in loans and deposits that we described in Chapter 12. For example, if we continue to assume a reserve requirement ratio of 0.2 for our illustration, the open-market purchase of bonds by the Bank of Canada eventually results in an increase of the public's deposits in chartered banks equal to $500,000. We need not repeat the details of that multiple expansion process. Our purpose here is only to explain how the Bank of Canada actually creates the initial increase in reserves that starts the expansion of the money supply. By a similar process, an open-market sale of government bonds by the Bank of Canada involves minus signs on the four entries in Table 13–2, and so leads to a multiple contraction of chartered bank loans and deposits.

Open-market operations constitute the major tool of monetary policy by which the Bank of Canada varies the rate of growth of the money supply.

The Bank of Canada buys bonds whenever it wants to increase the money supply; and it sells bonds whenever it wants to decrease the money supply.

To anticipate our discussion on exchange-rate policy in the next section of this chapter, we emphasize one important point now. *It does not matter what the Bank of Canada buys or sells; the effect on the money supply is the same.* Thus, as we shall see, Bank of Canada purchases of foreign exchange constitute an expansionary monetary policy, and Bank of Canada sales of foreign-exchange reserves constitute a contractionary monetary policy.

Controlling the Money Supply: Changes in Bank Rate

If the chartered banks ever get over-extended in loan operations and do not have the reserves required by the Bank Act, they can borrow the reserves from the Bank of Canada. The rate of interest charged by the Bank of Canada for these advances is called the **bank rate**. Since the chartered banks virtually never require an advance from the central bank, the bank rate is usually just employed as a summary signal, so that the private sector is aware of the behind-the-scenes operations of the Bank. For example, if the Bank has been selling government bonds, and intends to continue this action, it raises the bank rate. This represents an easily understood signal that the Bank is trying to reduce the money supply and tighten credit. Thus, changes in the bank rate merely reflect the stance of monetary policy as defined by the more basic tool of open-market operations.

The **bank rate** is the rate of interest charged by the Bank of Canada when reserves are loaned to the chartered banks (advances from the central bank). It is used as a signal of the direction of monetary policy.

Many people misunderstand the role of bank-rate announcements, since these changes are often *followed by* adjustments in the prime lending rates charged by chartered banks. Given this observed sequence of events, it appears that the bank rate is the fundamental causal influence. In fact, the Bank of Canada's contraction of reserves (due to open-market bond sales) is the real cause of loans becoming scarce and chartered bank loan rates increasing. However, the chartered banks can achieve a gain in public relations by waiting for the central bank to raise the bank rate before increasing their loan rates. Then they can talk about necessarily having to "pass on cost increases."

Before 1979, the bank rate was changed by the Bank of Canada on a relatively infrequent basis. In the autumn of 1979, the true role of the bank rate became more transparent as the Bank of Canada adopted a policy of weekly adjustments in the bank rate. Every week the federal government auctions its new issue of treasury bills, a type of bond that it uses to obtain operating funds. The yield on the treasury bills is determined in a free market by supply and demand. The bank rate is now set every week at one-quarter of one percentage point above that week's treasury bill yield. This arrangement makes explicit what has been true for years: The bank rate is set to be *consistent with* going market interest rates; it *does not determine* market interest rates. Monetary policy has its fundamental effects on market interest rates by affecting the quantity of bonds and reserves that are available to the private sector through open-market operations.

Flexible Exchange Rates: A Prerequisite for Independent Control of the Money Supply

The Bank of Canada intervenes in the foreign-exchange market on a daily basis, in order to control the value of the Canadian dollar. Since this intervention involves either buying or selling foreign exchange, the quantity of central-bank liabilities outstanding becomes residually determined. This means that the more the Bank tries to fix a particular price for the Canadian dollar (the exchange rate), the more it loses the ability to fix the nation's money supply at any particular value. Thus, exchange-rate policy and monetary policy are one and the same. Because of this connection, we now give a detailed explanation of exchange rates, and how they can be fixed by the central bank.

What Are Exchange Rates?

While we have mentioned exchange rates at numerous points in earlier chapters, it is now time for a more thorough discussion. In the next several pages we will explain the distinction between a policy of fixed exchange rates and one of floating exchange rates. Then we will discuss how the choice of policy affects the ability of the Bank of Canada to control the nation's money supply.

International trade is more complicated than domestic trade. There are no national borders to be crossed when, say, apples from British Columbia are shipped to Ontario. The consumer in Ottawa pays with *dollars*, just the currency that the farmer in the Okanogan wants. But if that same farmer ships his apples to Japan, consumers there will have only Japanese *yen* with which to pay, rather than the dollars the farmer in B.C. wants. Thus, if international trade is to take place, there must be a way to transform one currency (yen) into another (dollars). The rates at which such transformations are made are called **exchange rates**.

The **exchange rate** states the price, in terms of one currency, at which another currency can be bought.

There is an exchange rate between every pair of currencies. For example, $1 Canadian is currently the equivalent of about 6 French francs. The exchange rate between the franc and the dollar, then, may be expressed as "6 francs to the dollar" (meaning that it costs 6 francs to buy a dollar) or about "16 cents to the franc" (meaning that it costs 16 cents to buy a franc). Although exchange rates change all the time, Table 13–3 gives an indication of exchange rates prevailing in June 1984, showing how many Canadian dollars it cost at that time to buy each unit of foreign currency.

A nation's currency is said to **appreciate** when exchange rates change so that a unit of its own currency can buy more units of foreign currency. The currency is said to **depreciate** when exchange rates change so that a unit of its currency can buy fewer units of foreign currency.

Under our present system, currency rates change frequently. When other currencies get more expensive in terms of dollars, we say that they have **appreciated** relative to the dollar. Alternatively, we can look at this same event in terms of the dollar buying less foreign currency, meaning that the dollar has **depreciated** relative to another currency.

What is a depreciation to one country must be an appreciation to the other.

For example, if the dollar cost of a German mark rises from 48 cents to 60 cents,

Table 13-3

EXCHANGE RATES WITH THE CANADIAN DOLLAR, JUNE 1984
(dollars per unit of foreign currency)

COUNTRY	CURRENCY UNIT	SYMBOL	COST IN CANADIAN DOLLARS
Australia	dollar	$	1.17
France	franc	FF	0.16
Germany	mark	DM	0.48
Italy	lira	L	0.00079
Japan	yen	¥	0.0056
Mexico	peso	$	0.0068
Sweden	krona	Kr	0.16
Switzerland	franc	S. Fr.	0.58
United Kingdom	pound	£	1.82
United States	dollar	$	1.30

SOURCE: *The Financial Post*

the cost of a Canadian dollar in terms of marks simultaneously falls from just over 2 marks to 1.67 marks. The Germans have had a currency *appreciation* while we have had a currency *depreciation*.

Notice also that, when many currencies are changing in value, the dollar may be appreciating with respect to one currency but depreciating with respect to another. Consider, for example, this set of actual recent exchange rates:

	ACTUAL EXCHANGE RATES	
	January 1982	**June 1984**
British pound	1 pound = $2.23	1 pound = $1.82
U.S. dollar	1 U.S. dollar = $1.19	1 U.S. dollar = $1.30

Between January 1982 and June 1984, the Canadian dollar *depreciated* relative to the U.S. dollar but *appreciated* relative to the pound.

While this is the terminology used to describe movements of exchange rates in free markets, another set of terms is used to describe decreases and increases in currency values when these values are set by government decree. When an officially set exchange rate is altered so that a unit of a nation's currency can buy *fewer* units of foreign currency, we say there has been a **devaluation** of that currency. When the exchange rate is altered so that the currency can buy *more* units of foreign currency, we say there has been a **revaluation**.

Exchange-Rate Determination in a Free Market

Why is it that a German mark costs 48 cents and not 40 cents or 55 cents? In a world of **floating exchange rates** (also called **flexible exchange rates**), with no government interferences, the answer would be fairly straightforward. Exchange rates would be determined by the forces of supply and demand, just like the prices of apples, or typewriters, or haircuts.

In a leap of abstraction, imagine that Canada and West Germany were the only countries on earth, so there was only one exchange rate to be determined. Figure 13-1 depicts the determination of this exchange rate at the point (denoted *E* in the figure) where demand curve *DD* crosses supply curve *SS*. At this price (48 cents per mark), we know that the number of marks demanded is equal to the number of marks supplied.

In a free market, exchange rates are determined by the law of supply and demand. If the rate were below the equilibrium level, the quantity of marks

A **devaluation** is a reduction in the official value of a currency.

A **revaluation** is an increase in the official value of a currency.

Floating exchange rates (also known as **flexible exchange rates**) are rates determined in free markets by the law of supply and demand.

Figure 13-1

DETERMINATION OF EXCHANGE RATES IN A FREE MARKET

Like any price, an exchange rate will be determined by the intersection of the demand and supply curves in a free market. Point *E* depicts this point for the exchange rate between the Canadian dollar and the German mark, which settles at 48 cents per mark in this example.

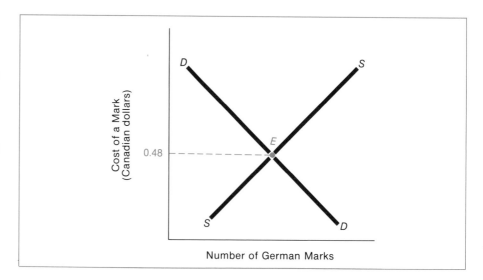

demanded would exceed the quantity of marks supplied, and the price of a mark would be bid up. If the rate were above the equilibrium level, quantity supplied would exceed quantity demanded, and the price of a mark would fall. Only at the equilibrium exchange rate is there no tendency for the exchange rate to change.

As usual, supply and demand determine price. What we must ask in this case is: Where do the supply and demand come from? Why does anyone demand a German mark?

1. **International trade in goods and services.** If, for example, Jane Doe, a Canadian, wants to buy a German automobile, she will first have to buy marks with which to pay the dealer in Munich.[2] So Jane's demand for a German *car* leads to a demand for German *marks*. In general, *demand for a country's export goods and services leads to a demand for its currency.*

2. **International trade in financial instruments like stocks and bonds.** For example, if Canadian investors want to purchase German stocks, they will first have to acquire the marks that the sellers will insist on. In this way, demand for German financial assets leads to demand for German marks. Thus, *demand for a country's financial assets leads to a demand for its currency.*

3. **Purchases of physical assets like factories and machinery overseas.** If a company in Canada wants to buy out a small German manufacturer, the owners will no doubt want to receive marks. So the Canadian company will first have to acquire German currency. In general, *direct foreign investment leads to a demand for a country's currency.*

Now, where does the supply come from? To answer this, we need only turn all of these transactions around. Germans wanting to buy Canadian goods and services, or to invest in Canadian financial markets, or to make direct investments in Canada will have to offer their marks for sale in the foreign-exchange market (which is similar to the stock market) to acquire the needed dollars. To summarize:

The *demand* for a country's currency is derived from the demands of foreigners for its export goods and services and for its assets, including financial assets, factories,

[2]Actually she will not do this because banks generally handle foreign-exchange transactions for consumers. A Canadian bank probably will buy the marks for her. But the effect is exactly the same as if Jane had done it herself.

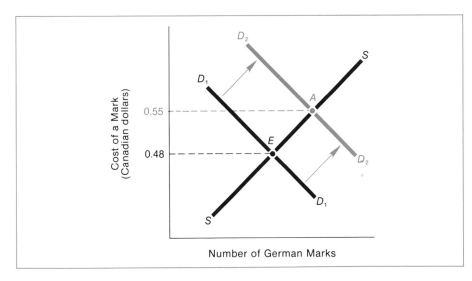

Figure 13-2
THE EFFECT OF AN
ECONOMIC BOOM ON THE
EXCHANGE RATE
If the Canadian economy
suddenly booms, Canadians will
spend more on imports from
Germany. Thus, the demand
curve for German marks will rise
from D_1D_1 to D_2D_2 as Canadians
seek to acquire the marks they
need. The diagram shows that
this will cause the mark to
appreciate, from 48 cents to 55
cents, as equilibrium shifts from
point E to point A. Looked at from
the Canadian perspective, the
dollar will depreciate.

and machinery. The *supply* of a country's foreign currency to individuals and firms in the rest of the world arises from its imports, and from foreign investment by its own citizens.

To appreciate the usefulness of even this simple supply and demand analysis, let us consider how the exchange rate between the Canadian dollar and the mark would change if there were an economic boom in Canada. One important effect of such a boom would be to stimulate Canadian demand for German products, such as automobiles, cameras, and wines. In terms of the supply-demand diagram shown in Figure 13-2, the increased desires of Canadians for German products would shift the demand curve for German marks out from D_1D_1 (the black line in the figure) to D_2D_2 (the blue line). Equilibrium would shift from point E to point A, and the exchange rate would rise from 48 cents per mark to 55 cents per mark. In a word, the increased demand for marks by Canadian citizens causes the mark to appreciate relative to the dollar.

EXERCISE
Test your understanding of the supply and demand analysis of exchange rates by showing why each of the following events would lead to a depreciation of the mark (appreciation of the dollar) in a free market:

1. A recession in Canada cuts Canadian purchases of German goods.
2. German investors are attracted by prospects for profit in the Canadian stock market.
3. Interest rates on government bonds rise in Canada but are stable in Germany. (*Hint*: Which country's citizens will be attracted by high interest rates to the other country?)

We will discuss the other important factors that shift the supply and demand curves for foreign exchange in Chapter 16. Here our focus is on the way central banks limit the flexibility of exchange rates (no matter what shifts the supply and demand curves for foreign exchange).

Fixed Exchange Rates

History records rather few instances of truly free exchange rates, determined by supply and demand without government interference. Much more typical are cases where governments have resisted market forces and kept their exchange rates either above or below the equilibrium price for long periods of time. For this reason, we turn our attention next to the opposite of floating exchange rates, a system of **fixed exchange rates**, or rates that are set by governments. Naturally, under such a system the exchange rate, being fixed, is not closely watched. Instead, international financial specialists focus on a country's **balance of payments**—a term we are now ready to define.

To understand what the balance of payments is, look at Figure 13-3, which depicts a situation that might represent, say, Great Britain before its major devaluation in 1967—an *overvalued* currency. While the supply and demand curves for British pounds indicate an equilibrium exchange rate of $2.60 to the pound (point *E*) the British government is keeping the rate at $3.00. Notice that at $3.00 more people are supplying pounds than are demanding them. In the example, suppliers are selling £22 billion per year, but demanders are purchasing only £20 billion.

This gap between the £22 billion that some people sell and the £20 billion that other people buy is what we mean by Britain's **balance of payments deficit**—£2 billion per year in this case. It is shown by the horizontal distance between points *A* and *B* in Figure 13-3.

How can market forces be flouted in this way? Since sales and purchases on any market must be equal, as a simple piece of arithmetic, the excess of quantity supplied over quantity demanded of British currency (£2 billion per year in this example) must be bought by the Bank of England, Britain's central bank. In buying these pounds, it must give up some of the gold and foreign currencies that it keeps as *foreign-exchange reserves*. Thus, the Bank of England would be losing £2 billion in reserves per year as the cost of keeping the pound at $3.00.

Naturally, this cannot go on forever; the reserves eventually will run out. And this is the fatal flaw in the system of fixed exchange rates. Once speculators become convinced that the exchange rate can be held only a short while longer, they will sell pounds in massive amounts rather than hold on to a currency whose value they soon expect to fall sharply. The supply curve of pounds will shift outward drastically, as shown in Figure 13-4, causing an astronomical rise in the balance of payments deficit (from £2 billion to £4 billion in the example). This is called a "run" on the currency. Lacking sufficient reserves, the Bank of England will have to permit the exchange rate to fall to its equilibrium level, and this

Fixed exchange rates are rates that are set by government decisions and maintained by central bank actions.

The **balance of payments deficit** is the amount by which the quantity supplied of a country's currency (per year) exceeds the quantity demanded. Balance of payments deficits arise whenever the exchange rate is pegged at an artificially high level.

Figure 13-3
A BALANCE OF PAYMENTS DEFICIT
At a fixed exchange rate of $3.00 per pound, which is well above the equilibrium level of $2.60 per pound, England's currency is overvalued in this example. As a consequence, more pounds will be supplied (point *B*) than are demanded (point *A*). The difference—distance *AB*, or £2 billion per year—represents Britain's balance of payments deficit.

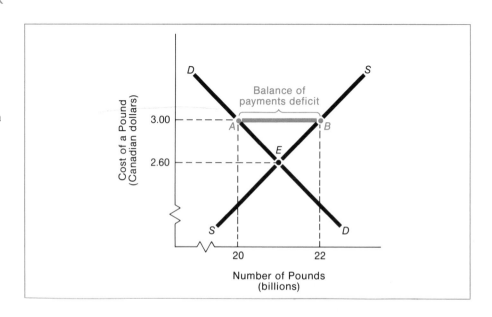

might amount to an even larger devaluation than would have been required before the speculative run on the pound began.

For an example of the reverse case, a severely *undervalued* currency, let us consider Germany in 1973. Figure 13-5 depicts demand and supply curves for marks that intersect at an equilibrium price of 40 cents per mark (point *E* in the diagram). Yet, in the example, we suppose that the German authorities are holding the rate at 35 cents. At this rate, the quantity of marks demanded (50 billion) greatly exceeds the quantity supplied (40 billion). The difference is Germany's **balance of payments surplus**, and is shown by the horizontal distance *AB*.

Germany can keep the rate at 35 cents only by providing the marks that foreigners want to buy: 10 billion marks per year in this example. In return, it receives U.S. dollars, British pounds, French francs, gold, and so on. All of this serves to increase Germany's reserves of foreign currencies. But notice the important difference between this case and Britain's overvalued pound.

The **balance of payments surplus** is the amount by which the quantity demanded of a country's currency (per year) exceeds the quantity supplied. Balance of payments surpluses arise whenever the exchange rate is pegged at an artificially low level.

The accumulation of foreign-exchange reserves rarely will *force* a central bank to revalue in the way that depletion of reserves can force a devaluation.

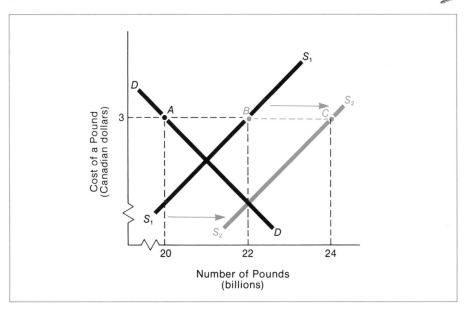

Figure 13-4

A SPECULATIVE RUN ON THE POUND

When speculators become convinced that a devaluation of the pound is in the offing, they will rush to sell all their pounds. Their actions shift the supply curve outward from S_1S_1 to S_2S_2 and, in the process, widen England's balance of payments deficit from *AB* to *AC*.

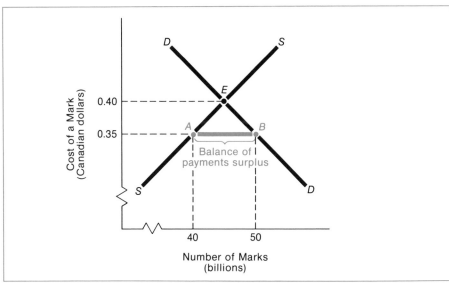

Figure 13-5

A BALANCE OF PAYMENTS SURPLUS

In this example, Germany's currency is undervalued at 35 cents per mark, since the equilibrium exchange rate is 40 cents per mark. Consequently, more marks are being demanded (point *B*) than are being supplied (point *A*). The gap between quantity demanded and quantity supplied—distance *AB*, or 10 billion marks per year— measures Germany's balance of payments surplus.

This was another weakness of the system of fixed exchange rates. In principle, imbalances in exchange rates could be cured either by a devaluation by the country with a balance of payments deficit or by an upward revaluation by the country with a balance of payments surplus. In practice, though, it was almost always the deficit countries that were forced to act.

Why did the surplus countries refuse to revalue? One reason was a simple misunderstanding of basic economics. They viewed the disequilibrium as the problem of the deficit countries and believed that the deficit countries, therefore, should take the corrective steps. This, of course, is nonsense. Some currencies are overvalued *because* some other currencies are undervalued. In fact, the two statements mean exactly the same thing.

The other reason is that exporters in Germany, Japan, and other surplus countries resisted upward revaluations because they knew that such actions would make their products more expensive to foreigners and thus cut into their export sales. And these exporters had the political clout to make that view stick. Meanwhile, since the values of the mark and the yen on world markets were artificially held down, German and Japanese consumers were put in the unenviable position of having to pay more for imported goods than they need have paid. Rather than buy these excessively expensive foreign goods, they watched domestically produced goods go overseas in return for pieces of paper (dollars, francs, pounds, and so on).

A more thorough investigation of the reasons why countries have tried to fix their exchange rates takes place in Chapter 16. Here we simply stress that fixing the exchange rate necessarily involves the country's central bank either buying up, or selling off, foreign exchange. Thus, pegging the exchange rate would involve the Bank of Canada performing an open-market operation in the foreign-exchange market, instead of the domestic bond market. The implications for the money supply are the same. This can be appreciated by simply moving the +$100,000 entry on the asset side of the Bank of Canada balance sheet in Table 13–2. The effect on chartered bank reserves is the same whether this entry is on the government-bond line or on the foreign-exchange line. Thus pegging the exchange rate involves allowing the growth in the Canadian money supply to be determined by the gap between the private demand and supply for foreign exchange.

The Bank of Canada can control our exchange rate or our money supply but not both.

The Money-Supply Mechanism: A Summary

This completes our discussion of the Bank of Canada's methods of controlling the money supply. We can now begin to integrate what we have just learned about the financial system into the macroeconomic model presented in Chapters 8 through 11, and to study how money affects the national economy. For this purpose, the analyses of the last chapter and the present one can be summed up in the following statement:

As interest rates rise, banks normally find it more profitable to expand their volume of loans and deposits, thus increasing the supply of money. This poses the danger that the money supply might expand rapidly during a period of inflation and economic boom and advance slowly, or even contract, during a period of recession—just the opposite from what stabilization policy requires.

However, the Bank of Canada can shift the relationship between the money supply and interest rates by employing its principal weapon of monetary control: open-market operations.

These ideas are depicted graphically in Figure 13–6. Part (a) shows a typical

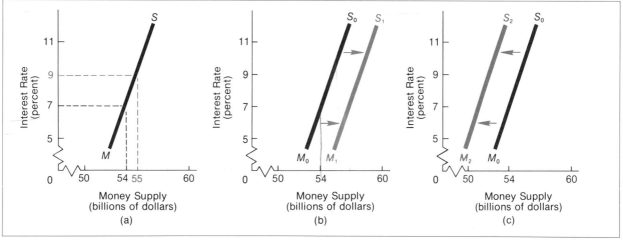

Figure 13-6

THE SUPPLY SCHEDULE FOR MONEY

Part (a) shows a typical supply schedule for money. It is rising as we move toward the right, meaning that banks will supply more money when interest rates are higher. Part (b) illustrates what happens to the money-supply schedule when the Bank of Canada purchases securities in the open market: The supply schedule shifts outward. Part (c) depicts the effect of a sale of bonds by the Bank of Canada. With this contractionary policy, the supply schedule shifts inward.

money-supply schedule labelled *MS*, illustrating that bank behaviour makes the money stock rise as interest rates rise. Notice that the sensitivity of the money supply to interest rates is rather weak in the diagram—a large rise in the rate of interest (from 7 percent to 9 percent) induces only a small increase in the supply of money (from $54 billion to $55 billion). The drawing is deliberately constructed that way because that is what the statistical evidence shows.

The curve in Figure 13-6(a) shows the money-supply schedule corresponding to some specific monetary policy. Figure 13-6(b) portrays how the money-supply schedule responds to an *expansionary change in monetary policy*, such as an open-market purchase of government bonds. The money-supply schedule shifts outward from M_0S_0 to M_1S_1, as indicated by the arrows. After banks have adjusted to the change, there is more money at any given interest rate. Figure 13-6(c) shows what happens in the reverse case—*contractionary monetary policy*, such as an open-market sale of securities. The money-supply schedule shifts inward from M_0S_0 to M_2S_2.

The diagrams make things look rather more precise than they actually are. Since the Bank of Canada's control over the money-supply schedule is imperfect in the short run, the actual *MS* schedule is obscured by a bit of fog. In what follows, we portray all the graphs as clean straight lines only for pedagogical simplicity. The Bank of Canada wishes things were so simple in the real world!

The Demand for Money

Just as we must know something about both the supply of and the demand for wheat before we can predict how much will be sold and at what price, it is necessary to know something about the **demand for money** if we are to understand the amount of money actually in existence and the prevailing interest rate.

The definition of money given in Chapter 12 suggests the most important reason why people hold money balances: The medium of exchange is needed to carry out purchases and sales of goods and services. Since the nominal gross national product (GNP) is considered to be the best measure of the total money value of all goods and services traded in the economy, it seems safe to assume that the higher the nominal GNP, the higher will be the demand for money. And, indeed, an impressive amount of statistical evidence supports this supposition. Notice that nominal GNP, and hence the demand for money, rises if *either* real output or the price level rises—a fact that will assume some importance in the next chapter.

But income is not the only factor affecting the demand for money; interest rates matter, too. At first, that may seem surprising because many forms of money, such as currency and some chequing deposits, pay no interest. Why, then, are interest rates relevant? They are relevant because money is only one of a variety of forms in which individuals can hold their wealth. Holders of money *give up* the opportunity to hold one of these other assets, such as government bonds, in order to gain the convenience of money. In so doing, they *give up* the interest that they could have earned on one of these alternative assets.

This is another example of the concept of *opportunity cost*.[3] On the surface, it seems virtually costless to hold money. But, *compared with the next best alternative*, this action is not costless at all. For example, if the next best alternative to holding $200 in cash is to put those funds into a government bond that pays 10 percent interest, then the opportunity cost of holding that money is $20 per year (10 percent of $200).

How, then, should the rate of interest influence the quantity of money that people demand? It is natural to assume that when interest rates are high people will make strenuous efforts to economize on their holdings of money balances, efforts that would not be worthwhile at lower interest rates. In a word, rational behaviour of consumers and business firms should make the demand to hold money *decline* as the interest rate *rises*. And once again, careful analysis of the data shows this to be true. To summarize:

People and business firms hold money primarily to finance their transactions. Therefore, the quantity of money demanded increases as real output rises or as prices rise. However, the quantity of money demanded decreases as the rate of interest rises because the rate of interest is the opportunity cost of holding money balances.

It is possible to portray the demand for money by a graphical device, as shown in Figure 13-7. There we show a downward-sloping demand schedule for money

[3]If you need to review this concept, see Chapter 3.

Figure 13-7

THE DEMAND SCHEDULE FOR MONEY

The downward-sloping curve *MD* is a typical demand schedule for money. It slopes down because money is a less-attractive asset when interest rates on alternative assets are higher. The entire curve is shifted if either the number of transactions (which is often measured by real GNP) or the average price of a transaction (which is measured by the price level) changes.

(the curve labelled *MD*)—the quantity of money demanded decreases as the rate of interest rises. But since the quantity of money demanded also depends on real output and the price level, we must hold both real output and the price level constant in drawing up such a curve. Changes in either of these variables will shift the *MD* curve in the manner indicated in the diagram because at higher levels of nominal GNP, demand for money is higher; and at lower levels of nominal GNP, it is lower.

Equilibrium in the Money Market When Foreign and Domestic Financial Markets Are Independent

As is usual in supply and demand analysis, it is useful to put both sides of the market together on a single graph. Figure 13–8 combines the money-supply schedule of Figure 13–6(a) (labelled *MS*) with the money-demand schedule of Figure 13–7 (labelled *MD*).

There is no curve representing foreigners' actions in this market, since, for the moment, we are assuming that funds cannot flow across international borders, so that interest rates in Canada can diverge from the level of U.S. interest rates. Point *E* is the equilibrium of the money market. The diagram thus shows that *given* real output and the price level (which locates the *MD* curve) and *given* the monetary policy (which locates the *MS* curve), the money market is in equilibrium at an interest rate (*r*) of 9 percent and a money stock (*M*) of \$55 billion.

Since the central bank can shift the *MS* curve, it can alter this equilibrium through its **monetary policy**. Expansionary monetary-policy actions involve purchasing government securities in the open market. This action provides additional excess reserves to the banking system, thus encouraging banks to increase their loans and deposits. As money becomes more plentiful, interest rates drop.

Our supply–demand analysis of the money market shows this in Figure 13–9(a). By shifting the money-supply schedule outward from M_0S_0 to M_1S_1, the central bank moves the market equilibrium from point *E* to point *A*—thus forcing the interest rate down.

Contractionary monetary-policy actions, such as selling securities in the open

Monetary policy refers to actions that the Bank of Canada takes in order to change the equilibrium of the money market, that is, to alter the money supply, move the exchange rate, or both.

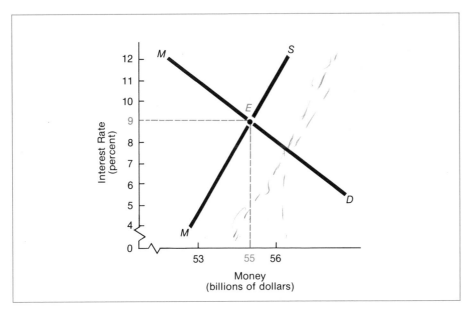

Figure 13-8
EQUILIBRIUM IN THE MONEY MARKET WITH FOREIGN TRANSACTIONS OMITTED
Equilibrium in the market for money is determined by the intersection of demand curve *MD* and supply curve *MS*. At point *E*, the interest rate is 9 percent, and the money supply is \$55 billion. At no other interest rate would the demand for and the supply of money be in balance.

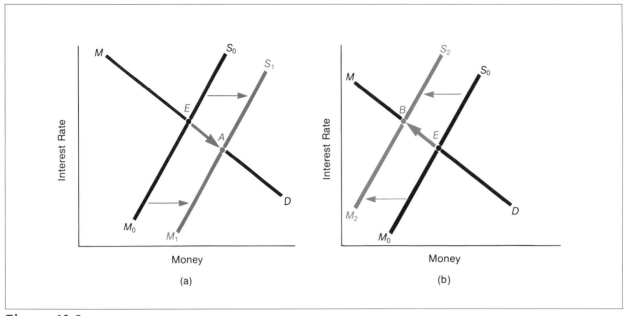

Figure 13-9

THE EFFECTS OF MONETARY POLICY ON THE MONEY MARKET

The two parts of this figure show the effects of monetary policy on the money supply (M) and the rate of interest (r). In part (a), expansionary monetary policies shift the supply schedule from $M_0 S_0$ to $M_1 S_1$ and push the equilibrium from point E to point A; M rises while r falls. In part (b), contractionary policies pull the supply schedule in from $M_0 S_0$ to $M_2 S_2$, causing equilibrium to move up from point E to point B; M falls as r rises.

market, have the opposite effect. They push interest rates up, as Figure 13-9(b) shows. Thus:

Monetary policies that expand the money supply normally lower interest rates. Monetary policies that reduce the money supply normally raise interest rates.

During the early 1980s the U.S. central bank rigidly restricted the growth of the U.S. money supply to fight inflation. The theory was that the resulting high interest rates would discourage investment spending and so decrease aggregate demand. Those high interest rates have caused much concern in Canada and other Western countries.

Equilibrium in the Money Market When Foreign and Domestic Financial Markets Are Integrated

In the previous section, we discussed the determination of the level of interest rates, without any reference to the level of foreign interest rates. While this analysis is useful for a country like the United States, it is unrealistic for Canada. Since it is so easy for Americans to buy Canadian bonds, and vice versa, and since Canadian bonds constitute such a small proportion of the North American financial market, the North American interest rate is essentially determined by U.S. monetary policy in the manner we have just described. Competition among sellers of bonds precludes a different rate of interest from being "made in Canada."

Figure 13-10, which reproduces the demand and supply curves from Figure 13-8, shows how this works. Assume that the value of the U.S. interest rate has just risen from 9 to 11 percent. Equilibrium in the Canadian market can no longer be at point E, since that outcome involves Canadians earning only 9 percent on their bonds, while 11 percent is available through buying U.S. bonds. Thus, households and firms will choose to be at point A on their demand-for-money curve.

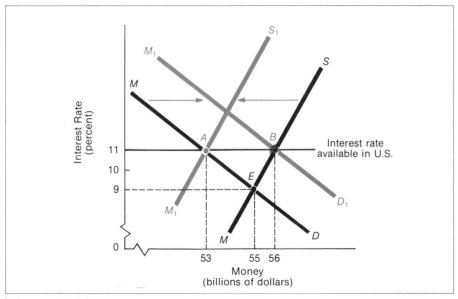

Figure 13-10

EQUILIBRIUM IN THE MONEY MARKET WHEN THE AVAILABILITY OF FOREIGN
BONDS PEGS THE RATE OF INTEREST

Under fixed exchange rates, the Bank of Canada must accept the otherwise unwanted Canadian
currency (given by distance AB). This decreases the amount of money in circulation so the money-
supply curve shifts left (to M_1S_1), and equilibrium obtains at point A. Under flexible exchange rates,
the Canadian dollar depreciates (because of the excess supply, AB). This raises import costs and
stimulates exports. The resulting increase in nominal GNP shifts the money-demand curve to the
right (to M_1D_1), and equilibrium obtains at point B.

Given this choice by demanders, and given the interest rate of 11 percent, there is
an excess supply of domestic money equal to the distance AB in Figure 13–10 ($3
billion in our example).

How is this disequilibrium resolved? There are two possible methods of
resolution, depending on whether the country has adopted a fixed or flexible
exchange-rate policy.

Fixed Exchange Rates

Under a fixed-exchange-rate regime, the Bank of Canada must intervene in the
money market to support the exchange rate. In this case, there is excess supply of
Canadian dollars, equal to $3 billion and shown by distance AB in the diagram.
The mirror image of this excess supply of Canadian dollars is the equivalent
excess demand for U.S. dollars, which savers need to buy the desired U.S. bonds.
Since the U.S. dollar is in demand, while the Canadian dollar is not, a fall in the
value of the Canadian dollar will occur unless the Bank intervenes. To avoid the
fall in the value of the Canadian dollar, the Bank of Canada must buy up the
otherwise unwanted $3 billion of Canadian dollars, by selling the corresponding
amount of U.S. dollars from the country's foreign-exchange reserves. As a result of
this foreign-exchange operation, there will be less Canadian money circulating
than before (by amount AB). So the money-supply curve will be shifted to the left
by this distance (to position M_1S_1), and all three curves intersect at point A. Thus,
a complete equilibrium can be obtained under fixed exchange rates but with an
adjustment that amounts to a contractionary monetary policy—an open-market
sale of foreign exchange.

A policy of fixed exchange rates involves giving up the ability to conduct an
independent monetary policy. Under fixed exchange rates, the private agents
involved in the foreign-exchange market dictate what open-market operation the
Bank of Canada must do to peg the exchange rate. Both the magnitude and
direction of this open-market operation is determined for the central bank.

Flexible Exchange Rates

How is full equilibrium achieved under a flexible-rate policy? Without intervention by the Bank of Canada, the attempt by private agents to trade away Canadian for U.S. dollars means that the Canadian dollar will depreciate in value. This makes our imports more expensive and so raises our price level. It also makes our exports cheaper for foreigners to buy, and so raises aggregate demand. Both of these influences raise nominal GNP in Canada, and so shift the money-demand curve to the right. The depreciation of the Canadian dollar continues until the excess supply of Canadian dollars is eliminated by the demand-for-money curve shifting to position M_1D_1 in Figure 13-10. Thus, a complete equilibrium is obtained under flexible exchange rates at point B, and the adjustment involves inflation and an increase in aggregate demand.

When foreign interest rates increase, competition forces Canadian interest rates to increase. Our only policy choice is whether we want aggregate demand to expand or contract along with this rise in interest rates. Contraction follows if the Bank of Canada fixes the exchange rate, since the bank must absorb the excess supply of Canadian dollars that results from bond-holders switching to foreign bonds. The bank can refuse to supply foreign currency in exchange for the Canadian dollars that bond-holders want to sell, but then the Canadian dollar depreciates. This raises the price of imports and stimulates aggregate demand, and so leads to inflation.

The applicability of this analysis can be demonstrated in two ways. First, we can illustrate the direct connection between Canadian and U.S. interest rates that exists in the data; and second, we can consider the annual report of the Bank of

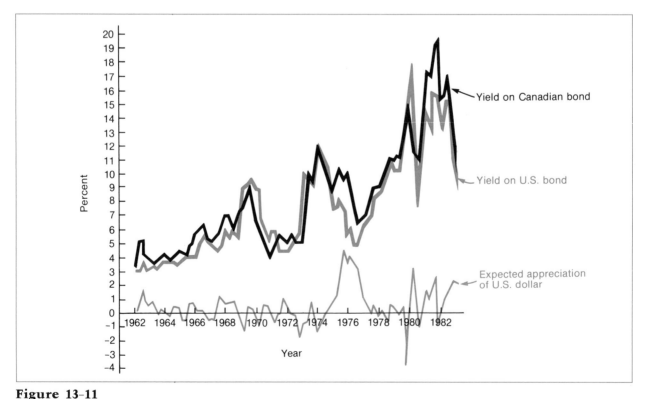

Figure 13-11
CANADIAN AND U.S. INTEREST RATES AND THE EXPECTED APPRECIATION OF THE U.S. DOLLAR, 1962–1982
This graph shows that a significant interest-rate differential has only emerged when a significant change in the exchange rate was expected by market participants. SOURCE: Cansim

Bank of Canada Policy

The following article from *The Globe and Mail* illustrates how directly the Bank of Canada relies on the economic analysis that we have covered in this chapter.

OTTAWA—Bank of Canada Governor Gerald Bouey says he cannot ease up on high interest rates at the expense of the Canadian dollar because this would risk further inflation....

In the Bank of Canada's annual report ... Mr. Bouey said that he will do everything within reason to fight rising prices—including resisting "sharp downward movements" in the value of the Canadian dollar.

The Bank of Canada allowed interest rates to rise on Thursday, in order to attract liquid capital into Canada and thus keep the value of the dollar up....

... at a press conference in which he released the annual report, Mr. Bouey told reporters that the central bank had little choice except to let interest rates go up.

He said the Bank of Canada would have had to print $2-billion worth of money on Thursday and buy up all government treasury bills to keep interest rates down. (The central bank lending rate is set at a weekly auction of these government treasury bills.)...

"I don't want a serious devaluation of the Canadian dollar. That is a sure way to inflation."

In his report, the central bank chief warned that it would be folly for the Government to deliberately try to devalue the currency in order to lower interest rates and create jobs. Such a move could only weaken private sector confidence in the Government's determination to bring down inflation.

If that were to happen, he said, interest rates might dip for a short period but then they would rise again....

Mr. Bouey said interest rates in Canada can come down significantly only if the United States lowers its federal deficit. This, by alleviating fears of inflation among Wall Street financiers, would let U.S. interest rates, and thus Canadian rates, come down.

He said that while he supports the idea of reducing the Canadian deficit, such a reduction would lower interest rates only minimally. Canadian interest rates, he said, are in large measure set in the U.S.

SOURCE: *The Globe and Mail*, Toronto, March 17, 1984, page 1.

Canada. Figure 13–11 certainly verifies that Canada has had to accept the high and volatile interest rates that have followed from U.S. monetary policy in the 1980s. The graph demonstrates that a significant interest-rate differential has only emerged when a significant change in the exchange rate was expected by market participants.

The only policy decision that exists for the Bank of Canada is whether we follow a fixed or a flexible exchange-rate policy. As the accompanying box explains, the Bank of Canada relies on this analysis and has chosen to fight inflation rather than unemployment, and therefore to resist depreciation of the Canadian dollar. It is possible to criticize the Bank for caring too much about inflation, but it cannot be blamed for the high interest rates.

Conclusion and Preview

We now understand how the Bank of Canada is organized, what tools it has available for regulating the money supply, how monetary policy is connected with exchange-rate policy, and how interest rates and exchange rates are determined. We can now investigate how these monetary-policy decisions affect unemployment, inflation, and the overall state of the economy, a task to which we turn in the next chapter.

Summary

1. The Bank of Canada is our central bank, which serves as a bank for the chartered banks. It is the institution that conducts Canada's monetary and exchange-rate policy.
2. The Bank of Canada uses open-market operations to change the reserves available to the chartered banks.
3. Open-market purchases of government bonds or foreign exchange by the Bank of Canada increase the money supply. Open-market sales of government bonds or foreign exchange by the Bank decrease Canada's money supply.
4. Bank rate is the rate the chartered banks must pay the Bank of Canada if they need to borrow reserves. Since very little borrowing of reserves occurs, the weekly adjustment in the bank rate serves only as a signal of the direction of monetary policy. A decrease in the bank rate indicates that the Bank of Canada has been conducting policies that increase the money supply.
5. The Bank of Canada does not have perfect control over the money supply in the short run, because it cannot predict perfectly how far the process of deposit creation or destruction will go.
6. Exchange rates state the value of one currency in terms of another, and thus influence the patterns of world trade in important ways.
7. If governments do not interfere, exchange rates will be determined in free markets by the usual laws of supply and demand. Such a system is called floating or flexible exchange rates.
8. Demand for a nation's currency is derived from foreigners' desires to purchase that country's goods and services or to invest in its assets. Any change that increases the demand for a nation's currency will cause its exchange rate to appreciate under floating rates.
9. Supply of a nation's currency is derived from the desire of that country's citizens to purchase foreign goods and services or to invest in foreign assets. Any change that increases the supply of a nation's currency will cause its exchange rate to depreciate under floating rates.
10. Exchange rates can be fixed at non-equilibrium levels by governments that are willing and able to mop up any excess of quantity supplied over quantity demanded, or provide any excess of quantity demanded over quantity supplied. In the first case, the country is suffering from a balance of payments deficit because of its overvalued currency. In the second, an undervalued currency has given it a balance of payments surplus.
11. When the Bank of Canada fixes the exchange rate, it performs an open-market operation in the foreign-exchange market instead of the domestic bond market. As a result, the central bank cannot set both the money supply and the exchange rate.
12. The money-supply schedule shows that more money is supplied at higher interest rates because, as interest rates rise, banks find it more profitable to expand their loans and deposits. This schedule can be shifted by Bank of Canada policy.
13. The money-demand schedule shows that less money is demanded at higher interest rates because interest is the opportunity cost of holding money. This schedule shifts when output or the price level changes.
14. The equilibrium money stock (M) and the equilibrium rate of interest (r) are determined by the intersection of the money-supply and money-demand schedules, as long as foreign and domestic financial markets are independent.
15. Central bank policy can shift this equilibrium. Expansionary policies cause M to rise and r to fall. Contractionary policies reduce M and increase r.
16. Canadian interest rates are determined in the United States. Increased foreign interest rates are accompanied by inflation if we let the Canadian dollar depreciate, and by a contraction in the money supply and aggregate demand if the Bank of Canada pegs the exchange rate.

Concepts for Review

Bank of Canada
Reserve requirements
Exchange rate
Appreciation
Depreciation
Devaluation
Revaluation
Supply of and demand for foreign exchange

Floating, or flexible, exchange rates
Open-market operations
Contraction and expansion of the money supply
Bank rate
Fixed exchange rates
Balance of payments deficit and surplus
Interest-rate differential

Supply of money
Demand for money
Equilibrium in the money market
Controlling M versus controlling exchange rate

Questions for Discussion

1. Why does a modern industrial economy need a central bank?
2. Do you think it is a good idea to have an independent central bank? Explain your reasons.
3. Suppose there is $80 billion of cash in existence, and that all of it is held in bank vaults as *required* reserves (that is, banks hold no *excess* reserves). How large will the money supply be if the required reserve ratio is $16\frac{2}{3}$ percent? 20 percent? 25 percent?
4. Show the balance-sheet changes that would take place if the Bank of Canada purchased an office building from the Bank of Commerce for a price of $100 million. Compare this to the effect of an open-market purchase of securities shown in Table 13–2. What do you conclude?
5. Suppose that the Bank of Canada purchases $5 million worth of government bonds from E.P. Taylor who banks at the Bank of Montreal. Show the effects on the balance sheets of the central bank, the Bank of Montreal, and E.P. Taylor. (*Hint*: What will Taylor do with the $5 million cheque he receives from the Bank of Canada?) Does it make any difference if the Bank of Canada buys bonds from a bank or from an individual?
6. Why would the Bank of Canada's control over the money supply be tighter if all chartered bank deposits were subject to the same reserve requirements?
7. Explain why Governor Bouey has stated that he would resign rather than carry out written instructions from the government to try to lower interest rates by allowing the Canadian dollar to depreciate.

assets   B. of Comm   Liabs

$+ 100$

$- 100$

Bank of Canada

ass

$+ 100$

$- 100$

$$\frac{80}{x} = \frac{16.67}{100}(x)$$

$$\frac{80}{x} = \frac{20}{100} \cdot \frac{1}{5}$$

$$x = 400$$

Liabs

-100

Stabilization Policy: Without International Capital Flows

In this chapter and the next, we bring together our analysis of income determination and the price level from Chapters 7 through 11 and our analysis of money and monetary policy from Chapters 12 and 13. In doing so, we complete the construction of our model of the entire macroeconomy. We will then use this model to see how and to what extent the Bank of Canada's ability to manage the money supply also enables it to manage the level of aggregate demand—and hence to influence unemployment and inflation.

We begin the chapter by integrating the financial system into the Keynesian $C + I + G + X - IM$ model described in Chapters 7 through 11. The mechanisms by which monetary policy affects aggregate demand are spelled out and analysed, and we learn an additional reason why the aggregate-demand curve slopes downward.

Then we turn to a very old and very simple macroeconomic model—the *quantity theory of money*, and its modern reincarnation, *monetarism*—for an alternative view of the effects of money on the economy. Although the monetarist and Keynesian theories seem to be two contradictory views of how monetary and fiscal policy work, we will see that the conflict is more apparent than real. In fact, the disagreement is akin to hearing a Briton say, "Yes," and a Frenchman say, "Oui." The uninitiated hear two different languages, but knowledgeable listeners understand that they mean the same thing.

However, while a major objective of this chapter is to show that the differences between the two theories are greatly exaggerated, there *are* significant differences between the two schools of thought—not outright contradictions but differences in emphasis. These differences occupy the rest of this chapter.

The analysis in this chapter rests on the unrealistic but simplifying assumption that Canada's financial markets operate independently of foreign financial markets. That is, we assume that Canadian interest rates can diverge from the level of U.S. interest rates. This is *not* realistic, but for the sake of clearer exposition we discuss the Keynesian–monetarist controversy and the foreign-exchange market complications in two separate steps. We will consider the more realistic case of integrated financial markets in Chapter 15.

A Study Hint

Because it integrates so many aspects of the macroeconomic theory we have already constructed, this chapter requires you to keep many things in mind at the same time. In this respect, it requires careful study. Fortunately, however, it does not introduce any new technical apparatus. Literally everything we need can be borrowed from earlier chapters. The following is a list of the things we will be referring to in the pages to come, indicating where you should look if you need to review any of them:

- How aggregate supply and aggregate demand interact to determine the price level (Chapters 5 and 10).
- How the circular flow of income and expenditure determines equilibrium output (Chapter 8).
- The analysis of the multiplier (Chapters 9 and 11).
- The workings of fiscal policy (Chapter 11).
- How the supply of and the demand for money interact to determine the quantity of money and the interest rate, and how the central bank can influence this equilibrium (Chapter 13).

Money and Income: The Important Difference

First, a review of some important vocabulary. As pointed out in Chapter 1, the words "money" and "income" are used almost interchangeably in common parlance. This is a pitfall we must learn to avoid.

Money is a snapshot concept. It is the answer to questions like: "How much money do you have right now?" or "How much money did you have at 3:32 P.M. on Friday, November 5th?" To answer questions like these, you would add up the cash you are (or were) carrying and whatever bank balances you have (or had), and answer something like: "I have $126.33," or "On Friday, November 5th, at 3:32 P.M., I had $31.43."

Income, by contrast, is more like a motion picture; it comes to you only over a period of time. If you are asked "What is your income?" you must respond by saying "$300 *per week*," or "$1200 *per month*," or "$14,400 *per year*," or something like that. Notice that there is a unit of time attached to each of these responses. If you just say "My income is $452.19," without indicating whether it is per week or per month or per year, no one will understand what you mean.

That the two concepts are very different is easy to see. A typical Canadian family has an income of about $32,000 per year, but its holdings of *money* at any point in time (using the M1 definition) are $4500. Similarly, at the national level, nominal GNP in 1983 was about $389 billion, while the money stock (M1) was only about $30 billion.

While money and income are very different, they are certainly related. This chapter is precisely about that relationship. Specifically, we will look at how the stock of *money* in existence at any moment of time influences the rate at which people will be earning *income*, that is, how money affects the GNP.

Money and Total Expenditure in the Keynesian Model

To begin, we go back to the analysis of Chapters 7–11, where we learned that aggregate demand is the sum of consumption spending (C), investment spending (I), government purchases of goods and services (G) and net exports (X – IM). We know that *fiscal policy* controls G directly and exerts influence over both C and I through the tax laws. We now want to find out how *monetary policy* influences $C + I + G + X - IM$.

Most economists agree that, of the four components of aggregate demand, investment (I) is the most sensitive to monetary policy. *Business investment* in new factories and machinery is sensitive to interest rates for reasons that have been explained in earlier chapters.[1] Since the rate of interest that must be paid on borrowings is one element of the cost of making an investment, business executives will find investment prospects less attractive as interest rates rise. Therefore, they will spend less. For similar reasons, *investment in housing* by individuals may also be deterred by high interest rates. Since the interest cost of a home mortgage is the major component of the total cost of owning a home, fewer families will want to buy a new home when interest rates are high than when interest rates are low. We conclude that:

Higher interest rates lead to lower investment spending. But investment (*I*) is a component of total spending ($C + I + G + X - IM$). Therefore, when interest rates rise, total spending falls. In terms of the 45° line diagram of previous chapters, a higher interest rate leads to a lower $C + I + G + X - IM$ schedule. Conversely, a lower interest rate leads to a higher $C + I + G + X - IM$ schedule (see Figure 14–1).

Monetary Policy in the Keynesian Model

The effect of interest rates on spending provides the mechanism by which monetary policy affects aggregate demand in the Keynesian model. We know from our analysis of the money market in Chapter 13 that monetary policy can have a profound effect on the rate of interest. Let us, therefore, outline the effects of monetary policy in the Keynesian model, starting first on the demand side of the economy.

Suppose the Bank of Canada, seeing the economy stuck with unemployment and a recessionary gap, raises the money supply. We learned in Chapter 13 that it normally would do this by purchasing government securities in the open market. With the demand schedule for money (temporarily) fixed, such an increase in the supply of money has the effect that an increase in supply always has in a free market—it lowers the price. In this case, the price of renting money is the rate of interest, *r*; so *r* falls.

Next, for reasons we have just outlined, investment spending (*I*) rises in response to the lower interest rates. But, as we learned in Chapter 9, such a rise in

[1]See, for example, Chapter 8, page 142.

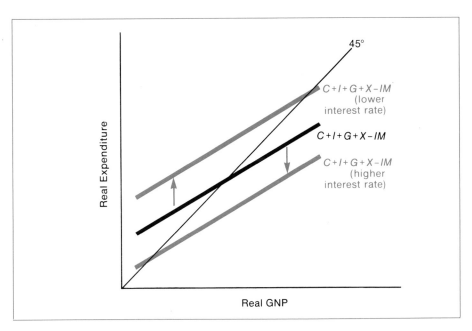

Figure 14–1

THE EFFECT OF INTEREST RATES ON AGGREGATE DEMAND

Because interest rates are an important determinant of investment spending, *I*, the $C + I + G + X - IM$ schedule shifts whenever the rate of interest changes. Specifically, as shown here, lower interest rates shift the curve upward and higher interest rates shift it downward.

investment kicks off a multiplier chain of increases in output and employment. Thus, finally, we have completed the links from the money supply to the level of aggregate demand. In brief, monetary policy works as follows:

A higher money supply leads to lower interest rates, and these lower interest rates encourage investment, which has multiplier effects on aggregate demand.

The process operates equally well in reverse. By contracting the money supply, the Bank of Canada can force interest rates up, causing investment spending to fall and pulling down aggregate demand via the multiplier mechanism.

This, in outline form, is how monetary policy operates in the Keynesian model. Since the chain of causation is fairly long, the following schematic diagram may help clarify it.

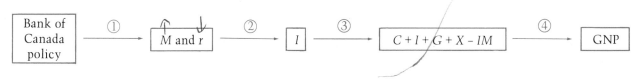

In this causal chain, link 1 indicates that the actions of the Bank of Canada affect money and interest rates. Link 2 stands for the effect of interest rates on investment. Link 3 simply notes that investment is one component of total spending. And link 4 is the multiplier, relating an autonomous change in investment to the ultimate change in aggregate demand.

Let us next review what we have learned about each of these links in previous chapters. In the process, we will see what Keynesians must study if they are to estimate the effect of monetary policy.

Link 1 was the subject of the last chapter, and Figure 14–2 reviews the analysis. Given the initial level of real GNP and prices, the demand schedule for money is shown by curve MD. The Bank of Canada's expansionary action shifts the supply schedule out from M_0S_0 to M_1S_1, resulting in an increase in the money stock from $55 billion to $59 billion in this example, and a decline in the interest rate from 9 percent to 7 percent. Thus the first thing a Keynesian economist must know is how sensitive interest rates are to changes in the supply of money.

Figure 14-2

THE EFFECT OF EXPANSIONARY MONETARY POLICY ON THE MONEY SUPPLY AND RATE OF INTEREST

An expansionary monetary policy pushes the money-supply schedule outward from M_0S_0 to M_1S_1, causing equilibrium in the money market to shift from point E_0 to point E_1. The money supply rises from $55 billion to $59 billion, while the interest rate falls from 9 percent to 7 percent.

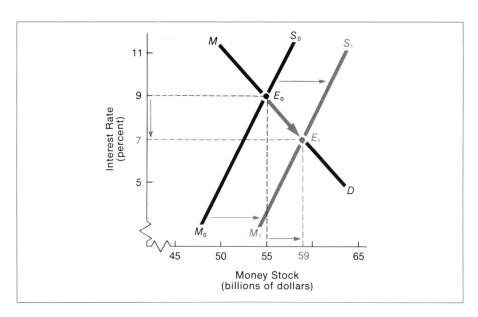

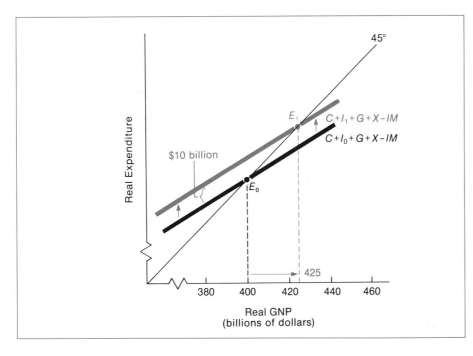

Expansionary monetary policies,
which lower the rate of interest, will
cause the $C + I + G + X - IM$
schedule to shift upward from $C + I_0 + G + X - IM$ to $C + I_1 + G + X - IM$ as shown here. In this example,
since the multiplier is 2.5, a $10
billion rise in investment leads, via
the multiplier process, to a $25
billion rise in GNP.

Link 2 translates the drop in the interest rate into an increase in investment spending (I), which we take to be $10 billion in this example. To estimate this effect in practice, a Keynesian economist must study the sensitivity of investment to interest rates.

Link 3 instructs us to enter this $10 billion rise in I as an autonomous shift in the $C + I + G + X - IM$ schedule of a 45° line diagram. Figure 14-3 carries out this step. The expenditure schedule rises from $C + I_0 + G + X - IM$ to $C + I_1 + G + X - IM$.

Finally, link 4 applies multiplier analysis to this vertical shift in the expenditure schedule in order to predict the eventual increase in real GNP demanded. In this example, we assume a multiplier of 2.5, so multiplying $10 billion by 2.5 gives the final effect on aggregate demand—a rise of $25 billion. This is shown in Figure 14-3 as a shift in equilibrium from E_0 (where GNP is $400 billion) to E_1 (where GNP is $425 billion). Of course, the size of this multiplier itself must also be estimated. To summarize:

The effect of monetary policy on aggregate demand depends on the sensitivity of interest rates to the money supply, on the responsiveness of investment spending to the rate of interest, and on the size of the multiplier.

Money and the Price Level: The Complete Keynesian Model

One need only recall the inflation of past decades to realize that we have forgotten something. What happens to the price level? To answer this, we must simply remember once again that prices and output are determined jointly by aggregate supply *and* aggregate demand. The analysis of monetary policy that we have completed so far has shown us how an increase in the money supply shifts the aggregate-demand curve; that is, increases the *aggregate quantity demanded at any given price level.* But to learn what happens to the price level and to real output, we must bring *aggregate supply* into the picture as well.

Specifically, in considering shifts in aggregate demand caused by *fiscal* policy in Chapter 11, we noted that an upsurge in total spending normally induces firms to increase output somewhat *and* to raise prices somewhat. This is just what an aggregate-supply curve shows. Whether prices or real output exhibit the greater response depends mainly on the degree of capacity utilization. An economy operating near full employment has only a limited ability to increase production; it therefore responds to greater demand mainly by raising prices. On the other hand, an economy with a substantial amount of unemployed labour and unused capital is able to increase output a great deal without raising prices.

Now this analysis of output and price responses applies equally well to monetary policy or, for that matter, to anything else that raises aggregate demand. We conclude, then, that:

Expansionary monetary policy causes some inflation under normal circumstances. But how much inflation it causes depends on the state of the economy. If the money supply is expanded when unemployment is high and there is much unused industrial capacity, then the result may be little inflation. If, however, increases in the money supply occur when the economy is fully employed, then the main result is inflation.

The effect of a rise in the money supply on the price level is depicted graphically on an aggregate-supply-and-demand diagram in Figure 14-4. The curved shape of aggregate-supply curve SS reflects the assumptions that output rises with little inflation when the economy is depressed, while prices rise with little gain in output when the economy is near full employment.

In the example we have been using, the Bank of Canada's actions raise the money supply by $4 billion, and this increases aggregate demand (through the multiplier) by $25 billion. We enter this in Figure 14-4 as a horizontal shift of $25 billion in the aggregate-demand curve, from D_0D_0 to D_1D_1. The diagram shows that this expansionary monetary policy raises the economy's equilibrium from point E to point B—the price level therefore rises from 100 to 103, or 3 percent. The diagram also shows that real GNP rises by only $20 billion, which is less than the $25 billion stimulus to aggregate demand. The reason, as we know from earlier chapters, is that rising prices stifle demand.

By taking account of the effect of an increase in the money supply on the price level, we have completed our story about the role of monetary policy in the Keynesian model. We can thus expand our schematic diagram of monetary policy as follows:

Figure 14-4

THE INFLATIONARY
EFFECTS OF EXPANSIONARY
MONETARY POLICY

Raising the money supply normally causes inflation. When expansionary monetary policy causes the aggregate-demand curve to shift outward from D_0D_0 to D_1D_1, the economy's equilibrium shifts from point E to point B. Real output expands (in this case by $20 billion), but prices also rise (in this case by 3 percent).

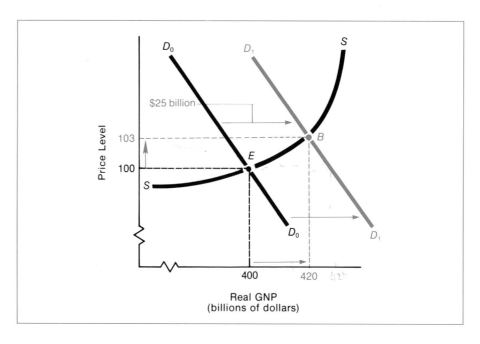

$$\boxed{\begin{array}{c}\text{Bank of}\\\text{Canada}\\\text{policy}\end{array}} \xrightarrow{\;\;①\;\;} \boxed{M \text{ and } r} \xrightarrow{\;\;②\;\;} \boxed{I} \xrightarrow{\;\;③\;\;} \boxed{C + I + G + X - IM} \xrightarrow{\;\;④\;\;} \boxed{Y \text{ and } P}$$

The last link now recognizes that *both* output *and* prices normally are affected by changes in the money supply.

Why the Aggregate-Demand Curve Slopes Downward

This analysis of the effect of money on the price level puts us in a better position to understand why higher prices reduce aggregate quantity demanded; that is, why the aggregate-demand curve slopes downward. In earlier chapters, we explained this phenomenon by observing that rising prices reduce the purchasing power of certain assets held by consumers, especially money and government bonds, and that this in turn retards consumption spending. There is nothing wrong with this analysis. But higher prices have much more important effects on aggregate demand through channels that we are now in a position to understand.

Money is demanded primarily to conduct transactions, and we saw in Chapter 13 that a rise in the *average money cost* of each transaction—as a result of a rise in the price level—will increase the quantity of money demanded. It simply takes more cash to buy a given amount of goods at higher prices. This means that when expansionary policy of any kind pushes the price level up, more money will be demanded at any given interest rate.

But, if the supply of money is *not* increased, an increase in the quantity of money demanded at any given interest rate must force the cost of borrowing money—the rate of interest—to rise. As we know, increases in interest rates reduce investment and, hence, reduce aggregate demand. This, then, is the main reason why the economy's aggregate-demand curve has a negative slope, meaning that aggregate quantity demanded is lower when prices are higher.

At higher price levels, the quantity of money demanded is greater. Given a fixed supply schedule, a higher price level must lead to a higher interest rate. Since high interest rates discourage investment, aggregate quantity demanded is lower when the price level is higher. That is, the aggregate-demand curve slopes downward to the right.

There exists yet another reason for the downward slope of the aggregate-demand curve. The higher the domestic price level, the more expensive are our goods relative to foreign products. As a result, both domestic residents and foreigners buy fewer Canadian-produced goods. This means that net exports $(X - IM)$ fall, leading to an overall drop in aggregate-demand when our price level rises.

Velocity and the Quantity Theory of Money

We have now seen how money influences real output and the price level in the Keynesian model. But there is another way to look at these matters using a model that is much older than the Keynesian model, and yet is at the heart of some very modern critiques of Keynesian economics. This model is known as the **quantity theory of money**, and it is easy to understand once we have introduced one new concept—*velocity*.

We learned in Chapter 12 that because barter is so cumbersome, virtually all economic transactions in advanced economies are conducted by the use of money. This means that if there are, say, $350 billion worth of transactions in the economy during a particular year, and there is an average money stock of $70 billion during that year, then each dollar of money must get used an average of five times during the year (since 5 × $70 billion = $350 billion).

The number 5 in this example is called the **velocity of circulation**, or just **velocity** for short, because it indicates the speed at which money circulates.

Velocity indicates the number of times per year that an "average dollar" is spent on goods and services. It is the ratio of nominal GNP to the number of dollars in the money stock. That is:

$$\text{Velocity} = \frac{\text{Nominal GNP}}{\text{Money stock}}.$$

For example, a particular dollar bill might be used to pay for a haircut in January; the barber might use it to buy a sweater in March; the storekeeper might then use it to buy gasoline in May; the gas station owner could pay it out to a painter who paints his house in October; and the painter might spend it on a Christmas present in December. This would mean that the dollar was used five times during the year. If it were used only four times during the year, its velocity would be only 4, and so on. Similarly, a $20 bill circulating with a velocity of 4 would be the monetary instrument used to finance $80 worth of transactions in that year.

As we noted in Chapter 13, the gross national product in current prices (nominal GNP) is the most widely used measure of the value of the economy's total transactions (the number of dollars changing hands in a year). This measure leads to a concrete definition of velocity as the ratio of nominal GNP to the number of dollars in the money stock. Since nominal GNP is the product of real GNP times the price level, we can write this definition in symbols as:

$$V = \frac{\text{Value of transactions}}{\text{Money stock}} = \frac{\text{Nominal GNP}}{M} = \frac{P \times Y}{M}.$$

The **equation of exchange** states that the money value of GNP transactions must be equal to the product of the average stock of money times velocity. That is: $M \times V = P \times Y$.

By multiplying both sides of the equation by M, we arrive at an identity called the **equation of exchange** that relates the money supply and nominal GNP:

Money supply × Velocity = Nominal GNP.

Alternatively, stated in symbols, we have:

$$M \times V = P \times Y.$$

Here we have quite an obvious link between the stock of money, M, and the nominal value of the nation's output. But it is only a matter of arithmetic, not of economics. For example, it does not imply that the Bank of Canada can raise nominal GNP by increasing M. Why not? Because V might simultaneously fall by enough to prevent $M \times V$ from rising. That is, if there were more dollar bills in circulation than before, but each bill changed hands more slowly, total spending would not necessarily rise.

The *quantity theory of money* transforms the equation of exchange from an accounting identity into an economic model *by assuming* that changes in velocity are so minor that, for practial purposes, velocity can be taken to be a constant.

You can see that if V never changed, the equation of exchange would be a marvellously simple model of the determination of nominal GNP—one that is far simpler than the Keynesian model. To see this, we need only to turn the equation of exchange around to read,

$$P \times Y = V \times M.$$

This equation says, for example, that if the Bank of Canada wants to increase nominal GNP by 12.7 percent, it need only raise the money supply by 12.7 percent. In such a simple world, economists could use the equation of exchange to *predict* nominal GNP simply by predicting the quantity of money. And policy-makers could *control* nominal GNP simply by controlling the money supply.

In the real world things are not so simple, because velocity is not a fixed number. But this does not necessarily destroy the usefulness of the quantity theory. We explained in Chapter 1 why all economic models make assumptions that are at least mildly unrealistic—without such assumptions they would not be models at all, just tedious descriptions of reality. The question is really whether

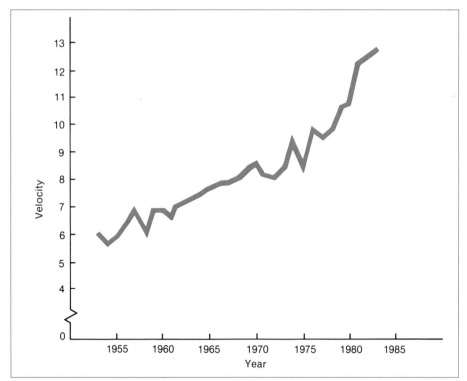

Figure 14-5
VELOCITY OF CIRCULATION,
1953–1983
Velocity displays both a trend and
short-run fluctuations.
SOURCE: Historical Statistics of Canada
(series J22), and Bank of Canada
Review, selected issues.

the assumption of constant velocity is a useful abstraction from annoying detail
or a gross distortion of facts.

Figure 14–5 sheds some light on this question by showing the behaviour of
velocity since 1953. You will undoubtedly notice an upward trend throughout this
period. Quite clearly, *velocity is not constant over long periods of time.* Also we
see some rather substantial fluctuations of velocity about its trend. Such fluctuations have led most economists to the conclusion that *velocity is not constant in
the short run either.* Nor have predictions of nominal GNP based on the product of
V times M fared very well. It seems, then, that the strict quantity theory of money
is not an adequate model of aggregate demand.

The Determinants of Velocity

Since it is abundantly clear that velocity is a variable, not a constant, we can use
the equation of exchange as a model of GNP determination only by examining the
determinants of velocity. What factors decide whether *V* will be 6 or 8 or 10; that
is, whether a dollar will be used to buy goods and services six or eight or ten times
a year?

Perhaps the principal factor is the *frequency with which paycheques are
received.* This can best be explained through a numerical example. Consider a
worker who earns $12,000 a year, paid to her in 12 monthly *paycheques* of $1000
each. Suppose that she spends the whole $1000 over the course of each month and
maintains a minimum balance in her chequing account of $500. Each payday her
bank balance will shoot up to $1500 and then be gradually whittled down as she
makes withdrawals to purchase goods and services. Finally, on the day before her
next paycheque arrives, her chequing balance will be just $500. Over the course of
a typical month, then, her average chequing account balance will be $1000 (halfway
between $1500 and $500).

Now suppose her employer switches to a twice-a-month payroll. Her paycheques come twice as often but are reduced to $500 each. There is no reason for her rate of spending to change, but her *cash balances* will change. For now her chequing balance will rise only to $1000 on payday (the $500 minimum balance plus the $500 paycheque), and it will still be drawn down gradually to $500. Her average cash balance will therefore decline to $750 (halfway between $1000 and $500). Why is this so? Because, with the next paycheque coming sooner than before, it is not necessary to keep as much cash in the bank in order to carry out a given quantity of transactions.

But what does this have to do with velocity? Notice that when she was on a monthly payroll, this worker's personal velocity was:

$$V = \frac{\text{Annual income}}{\text{Average cash balance}} = \frac{\$12,000}{\$1000} = 12.$$

When she switched to a semimonthly payroll, velocity rose to:

$$V = \frac{\text{Annual income}}{\text{Average cash balance}} = \frac{\$12,000}{\$750} = 16.$$

The general lesson to be learned is that:

More frequent wage payments mean that people can conduct their transactions with lower average cash balances. Since they will want to hold less cash, money will circulate faster. In other words, velocity will rise.

A second factor influencing velocity is the *efficiency of the payments mechanism*, including how quickly cheques clear through banks, the use of credit cards, and other methods of transferring funds. It is easy to see how this works.

The example in the previous paragraph assumed that our worker holds her entire paycheque in the form of money until she uses it to make a purchase. But, given that many forms of money pay little or no interest, this method may not be the most rational behaviour. If it is possible to convert interest-bearing assets into money on short notice and at low cost, a rational individual might use her paycheque to purchase such assets and then use credit cards for most purchases, making periodic transfers to her chequing account as necessary. For the same amount of total transactions, then, she would require lower money balances. This means that money would circulate faster: Velocity would rise.

The incentive to limit cash holdings depends on the ease and speed with which it is possible to exchange money for other assets. This is what we mean by the "efficiency of the payments mechanism." As computerization has speeded up the bookkeeping procedures of banks, as financial innovations have made it possible to transfer funds rapidly between chequing accounts and other assets, and as credit cards have come to be used instead of cash, the need to hold money balances has declined. By definition, then, velocity has risen.

Fortunately such basic changes in the payments mechanism usually take place only gradually, and thus often are easy to predict. But this is not always so. For example, a host of financial innovations in the 1980s—some of which were mentioned in Chapter 12's discussion of the definitions of money—gave analysts fits in predicting velocity.

A third determinant of velocity is the *rate of interest*. The basic motive for economizing on money holdings is that most money (at least M1) pays little or no interest, while many alternative stores of value pay higher rates. The higher these alternative rates of interest, the greater the incentive to economize on holding money. Therefore, as interest rates rise, people want to hold less money. So the existing stock of money circulates faster, and velocity rises.

It is this factor that most directly undercuts the usefulness of the quantity theory of money as a guide for monetary policy. For in the last chapter we learned that expansionary monetary policy, which increases M, normally also decreases the interest rate. But if interest rates fall, other things equal, velocity (V) will also fall. Thus, when the central bank raises the money supply (M), the product $M \times V$ may go up by a smaller percentage than does M itself.

One component of the interest rate is worth singling out for special attention: *the expected rate of inflation.* We explained in Chapter 6 why an "inflation premium" equal to the expected inflation rate often gets built in to market interest rates.[2] Thus, in many instances, high inflation is the principal cause of high nominal interest rates. High rates of inflation, which erode the purchasing power of money, therefore lead both individuals and businesses to hold as little money as they can get by on—actions that increase velocity. To summarize this discussion of the determinants of velocity:

Velocity is not a strict constant but depends on such things as the frequency of payments, the efficiency of the financial system, the rate of interest, and the rate of inflation. Only by studying these determinants of velocity can we hope to predict the level of nominal GNP from knowledge of the money supply.

Monetarism: The Quantity Theory Modernized

The foregoing does not mean, however, that the equation of exchange cannot be a useful framework within which to organize macroeconomic analysis. It can be. And during the past 30 years a group of economists called *monetarists* have convincingly demonstrated that this is so.

Monetarists recognize that velocity is not a constant. But they stress that it is fairly *predictable*—certainly in the long run and probably also in the short run. This leads them to the conclusion that the best way to study economic activity is to start with the *equation of exchange:* $M \times V = P \times Y$. From here, careful study of the determinants of M (which we provided in the previous two chapters) and of V (which we just completed) can be used to *predict* the behaviour of nominal GNP. Similarly, given an understanding of movements in V, control over the money supply gives the central bank *control* over nominal GNP.

These are the central tenets of **monetarism**. When something happens in the economy, monetarists ask two questions:

1. What does this event do to the stock of money?

2. What does this event do to velocity?

From the answers, they assert that they can predict the path of nominal GNP.

By comparing the monetarist approach with the Keynesian approach that we described earlier in this chapter, we can put both doctrines into perspective and understand the limitations of each. As we mentioned earlier, they differ more in style than in substance. Keynesians, as we learned in earlier chapters, divide economic knowledge into four neat compartments—marked "C," "I," "G," and "$X - IM$"—and unite them all with the equilibrium condition that $C + I + G + X - IM = Y$. In Keynesian analysis, money affects the economy by first affecting interest rates.

Monetarism is a mode of analysis that uses the equation of exchange to organize macroeconomic data.

[2]If you need review, turn back to pages 100–101.

Monetarists on the other hand, organize their knowledge into two alternative boxes—labelled "M" and "V"—and then use a simple identity that says $M \times V = P \times Y$ to bring this knowledge to bear in predicting aggregate demand. The role of money in the national economy is not necessarily limited to working through interest rates in the monetarist model.

The bit of arithmetic that multiplies M by V to get P multiplied by Y is neither more nor less profound than the one that adds C, I, G, and $X - IM$ to get Y. And certainly both approaches are correct. The only substantive difference is that the monetarist equation leads to a prediction of *nominal* GNP, that is, the demand for goods and services measured in money terms, whereas the Keynesian equation leads to a prediction of *real* GNP, that is, the demand for goods and services measured in dollars of constant purchasing power.

Why, then, do we not simply mesh the two theories—using the monetarist approach to study nominal GNP and the Keynesian approach to study real GNP? It seems that by doing so we could use the separate analyses of real and nominal GNP to obtain a prediction of the future behaviour of the price level, which, of course, is the source of any difference in behaviour between real and nominal GNP.

The reason that this appealing procedure will not work helps point out the major limitation of each theory. *Taken by itself, either theory is incomplete.* Each gives us a picture of the *demand* side of the economy without saying anything about the *supply* side. To try to predict both the price level and real output solely from these demand-oriented models would be like trying to predict the price of spinach by studying only the behaviour of consumers and ignoring that of farmers. It just will not work. In terms of our earlier aggregate-supply-and-demand analysis:

Both the monetarist and Keynesian analyses are ways of studying the *aggregate-demand curve*. In neither case is it possible to learn anything about both output and the price level without also studying the *aggregate-supply curve*.

Economists thus are forced to choose between two alternative ways of predicting aggregate demand. If the monetarist route is chosen, the economist will use velocity and the money supply to study the demand for *nominal* GNP, and then turn to the supply side to estimate how any predicted change in nominal income gets apportioned between changes in production and changes in prices. The schematic diagram on page 271, with its emphasis on interest rates, plays little role in the monetarist analysis of the transmission mechanism for monetary policy.

On the other hand, an economist working with the Keynesian $C + I + G + X - IM$ approach will start by using the schematic diagram on page 271, to predict how monetary policy affects the demand for *real* GNP. Then he will turn to the aggregate-supply curve to estimate the inflationary consequences of this real demand.

Which approach works better? There is no generally correct answer for all economies in all periods of time. Therefore, it is not surprising that some economists prefer one approach while others favour the alternative.

Reconciling the Keynesian and Monetarist Views

We have already come quite a long way toward reconciling the Keynesian and monetarist views of how the economy operates. Keynesian analysis lends itself naturally to the study of fiscal policy, since G is a part of $C + I + G + X - IM$. But we have learned in this chapter that Keynesian economics also provides a powerful and important role for monetary policy: An increase in the money supply reduces interest rates, which, in turn, stimulates the demand for investment.

Monetarist analysis provides an obvious and direct route by which monetary policy influences both output and prices. But can the monetarist approach also handle fiscal policy? It can, because fiscal policy has an important effect on the rate of interest. And it is not hard to understand how this effect operates.

Let's see what happens to real output and the price level following, say, a rise in government purchases of goods and services. We learned in Chapter 11 that both real GNP (Y) and the price level (P) rise. But Chapter 13's analysis of the demand for money taught us that rising Y and P push the demand curve for money outward to the right. With no change in the supply curve for money, the rate of interest must rise. So expansionary fiscal policy raises interest rates.

If the government uses its spending and taxing weapons in the opposite direction, the same process works in reverse. Falling output and (possibly) falling prices shift the demand curve for money inward to the left. With a fixed supply curve for money, equilibrium in the money market leads to a lower interest rate. Thus:

Monetary policy is not the only type of policy that affects interest rates. Fiscal policy also affects interest rates. Specifically, increases in government spending or tax cuts normally push interest rates higher, whereas restrictive fiscal policies normally pull interest rates down.

The fact that fiscal policy affects interest rates gives it a role in the monetarist model despite the fact that the equation of exchange, $M \times V = P \times Y$, does not include either government spending or taxation among its variables. The way it works is that a rise in government spending, for example, pushes up the rate of interest. And rising interest rates push up velocity because people want to hold less money when the interest they can earn on alternative assets increases. So it is through the V term in $M \times V$ that fiscal policy does its work in the monetarist framework.

Any of the government policies that a Keynesian would call expansionary—higher spending, lower taxes, and so on—forces interest rates higher, thus increasing V. The equation of exchange, $M \times V = P \times Y$, then implies that nominal GNP must rise when government spending increases, even if M is fixed. The given supply of money can finance more transactions when velocity is higher.

Conversely, restrictive fiscal policies, like tax increases and expenditure cuts, reduce the quantity of money demanded and lower interest rates. The consequent drop in velocity lowers income through the equation of exchange, because the money supply circulates more slowly.

The translation, then, seems to be complete. The Keynesian story about how fiscal policy works can be phrased in the monetarist dialect. And the monetarist tale about monetary policy can be told with a Keynesian accent. Furthermore, both modes of analysis help only to explain the mysteries of aggregate *demand*, and must be supplemented by an analysis of aggregate *supply* to be complete. We must conclude then, that:

The differences between Keynesians and monetarists have been grossly exaggerated by the news media. Indeed, when it comes to matters of basic economic theory, there are hardly any differences at all.

But this does not mean that Keynesians and monetarists must agree on everything any more than the fact that English prose can be translated into French implies that the English and the French always see eye to eye. There are important differences of emphasis and policy that we will take up in the remainder of this chapter.

The Multiplier Formula Once Again

But first, the fact that expansionary fiscal policy pushes up interest rates has another important consequence that we should mention. Recall that higher interest rates deter private investment spending. This means that when the government raises the G component of $C + I + G + X - IM$ one of the side effects of its action will be to reduce the I component (by raising interest rates). Consequently, the sum $C + I + G + X - IM$ will not rise as much as simple multiplier analysis might suggest. In a word, the surge in government demand (G) discourages some private demand (I). This phenomenon provides another reason why the oversimplified multiplier formula, $1/(1 - MPC)$, exaggerates the size of the multiplier:

Because any rise in G (or, for that matter, any autonomous rise in C or I or $X - IM$ pushes interest rates higher, and hence deters some investment spending, the increase in the sum $C + I + G + X - IM$ is smaller than what the oversimplified multiplier formula predicts.

Combining this observation with our previous analysis of the multiplier, we now have a more complete list of:

REASONS WHY THE OVERSIMPLIFIED MULTIPLIER FORMULA IS WRONG

1. It ignores price-level changes, which reduce the size of the multiplier.

2. It ignores the income tax, which reduces the size of the multiplier.

3. It ignores imports, which reduce the size of the multiplier.

4. It ignores the rising interest rates that accompany any autonomous increase in spending, which also reduce the size of the multiplier.

Keynesians Versus Monetarists: Fiscal Versus Monetary Policy

Although the Keynesian and monetarist approaches can be thought of as two languages, it is well known that language can influence attitudes in many subtle ways. And it must be admitted that Keynesians and monetarists have not lacked things to argue about.

For years they conducted a spirited, and well-publicized, debate over whether the government should rely mainly on fiscal policy or monetary policy to manage aggregate demand. While one would guess from reading the newspapers that this is the most important issue in the Keynesian–monetarist debate today, it is in fact the *least* important. It is unimportant because, as we have seen, each approach allows a role for each type of policy.

None the less, the Keynesian language biases things subtly toward thinking that fiscal policy is very important simply because fiscal actions influence aggregate demand so directly. G is, after all, a part of $C + I + G + X - IM$. Monetarists, on the other hand, see a more indirect channel that works through interest rates and velocity, and they wonder if something might not go wrong along the way.

The roles are reversed in the analysis of monetary policy. To monetarists, the effect of the money supply on aggregate demand is simple—it follows directly from velocity through the equation of exchange: $M \times V = P \times Y$. While monetary policy also affects aggregate demand in the Keynesian model, the mechanisms are rather complex, and there is obviously room for a slip-up. Monetary expansion might not affect the interest rate very much, or a fall in the interest rate might not induce much additional investment. Thus some Keynesians have their doubts when monetarists attribute great stabilizing powers to monetary policy.

During the 1960s and early 1970s the choice between fiscal and monetary policy dominated the debate between the more partisan Keynesians and monetarists. Extreme monetarists claimed that fiscal policy was futile, while extreme Keynesians countered that monetary policy was useless. We shall see in the next chapter that these conclusions can be perfectly correct, *if* the country's financial markets are integrated with those of the rest of the world (as Canada's are). It turns out that monetary policy cannot have a significant effect on aggregate demand if a country follows a fixed exchange-rate policy, while fiscal policy has no significant effect on aggregate demand if a flexible exchange-rate policy is followed. However, a country such as the United States is much more capable of setting its own level of interest rates, and for it, the analysis of this chapter is directly relevant. U.S. evidence has rejected the extreme claims of both Keynesians and monetarists, so that now both groups agree that both fiscal and monetary policy have significant effects on aggregate demand. However, Keynesians still tend to look more toward fiscal policy while monetarists tend to rely more on monetary policy.

Keynesians Versus Monetarists: Lags in Fiscal and Monetary Policy

More important than the issue of which type of policy is more *powerful* is the related question: Which type of medicine—fiscal or monetary—cures the patient more *quickly*? In our discussions of fiscal and monetary policy so far, we have ignored such subtle questions of timing and proceeded as if the authorities instantly noticed the need for stabilization policy, decided upon a course of action, and administered the appropriate medicine. In reality, each of these steps is time consuming.

First, delays in data collection and processing mean that the latest macro-economic data pertain to the economy as it was a few months ago. Second, one of the prices of democracy is that the government often takes a good deal of time to decide what should be done, to muster the necessary political support, and to put its decisions into effect. Finally, our economy is a bit like a sleeping elephant—it reacts rather sluggishly to moderate fiscal and monetary prods. As it turns out, these **lags in stabilization policy**, as they are called, play a pivotal role in the choice between fiscal and monetary policy. It is not hard to see why.

The main policy tool for manipulating consumer spending (*C*) is the personal income tax, and Chapter 7 documented why the fiscal-policy planner can feel fairly secure that each $1 of tax reduction will lead to about 90¢ of additional spending *eventually*. But not all of this will happen at once.

First, consumers must learn about the tax change. Then, more time may elapse before many consumers are convinced that the change is permanent. Finally, there is the simple force of habit: Households need time to adjust their spending habits when circumstances change. For all these reasons, consumers may increase their spending by only 30¢ to 50¢ for each $1 of additional income within the first few months after a tax cut. Only gradually, over a period of perhaps several years, will they raise their spending until they are finally consuming 90¢ of each additional dollar of income.

Lags are much longer for investment (*I*), which, while it also can be influenced by fiscal policy (tax incentives), provides the main vehicle by which monetary policy affects aggregate demand. Planning for capacity expansion in a large corporation is a long, drawn-out process. Ideas must be submitted and approved. Plans must be drawn up, funding acquired, orders for machinery or contracts for new construction placed. And most of this occurs *before* any appreciable amount of money is spent. Economists have found that most of the response of investment to changes in interest rates or tax provisions is delayed for several years.

The fact that *C* responds more quickly than *I* has important implications for the choice among alternative stabilization policies. The reason is that the most common varieties of fiscal policy affect aggregate demand either directly (G is a component of $C + I + G + X - IM$) or work through consumption with a relatively short lag, while monetary policy has its major effects on investment. Therefore:

Conventional types of fiscal-policy actions, such as changes in G or in personal taxes, probably affect aggregate demand much more promptly than do monetary-policy actions.

Notice that the statement says nothing about which instrument is more *powerful*. It simply asserts that the fiscal weapon, whether it is stronger or weaker, acts more *quickly*. This important fact has been used to build a case that fiscal policy should bear the major burden of economic stabilization. But before you jump to such a conclusion, you should realize that the sorts of lags we have been discussing are not the only ones affecting the timing of stabilization policy.

Apart from these lags in expenditure, which are beyond the control of policy-makers, there are further lags that are due to the behaviour of the policy-makers themselves! We are referring here to the delays that occur while the policy-makers are studying the state of the economy, contemplating what steps they should take, and putting their decisions into effect. And here most observers believe that monetary policy has an important edge; that is:

Policy lags are normally shorter for monetary policy than for fiscal policy.

The reasons are apparent. The Governor of the Bank of Canada meets frequently with his advisors, so monetary-policy decisions are made almost every month. And once the Bank of Canada decides on a course of action, it normally can be executed almost instantly by buying or selling bonds on the open market.

Contrast this with fiscal policy. Federal budgeting procedures operate on an annual budget cycle. Except in rare circumstances, then, *major* fiscal-policy initiatives that affect spending can occur only at the time of the budget. Tax laws can be changed at any time, but the wheels of Parliament grind slowly and it may take many months before Parliament acts on a bill to change taxes. In sum, one has to be very optimistic to suppose that important fiscal-policy actions can be taken on short notice.

Where does the combined effect of expenditure lags and policy lags leave us? With nothing conclusive, we are afraid. As the late Arthur Okun put it, the debate over whether the nation should rely only on monetary policy or only on fiscal policy is a bit like arguing whether a safe car is one with good headlights or one with good brakes. It is not very wise to drive at night unless you have both.

Keynesians Versus Monetarists: The Aggregate-Supply Curve

But the Keynesian–monetarist battles did not end there. As the debate over fiscal versus monetary policy fizzled, the two schools of thought regrouped along new, and more productive, battle lines.

One major controversy that is very much alive today is over whether the government should conduct *any* stabilization policy at all, be it monetary or fiscal. This argument is not surprising given the political differences between the two groups. As it happens, monetarists tend to be conservative politically and Keynesians tend to be liberal, which helps explain why the two schools differ markedly in the degree to which they think the government should try to manage the economy. Since this important and controversial issue transcends the Keynesian–monetarist debate, we defer discussion of it until Chapter 19.

Another major battleground in the Keynesian–monetarist debate today is over the shape of the economy's aggregate-supply curve. As we have noted, either the Keynesian or the monetarist model must be supplemented by an aggregate-

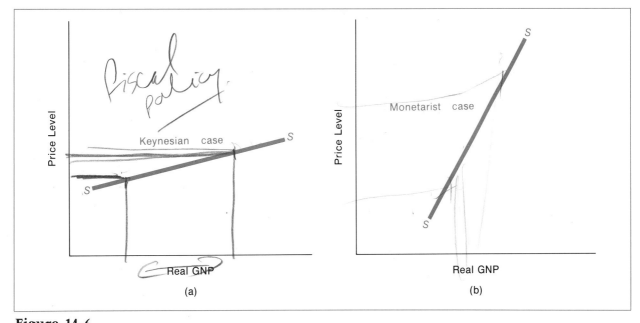

Figure 14-6

ALTERNATIVE VIEWS OF THE AGGREGATE-SUPPLY CURVE

Keynesians tend to think of the economy's aggregate-supply schedule as very flat, as in part (a), whereas monetarists tend to think of it as quite steep, as in part (b).

supply curve if it is to tell us anything about output and prices. Most Keynesians tend to think of the aggregate-supply curve as fairly flat in the short run, as in Figure 14–6(a), so that large increases in output can be achieved with rather little inflation. Monetarists, by contrast, picture the supply curve as quite steep, as in Figure 14–6(b), so that prices are very responsive to changes in output. The differences for public policy are substantial.

In the Keynesian view, expansionary fiscal or monetary policy that raises the aggregate-demand schedule can buy large gains in real GNP at little cost in terms of inflation. This is shown in Figure 14–7(a). Here, stimulation of demand raises the aggregate-demand curve from D_0D_0 to D_1D_1 and moves the economy's equilibrium from point E to point A. There is a substantial rise in output ($40 billion) with only a pinch of inflation (1 percent).

Conversely, when the supply curve is so flat, a restrictive stabilization policy is not a very effective way to cure inflation; instead, it serves mainly to reduce real output, as Figure 14–7(b) shows. Here, a leftward shift of the aggregate-demand curve moves equilibrium from point E to point B, lowering real GNP by $40 billion, but cutting the price level merely 1 percent.

The monetarists see things differently. To them, the aggregate-supply curve is so steep that expansionary fiscal or monetary policies are likely to cause a good deal of inflation without adding much to real GNP. [See Figure 14–8(a), where expansionary policies shift equilibrium from E to A.] Similarly, contractionary policies are effective ways of bringing down the price level without much sacrifice of real output, as shown by the shift from E to B in Figure 14–8(b).

The resolution of this debate is of fundamental importance for the proper conduct of stabilization policy. If the Keynesian view is right, stabilization policy is much more effective at combating recession than inflation. If the monetarist view is correct, the reverse is true.

Why, then, does the argument persist? Why cannot economists determine whether the aggregate-supply curve is flat or steep, and stop arguing? The answer is that supply conditions in the real world are far more complicated than our simple diagrams suggest. Some industries may have flat supply curves while others have

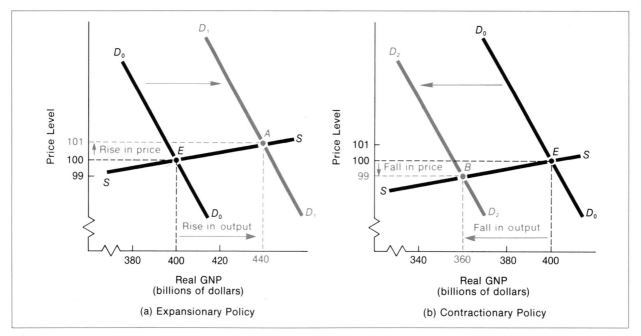

Figure 14–7

STABILIZATION POLICY WITH A FLAT AGGREGATE-SUPPLY CURVE: THE KEYNESIAN CASE

These two diagrams show that stabilization policy is much more effective as an anti-recession policy than as an anti-inflation policy when the aggregate-supply curve is very flat. In part (a), monetary or fiscal policies push the aggregate-demand curve outward from D_0D_0 to D_1D_1, causing equilibrium to shift from point E to point A. It can be seen that output rises substantially (from $400 billion to $440 billion), while prices rise only slightly (from 100 to 101, or 1 percent). So the policy is quite successful. In part (b), contractionary policies are used to combat inflation by pushing the aggregate-demand curve inward from D_0D_0 to D_2D_2. Prices do fall slightly (from 100 to 99) as equilibrium shifts from point E to point B, but real output falls much more dramatically (from $400 billion to $360 billion); so the policy has had little success. Keynesians tend to believe in this case.

steep ones. For reasons explained in Chapter 10, supply curves change over time. And, unlike many laboratory scientists, economists cannot perform the controlled experiments that would reveal the shape of the aggregate-supply curve directly. Instead, they must use statistical inference to make educated guesses.

Although empirical research on aggregate supply is proceeding, our understanding of aggregate supply remains much less settled than our understanding of aggregate demand. Nevertheless, many economists believe that the dim outline of a consensus view is emerging. This view stresses that the steepness of the aggregate-supply schedule depends on the degree of slack in the economy.

If industry has a great deal of spare capacity, then increases in demand will not call forth large price increases. Similarly, when many workers are unemployed, employment can rise without causing much acceleration in the rate at which wages are growing. In a word, the aggregate-supply curve is quite flat. On the other hand, when businesses are producing near capacity and unemployment is near the frictional level, greater demand for goods will induce firms to raise prices; and greater demand for labour will push wages up faster. In brief, the aggregate-supply schedule will be steep.

Figure 14–9 shows a version of the aggregate-supply curve that embodies these ideas. It has the same general shape as most of the supply curves that we have used in this book. At low levels of GNP, like Y_1, it is nearly horizontal; then its slope starts to rise gradually until at very high levels of GNP, like Y_2, it becomes almost vertical. The implication is that any change in aggregate demand will have most of its effect on *output* when economic activity is slack (the Keynesian case) but on *prices* when the economy is operating near full employment (the monetarist case). In summary:

1. Keynesians believe that the aggregate-supply curve is rather flat in many

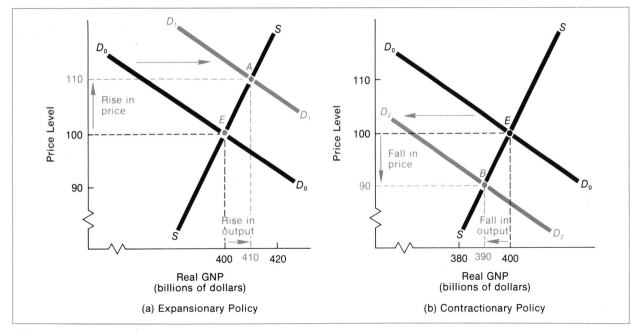

Figure 14-8

STABILIZATION POLICY WITH A STEEP AGGREGATE-SUPPLY CURVE: THE MONETARIST CASE

These two diagrams show that stabilization policy is much more effective at fighting inflation than at fighting recession when the aggregate-supply curve is very steep. In part (a), expansionary policies that push aggregate demand outward from $D_0 D_0$ to $D_1 D_1$ raise output by only $10 billion but push up prices by 10 percent, as equilibrium moves from point E to point A. So demand management is not a good way to end a recession. In part (b), contractionary policies that pull aggregate demand inward to $D_2 D_2$ are successful in that they lower prices quite markedly (from 100 to 90, or about 10 percent) but reduce output only slightly (from $400 billion to $390 billion). Monetarists tend to believe in this case.

circumstances, especially when the economy is operating at low levels of resource utilization. They therefore stress the effects of demand management on output, and belittle the effects on prices.

2. Monetarists believe that the aggregate-supply curve is rather *steep* in many circumstances, especially when the economy has little slack. They therefore

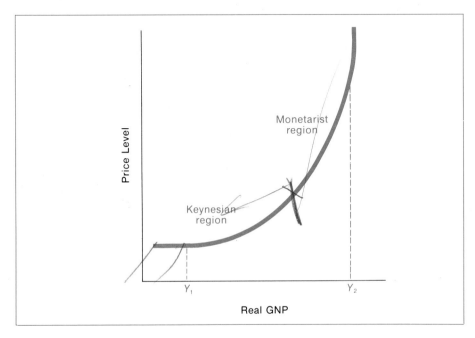

Figure 14-9

AN AGGREGATE-SUPPLY CURVE WITH BOTH STEEP AND FLAT REGIONS

As this diagram suggests, either the Keynesians or the monetarists may be right under the appropriate circumstances. The Keynesian view of a flat supply curve is likely to be most accurate when there is much unemployment and unused capacity. The monetarist view of a steep supply curve is likely to be more accurate when there is full employment and high capacity utilization.

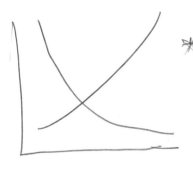

emphasize the effects of demand management on prices, and belittle the effects on real output.

3. A middle-of-the-road view would hold that the Keynesian case is quite strong when there is a great deal of unemployment, while the monetarist case is stronger when the economy is near full employment. Not all economists accept this middle-of-the-road view, but many do.

Since the nature of the trade-off between output gains (which reduce unemployment) and inflation, as embodied in the slope of the aggregate-supply schedule, plays such a fundamental role in the design of an appropriate stabilization policy, we shall devote all of Chapter 18 to an exploration of this trade-off.

Summary

1. Monetarist and Keynesian analyses are two different ways of studying the determination of aggregate demand. Neither is a complete theory of the behaviour of the economy until aggregate supply is brought into the picture.
2. Investment spending (I), including business investment and investment in new homes, is sensitive to interest rates (r). Specifically, I is lower when r is higher.
3. This fact explains how monetary policy works in the Keynesian model. Raising the money supply (M) leads to lower r; the lower interest rates stimulate more investment spending; and this investment stimulus, via the multiplier, then raises aggregate demand.
4. However, prices are likely to rise as output rises. The amount of inflation caused by increasing the money supply depends on the levels of unemployment and of capacity utilization. There will be much inflation when the economy is near full employment, but little inflation when there is a great deal of slack.
5. An important reason why the aggregate-demand curve slopes downward is that higher prices increase the demand to hold money in order to finance transactions. Given the money supply, this pushes interest rates up; and this, in turn, discourages investment.
6. A second reason why the aggregate-demand curve slopes downward is that higher domestic prices make our exports less competitive internationally so net export demand falls.
7. Velocity (V) is the ratio of nominal GNP to the stock of money. It indicates how quickly money circulates, that is, how many times money changes hands in a year.
8. Among the determinants of velocity is the rate of interest (r). At higher interest rates, people find it less attractive to hold money because most money pays no interest. Thus, when r rises, money circulates faster, and V rises.
9. Monetarism is a type of analysis that focuses attention on velocity and the money supply (M). Though monetarists realize that V is not constant, they

believe that it is predictable enough to make it a useful tool for policy analysis and forecasting.
10. Because it raises output and prices, and hence increases the demand for money, expansionary fiscal policy pushes interest rates higher. This is how a monetarist explains the effect of fiscal policy. Because higher r leads to higher velocity, it leads to a higher product $M \times V$ even if M is unchanged.
11. While Keynesian and monetarist theories both lead us to expect that fiscal *and* monetary policies can each affect aggregate demand, Keynesians tend to believe more in the effectiveness of fiscal policy while monetarists tend to believe more in the effectiveness of monetary policy.
12. Because fiscal-policy actions affect aggregate demand either directly through G or indirectly through C, the expenditure lags between fiscal actions and their effects on aggregate demand are probably fairly short. By contrast, monetary policy operates mainly on investment, I, which responds very slowly to changes in interest rates.
13. However, the policy-making lag normally is much longer for fiscal policy than for monetary policy. Hence, when the two lags are combined, it is not clear which type of policy acts more quickly.
14. Keynesians believe that the aggregate-supply curve is rather flat in the short run. This means that increases in aggregate demand will add much to the nation's real output and add little to the price level. Stabilization policy thus has much to recommend it as an anti-recession device, but it has little power to combat inflation.
15. Monetarists believe that the aggregate-supply curve is very steep. This means that increases in aggregate demand increase real output rather little and succeed mostly in pushing up prices. Consequently, while stabilization policy can do much to fight inflation, it is not a very effective way to cure unemployment.
16. The Keynesian view probably is most applicable to an economy with much unemployment, while the monetarist view applies best to an economy producing near capacity levels.

Concepts for Review

Why the aggregate-demand curve
   slopes downward
Quantity theory of money
Velocity
Equation of exchange

Effect of interest rate on velocity
Monetarism
Effect of monetary policy on
   inflation
Effect of fiscal policy on interest
   rates

Lags in stabilization policy
Shape of the aggregate-supply
   curve

Questions for Discussion

1. How much money (including cash and chequing account balances) do you typically have at any particular moment? Divide this into your total income over the past 12 months to obtain your own personal velocity. Are you typical of the nation as a whole?

2. Just below you will find data on nominal gross national product and the money supply (M1 definition) for selected years. Compute velocity in each year. Can you see any trend?

YEAR	NOMINAL GNP (billions of dollars)	MONEY SUPPLY (M1) (billions of dollars) (end of year)
1963	46.0	6.3
1973	123.6	14.5
1983	388.7	30.2

3. Use the concept of opportunity cost to explain why velocity is higher at higher interest rates.

4. How does monetarism differ from the quantity theory of money? How does it differ from Keynesian analysis?

5. Explain why both business investments and purchases of new homes are expected to decline when interest rates rise.

6. Explain what a $60 billion increase in the money supply will do to real GNP under the following assumptions:
   a. Each $20 billion increase in the money supply reduces the rate of interest by 1 percentage point.
   b. Each 1 percentage point decline in interest rates

stimulates $40 billion of new investment spending.
   c. The expenditure multiplier is 2.
   d. There is so much unemployment that prices do not rise noticeably when demand increases.

7. Explain how your answer to Question 6 would differ if each of the assumptions were changed. Specifically, what sorts of changes in the assumptions would make monetary policy very weak?

8. Explain why the aggregate-demand curve has a negative slope.

9. Distinguish between the expenditure lag and the policy lag in stabilization policy. Does monetary policy or fiscal policy have the shorter expenditure lag? What about the policy lag?

10. Explain why their contrasting view on the shape of the aggregate-supply curve lead Keynesians to argue much more strongly for stabilization policies to fight unemployment while monetarists argue much more strongly for stabilization policies to fight inflation.

11. (More difficult.) Consider an economy in which government purchases, taxes, and net exports are zero; the consumption function is:

$$C = 100 + 0.8\ Y,$$

and investment spending (I) depends on the rate of interest (r) in the following way:

$$I = 500 - 800\ r.$$

Find the equilibrium GNP if the central bank makes the rate of interest (a) 5 percent ($r = 0.05$), (b) 10 percent, (c) zero.

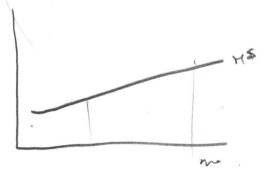

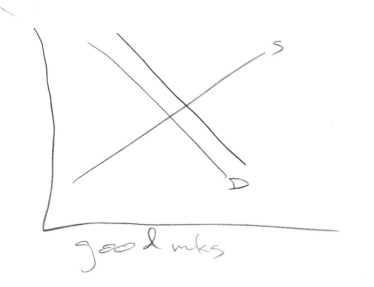

good mkts

money mkt

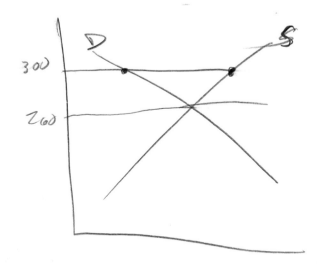

300

260

Stabilization Policy: With International Capital Flows

15

> The truth is never pure
> and rarely simple.
> OSCAR WILDE

In Chapter 14 we explained how fiscal and monetary policy affect GNP, the price level, and the level of interest rates. We now must admit, however, that we cut the story short by assuming that Canadian interest rates can move independently of foreign interest rates. On the contrary, as we stressed in Chapter 13, interest-rate differentials cause large flows of funds across the border as asset holders strive to acquire bonds giving a higher yield. These flows of funds represent shifts in the demand and supply curves for foreign exchange. Such shifts must result in one of two things: either a movement of the exchange rate (if we are on a flexible-rate policy) so that net exports will change; or a change in the domestic money supply (if we are on a fixed exchange-rate policy). In either case, there are further effects on aggregate demand. We now complete the analysis by examining four separate cases:

1. Fiscal policy under fixed exchange rates.
2. Fiscal policy under flexible exchange rates.
3. Monetary policy under fixed exchange rates.
4. Monetary policy under flexible exchange rates.

Our conclusion is that the usefulness of monetary and fiscal policies as demand-management tools depends critically on the government's exchange-rate policy. Thus, although this is one of the shorter chapters in the book, it is indispensible to a proper understanding of macroeconomic policy.

Fiscal Policy Under a Fixed Exchange-Rate Regime

Consider an increase in government spending. Our earlier analysis suggested that this policy leads to an increase in GNP and the price level, and that the higher nominal value of transactions induces households and firms to try to acquire more money. As a result, the money-demand curve shifts to the right, and there is an increase in the Canadian interest rate. This review of our earlier analysis is summarized by the shift from point *A* to point *B* in both panels of Figure 15–1.

Both real GNP and the price level increase, from $400 billion to $420 billion and from 100 to 105 in this example; and there is what we now recognize as a *temporary* increase in the Canadian interest rate to 11 percent. Canadian interest rates now exceed foreign interest rates by two percentage points in this example.

Now let us trace through the international effects of the higher Canadian interest rate depicted in Figure 15–1(b). It causes foreign investors to send more funds into Canada as they shift their portfolios of assets to acquire more of the now-appealing high-yield Canadian bonds. To acquire our bonds, they need our currency; therefore, they sell foreign exchange to obtain our currency. Similarly, Canadians reduce their demand for foreign exchange as they have increased incentive to hold their own bonds.

The net effect on the foreign-exchange market is that the Canadian dollar is more in demand so Canada's balance of payments must move in the direction of a surplus. Under a fixed exchange-rate regime, the Bank of Canada avoids any appreciation of the Canadian dollar by buying up the otherwise unwanted quantity of foreign exchange, thereby issuing more Canadian money.

The higher quantity of domestic money is shown by a shift to the right of the money-supply line in Figure 15–1(b) from M_0S_0 to M_1S_1. This easing of domestic credit conditions, which necessarily follows from the Bank of Canada's intervention in the foreign-exchange market, eliminates the interest-rate differential. The final outcome in the domestic-money market is given by point C in Figure 15–1(b). The return of the Canadian interest rate to its original level reverses any cut-back of investment spending that originally occurred, so aggregate demand is stimulated further, as shown by the aggregate-demand curve shifting further to position D_2D_2 in Figure 15–1(a).

We conclude that the initial direct expansionary effect of the fiscal policy (the movement from point A to point B in Figure 15–1) is *reinforced* by the subsequent effects of the policy that are induced by the Bank of Canada's intervention to keep the exchange rate fixed (the movement from point B to point

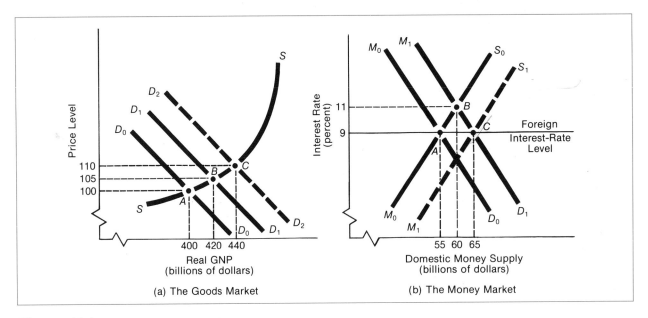

Figure 15–1

FISCAL POLICY WITH INTERNATIONAL CAPITAL FLOWS

An increase in government spending shifts the aggregate-demand curve from D_0D_0 to D_1D_1. The resulting higher nominal GNP shifts the money-demand curve from M_0D_0 to M_1D_1. The higher rate of interest attracts foreign funds into Canada so that: either the Canadian dollar appreciates (and net exports fall, returning the demand curves to D_0D_0 and M_0D_0) under flexible exchange rates, or the Bank of Canada buys the incoming foreign funds (so that the domestic money supply increases to M_1S_1, and aggregate demand is further stimulated to D_2D_2) under fixed exchange rates.

C in Figure 15–1). In our example then, the expansionary fiscal policy raises real GNP from $400 billion to $440 billion and raises the price level from 100 to 110. The reason for these large effects is that the Bank of Canada was forced, by its commitment to fix the exchange rate, to perform a complementary monetary policy. The open-market purchase of foreign exchange increases the Canadian money supply (to $65 billion in our example). The interest rate only rises from 9 percent to 11 percent *temporarily*; in the end, the Canadian interest rate has returned to the level of foreign interest rates.

Fiscal Policy Under a Flexible Exchange-Rate Regime

Now consider the same increase in government spending when exchange rates are floating freely. The initial effects are the same as in Figure 15–1 (to which we continue to refer): higher GNP (shown by the move from *A* to *B*), Canadian interest rates rising above foreign rates, and an increased demand for Canadian dollars on the foreign-exchange market. Under flexible exchange rates, the Bank of Canada makes no attempt to buy up the otherwise unwanted quantity of foreign exchange, so the Canadian dollar appreciates in value. With no transactions by the Bank of Canada, the money supply is constant so the money-supply schedule remains at position M_0S_0 in Figure 15–1(b). But the appreciating Canadian dollar makes our imports cheaper, and foreigners find our exports more expensive. As a result, *net exports fall*, and so the aggregate-demand curve shifts back to the left from D_1D_1 toward D_0D_0 in Figure 15–1(a).

How far will this process go? The induced appreciation of the Canadian dollar must continue as long as the Canadian interest rate remains above foreign rates. Hence, the process can come to an end only when the aggregate-demand curve has shifted leftward enough to re-establish the original equilibrium point *A*. With prices and real output back at their original levels, the demand-for-money curve will be back at its original position, so Canadian interest rates will be back down to the level of foreign interest rates. At this point, the shift of funds across the border by savers stops. In the end, then, the initial direct expansionary effect of fiscal policy is eventually completely eliminated by the induced exchange-rate effects.

The effort to raise GNP by government spending fails under flexible exchange rates; aggregate demand is only affected temporarily, since all that the higher government spending does is *replace* pre-existing export demand for Canadian products.

This scenario is a perfect description of the Canadian situation during the late 1950s and early 1960s. We were in a recession, with unemployment in excess of 7 percent and very little inflation. James Coyne, the governor of the Bank of Canada, felt that unemployment was not a concern of the central bank. Technically he was right; the Bank Act states that the Bank of Canada's job is to preserve the value of our currency, and that means keeping the purchasing power of our dollar from being eroded by inflation. Coyne tried to ensure that this would not occur by restricting the quantity of money in the system. This policy put upward pressure on interest rates, and the resulting increase in the foreign demand for our bonds pushed up the value of the Canadian dollar. The problem was that both the temporarily higher interest rates and the more expensive Canadian dollar made the unemployment problem worse. The Department of Finance ran large deficits in an attempt to lessen unemployment, but as we have just learned, there is no lasting effect on aggregate demand from fiscal policy under flexible exchange rates. It is no wonder that the Diefenbaker government wanted Coyne to resign; they were left with fiscal policy as the only tool for "curing" the recession, and it is

essentially a useless tool in a flexible exchange-rate setting. It is not surprising that major Canadian economists ran a full-page item in leading newspapers at the time, urging the Bank of Canada to relieve the constraint it had placed on stabilization policy.

Monetary Policy Under a Fixed Exchange-Rate Regime

We now consider monetary policy in each of the polar case exchange-rate regimes. Suppose the Bank of Canada wants to fight inflation and so decreases the domestic money supply. The analysis in Chapter 14 suggested that this policy leads to a decrease in GNP and the price level, and a higher interest rate due to tighter credit conditions. This is illustrated in Figure 15–2. The decrease in the domestic money supply is shown by the leftward shift of the money-supply line (from M_0S_0 to M_1S_1) in Figure 15–2(b). The resulting tighter credit conditions are indicated by the fact that Canadian interest rates have risen from 9 percent to 11 percent, at point B in panel (b). The higher borrowing costs mean lower investment spending by firms, so the aggregate-demand curve shifts left from D_0D_0 to D_1D_1 in panel (a). Thus, the economy moves from point A to point B in both panels of Figure 15–2. The initial effects of the contractionary monetary policy in this example are to reduce real GNP from \$400 billion to \$380 billion, to reduce the price index from 100 to 95, and to raise borrowing costs from 9 percent to 11 percent. As we have seen before, however, the resulting gap between foreign and domestic interest rates cannot last.

The interest-rate differential causes portfolio shifts on the part of bond-holders toward Canadian bonds. Foreigners will supply more foreign exchange to the trading market, to get the Canadian dollars that are required to pay for the high-yield Canadian bonds. Canadians will demand less foreign exchange, since they now have a decreased demand for foreign financial assets. These reactions to the temporary interest-rate differential mean upward pressure on the value of the

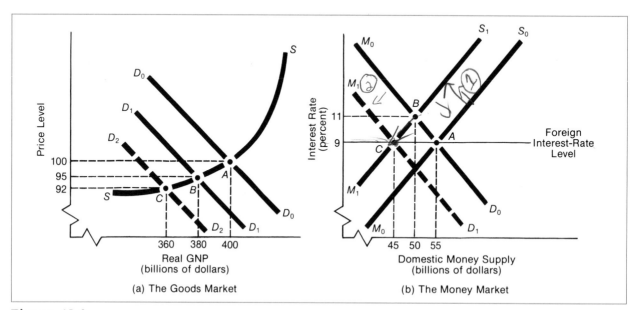

Figure 15-2

MONETARY POLICY WITH INTERNATIONAL CAPITAL FLOWS

A decrease in the money supply shifts the money-supply curve from M_0S_0 to M_1S_1. The resulting higher borrowing costs reduce aggregate demand from D_0D_0 to D_1D_1. The higher rate of interest also attracts foreign funds into Canada so that: either the Canadian dollar appreciates (and net exports fall, pushing aggregate demand down to D_2D_2) under flexible exchange rates, or the Bank of Canada buys the incoming foreign funds (so that the domestic money supply increases back to supply-curve position M_0S_0) under fixed exchange rates.

Canadian dollar. Under a fixed exchange-rate regime, the Bank of Canada precludes this appreciation of the dollar by buying the otherwise unwanted quantity of foreign exchange. That is, Canada sustains an increase in the balance-of-payments surplus, and the Bank of Canada issues more domestic currency to pay for this accumulation of foreign-exchange reserves. Since the money supply increases automatically as a result of this open-market purchase of foreign exchange, the money-supply curve in Figure 15–2(b) shifts back to the right. This easing of credit conditions causes Canadian interest rates to start falling back down from 11 percent, and as a result, the aggregate-demand curve starts to shift back to the right, from position D_1D_1 in Figure 15–2(a). Thus, the original decreases in real GNP and the price level are reversed.

How far will this process go? The increase in the money supply that is induced by the flow of foreign funds into Canada must continue as long as the Canadian interest rate is significantly above foreign rates. Hence, the process comes to an end when the money-supply line shifts far enough to the right that it returns to position M_0S_0, and the interest rate is 9 percent, at point A in Figure 15–2(b). But if borrowing costs return to their original level, investment spending by firms will be restored to its initial level. Thus, the aggregate-demand curve will return to its starting position, D_0D_0, in Figure 15–2(a). In the end, then, we return to point A in both panels of Figure 15–2, and there is no lasting effect of monetary policy.

By committing themselves to issue or withdraw money according to the outcome in the foreign-exchange market, the authorities have relinquished the ability to set the domestic money supply at any independently specified value.

In spite of the fact that the flexible exchange-rate version of this model explained the "Coyne Affair" so well, the Bank of Canada ignored it again by trying a rather dramatic contractionary monetary policy in 1969, while we were then still in a fixed exchange-rate regime. This move was part of the Trudeau government's fight against inflation. The money supply was cut in mid-1969, and Canadian interest rates rose. The effect on the balance of payments was dramatic. We had a surplus of $65 million in 1969; then, with the foreign currency attracted by high Canadian interest rates, the balance-of-payments surplus rose to $1663 million in 1970, and the Bank had only maintained the fixed exchange-rate policy until May of that year! The Bank tried to insulate the domestic money supply from the balance-of-payments surplus by using open-market operations in the bond market. That is, as rapidly as it was issuing new Canadian money to buy the incoming foreign exchange, it tried to balance this by selling government bonds to decrease chartered bank reserves. However, the Bank soon realized that selling bonds to the general public (to get the new money back out of the system) produced a vicious circle. Big bond issues are only purchased if the interest rate involved is favourable. Thus, the big bond sales further raised interest rates, caused a larger inflow of foreign exchange (resulting in an even larger balance-of-payments surplus), and forced the government to sell even more bonds, etc., etc., if the money supply was to remain contracted.

The government finally realized it was trapped in this vicious circle, and it broke the chain in May 1970 by removing the promise to fix the exchange rate. As the model predicts, the value of the Canadian dollar increased noticeably immediately following this decision. It is ironic that after moving to a floating-rate policy (which we have just shown to be a necessary condition for conducting a successful monetary policy), the Bank gave up its fight against inflation and embarked on an expansionary monetary policy. This was "effective" (given the new floating exchange-rate environment), and the acceleration of inflation was the result.

Monetary Policy Under a Flexible Exchange-Rate Regime

To discuss monetary policy under flexible exchange rates we consider the same decrease in money supply and continue to refer to Figure 15–2. The initial effects are the same: lower GNP, lower price level, the Canadian interest rate going higher than foreign rates, and the interest-rate differential causing foreign funds to flow into Canada. The difference is that without the Bank of Canada's involvement in the foreign-exchange market there is no further move in the position of the money-supply curve from M_1S_1. Instead, the Canadian dollar appreciates as the foreign funds enter the country, and this makes our imports cheaper to buy, and our exports more expensive for foreigners to buy. As our net exports fall, the aggregate-demand curve shifts leftward in the direction of D_2D_2, so the price level and real GNP are further reduced.

How far will this process go? The appreciation of the Canadian dollar must continue as long as the Canadian interest rate is significantly above foreign interest rates. The process ends when the aggregate-demand curve has shifted down enough to lower nominal GNP enough to shift the demand-for-money curve to position M_1D_1 in panel (b). At this stage, the economy is at point C in both panels of Figure 15–2. In our example, the price index has fallen from 100 to 92, and real GNP has fallen to $360 billion. The money supply has fallen to the $45 billion level, and the interest rate has returned to its original value of 9 percent, which is the level of foreign interest rates. Since the interest rate differential is eliminated, we see that:

Monetary policy works through the sensitivity of net exports to the exchange rate, not the sensitivity of investment spending to the interest rate.

We have analysed a *contractionary* monetary policy in the flexible exchange-rate case, so you can directly compare the effects to the earlier discussion of actual policy taken in 1969–70 under fixed exchange rates. As a matter of fact, however, the 1971–74 period was characterized by *expansionary* monetary policy. The same reasoning can be used in reverse to explain how this does have a lasting expansionary effect on aggregate demand, but only under floating rates.

Monetary policy certainly was expansionary in the early 1970s. The rate of growth of Canada's money supply rose from 4.7 percent in 1969 to 19.9 percent in 1974. Given that the average annual growth in Canada's real GNP since 1953 has been less than 4.7 percent, this policy clearly involved an excessive stimulation of spending.

The Bank of Canada accepted this interpretation and, in September 1975, reversed its policy position. During the 1975–82 period, the Bank emphasized repeatedly that it was attempting to ensure that Canada's money supply did not increase at more than a specified rate (to be lowered systematically so that inflation could be gradually reduced). The news media referred to this period as "Canada's experiment with monetarism." One interesting question is why the Bank permitted the overstimulation of aggregate demand in the 1971–74 period. The answer to this question will make clear the underlying cause of inflation.

The key to the answer is found in the 1971 *Annual Report* of the Bank of Canada. The report notes that the expansion in Canada's money supply was needed to "avoid contributing to undue appreciation of our currency," which would have "exacerbated the difficulties of important export and import competing industries and impeded the expansion of economic activity." Essentially, the Bank was concerned about unemployment, not inflation, and felt that rising interest rates and the resulting increase in the foreign value of the Canadian dollar would aggravate unemployment.

It is true that *if* foreign countries were not inflating, the higher value of the Canadian dollar would have hurt our exports, since a given amount of foreign currency earned as sales receipts would translate into fewer Canadian dollars to be used for financing domestic production costs. This is what the Bank of Canada was trying to avoid, and they probably regarded this possibility with particular concern since this is exactly what happened in the 1958–61 period of tight monetary policy, that is, during the "Coyne Affair." However, there was an important difference in the 1970s: foreign countries *were* inflating. Thus, as long as the rate at which the Canadian dollar appreciated was no larger than the rate of foreign inflation, Canadian exporters would *not* be subject to a cost squeeze *at all*. Given the foreign environment, then, the Bank's inappropriate resistance to currency appreciation led to the overly expansive aggregate-demand policy in the 1971–74 period.

Review of Aggregate-Demand Policy Options

1. Fiscal policy has a lasting effect on aggregate demand under fixed exchange rates. The temporary rise in interest rates following the expansion attracts foreign funds, which the Bank of Canada must absorb to peg the exchange rate. The increase in the domestic money supply that the Bank must allow to buy the incoming foreign exchange reinforces the initial fiscal expansion.

2. Fiscal policy has no lasting effect on aggregate demand under a floating exchange rate. Any initial expansion of demand just causes temporarily higher interest rates, which attract foreign funds. The Canadian dollar appreciates, forcing a contraction in net export demands.

3. Monetary policy has no lasting effect on aggregate demand under fixed exchange rates. Any initial expansion of demand involves temporarily lower domestic interest rates, which cause foreign funds to leave the country. The Bank of Canada must accept the domestic currency that is relinquished as foreign exchange is purchased to buy foreign bonds. The resulting decrease in domestic money circulating counteracts the original policy.

4. Monetary policy has a lasting effect on aggregate demand under a floating exchange rate. An expansion of demand by the central bank initially involves lower domestic interest rates. As foreign funds leave the country, the Canadian dollar depreciates. The resulting stimulation of net exports reinforces the initial expansionary monetary policy.

These strong conclusions depend on the assumption that Canada has absolutely no ability to maintain interest rates at values that differ significantly from those in the United States. This assumption is not literally true, but as we noted in Chapter 13 (pages 258–59) it is very close to being completely true. Thus, while the aggregate-demand effects summarized above are *far* more relevant than those discussed in Chapter 14, we should probably temper them a little bit. Capital flows across the U.S.–Canadian border are not instantaneous. The following summary table gives the conclusions in this slightly weaker form.

To utilize this summary table, we must know what Canada's exchange-rate policy is. However, there is no simple answer to this question. We had a flexible

EFFECTS ON AGGREGATE DEMAND OF:		
	FISCAL POLICY	MONETARY POLICY
Under a fixed exchange-rate regime	Strong	Weak
Under a flexible exchange-rate regime	Weak	Strong

exchange-rate regime in the 1950s, a fixed exchange-rate regime in the 1960s, and a mixture of the two since 1970.[1]

Canada is currently following a policy of heavily managing the exchange rate. While the exchange rate is not absolutely fixed, intervention by the Bank of Canada is dramatic at times. Only limited variation in the exchange rate around its ongoing trend of depreciation (a trend that has occurred since 1976) is permitted. Thus, it is probably best to take the conclusions contained in the fixed exchange-rate row of the summary table as being roughly appropriate.

As an example of the use of the summary table, let us consider the Foreign Investment Review Agency (FIRA) and the National Energy Policy (NEP), which were introduced by the Trudeau government at the start of the 1980s. Most analysts have concluded that these policies discouraged investment spending by foreign-owned firms in Canada. As a result, these policies shifted the total-expenditure ($C + I + G + X - IM$) line down, in the same manner as would a decrease in government expenditure. To use the summary table, then, we consult the entry for fiscal policy under a fixed exchange-rate regime. The "strong" entry means that our model supports those who claimed that FIRA and the NEP had contractionary effects on the Canadian economy.

Defenders of these policies can react in two ways. First, they can claim that significant depreciation of the Canadian dollar has occurred during the 1980s, so perhaps the flexible exchange-rate row of the summary table is more appropriate. As we see, this entry says the contractionary effects of FIRA and NEP are weak, but this is because they would have contributed to the weaker dollar. Second, the defenders can claim that certain microeconomic benefits of these policies are worth the macroeconomic costs.

Exchange Rates and Aggregate Supply

We emphasized in Chapter 11 that the exchange rate is a shift variable for the aggregate-supply curve. Since some imports are intermediate products, an appreciating Canadian dollar lowers one component of domestic costs and shifts the aggregate-supply curve down. Similarly, a depreciating Canadian dollar raises this component of domestic costs and shifts the aggregate-supply curve up. With this reminder, we are in a position to extend our discussion beyond aggregate demand and to derive the complete real GNP and price-level effects of monetary and fiscal policies under each exchange-rate regime.

An increase in government spending under fixed exchange rates is shown in Figure 15–3(a). We have already shown that there is a lasting effect on aggregate demand in this case, and this is indicated by the rightward shift of the aggregate-demand curve from D_0D_0 to D_1D_1. Since the exchange rate is fixed, the aggregate-supply curve does not move. We conclude that expansionary fiscal policy under fixed exchange rates raises both prices and real output.

The same increase in government spending under flexible exchange rates is shown in Figure 15–3(b). We discovered earlier that there is no lasting effect on aggregate demand in this case, so there is no rightward shift of the aggregate-demand curve. The reason for this is that the appreciation of the Canadian dollar reduces net exports and lowers aggregate demand by as much as the higher government spending raises demand. There is nothing to counteract the cost-saving effect of the currency appreciation, however, so the aggregate-supply curve shifts down from S_0S_0 to S_1S_1. We conclude that expansionary fiscal policy under flexible exchange rates raises real GNP and lowers the price level.

An increase in the domestic money supply is considered in the remaining two panels of Figure 15–3. Since there is no lasting effect on aggregate demand under

[1]The historical development of the international monetary system is discussed in the next chapter.

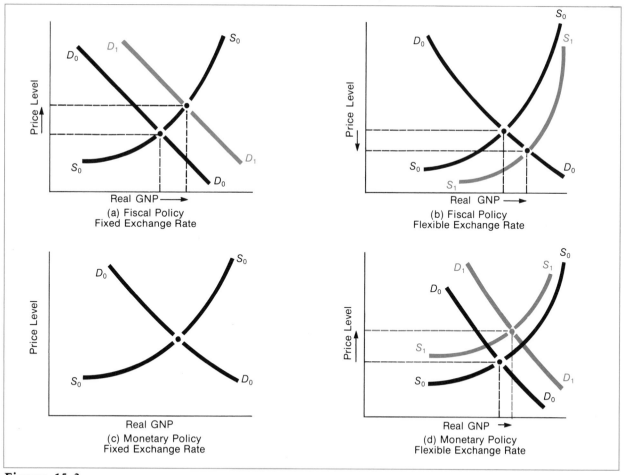

Figure 15-3

FISCAL AND MONETARY EFFECTS ON AGGREGATE DEMAND AND SUPPLY

Both monetary and fiscal policies have direct aggregate-supply effects under a floating exchange-rate regime, since the exchange rate affects the costs of imported intermediate products.

fixed exchange rates, nor any shift in the supply curve without an exchange-rate change, neither curve is shifted in Figure 15–3(c). We conclude that monetary policy has no effect on real GNP or the price level under fixed exchange rates. A more accurate description of this outcome is that an independent monetary policy cannot be set if the central bank has already committed the money supply to be whatever is required to peg the exchange rate.

An increase in the money supply is possible if the central bank does not intervene in the foreign-exchange market. This policy is considered in Figure 15–3(d). Since there is a lasting effect of the monetary expansion on aggregate demand, the demand curve shifts to the right from D_0D_0 to D_1D_1. However, the reason for this is that the depreciation in the Canadian dollar raises net exports. This depreciation also raises business costs, so the aggregate-supply curve shifts up from S_0S_0 to S_1S_1. We conclude that expansionary monetary policy under flexible exchange rates results in higher prices, and (at best) in only a small increase in real GNP.

Review

Before an informed opinion concerning the effects of government policy on unemployment and inflation can be had, we must know what the government's exchange-rate policy is. Although a noticeable depreciation of the Canadian dollar has taken place during the early 1980s, the government's policy has been one of significant management of the exchange rate. Thus we can take the fixed exchange-rate predictions of our analysis as roughly appropriate. As a result, we cannot expect Canada to have a monetary policy that is much different from that in the United States. Fiscal policy can be used as an independent instrument, but it involves the standard trade-off between the real GNP and price-level goals.

Foreign Interest-Rate Increases and Aggregate Supply

We considered the aggregate-demand effects of an increase in foreign interest rates in Chapter 13 (pages 258–60). Here we bring in the aggregate-supply effects that are involved if the exchange rate is allowed to float.

Until Canadian interest rates are pulled up to the level of foreign interest rates through competition, investors will sell Canadian bonds, to buy the higher-yield foreign bonds. To accomplish this shift, investors must buy foreign currency by selling Canadian dollars. If the exchange rate is flexible, this shift causes a fall in the value of the Canadian dollar. The depreciation of the Canadian dollar stimulates foreign demand for our exports, so that the aggregate-demand curve shifts out from D_0D_0 to D_1D_1 in Figure 15–4(a). The depreciated Canadian dollar also increases business costs, so the aggregate-supply curve moves from S_0S_0 to S_1S_1. The net result is significant upward pressure on the price level, and perhaps even a decrease in production.

A lower level of production is particularly likely in the short run, since the increase in business costs occurs without a lag. In contrast to this, there is often a

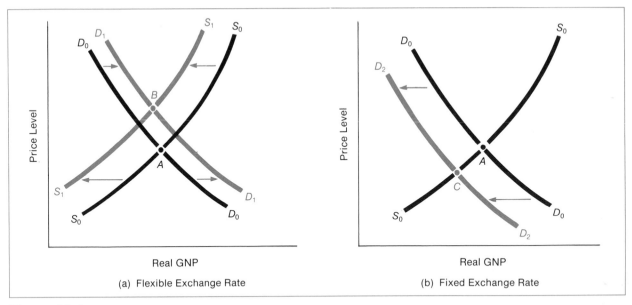

Figure 15-4

AGGREGATE-DEMAND AND AGGREGATE-SUPPLY EFFECTS OF FOREIGN INTEREST-RATE INCREASES

Foreign interest-rate increases lead investors to trade Canadian bonds for foreign bonds, and this requires exchanging Canadian dollars for foreign currencies. If there is a floating exchange rate, the depreciation of the Canadian dollar stimulates export demand (so demand shifts from D_0D_0 to D_1D_1) and increases business costs (so supply shifts from S_0S_0 to S_1S_1). We move from point A to point B in panel (a). If the exchange rate is fixed, the Bank of Canada buys the previously circulating Canadian currency to avoid depreciation, so the domestic money supply shrinks and aggregate demand shifts from D_0D_0 to D_2D_2. Without a change in the exchange rate, there is no direct effect on business costs, so no shift in the aggregate-supply curve. We move from point A to point C in panel (b). Output can fall under either exchange-rate regime, but more inflation occurs under a floating rate.

significant lag following an exchange-rate change, before foreign buyers decide that a change is permanent enough to warrant switching orders from one country to another.

To maintain a fixed exchange rate after an increase in foreign interest rates, the Bank of Canada must sell foreign exchange. Investors who desire high-yield bonds will be trading in Canadian dollars to get the necessary foreign exchange. As the previously circulating Canadian dollars are absorbed by the Bank of Canada (in payment for its sales of foreign exchange), the domestic money supply shrinks. As a result, the aggregate-demand curve shifts in from D_0D_0 to D_2D_2 in Figure 15–4(b). With no change in the exchange rate under a fixed exchange-rate policy, there is no direct effect on business costs, so there is no shift in the aggregate-supply curve.

To summarize, an increase in foreign interest rates leaves Canada with the following alternatives:

1. Peg the exchange rate, so the higher interest rate is accompanied by lower output and downward pressure on prices (a move from point A to point C in Figure 15–4(b)); or

2. Float the exchange rate, so the higher interest rate is accompanied by higher prices, and probably a mild slump in output (a move from point A to point B in Figure 15–4(a)).

One's choice between these alternatives depends (among other things) on one's beliefs concerning the relative sizes of the costs of unemployment and inflation.

As we learned in Chapter 13, the Bank of Canada has permitted some depreciation of the Canadian dollar in the face of U.S. interest-rate increases in the early 1980s, but the exchange rate has been heavily managed. The Bank has followed this policy since it regards the costs of inflation to be very high.

Summary

1. The usefulness of monetary and fiscal policies as tools of demand management depends critically on the government's exchange-rate policy.

2. Fiscal policy has no lasting effect on aggregate demand under a floating exchange rate. Any initial expansion of demand just causes temporarily higher interest rates, which attract foreign funds. The Canadian dollar appreciates, forcing a contraction in net export demands. The truth of this proposition was dramatically illustrated by the conflict between the Bank of Canada and the Diefenbaker government, known as the "Coyne Affair."

3. Fiscal policy has a lasting effect on aggregate demand under fixed exchange rates. The temporary rise in interest rates following the expansion attracts foreign funds, which the Bank of Canada must absorb to peg the exchange rate. The increase in the domestic money supply which the Bank must allow to buy the incoming foreign exchange reinforces the initial fiscal expansion.

4. Monetary policy cannot be used as an independent instrument in a fixed exchange-rate regime. Any initial expansion of demand involves temporarily lower domestic interest rates, which cause foreign funds to leave the country. The Bank of Canada must accept the domestic currency that is relinquished as foreign exchange is purchased to buy foreign bonds. The resulting decrease in domestic money circulating counteracts the original policy. The truth of this proposition was dramatically illustrated in the 1969–70 period. Canada tried a contractionary monetary policy with a pegged exchange rate, while the U.S. policy was expansionary due to the Vietnam war.

5. Monetary policy has a lasting effect on aggregate demand under a floating exchange rate. An expansion of demand by the Bank of Canada initially involves lower domestic interest rates. As foreign funds leave the country, the Canadian dollar depreciates. The resulting stimulation of net exports reinforces the initial expansionary monetary policy.

6. Both monetary and fiscal policies can have direct aggregate-supply effects under a floating exchange-rate regime. Since the exchange rate affects the costs of imported intermediate products, it affects business costs and shifts the position of the aggregate-supply curve.

7. The Bank of Canada has followed a policy of heavily managing the exchange rate during the 1980s. As a result, our monetary policy is largely determined in the United States. Fiscal policy remains an in-dependent instrument that can be used for demand management, but it involves the standard short-run trade-off: Higher levels of real GNP can be had only with increases in the price level.

Concepts for Review

Interest-rate differential
Foreign exchange market
    intervention
Floating, or flexible, exchange rates

Questions for Discussion

1. Why did the Bank of Canada resist appreciation of the Canadian dollar in the early 1970s?
2. Why did the Bank of Canada resist depreciation of the Canadian dollar in the early 1980s?
3. In the text we examined an expansionary fiscal policy and a contractionary monetary policy, under both exchange-rate regimes. Show that the conclusions in the table on page 293 are equally valid for a contrac-tionary fiscal policy and an expansionary monetary policy.
4. Does exchange-rate policy make a difference for the effects of a foreign tariff on the Canadian economy?

The International Monetary System

16

All decent people live beyond
their incomes nowadays, and
those who aren't respectable live
beyond other people's. A few gifted
individuals manage to do both.

SAKI

This chapter takes a look at the system that has been set up to handle the international movement of money—the **international monetary system.** We have already discussed the two polar forms of international monetary arrangements—the fixed and flexible exchange-rate regimes, at least from one country's point of view. In the first part of this chapter, we continue our investigation of these two exchange-rate regimes. First, we examine why some countries' currencies appreciate while others depreciate. Second, in discussing fixed exchange rates, we consider how the *balance of payments* is measured.

But the two polar exchange-rate systems are studied to illustrate some important principles, *not* to describe the actual international monetary system as it is now. Therefore, in the remainder of the chapter we turn to more realistic intermediate systems that have elements of both pure forms, including the old *gold standard*, the so-called *gold-exchange system* that prevailed from 1944 until 1971, and the current *mixed* system—a system that defies any short description because each country, it seems, handles its international monetary relations somewhat differently.

What Determines Exchange Rates?

When exchange rates are flexible, they are determined by the forces of supply and demand. But what factors move the supply and demand curves? Economists believe that the principal determinants of exchange-rate movements are rather different in the long, medium, and short runs. So we turn in the next three sections to the analysis of exchange-rate movements over these three "runs." We begin with the long run.

The Purchasing-Power Parity Theory: The Long Run

As long as there is free trade across national borders, exchange rates should eventually adjust so that the same product costs the same number of dollars (or the same amount of any other currency) in every country, except for differences attributable to transportation costs and the like. This simple statement forms the basis of the major theory of exchange-rate determination in the long run.

The **purchasing-power parity theory of exchange-rate determination** holds that the exchange rate between any two national currencies adjusts to reflect differences in the price levels in the two countries.

An example will bring out the basic truth in this theory and also suggest some of its limitations. Suppose that Swedish and Canadian steel are identical and that these two nations are the only producers of steel for the world market. Suppose further that steel is the only tradable good that either country produces.

Question: If Canadian steel costs $120 per ton and Swedish steel costs 1000 kronor per ton, what must be the exchange rate between the dollar and the krona?

Answer: Since 1000 kronor must be the equivalent of $120, each krona must be worth 12 cents. Why? Because if a krona cost 15 cents, then Swedish steel would cost $150 per ton (1000 kronor at 15 cents each) while Canadian steel would cost $120 per ton, and all foreign customers would shop for their steel in Canada. The exchange rate of 15 cents per krona would be too high.

EXERCISE
Show why an exchange rate of 10 cents per krona is too low.

The purchasing-power parity theory is used to make long-run predictions about the effects of inflation on exchange rates. To continue our example, suppose that over a five-year period, prices in Canada rise by one-third while prices in Sweden rise by 60 percent. The purchasing-power parity theory predicts that the krona would depreciate relative to the dollar. It also predicts the amount of the currency depreciation. Say that after the inflation, Canadian steel costs $160 per ton (one-third more than $120), while Swedish steel costs 1600 kronor per ton (60 percent more than 1000 kronor). For these two prices to be equivalent, 1600 kronor must be worth $160, or one krona must be worth 10 cents. The value of the krona, therefore, must have fallen from 12 cents to 10 cents.

According to the purchasing-power parity theory, differences in domestic inflation rates are a major cause of adjustments in exchange rates. For instance, if one country has a faster rate of inflation than another, then its exchange rate must be depreciating.

For many years, the theory seemed to work tolerably well. While precise numerical predictions based on purchasing-power parity calculations were not very accurate (see the accompanying box), nations with higher inflation did at least experience depreciating currencies. But in the early 1980s even this theory broke down. For example, while the U.S. inflation rate was slightly higher than West Germany's and much higher than Japan's between 1980 and 1983, the U.S. dollar none the less rose relative to both the mark and the yen during this period. Clearly, the theory is missing something. There are a number of complications that the purchasing-power theory ignores.

First, changes in any of the interferences with free trade, such as tariffs and quotas, can upset simple calculations based on purchasing-power parity. For example, if Swedish prices rise faster than Canadian prices but, at the same time, foreign countries erect tariff barriers to keep Canadian (but not Swedish) steel out, then the krona might not have to depreciate.

Second, some goods and services cannot be traded across national frontiers. Land and buildings are only the most obvious examples; most services can be traded only to a limited extent (as when tourists from one country have their hair cut in another). Inflation rates for goods and services that are *not tradable* have little bearing on exchange rates.

Third, few of the goods that different nations produce and trade are as uniform

Purchasing-Power Parity and the Big Mac

In July 1983, *The New York Times* used a well-known international commodity to assess the purchasing-power parity theory. As this article shows, the theory did not work very well.

The French have been most vociferous in complaining that the U.S. dollar's value has been too high. But if the cost of lunch at McDonald's is any guide, it is the franc, more than the dollar, that should be devalued.

Theoretically, at least, if all exchange rates were where they should be, prices of the same goods should be identical in every country. Using McDonald's as an example, exchange rates, indeed, are out of line and the dollar is overvalued against all the major currencies, except the franc.

Last Wednesday, in New York, it cost $3.39 to buy a Big Mac, a small order of fries, and a small Coke. This was substantially higher than the cost of a comparable McDonald's lunch in five major foreign cities.

In Paris, however, the dollar-equivalent price was $3.82, based on the franc's June 28 value of 13.08 cents. The biggest bargain was in Amsterdam, where the price of a McDonald's lunch was only $2.40. In Switzerland, the cost of a comparable meal was $3.23; in Tokyo, $2.62; in Germany, $2.57, and in London, $2.40.

If the seven currencies were to be made equal on the "MacIndex," using the New York price as the yardstick, the Swiss franc would have to be revalued upward by 4.7

percent against the dollar; the Japanese yen 22.7 percent; the German mark 24 percent; the British pound 25.7 percent; and the Dutch guilder 29.2 percent. The French franc would have to be devalued 11.3 percent.

SOURCE: *The New York Times*, July 3, 1983.

AUTHORS' NOTE: Actually, the theory did not do all that badly. Over the next several months, the French franc depreciated 10.9 percent relative to the U.S. dollar.

---

as the Swedish and Canadian steel in our example. A Volvo and a Buick, for example, are not identical products. So the price of a Volvo *in Canadian dollars* can rise faster than the price of a Buick without driving Volvos out of the market entirely. On balance:

Most economists believe that other factors are much more important than relative price levels for exchange-rate determination in the short run. But in the long run, purchasing-power parity plays an important role.

Economic Activity and Exchange Rates: The Medium Run

Consumer spending increases quite regularly when income expands, and decreases when income contracts, and the same is true for imported goods. Thus, as we stressed in Chapter 11:

A country's imports will rise quickly when its economy is booming and slowly when its economy is stagnating.

A boom in Canada would shift the demand curve for marks outward and therefore lead to an appreciation of the mark (depreciation of the dollar) and Canadian imports from Germany would surge. However, if Germany were booming at the same time, German citizens would be buying more Canadian exports, which would shift the supply curve of marks outward. On balance, the value of the dollar might or might not fall. What matters is whether exports are growing faster than imports. The general lesson is that:

Holding other things equal, a country that grows faster than the rest of the world normally finds its currency depreciating because its imports grow faster than its exports, so that its demand curve for foreign currency shifts outward more rapidly than its supply curve.

The exchange rate between the U.S. dollar and the mark in the 1970s (but not in the 1980s!) is a case in point. During the recovery from the worldwide recession of 1974–76, the U.S. economy expanded quite a bit more rapidly than the German economy. This is one reason why the dollar depreciated and the mark rose in value from late 1976 to late 1978.

Interest Rates and Exchange Rates: The Short Run

While economic activity is very important for exchange-rate determination in the medium run, "other things" often are not equal in the very short run. Specifically, one factor that often seems to call the tune in determining exchange rates in the short run is *interest-rate differentials*. There is an enormous fund of so-called "hot money"—owned by banks, multinational corporations, and wealthy individuals of all nations, and amounting to perhaps $500 billion to $700 billion—that travels around the globe in search of the highest interest rates.

Thus, suppose that British government bonds are paying a 10 percent rate of interest when yields on equally safe Canadian government securities rise to 15 percent. British investors will be attracted by the high interest rates in Canada and will offer pounds for sale in order to buy dollars, planning to use those dollars to buy Canadian securities. At the same time Canadian investors will find investing in Canada more attractive than ever, so fewer pounds will be demanded by Canadians.

When the demand schedule falls and the supply curve rises, the effect on price is quite predictable: the pound will depreciate, as Figure 16–1 shows. In the figure, the supply curve of pounds shifts outward from S_1S_1 to S_2S_2 when British investors seek to sell pounds in order to purchase Canadian securities. At the same time, Canadian investors wish to buy fewer pounds because they no longer

Figure 16–1

THE EFFECT OF A RISE IN CANADIAN INTEREST RATES
When Canada raises its interest rates, more English investors will want to buy Canadian bonds, and so the supply curve of pounds will shift outward from S_1S_1 to S_2S_2. At the same time, fewer Canadians will seek to buy British bonds, so the demand curve for pounds will shift inward from D_1D_1 to D_2D_2. The combined effect of these two shifts is to move the market equilibrium from point E_1 to point E_2. The British pound depreciates, and the dollar appreciates.

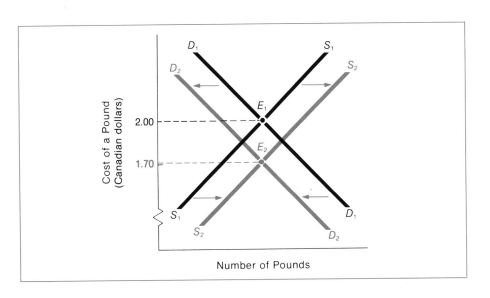

wish to invest in British securities. Thus, the demand curve shifts inward from D_1D_1 to D_2D_2. The result, in our example, is a depreciation of the pound from $2.00 to $1.70. In general:

Holding other things equal, countries with high interest rates are able to attract more capital than are countries with low interest rates. Thus a rise in interest rates often will lead to an appreciation of the currency, and a drop in interest rates will lead to a depreciation.

The Canadian dollar in 1981–83 provided a vivid example of the power of this phenomenon when high U.S. interest rates caused a sharp appreciation of the U.S. dollar and a depreciation of the Canadian dollar. Most experts in international finance agree that international money is so volatile that interest-rate movements are the chief determinant of exchange-rate fluctuations in the short run.

Market Determination of Exchange Rates: Summary

We can summarize this discussion of exchange-rate determination in free markets as follows:

1. Currencies generally will be *appreciating* in countries whose inflation rates are lower than the rest of the world, for otherwise it would be increasingly difficult for the other countries to market their goods.

2. Exchange rates would also be expected to rise in countries whose levels of economic activity are lower than average, because these countries will be importing rather little.

3. We expect to find appreciating currencies in countries whose interest rates are high because these countries will attract capital from all over the world.

Reversing each of these, we expect that currencies will be *depreciating* in countries with relatively high inflation rates, or high levels of economic activity, or low interest rates. *becoming*

Fixed Exchange Rates and the Definition of the Balance of Payments

From our discussion of fixed exchange rates in Chapter 13 (pages 248–54) it may seem that measuring a nation's balance-of-payments position is a simple task: We simply count up the private demand for and supply of its currency and subtract quantity supplied from quantity demanded. Conceptually, this is all there is to it. But, in practice, the difficulties are great because we never have statistics on the number of dollars demanded and supplied. There is no way to observe these directly.

If we look at actual market transactions, we will see that the number of Canadian dollars actually *purchased* and the number of Canadian dollars actually *sold* on the foreign-exchange market are identical. Unless someone has made a bookkeeping error, this must always be so. How, then, can we recognize a balance-of-payments surplus or deficit? Easy, you say. Just look at the transactions of the central bank, whose purchases or sales must make up the difference between private demand and private supply. If the Bank of Canada is buying Canadian dollars, its purchases measure our balance-of-payments deficit. If it is selling, its sales represent our balance-of-payments surplus. Thus, we measure the balance of payments by *excluding official transactions among governments.*

The Canadian Balance-of-Payments Accounts

Using 1983 as an example, Table 16-1 shows the official Canadian balance-of-payments accounts. The top section of the table summarizes Canada's trade in currently produced goods and services—the so-called *current account*. The positive or negative sign attached to each entry indicates whether the transaction represented a *gain* (+) or a *loss* (–) of foreign currency.

Looking first at the top of the table, we see that in merchandise transactions Canadians exported about $18 billion more than they imported, leading to a surplus in merchandise trade (lines 1–3). Almost as big an amount, but in this case a deficit, took place in the trade of services. Lines 4 and 5 indicate that Canadians spent more on foreign travel and on making interest payments to foreigners to service our international debt than we received from foreign tourists and from our investments abroad. The transfer payments in line 6 include items such as gifts and foreign aid. Line 7 gives the net result of all trading in goods and services—the balance on current account. The entry means that Canada received $1.6 billion more than it spent during 1983.

Lines 8–11 record trades of financial assets, and this section is called the *capital account* of the balance of payments. Line 8 indicates that Canadians purchased more shares in foreign companies than foreigners purchased in Canadian companies in 1983. Much of this is due to our banks and real estate companies, and the Canadianization that has taken place in the energy industry. Lines 9 and 10 indicate that Canadians sold $7.1 billion of long- and short-term bonds to foreigners, more than foreigners sold to Canadians. The balance on the capital account is given in line 11. It indicates that $5.5 billion entered Canada during 1983, as a result of all the recorded trades of stocks and bonds that took place across the border that year.

One would think that with a surplus on both the current and capital accounts,

Table 16-1

CANADIAN BALANCE-OF-PAYMENTS ACCOUNTS, 1983 (billions of dollars)

Current Account

1) Merchandise exports	+91.3		
2) Merchandise imports	−73.3		
3) Balance of merchandise trade		+18.0	
4) Service exports			
(Foreign travel in Canada, Canadian interest and dividend receipts from abroad)		+16.9	
5) Service imports			
(Canadian travel abroad, foreign interest and dividend receipts from Canada)		−34.2	
6) Net transfer payments		+0.9	
7) Balance on current account			+1.6

Capital Account

8) Net direct foreign investment in Canada		−1.6	
9) Net long-term portfolio investment in Canada		+4.4	
10) Net short-term investment in Canada		+2.7	
11) Balance on capital account			+5.5

Summary

12) Errors and omissions			−6.6
13) Balance of payments			
(Change in official foreign-exchange reserves)			−0.5

SOURCE: Bank of Canada *Review*

Where Has All the Money Gone?

Canada is not the only country that cannot balance its international books. As the following news report indicates, "statistical discrepancies" are causing problems all over the world—and the problem is getting worse.

WASHINGTON, July 29—Somewhere, in ships on the high seas, in the mails, in secret bank deposits, in some countries' ill-kept accounts and in a multitude of other places, about $100 billion a year is disappearing from the books of the world economy.

The figure represents the disparity in the sums of all countries' payments to each other for all the business they conduct across their borders—everything from sales of automobiles and airline tickets to the dividends a company in one country pays to stockholders in another.

A payment made in one country should show up as a receipt for an equal amount on the other country's books. And at the end of the year, the final accounting of all countries' payments on one side, and receipts on the other, should be equal, even though some individual countries have deficits and some have surpluses.

But lately, the figures have not come close.

"The world balance of payments doesn't add up," said Henry C. Wallich, a governor of the Federal Reserve Board and an expert on international commerce. "This question irritates a lot of people who can't answer it."

The country showing the largest shortfall is the United States.

According to economists for the international lending agency, the discrepancy is growing fastest in the category called "other services." These include construction and other contractual work that rapidly developing nations—recently, members of the Organization of Petroleum Exporting Countries—purchase from foreign companies and individuals. Payments go to some individuals "who have fiscal incentives for under-reporting or routing payments via tax havens," the I.M.F. reported in a seven-page appendix on the subject in last month's 1983 outlook.

Many other transactions bypass the world's bookkeepers entirely. When a ship that flies a flag of convenience picks up a cargo, one country makes note of payment of the shipping fees, but none records receipt of the payment.

C. Fred Bergsten, head of the Institute for International Economics, a research centre here, suspects that many travel transactions are inadequately reported as spendthrift American tourists, for example, travel across Europe.

"It's very important, because if everybody thinks he has a deficit and nobody thinks he has a surplus, then somebody thinks his problem is worse than it is," Mr. Bergsten said. "Right now, there's no one on the surplus side except Japan to take balancing action."

SOURCE: Peter T. Kilborn, "Global Trade Mystery: A Vanishing $100 Billion," *The New York Times*, July 30, 1983.

Canada would have had an overall balance-of-payments surplus in 1983. That is, official exchange reserves would increase as foreign exchange flowed into Canada. However, there is one other line in the table—line 12, errors and omissions. This entry shows that during 1983, $6.6 billion flowed out of Canada in unidentified forms.

While part of this huge discrepancy simply comes from errors in data collection and computation, the lion's share reflects the Canadian government's inability to monitor all the flows of money, goods, and services across its borders. (See the accompanying boxed insert.)

As a result, the official balance of payments shows a small deficit of $0.5 billion, so our foreign-exchange reserves decreased by this amount in 1983.

A Bit of History: The Gold Standard

About the only time exchange rates were truly fixed was under the old **gold standard**, at least when it was practised in its ideal form.[1]

Under the gold standard, fixed exchange rates were maintained by an automatic equilibrating mechanism that went something like this: All currencies were defined in terms of gold; indeed, some were actually made of gold. When a nation had a deficit in its balance of payments, this meant, essentially, that more gold was flowing *out* than was flowing *in*. Since the domestic money supply was based on gold, losing gold to foreigners meant that the quantity of money automatically fell. Thus, "monetary policy" *automatically* turned restrictive, and interest rates rose, attracting foreign capital. At the same time, the restrictive monetary policy pulled down national output and prices, thus discouraging imports and encouraging exports. The balance-of-payments problem quickly rectified itself. This means, however, that:

Under the gold standard, no nation had control of its domestic monetary policy, and therefore no country could control its domestic economy very well.

At least in principle, the effects on surplus countries were perfectly symmetrical under the gold standard. A balance-of-payments surplus led, via gold inflows, to an increase in the domestic money supply whether the surplus country liked the idea or not. This raised prices (which decreased exports) and raised real GNP (which increased imports). And it also lowered interest rates, thereby encouraging outflows of capital. Because of these automatic adjustments, nations rarely reached the point at which devaluations or revaluations were necessary. Exchange rates were fixed as long as countries abided by the rules of the gold-standard game.

In addition to the complete loss of control over domestic monetary conditions, the gold standard posed one other serious difficulty.

A fundamental problem with the gold standard was that the world's commerce was at the mercy of gold discoveries.

Discoveries of gold meant higher prices in the long run and higher real economic activity in the short run, through the standard monetary-policy mechanisms that we studied in Chapters 12–14. And when the supply of gold did not keep pace with growth of the world economy, prices had to fall in the long run and employment had to fall in the short run.

An examination of the periods containing the world's great gold discoveries during the last several centuries provides a direct test of our understanding of these arrangements. These periods are precisely the times when there were major world inflations, just as our analysis suggests.

The Bretton Woods System and the International Monetary Fund

The gold standard, which had faltered many times before, finally collapsed amid the financial chaos of the Great Depression of the 1930s. Without it, the world struggled through nearly 15 years of almost complete breakdown in international trade.

Then, as World War II drew to a close, with much of Europe in ruins and with the United States holding the lion's share of the free world's reserves, officials of

---

[1]As a matter of fact, while the gold standard lasted (on and off) for hundreds of years, it was rarely practised in its ideal form. Except for a brief period of fixed exchange rates in the late nineteenth and early twentieth centuries, there were periodic adjustments of exchange rates even under the gold standard.

the industrial nations met at Bretton Woods, New Hampshire, in 1944 to try to establish a stable monetary environment that would facilitate world trade. And since the U.S. dollar was the only "strong" currency at that time, it was natural for them to turn to the dollar as the basis of the new international economic order.

That is just what they did. The Bretton Woods agreements re-established a system of fixed exchange rates based not on the old gold standard but on the free convertibility of the U.S. dollar into gold. The United States agreed to buy or sell gold to maintain the $35 per ounce price that had been established by President Franklin Roosevelt in 1933. And the other signatory nations, which had almost no gold in any case, agreed to buy and sell U.S. dollars to maintain their exchange rates at agreed-upon levels. Thus all currencies were indirectly on a modified "gold standard." A holder of French francs, for example, could exchange these for U.S. dollars at (roughly) 5 francs per dollar and then exchange these into gold at $35 per ounce. In this way, the value of the franc was fixed at 175 francs per ounce of gold (5 francs per dollar times 35 dollars per ounce). The new system was dubbed the **gold-exchange system**, and often referred to as the **Bretton Woods system**.

The **International Monetary Fund (IMF)** was set up to police and manage this new system. Using funds that had been contributed by member countries, the IMF was empowered to make loans to countries that were running low on reserves. Only in the case of a "fundamental disequilibrium" in a nation's balance of payments was a change in exchange rates to be permitted. For it was believed that only relatively fixed exchange rates could provide the stable climate needed to restore world trade.

Of course, the Bretton Woods conferees did not define clearly what a "fundamental disequilibrium" was, nor could they have. As the system evolved, it came to mean a chronic deficit in the balance of payments of sizable proportions. Such nations would then *devalue* relative to the U.S. dollar; that is, they would reduce the value of their currencies in terms of U.S. dollars. So the system was not really one of fixed exchange rates but rather one where rates were "fixed until further notice."

Several flaws in the Bretton Woods system were evident in our discussion of the pure system of fixed exchange rates in Chapter 13 (pages 251–54). First, since devaluations were permitted only after a long run of balance-of-payments deficits, these devaluations (a) could be clearly foreseen, and (b) normally had to be quite large. Speculators then saw opportunities for profit and would "attack" weak currencies with a wave of selling.

This problem led many economists to question whether the system of fixed exchange rates was really providing the stable climate for world trade that had been intended. Was a system where rates were constant for long periods and then altered by very large amounts really more conducive to international trade than one where overvalued currencies would gradually depreciate, as they would under a system of floating rates?

The second problem arose from the custom that deficit nations were expected to devalue when forced to, while surplus nations (mainly Germany and Japan) could resist upward revaluations. Since the U.S. dollar defined the monetary value of gold (at $35 per ounce), the United States was the one nation in the world that had no way to devalue its currency relative to gold, no matter how "fundamental" the disequilibrium became. The only way exchange rates between the U.S. dollar and foreign currencies could change was if the surplus nations revalued their currencies upward relative to the U.S. dollar. They did not do this frequently enough, so the United States, with its chronically overvalued currency, ran persistent balance-of-payments deficits.

This represented an adjustment problem for the system as a whole, but it was a benefit for the United States. Whenever other countries had large balance-of-payments deficits, they had to do something about it before they ran out of foreign-exchange reserves. But the United States could not run out of "foreign exchange," since they could simply print more. It certainly was convenient for the United States. They could import more than they exported and could buy up ownership in companies operating in other countries, and all they had to give in return were U.S. dollars, which they could print at essentially no cost.

Adjustment Mechanisms Under the Bretton Woods System

Under the Bretton Woods system, devaluation was viewed as a last resort, to be used only after other methods of adjusting to payments imbalances had failed. What were these other methods?

We have already encountered most of them in our discussion of exchange-rate determination in free markets (see Chapter 13, pages 260–61). Any factor that increases the demand for, say, British pounds or that reduces the supply will push the exchange rate upward if it is free to adjust. If, however, the exchange rate is pegged, it is the balance-of-payments deficit rather than the exchange rate that will adjust when supply of or demand for a nation's money changes. Specifically, the British balance-of-payments deficit will shrink if either the demand for pounds increases or the supply decreases.

The two panels of Figure 16–2 illustrate this adjustment. In each case, the United Kingdom has a payments deficit, since the official exchange rate ($3.00) exceeds the equilibrium rate ($2.60). The deficit starts at AB in each diagram. Then either the demand curve moves outward as in part (a), or the supply curve moves inward as in part (b). With the exchange rate held at $3.00, the balance-of-payments deficit shrinks—to CB in part (a) or AC in part (b).

Referring back to our earlier discussions of the factors that underlie the demand and supply curves, then, we see that one way a deficit nation can improve its balance of payments is to *reduce its aggregate demand*, thus discouraging imports and cutting down its demand for foreign currency. Another is to *slow its*

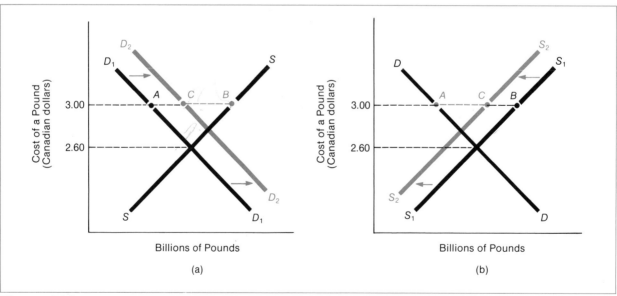

Billions of Pounds

(a)

Billions of Pounds

(b)

Figure 16–2

ADJUSTING TO BALANCE-OF-PAYMENTS DEFICITS

The two parts of this diagram illustrate alternative ways to cut Britain's balance-of-payments deficit while maintaining the exchange rate at $3.00 per pound. Part (a) might represent a reduction in British inflation, which would increase world demand for her export products. Or it could represent a rise in British interest rates, which would attract foreign capital. Part (b) might represent a reduction in British incomes, which would diminish English appetites for foreign goods. In either case, whether demand rises or supply falls, the balance-of-payments deficit is reduced: from AB to CB in part (a) and from AB to AC in part (b).

rate of inflation, thus encouraging exports and discouraging imports. Finally, it can raise its interest rates in order to attract more foreign capital.

In a word, deficit nations were expected to follow restrictive monetary and fiscal policies *voluntarily* just as they would *automatically* have done under the old gold standard. However, just as under the gold standard, this medicine was often unpalatable, so deficit nations frequently resorted to a bewildering variety of **exchange controls**—laws and regulations that made it very difficult for its nationals to sell their own currency to get foreign exchange. Many countries still have such controls.

Exchange controls are laws restricting the exchange of one nation's currency for another's.

Surplus nations could, of course, have taken the opposite measures: pursuing expansive monetary and fiscal policies to increase economic growth and lower interest rates. But they often did not relish the inflation that would come with such actions, and, once again, left the burden of adjustment to the deficit nations. The general point about fixed exchange rates is that:

Under a system of fixed exchange rates, the government of a country loses some control over its domestic economy. There may be times when balance-of-payments considerations force it to contract its economy in order to cut down its demand for foreign currency, even though domestic needs are calling for expansion. Conversely, there may be times when the domestic economy needs to be reined in, but balance-of-payments considerations suggest expansion.

The system worked fairly well for a number of years, but it finally broke down over its inability to "devalue" the U.S. dollar with respect to the other world currencies. During the mid-1960s, the size of the U.S. balance-of-payments deficit grew tremendously. This was primarily due to their large expenditures on the Vietnam war and on domestic social programs, and on the fact that the stock of U.S. dollars in foreign hands had reached a level that was many times larger than the U.S. government's holdings of gold. The demand for U.S. dollars fell, and the demand for gold rose, as many speculators anticipated that the United States would effectively increase their reserves of gold by raising the official price above $35 per ounce. But the larger U.S. balance-of-payments deficits meant that the *world money supply was growing very rapidly.* So the late 1960s was just like one of the earlier periods of large gold discoveries, and just like in those periods, a world inflation ensued. Since the other nations had no way of stopping the overly expansive U.S. monetary policy, the only way they could control their own inflation rate was to cut the link with the U.S. dollar. Many countries floated their exchange rate, as Canada did in 1970. The Bretton Woods system ended when the monetary policy of the base-currency country, the United States, became irresponsible in the eyes of the other countries.

In August 1971, President Nixon formally abolished the Bretton Woods system by announcing that the United States would no longer peg the value of the dollar by buying and selling gold. Actually, the system had already ended.

Most observers today agree that the gold-exchange system could not have survived the incredible events of the 1970s in any case. The worldwide inflationary boom of 1972, the poor food harvests in 1972–74, the huge increases in the price of oil in 1973–74 and again in 1979–80, and the great worldwide recession of 1974–76 all helped create a world in which the major countries were experiencing dramatically different inflation rates.

For example, between 1972 and 1982 inflation averaged 5 percent per year in Germany, 9 percent in the United States, and 16 percent in Italy. As the purchasing-power theory reminds us, large differences in inflation rates call for *major* changes in currency values. And the Bretton Woods system was ill-suited to handle such major changes.

Why Try to Fix Exchange Rates?

In view of these and other severe problems with the Bretton Woods system, why did the international financial community work so hard to maintain fixed rates for so many years? The answer is that floating exchange rates, determined in free markets by supply and demand, also pose problems.

Chief among these is the possibility that freely floating rates might be highly variable rates, which add an unwanted element of riskiness to foreign trade. For example, if the exchange rate is 16 cents to the French franc, then a 2000-franc Parisian dress will cost $320. But should the franc appreciate to 20 cents, this same dress would cost $400. A Canadian department store thinking of buying this dress may need to place its order far in advance and will want to know the cost *in dollars*. It may be worried about the possibility that the value of the franc will rise, so that the dress will cost more than $320. And such worries might inhibit trade.

There are two answers to this worry. First, we could hope that freely floating rates would prove not to be very volatile. Prices of many domestic consumer goods, for example, are determined by supply and demand in free markets and yet do not fluctuate unduly. Second, speculators might relieve business firms of exchange-rate risks—for a fee, of course. Consider the department store example. If French francs cost 16 cents today, the department store manager can assure herself of paying exactly $320 for the dress several months from now by arranging for a speculator to deliver francs to her at 16 cents on the day she needs them. If the franc appreciates in the interim, it is the speculator, not the department store, that will take the financial beating. (And, of course, if the franc depreciates, the speculator will pocket the profits.)

This role of speculation is described more fully in our discussion of the stock market in *Microeconomics*, Chapter 9. The widespread fears that speculative activity in free markets will lead to wild gyrations in prices, while occasionally valid, are more often unfounded. The reason is quite simple. International currency speculators, if they are to make profits, must buy a currency when its value is low (thus helping to support the currency by pushing up its demand curve) and sell it when its value is high (thus holding down the price by adding to the supply curve).

This means that, if they are successful, speculators will be coming into the market as *buyers* just when demand is weak (or when supply is strong), and coming in as *sellers* just when demand is strong (or supply is scant). In doing so, they will help limit price fluctuations. Looked at the other way around, speculators can destabilize prices only if they are systematically willing to lose money.

Notice the stark contrast to the system of fixed exchange rates in which speculation often led to wild "runs" on currencies that were on the verge of devaluation. Speculative activity, which may very well be destabilizing under fixed rates, is likely to be stabilizing under floating rates.

We do not mean to imply here that there are no difficulties at all under floating exchange rates. Indeed, it may prove impossible to eliminate all exchange-rate risks through speculation. And at the very least, speculators will demand a fee for their services—a fee that adds to the costs of trading across national borders. We only suggest that life is liable to be more placid than is commonly supposed.

The experience under floating rates since 1973 has delivered clear verdicts on these two issues. First, exchange rates have in fact proven to be quite volatile—more volatile than many of the advocates of floating rates anticipated. Second, however, international trade has flourished despite this volatility. Speculators, we may surmise, are doing their job.

The Current Mixed System

Our current international financial system—where some currencies are still pegged in the old Bretton Woods manner, others are floating freely, and many more are

"Then it's agreed. Until the dollar firms up, we let the clamshell float."
Drawing by Ed Fisher
© 1971, The New Yorker Magazine, Inc.

floating subject to government interferences—has evolved gradually since 1971. Though it continues to change and adapt, at least three features are quite evident.

The first is the decline in the notion that exchange rates should be fixed for relatively long periods of time. The demand by many countries in the early 1970s that the world quickly return to fixed exchange rates had largely subsided by the mid-1970s. Even where rates are still pegged to the U.S. dollar, devaluations and revaluations are now much more frequent—and smaller—than they were in the 1944–71 period. Most free-world currency rates change very slightly on a day-to-day basis, and market forces generally determine the basic trends, up or down.

Second, however, some central banks do not hesitate to intervene to moderate exchange movements whenever they feel that such actions are appropriate. Typically, these interventions are aimed at ironing out transitory fluctuations. But there have been instances in which central banks have, for a time, opposed basic trends in exchange rates. Deficit nations have bought their own currencies to prevent them from depreciating. Surplus nations have sold their own currencies to prevent them from appreciating. While we certainly no longer have many fixed exchange rates, many of the major currencies are floating less than freely. The terms "dirty float" or "managed float" have been coined to describe this mongrel system.

Figure 16–3 illustrates these tendencies in Canada. The decade of the 1960s was rather tranquil. Despite Canada's maintaining a fixed exchange rate from 1962 to 1969, our balance-of-payments surpluses and deficits were small. In the 1970s and 1980s, there were quite dramatic changes in the exchange rate *and* much larger balance-of-payments surpluses and deficits. The balance-of-payments data show that the Bank of Canada limited the fluctuations in the exchange rate. The

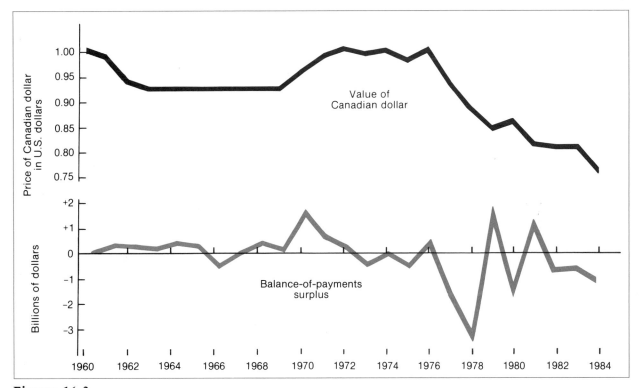

Figure 16-3

CANADA'S BALANCE OF PAYMENTS AND THE VALUE OF THE CANADIAN DOLLAR

This graph shows that the Bank of Canada has resisted movements in the exchange rate. The balance-of-payments surpluses in the early 1970s indicate that the Bank was accumulating foreign-exchange reserves (that is, selling Canadian dollars) to limit the rise in the Canadian dollar that took place. Also, balance-of-payments deficits occurred in 1976-78 and 1982-84, since the Bank was buying up Canadian dollars to limit the fall in our currency's value that was taking place.

surpluses in the early 1970s prove that the Bank of Canada was accumulating foreign-exchange reserves (that is, selling Canadian dollars) to limit the rise in the value of the Canadian dollar that did take place. Similarly, the deficits during 1976–78 and 1982–84 prove that the Bank of Canada was selling off foreign-exchange reserves (that is, buying Canadian dollars) to limit the fall in the value of the Canadian dollar.

Incidentally, most analysts attribute the rise in the Canadian dollar in the 1969–70 period to the temporarily higher interest rates, and the lower inflation rate in Canada (compared to the United States). Similarly, the fall in the Canadian dollar in the later 1970s and the 1980s is due to the higher inflation rate in Canada, and our attempt to maintain interest rates lower than the United States.

The third unmistakable feature of the present international monetary system is the virtual elimination of any role for gold. The trend away from gold actually began before President Nixon's dramatic announcement in 1971, and by now it is only a minor exaggeration that gold plays no role in the world's financial system.

Nowadays there is a *free market* in gold, which enables those who wish to invest in gold—dentists, jewelers, industrial users, speculators, and ordinary citizens who think of gold as a good store of value—to buy or sell as they wish. The price of gold, determined each day by the law of supply and demand, has proved to be quite volatile. Fortunes have been made and lost by investors in gold.

Developments in International Financial Markets Since 1973

Oil Prices and "Petrodollars"

The system of "dirty floating" is generally dated from early 1973. It received its first test in late 1973 and early 1974, when the Organization of Petroleum Exporting Countries (OPEC) quadrupled the price of oil. This naturally led to huge surpluses in the current accounts of the OPEC nations: Their combined surplus in 1974, for example, was a colossal $70 billion (U.S.). Because the sum of the current-account balances of all nations must necessarily be zero (since the country's exports are another's imports), this meant that the rest of the world had a combined deficit of $70 billion. And since this $70 billion (U.S.) total deficit was distributed quite unevenly across the nations of the world, it is hard to imagine how fixed exchange could have been maintained.

In particular, with OPEC earning so much more foreign currency than it was spending, it had to find places to invest its unspent revenues. Since OPEC invested mainly in New York, Zurich, and other financial centres, a problem arose that journalists dubbed "recycling petrodollars." Specifically, while the advanced industrial nations were paying more for oil, they were also receiving capital inflows from OPEC. So they found their balance-of-payments problems manageable. But the less developed countries (LDCs) had no such luck. They needed more foreign exchange to pay OPEC for oil but did not receive any through capital inflows.

The problem, then, was clear: How could OPEC's savings be channelled to the LDCs that needed the funds? At first, the IMF took the lead in this "recycling" effort. But soon the job was taken over by the big international banks, especially American banks, which received funds from OPEC and made loans to less developed countries. The short-term problem was solved, but a long-term problem was created: How were the less developed countries ever going to repay the loans?

The LDC Debt Problem*

Before anyone had an answer, OPEC struck again. The price of oil more than doubled during 1979, and the combined current-account surplus of the OPEC

---

*For more on this problem, see Chapter 22, especially page 436.

nations (the rest of the world's deficit) skyrocketted to $111 billion (U.S.) in 1980. As in 1974, the currencies of the developed countries withstood the shock fairly well; they once again financed their oil deficits through capital inflows. And the non-oil-developing nations again turned to borrowing on the private market; but the debts were getting unmanageably large.

Then two further problems beset the LDCs. First, the worldwide recession of 1981–83 made it harder for them to earn foreign currency by exporting goods to the industrial countries. Second, real interest rates rose dramatically, making the burden of paying interest on the debt much harder to bear. As a result, the 1980s so far have been marked by a series of near-crises in the international financial system as Mexico, Argentina, Brazil, and other nations have encountered difficulty in meeting their debt obligations.

To date, a series of special arrangements negotiated by governments and banks have kept the system afloat and avoided a panic. But no one is declaring the problem solved. And there is continued concern that major defaults on loans by LDCs could threaten the solvency of some banks in the developed countries.

The European Monetary System

As noted earlier, floating exchange rates are no magical cure-all. One particular problem beset the members of the European Economic Community (EEC). These Common Market countries seek a unified large market like the United States and have a long-range goal of establishing a single currency for all member countries. Floating rates would make this goal impossible. So in 1973 some of the member countries entered into an agreement whereby exchange rates among their currencies could remain relatively *fixed* while Common Market currencies as a group would rise or fall *relative to the rest of the world*.

Within a short time, however, both Britain and Italy found themselves unable to maintain parity with the strong currencies of Germany and the Netherlands. Britain was the first to let the pound float, but soon Italy and France also had to devalue relative to the mark. In 1979 the arrangement was strengthened and formalized in the **European Monetary System (EMS)**, which currently has eight member nations. The EMS includes detailed provisions for coping with exchange rates that threaten to get out of line with the others, and it is widely regarded as the first step, albeit a small one, toward a unified European currency.

Concluding Remark: Summits and Precipices

The past 15 years have been tumultuous ones for the international monetary system. Several crises have been faced and several changes have been made. No doubt, we will have more of both in the coming years.

Since 1975, the leaders of the major industrial nations have held annual summit meetings to discuss international economic problems. Sometimes these discussions are frank and fruitful. Sometimes they are public-relations exercises that paper over disagreements rather than resolve them. But most observers find the summits a useful and productive enterprise in any case. In today's small world, the major economies are too interrelated to ignore the need for international co-operation.

No one can predict with confidence the agendas for summit meetings to come. But it would be surprising indeed if the issues dealt with in this chapter did not arise again and again.

Summary

1. Several factors are important in the determination of exchange rates. In the long run, purchasing-power parity plays a major role in exchange-rate movements. The purchasing-power parity theory states that relative price levels in any two countries determine the exchange rate between their currencies. Therefore, countries with relatively low inflation rates normally will have appreciating currencies.

2. Over shorter periods, the pace of economic activity and the level of interest rates exert a greater influence on the exchange rate.

3. The balance of payments is difficult to measure, since many transactions across borders are difficult to monitor. However, the estimated accounts show that Canada typically has a surplus on merchandise trade, a deficit on the services account (which is due mostly to the interest payments on our foreign debt), and a surplus on the capital account (which is due to the fact that our foreign debt is increasing).

4. In the early part of this century, the world was on a particular system of fixed exchange rates called the gold standard, in which the value of every nation's currency was fixed in terms of gold. But this created problems because nations could not control their own money supplies and because the world could not control its total supply of gold.

5. After World War II, the gold standard was replaced by the gold-exchange (or Bretton Woods) system where rates were again fixed, or rather, fixed until further notice. In this system, the U.S. dollar was the basis of international currency values.

6. The gold-exchange system served the world well and helped restore world trade, but it got into trouble when U.S. monetary policy became overly expansionary, making the U.S. dollar overvalued. The system provided no way to remedy this situation.

7. Since 1971, the world has gradually been moving toward a system of relatively free exchange rates, though there are plenty of exceptions. We now have a thoroughly mixed system of "dirty" or "managed" floating, which continues to evolve and adapt.

8. Canada's managed exchange rate has fallen since 1976, mostly because of our relatively inferior inflation performance, and because we have tried to maintain slightly lower interest rates than those in the United States.

9. Floating rates are not without their problems; importers and exporters justifiably worry about fluctuations in exchange rates. But these problems seem manageable, if not completely solvable, and few people think that a return to fixed exchange rates is likely.

10. Under floating exchange rates, investors who speculate on international currency values provide a valuable service by assuming the risks of those who do not wish to speculate. Normally, speculators stabilize rather than destabilize exchange rates, because that is how they make profits.

Concepts for Review

Purchasing-power parity	Gold-exchange system (Bretton Woods system)	The LDC debt problem
Current account	International Monetary Fund (IMF)	The European Monetary System (EMS)
Capital account	Exchange controls	
Balance of payments	"Dirty" or "managed" floating	
Gold standard		

Questions for Discussion

1. What items do you own, or routinely consume, that are produced abroad? What countries do these come from? How have your purchases affected the exchange rates between the dollar and these currencies?

2. If the Canadian dollar appreciates relative to the Japanese yen, will the Sony stereo you have longed for become more or less expensive? What effect do you imagine this will have on Canadian demands for Sonys? Does the demand curve for yen, therefore, slope upward or downward? Explain.

3. Inflation in West Germany has generally been below that in Canada. What, then, does the purchasing-power parity theory predict should have happened to the exchange rate between the mark and the dollar? Ask your instructor what actually has happened.

4. Use supply and demand diagrams to analyse the effect on the exchange rate between the Canadian dollar and the British pound if:
   a. Britain's flow of North Sea oil ceases.
   b. British dockworkers refuse to unload ships that arrive with cargo from Canada but continue to load ships that sail from Britain.
   c. Both Britain and Canada slip into recession, but the Canadian recession is far more severe.
   d. Polls suggest that Mrs. Thatcher's government will be replaced by radicals who vow to nationalize all foreign-owned assets.

5. How are the problems of a country faced with a

balance-of-payments deficit similar to those posed by a government regulation that holds the price of milk above the equilibrium level? (*Hint*: Think of each in terms of a supply–demand diagram.)

6. Look at the Canadian balance-of-payments accounts table in the text (Table 16–1 on page 304). Figure out where each of the following actions you could have taken in 1983 would have been recorded in these accounts:
   a. You spent the summer travelling in Europe.
   b. Your uncle in France sent you $50 as a birthday present.
   c. You bought a new Toyota.
   d. You bought stock on the Japanese stock market.
   e. You drove over the American border carrying Canadian records in your truck and sold them to a friend in the United States. (*Hint*: Would your sale have been recorded anywhere?)

7. For each of the transactions listed in Question 6, indicate how it would affect:
   a. The Canadian balance of payments, if exchange rates were fixed.
   b. The international value of the Canadian dollar, if exchange rates were floating.

8. Explain why the members of the Bretton Woods conference in 1944 wanted to establish a system of fixed exchange rates. What was the flaw that led to the ultimate breakdown of the system in 1971?

9. Suppose you want to reserve hotel rooms in Rome for the coming summer but are worried that the value of the lira may rise between now and then, making the rooms too expensive for your budget. Explain how a speculator could relieve you of this worry. (Don't actually try it. Speculators deal only in very large sums!)

10. On page 310, it is pointed out that successful speculators buy a currency when demand is weak and sell it when demand is strong. Use supply and demand diagrams for two different periods (one with weak demand, the other with strong demand) to show why this will limit price fluctuations.

Budget Deficits and the National Debt: Fact and Fiction

17

Blessed are the young, for they shall inherit the national debt.

HERBERT HOOVER

There is a widespread belief that there is something inherently wrong with government budget deficits. Public-opinion polls consistently show that the public wants the budget balanced, and politicians of all parties constantly rail against deficits. Yet the federal budget has shown a deficit in 18 of the last 26 years.

Why is the federal budget so frequently in the red? What kinds of problems do large deficits pose for the economy, both now and in the future? Should we strive to balance the budget? And, if so, by what means? These are the questions to be addressed in this chapter.

We begin by explaining why the principles of stabilization policy that we learned in Part Three do not lead to the conclusion that the budget should always be balanced. (Neither, however, do they lead to the conclusion that it should always be in deficit!) Then we try to get the facts straight. We discuss the size of the national debt, and how it grew so large. Then we turn to the federal budget deficit and why some economists claim that it is badly mismeasured.

With the facts established, we examine the alleged ill effects of deficits. We shall see that many popular arguments against deficits are based on faulty reasoning. But not all are. In particular, we devote special attention to two potentially severe costs of deficit spending: It can be inflationary, and it can "crowd out" private investment spending or export sales.

Should the Budget Be Balanced?

The basic principles of fiscal policy that we discussed in Chapter 11 certainly do not lead to the conclusion that the government should always balance its budget. Instead, they point to the desirability of budget *deficits* when private demand ($C + I + X - IM$) is too weak and budget *surpluses* when private demand is too strong. The budget should be balanced, according to these principles, only when $C + I + G + X - IM$ approximately equals the full employment level of output. This may sometimes occur, but it will not necessarily be the norm.

In brief, according to this approach, the focus of fiscal policy should be on *balancing aggregate supply and aggregate demand*, not on balancing the budget. The reason why a balanced budget may not achieve a balanced economy is clear from our earlier discussion of stabilization policy.

Consider the fiscal policy that would be followed by a government that believed in balanced budgets. If private spending sagged for some reason, the multiplier would pull GNP down. Since personal and corporate tax receipts fall sharply when GNP declines, the budget would inevitably swing into the red. To a true budget-balancer, this would be a signal either to reduce spending or to raise taxes—exactly the opposite of the appropriate policy response.

Thus, budget balancing—as was practised during the early part of the Great Depression—will prolong and deepen recessions.

Budget balancing can also lead to inappropriate fiscal policy when an economic boom begins. If rising tax receipts induce a budget-balancing government to spend more or cut taxes, fiscal policy will accentuate the boom—with inflationary consequences. Fortunately, believers in budget balancing usually are not alarmed by surpluses.

This analysis explains why a balanced budget should not be expected to be the norm. But it does not explain why all of the last nine budgets have shown deficits. Why not, for example, five deficits and four surpluses? That is a good question, but a complicated one. So, before attempting an answer, we should get the facts straight.

Deficits and Debt: Some Terminology

First some critical terminology. The title of this chapter contains two terms that seem similar but mean different things: *budget deficits* and the *national debt*. We must learn to distinguish between the two.

The **budget deficit** is the amount by which the government's expenditures exceed its receipts during some specified period of time, usually one year. For example, during fiscal year 1983–84, the federal government raised about $58.6 billion in taxes but spent almost $90.1 billion, leaving a deficit of almost $31.5 billion.[1]

The **national debt**, also called the public debt, is the total value of the government's indebtedness at a moment in time. Thus, for example, the national debt at the end of fiscal year 1983–84 was $151 billion.

The two concepts—debt and deficit—are closely related because the government accumulates *debt* by running *deficits* or reduces its debt by running surpluses. The relationship between the debt and the deficit can be explained by a simple analogy. As you run water into a bathtub ("run a deficit"), the level of water in the tub ("the debt") rises. Alternatively, if you let water out of the tub ("run a surplus"), the level of the water ("the debt") falls. Analogously, budget deficits raise the national debt while budget surpluses lower it.

Having made this distinction, let us look first at the size and nature of the accumulated public debt, and then at the annual budget deficit.

Some Facts About the National Debt

How large a public debt do we have? How did we get it? Who owns it? Is it really growing rapidly?

To begin with the simplest question, the public debt is enormous. At the end of fiscal 1983–84 it amounted to more than $151 billion, over $6,000 for every man, woman, and child in Canada. When we compare the debt with the gross national product—the volume of goods and services our economy produces in a year—it does not seem so large after all. With a nominal GNP of $390 billion in

The **budget deficit** is the amount by which the government's expenditures exceed its receipts during a specified period of time, usually one year.

The **national debt** is the federal government's total indebtedness, which has resulted from previous deficits.

---

[1]*Reminder*: The fiscal year of the Canadian government ends on March 31. Thus, fiscal year 1983–84 ran from April 1, 1983, to March 31, 1984.

fiscal 1983–84 the debt was about 39 percent of the nation's yearly income. By contrast, many families who own homes owe *several years'* worth of income to the bank that granted them a mortgage. Many corporations also owe their bondholders much more than 39 percent of a year's sales.

But before these analogies make you feel too comfortable, we should point out that simple analogies between public and private debt are almost always misleading. A family with a large mortgage debt also owns a home with a value that presumably exceeds the mortgage. A solvent business firm has assets (factories, machinery, inventories, and so forth) that far exceed its outstanding bonds in value.

Is the same thing true of the Canadian government? Nobody knows for sure. How much are the parliament buildings worth? Or the national parks? Simply because these government assets are *not* sold on markets, no one can tell whether the federal government's assets exceed its debt or not.

Figure 17–1 charts the increase in the national debt from 1927 to 1984. You will notice that most of the debt was acquired during World War II, during the deep recession of 1958–62, or since 1973. The recent years have included a very severe recession. When economic activity falls, tax receipts of the federal government fall because of the heavy reliance on income taxes. As we shall see later, the *cause* of the debt is quite germane to the question of whether or not the debt is a burden. So it is important to remember that except for the years since 1973:

Much of the Canadian national debt stems from financing the war and from losses of tax revenues that accompany recessions.

But not all of the increase in the debt since 1973 can be blamed on the existence of recessions. A major cause is the indexation of the personal income-tax system in 1973 (by John Turner, then Minister of Finance). This scheme dramatically reduced

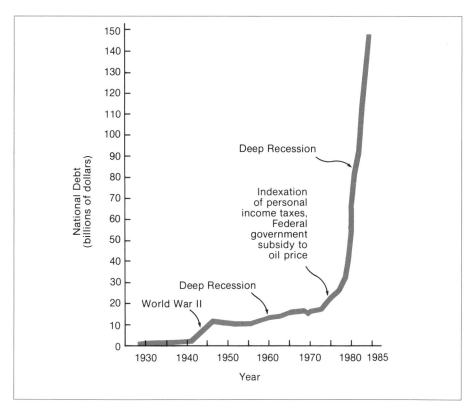

Figure 17-1
THE CANADIAN NATIONAL DEBT, 1927–1984
This graph charts the behaviour of the public debt in Canada. Until recently most of the increase can be accounted for by World War II and the severe recession during the Diefenbaker–James Coyne period (late 1950s and early 1960s). But since the early 1970s, the debt has grown very rapidly.
SOURCE: Department of Finance, *The Fiscal Plan* (1984), p. 62.

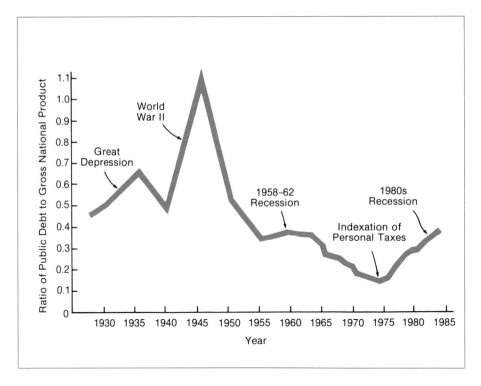

Figure 17-2

RATIO OF PUBLIC DEBT TO GROSS NATIONAL PRODUCT

This graph takes the data from Figure 17-1 and divides each year's debt by the gross national product of that year. We can see that the debt grew relative to GNP during the Great Depression, World War II, the recessions of 1958-62 and the 1980s, and in the period following the indexation of the personal income-tax system.
SOURCE: Department of Finance, *The Fiscal Plan* (1984), p. 62.

the government's revenue during inflationary times. The government did not reduce its expenditures by a similar amount. Indeed, it raised expenditures on such schemes as paying the very large difference between the domestic and world oil prices for consumers in eastern Canada.[2]

The growth of the debt looks enormous in Figure 17-1. But we must remember that everything grows in a growing economy. Private debt and business debt have grown rapidly since 1927 also, so it would be surprising indeed if the public debt had not grown too.

In addition, the debt is measured in dollars and, in an inflationary environment, the amount of purchasing power that each dollar represents is declining each year. A good way to put the numbers into some perspective is to express each year's national debt as a fraction of that year's nominal GNP. This is done in Figure 17-2. Here, in contrast to Figure 17-1, we see an unmistakable downward trend from the dizzying heights of World War II until 1975. In 1947, the national debt was the equivalent of 13 months' national income. By 1975, this figure had been whittled down to less than two months' income. If we use this as a crude indicator of the nation's ability to "pay off" its debt, then the burden of the debt was certainly far smaller in 1975 than it was in 1947.

However, in the last few years, the national debt has been growing very fast. In less than a decade since 1975, the debt has become greater than 4.5 months of GNP. According to the government's projections, it should rise to 6.3 months of GNP by 1988. This is one reason why many economists are alarmed by the continued large budget deficits of the 1980s.

Interpreting the Budget Deficit

We have seen that the national debt has grown unusually rapidly in the 1980s. The reason, of course, is that the federal government's annual budget deficits have been much larger than they had been previously.

[2]Indexing the tax system is explained on page 104, and the energy policy is explained in *Microeconomics*, Chapter 20, pages 384–86.

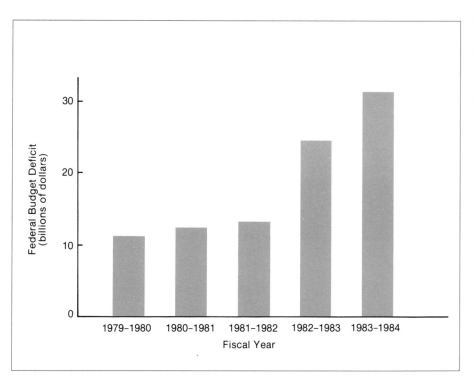

Figure 17-3
FEDERAL BUDGET
DEFICITS, 1979-1984.
The federal deficit almost tripled
during this period.
SOURCE: Department of Finance, *The Fiscal Plan* (1984), p. 6.

As Figure 17-3 shows, the budget deficit for fiscal 1979-80 was $11.5 billion. By fiscal 1983-84 it had grown to a record $31.5 billion. These are enormous numbers. But what do they mean? In interpreting them, we begin with what many economists view as a serious measurement problem—the way interest payments are treated in the government's budget.

Inflation Accounting for Interest Payments*

At first blush, government accountants seem to treat interest payments in the sensible way: Every dollar of interest that the government pays on the national debt is counted as a dollar of spending—just like purchases of supplies, old age security payments, and the salaries of civil servants. This seems the natural thing to do. But it ignores the fundamental distinction between real and nominal interest rates that we emphasized in Chapter 6. To review the analysis:

> The **real interest rate** tells us the amount of purchasing power the borrower turns over to the lender for the privilege of borrowing. To this we must add an **inflation premium**, equal to the expected rate of inflation, to get the **nominal interest rate**. The inflation premium compensates the lender for the expected erosion of the purchasing power of his money, and is best thought of as repayment of principal.[3]

The last sentence has important implications for the government budget—implications that very few people understand.

From an economic point of view, the portion of the government's interest payments that merely compensates lenders for inflation should be counted as *repayment of principal*, not as *interest expense*, because it simply returns to lenders the purchasing power of their original loans. Only the *real* interest that the government pays should be treated as an expenditure item in the budget. Breaking up interest payments in this way is called **inflation accounting**. Since even

Inflation accounting means adjusting standard accounting procedures for the fact that inflation lowers the purchasing power of money.

---

*This section contains difficult material which may be skipped in shorter courses.
[3]If you need further review, see pages 99-101.

Table 17–1

ACCOUNTING FOR A $1000 LOAN AT A 2 PERCENT REAL INTEREST RATE

	(1)	(2)	(3)
		AT 10 PERCENT INFLATION	
ITEM	AT ZERO INFLATION	CONVENTIONAL ACCOUNTING	INFLATION ACCOUNTING
Interest (included in budget)	$ 20	$ 122	$ 22
plus			
Principal (excluded from budget)	1000	1000	1100
equals			
Total payment	$1020	$1122	$1122

quite sophisticated people have trouble understanding inflation accounting, it is worth taking the time to illustrate the idea with an analogy and a simple example.

Imagine that you lend a roommate, who is enrolled in a chemistry course, a bar of radium that you happen to own. Your roommate uses the radioactive bar in experiments for a year and then returns it to you. Has your loan been repaid in full? Certainly not. Because of the natural process of radioactive decay, the bar you get back is smaller than the bar you originally loaned. To pay you back in full, your roommate must give you enough additional radium to replace the portion that eroded during the year.

The analogy to interest rates on loans is straightforward: Inflation erodes the purchasing power of money just as radioactive decay erodes radium. So, in figuring out how many dollars constitutes repayment of principal, we must take inflation into account. Let's illustrate this by a concrete example, comparing a loan made at zero inflation (no decay) with a loan made at 10 percent inflation (rapid decay).

First, suppose the government borrows $1000 for a year when the inflation rate is zero, paying 2 percent interest. At the end of the year it must pay back $1000 in principal and $20 in interest, for a total of $1020. Of this, only $20—the interest payment—is an expenditure item in the budget. The repayment of principal does not appear in the budget since it is not spending. The loan transaction is summarized quite simply in column 1 of Table 17–1.

Now, let us see how inflation (radioactive decay of money) complicates the accountant's job. Suppose the same transaction takes place when the rate of inflation is 10 percent. If the real rate of interest is still 2 percent, the nominal rate of interest must be about 12 percent.

Specifically, to compensate the lender for 10 percent inflation, and nothing more, the government must return $1.10 for each dollar originally borrowed. A real interest rate of 2 percent means that the government must return 2 percent more than this, or $1.02 \times \$1.10 = \$1.122$ per dollar borrowed. Thus, each dollar of lending earns 12.2 cents in interest, making the nominal interest rate 12.2 percent.

If the nominal interest rate is 12.2 percent, a government that borrows $1000 at the start of the year will have to repay $1,122 at year's end. Conventional accounting procedures will treat $1000 of this as repayment of principal (and hence not as an expenditure) and $122 as interest (which is an expenditure). This conventional accounting treatment is indicated in column 2 of Table 17–1.

But these numbers are misleading since $1000 at the end of the year is not adequate repayment of principal because inflation has eroded the real value of money. The correct inflation accounting treatment recognizes that it takes $1100 at the end of the year to buy what $1000 bought at the beginning of the year. So

Table 17-2

INFLATION ACCOUNTING AND THE DEFICIT

YEAR	ACTUAL DEFICIT* (billions of dollars)	INFLATION ADJUSTMENT (billions of dollars)	INFLATION-ADJUSTED DEFICIT (-) OR SURPLUS (+) (billions of dollars)
1980	-9.9	+4.7	-5.2
1981	-7.0	+6.2	-0.8
1982	-20.5	+5.6	-14.9
1983	-24.3	+4.2	-20.1
1984	-26.6	+6.7	-19.9

*Measured on a national-accounts basis. The deficit data reported in Figure 17-3 are on a public-accounts basis, as reported to Parliament on a fiscal-year basis. The deficits reported in this table are defined on a national-accounts basis since the government has calculated its inflation adjustments with deficits measured on a national-accounts basis. The main differences in the two methods are that the national-accounts procedure involves the calendar year, and its revenue items are recorded on the basis of when revenues were earned (not when they were actually paid).

SOURCE: Department of Finance, *The Fiscal Plan* (1984), page 58.

$1100 is treated as repayment of principal, leaving only $22 ($1122 – $1100) to be treated as interest. The correct inflation accounting treatment of the loan is shown in column 3 of Table 17-1.

To recapitulate, the proper economic treatment of a loan in an inflationary environment must recognize that more dollars (in our example, $1100) must be returned to the lender in order to give back the purchasing power of the original loan ($1000). Only the excess of the nominal interest payment ($122) over the compensation for inflation ($100) should be counted as interest.

This example holds the following lesson for interpreting budget-deficit figures:

Inflation distorts the government budget under conventional accounting procedures by exaggerating interest expenses.

The example also suggests how this error can be corrected:

To correct the deficit for inflation, we must subtract the inflation premium from the interest paid on the national debt, thereby counting only *real* interest payments.

This treatment, by the way, corresponds exactly to the way inflation accounting is done by major corporations.

As Table 17-2 shows, making the inflation adjustment to interest payments would have reduced reported deficits by an average of about $5 billion in recent years. Starting in 1982, the federal government began running large deficits even after correction for inflation accounting.

The High-Employment Budget

The second major issue in making sense of the budget deficit is not a problem of measurement, but rather one of interpretation.

As we learned in Chapter 11, the government's taxing and spending decisions affect the level of economic activity. For example, higher spending or lower taxes lead—via the multiplier process—to higher aggregate demand and therefore to a higher GNP. This makes it natural to think that big deficits signify expansionary fiscal policy.

But that view may be incorrect because the state of the economy also affects the budget. In particular, recessions tend to enlarge the budget deficit. The reason is simple. Remember that the deficit is the difference between government expenditures and tax receipts, that is:

$$\text{Deficit} = G + \text{Transfers} - \text{Taxes}.$$

The government's most important sources of tax revenue—income taxes, corporate profit taxes, sales taxes, and payroll taxes—all shrink when GNP falls because firms and people pay less tax when they earn less. Similarly, some government spending, notably transfer payments like unemployment benefits, rise when GNP falls because more people are out of work. Since spending goes up and tax receipts go down as GNP falls:

The deficit rises in a recession (and falls in a boom), even when there is no change in fiscal policy.

The **high-employment budget** is the hypothetical budget we *would have* if the economy were operating near full employment.

Because the deficit changes even when policy does not, the deficit is a poor measure of the government's fiscal policy. For this reason, many economists feel that we should pay less attention to the actual deficit or surplus and more attention to the deficit or surplus in what is called the **high-employment budget**. This is a hypothetical construct that replaces both the spending and taxes in the *actual* budget by estimates of how much the government *would be* spending and receiving, given current tax rates and expenditure rules, if the economy were operating near full employment.

Since it is based on the spending and taxing the government would be doing at full employment, rather than on actual expenditures and receipts, the high-employment budget is not sensitive to the state of the economy. It will change only when policy changes. For this reason, most economists believe it is a better measure of the thrust of fiscal policy than the actual deficit. Using this new concept, we can provide a useful restatement of our previous conclusion about the effect of a recession on the budget deficit:

When unemployment rises, the actual budget deficit grows larger even if the high-employment budget is unchanged.

This simple observation helps us understand the genesis of the large budget deficits of the early 1980s: They were partly attributable to the consistently high unemployment rates that marked this period. Table 17-3 shows just how important

Table 17-3

UNEMPLOYMENT AND THE FEDERAL DEFICIT

YEAR	DEFICIT* (billions of dollars)	ADJUSTMENT TO HIGH EMPLOYMENT† (billions of dollars)	HIGH-EMPLOYMENT DEFICIT (billions of dollars
1980	-9.9	+2.4	-7.5
1981	-7.0	+1.9	-5.1
1982	-20.5	+9.2	-11.3
1983	-24.3	+11.6	-12.7
1984	-26.6	+10.2	-16.4

*Measured on a national-accounts basis.
†Based on a 7 percent unemployment rate.

SOURCE: Department of Finance, *The Fiscal Plan* (1984), pages 54, 56, 58, 63.

the distinction between the actual deficit and the high-employment deficit has been in recent years. For 1982 through 1984, the deficits in the high-employment budget were rather small even though the deficits in the actual budget were quite large. Nevertheless, even the high-employment budget has been deeply in the red.

Other Measurement Issues

There are many other complicated issues in measuring and interpreting the federal budget deficit. We conclude this section by mentioning just three of them.

1. *Junior-level government budget surpluses.* Some analysts argue that it is the combined deficit of all levels of government that matters, not just the federal deficit. In this regard, it is useful to realize that the junior-level governments together have been running surpluses in recent years—averaging $3 billion per year throughout the 1980–84 period. Part of the reason for these surpluses—and for the federal deficit—is that the federal government gives a good deal of money to the provincial governments in the form of grants each year.

2. *Capital expenditures.* A further point is that some federal spending goes to purchase capital of various sorts—government buildings, military equipment, and so on. There is nothing unusual about borrowing to purchase assets. Private businesses and individuals do it all the time. For this reason, many people have suggested that the federal government compile a separate capital budget—which is precisely what municipal governments do.

3. *Off-budget activities.* Another source of ambiguity stems from the lending activities of the so-called "off-budget" agencies. (A familiar example is loans for low-income housing.) In recent years, these agencies have run deficits that are not included in the official budget deficit.

Conclusion: What's New About the Recent Deficits?

Table 17–4 puts our two major adjustments—for inflation accounting and for unemployment—together and compares recent deficits (column 1) with corresponding figures on the high-employment, inflation-corrected deficit (column 4). The difference between the two columns is startling. Only since 1982 has the high-employment, inflation-corrected budget been in substantial deficit. But this does represent a major swing in the federal budget position. Much of the actual deficit is understandable, given the high levels of inflation and recession prevailing in the early 1980s. But these considerations account for only about 66 percent of the 1984 federal deficit. It is because the *corrected* deficit has never been near these levels in peace time that there has been such concern.

Table 17-4
ACTUAL AND ADJUSTED BUDGET DEFICITS

YEAR	(1) ACTUAL DEFICIT* (billions of dollars)	(2) ADJUSTMENT FOR INFLATION (billions of dollars)	(3) ADJUSTMENT TO HIGH EMPLOYMENT (billions of dollars)	(4) ADJUSTED DEFICIT (-) OR SURPLUS (+) (billions of dollars)
1980	-9.9	+4.7	+2.4	-2.8
1981	-7.0	+6.2	+1.9	+1.1
1982	-20.5	+5.6	+9.2	-5.7
1983	-24.3	+4.2	+11.6	-8.5
1984	-26.6	+6.7	+10.2	-9.7

*Measured on a national-accounts basis.

SOURCE: Tables 17-2 and 17-3.

Bogus Arguments About the Burden of the Debt

Having gained some perspective on the facts, let us now turn to some of the arguments advanced by those who claim that by running budget deficits we are placing an intolerable burden on future generations.

Argument 1: Our children and grandchildren will be burdened by heavy interest payments. To meet these payments there will have to be higher taxes.

Answer: It is certainly true that a higher debt will necessitate higher interest payments and, other things being equal, this will lead to higher taxes paid by our children and grandchildren. But think who will receive the higher interest payments as income: our children and grandchildren! Thus one group of future Canadians will, essentially, be making interest payments to another group of future Canadians. While some people will gain and others will lose, the future generation as a whole will come out even. We conclude that:

As long as the national debt is owned by domestic citizens, the future interest payments merely shuffle money from one group of Canadians to another. These transfers may or may not be desirable, but they hardly constitute a burden to the nation as a whole.

However, this argument *is* valid for that portion of our debt that is held by foreigners. To pay the interest on this portion of the debt *will* be a burden on future generations of Canadians.

Argument 2: It will ruin the nation when we have to repay the enormous debt.

Answer: A first answer to this merely rephrases the answer to the previous argument: Only the part owned by foreigners involves any burden; the rest is paid by one group of Canadians to another. But there is a much more fundamental point. *Unlike a private family, the nation need never pay off its debt.* Instead, each time the principal is due, the government can simply "roll it over" by floating more debt. Indeed, this is precisely what the government does.

Is this a bit of chicanery? How can the government get away with making loans that it never intends to pay back? The answer is found by recognizing the fallacy of comparing the government to a family or individual. People cannot be extended credit in perpetuity because they will not live that long. Sensible lenders will not extend long-term credit to very old people because their heirs cannot be forced to pay up. But the Canadian government will never "die"; at least, we hope not! So this factor does not arise. In this respect, the government is in much the same position as a large corporation. General Motors never worries about paying off its debt. It too rolls it over by floating new debt all the time.

Argument 3: It will bankrupt the nation. Like any family or any business firm, a nation has a limited capacity to borrow. If it exceeds this limit, it is in danger of being unable to pay its creditors. It may go bankrupt with calamitous consequences for everyone.

Answer: This is another example of a false analogy. What is claimed about private debtors is certainly true. But the Canadian government need never fear defaulting on its debt. Why? First, because it has enormous power to raise revenues by taxation. If you had such power, you would never have to fear bankruptcy either.

Furthermore, a good part of the Canadian national debt is an obligation to pay *Canadian* dollars: Each debt certificate obligates the government to pay the holder so many Canadian dollars on a prescribed date. But the Canadian government is the source of these dollars; it prints them! *No nation need ever fear defaulting on debts that call for repayment in its own currency.* At the very worst, it can always print whatever money it needs to pay off its creditors.

It does not follow, however, that acquiring debt through budget deficits is therefore always a good idea. Sometimes it is clearly a very bad idea. Printing money to pay the debt will expand aggregate demand and cause inflation, and this often will be undesirable. The point is not that budget deficits are either good or bad—we already know that they can be either under the appropriate circumstances. Rather, the point is that worrying about a possible default on the national debt is quite unnecessary, unless a very significant portion of that debt, or the debts of the nation's households and firms, are obligations to pay *foreign* currencies. A large foreign debt cannot be paid by simply printing more domestic currency. This is a problem for a number of less-developed countries, but Canada's foreign debt is not at such levels.

Having cleared the air of these fallacious arguments, we are now in a position to explore some real problems that may arise when the government spends more than it takes in through taxation.

Budget Deficits and Inflation

One indictment of deficit spending that certainly *does* have validity under most circumstances is the charge that it is inflationary. Why? Because when government policy pushes up aggregate demand, firms may find themselves unwilling or unable to produce the higher quantities that are being demanded at the going prices. Prices will therefore have to rise.

Figure 17-4 is an aggregate-supply-and-demand diagram that shows this analysis graphically. Initially, equilibrium is at point E_0—where demand curve D_0D_0 and supply curve SS intersect. Output is $400 billion, and the price index is at 100. The diagram indicates that the economy is operating below full employment; there is a recessionary gap. If the government does nothing to reduce the resulting unemployment, we know from Chapter 10 that this recessionary gap will linger for a long time. The economy will suffer through a prolonged period of unemployment.

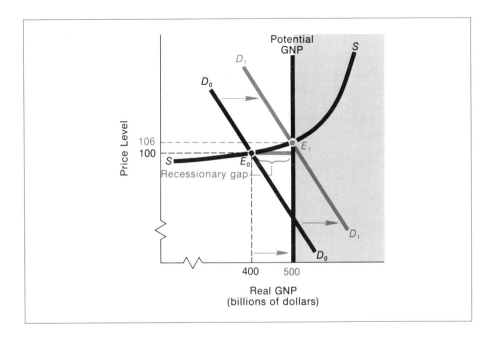

Figure 17-4

THE INFLATIONARY EFFECTS OF DEFICIT SPENDING

In this diagram, expansionary fiscal policy pushes the aggregate-demand curve out from D_0D_0 to D_1D_1, causing equilibrium to move from E_0 (where there is unemployment) to E_1 (where there is full employment). But because aggregate-supply curve SS slopes upward, the price level is pushed up from 100 to 106; that is, there is a 6 percent inflation.

Figure 17-5

FISCAL EXPANSION AND
INTEREST RATES

If expansionary fiscal policy
pushes real GNP and the price
level higher, the demand curve for
money will shift outward from
M_0D_0 to M_1D_1. Equilibrium in the
money market shifts from point A
to point B, so interest rates rise.

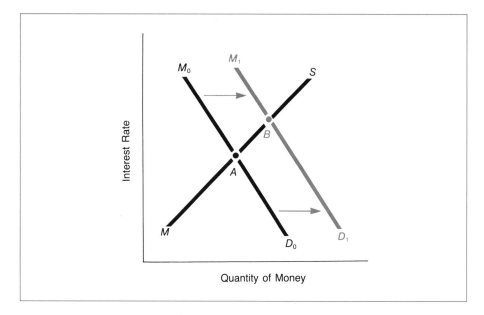

Rather than permit such a long recession, we know that the government can raise its spending or cut its taxes enough to shift the aggregate-demand schedule upward from D_0D_0 to D_1D_1. Such a policy can wipe out the recessionary gap and the associated unemployment—but not without an inflationary cost. The diagram shows that the new equilibrium price level is at 106—6 percent higher than before the government acted.

Thus the cries that budget deficits are "inflationary" have the ring of truth. How much truth, of course, depends on the slope of the aggregate-supply curve. Deficit spending will not cause much inflation if the economy has lots of slack and the aggregate-supply curve consequently is flat. But deficit spending will be highly inflationary in a fully employed economy with a steep aggregate-supply curve.

The Monetization Issue

Some people worry about the inflationary consequences of deficits for a rather different reason. They fear that the Bank of Canada may have to "monetize" part of the deficit, by which they mean that the Bank may feel compelled to purchase some of the newly issued government debt. Let us explain, first, why the Bank might make such purchases, and second, why these purchases are called **monetizing the deficit**.

The central bank is said to
monetize the deficit
when it purchases the bonds
that the government issues.

Deficit spending, we have just noted, normally drives up both real GNP and the price level. As we have emphasized before, such an economic expansion shifts the demand curve for money outward to the right—as depicted in Figure 17-5. The figure shows that, if the Bank of Canada takes no actions to shift the money supply curve, interest rates will rise.

Suppose now that the Bank does not want interest rates to rise. What can it do? To prevent the incipient rise in r, it must engage in expansionary monetary policies that shift the supply curve for money outward to the right—as indicated in Figure 17-6. And, as noted in Chapter 13, expansionary monetary policies normally take the form of open-market purchases of government bonds. For this reason, deficit spending sometimes induces the Bank of Canada to increase its purchases of government bonds, that is, to buy up some of the newly issued debt.

Even if the Bank of Canada makes no explicit response to the pressure for higher interest rates, the reaction of foreign bond-holders forces the same result.

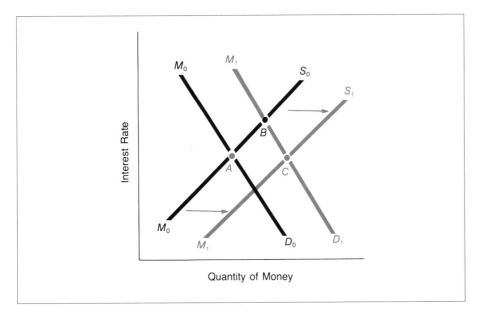

Figure 17-6
MONETIZATION AND
INTEREST RATES
If the Bank of Canada does not
want a fiscal expansion to raise
interest rates, it must increase the
money supply. In this diagram, the
fiscal expansion shifts the demand
curve for money from M_0D_0 to
M_1D_1, precisely as it did in Figure
17-5. To keep the rate of interest
constant, the Bank of Canada will
have to shift the money-supply
curve outward from M_0S_0 to M_1S_1.
Points A and C correspond to the
same rate of interest.

As foreigners move to acquire the relatively high-yield Canadian bonds, they must enter the foreign-exchange market to get the required amount of Canadian dollars to buy the bonds. This puts upward pressure on the value of the Canadian dollar. The Bank of Canada frequently resists any significant appreciation of the Canadian dollar, to avoid a potential squeeze on the profits of Canadian exporters. This requires intervention in the foreign-exchange market, to make available the additional Canadian dollars demanded by the foreign investors. Thus, the pursuit of maximum interest yields by foreign bond-holders keeps Canadian interest rates from rising significantly, and a fixed exchange-rate policy by the Bank of Canada means that the domestic money supply must increase following newly issued government debt.

Why is this process called *monetizing* the deficit? The reason is simple. As we learned in Chapter 13, open-market purchases of bonds by the central bank give the chartered banks more reserves, which leads, eventually, to an increase in the money supply. This is also shown in Figure 17–6: The outward shift of the money-supply schedule from M_0S_0 to M_1S_1 leads to an increase in the money supply. By this indirect route, then, larger budget deficits may lead to an expansion of the money supply. To summarize:

If the Bank of Canada takes no countervailing actions, an expansionary fiscal policy that raises the budget deficit will raise real GNP and prices, thereby shifting the demand curve for money outward and putting upward pressure on interest rates. If the Bank does not want either interest rates or the exchange rate to rise, it can engage in expansionary open-market operations, that is, purchase more government debt. If the Bank of Canada does this, the money supply will increase. In this case, we say that part of the deficit is *monetized.*

Monetized deficits are more inflationary than non-monetized deficits for the simple reason that expansionary monetary and fiscal policies together are more inflationary than expansionary fiscal policy alone. Figure 17–7 illustrates this conclusion. The aggregate-supply curve and aggregate-demand curves D_0D_0 and D_1D_1 are carried over without change from Figure 17–4. The shift from D_0D_0 to D_1D_1 represents the effect of expansionary fiscal policy (raising the budget deficit). If, in addition, the central bank monetizes part of the deficit, the aggregate-demand

Figure 17-7

MONETIZED DEFICIT
SPENDING

Expansionary fiscal policies that
raise the budget deficit push the
aggregate-demand curve outward
from D_0D_0 to D_1D_1. If the Bank of
Canada monetizes some of the
deficit, then expansionary
monetary policy pushes the
aggregate-demand curve out even
further—to D_2D_2. Monetized
deficits (point C) are therefore
more inflationary than deficits that
are not monetized (point B).

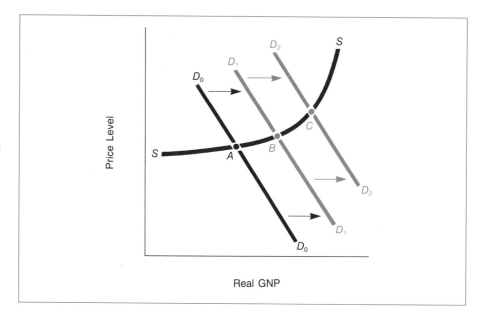

curve will shift out still further—perhaps to the position indicated by D_2D_2. Thus,
the price level will rise even more (compare points B and C).

Many economists and business leaders have been concerned about monetization in the 1980s. The reason is simple arithmetic. When budget deficits are
extremely large, even a small percentage of monetization can lead to a substantial
increase in bank reserves and the money supply.

Deficits, Interest Rates, and Crowding Out

So far we have been looking for possible burdens of the national debt on the
demand side of the economy. But a serious burden also comes on the *supply* side
because large budget deficits discourage investment and therefore retard the
growth of our nation's capital stock. The mechanism is easy to understand.

We have just seen that budget deficits create pressure for higher interest rates
unless the Bank of Canada engages in substantial monetization. But the rate of
interest (r) is a major determinant of investment spending (I). In particular, higher r
leads to lower I. And if we do less spending on I today, we will have a smaller
capital stock tomorrow. This, according to most economists, is the true sense in
which a large national debt may put a burden on future generations:

Because of the large national debt, we may bequeath less physical capital to future
generations. If they inherit less plant and equipment, these generations will be
burdened by a lower productive capacity—a lower potential GNP.

Crowding out occurs
when deficit spending by the
government forces private
investment spending or
exports to contract.

There is another way of looking at this problem—a way that explains why it
is often called the **crowding-out effect**. Consider what happens in financial
markets when the government engages in deficit spending. When it spends more
than it takes in through tax revenues, the government must borrow the balance
from private citizens. It does this by issuing bonds, and these bonds compete with
corporate bonds and other financial instruments for the available supply of funds.
When some private savers are persuaded to buy government bonds, there must be
a decline in the funds remaining to invest in private bonds. Thus some private
borrowers will get "crowded out" of the financial markets as the government
claims an increasing share of the economy's total pool of saving.

Some critics of deficits who have taken this lesson to its illogical extreme argue that each $1 of deficit spending by government crowds out exactly $1 of private spending, so that expansionary fiscal policy has no net effect on total demand. In their view, when G rises, I falls by the same amount, so that $C + I + G + X - IM$ is unchanged.

Other analysts feel that as long as a severe recession exists, firms will not be borrowing to expand anyway. According to this view, crowding out becomes a real issue only if the deficit remains large after the economy improves.

Some analysts challenge the relevance of the crowding-out problem even when the economy is recovering. They argue that the notion of "room in the bond market" for both government and private borrowing makes limited sense for Canada. We always have the option of foreign borrowing, so the relevant bond market is very big relative to all Canadian participants. With the option of foreign borrowing, there should be little increase in interest rates following deficit finance, so there should be little crowding out of investment.

We must remember, however, that foreign borrowing involves foreign exchange entering the country. This foreign exchange must be converted to domestic currency to finance the increased domestic expenditures. If the exchange rate is flexible, it is the international value of the Canadian dollar that gets bid up, not the domestic rate of interest. But an appreciating Canadian dollar makes our exports more expensive to foreigners, so there is still a crowding out effect—exports are crowded out by the increase in government spending. Investment spending by these exporting firms also diminishes, without an increase in interest rates.

Exchange-rate crowding out can be avoided if the Bank of Canada fixes the exchange rate. Thus, we can summarize as follows:

Both interest-rate and exchange-rate reasons for crowding out can be avoided, but only by monetizing the deficit and/or by allowing the foreign-owned portion of the national debt to rise. Either option yields a burden: either inflation or large interest payment obligations to foreigners in the future.

The True Burden of the National Debt

With this analysis of crowding out, we are in a position to understand why budget deficits might, or might not, impose a burden on future generations: When government budget deficits take place in a high-employment economy, the crowding-out effect becomes important, so the deficits will exact a burden by leaving a smaller capital stock to future generations. However, deficits in a slack economy may well lead to more investment rather than less since economic activity is stimulated. In this case, the debt may be a blessing rather than a burden.

Which case applies to the Canadian national debt? To answer this, let us go back to the historical facts and recall how we have accumulated such a large debt. The first cause was the financing of World War II. This debt was contracted in a fully employed economy, and thus undoubtedly constituted a burden in the formal sense. It left future generations with less capital because some of our nation's resources were diverted from private investment into government production. The bombs, ships, and planes that it financed were used up in the war, not bequeathed as capital to future generations.

Yet what were the alternatives? We could have tried to finance the entire war by taxation, and thus placed the burden on consumption rather than on investment. But that would truly have been ruinous, and probably even impossible, given the colossal wartime expenditures. Or we could have printed money, but that would have unleashed an inflation that nobody wanted. Or we could have just done much less government spending and would therefore have contributed less toward winning the war. So, in retrospect, the generations alive today and in the future may not feel unduly burdened by the decisions of the people in power in the 1940s.

The second major contributor to the national debt has been a series of recessions. But these are precisely the circumstances under which increasing the debt might prove to be a blessing rather than a burden. So, if we look for the classic type of deficits to which the valid burden-of-the-debt argument applies—deficits acquired in a fully employed peacetime economy—we do not find many in the Canadian record *until after 1973*.

It is in this context that current budget deficits are a sharp departure from the past. Our examination of the inflation and high-employment adjustments showed that large deficits would exist today even if the Canadian economy had "full" employment and no inflation. This is not something that has happened before, at least on an on-going basis, and it poses a real threat of severe crowding out and a serious potential burden on future generations.

The Burden of the National Debt

Let us now summarize our evaluation of the burden of the national debt and thereby clarify one of the **12 Ideas for Beyond the Final Exam** introduced in Chapter 1. First, the arguments that a large national debt may lead the nation into bankruptcy, or unduly burden future generations who have to make onerous payments of interest and principal, are mostly bogus. They are important arguments only if the country is significantly in debt to foreigners. Second, the national debt *will* be a burden if it is contracted in a fully employed peacetime economy, because in that case it will reduce the nation's capital stock. Third, there are circumstances in which budget deficits are quite appropriate for stabilization reasons. Fourth, and finally, before 1973 the actual public debt of the Canadian federal government was mostly contracted as a result of the war and recessions—precisely the circumstances under which the valid burden-of-the-debt argument does not apply. However, the large deficits since 1973 are worrisome from this point of view.

Conclusion: What Should Be Done About the Deficit?

It is a matter of simple arithmetic that you close a budget deficit by raising taxes and/or reducing spending. Either of these routes is a contractionary fiscal policy, and will retard the growth of the real GNP. Given this fact of life, should we try to close the deficit? The correct answer would be "No," if the inflation-adjusted, high-employment deficit were zero. But even after these adjustments, the federal government deficit exists and is large, so some closing of the deficit is called for. Thus, one of the very real costs of the deficit is that it constrains the government's ability to undertake any job-creation policies.

Is there any way around the problem that moves to close the deficit are contractionary? The government has tried to lessen this problem by waiting until significant economic recovery before attempting to close the deficit. Another answer to this problem is that fiscal and monetary policies could be better co-ordinated. If fiscal policy must turn contractionary to reduce the deficit, monetary policy can turn expansionary to counteract the effects on aggregate demand. In this way, we can hope to shrink the deficit without shrinking the economy in the process. Such a change in the policy "mix" would put downward pressure on interest rates, since both tighter budgets and easier money tend to push interest rates down.

The problem with this policy mix is that it would lead to a depreciation in the foreign value of the Canadian dollar. Pressure for lower interest rates in Canada leads to foreign investors' selling off Canadian bonds in favour of higher yields elsewhere. A depreciated Canadian dollar *stimulates* aggregate *demand* (through higher net export sales), but it *contracts* aggregate *supply* (by raising business costs). Despite this unfavourable supply-side effect, quite a few economists, including those at the Economic Council of Canada, have advocated a shift in the policy mix toward tighter budgets and easier monetary policy. However, the history of the 1980s so far has given us precisely the opposite combination: loose fiscal policy and tight money. If this continues, deficits will persist and will become increasingly burdensome.

Summary

1. Rigid adherence to budget balancing would make the economy less stable by reducing aggregate demand (via tax increases and reductions in *G*) when private spending is low, and raising aggregate demand when private spending is high.

2. The national debt has grown dramatically since the early 1970s. Before then it grew only because of recessions and World War II.

3. Inflation makes the deficit look bigger than it really is because all nominal interest payments are counted as expenditures. Under inflation accounting, only real interest payments would count as expenditures, and the corrected deficit is seen to be much smaller than it appears.

4. Part of the reason for large budget deficits in recent years is the fact that the economy has operated well below full employment. The high-employment deficit, which uses estimates of what the government's receipts and outlays would be at full employment, has been much smaller than the official deficit.

5. If we correct the official deficit for inflation and adjust it to high levels of employment, we find that large deficits in the high-employment, inflation-corrected budget began only in 1982.

6. Arguments that the public debt will burden future generations, who will have to make huge payments of interest and principal, are based on false analogies. In fact, most of these payments are simply transfers from some Canadians to other Canadians. However, some of the debt is foreign-owned, and the associated interest obligations *do* represent a burden in the future.

7. Under normal circumstances, budget deficits are somewhat inflationary. They are even more inflationary if they are "monetized," that is, if the Bank of Canada buys some of the newly issued government debt in the open market to keep interest rates from rising or to fix the exchange rate.

8. Unless the deficit is substantially monetized, deficit spending forces interest rates higher and discourages private investment spending. This is called the crowding-out effect. If there is a great deal of crowding out, then deficits really do impose a burden on future generations by leaving them a smaller capital stock to work with.

9. Even if foreigners purchase most of the newly issued Canadian debt, so that interest rates do not rise, the increased foreign demand for Canadian dollars results in an appreciation of the Canadian dollar so that export demand is crowded out.

10. Crowding out may not be very important when unemployment is high. Indeed, higher output levels may induce firms to raise investment spending. But when the economy is near full employment, the proponents of the crowding-out hypothesis are probably right: High government spending just displaces private investment and exports.

11. Whether or not deficits are a burden depends on how and why the government ran these deficits in the first place. If deficits are contracted to fight recessions, it is possible that more investment is actually stimulated. Deficits contracted to carry on wars certainly impair the future capital stock, though they may not be considered a burden for non-economic reasons. Since these two cases account for most of Canada's national debt that was incurred before 1973, this debt cannot reasonably be considered a serious burden. However, a noticeable part of the debt incurred since 1973 does represent an overly expansionary fiscal policy.

12. Since the size of the deficit depends on the state of the economy, and since the state of the economy is affected by the deficit, simple correlations between the deficit and other economic variables cannot be used to deduce causation.

Concepts for Review

Budget deficit
National debt
Real versus nominal interest rates

Inflation accounting
High-employment budget
Monetization of deficits

Interest-rate crowding out
Exchange-rate crowding out
Burden of the national debt

Questions for Discussion

1. Explain the difference between the budget deficit and the national debt. If we reduce the deficit, will the debt stop growing?

2. Explain how the Canadian government has managed to accumulate a debt of more than $150 billion. To whom does it owe this debt? Can this debt be considered a burden on future generations?

3. Comment on the following: "Deficit spending paves the road to ruination. If we keep it up, the whole nation will go bankrupt. Even if things do not go this far, what right have we to burden our children and grandchildren with these debts while we live high on the hog?"

4. Calculate the budget deficit and the inflation-corrected deficit for an economy with the following data:
   Government expenditures other than interest = $80
   Tax receipts = $85
   Interest payments = $60
   Interest rate = 12 percent
   Inflation rate = 10 percent
   National debt at start of year = $500.
   (*Note*: 12 percent interest on a $500 debt is $60.)

5. Explain why the high-employment budget might show a surplus while the actual budget is in deficit.

6. If the Bank of Canada begins to increase the money supply more rapidly than before, what will happen to the government budget deficit? (*Hint*: What will happen to tax receipts and interest expenses?) If the government wants to offset the effects of the Bank's actions on aggregate demand, what might it do? How will this affect the deficit?

7. Given the current state of the economy, do you think the Bank of Canada should monetize a sizeable proportion of the deficit? (*Note*: There is no one correct answer to this question. It is a good question to discuss in class.)

8. Explain both interest-rate and exchange-rate mechanisms for crowding out. Given the current state of the economy, do you think crowding out is an issue?

9. Evaluate each of the following statements. (*Note*: The facts in each case are correct; concentrate on the conclusion that is reached.)
   a. "In 1978, we had a small deficit and strong GNP growth. In 1982, we had a huge deficit and a recession. Therefore, deficit spending does not stimulate the economy."
   b. "If we compare 1981 with 1983, we find a much larger deficit but much lower inflation in 1983. Therefore, it is clear that deficit spending is not inflationary."

The Trade-Off Between Inflation and Unemployment

All progress is precarious, and
the solution of one problem
brings us face to face with
another problem.

MARTIN LUTHER KING

etween 1980 and 1983 the rate of inflation, as measured by the deflator for GNP, declined from just over 11 percent to just under 6 percent, reversing a worrisome trend toward higher inflation rates. At the same time, the economy suffered a severe recession and the unemployment rate climbed ominously, from 7.5 percent in 1980 to 11.9 percent in 1983.

Most economists believe that this conjunction of events was no coincidence. Rather, they insist, the period of high unemployment was the price we paid to reduce the rate of inflation. Although some optimists claim that it is possible to reduce inflation without suffering from unemployment, the Canadian economy clearly paid a heavy price for the disinflation of the early 1980s. Was this price inevitable, or could we have avoided it? That is the question for this chapter.

You may recall from Chapter 1 that the existence of an agonizing trade-off between inflation and unemployment is one of the **12 Ideas for Beyond the Final Exam**. The importance of this trade-off can hardly be overestimated. It is probably the one area of macroeconomics where confusion is most widespread. And because this confusion can have disastrous consequences for the conduct of stabilization policy, the trade-off merits the comprehensive examination that we give it in this chapter. Without a thorough understanding of the dimensions of this trade-off, it is impossible for a citizen to make an informed judgment about macroeconomic policy.

Demand-Side Inflation Versus Supply-Side Inflation: A Review

Let us begin our investigation of the trade-off by reviewing some of what we have learned about inflation in earlier chapters.

One major cause of inflation, though not the only one, is *excessive growth of aggregate demand*. What happens if, for some reason, consumers, investors, the government, or foreigners decide to increase spending? We know, first of all, that such an autonomous increase in spending will have a multiplier effect on aggregate

Figure 18–1

INFLATION FROM THE
DEMAND SIDE

An increase in aggregate demand,
whether it comes from consumers,
investors, the government, or
foreigners, shifts the aggregate-
demand curve outward from D_0D_0
to D_1D_1. The economy's
equilibrium moves from point A to
point B. Since point B corresponds
to a higher price level than does
point A, there is *inflation* (that is, a
rising price level) as the economy
moves from A to B.

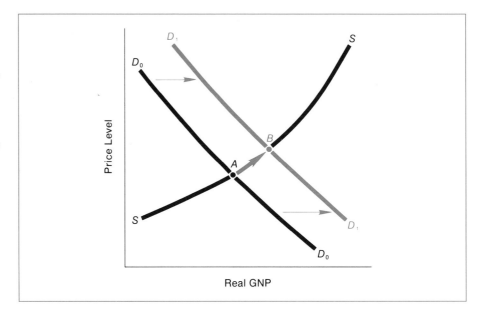

demand; that is, each additional \$1 of $C, I, G,$ or $X - IM$ will lead to perhaps \$2 of additional demand, assuming we are on a fixed exchange rate. Second, we know that such a stimulus to aggregate demand will normally pull up *both* real output *and* prices. The reason, to review our earlier findings, is that firms normally will find it profitable to supply the additional output only at higher prices.

Figure 18–1, which is familiar from earlier chapters, displays this conclusion. Initially, the economy is at point A, where aggregate-demand curve D_0D_0 intersects aggregate-supply curve SS. Then something happens to increase demand, and the aggregate-demand curve shifts horizontally to D_1D_1. The new equilibrium is at point B, where both prices and output are higher than they were at A.

The slope of the aggregate-supply curve measures the amount of inflation that accompanies any specified rise in output and therefore embodies the most important aspects of the trade-off between unemployment and inflation. We concluded in Chapter 14 that this trade-off will be favourable when the economy is operating at low levels of capacity utilization and high levels of unemployment. Under such circumstances, firms can expand their operations substantially without running into higher costs. On the other hand, if demand stimulus occurs in a fully employed economy, firms will find it quite difficult to raise output and so will respond mostly by raising prices. Thus, the trade-off is very unfavourable when unemployment is low.

But we have learned in this book (especially in Chapter 10) that inflation need not always emanate from the demand side. Restrictions in the growth of aggregate supply—caused, for example, by an increase in the price of foreign oil—can shift the economy's aggregate-supply curve inward (or upward). This is illustrated in Figure 18–2, where the aggregate-supply curve shifts from S_0S_0 to S_1S_1, and the economy's equilibrium consequently moves from point A to point B. Prices rise as output falls; we have *stagflation*. Thus, while inflation can be initiated from either the demand side or the supply side of the economy, there is a crucial difference. Demand-side inflation is normally accompanied by rising real GNP (see Figure 18–1), while supply-side inflation may well be accompanied by falling GNP (see Figure 18–2). This is an important distinction, as we shall see in this chapter.

Applying the Model to a Growing Economy

You may have noticed that our simple model of aggregate supply and aggregate demand determines an equilibrium *price level* and an equilibrium *level of real*

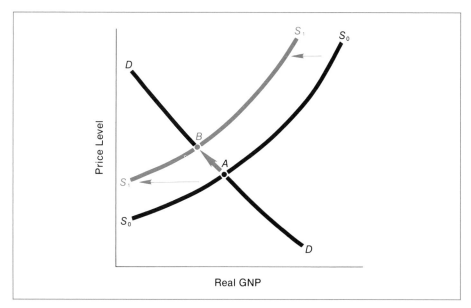

Figure 18-2
INFLATION FROM THE SUPPLY SIDE
A decrease in aggregate supply—which can be caused by such factors as an autonomous increase in wages, or by an increase in the price of foreign oil—can cause inflation. When the aggregate-supply curve shifts to the left, from S_0S_0 to S_1S_1, the equilibrium point moves from A to B. Comparing B with A, we see that the price level is higher, which means there must have been *inflation* (rising prices) in the interim. Notice also that adverse supply shifts make real output decline while prices are rising; that is, they produce *stagflation*.

GNP. But in the real economy, we do not see an unchanged price level and an unchanged level of real GNP for long periods of time. Instead, the price level and the level of real GNP change every year.

This is illustrated in Figure 18-3, which is a scatter diagram of the Canadian price level and the level of GNP for every year from 1960 to 1983. The points are labelled for your convenience, and it is quite clear that the general march of the economy through time is upward and to the right—toward higher prices and higher levels of output.

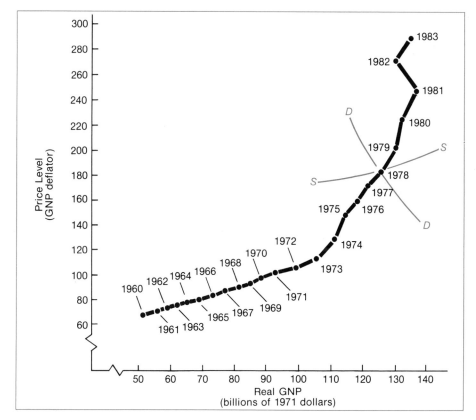

Figure 18-3
THE PRICE LEVEL AND REAL OUTPUT IN CANADA, 1960-1983
This scatter diagram shows, for each year from 1960 to 1983, the price level (GNP deflator) and real GNP for Canada. Clearly the normal state of affairs is for both variables to rise from one year to the next.
SOURCE: Statistics Canada

Figure 18-4

AGGREGATE SUPPLY AND
DEMAND ANALYSIS OF A
GROWING ECONOMY

This diagram illustrates how the
aggregate supply and demand
analysis of earlier chapters can be
applied to a real-world economy,
in which both the supply curve and
the demand curve normally shift
outward from one year to the next.
In this example, demand curve
D_0D_0 and supply curve S_0S_0
represent the Canadian economy
in late 1982. Equilibrium was at
point A, with a price level of 274
and real GNP of $130 billion.
Demand curve D_1D_1 and supply
curve S_1S_1 represent the end of
1983. During the year, the price
index rose by 16 points (about 6
percent) and output increased by
$4 billion (about 3 percent).

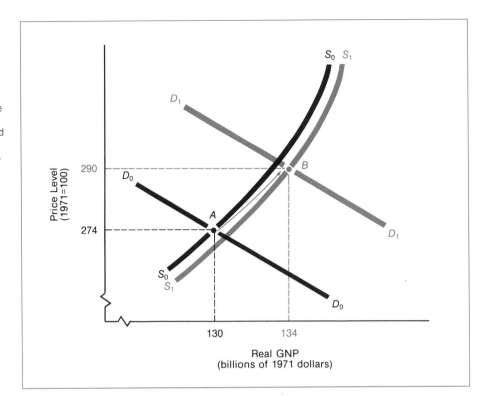

It is certainly no mystery why this occurs. The economy's aggregate-supply
and aggregate-demand curves change each year. Aggregate supply normally grows
because there are more workers, more machinery, and more factories each year,
and because technology is improving. Aggregate demand normally grows because,
with a growing population, there is more demand for both consumer and
investment goods by both domestic and foreign residents, and because the
government increases its spending and the Bank of Canada increases the money
supply. We can think of each point in Figure 18-3 as the intersection of an
aggregate-supply curve and an aggregate-demand curve for that particular year. To
help you visualize this, the curves for 1978 are sketched in the diagram.

One thing is clear from this diagram: If we want to apply our theoretical
model to the real world, we must recognize that the normal state of affairs is for
both the aggregate-demand curve *and* the aggregate-supply curve to shift to the
right each year. As a consequence, we expect to find both the price level and real
GNP rising from year to year.

Figure 18-4 illustrates this idea. The numbers are chosen so that curves D_0D_0
and S_0S_0 approximately represent the end of 1982, and the curves D_1D_1 and S_1S_1
approximately represent the end of 1983. Thus the equilibrium late in 1982 was at
point A, with real GNP of $130 billion (in 1971 dollars) and a price level of 274,
while the equilibrium one year later was at point B, with real GNP at $134 billion
and the price level at 290. The blue arrow in the diagram shows how equilibrium
moved during 1983. It points upward and to the right, meaning that both prices
and output increased.

Demand-Side Inflation and the Phillips Curve

Let us now use our theoretical model to rerun history. Suppose that during 1983
the aggregate-demand curve grew either faster or slower than it actually did. What
difference would this have made for the performance of the national economy?

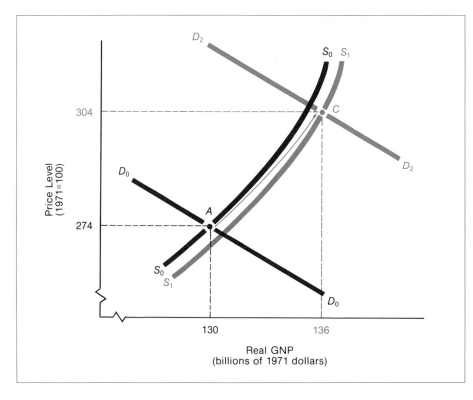

Figure 18-5

THE EFFECTS OF FASTER GROWTH OF AGGREGATE DEMAND

In this hypothetical example, we imagine that, because either private citizens spent more or the government pursued more expansionary policies, aggregate demand grew faster between late 1982 and late 1983 than it did in Figure 18-4. The consequence is that in this diagram the price level rises 30 points (about 11 percent) during 1983, compared with the 16 points (6 percent) in Figure 18-4. Growth of real output is also greater. $6 billion here and only $4 billion in the previous figure.

The next two figures are intended to provide the answers.

In Figure 18–5 we imagine that aggregate demand grew even *faster* during 1983 than it actually did. Thus, the demand curve D_0D_0 and both supply curves are exactly as they were in the previous diagram, but the demand curve D_2D_2 in Figure 18–5 is farther to the right than the demand curve D_1D_1 in Figure 18–4. Equilibrium is at point A late in 1982 and point C late in 1983. Comparing point C in Figure 18–5 with point B in Figure 18–4, we see that output would have increased more during 1983 ($6 billion versus $4 billion) and prices would also have increased more (to 304 instead of 290); that is, there would have been more inflation. This is generally what happens when the growth rate of aggregate demand speeds up.

For any given rate of growth of the aggregate-supply curve, a faster rate of growth of the aggregate-demand curve will lead to more inflation and faster growth of real output.

Figure 18–6 illustrates the opposite case. Here we imagine that the aggregate-demand curve shifted outward *less* than in Figure 18–4. That is, demand curve D_3D_3 in Figure 18–6 is to the left of demand curve D_1D_1 in Figure 18–4. The consequence, we see, is that the shift of the economy's equilibrium during 1983 (from point A to point E) would have entailed *less inflation* and *slower growth of real output* than actually took place. This again is generally the case.

For any given rate of growth of the aggregate-supply curve, a slower rate of growth of the aggregate-demand curve will lead to less inflation and slower growth of real output.

If we put these two findings together, we have a very clear prediction from our theory:

If fluctuations in the economy's real growth rate from year to year are caused

Figure 18-6

THE EFFECTS OF SLOWER GROWTH OF AGGREGATE DEMAND

Here, the aggregate-demand curve is assumed to shift outward less than it did in Figure 18-4. Consequently, the movement from equilibrium point *A* to equilibrium point *E* during 1983 entails a smaller rise in the price level and a smaller increase in real output than actually occurred.

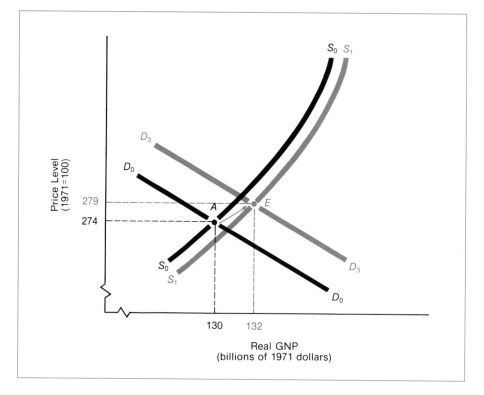

primarily by variations in the rate at which the aggregate-demand curve shifts outward, then the data should show that the most rapid inflation occurs during years when output expands most rapidly, and the slowest inflation occurs when output expands more slowly.

Does the theory fit the facts? We will put it to the test in a moment, but first let us translate it into a prediction about the relationship between inflation and unemployment. Faster growth of real output naturally means faster growth in the number of jobs and, hence, *lower unemployment*. Conversely, slower growth of real output means slower growth in the number of jobs and, hence, *higher unemployment*. Thus, the unemployment rate and the growth rate of output should be inversely related—the faster the economy grows the lower the unemployment rate, and the slower the economy grows the higher the unemployment rate.

Figure 18-7 illustrates this idea. The actual unemployment rate in Canada in 1983 was about 12 percent, and the inflation rate during the year was about 6 percent. This is point *b* in Figure 18-7, which corresponds to equilibrium point *B* in Figure 18-4. The faster growth rate of demand depicted by point *C* in Figure 18-5 would have led to higher inflation and lower unemployment. For the sake of a concrete example, we suppose that unemployment would have been 10 percent and inflation would have been 11 percent; this is point *c* in Figure 18-7. Point *E* in Figure 18-6 summarized the results of slower growth of aggregate demand: Unemployment would have been higher and inflation lower. In Figure 18-7, this is represented by point *e*, with an unemployment rate of 15 percent and an inflation rate of 2 percent. This figure shows quite graphically the principal empirical implication of our theoretical model:

If fluctuations in economic activity are primarily caused by variations in the rate at which the aggregate-demand curve shifts outward from year to year, then the data should show that low unemployment rates are associated with high inflation rates and high unemployment rates are associated with low inflation rates.

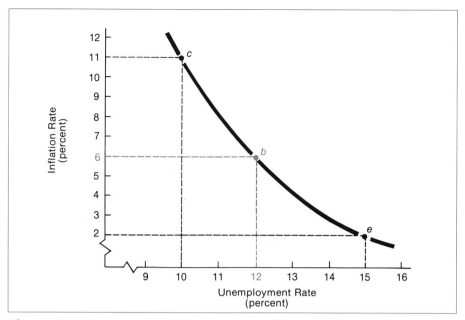

Figure 18-7

ORIGINS OF THE PHILLIPS CURVE

The three previous diagrams indicated three different rates of growth of real GNP between late 1982 and late 1983 and three different inflation rates. Since each different real growth rate corresponds to a different rate of unemployment, we can put the information contained in the three preceding diagrams together in a scatter diagram to show the relationship between inflation and unemployment. Points *b*, *c*, and *e* in this figure correspond to points *B*, *C*, and *E* in Figures 18-4, 18-5, and 18-6, respectively. The inflation numbers are read directly from the previous three graphs. The unemployment numbers are fabricated to represent the fact that faster growth (Figure 18-5) is associated with lower unemployment (point *c*) while slower growth (Figure 18-6) is associated with higher unemployment (point *e*). Scatter diagrams like this one are called "Phillips curves," after their inventor, A. W. Phillips.

Now we are ready to look at real data. Do we actually observe such an inverse relationship between inflation and unemployment? About 27 years ago, economist A. W. Phillips plotted data on unemployment and the rate of change of *wages* (not prices) for several extended periods of British history on a series of scatter diagrams, one of which is reproduced as Figure 18-8. He then sketched in a curve that seemed to "fit" the data. This type of curve, which is now called a **Phillips curve**, shows that wage inflation normally is high when unemployment is low and is low when unemployment is high. So far, so good.

Phillips curves have also been constructed for *price* inflation, and one of these for Canada in the 1950s and 1960s is shown in Figure 18-9. The curve appears to fit the data fairly well, although there are two exceptions, 1953 and 1955. As viewed through the eyes of our theory, these facts suggest that economic fluctuations in England between 1861 and 1913 and in Canada between 1952 and 1969 probably were accounted for primarily by changes in the growth of aggregate demand; that is, by changes in the spending habits of consumers, investors, foreigners, and the government. The simple model of demand-side inflation really does seem to describe what happened.

During the 1960s and early 1970s, economists often thought of the Phillips curve as a "menu" of the choices available to policy-makers. In this view, policy-makers could opt for low unemployment and high inflation—as was done in 1967. Or they might prefer higher unemployment coupled with lower inflation—as, for example, in 1961. The Phillips curve, it was thought, described the *quantitative* trade-off between inflation and unemployment. And, for a number of years, it worked rather well.

Then something happened. The economy in the 1970s behaved far worse than

A **Phillips curve** is a graph depicting the rate of unemployment on the horizontal axis and either the rate of inflation or the rate of change of money wages on the vertical axis. Phillips curves are normally downward sloping, indicating that higher inflation rates are associated with lower unemployment rates.

Figure 18-8

THE ORIGINAL PHILLIPS
CURVE

This scatter diagram, reproduced from the original article by A. W. Phillips, shows the rate of change of money wages and the rate of unemployment in the United Kingdom between 1861 and 1913. Each year is represented by a point in the diagram.

SOURCE: A. W. Phillips, "The Relationship Between Unemployment and the Rate of Change of Money Wages in the United Kingdom, 1861-1957." *Economica*, New Series, vol. 25, November 1958.

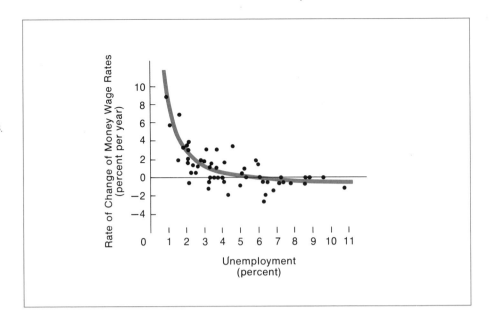

expected in terms of the Phillips curve shown in Figure 18-9. In particular, given the unemployment rates in each of those years, inflation was astonishingly high by historical standards. This is shown in Figure 18-10, which simply adds to Figure 18-9 the points for 1970-83. Clearly something had gone wrong with the old view of the Phillips curve as a menu for policy choices. As a result, a new view of the Phillips curve has emerged. We will discuss this "new view" next, and then return to the implications of the Phillips curve for the conduct of economic policy.

What the Phillips Curve Is Not

One view of what went wrong in the 1970s holds that policy-makers misinterpreted the Phillips curve and tried to pick combinations of inflation and unemployment that were not in fact on the menu. Specifically, the Phillips curve is a *statistical relationship* between inflation and unemployment that we expect to emerge *if*

Figure 18-9

A PHILLIPS CURVE FOR
CANADA

This Phillips curve relates price inflation (using the GNP price deflator rather than wage inflation) to the unemployment rate in Canada for the years 1952-69. Though it misses badly in two instances (1953 and 1955), it generally "fits" the data fairly well.

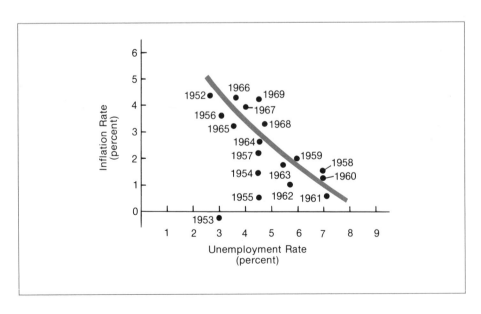

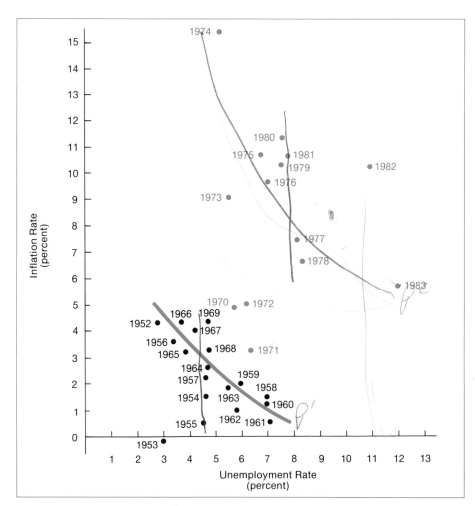

Figure 18-10
A PHILLIPS CURVE FOR CANADA?

This scatter diagram adds the points for 1970-83 to the scatter diagram shown in Figure 18-9. It is clear that inflation in each of those years was much higher than the Phillips curve would have led us to predict.

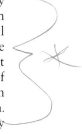

changes in the growth of aggregate demand are the predominant factor accounting for economic fluctuations. But the curve was widely misinterpreted as depicting a number of *alternative equilibrium points* that the economy could achieve and from which policy-makers could choose.

We can understand the flaw in this reasoning by quickly reviewing an earlier lesson. We know from Chapter 10 that the economy has a **self-correcting mechanism** that will cure both inflations and recessions *eventually* even if the government does nothing. Why is this relevant here? Because it tells us that many combinations of output and prices cannot be maintained indefinitely. Some will "self-destruct." Specifically, if the economy finds itself far away from the normal "full-employment" level of unemployment, forces will be set in motion that tend to erode the inflationary or recessionary gap.

For example, consider the case of a recessionary gap where aggregate-supply curve S_0S_0 intersects aggregate-demand curve DD as in Figure 18-11. With equilibrium output well below potential GNP at point A, there is unused industrial capacity and unsold output. So firms will not raise prices very much. At the same time, the availability of unemployed workers eager for jobs limits the rate at which labour can push up wage rates. But wages are the main component of business costs, so when wages decline (relative to what they would have been without a recession) so do costs. And lower costs stimulate greater production. This idea is depicted in Figure 18-11 as an outward shift of the aggregate-supply curve—from S_0S_0 to S_1S_1.

Figure 18-11

THE ELIMINATION OF A
RECESSIONARY GAP
When the aggregate-supply curve
is S_0S_0 and the aggregate-demand
curve is DD, the economy will
reach an equilibrium with a
recessionary gap (point A). The
resulting deflation of wages will
cause the aggregate-supply curve
to shift outward (downward) from
S_0S_0 to S_1S_1 and eventually to
S_2S_2. Here, with equilibrium at
point C, the recessionary gap is
gone and the economy is back at
"full employment."

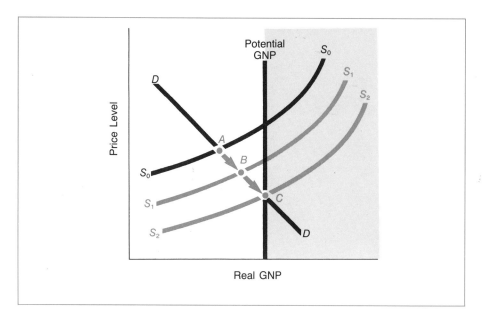

As can be seen in the figure, the outward shift of the aggregate-supply curve
brought on by the recession causes equilibrium output to rise as the economy
moves from point A to point B. Thus the recessionary gap begins to shrink. This
process continues until the aggregate-supply curve reaches the position indicated
by S_2S_2 in Figure 18-11. Here wages have fallen enough to eliminate the
recessionary gap, and the economy has reached a full-employment equilibrium at
point C.[1]

So far this is all review. Now let us relate it to our discussion of the origins of
the Phillips curve. Figure 18-12, which is a hypothetical Phillips curve, will help
us do this.

Point a in Figure 18-12 corresponds to point A in Figure 18-11: It shows the
initial recessionary gap with unemployment (at 9 percent) above full employment,
which we assume to occur at 7 percent. But we have just seen that point A in
Figure 18-11—and therefore also point a in Figure 18-12—is not sustainable. The
economy tends to rid itself of the recessionary gap through the process of
disinflation that we have just described. The adjustment path from A to C that we
analysed in Figure 18-11 would appear on our Phillips curve diagram as a
movement toward less inflation and less unemployment—something like the blue
arrow from point a to point c in Figure 18-12.

Similarly, points representing inflationary gaps—such as point d in Figure
18-12—are not sustainable. They are also gradually eliminated by the self-
correcting mechanism that we studied in Chapter 10. To review briefly, wages are
forced up by the abnormally low unemployment, and this in turn pushes prices
higher. Higher prices deter export spending by foreigners, and they reduce
investment spending by forcing up interest rates. And they also deter consumer
spending by lowering the purchasing power of consumer wealth. The inflationary
process continues until the amount people want to spend is brought into balance
with the amount firms want to supply at normal full employment. During such an
adjustment period, unemployment and inflation are both rising—as indicated by
the blue path from point d to point f in Figure 18-12.

[1]This simple analysis assumes that the aggregate-demand curve does not move during the
adjustment period. If it is shifting to the right, the recessionary gap will disappear even faster, but
inflation will not slow down as much. *Exercise*: Construct the diagram for this case by adding a
shift in the aggregate-demand curve to Figure 18-11.

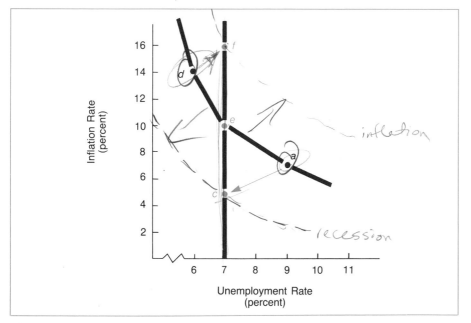

Figure 18-12

THE VERTICAL LONG-RUN PHILLIPS CURVE

In the long run, points like *a*, where unemployment is above the normal "full-employment" unemployment rate, are unsustainable. The economy's natural self-correcting mechanism (which was described in Figure 18-11) will erode the recessionary gap by reducing both inflation and unemployment. In the diagram, this will force the economy toward a point like *c*. The long-run choices, therefore, are among points like *c* and *f*, which constitute what is called the *vertical (long-run) Phillips curve*, not among points like *d* and *a* on the downward-sloping (short-run) Phillips curve.

Putting these two conclusions together, we see that:

On a Phillips curve diagram, neither points corresponding to an inflationary gap (like *d* in Figure 18–12) nor points corresponding to a recessionary gap (like *a* in Figure 18–12) can be maintained indefinitely. Inflationary gaps lead to rising unemployment and rising inflation. Recessionary gaps lead to falling inflation and falling unemployment. All the points that are sustainable in the long run (such as *c*, *e*, and *f* in Figure 18–12) correspond to the same rate of unemployment, which is therefore called the **natural rate of unemployment**. The natural rate corresponds to what we have so far been calling the "full-employment" unemployment rate.

Now we can see why the Phillips curve connecting points *d*, *e*, and *a* does not represent a menu of policy choices. While we can move from a point like *e* to a point like *d* by stimulating aggregate demand sufficiently, there is no way that we can *stay* at point *d*. Unemployment cannot be kept this low indefinitely. Instead, policy-makers must choose from among points like *e*, *f*, and *c*, all of which are vertically above one another at the natural rate of unemployment. For rather obvious reasons, the line connecting these points has been dubbed the **vertical (long-run) Phillips curve**. It is this vertical Phillips curve (connecting points like *e*, *f*, and *c*) that represents the true long-run "menu" of policy choices.

Our conclusions about the Phillips curve can be summarized in three statements:

SUMMARY

1. To the extent that economic fluctuations emanate from the demand side, we expect to find an inverse relationship between unemployment and inflation—a downward-sloping Phillips curve.

> The economy's self-correcting mechanism always tends to push the unemployment rate back toward a specific rate of unemployment that we call the **natural rate of unemployment**.

> The **vertical (long-run) Phillips curve** shows the menu of inflation/ unemployment choices available to society in the long run. It is a vertical straight line at the natural rate of unemployment.

2. In the short run, it is possible to "ride up the Phillips curve" toward lower levels of unemployment by stimulating aggregate demand. Conversely, by restricting the growth of demand, it is possible to "ride down the Phillips curve" toward lower rates of inflation (see, for example, point *a* in Figure 18–12). There is, thus, a *trade-off between unemployment and inflation.* Stimulating demand will improve the unemployment picture but worsen inflation; restricting demand will lower inflation but aggravate the unemployment problem.

3. However, there is no such trade-off in the long run. The economy's self-correcting mechanism ensures that unemployment eventually will return to the "natural rate," no matter what happens to aggregate demand. In the long run, faster growth of demand leads only to higher inflation, not to lower unemployment; and slower growth of demand leads only to lower inflation, not to higher unemployment.

Fighting Inflation with Fiscal and Monetary Policy

Let us now apply this analysis to a concrete policy problem, one that has vexed our ministers of finance for years. How should the government's ability to manage aggregate demand through fiscal and monetary policy be used to fight inflation?

We have already spent many chapters discussing how the government's monetary and fiscal policy tools—tax rates, government spending, open-market operations, and so on—can be used to increase or decrease aggregate demand. We have also discussed some of the practical problems that arise in using each of these weapons and some of the issues involved in choosing among them. Rather than repeat all this, let us just suppose that the government somehow controls aggregate demand and wishes to use this ability to fight inflation. What has our discussion of the trade-off between inflation and unemployment taught us about this problem?

To create a somewhat realistic example, let us imagine that a new government takes office when the inflation rate is 10 percent and the unemployment rate is 7 percent—point *e* in Figure 18–12. Suppose the new government adopts a policy of restricting the growth of aggregate demand by contractionary fiscal and monetary policies, thereby opening up a recessionary gap. In a word—though no politician would ever use such blunt language—he decides to fight inflation by causing a recession.

At first, the economy "rides down" the short-run Phillips curve from point *e* to point *a* in Figure 18–12. The recession pushes unemployment up from 7 percent to 9 percent but reduces inflation from 10 percent to 7 percent. Lower inflation has been "bought" by causing higher unemployment. This scenario roughly describes what happened in Canada between 1980 and 1982, except that the recession was much more severe in reality than in the example.

But the anti-inflation dividends of recession do not end there. The economy's self-correcting mechanism begins to work and gradually erodes the recessionary gap. Inflation continues to decline as the economy recovers and unemployment falls. In the example, inflation falls from 7 percent to 5 percent as the economy recovers along the path from *a* to *c* in Figure 18–12. In the actual Canadian case, inflation continued to decline as recovery progressed in 1983, but the economy had still not returned to full employment when this book went to press.

When all the dust has settled, the economy in our hypothetical example has moved from point *e* to point *c* in Figure 18–12. Comparing these two points shows that, in the end, there is less inflation and no more unemployment. In what sense, then, do policy-makers have to face up to a trade-off between inflation and unemployment? The answer is that:

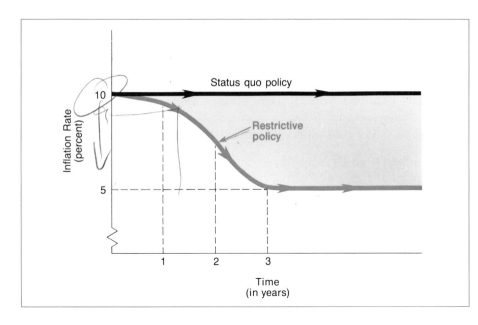

Figure 18-13
THE PAYOFF TO ANTI-INFLATION POLICY
If a recession is caused by restrictive fiscal and monetary policy, the inflation rate will not respond very much at first. Gradually, however, inflation will yield to the slack caused by the restrictive policy. In this example the inflation rate begins at 10 percent, falls only to 9 percent after one year, but is down to 7½ percent after two years, and 5 percent after three years. The shaded area indicates the gains that the policy has reaped on the inflation front.

The cost of reducing inflation by restrictive fiscal and monetary policies is a *temporary* rise in unemployment.

Figures 18-13 and 18-14 are intended to give the flavour of what the real menu of choices looks like to a policy-maker who is considering embarking on such a program. Figure 18-13 contrasts the behaviour of the inflation rate over time under a "status quo policy" (which makes the unemployment rate unchanged at 7 percent) with the behaviour under a restrictive anti-inflationary policy (which deliberately slows the growth rate of aggregate demand and makes unemployment rise).

Inflation will continue at 10 percent per year if the government does not restrain the growth of demand and unemployment remains at 7 percent. This is the status quo policy path shown in black in Figure 18-13. It corresponds to the case where the economy remains indefinitely at point *e* in Figure 18-12.

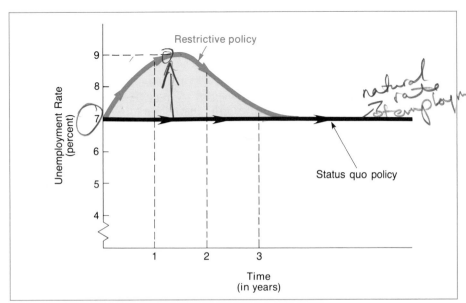

Figure 18-14
THE COST OF ANTI-INFLATION POLICY
The inflation gains depicted in the preceding figure do not come to us without cost. The restrictive policy increases unemployment for a period; that is, it induces a recession. In this example, the unemployment rate takes about a year to rise from 7 percent to 9 percent (the recession period), and then takes over two years to return to 7 percent (the recovery period). The shaded area indicates the extra unemployment that must be endured in order to get the inflation rate down from 10 percent to 5 percent.

On the other hand, if a restrictive policy is followed and the growth of aggregate demand is restrained, inflation will begin to fall, slowly at first but then with increasing speed. In the example, we suppose that the inflation rate falls little in the first year, more in the second year, and is essentially down to 5 percent after three years. This is the restrictive-policy path shown in blue in Figure 18-13. It corresponds to the path from *e* to *a* to *c* in Figure 18-12.

The shaded area in the figure summarizes the difference between these two paths, and therefore depicts the payoff to anti-inflation policy. But there are also costs.

Figure 18-14 gives a rough impression of how the unemployment rate might behave under the two alternative policies. The status quo policy keeps the unemployment rate at 7 percent, which is the natural rate. The restrictive policy results in a recession: Unemployment rises gradually from 7 percent to 9 percent and then gradually falls back to the natural rate of 7 percent. The shaded area in Figure 18-14 shows what it costs to get the inflation rate down: For over three years unemployment is above the natural rate.

Notice the differences in timing between Figure 18-13 and Figure 18-14. In the early stages of the disinflation program (say, the first year), progress against inflation is meagre even though the losses on the unemployment front are substantial. This reflects an underlying reality that we have mentioned before: Inflation gives way only grudgingly to economic slack. Because of this, policymakers who embark on a disinflationary course must be patient. The costs in terms of unemployment, although temporary, come sooner. The gains on the inflation front, though more durable, appear later.

What Should Be Done?

Should the government pay the recessionary cost of fighting inflation? When the benefits depicted in Figure 18-13 are balanced against the costs shown in Figure 18-14, have we made a good bargain? While each of you will have to answer this question for yourself, our analysis has highlighted three critical issues on which your answer should rest.

The Costs of Inflation and Unemployment

We spent an entire chapter early in the book (Chapter 6) examining the social costs of inflation and unemployment. Most of the costs of the extra unemployment depicted in Figure 18-14, we concluded, are easy to translate into dollars and cents. Basically, we only need to estimate the real GNP that is lost each year. However, the costs of inflation are harder to put a price tag on, and hence the benefits from reducing inflation are harder to measure. Thus, there is considerable controversy over the costs and benefits of using recession to fight inflation.

Some economists and public figures believe that inflation is extremely costly, and so they look with favour on the trade-off that is embodied in Figures 18-13 and 18-14. Others have a lower estimate of the costs of inflation and find recession a terribly high price to pay. Thus, in particular, some observers believe that we paid an excessively high price to reduce inflation from 11 percent to 6 percent in 1980-83, while others applaud the policy and maintain that the price was worth paying.

The Position of the Economy

We have stated several times in this book that the shape of the economy's aggregate-supply curve, and hence the shape of the short-run Phillips curve, depends very much on the degree of resource utilization. If resources are virtually fully employed, the aggregate-supply curve (and thus the Phillips curve) will be rather steep, which means that the inflation gains will be substantial and the unemployment costs will be minimal. On the other hand, if there is a great deal of unemployed labour and unutilized industrial capacity, the aggregate-supply curve (and hence the short-run Phillips curve) may be nearly horizontal. In that case, a great deal of unemployment will be needed to achieve even a slight reduction in inflation. The Phillips curves we have drawn in this chapter have this characteristic shape.

Because the Phillips curve is shaped this way the trade-off depicted in our last two diagrams will look more favourable when the economy is in a boom and less favourable when there is already a good deal of unemployment.

The Efficiency of the Economy's Self-Correcting Mechanism

We have stressed that once government policy causes a recession, it is the economy's natural self-correcting mechanism that cures the recessionary gap. The obvious question here is: How long do we have to wait? If the self-correcting mechanism—which works through reductions in the rate of wage inflation—is slow and halting, the costs of fighting inflation will be enormous. On the other hand, if wage inflation responds promptly, the recession necessary to bring down inflation may not be very severe.

This is another issue that is surrounded by controversy. Most economists believe that the weight of the evidence points to very sluggish wage behaviour. The rate of wage inflation appears to respond only slowly to economic slack. In terms of our Figure 18–12 (page 345), this means that the economy will traverse the path from *a* to *c* at an agonizingly slow pace, so that a very long recession will be necessary if there is to be any appreciable effect on inflation.

But a significant minority opinion finds this assessment far too pessimistic. Economists in this group argue that the costs of reducing inflation are not nearly so severe and that the key to a successful anti-inflation policy is its effect on people's *expectations*. But, to understand this argument, we must first examine why expectations are relevant to the Phillips curve trade-off.

Inflationary Expectations and the Phillips Curve

The explanation starts with some more review. Recall from Chapter 10 that the main reason why the economy's aggregate-supply curve slopes upward—that is, why output increases as the price level rises—is that businesses typically purchase labour and other inputs under long-term contracts that stipulate the cost of the input in *money* terms (for example, the nominal wage rate). If such contracts are in force when prices go up, then *real* wages fall as prices rise. From businesses' point of view, labour becomes cheaper in real terms, and firms are induced to expand employment and output. Buying cheaply and selling dearly is, after all, the route to higher profits. Long-term contracts that set the nominal wage rate, then, explain why higher prices lead to more output; that is, why the aggregate-supply curve slopes upward.

Table 18–1 illustrates how this works in a concrete example. We suppose that workers and firms agree today that the money wage to be paid a year from now will be $10 per hour. The table then shows the real wage that corresponds to each alternative rate of inflation.[2] Clearly, the higher the inflation rate, the higher the price level at the end of the year and the lower the real wage.

Lower real wages provide an incentive for the firm to increase output, as we have just noted. But lower real wages also impose losses of purchasing power on workers. Thus, there is a sense in which workers are being "cheated" by inflation if

[2] Each real-wage figure is obtained by dividing the $10 nominal wage by the corresponding price level a year later and multiplying by 100. Thus, for example, when the inflation rate is 4 percent, the real wage at the end of the year is ($10/104) × 100 = $9.62.

Table 18-1

MONEY AND REAL WAGES UNDER INFLATION

INFLATION RATE (percent)	PRICE LEVEL ONE YEAR FROM NOW	MONEY WAGE ONE YEAR FROM NOW (dollars per hour)	REAL WAGE ONE YEAR FROM NOW (dollars per hour)
0	100	10.00	10.00
4	104	10.00	9.62
8	108	10.00	9.26
12	112	10.00	8.93

they sign a contract specifying a fixed money wage in an inflationary environment.

Many economists wonder why workers would sign such a contract if they can see inflation coming. Would it not be more reasonable, these economists ask, to insist on being compensated for inflation in advance? After all, firms should be willing to provide compensation for expected inflation because they realize that it does not raise real wages.

Table 18-2 illustrates how the money wage specified in a contract can be adjusted for expected inflation. For example, if 4 percent inflation is expected, the contract could stipulate that the wage rate be increased to $10.40 (which is 4 percent more than $10) at the end of the year. That would keep the real wage at $10, the same as it would be under zero inflation. The remaining money wage figures in Table 18-2 are derived similarly.

If workers and firms actually adjust money wages in the way suggested in Table 18-2, then the expected real wage will not decline as the expected price level rises. (In the example, the expected future real wage is always $10 per hour.) Then, if expectations prove correct, prices and wages will go up together, leaving the real wage unchanged. Workers will not lose from inflation and firms will not gain. But, of course, that means that there will be no special incentive for firms to produce more as prices rise. In a word, the aggregate-supply curve would become *vertical.* In general:

 If workers can see inflation coming, and if they receive compensation for it in advance so that inflation does not erode *real* wages, then the economy's aggregate-supply curve will not slope upward. It will be a vertical line at the level of output corresponding to potential GNP.

Such a curve is shown in part (a) of Figure 18-15. Since we derived the Phillips curve from the aggregate-supply curve earlier in the chapter, it follows that even the *short-run* Phillips curve will become vertical under these circumstances [see part (b) of Figure 18-15].[3]

[3]See Discussion Question 10 at the end of the chapter.

Table 18-2

MONEY AND REAL WAGES UNDER EXPECTED INFLATION

EXPECTED INFLATION RATE (percent)	EXPECTED PRICE LEVEL ONE YEAR FROM NOW	MONEY WAGE ONE YEAR FROM NOW (dollars per hour)	EXPECTED REAL WAGE ONE YEAR FROM NOW (dollars per hour)
0	100	10.00	10.00
4	104	10.40	10.00
8	108	10.80	10.00
12	112	11.20	10.00

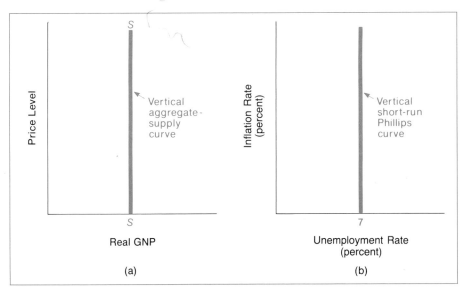

If workers foresee inflation, and if
they also receive full
compensation for it in advance,
then inflation will no longer erode
real wages. In that case, firms will
have no incentive to raise
production as prices rise, and the
aggregate-supply curve will be
vertical as in part (a). Since we
derived the short-run Phillips curve
from the aggregate-supply curve,
the short-run Phillips curve will
also become vertical [part (b)].

If this analysis is correct, it has profound implications for the trade-off and for the costs and benefits of inflation-fighting. This can be seen by referring back to Figure 18-12 on page 345, where we depicted the strategy of fighting inflation by causing a recession. We concluded there that in order to move from point *e* (representing 10 percent inflation) to point *c* (representing 5 percent inflation), the economy would have to take a detour through point *a*; that is, it would have to endure a recession. If, however, even the *short-run* Phillips curve were *vertical* rather than downward sloping, this detour would not be necessary. It would be possible for inflation to fall without unemployment rising. The economy could jump directly from point *e* to point *c*.

Is this analysis correct? Can we really slay the inflationary dragon so painlessly? As a piece of pure logic, the argument is impeccable. Yet things do not seem to have worked out this way. In practice, inflation fighting has been very costly. We must, therefore, ask ourselves whether the premises on which the analysis rests are realistic. There are several reasons why many economists think the expectations argument should not be applied uncritically to the modern economy.

Point 1. The argument is predicated on the notion that inflation can be accurately foreseen. But many contracts for labour and other raw materials cover such long periods of time that the expectations that were held when the contracts were written may be very different from the current reality. If a restrictive policy reduces inflation below the rate firms and workers were expecting when they made their wage agreement, real wages will wind up higher than was intended, and hence firms will want to reduce employment and produce less.

Point 2. Many people believe that inflationary expectations are quite sluggish, that they do not adapt quickly to changes in the economic environment. If, for example, the government embarks on an anti-inflation policy, workers will continue to expect high inflation for quite a while. Thus they will continue to insist on high rates of increase in money wages. Then, if inflation actually slows down, real wages will wind up rising faster than anyone expected. Firms will therefore find labour "too expensive" relative to current selling prices, and unemployment will result. With lags in the reaction of expectations, then, the short-run Phillips curve retains its downward slope and inflation-fighting is costly.

The Theory of Rational Expectations

These two points, and others we have not mentioned, have persuaded most economists that the expectations argument, while valid in part, should not be taken to extremes. Most economists nowadays accept the notion that the Phillips curve is downward sloping in the short run, and hence that a short-run trade-off does exist.

But a vocal minority of economists disagrees. This group, believers in the doctrine of **rational expectations**, insists that the only type of inflation that leads to *increases* in output is *unexpected* inflation, because only unexpected inflation will reduce real wages. (To see this, compare Tables 18-1 and 18-2.) Similarly, they argue, the only type of reduction in inflation that leads to recession is an *unexpected* reduction.

To explain this point of view, we must first explain what rational expectations are. Then, we will be in a position to understand why the hypothesis of rational expectations has such radical implications for the Phillips curve.

What Are Rational Expectations?

In many economic problems, people must formulate expectations about what the future will bring. For example, those who invest in the stock market need to forecast the future prices of the stocks they buy and sell. And we have just discussed why workers and businesses may want to forecast the future price level before they agree on a money wage. *Rational expectations* is a controversial hypothesis about how such forecasts are made.

As used by economists, a forecast (an "expectation") of a future variable is considered rational if the forecaster makes *optimal* use of all information that is both *available* and *relevant*. Let us elaborate on the italicized words in this definition, using as an example a hypothetical stock-market investor who has rational expectations.

First, believers in the doctrine of rational expectations recognize that *information is limited*. An investor who is interested in buying Canadian Pacific stock would like to know how much profit the company will make in the coming years. Armed with such information, she could predict the future price of CP stock more accurately. But that information is not available; no one knows it. Her forecast of the future price of CP stock is not "irrational" just because she does not know CP's future profits. On the other hand, if CP stock normally goes down on Fridays and up on Mondays, she should be aware of this fact.

Second, *not all information is important.* Some publicly available facts may be irrelevant to predicting the variables of interest. If so, a rational forecaster can afford to be ignorant of them. For example, anyone who cares to can find out how many babies were born last year in Fredericton. But this fact may not tell you much about the future performance of Canadian Pacific. So our investor need not have this information to be rational. However, if there is a clear Friday/Monday pattern in CP stock prices, she had better know what day of the week it is!

Finally, we have the word *optimal*. As used by economists, this means using proper statistical inference to process all the relevant information that is available before making a forecast. Thus, to have rational expectations, your forecasts do not have to be correct, but they cannot have systematic errors that could have been avoided by applying better statistical methods. This requirement, while exacting, is not quite as outlandish as it may seem. A good billiards player makes expert use of the laws of physics, even though he may have no understanding of the theory. Similarly, an experienced stock-market investor may make good use of information even without formal training in statistics.

Rational Expectations and the Trade-Off

Let us now see how the doctrine of rational expectations has been applied to deny that there exists any trade-off between inflation and unemployment—even in the short run.

Even though they recognize that inflation cannot always be predicted accurately, rational expectationists claim that workers will not make *systematic* errors in forecasting inflation. Note that Point 2 above suggests that inflationary expectations are typically *too low* when inflation is rising and *too high* when inflation is falling. Rational expectationists deny that this is possible. Workers, they argue, will always make the best possible forecast of inflation, using all the latest data and the best available economic models. Such forecasts will not err systematically in one direction or the other regardless of whether inflation is rising or falling. Consequently:

If expectations are rational, the difference between the *actual* rate of inflation and the *expected* rate of inflation (the forecasting error) will be a pure random number.

Now recall that the basic expectationist argument summarized in the previous section claims that employment is affected by inflation only to the extent that inflation differs from what was expected. It follows, therefore, that:

If expectations are rational, and there are no long-term contracts, the inflation rate can be reduced without the need for a period of high unemployment.

Except for some random—and totally unpredictable—gyrations due to forecasting errors, unemployment will always remain at the natural rate.

The implications of rational expectations for the conduct of economic policy are really quite revolutionary, at least when long-term contracts are not important. According to this view, the government's ability to manipulate aggregate demand does not give it any control over real output and unemployment because the aggregate-supply curve is vertical—even in the short run. [To see why, experiment by moving an aggregate-demand curve when the aggregate-supply curve is vertical as in Figure 18–15(a).] Any *predictable* change in aggregate demand will lead to a change in the expected rate of inflation, and hence will leave real wages unaffected.

The government can influence output only by making *unexpected* changes in aggregate demand. But this is not easy to do when expectations are rational because people are well informed about what policy-makers are up to. According to the rational expectationists, if the monetary and fiscal authorities typically react to high inflation by reducing aggregate demand, people will soon come to anticipate this reaction. And, as just mentioned, anticipated reductions in aggregate demand will not affect unemployment because they will not cause *unexpected* changes in inflation.

An Evaluation

The hypothesis of rational expectations is now embraced by many economists, but the proposition that inflation can be reduced without significant output losses is not. There are many reasons for this.

For one, Point 1 above remains valid even if expectations are rational. When long-term contracts are made, people get locked into provisions that, while rational when they were made, may seem irrational from today's point of view. For example, consider a labour contract drawn up in 1980 that specified a money wage rate to be paid in 1983. Given what people knew in 1980, it may have been rational to expect the 1983 price level to be 30 percent higher than the 1980 price level. So the money wage may have been set to rise 33 percent over the three years. Then inflation slowed dramatically. If the money wage specified in the contract was actually paid, the real wage was higher than had been intended. But no one behaved irrationally. Thus, the hypothesis of rational expectations is a *necessary* assumption for defending the proposition that inflation can be reduced without a recession, but it is *not sufficient*. There must also be no long-term contracts.

Since long-term contracts do exist, it is perhaps not surprising that the facts have not been kind to the costless disinflation proposition. The theory suggests that unemployment should hover around the natural rate most of the time. Yet this does not seem to be the case. The theory also denies that predictable monetary- and fiscal-policy actions will have effects on real output. Yet most observers think they can identify episodes in the past, such as the policy-induced recession of the early 1980s, where such actions had significant effects on real GNP and unemployment. Finally, some direct tests of the rationality of expectations have cast some doubt on the hypothesis.

At this writing, there is a great deal of controversy over how best to apply the idea of rational expectations to macroeconomic issues. The issues are far from resolved. But the evidence to date has led most economists to reject the extreme costless disinflation proposition and to affirm the existence of a short-run trade-off between inflation and unemployment.

Fighting Recessions with Fiscal and Monetary Policy

We have covered a lot of ground in this chapter already, and we have introduced a number of new concepts. At this point it may be useful to pause and take stock of what we have learned. A good way to test your understanding is to run the analysis in reverse. Up to now we have been considering the use of monetary and fiscal policies to combat *inflation*. Let us now suppose instead that the crucial macroeconomic problem is *unemployment*.

We again turn to the Phillips curve diagram, Figure 18–12 on page 345, for a concrete example. Suppose that the economy somehow finds itself at a point like *a*, in a recession. And suppose that the government wants to get the economy back to full employment. What should it do?

We already know from our previous analysis what will happen if the current rate of growth of aggregate demand is simply maintained. Point *a* on the short-run Phillips curve represents a recessionary gap, so the economy's self-correcting mechanism starts to work. High unemployment slows the rate of increase of money wages, which tends to push the aggregate-supply curve downward (compared with where it would have been if full employment were maintained). This both puts a brake on inflation and encourages employment. The economy slowly travels down the path indicated by the blue arrow in Figure 18–12, from point *a* to point *c*. But, as we have noted before, the road from *a* to *c* may be slow and bumpy.

Is there a better way out of our economic problems? Perhaps. As we have learned, expansionary measures such as tax cuts, increases in government spending, or open-market purchases of government securities can speed up the rate at which the aggregate-demand curve moves to the right. (Compare Figure 18–5 and Figure 18–4.) Such a policy would enable the economy to "ride up" the short-run Phillips curve toward point *e*.

Let us compare this active anti-recession policy with the more passive "status quo policy." Figures 18–16 and 18–17 will assist in the comparison. Under the status quo policy of relying on the economy's self-correcting mechanism, the unemployment rate gradually falls from the 9 percent that corresponds to point *a* on the Phillips curve to the 7 percent that corresponds to point *c*. But progress is agonizingly slow. The status quo policy path shown in black in Figure 18–16 indicates that it takes three uncomfortable years to return to full employment.

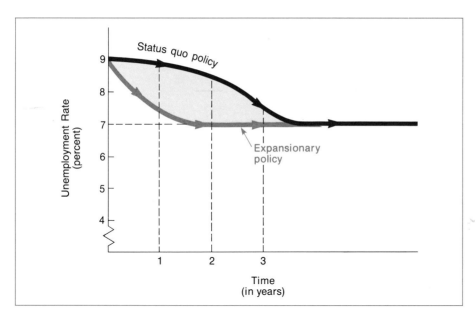

Figure 18-16
THE PAYOFF TO ANTI-
RECESSION POLICY
By stimulating aggregate demand
through monetary and fiscal policy,
the government can reduce
unemployment more rapidly. If it
relies exclusively on the
economy's ability to right itself,
unemployment will follow the black
"status quo policy" path. If,
instead, the government takes an
active hand in fighting the
recession, unemployment will
follow the blue "expansionary-
policy" path. The shaded area
measures the reduction in
unemployment that the
expansionary policy achieves.

By contrast, if expansionary monetary- and fiscal-policy actions are taken, the
return to full employment is much quicker. According to the blue "expansionary-
policy" path in Figure 18-16, we get there in about one and one-half years. The
shaded area in the figure measures the payoff to anti-recession policy; it shows
how much unemployment we save during the three-year period.

But, as we have by now come to expect, these gains are made at some cost.
The black status quo policy path in Figure 18-17 shows the likely behaviour of the
inflation rate under the policy of waiting for the economy's self-corrective forces
to work. Inflation falls gradually from the 7 percent rate that corresponds to point
a on the Phillips curve to the 5 percent rate that corresponds to point *c*. But if the
expansionary policy is pursued, inflation will not creep downward; instead it will
creep upward, as indicated by the blue expansionary-policy path in Figure 18-17.
The shaded area in this figure shows the cost of fighting recession with monetary
and fiscal policy: We wind up with more inflation.

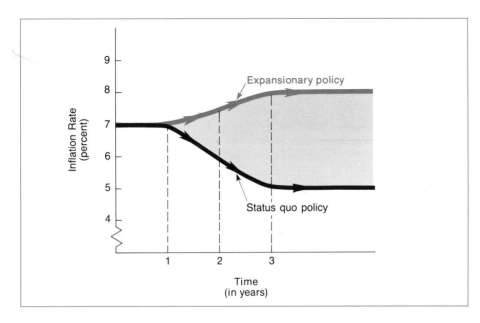

Figure 18-17
THE COST OF ANTI-
RECESSION POLICY
The unemployment gains depicted
in the previous figure are not
obtained without cost. By
stimulating the economy, the
government policies cause a rise
in the inflation rate—as shown by
the blue "expansionary-policy"
path. If, instead, the government
had simply waited for the
economy's natural self-correcting
mechanism to work, inflation would
have fallen—see the black "status
quo policy" path. The difference
between these two paths (the
shaded area) represents the
inflationary cost of fighting the
recession.

> In considering whether or not to fight a recession, policy-makers face a trade-off between unemployment and inflation. If they take expansionary actions to reduce unemployment, they may end up with a higher inflation rate.

Are the inflationary costs depicted in Figure 18–17 worth the benefits of the lower unemployment shown in Figure 18–16? This is not a question that can be answered with any assurance. The answer hinges on the same three issues we isolated before when considering anti-inflation policy:

1. *The social costs of inflation and unemployment*. Those who regard inflation as very costly will not want to pay the price of shortening the recession. Those who are more concerned with unemployment will find recession-fighting a good idea.

2. *The position of the economy*. As we have noted, the Phillips curve is likely to be flatter at higher rates of unemployment. As you can see by studying Figure 18–12, if the Phillips curve is rather flat, the extra inflation caused by fighting a recession will be minimal. On the other hand, if the short-run Phillips curve is steep, the inflationary price tag will be high. Thus the case for fighting deep recessions is stronger than the case for fighting shallow ones.

3. *The efficiency of the economy's self-correcting mechanism*. Naturally, if the economy's self-corrective forces worked rapidly, there would be little reason for the government to try to speed things up. On the other hand, if the mechanism is slow and unreliable or, worse yet, if it breaks down entirely, the case for government intervention is much stronger.

Why Economists (and Politicians) Disagree

These three factors help explain why economists sometimes differ so radically from one another in their recommendations as to the proper conduct of national economic policy. And they also help account for disagreements among politicians.

The question is: When a recession occurs, should the government take actions to bring it to a rapid end? You will say *yes* if you believe that (1) unemployment is more costly than inflation, (2) the short-run Phillips curve is rather flat, and (3) the economy's self-correcting mechanism—which works as unemployment slows the rate of growth of wages—is slow and unreliable. These views on the economy tend to be associated with economists of the Keynesian school and with the (generally liberal) politicians who listen to them.

But you will say *no* if you believe that (1) inflation is more costly than unemployment, (2) the short-run Phillips curve is quite steep, and (3) the self-correcting mechanism works smoothly and quickly. These views are held by most monetarists and rational expectationists, so it is not surprising that the (generally conservative) politicians who follow their advice typically oppose strong measures to fight recessions.

The tables turn, however, when the question is whether or not to use policy to fight inflation. The Keynesian view of the world—that unemployment is costly, that the short-run Phillips curve is flat, and that the self-correcting mechanism is unreliable—leads to the conclusion that the costs of fighting inflation are high while the benefits are low. The monetarist and rational-expectationist positions on these three issues are just the reverse, and so are the policy conclusions.

Supply-Side Inflation and the Phillips Curve

Let us now return to the question posed early in the chapter: Why did the Phillips curve, which worked reasonably well in the 1950s and 1960s, seem to fall apart in the 1970s? (It may be useful to refer back to Figure 18–10 on page 343 to see the

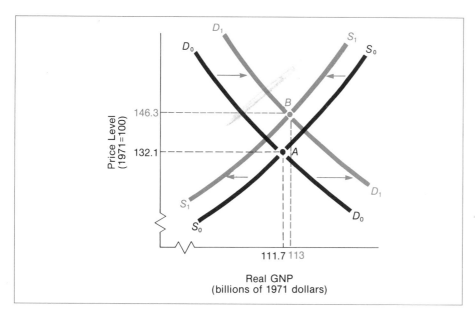

Figure 18-18
STAGFLATION FROM A
SUPPLY SHOCK
Instead of shifting outward as it
normally does, the aggregate-
supply curve shifted inward—from
S_0S_0 to S_1S_1—between 1974 and
1975. Coupled with some growth
of the aggregate-demand curve—
from D_0D_0 in 1974 to D_1D_1 in
1975—equilibrium moved from
point A to point B. There was only
a very slight increase in real
output, and prices rose rapidly.

evidence.) The analysis that we have provided in this chapter so far gives one answer: Economists and policy-makers at that time mistakenly viewed the Phillips curve as a menu of *long-run* policy choices. Wanting to lower unemployment, the government adopted policies that pushed the economy up the Phillips curve. But, as we know, unemployment rates below the natural rate are not sustainable, and these policy-makers got much more inflation than they had bargained for.

There is another answer that operates along with the first effect. This answer is that some of the inflation of the 1970s did not emanate from the demand side. Instead, the 1970s contained adverse "supply shocks," events that pushed the economy's aggregate-supply curve inward, to the left. What kind of Phillips curve will be generated when economic fluctuations come from the supply side?

Figure 18-2 already gives us the answer: The price level increases, and real output falls. Falling output means fewer jobs available, so unemployment increases. Thus:

If fluctuations in economic activity emanate mainly from the supply side, higher rates of inflation will be associated with higher rates of unemployment, and lower rates of inflation will be associated with lower rates of unemployment.

There were numerous supply shocks during the 1970s. Food prices boomed between 1972 and 1974 and again in 1978. World energy prices soared in 1973–74 and again in 1979–80. The Canadian government shielded our economy from some of these shocks (as we discussed in Chapter 10), but we were not completely insulated. The government also increased aggregate demand in reaction to these shocks, in an attempt to keep unemployment from rising. The combined effect of the supply-side shock and the expansion in aggregate demand can be clarified by considering a specific example. In Figure 18–18, aggregate-demand curve D_0D_0 and aggregate-supply curve S_0S_0 represent the economic situation in 1974. Equilibrium was at point A, with a price level of 132.1 and real output of $111.7 billion. In 1974, OPEC raised the world price of oil by a factor of four. The Canadian price of oil increased but not to this extent. As a result, instead of shifting to the *right* as it normally does from one year to the next, the aggregate-supply curve shifted to the *left* during 1974, to S_1S_1.

By 1975, the aggregate-demand curve had shifted out to the position indicated by D_1D_1. The equilibrium for 1975 (point B in the figure), therefore wound up almost vertically above the equilibrium point for 1974. Real output only increased slightly. Prices rose rapidly (10.7 percent).

Now, in a growing population with more people looking for jobs each year, a stagnant economy that is not generating new jobs will suffer a rise in the unemployment rate. This is precisely what happened in Canada; the unemployment rate averaged 5.4 percent in 1974 and 6.9 percent in 1975. Thus the inflation rate and the unemployment rate increased at the same time. The Phillips curve was upward sloping! We conclude that a model involving both demand-side *and* supply-side inflation shocks can easily explain our unemployment and inflation experience since 1970.

The Dilemma of Demand Management

We have just learned that when inflation comes from the supply side, inflation and unemployment will be *positively* associated: We will suffer from more of both or enjoy less of each. Does this mean that monetary and fiscal policy-makers can escape the trade-off between inflation and unemployment? Certainly not.

Adverse shifts in the aggregate-supply curve can cause both inflation and unemployment to rise together and thus can destroy the Phillips curve relationship. Nevertheless, anything that monetary and fiscal policy can do will make unemployment and inflation move in opposite directions. The reason is that monetary and fiscal policy only gives the government control over the *aggregate-demand* curve, not the *aggregate-supply* curve. If the government stimulates demand to cut down on unemployment, it will make inflation worse; if it restricts demand to fight inflation, it will increase unemployment.

Thus, no matter what the source of inflation, and no matter what happens to the Phillips curve, the makers of monetary and fiscal policy must still face up to the disagreeable trade-off between inflation and unemployment. This is a principle that many policy-makers have failed to recognize and one of the **12 Ideas** that we hope you will remember well **Beyond the Final Exam**.

Naturally, the unpleasant nature of this trade-off has led to a vigorous search for a way out of the dilemma. Both economists and public officials have sought a policy that might offer improvements on both fronts simultaneously, or that might ease the pain of either unemployment or inflation. The next chapter will consider some of these ideas.

Summary

1. Inflation can be caused either by rapid growth of aggregate demand or by sluggish growth of aggregate supply.

2. When fluctuations in economic activity emanate from the demand side, prices will rise rapidly when real output grows rapidly. Since rapid growth means more jobs, unemployment and inflation will be inversely related.

3. This inverse relationship between unemployment and inflation is called the Phillips curve. It explains Canadian data for the 1950s and 1960s rather well but fails miserably to account for the 1970s.

4. One reason for this failure is that the Phillips curve was misinterpreted as a menu of *long-run* policy choices for the economy. This view is incorrect because the economy's self-correcting mechanism guarantees that neither an inflationary gap nor a recessionary gap can last indefinitely.

5. Because of the self-correcting mechanism, the economy's true long-run choices lie along a *vertical* Phillips curve, which shows that the so-called *natural rate of unemployment* is the only unemployment rate that can persist indefinitely.

6. In the short run, the economy can move up or down its short-run Phillips curve. *Temporary* reductions in unemployment can be achieved at the cost of higher inflation. Similarly, *temporary* increases in unemployment can be used to fight inflation.

7. Whether it is advisable to use unemployment to fight inflation depends on three principal factors: The relative social costs of inflation versus unemployment; the efficiency of the economy's self-correcting mechanism; and the current position of the economy (which influences the shape of the short-run trade-off between inflation and unemployment).

8. Since controversy surrounds each of these three factors, both economists and politicians often disagree on the proper conduct of stabilization policy.

9. If workers expect inflation to occur, and if they demand (and receive) compensation for inflation, output will be independent of the price level. Both the aggregate-supply curve and the short-run Phillips curve are vertical in this case.

10. However, errors in predicting inflation will still change real wages and hence will still change the quantity of output that firms wish to supply. Thus, *unpredicted* movements in the price level will lead to the normal sort of upward-sloping aggregate-supply curve.

11. According to the doctrine of rational expectations, errors in predicting inflation will be purely random. This, means that, except for some random (and uncontrollable) gyrations, the aggregate-supply curve is vertical even in the short run.

12. Many economists reject the rational expectations view of the world. Some deny that expectations are "rational," and believe instead that people tend, for example, to underpredict inflation when it is rising. Others point out that contracts signed years ago cannot possibly embody expectations that are "rational" in terms of what we know today.

13. When fluctuations in economic activity are caused by shifts of the aggregate-supply curve, output will grow slowly (causing unemployment to rise) when inflation speeds up. Hence, the rates of unemployment and inflation will be positively related.

14. Many observers feel that the adverse supply shifts during the 1970s help explain why the Phillips curve collapsed.

15. Even if inflation is initiated by supply-side problems, so that inflation and unemployment occur together, the monetary and fiscal authorities still face this trade-off: Anything they do to improve unemployment is likely to worsen inflation, and anything they do to reduce inflation is likely to aggravate unemployment. The reason is that monetary and fiscal policy mainly influences the aggregate-demand curve, not the aggregate-supply curve. This is one of our **12 Ideas for Beyond the Final Exam**.

Concepts for Review

Demand-side inflation
Supply-side inflation
Phillips curve
Self-correcting mechanism
Natural rate of unemployment

Vertical (long-run) Phillips curve
Trade-offs between unemployment
    and inflation in the short run
    and in the long run
Inflationary expectations

Rational expectations
Stagflation caused by supply
    shocks

Questions for Discussion

1. Some observers during the 1970s claimed that policy-makers no longer faced a trade-off between inflation and unemployment. Why did they think this? Were they correct?

2. "There is no sense in trying to shorten recessions through fiscal and monetary policies because the effects of these policies on the unemployment rate are sure to be temporary." Comment on both the truth of this statement and its relevance for policy formulation.

3. Why is the economy's self-correcting mechanism more efficient at eliminating inflationary gaps than it is at eliminating recessionary gaps?

4. Why is it said that decisions on fiscal and monetary policy are, at least in part, political decisions that cannot be made on "objective" economic criteria?

5. Does the economy have a recessionary gap or an inflationary gap today? What should be done about this? What facts would you want to know in preparing an answer to this question?

6. What is a "Phillips curve"? Why did it seem to work so much better in the 1950s and 1960s than it did in the 1970s?

7. Explain the dilemma that policy-makers face when there is an episode of supply inflation. What would you recommend if there were a severe bout of supply inflation today?

8. Why do expectations about inflation affect the wages resulting from labour–management bargaining?

9. What is meant by "rational" expectations? Why does the doctrine of rational expectations have such stunning implications for economic policy? Would believers in rational expectations want to shorten a recession by expanding aggregate demand? Would they want to fight inflation by reducing aggregate demand?

10. Show that, if the economy's aggregate-supply curve is vertical, fluctuations in the growth of aggregate demand produce only fluctuations in inflation with no effect on output. Relate this to your answer to the previous question.

Further Controversies Over Stabilization Policy

19

Where there is much desire to learn, there of necessity will be much arguing.

JOHN MILTON

We have pointed out that stabilization-policy decisions are inherently political and, as a consequence, are usually immersed in controversy. Several of these controversies were examined in the preceding chapters, and we now turn our attention to two others.

In the first part of the chapter, we investigate a number of suggestions that have been offered to improve the trade-off between inflation and unemployment or, better yet, to eliminate it entirely. Some of these plans have actually been tried; others are still untested ideas. They range from governmental exhortations to hold down inflation to outright prohibition of wage or price increases. They include efforts to improve the functioning of labour markets, plans to enlist the tax system in the battle against inflation, and institutional changes designed to rob inflation of its social costs. Although each of these ideas is worthy of consideration, we must emphasize in advance that all are controversial and none is a panacea.

The second part of the chapter turns to an even more fundamental question: Should the government conduct any stabilization policy at all? Much that we have said in earlier chapters seems to indicate that it should. But, as we shall see, there are several important factors that point in the opposite direction—factors that we have not yet considered. These factors lead a number of economists, many of them monetarists, to conclude that it is unwise to try to stabilize the economy through monetary and fiscal policy.

Can We Improve the Trade-Off Between Inflation and Unemployment?

In the last chapter, we learned that one way to fight inflation is to create economic slack by slowing the growth of aggregate demand; that is, to use recession to fight inflation. Though it is a genuine alternative, politicians react to it somewhat like children react to spinach. For, in addition to its obvious economic costs, fighting inflation by causing unemployment is politically unpopular.

Because of the agonizing nature of the Phillips curve trade-off, economists and politicians have been searching for years for policies that promise to improve the terms of the trade-off a bit. Since the long-run Phillips curve is believed to be approximately vertical, such policy initiatives in effect seek to *reduce the natural rate of unemployment.*

Attempts to Reduce the Natural Rate of Unemployment

One class of policies that attempts to reduce the natural rate of unemployment is vocational training and retraining programs. When successful, they help unemployed workers with obsolete skills acquire abilities that are currently in demand. In doing so, they help alleviate upward pressures on wage rates in jobs where qualified workers are in short supply. For example, if an unemployed steelworker is taught to assemble computers, then progress is made against both inflation and unemployment, since one former steelworker leaves the ranks of the unemployed while one new worker helps alleviate the shortage of skilled labour in the computer industry.

Although the idea sounds appealing and has attracted many adherents, successes achieved through training programs have, in practice, been rather limited. Too often, people are trained for jobs that do not exist by the time they finish their training—if indeed they ever existed. Even when successful, these programs are quite expensive, which restricts the number of workers that can be accommodated. Despite these difficulties, revised versions of these retraining schemes continue to be developed. A recent scheme is the National Training Program, introduced in August 1982.

The Canada Employment Centres also try to improve the match of workers to jobs but not by retraining workers. Instead, they seek to funnel information from prospective employers to prospective employees. Firms are encouraged to list their job vacancies with the centres and to inspect the centres' lists of people looking for work. Unemployed workers, or people wanting to change jobs, are encouraged to register with the Canada Employment Centres and to study its lists of openings. In this way, it is hoped, the simultaneous occurrence of unemployed workers and unfilled jobs will be reduced.

The centres also co-ordinate recent initiatives such as the New Employment Expansion Development (NEED) program, and other direct job-creation schemes, which are intended to provide jobs for persons whose unemployment insurance has run out. The federal government also operates the Industry and Labour Adjustment Program (ILAP), which pays two-thirds of workers' former wages (after their unemployment insurance has expired—until retirement if necessary) if the workers are over 45 years of age and have been released by declining, low-productivity industries. This experimental program may be a useful way to raise aggregate productivity, since it is a substitute for continually propping up industries in which Canada is not competitive.

Another federal government program aimed at reducing frictional unemployment is one involving relocation grants. If the unemployed live in one province and job vacancies occur in others, the government moving allowance permits the family to move and therefore to take the job. Some analysts argue that other grants to high-unemployment regions tend to cancel out the effectiveness of the moving allowances. While it may not be due to any government programs, it is noteworthy that Newfoundland, Prince Edward Island, and Nova Scotia all experienced net immigration during the 1970s.

Despite the many government programs that are aimed at improving the functioning of the labour market, unemployment insurance still represents the major commitment of funds. During the 1982–83 fiscal year, the government spent $9.7 billion on unemployment insurance and $1.6 billion on all other job creation, training, and related employment services.

While these government programs are intended to improve the Phillips curve, many other schemes—such as government regulations ranging from agricultural price supports, to control of airline-passenger fares, to requirements that trucks return empty after delivering their loads—have been criticized on the grounds that they make prices higher at any given level of unemployment. Over recent years many of these government interferences with free-market processes have come under vigorous verbal assault, with the result that some deregulation has now occurred in the airline, trucking, and telecommunications industries.

An added impetus for deregulation in Canada has been provided by the Reagan administration in the United States, which made deregulation one of its top priorities. It has deregulated the airline and telecommunications industries, expedited the demise of price controls on energy products, halted the rise of the minimum wage, and generally reduced the amount of red tape imposed on businesses.[1] It has also sparked several acrimonious debates by slackening federal enforcement efforts in the areas of environmental protection and occupational health and safety.

Incomes Policy

Yet another way to improve the trade-off, an approach that has been tried intermittently in Canada, is **incomes policy**. As practised in this country during the last 20 years, incomes policy has run the gamut from verbal admonitions all the way to outright prohibition of wage and price increases beyond a certain guideline (in the 1975–78 period). In some foreign countries that rely upon incomes policy more heavily than we do, a still more bewildering variety of alternative measures has emerged. Indeed, there may be only one common thread linking these disparate policies: No hard evidence exists that any of them has succeeded *permanently* in improving the trade-off between unemployment and inflation. Note that the emphasis here is on the word "permanently," for many attempts at incomes policy—including some in this country—have had temporary success.

The Canadian 1975–78 episode stands out as perhaps the most successful use of incomes policy ever tried in a Western economy since World War II. All studies show that our controls program lessened the magnitude of the temporary increases in unemployment that accompanied the contractionary aggregate-demand policy at the time. The reason for the relative success of the Canadian experience is given later in this chapter.

Incomes policy is a generic term used to describe a wide variety of measures aimed at curbing inflation *without* reducing aggregate demand.

Jawboning

The mildest form of incomes policy is commonly referred to as **jawboning**. The term is descriptive. It is meant to conjure up in your mind an image of the Prime Minister's Office communicating directly with corporate executives, applying pressure to limit price increases deemed to be contrary to the national interest. Since corporate executives may feel somewhat threatened under these circumstances, jawboning has occasionally enjoyed some success.

The main argument in favour of jawboning is that it is a relatively painless way to try to improve the trade-off between inflation and unemployment. Large corporations, it is argued, have the market power to raise prices even when price rises are not justified by cost increases. But, since these corporate giants are also very conscious of their public-relations images, proponents of jawboning argue, why not use the prestige of the federal government to dissuade them from exercising their market power?

Opponents of jawboning respond that market power, which undoubtedly exists, can explain *high* prices. But why, they ask, would a firm with market power wait until this month to raise prices when it could have done so last month, or the month before? They answer that large corporations raise prices only when changes

Jawboning refers to informal pressures on firms and unions to slow down the rates at which prices and wages are rising.

[1] For a full discussion of regulation and deregulation, see *Microeconomics*, Chapter 15.

in demand or cost considerations make it profitable to do so, not because they have a residue of unused market power. Furthermore, there is an inevitable element of inequity in jawboning. By its very nature it must be discriminatory, picking on some firms while letting others go scot-free.

On balance, a fair assessment of jawboning would probably conclude that it does little good and little harm.

Wage–Price Guidelines

The next step up from jawboning is the establishment of an official standard for "permissible" rates of increase in wages and prices. This was the Canadian approach in the late 1960s, when the Prices and Incomes Commission was set up. However, lacking any enforcement mechanism, there was no chance that the **wage-price guidelines** could be effective in the face of the excessive aggregate demand that characterized this period.[2]

The logic behind guidelines is both simple and compelling. In an ideally functioning economy, if worker productivity rises by 2 percent a year, then wages can rise by 2 percent a year with no increase in costs or prices. Alternatively, wages can increase at a 4 percent annual rate while prices rise at 2 percent a year, and so on. In general, price inflation proceeds at a rate roughly 2 percentage points below wage inflation. A set of wage–price guidelines is obtained by picking a target rate of inflation, say 4 percent a year, and adding 2 percent to get a consistent target for wage increases—6 percent in this example. The government then announces that (a) wage increases that exceed this standard will be deemed "inflationary," (b) firms enjoying productivity increases faster than the national average are expected to raise their prices more slowly than 4 percent a year while, (c) firms obtaining sub-par productivity improvements are allowed to have higher-than-average price increases so that, (d) the overall price level can increase at a rate of 4 percent a year.

As noted, guidelines are quite logical. The problem comes in deciding what to do if some union or corporation violates them. Experience shows that voluntarism goes only so far when economic self-interest is threatened. If the government responds by jawboning we are back to the first type of incomes policy, but with one important difference. The uniformity of the guidelines means that the firms or unions singled out for public scrutiny earned that status. Official guidelines remove much of the element of capriciousness from an *ad hoc* jawboning policy. An alternative approach is to give the guidelines the force of law, which brings us to the next variety of incomes policy.

Wage–Price Controls

Once the government is given the legal authority to *force* labour and industry to adhere to a set of guidelines, we have moved to a system of mandatory **wage-price controls**. Canada used such a policy during World War II and during the 1975–78 period, when the Anti-Inflation Board (AIB) was in existence.

A major justification for controls is that inflation gathers substantial momentum once workers, consumers, and business managers begin to expect that it will continue. **Inflationary expectations** encourage workers to demand higher wage increases. Firms, in turn, are willing to grant the workers' demands because they believe they will be able to pass the cost increases on to consumers in a general inflationary environment. Consumers contribute their part to the shell game by purchasing durable goods ahead of their needs in anticipation of higher prices in the future, an action that increases demand and helps fuel the inflation engine. Thus, to a great extent, *inflation occurs because people expect it to occur.*

---

[2] By mid-1969, Prime Minister Trudeau gave up on the Commission and tried a contractionary monetary policy to solve inflation. However, this was attempted during a fixed exchange-rate period—a policy error that we described in Chapter 15.

Wage-price guidelines are numerical standards for permissible wage and price increases.

Wage-price controls are legal restrictions on the ability of industry and labour to raise wages and prices.

In terms of our aggregate supply and demand analysis, inflationary expectations shift the aggregate-supply curve upward because workers insist on—and get—higher money wages to compensate them for the coming inflation.[3] Phrased in terms of the Phillips curve, this means that *inflationary expectations shift the Phillips curve upward*, so that any given rate of unemployment corresponds to a higher rate of inflation.

This analysis provides the best intellectual case for controls. A tough and thorough program of wage and price controls, it is argued, can break the vicious cycle of inflationary expectations. By announcing a controls program, the government serves notice on workers that they do not need anticipatory wage increases to preserve their purchasing power. Firms are warned that they may not be able to pass on higher costs to consumers. And consumers may conclude that buying now to beat future price increases is a poor strategy. By breaking inflationary expectations, supporters argue, a controls program can shift the Phillips curve down and reduce the rate of inflation. Under the right conditions, this argument may be correct. However, many economists question whether this line of reasoning is generally valid. For example, it may be that astute workers, business executives, and consumers realize that no controls program can remain in force forever—at least not in a free-market economy like ours. They may then view the temporary dip in the inflation rate caused by controls as an aberration soon to be corrected and therefore not as a major event that warrants changing their long-term expectations.

Why cannot wage–price controls be a permanent feature of the Canadian economy? We learned the answer to this back in Chapter 4. When price ceilings are effective, they force the price below the equilibrium price, so that quantity demanded exceeds quantity supplied. This is shown in Figure 19–1, where the equilibrium price of hamburgers is assumed to be $1. If controls do not allow the price of hamburgers to rise above 75¢, quantity demanded will exceed quantity supplied by one million hamburgers.

With price no longer serving as the rationing device, some other method of rationing is necessary. One possibility is long lines of eager eaters waiting their turn for hamburgers. Scenes like this are quite typical in the Soviet Union and were witnessed in the United States at gas stations during 1979, when gasoline

[3]To review this idea, refer back to pages 349–51 in Chapter 18.

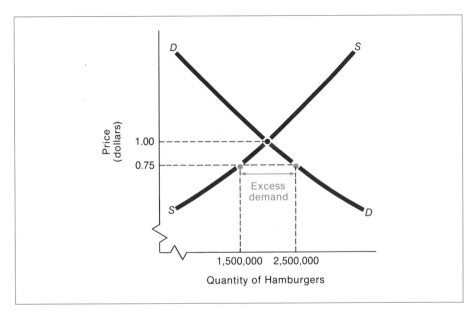

Figure 19-1
THE EFFECTS OF PRICE CONTROLS
This diagram portrays the market for hamburgers under an effective price-control system. Since the equilibrium price is $1 per hamburger, a regulation that holds the price at 75¢ makes the quantity of hamburgers demanded (2,500,000 per year) exceed the quantity supplied (1,500,000 per year). There is a shortage of one million hamburgers per year, and some sort of rationing scheme probably will be necessary.

was in short supply. Another is government ration coupons, giving the owner the right to buy a hamburger—a device used successfully for many goods during World War II. Neither of these measures is likely to be popular with the electorate in peacetime. And both are likely to spawn a black market, which erodes respect for law and order at the same time that it abrogates the effects of controls. As critics of controls are fond of pointing out, controls give law-abiding citizens an incentive to become criminals by participating in illicit black-market activities.

And the problems spawned by price controls go deeper than this. Among the principal factors determining the equilibrium price of hamburgers are the prices of various raw agricultural commodities such as beef. But prices of raw agricultural commodities cannot be controlled by the government because they are so dependent on the weather and other acts of nature. If price controls hold the price of hamburgers at 75¢ while the price of beef skyrockets, it may become unprofitable to sell hamburgers. If so, firms will start leaving the hamburger industry.

With hamburgers unavailable, consumers will increase their purchases of others goods, thereby putting upward pressure on the prices of goods such as fish and soybeans. Thus, price controls on hamburgers will cause the hamburger industry to contract and necessitate additional price controls on fish and soybeans. And so it goes. Each extension of price controls to a new commodity requires additional controls to support it, in a never-ending chain. Thus, for price controls to be effective, they must be nearly universal—which is, of course, next to impossible.

This analysis also explains why wage and price controls have almost always failed to work. Most governments who used controls (for example, the British during the 1960s and 1970s) saw them as "solving" the inflation problem and thereby freeing monetary and fiscal policy to be used without restraint for achieving employment objectives. As a result, aggregate-demand policy and incomes policy were often inconsistent. Monetary and fiscal policy pushed demand curves to the right, while the incomes policy made it unlawful for the prices to adjust to equilibrium. Most analysts have likened these policy episodes to putting a pot of water on the stove and trying to wire on the lid while the burner is turned on high. Little steam emerges for a while but eventually it all blasts out. This is exactly what happened with the many European experiments with controls, and with the Nixon controls in the United States. Lower inflation rates prevailed while the controls were in effect, but these were counterbalanced by higher inflation rates during the year or so after controls were lifted. Instead of improving the trade-off, the controls just managed to increase the *variability* of inflation. In Chapter 6 we pointed out that the *variability* of inflation often exacts more serious social costs than the *average level*. In this sense, then, these control programs were counter productive, and this is why most economists say that they "failed."

The Canadian AIB experiment avoided this problem to some degree, since it was imposed as a *complement* to, not a *substitute for*, contractionary aggregate-demand policy. During this period, the government used monetary and fiscal policy to limit the rightward shifts of demand curves, and the controls were only intended to shorten the lags in the downward revision of inflationary expectations.

Wage–Price Freezes

A **wage-price freeze** is an outright ban on wage or price increases.

An extreme case of mandatory controls is a **wage-price freeze**—a statute making it illegal to increase wages or prices above their levels on some specified date. Nixon ushered in his U.S. controls program with a three-month freeze beginning in mid-August 1971. Such an action cannot be considered a constructive incomes policy; it is meant to be a shock treatment—a dramatic action intended to break inflationary expectations. A wage–price freeze also gives an administration contemplating controls some breathing space to plan a rational program. Nothing could be worse than letting people know today that a controls program is on the way. News reports that a controls program *may* begin can cause price increases just in case. According to the U.S. Secretary of the Treasury an epidemic of rumours of impending controls forced President Nixon's hand in 1971.

Incomes Policies in the Future

There are many problems with incomes policies. They limit relative price adjustments and so diminish the effectiveness of the market mechanism for allocating scarce resources. It is difficult to command lasting commitment for an incomes policy when the freedoms of individuals and firms are curtailed and when import prices cannot be controlled. Furthermore, since wage rates are easier to control than managerial salaries or prices, many feel that controls hurt the real income position of the lower-income groups. Also, the administrative costs become horrendous the longer the controls are left in place.

One implementation issue in Canada is a constitutional one. Before the AIB, most economists and lawyers regarded a wage-and-price-control scheme imposed by the federal government as illegal. The BNA Act stipulates that provincial governments have the power to oversee the setting of domestic wages. Because of this, and because the AIB was expected to control wages more effectively than prices, organized labour tested the legality of the AIB in the Supreme Court. The only possible argument the federal government could give for the legality of the AIB was that Canada faced a "national emergency" without it. (The constitution provides a justification for virtually any federal government action, if this claim can be sustained.)

The analysis submitted to the Supreme Court showed that no emergency existed, in the sense that Canada's inflation was not extraordinary by historical standards, nor when compared to that of other countries. Nor was there a crisis in the sense that alternative anti-inflation policies did not exist. Nevertheless, the Supreme Court ruled that while an emergency may not have existed in 1975, one would exist if the controls were lifted before their intended expiry date. It would seem that legal precedent now exists for the future wage–price control programs.

While the economics profession maintains a healthy skepticism about inordinate reliance on incomes policies, the general public seems more optimistic. When a Gallup poll released in April 1982 indicated that a majority of Canadians favoured wage and price controls, the federal government responded with the "6 and 5" program in the June 1982 budget. This program limited wage increases in the public sector to 6 percent for the first year and 5 percent in the second year. Also, the program involved a form of jawboning, as government contracts only went to firms who respected the 6 and 5 guidelines in their wage settlements. It is difficult to know whether the 6 and 5 program made any significant addition to the effect of the severe recession on lowering inflation during the early 1980s. Nevertheless, incomes policies seem to command much general acceptance, despite administrative and other costs.

Primarily because of the resource-misallocation problems, many economists oppose incomes policies. They agree with the summary of incomes policies given by the famous Canadian economist Harry Johnson, who likened incomes policies to a farmer's attempts to make his donkey behave. The policy always begins as gentle ear-stroking but seems eventually to turn into ear-twisting and then attempts to grope for more sensitive parts of the animal.

A more constructive incomes policy is one that does not try to force the donkey to ignore its private interest but to change the signals facing the donkey so that its private interest and the public interest coincide. This is the idea behind tax-based incomes policies.

Tax-Based Incomes Policy

Tax-based incomes policy uses the tax system to provide incentives favouring non-inflationary behaviour.

Advocated originally by Governor Henry Wallich of the U.S. Federal Reserve System, Professor Sidney Weintraub of the University of Pennsylvania, and the late Arthur Okun of the Brookings Institution in Washington, **tax-based incomes policy (TIP)** seeks to use the tax system to fight inflation. The idea behind TIP is simple, though its implementation might be quite complex in practice. TIP would give employers and employees a financial stake in fighting inflation by lowering taxes for firms or workers who abided by national guidelines for wage–price behaviour, or by raising taxes for those who violated them.

While there are many TIP plans, one particular example will bring out the flavour of all of them. Suppose the government wants to limit wage increases to 5 percent a year. It could pass legislation granting a 2 percent *decrease* in payroll taxes to all employees of firms in which average wages increased by no more than 5 percent. Then, for example, workers who settled for a (non-inflationary) 4½ percent raise would actually wind up with *more* after-tax income than those who settled for an (inflationary) 6 percent raise. They would get 4½ percent more from their employers, plus 2 percent more from the government in the form of lower taxes, for a total gain of 6½ percent. This incentive, it is hoped, would lead labour and management to settle for slower growth in wages; and these slower wage increases, in turn, would lead to slower price increases.

Other TIP plans focus on corporation taxes rather than on payroll taxes, or utilize the "stick" rather than the "carrot" by penalizing the violators of the wage–price guidelines rather than rewarding those who obey. But the basic goal is always the same: to make non-inflationary behaviour profitable for either firms or workers, or both.

Is TIP workable? We really have no way of knowing because it has never been tried. In 1978, President Carter asked the U.S. Congress to enact a modified version of TIP, but Congress never gave the idea serious consideration. The Economic Council of Canada has suggested that TIPs warrant further study.

Making Wages More Flexible

Other countries seem to have had success in eliminating some of the downward inflexibility in wage rates. This makes the economy's self-correcting mechanism work faster, so that anti-inflation policy involves a smaller and less prolonged recession. For example, the West Germans have a "concerted-effort program," which involves regular discussions between unions, firms, and the government. The intention is to reach a consensus on how income can be divided up without inflation. For example, if all participants agree that a recession is coming, slower wage-and-price growth can be agreed upon *in advance*, thereby lessening the recession.

Japan provides another example, which the Canadian government considered within the "gain-sharing" proposals of the 1984 Federal Budget. Workers in Japan receive a regular wage plus a bonus every six months that is geared to the employer's profits. Since profits are high in the good years, but very low during recessions, this system makes total wages go up and down dramatically over the cycle, too. The much lower wages during the recession result in fewer job losses.

Indexing

Indexing refers to provisions in a law or a contract whereby monetary payments are automatically adjusted whenever a specified price index changes. Wage rates, pensions, interest payments on bonds, income taxes, and many other things can be indexed in this way, and have been. Sometimes such contractual provisions are called *escalator clauses*.

A very different approach to the inflation–unemployment dilemma is **indexing**. Indexing refers to provisions in a law or a contract whereby monetary payments are automatically adjusted whenever a specified price index changes. The idea behind indexing is to lessen the magnitude of the temporary recession that results from standard contractionary aggregate-demand policies, and to reduce the social costs of inflation at the same time.

The mechanics of indexing can be explained best through an example. In Canada the most common form of indexed contract is an *escalator clause* in a wage agreement. An escalator clause provides for an automatic increase in money wages—without the need for new contract negotiations—any time the price level rises by more than a specified amount. Suppose that with the Consumer Price Index (CPI) sitting at 300, a union and a firm agree on a three-year contract setting wages at $7 per hour this year, $8 next year, and $9 in the third year. They might then add an escalator clause stating that wages will be increased above these stipulated amounts by 5 cents per hour for each point by which the CPI exceeds 330 in any future year of the contract. Then, if the CPI in year three of the contract reaches 340, workers will receive an additional 50 cents per hour (5 cents for each of the 10 points by which 340 exceeds 330), for a total wage of $9.50 per hour. In this way, workers are partly protected from inflation. Nowadays, more than half of all workers employed by large unionized firms in Canada are covered by some sort of escalator or cost-of-living clause.

Interest payments on bonds or savings accounts can also be indexed, although this is not currently done in Canada.[4] The mechanics here are quite simple. If you had an indexed savings account, your bank might guarantee you a 1 percent *real interest rate* on your savings by automatically increasing your balance by the amount of inflation. For example, suppose you deposited $1000 on January 1 and withdrew it on December 31. An ordinary savings account, paying 6 percent interest, would pay you $1060 at the end of the year—your original $1000 plus 6 percent interest. But if this were an indexed bank account paying 1 percent, and prices rose by 10 percent during the year, your balance at year-end would be $1110—your original $1000 plus 1 percent real interest ($10) plus 10 percent ($100) to compensate you for your loss of purchasing power. The *nominal interest rate* would thus be 11 percent.[5] In general, the nominal rate would be 1 percent *plus* the rate of inflation. Thus, if inflation turned out to be less than 5 percent that year, you would receive less than $1060.

Indexing is not designed to keep interest rates *high*, but to make real interest payments independent of inflation—to cut down the chances that the purchasing power of savings will be eroded by inflation.

With a conventional 6 percent savings account you get a real interest rate of 6 percent if there is zero inflation, 2 percent if there is 4 percent inflation, –2 percent if there is 8 percent inflation, and so on. With an imaginary 1 percent indexed account, you would receive 1 percent real interest no matter what the inflation rate. Indexing thus enables the saver to avoid gambling on inflation. For this reason, some economists have advocated that the Canadian government issue an indexed savings bond that small savers could use to protect themselves against inflation. This idea was proposed by Conservative leader Robert Stanfield in the early 1970s, but the government opted for the arbitrary $1000 interest-income exemption instead. While the personal deduction and tax bracket cut-offs in the personal income-tax system have been indexed since 1973, the interest-income exemption is not indexed. Thus its real value has shrunk dramatically over the last decade.

Indexing and the Social Costs of Inflation

The most extensive government use of indexing to be found in Canada today is in transfer payments and the personal income-tax system. Canada Pension Plan

---

[4]Some other countries, with much higher inflation than ours, do extensive indexing of interest rates. Brazil and Israel are notable examples.

[5]The distinction between real and nominal interest rates, one of our 12 Ideas for Beyond the Final Exam, was discussed in detail in Chapter 6.

benefits are fully indexed so that retirees are not victimized by inflation. A variety of government income-maintenance and social-insurance programs also pay benefits that are tied directly to prices. Some economists believe that Canada should adopt a much more widespread system of indexing. Why? Because, they argue, it would take most of the sting out of inflation. To see how indexing would accomplish this, let us review some of the social costs of inflation that we enumerated in Chapter 6.

One important cost is the capricious redistribution of income caused by unexpected inflation or deflation. We saw that borrowers and lenders normally incorporate an *inflation premium* equal to the *expected rate of inflation* into the nominal interest rate. Then, if inflation turns out to be higher than expected, the borrower has to pay to the lender only the agreed-upon nominal interest rate, including the premium for expected inflation; he does not have to compensate the lender for the (higher) actual inflation. Thus the borrower enjoys a windfall gain and the lender loses out. The opposite happens if inflation turns out to be lower than was expected. Again the borrower pays the lender the agreed-upon nominal interest rate, but now his rate includes an inflation premium that overcompensates the lender for the actual inflation. But if interest rates on loans were indexed, none of this would occur. Borrowers and lenders would agree on a fixed *real* rate of interest, and then the borrower would compensate the lender for whatever *actual inflation* occurred. No one would have to guess what the inflation rate would be.

A second social cost we mentioned in Chapter 6 stems from the fact that our tax system levies taxes on nominal interest and nominal capital gains. As we learned, this flaw in the tax system leads to extremely high effective tax rates in an inflationary environment. But indexing could fix this problem easily. We need only rewrite the tax code so that only real interest payments and real capital gains are taxed.

A final problem noted in Chapter 6 is that uncertainty over future price levels makes it difficult to enter into long-term contracts—rental agreements, construction agreements, and so on. One way out of this problem is to write indexed contracts, which specify all future payments in real terms.

In the face of all these benefits, and others we have not mentioned here, why do many economists oppose a move toward more complete indexing? One reason is the fear that indexing will lead to an acceleration of inflation. With the costs of inflation reduced so markedly, they argue, what will persuade governments to pay the price of fighting inflation? What will stop them from inflating more and more? They fear that the answer to these questions is, Nothing. Voters who stand to lose nothing from inflation are unlikely to pressure their legislators to stop it. Opponents of indexing worry that a mild inflationary disease could turn into a ravaging epidemic in a highly indexed economy. Hyperinflation often involves dramatic political changes.

Can We Conduct a Successful Stabilization Policy?

It seems fitting to conclude Part Three by considering what may be the most fundamental and controversial issue of all: Is it likely that the government can conduct a successful stabilization policy? Or are its well-intentioned efforts likely to be harmful, so that it would be better to adhere to *fixed rules*?

This controversy has raged for several decades now, with no clear resolution of the issue. Often the protagonists in the debate have been monetarists arguing for fixed rules, against Keynesians arguing for discretionary adjustments of policy.

Monetarists point to the lags and uncertainties that surround the operation of both fiscal and monetary policies—lags and uncertainties that we have stressed repeatedly in earlier chapters. Will the Bank of Canada's actions have the desired effects on the money supply? How long will these actions have significant effects on interest rates? How will they affect spending, and how long will it take before the effects appear? Can fiscal-policy actions be taken promptly? Will consumers view tax changes as temporary or permanent? How large is the expenditure multiplier? The list could go on and on.

Monetarists look at this formidable catalogue of difficulties, add a dash of skepticism about our ability to forecast the economy's future, and conclude that stabilization policy is likely to do more harm than good. They advise both the fiscal and monetary authorities to pursue a passive policy rather than an active one—adhering to fixed rules that, while they will not iron out all the bumps in the economy's growth path, will at least keep it roughly on track in the long run.

Keynesians, though they admit that perfection is unattainable, are much *more optimistic* about the possibility of achieving a successful stabilization policy. And they are much *less optimistic* than the monetarists about how smoothly the economy would function in the absence of demand management. They therefore advocate discretionary increases in government spending (or decreases in taxes) and more rapid growth of the money supply when the economy has a recessionary gap. By this policy mix, they believe, government can keep the economy closer to its full-employment growth path.

Naturally, each side can point to evidence that buttresses its own view. Keynesians like to remind us of the U.S. government's tax cut of 1964 and the sustained period of economic growth that it helped usher in. Monetarists remind us of the government's refusal to curb what was obviously a situation of runaway demand during the late 1960s.

The historical record of fiscal and monetary policy is far from glorious. It shows that while there were many instances in which appropriate stabilization policy could have been helpful, the authorities instead either took inappropriate steps or did nothing at all. We examined some of these mistakes in Chapter 15. It seems, therefore, that the question of whether the government should adopt passive rules or attempt an activist stabilization policy merits a closer look. As we shall see, the lags in the effects of policy play a pivotal role in the debate.

Lags and the Rules-Versus-Discretion Debate

The reason that lags lead to a fundamental difficulty for stabilization policy—a difficulty so formidable that it has led many economists to conclude that attempts to stabilize economic activity are likely to do more harm than good—can be explained best by reference to Figure 19–2. Here we chart the behaviour of both actual and potential GNP over the course of a business cycle in a hypothetical economy in which no stabilization policy is attempted. At point *A*, the economy begins to slip into a recession and does not recover to full employment until point *D*. Then, between points *D* and *E*, it overshoots and is in an inflationary boom.

The case for stabilization policy runs like this. The recession is recognized to be a serious problem at point *B*, and appropriate actions are taken. These have their major effects around point *C* and thus curb both the depth and length of the recession.

But suppose the lags are really much longer than this. Suppose, for example, that delays in taking action postpone policy initiatives until point *C* and that stimulative policies do not have their major effects until after point *D*. Then policy will be of little help during the recession, and will actually do harm by overstimulating the economy during the ensuing boom. Thus:

In the presence of long lags, attempts at stabilizing the economy can actually succeed in destabilizing it.

Figure 19-2

A TYPICAL BUSINESS CYCLE
This is a stylized representation of the relationship between actual and potential GNP during a typical business cycle. The imaginary economy slips into a recession at point *A*, bottoms out around point *B*, and is in a recovery period until point *D*. After point *D*, it enters an inflationary boom that lasts until point *E*.

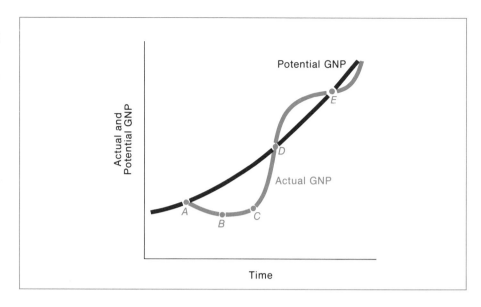

Because of this, some economists, like Milton Friedman, have argued that we are better off letting the economy alone and relying on its natural self-corrective forces to cure recessions and inflations. Instead of embarking on periodic programs of monetary and fiscal stimulus or restraint, they advise policy-makers to stick to fixed rules; that is, to rigid formulas that ignore current economic events.

The rule most emphasized by monetarists is that the Bank of Canada simply keep the money supply growing at a constant rate. The corresponding rule for fiscal policy is to *keep the high-employment budget in balance.*

The concept of the high-employment budget was introduced and explained in Chapter 17 (pages 323–25). Under this rule for fiscal policy, the actual budget would swing from surplus to deficit during a recession and from deficit to surplus during an inflationary boom. The main reason is that tax receipts automatically rise when GNP rises and fall when GNP falls. In addition, some items of government expenditure, such as transfer payments, automatically increase when unemployment rises and decrease when unemployment falls. So fiscal policy automatically swings toward expansion when the economy sags and toward contraction when the economy booms.

Automatic Stabilizers

An **automatic stabilizer** is any arrangement that automatically serves to support aggregate demand when it would otherwise sag and to hold down aggregate demand when it would otherwise surge ahead. In this way, an automatic stabilizer reduces the sensitivity of the economy to shifts in demand.

This discussion actually illustrates a general class of mechanisms called **automatic stabilizers**—features of the economy that reduce its sensitivity to shocks. Examples of automatic stabilizers are not hard to find in the federal budget. The personal income tax is the most obvious example.

The ability of the income tax to act as a shock absorber derives from the fact that it makes disposable income, and thus consumer spending, less sensitive to fluctuations in GNP. When GNP rises, disposable income (*DI*) rises also, but by less than the rise in GNP because part of the income is siphoned off by the government. This helps limit the upward fluctuation in consumption spending. And when GNP falls, *DI* falls less sharply because part of the loss is absorbed by the government rather than by consumers. So consumption does not drop as much as it otherwise might. Thus, although everybody likes to grumble about it, the personal income tax—which affected very few families in 1929, but affects almost everyone now—is one of the many modern institutions that helps ensure us against a repeat performance of the Great Depression.

There are many other automatic stabilizers in our economy. For example, in Chapter 6 we studied the Canadian system of unemployment insurance. This serves as an automatic stabilizer in a similar way. When GNP begins to fall and people lose their jobs, unemployment benefits prevent the disposable incomes of the jobless from falling as much as their earnings. As a result, unemployed workers can maintain their spending, and consumption need not fluctuate as dramatically as employment.

And the list could continue. The basic principle is the same: Each of these automatic stabilizers, in one way or another, serves as a shock absorber, and each does so without the need for any decision-maker to take action. In a word, they work *automatically*.

Stabilization Policy: Discretionary Measures or Fixed Rules?

Believers in fixed rules assert that we should forget about discretionary policy and rely solely on automatic stabilizers and the economy's natural self-correcting mechanisms. Are they right? As usual, the answer depends on many factors.

How Fast Does the Economy's Self-Correcting Mechanism Work?

We stressed in Chapter 10 that the economy does have a self-correcting mechanism. If the economy can cure recessions and inflations very quickly by itself, then the case for intervention is weak. For if such problems typically last only a short time, then lags in discretionary stabilization policy mean that the medicine will often have its major effects only after the disease is over. (In terms of Figure 19–2, this would be a case where point D comes very close to point A.)

While the more extreme advocates of rules argue that this is what indeed happens, most economists agree that the economy's self-correcting mechanism is slow and not terribly reliable, even when supplemented by the automatic stabilizers. On this count, then, a point is scored for discretionary policy.

How Long Are the Lags in Stabilization Policy?

As we explained, long lags before stabilization measures are adopted or can take effect make it unlikely that policy can do much good, while short lags point in the other direction. Thus, advocates of fixed rules emphasize the length of lags while proponents of discretion discount them.

Who is really right depends on the circumstances. In the most optimistic scenario, fiscal-policy actions are taken promptly, and the economy feels much of the stimulus from expansionary policy in less than a year after slipping into a recession. While far from an instant curve, these actions certainly are felt soon enough to do a lot of good. But, as we have seen, more pessimistic scenarios raise the possibility that policy may actually be destabilizing. History offers examples of both types of scenarios. No general conclusion can be drawn.

How Accurate Are Economic Forecasts?

One way to cut down the policy-making lag is to have good economic forecasts. If we could see a recession coming a full year ahead of time (which we certainly *cannot* do), even a rather slow-acting policy response would still be timely. (In terms of Figure 19–2, this would be a case where the coming recession is predicted well before point A arrives.) Unfortunately, however, to forecast Canadian economic performance, we must be able to predict U.S. interest rates, foreign-government policies that affect our export performance, and such intangibles as inflationary expectations. The evidence is that forecasting is certainly not good enough to support so-called "fine tuning," that is, attempts to keep the economy always within a hair's breadth of full employment. But it probably is good enough if our interest in using discretionary stabilization policy is simply to avoid sizable gaps between actual and potential GNP.

Other Dimensions of the Rules-Versus-Discretion Debate

While lags and forecasting play major roles in the debate between advocates of rules and advocates of discretionary policy, these are not the only battlegrounds.

The Size of Government

One bogus argument that is none the less quite often heard is that an activist fiscal policy must inevitably lead to a growing public sector. Since proponents of fixed rules tend also to be opponents of big government, they view this as undesirable. Of course, others think that a large public sector is just what society needs. This argument is, however, completely beside the point, as we pointed out in Chapter 11 (pages 209–210).

One's opinion about the proper size of government should have nothing to do with one's view on stabilization policy. When recessions occur, advocates of big government can call for greater spending while advocates of small government can insist on tax cuts. Similarly, if there is a need to contract aggregate demand to fight inflation, we can make the public sector smaller by cutting expenditures or bigger by raising taxes. While such choices may be quite momentous from other points of view, they simply do not bear on the question of whether we should fight the recession or the inflation.

A particularly clear example of this point came in the early days of the Reagan administration. Reagan embarked on an extremely *activist* stabilization policy based on *shrinking* the size of the public sector through reductions in both taxes and government spending.

Uncertainties Caused by Government Policy

Advocates of rules are on stronger ground when they argue that frequent changes in tax laws, government spending programs, or monetary conditions will make it difficult for firms and consumers to formulate and carry out rational plans. They argue that by adhering to fixed rules, which are known to businesses and consumers, the authorities can provide a more stable environment for the private sector. One of the points stressed by advocates of rules is that the downward flexibility of wages and prices has been undermined by the government's commitment to activist stabilization policy. Why lower your wage or price during a recession, if you expect that the government is about to stimulate demand?

Supporters of discretionary policy tend to ignore this issue and instead stress the difference between stability in the government budget (or in Bank of Canada operations) and stability in the economy. The goal of stabilization policy is to help *prevent* gyrations in the pace of economic activity by *causing* timely gyrations in the government budget (or in monetary policy). Which atmosphere is better for business, they ask, one in which fiscal and monetary rules keep things peaceful on Parliament Hill and at the Bank of Canada while recessions and inflation hit the economy, or one in which policy instruments are changed abruptly on occasion but the economy grows more steadily? They think that the answer is self-evident.

A Political Business Cycle

A final argument used by advocates of rules is political rather than economic in nature. Fiscal policy, they note, is decided upon by elected politicians. At least when elections are on the horizon, these men and women are likely to be at least as concerned with keeping their offices as with doing what is right for the economy. This leaves fiscal policy subject to all sorts of political manipulations, meaning that inappropriate actions may be taken to attain short-run political goals. In a system of purely automatic stabilization, its proponents argue, a rule of law would replace the rule of men, and this peril would be eliminated.

There is certainly a *possibility* that politicians could deliberately *cause*

Political Business Cycles

Since the Phillips curve trade-off is reasonably favourable in the short run (so that lower unemployment can be bought rather cheaply in terms of inflation), and since elected officials tend to have a hard time seeing past the next election, there is the possibility that politicians might deliberately cause business cycles in order to promote their own political ends.

Let us see how this might work with a hypothetical scenario. In January 1993, Les Scruples, a clever politician, takes office. The inflation rate is 8 percent and the unemployment rate is 7 percent (see the accompanying figure). Scruples remembers from his university political science course that (a) voters tend to blame the government when economic conditions are bad and reward them when economic conditions are good, and (b) voters have very short memories when they go to the polls. In fact, Scruples has seen studies that suggest that voters care only about the economy's real growth rate in the *one year prior to election day*. (This, in fact, is what the studies do suggest.)

This gives Scruples an idea. "By wringing inflation out of the system with a recession early in my term, and then stimulating demand near the end of my term, I should be able to stand for re-election with the inflation rate well below 8 percent and the unemployment rate well below 7 percent. Sounds great. I wonder if I can do it?" Scruples consults his economic advisers who explain to him that while the long-run Phillips curve is vertical, the short-run Phillips curve is probably quite flat, so his plan should work.

During his first year in office Scruples raises taxes and cuts government spending. A serious recession ensues: unemployment rises to 10 percent (again, see the accompanying figure). During the second, third, and fourth years of his term, the economy's natural self-

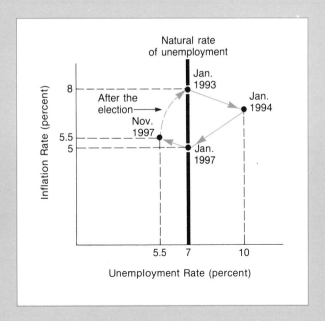

correcting mechanism slowly and painfully erodes the recessionary gap, so that by January 1997—an election year—inflation is down to 5 percent and unemployment is back to 7 percent (see the figure).

Now Les Scruples opens the sluice gates of federal spending and enacts a huge tax cut. The economy travels leftward along its short-run Phillips curve until, on election day 1997, the unemployment rate is down to 5½ percent and inflation is only 5½ percent. Scruples runs "on his record" as the prime minister who brought down both inflation and unemployment. His party is re-elected in a landslide. After the election, inflation accelerates and unemployment rises.

economic instability to help their own re-election. (See the boxed insert above.) And some observers of these "political business cycles" have claimed that several leaders have taken full advantage of the opportunity. Furthermore, even if there is no insidious intent, politicians may take the wrong actions for perfectly honourable reasons. Decisions in the political arena are never clear-cut, and it certainly is easy to find examples of large errors in the history of Canadian stabilization policy. Again, we refer the reader to Chapter 15, which described the government's attempts to use fiscal policy in a floating exchange-rate regime, and its attempts to use monetary policy in a fixed exchange-rate regime.

So, taken as a whole, the political argument against discretionary policy seems to have a great deal of merit. But what are we to do about it? It is foolhardy to believe that fiscal and monetary decisions could or should be made by a group of objective and non-partisan technicians. Steering the economy is not like steering a rocket to the moon. Because policy actions that help on the employment front normally do harm on the inflation front, and vice versa, the "correct" policy action is almost always an inherently political matter. In a political democracy, if we take such decisions out of the hands of elected officials, in whose hands shall we put them?

Ethical Reflections on the Economic Crisis

Many Canadians have been shocked by the depth of the recession of the 1980s. The Canadian Conference of Catholic Bishops made public its *Ethical Reflections on the Economic Crisis* in January 1983 and much public discussion followed. The following three statements capture the general thrust of the Bishops' views:

1. Unemployment rather than inflation should be recognized as the number-one problem, and expansion in aggregate demand is warranted.
2. Wage and price controls represent a more balanced and equitable means of controlling inflation than does contractionary demand policy.
3. Investment should take place in labour-intensive, not capital-intensive, industries.

All of these comments stem from the Bishops' deep concern for the poor. But each statement involves both a positive and a normative element; that is, each involves an economic issue (that may be true or false) and a moral issue (upon which the Bishops can comment). Economists, in their role as technical advisers, must limit their evaluation of these policy suggestions to the positive, or factual, aspects. We consider each statement in turn.

1. Statement One involves the proposition that unemployment can be traded-off with inflation (a factual issue) and the view that the costs of unemployment are more important than the costs of inflation. We have learned that it is very unlikely that unemployment and inflation can be traded off in the long run, so that *in the long run* (but not the short run!), moral disagreements concerning the relative burdens of unemployment and inflation are not critical for the conduct of policy.
2. Statement Two involves the assumption that wage and price controls work, even when aggregate-demand policy is expansionary (the factual question), and the view that unemployment is more important than the misallocation of resources that follows from controls (the moral question). Unfortunately, history has given a very clear answer regarding the factual question: While controls can work for a year or two, they have *never* provided *any lasting* help in fighting inflation when used as a substitute for (rather than a complement to) contractionary demand policy. If controls do not work, moral debates concerning their costs are beside the point.
3. Statement Three involves the assumption that jobs created by new industries involve less total employment than jobs that are lost during the adjustment period that follows automation. This is the factual issue. The moral proposition is that jobs are more important than cost-saving techniques. Regarding the economic issue, history has shown that the industrial revolution led to more jobs *and* higher income standards. Again, it seems that in the *long run*, the moral issue may not arise.

The point of this discussion is to emphasize that while economists *cannot* referee moral disputes, they can contribute toward minimizing them by drawing attention to, and commenting on, the positive aspects of policy disagreements. As we have seen in these examples, the factual issue *can* be logically prior to the moral question. Nevertheless, the current state of economic analysis *only* permits this strong conclusion if one is prepared to stress the *longer run*. In the short run, there *is* an unemployment–inflation trade-off, controls do slow inflation temporarily, and automation does cause significant dislocation. Regarding short-run policy options then, heated debate will continue even if all participants are careful to separate positive and normative issues.

This harsh fact may seem worrisome in view of the possibilities for political chicanery, but it should not bother us any more (or any less!) than similar manoeuvring in other areas of policy-making. After all, the same thing applies to international relations, formulation of the law, and so on. Politicians make all these decisions for us, subject only to sporadic accountability at election times. Is there really any reason why economic decisions should be different?

Conclusion: What Should Be Done?

Where do all these considerations leave us? On balance, is it better to conduct discretionary policy as best we can, knowing full well that we will never do it perfectly? Or is it wiser to rely on fixed rules and automatic stabilizers?

In weighing the pros and cons that we have discussed in this chapter, one's basic view of the economy is very important. Some economists believe that the economy, if left unmanaged, would generate a series of ups and downs that are hard to predict, but that it would correct each of them by itself in a relatively short period of time. They conclude that, because of long lags and poor forecasts our ability to anticipate whether the economy will be heading up or down by the time policy actions have their effects is quite limited. And so they are led to advocate fixed rules.

Other economists liken the economy to a giant glacier with a great deal of inertia. This means that if we observe an inflationary or recessionary gap today, it is likely still to be there a year or two from now because the self-correcting mechanism is so slow. In such a world, accurate forecasting is not imperative, even if policy lags are long. If we base policy on a forecast of a $10 billion gap between actual and potential GNP a year from now, and the gap turns out to be only $5 billion, then we still will have done the right thing despite the horrible forecast. Holders of this view of the economy, then, are likely to advocate the use of discretionary policy.

While there is no consensus on this issue either among economists or among politicians, a prudent view might be that:

The case for active discretionary policy is strong when the economy has a serious deficiency or excess of aggregate demand. However, advocates of fixed rules are right that it is unwise to try to iron out every little wiggle in the growth path of GNP.

But the decision cannot be made solely on economic grounds. Political judgments enter as well. In the end:

The question of whether the government should take an active hand in managing the economy, which is one of the main bones of contention between Keynesians and monetarists today, is as much a matter of ideology as of economics. Liberals have always looked to government activism to solve social problems, while conservatives have consistently pointed out that many efforts of government fail despite the best of intentions.

Since no one can decide whether liberal or conservative political attitudes are the "correct" ones on purely objective criteria, the rules-versus-discretion debate is likely to go on for quite some time.

Summary

1. Policies that improve the functioning of the labour market—including retraining programs and various types of employment services—can improve the trade-off between inflation and unemployment by lowering the natural rate of unemployment. To date, however, Western governments have had only modest success with these measures.

2. Some small amount of progress against inflation may also be made by eliminating some of the government regulations that keep prices high.

3. Many varieties of incomes policies have been used in this and other countries in an effort to improve the trade-off between inflation and unemployment. While some have led to notable temporary improvements, a surge of inflation often follows the controls period.

4. The weakest varieties of incomes policies simply set up standards for permissible wage and price increases (wage-price guidelines) and apply verbal admonitions against violators (jawboning). Stronger variants may actually set legal limits on wage and price increases or even ban them outright (a wage-price freeze). But such policies seriously interfere with the workings of our market economy.

5. One argument in favour of short-term wage-price controls is that they can reduce inflationary expectations and thereby rob inflation of some of its momentum and reduce the magnitude of the temporary recession that must accompany contractionary aggregate-demand policy. The Canadian AIB made a significant contribution in this regard.

6. A new and different approach to incomes policy would use tax incentives to encourage more moderate wage and price increases. This so-called "tax-based incomes policy" has yet to be tried.

7. Indexing is another way to approach the trade-off problem. Instead of trying to improve the trade-off, it concentrates on reducing the social costs of inflation.

Opponents of indexing worry, however, that the economy's resistance to inflation may be lowered by indexing.

8. When there are long lags in the operation of fiscal and monetary policy, it becomes possible that attempts to stabilize economic activity may actually succeed in destabilizing it.

9. The Canadian economy has a number of automatic stabilizers that make it less vulnerable to shocks than it would otherwise be. Among these are the personal income tax and unemployment benefits.

10. Many monetarists believe that our imperfect knowledge of the channels through which stabilization policy works, and the long lags involved, make it unlikely that discretionary stabilization policy can succeed.

11. Keynesians recognize these difficulties but do not believe they are as serious as monetarists think. On the other hand, Keynesians place much less faith in the economy's ability to cure recessions and inflations on its own. They therefore think that discretionary policy is not only advisable, but essential.

Concepts for Review

Incomes policy	Anti-Inflation Board (AIB)	Indexing (escalator clauses)
Jawboning	Inflationary expectations	Real versus nominal interest rates
Wage-price guidelines	Wage-price freezes	Rules versus discretionary policy
Wage-price controls	Tax-based incomes policy (TIP)	Automatic stabilizers

Questions for Discussion

1. Do you think it is proper for the Prime Minister's Office to "jawbone" some corporations into reducing their price increases?

2. Explain some of the differences between wage-price guidelines and wage-price controls.

3. Suppose that a program of wage-price controls is under consideration by the government. What are the possible benefits to the nation from such a program? What are the possible costs? How would you go about balancing the benefits against the costs?

4. Explain the basic idea behind "TIP" (tax-based incomes policy). Try to devise a TIP plan of your own. Can you foresee some practical difficulties with your plan?

5. At the time of writing (late 1984), ordinary savings accounts paid approximately 8 percent *nominal* interest. Would you prefer to trade yours in for an indexed bank account that paid a zero *real* rate of

interest? What if the real interest rate offered were 2 percent? What if it were –2 percent? What do your answers to these questions reveal about your personal attitudes toward inflation?

6. Explain why lags make it possible for policy actions intended to stabilize the economy to actually destabilize it instead.

7. Name some automatic stabilizers and explain how and what they "stabilize."

8. Which of the following events would strengthen the argument for the use of discretionary policy, and which would strengthen the argument for rules?
   a. Structural changes make the economy's self-correcting mechanism faster and more reliable than before.
   b. New statistical methods are found that improve the accuracy of economic forecasts.

IV

Productivity, Trade, and Growth

Productivity Problems

20

Japan commercially, I regret to say, does not bear the best reputation for executing business. Inferior goods, irregularity and indifferent shipments have caused no end of worry ... you are a very satisfied easy-going race who reckon time is no object. When I spoke to some managers they informed me that it was impossible to change the habits of national heritage.

(FROM A REPORT OF AN AUSTRALIAN EXPERT FOR THE JAPANESE GOVERNMENT, 1915)

Productivity is a measure of the amount of output obtained from a given amount of input. So productivity grows if innovation, improved education, or other influences increase the number of cars or the number of watches produced by an hour of work.

Only rising productivity can raise standards of living in the long run. Indeed, as we pointed out in our list of **12 Ideas for Beyond the Final Exam:**

It is hardly an exaggeration to say that, in the long run, almost nothing counts for the determination of a nation's standard of living but its *rate of productivity growth.*

Over long periods of time, small differences in rates of productivity growth compound, like interest in a bank account, and can make an enormous difference to a society's prosperity. Nothing contributes more to reduction of poverty, to increases in leisure, and to the country's ability to finance education, public health, environmental protection, and the arts.

To take a rather exaggerated example, let us assume that productivity data for the year 1800 were available for Canada. If productivity had increased at a rate of 1 percent per year between then and now, the average Canadian today would command about six times as many goods and services as his forebears did in 1800. If productivity growth had been 3 percent, the average living standard would be an incredible *137* times as high as it was in 1800.

Consequently, productivity growth can make an enormous difference for a nation's standing in the hierarchy of the world's economies. It has been remarked that the success of the United States in keeping its annual productivity growth about one percent ahead of England's for about a century transformed America from a minor, developing country into a superpower and transformed the United Kingdom from the world's pre-eminent power into a second-rate economy.

Unfortunately, productivity growth in Canada in recent years has been very slow, in comparison with both its earlier record and that of many other countries. This chapter reviews the recent record of Canadian productivity performance and summarizes some of the explanations that have been offered for our productivity problems, though the evidence is very unclear. Much of the chapter is devoted to productivity policy—what is being done and what other measures are possible.

A Puzzle: Productivity Growth Lags, Foreign Competition, and Employment

A common view of the dangers of the lag in Canadian productivity growth is that as foreign producers become more efficient in comparison with ours, they will capture more of our industries' markets at home and abroad. First our steel industry, then our telecommunications industry, and, perhaps, our automobile industry will fall victim to the growing productivity of the Japanese. This conjures up the vision of Canada's industries being driven out of almost all their export markets, and Japanese exports taking over an increasing share of Canadian consumer purchases of manufactured goods. The result, it would seem, will be growing unemployment and an increasing Canadian debt to foreigners.

Yet British history suggests that this will not happen. Despite a century of lag in productivity growth, Britain has shown no long-term trend toward increasing unemployment, and its foreign debt, while sometimes large, certainly has not shown an extraordinarily rising trend. In the 1960s and 1970s, British unemployment was extremely low, and in a number of recent years the value of the goods and services Britain sold to foreigners was greater than the value of the items imported. Why did the steady decline in British efficiency compared to many other countries not cause it to lose its export markets and its demand for employment? What does this mean for Canada? We will return to this subject later in the chapter.

Measuring Productivity

Labour productivity is a measure of total output divided by the amount of labour that was used to produce it. It is a measure of output per unit of labour employed.

Most productivity statistics report **labour productivity**; that is, output per worker. One can measure the labour productivity of a single factory, an industry, or an entire economy. Since output consists of a mixture of very different items—automobiles, shoes, computers, and telephone calls—one runs into the problem of adding apples and oranges in measuring its total amount. Statistics that weight outputs by relative prices, such as GNP or national income, are usually used as the output data in measuring the labour productivity of a country. Analogous price-weighted sums are used for industries or individual factories that turn out more than one output. It is also generally agreed that quantity of labour is best measured as number of hours worked rather than number of persons employed.

Dimensions of the Canadian Productivity Problem

Canada actually has not one, but two, different productivity problems. First, our own productivity growth has slowed substantially since the 1960s. Second, for nearly twenty years, our productivity growth rate has been much lower than that of most industrialized and industrializing countries in Europe and the Far East. We will refer to the second of these problems as the Canadian **productivity growth gap**. The two problems probably have somewhat different explanations, almost certainly have different consequences for the welfare of our country, and may require somewhat different policy responses.

What are the magnitudes of these problems? From 1946 to 1982, labour productivity in Canadian manufacturing grew at about 4 percent per year, on the average. But the performance of recent years has been pulling this average down, since the average annual rate of change for the 1979–82 period was approximately *minus* one percent. Indeed, the rate of growth figure for 1982 alone—*minus* 2.7 percent—represents the largest decrease that has been recorded since the series on the growth in manufacturing output per man hour began in 1946.[1]

---

[1]Statistics Canada, *Aggregate Productivity Measures 1982* (Catalogue 14-201), page 8.

It should be noted that throughout most of this period the *level* of productivity continued to improve. In almost every year, it was higher than the last. But the *rate* of improvement has steadily slowed from a gallop to a walk, and finally to a crawl.

The second Canadian productivity problem—the gap in Canadian productivity growth relative to other industrial countries—should be analysed in two steps. First, our performance must be compared to that of our major trading partner, the United States, then it must be compared to that of other industrialized countries.

For the 1946–82 period as a whole, productivity growth in Canadian manufacturing exceeded that in the United States: 4 percent per year in Canada versus 2.5 percent in the United States. But for the years since 1970, we are tied with U.S. manufacturing—both countries have averaged 2 percent annually for this later period. However, the 1982 productivity growth rate of minus 2.7 percent in Canadian manufacturing was well below the United States' rate of minus 1 percent. Thus, while Canada might be considered the overall "winner" in the productivity race in the past, a concern for our current competitiveness is indeed warranted. This is especially true since increases in compensation per man hour in Canada have typically exceeded those in the United States.

At the broader international level, Figure 20-1 presents data comparing overall productivity growth for various countries for the period 1973–79. Note that Canada and the United States trail the pack.

Clearly, Canadian productivity growth has been in trouble in comparison with both its own record and that of other countries.

The Canadian productivity growth rate has fallen drastically from where it was right after World War II, and it is far behind productivity growth rates in a number of other countries.

The analogy between recent Canadian productivity statistics and those relating to Great Britain during the period when it lost its economic pre-eminence is disturbing. Historians date the British decline between 1870 and 1914. By no coincidence, British labour productivity growth in industry fell fairly steadily from 1.2 percent per year between 1870 and 1880 to 0.2 percent between 1890 and

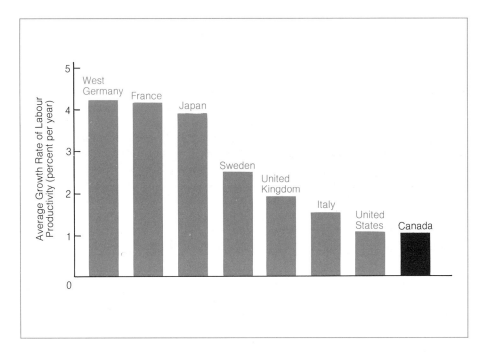

Figure 20-1
AVERAGE LABOUR PRODUCTIVITY GROWTH RATES, 1973-1979, FOR EIGHT COUNTRIES
Each country's productivity growth has fallen relative to earlier periods. Nevertheless, Canada is at the bottom.
SOURCE: New York Stock Exchange

1913.[2] During this same period, British productivity growth lagged slightly behind that of France and well behind the American and German performances.[3] What happened in Britain can happen here.

Why Did Canadian Productivity Growth Slow Down?

Many statisticians and economists have worked very hard to determine why Canadian productivity growth has fallen so much since the mid-1960s. But because so many things have changed at once, no clear and easy answers have emerged. But several culprits have been identified.

Low Investment

Probably most widely cited as a cause of the slowdown is what many regard as insufficient investment in plant and equipment. The more a society invests, the more plant and equipment an average member of the labour force has available to work with. More and better equipment enables her to turn out more output per hour, so productivity grows. Also, new machines usually incorporate the latest designs; conversely, obsolete equipment tends to be kept longer when investment lags. Thus investment and the savings that make investment possible are crucial for productivity growth.

After World War II, business investment in Canada actually rose faster than GNP for a while. However, investment was not large enough to keep pace with the rapidly expanding labour force. Consequently, the amount of capital each worker had to work with fell. Because of differences in measurement procedures, there is some disagreement about the actual magnitude of this decline, but analysts agree that lagging investment played a definite role in the general decline in Canadian productivity growth.

Low Research and Development Expenditure

Another prime suspect in the slowing of Canadian productivity growth is expenditure on applied research. Innovation is one of the main sources of productivity growth. New and more efficient productive procedures—from the steam engine to robotics—have multiplied the output a worker is capable of producing. However, innovation requires more than a new idea. It usually needs careful research to get out the "bugs" and to make the new procedures operational. This work is called **research and development (R & D)**. About half of Canada's R & D expenditures are made by businesses, and the other half by government and non-profit institutions. Because R & D is a critical step between the original invention and its final adoption by business enterprise, a big drop in R & D expenditures can do substantial damage to productivity growth.

The ratio of R & D outlays to GNP has been rising since 1977. In that year, they accounted for 0.98 percent of GNP while in 1982 the percentage was 1.29. However, published data indicate that Canada has the lowest ratio of R & D outlays in relation to GNP of eight OECD countries. In fact, in 1979 Canada's was only 67 percent of that in the country with the second lowest ratio, France.

Why haven't R & D expenditures risen more rapidly in Canada? Why has innovation seemed to slow? No one really knows. One hypothesis is that a decade of stagflation just made innovation and research less attractive to business. Another holds that rising real wages of scientists and engineers discouraged R & D activity by making it more expensive.

[2] Derek H. Aldcroft and Harry W. Richardson, *The British Economy 1870–1939* (London: Macmillan, 1969), page 126.
[3] Trevor May, *The Economy 1815–1914* (London: Collins, 1972), page 163.

Government Regulation

Government regulation is also sometimes blamed for the slowdown. In the 1960s and 1970s, regulations for protection of the health and safety of workers and for defence of the environment were strengthened. These absorbed some of the investment outlays of business and increased the costs of production. Some business leaders believe that this has been a substantial impediment to productivity growth.

Shift to the Service Industries

Another possible culprit is the fact that the share of the nation's labour force employed in **service industries** has more than doubled since 1951. Historically, growth of productivity in many (but by no means all) of the services has been far lower than in manufacturing. This is so in part because for many services quality depends, or is believed to depend, directly on the amount of time the supplier devotes to the activity (for example, the time devoted by a doctor to an average patient, or the amount of faculty time per student). Also, many services (such as diagnosis and treatment of a sick person) cannot be standardized and put on an assembly line. When workers leave manufacturing, with its relatively rapid productivity growth, and go into those services whose productivity growth is slow, overall productivity growth slows down. How serious is this phenomenon? Unfortunately, statistical estimates vary enormously. We really are not sure.

In any event, the shift of the labour force toward the services cannot be considered an example of poor performance by our economy. Unlike lack of innovation, it is not something we must "cure."

A **service** is an industry that does not turn out any physical products. Telecommunications, medical care, teaching, police protection, and the work of lawyers are examples of service industries. Some, like telecommunications, use highly sophisticated equipment, and their productivity has grown rapidly. In many other services, such growth has been very slow.

Rising Energy Prices

Probably part of the slowdown in productivity growth resulted from the sharply rising price of energy, which led to many economic changes. The building insulation business grew. The demand for large, gas-guzzling cars plunged. Much plant and equipment had to be changed to adapt them to the new patterns of consumer and business demands induced by rising energy prices and to substitute fuel-efficient equipment for items that had been installed when energy was cheap.

Because energy constitutes a small proportion of the nation's total expenditure on inputs, most statistical studies suggest that higher energy prices did not contribute much to the slowdown. A typical estimate is that they account for about 15 percent of the total decline in productivity growth. Yet there are many, including the authors of this book, who suspect that energy may be responsible for more than that. The equipment that had to be replaced or modified to save on fuel probably used up a far from negligible portion of the country's investment.

Macroeconomic Conditions

Finally, some portion of the slowdown is probably attributable to the fact that the 1970s and early 1980s were not generally characterized by healthy business conditions. Several recessions and inflation of unprecedented severity and duration are not conditions that encourage business investment and innovation. There is no clear statistical evidence on the importance of this influence, but it is not hard to believe that it was important.

The causes of the slowdown in Canadian productivity growth are far from certain. Lagging investment, modest growth in R & D, government regulation, the shift to service industries, rising energy prices, and repeated recessions and protracted inflation probably all played a part.

Causes of the Canadian Productivity Growth Gap

As already indicated, Canada has two productivity problems: first, the slowdown from its previous growth performance (a problem we share with other countries) and, second, the productivity gap—the fact that our growth rate has been poorer than those of our main foreign competitors.

Five explanations have been offered for the gap in Canadian productivity growth: higher rates of saving and investment in some of the other countries than in Canada; a decline in Canadian entrepreneurship; special foreign institutions and cultural characteristics, such as an alleged superiority in the standards of workmanship in Japan; government programs to assist industrial growth in other countries; and the existence in Canada of plants operating at less than the most efficient level of production.

Investment and Saving

During the 1960s, capital investment in manufacturing as a percentage of output was 30 percent in Japan, 16 percent in West Germany, 14.4 percent in Canada, and 9 percent in the United States. One would expect the Canadian productivity growth gap to emerge, if this ranking of investment rates was maintained, and this is what has occurred. During the late 1970s and early 1980s, the average annual growth in capital formation was 4.7 percent in Japan, 5.2 percent in Germany, 2.3 percent in Canada, and 3.3 percent in the United States.[4]

While investment can be financed by borrowing from foreigners in the short run, the supply of domestic savings represents the ultimate constraint on what is available for firms to invest. Thus, it is not surprising that the ranking of countries by growth in investment is mirrored reasonably well in their ranking by savings rates. Total savings as a percentage of national income was 30.7 percent in Japan, 23.1 percent in Germany, 21.5 percent in Canada, and 18.3 percent in the United States in 1980 (the last year for which comparable international data were available when this book was written).

The differences in investment and saving rates means that workers in Japan and Germany (and in some other countries) have been supplied with increasing amounts of equipment relative to Canadian workers. Their equipment, having been acquired more recently, is generally more modern and more efficient than our own. According to one study, the Ford Motor Company turns out two car engines per day per employee, while Toyota produces nine. A U.S. colour TV set requires 3.5 to 4.5 labour hours while in Japan only 1.8 labour hours are required. It is hardly surprising, therefore, that studies have attributed as much as 80 percent of the superior Japanese growth record (compared to the United States) to Japan's persistently higher saving and investment.[5]

Entrepreneurial Activity

Entrepreneurship is also widely cited as a reason for the gap in productivity growth. No one knows how to measure **entrepreneurship**, and there is not even agreement on its definition. Roughly speaking, it refers to the imagination, daring, alertness, and skillful intuition of the men and women who innovate, take advantage of opportunities to enter fields where incumbent managements have performed badly, and generally keep bringing changes to the economy.

The prevailing legend (which, like many legends, may have a great deal of truth to it) is that, perhaps until the Great Depression of 1929, American entrepreneurship was unbeatable, setting an example of accomplishment that was

---

[4]Organization for Economic Cooperation and Development, *Economic Surveys 1982–83*.
[5]See, for example, J.R. Norsworthy, testimony before the U.S. Senate Subcommittee on Employment and Productivity (97th Congress, 2nd Session, April 2, 1982).

envied by the rest of the world. Because of our close connections with the American economy, Canadian business reflected the same drive.

Then, in the period after World War II, something happened. Some say entrepreneurs were gradually replaced by products of business schools who knew how to manage firms well, but whose style encouraged good organization and good routine rather than the constant upheaval that characterizes entrepreneurship. Others say businesses turned ever more toward the courts and regulators to protect them from the pressures of competition, relying on lawyers rather than engineers for their prosperity. Still others claim that the alleged decline in entrepreneurship reflects a general change in the attitudes of our society, involving a lower valuation of business success and less widespread appreciation of material rewards.

Whatever the explanation, the conclusion is that business leadership no longer resides in North America, but has been seized by the Far East: Japan, Hong Kong, Taiwan, Singapore, and South Korea. Historically, this would not be the first time such an event has occurred. In the seventeenth century, Holland was the economic and cultural leader of the world until Britain took over that position in the eighteenth century, only to be succeeded by the United States and Germany in the nineteenth century.

How valid is this view of declining entrepreneurship in North America? We simply do not know.

Institutional and Cultural Differences

The third factor widely blamed for the productivity gap is the difference in cultural characteristics. It has been said that Japanese culture, for example, tends to make workers very loyal to their firms and to lead to an emphasis on product quality. This may be true. But the organization of production in large Japanese and Canadian firms differs in ways designed to promote such attitudes.

Japanese workers change jobs from one company to another far less frequently than do Canadian workers. Perhaps one-third to half of the labour force is granted **lifetime employment** and is promoted steadily. At about age 55 these workers are automatically transferred to less responsible positions. Some observers believe that this lifetime employment system has made Japanese workers more willing than their North American and European counterparts to accept labour-saving innovations such as robotics.

The salaries of workers and management in Japan are closer to one another than those in Canada, and management is less likely to dine by itself in a separate, elegant dining room. Workers often organize themselves into small groups called **quality circles**, designed to improve productivity and product quality. Special rewards are given to such groups for outstanding achievements. (See the boxed insert on the next page.)

Emulating Japanese management techniques has recently become fashionable in North America. Delegations of North American executives stream to Japan to see for themselves how quality circles and other such things are run. Imitations have appeared in Canadian factories, and plants run by Japanese managers in the United States using American workers claim to be matching Japanese productivity standards.

Yet there are voices of caution. First, some people who have studied the issue question whether the methods that work in Japan can be transferred successfully to North America, with its different traditions and institutions. Moreover, the statistical evidence suggests that no more than 10 to 20 percent of the superior Japanese growth performance can be attributed to the Japanese management style. So this alone will not enable us to catch up.

Government Assistance

The fourth explanation for the gap in Canadian productivity growth is government assistance programs in other countries. In France and Japan, the government has

The Quality of Japanese Products

Before World War II the label "made in Japan" was generally taken to mean that the item was a shoddy product of poor workmanship and design. Clearly that is no longer true.

This issue has been studied in some detail by Peter G. Peterson, chairman of the National Commission on Productivity in the United States. According to Peterson, "One study found that 96 percent of [Japan's] automobiles leave the production line in fit shape for delivery, versus 75 percent of ours. American rent-a-car companies report that cars made in the United States require two to three times more servicing than comparable Japanese cars."

The accompanying figure shows the frequency of service calls for U.S. and Japanese television sets. According to the data, in 1973 about 3 percent of the Japanese sets required service calls during their warranty period, compared with about 20 percent of American sets. Since then, U.S. performance has improved substantially, and that of the Japanese has deteriorated slightly. By 1979, the most recent year for which figures are available, the U.S. servicing requirements were a bit less than twice as high as the Japanese, but the trend seems to be encouraging for the Americans.

Even more dramatic are the figures reported by Hewlett-Packard summarizing the differences in quality between integrated circuit chips from the United States and those from Japan. Three different manufacturers from each country were represented in the sample. On arrival, 0.16 percent of the American chips failed the acceptance test, but none of the Japanese chips did. When the chips

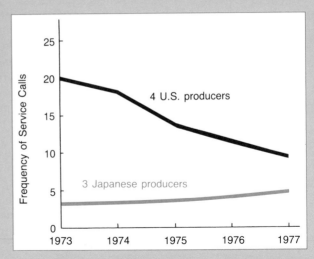

PERCENTAGE OF THE POPULATION OF COLOUR TV SETS REQUIRING SERVICE CALLS DURING THE WARRANTY STAGE, 1973-1977. (DATA ARE WEIGHTED EQUALLY AND REPRESENT THE AVERAGE FOR THE FIRST AND SECOND QUARTERS.)

were used in the field for 1000 hours, the Japanese failure rate was 0.014 percent; the U.S. failure rate was almost ten times as high.

SOURCE: The data are taken from Peter G. Peterson, "The U.S. Competitive Position in the 1980s—And Some Things We Might Do About It," speech presented to the Center for International Business, March 1981.

also taken on the task of guiding private investment toward fields that are judged promising for future growth. Thus, particular industries are singled out for assistance in obtaining capital, choice locations, and tax advantages. While much of the co-operation of private firms has been voluntary, the planning agencies have incentives that make it easier to persuade businesses to participate. There is a great deal of controversy about the effectiveness and the wisdom of these programs, and we will return to this issue later in the chapter, when we discuss "industrial strategy" proposals that call for similar programs in Canada.

Short Production Runs

Finally, productivity differentials between Canada and other countries have been linked to the fact that the Canadian tariff has protected some domestic industries from competitive pressures. Since some producers are insulated from these competitive pressures, there is nothing to force them to adjust the scale of plant so that the average cost of production is pushed down to its minimum possible point. Fixed costs are relatively important for firms operating for the small market in Canada. Furthermore, most technological improvements reduce variable costs more than fixed costs. Thus, technological improvements reduce average costs more for firms that are not in existence solely to service a small domestic market.

The Economic Council of Canada has emphasized this point in a recent study.

The study compared many industries in Canada to their counterparts in the United States, and the conclusion was that much of the lower productivity levels in Canada were due to the protected nature of the small Canadian markets.[6]

Several factors are responsible for the Canadian productivity gap. Our saving and investment rates are below those of many other countries. Canadian growth is also handicapped by relatively poor management–labour relations, by decline in the quality and quantity of entrepreneurship, and by the tariff. Labour's resistance to labour-saving innovation may also be greater in Canada than in the Far East, but it may be less than in Europe.

Why Encourage Productivity Growth?

The two different productivity problems have very different consequences for public welfare in Canada. Thus, the reasons for Canada to try to resume its past growth record are different from the reasons for trying to catch up with growth rates in other countries.

Consequences of the Decline in Canadian Productivity

The slowdown in Canadian productivity growth has had at least three unfortunate consequences, each of which can be ameliorated by increased productivity growth:

1. It has kept living standards from rising as rapidly.
2. It has impeded the expansion of social expenditures on, for example, public health, education, and protection of the environment.
3. It has contributed to inflation.

The first of the three consequences is the most obvious. Without rising output per worker, it is very difficult to increase the quantity of goods and services available to each consumer.

Besides holding down living standards, a decline in productivity growth makes it difficult politically and psychologically to finance a variety of social programs that many Canadians consider important. Improvements in health care, education, the arts, environmental protection, attempts to reduce poverty, and many other such activities generally require higher expenditures and therefore higher taxes. If productivity is growing rapidly, these taxes are not too painful because there is enough left over so that workers' take-home pay can still rise. But if productivity growth is slow, any substantial increase in expenditure for social purposes is likely to cut into workers' real incomes. So it was no accident that the slowdown in productivity created pressures to reduce spending on social programs.

Productivity also affects inflation in the long run. The arithmetic here is simple. Inflation rises if the growth of aggregate demand speeds up or if the growth of aggregate supply slows down. Aggregate supply, by definition, is the product of the number of labour hours available times productivity (the amount of output produced by each hour of labour). Thus, if productivity growth slows down, the growth rate of aggregate supply slows down and inflation is likely to rise.

The slowdown in Canadian productivity growth has aggravated inflation. It has made it harder to finance social programs such as public health, anti-poverty schemes, and environmental protection. Above all, it has held living standards almost level.

---

[6]J.R. Baldwin and P.K. Gorecki (with J. McVoy and J. Crysdale), "Trade, Tariffs and Relative Plant Scale in Canadian Manufacturing Industries: 1970-1979," Discussion Paper No. 232, Economic Council of Canada, Ottawa, May, 1983.

Consequences of the Gap in Canadian Productivity Growth

The relatively slow growth in Canadian productivity compared to that of many other countries has consequences that are different from those of the slowdown from earlier Canadian performance:

1. It causes painful shifts in the jobs done by Canadian workers, requiring retraining and geographic relocation, replacement of specialized plant and equipment, and other substantial readjustment costs using resources that might be better employed for other purposes;

2. While it does *not* threaten to drive Canadian products from the markets of the world or to create ever-growing unemployment rates, it can avoid this only by constant (and costly) restructuring of the composition of Canadian industry, and by driving the real wages of Canadian workers lower and lower relative to those of other countries.

The lag in Canadian productivity growth can be expected to cause continuous shifts in the products that Canada can turn out most profitably. For example, we have observed a decline in marketability of Canadian clothing, footware, steel, and automobiles relative to the products of other countries. Meanwhile, the demand for Canadian agricultural products, telecommunications equipment, energy, and other items has risen. In the long run, the decline of one industry, if accompanied by the rise of another, is not a bad thing. But in the shorter run it may be very costly and painful to the community. A young steelworker may be retrained if he loses his job, but it may involve months of unemployment. An older worker may find himself in far more serious trouble. Factories in dying industries must be abandoned and replaced by new plants to house the growing industries. Families must be uprooted, leaving friends and relatives, to follow the geographic movement of job opportunities. Flourishing communities sometimes are transformed into ghost towns. Thus, even if in the long run a new job arises for every one that was lost, the transition is a costly and painful process.

The Lag in Living Standards (The Puzzle Resolved)

A widespread but mistaken belief about the lag in Canadian productivity growth behind other countries is that it will enable foreigners to outcompete Canadian industries, causing catastrophic Canadian unemployment. This seems plausible enough, but neither history nor economic analysis provides any confirmation for this view. This is the puzzle that we encountered earlier in this chapter. If the Germans, the Japanese, and the Americans are growing ever more productive and efficient in comparison with Canada, why will they not eventually take all our markets away?

An answer is to be found in the laws of supply and demand, which tell us that if the productivity gap reduces foreign demand for Canadian products, the derived demand curve for Canadian labour will also shift downward. That, in turn, will reduce wages in Canada below what they would otherwise have been, until costs have been cut to the point where Canadian products again become competitive.

It should be clear that if the gap in Canadian productivity growth raises the relative cost of Canadian products to the point where its exports fall materially and widespread unemployment results, then real wages in Canada will indeed be forced to lag behind those in other countries that are encountering no difficulty in selling their products. That is precisely why real wages in Great Britain, though they have risen in the postwar period, have lagged far behind those in a number of other countries.

To complete the story, that is, to explain how Canadian products as a group will regain their export market despite the productivity gap, it only remains to confirm that lagging wages are an effective substitute for productivity growth as a

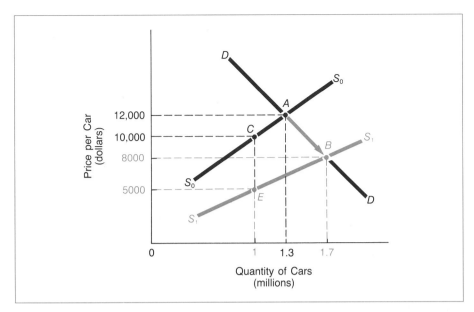

Figure 20-2
SUPPLY, PRODUCTIVITY
AND REAL WAGES
The supply curve of a product can
be shifted to the right, and product
price can be decreased, either by
a rise in productivity or by a fall in
wages. Thus, a country that suffers
from a productivity gap must
compete by providing cheap
labour.

means to preserve international competitiveness. That is, one country may retain the market for its exports through rapid productivity increases while another can keep its market by means of lagging real wages.

Figure 20-2 explains how this works. First, consider the case of a hypothetical Japanese industry whose productivity is assumed to double over a ten-year period. For simplicity we also assume that Japanese real wages remain unchanged over the decade in question. Let S_0S_0 be Japan's supply curve of the product, call it cars, at the beginning of the decade. We see (point C) that to induce the industry to produce one million cars, it must receive $10,000 per car. But as productivity doubles, it takes half the quantity of inputs to produce a given quantity of cars that it required ten years earlier. Thus, to get Japan to produce one million cars at the end of the decade, a price of only $5,000 is required (point E). This means that the Japanese supply curve will have shifted downward from S_0S_0 to S_1S_1. With the demand curve DD unchanged, the equilibrium point will move from A to B. The number of cars produced by Japan will rise from 1.3 million to 1.7 million and the market price per car will fall from $12,000 to $8,000.

Can Canada match this performance despite the gap in its productivity growth? It can if its wages and other input prices fall sufficiently. If productivity growth in Canada is zero, but input prices fall 50 percent over the same period, it can match the Japanese cost performance precisely. If it started out with the same supply and demand curves as Japan, it too will be able to cut the cost per car (when producing one million cars) from $10,000 to $5,000. That is, the corresponding point on its supply curve will move from C to E. Consequently, the Canadian supply curve will also shift from S_0S_0 to S_1S_1, just as Japan's did. The Canadian equilibrium will also move from point A to point B, and its prices and outputs will change just like Japan's.

That may sound easy and painless, but it is really a disaster for Canada. It is a mechanism for the impoverishment of Canadian workers. In effect, it enables the country to compete through low real wages rather than efficiency. By giving Canadian workers smaller and smaller quantities of goods for their efforts, it brings on the day when the rest of the world becomes afraid of the "unfair competition of cheap Canadian labour"—precisely the danger many Canadians once feared from competition with Japan and other countries in the Far East.

In practice, the process will, however, not affect all Canadian export industries similarly. Some traditional export industries will become unprofitable while others will arise to take their place. There are two reasons: First, productivity growth inevitably lags more severely in some industries than in others. Canadian investment will then move away from those industries in which the Canadian lag is greatest, toward industries in which it is smallest relative to other countries. Second, the fall in relative Canadian wages will not reduce the costs of all Canadian industry equally. Cheaper labour will reduce costs most heavily in handicraft activities in which other inputs play a comparatively minor role, and the wage lag will provide less of a cost advantage to high-tech industries with heavy capital–labour ratios. Both of these forces will depress some industries and benefit others, bringing about the painful transition problems of moving labour from one industry to another that were discussed earlier.

Falling real wages is not the only mechanism involved in preserving the markets for Canadian exports. Chapter 16, on the international monetary system, shows how the value of the dollar in relation to other currencies will always adjust in the long run to restore the foreign market for Canadian exports. Moreover, the law of comparative advantage (which will be discussed in detail in the following chapter) tells us that as Canada loses its competitiveness in some industries there must necessarily be other industries in which its *comparative* advantage increases; that is, in which it becomes comparatively less *inefficient*. It is industries in the latter category that will then produce Canada's exports.

The lag in Canadian productivity behind other countries does not threaten to cause cumulatively growing unemployment or to drive all Canadian industries from world markets. But the cost is nevertheless very high. It can lead to lower relative incomes for Canadians, transforming Canada into a cheap labour country. It can also cause shifts among industries, with some declining or dying and others rising to take their place, causing costly and painful transition problems.

Toward Remedies

No one has yet devised a foolproof set of prescriptions to raise productivity growth. However, a number of policy changes can be helpful. We will first discuss more or less obvious approaches designed primarily to encourage investment and innovation. Then we will turn to two highly publicized approaches with some political overtones—*supply-side economics* and *industrial strategy*. Each of these has a kernel of truth, but each has been badly oversold and suffers from serious practical shortcomings.

Encouragement of Saving and Investment

No one is sure exactly why Canadians save and invest so much less of their incomes than the Japanese. But some Canadian laws clearly discourage industrial investment; and others encourage investment in non-industrial items such as housing. Obviously, if one wants to increase the growth of labour productivity by stimulating industrial investment, these disincentives should be reversed. Here are two noteworthy proposals.

A **capital gain** is the difference between the price at which a piece of capital is sold and the price for which it was bought earlier. The **nominal capital gain** is calculated in current dollars without adjustment for inflation. The **real capital gain** is obtained after the price is adjusted for inflation; it is calculated in dollars of constant purchasing power.

1. Tax real capital gains. If a firm invested $100,000 in a machine in 1970 and sold it ten years later for $140,000, it would seem to have earned a **capital gain** of 40 percent. However, because the price level roughly doubled during this period, the $140,000 received in 1980 had the purchasing power of only $70,000 in 1970 dollars. In other words, the firm had spent 100,000 1970 dollars and received only 70,000 1970 dollars in return—an actual capital loss of 30 percent. We say that the firm earned a **nominal** capital gain of 40 percent but suffered a **real** capital loss of 30 percent.

   It is the real capital loss that matters to the investor. But, in Canada, taxes on investments are based on *nominal* capital gains instead. The firm in our example would be taxed on its 40 percent paper profit, even though it suffered a 30 percent real loss.

Such a tax provision means that even if an investor loses out on an investment in terms of purchasing power, she may nevertheless have to pay a tax besides—just as if she had made a profit. Obviously, this can discourage investment during an inflationary period. Many observers believe that a switch from taxation of nominal capital gains to taxation of real capital gains can make a major contribution to investment, encouraging construction of plant and equipment. However, as we noted in Chapter 11 (page 217), it is difficult for Canada to act alone in the corporate tax area. For branch companies of multinationals, tax reductions here often just mean taxes transferred to the government where the parent company is based.

2. Eliminate tax subsidies to housing. Homebuilding clearly takes resources that could be used to build factories instead. Investment in housing has for many years been accorded preferential tax treatments, such as the RHOSP program, the government allowance for first-time home buyers, and the exemption from any tax on the implicit rents received by house owners living in their own homes (see *Microeconomics*, Chapter 18, page 337). Many economists believe that elimination of some of these tax subsidies to housing can contribute to business investment by redirecting resources from home construction to industrial investment.

Savings and investment can be encouraged by policies such as reduced subsidies for private housing construction and taxation of real rather than nominal capital gains.

Encouragement of Innovation

Besides stimulating investment, one can seek to increase productivity by facilitating innovation through more government financing of basic research. Basic research is one of the mainstays of innovation and long-term productivity growth. Electronics, computers, and a variety of other technological innovations would not have been possible without **basic research**.

Most basic research is already financed by government, and only a little by private industry. The reason is that, while basic research generally has large payoffs, the researcher may not benefit from his or her ideas. Basic research in mathematics made modern automation possible many decades later. Basic research in physics made nuclear energy possible much later. But there was no practical way for the pioneering researchers to receive payment from the then unidentified future entrepreneurs who would profit from their work.

Thus, basic research is said to suffer from the **free-rider problem**—that is, those who benefit obtain their benefits free. Basic research is therefore unprofitable; and so private industry cannot be expected to invest a great deal in it. Consequently, basic research is usually financed by governments. It has been suggested that government funding of basic research should be increased.

Supply-Side Economics

We come, finally, to two controversial packages of proposals that have been widely advertised by their advocates as means to stimulate productivity.

Since **supply-side economics** has already been discussed in Chapter 11, we can deal with it rather briefly here. In a sense, any plan for the encouragement of productivity must be a supply-side measure in that it seeks to raise output primarily through its effect on supply rather than through any effects on demand. But serious questions have been raised about whether the measures advocated by supply-siders (many of which were described in Chapter 11) can really be expected to make an appreciable difference to productivity.

Careful examination of the bundle of measures that the United States

Basic research is research carried out to increase knowledge, without any particular practical use in mind. For example, what is the structure of the atom?

The **free-rider problem** arises whenever provision of a service to one individual or group automatically benefits others (the free riders) whether or not the others make any contribution to the costs. For example, if individual A on a private street builds drains to reduce flooding, all others who live on the street will automatically benefit.

Congress passed in the early 1980s under the supply-side banner gives a somewhat mixed picture. There were a number of targetted incentives of the sort discussed in this chapter; for example, tax breaks for increased investment and for retirement savings. But the mainstay of the program was simply a set of reductions in the taxes paid by individuals and business firms, in the hope that tax cuts will induce individuals to work harder and firms to pursue profits through growth.

Critics of Reaganomics question whether the tax cuts will make much difference. An analogy will illustrate the issue: Consider two firms which want to increase their sales. Firm A simply raises each salesperson's base wages by a flat 25 percent, no matter how much or how little she sells. Firm B, instead, increases the commission it pays on each item that an individual sells by 25 percent. At firm B, but not firm A, the more a salesperson manages to sell, the higher will be the rise in that individual's take-home pay. Which of the two companies do you think will end up with the larger increase in sales? The point is that a general tax reduction is very much like the approach taken by firm A in our example. The benefits are not, in general, contingent on the amount the firm or the individual does to increase productivity.

Industrial Strategy

Over the past decade, a very different approach to productivity stimulation has been advocated by a number of university researchers and embraced by many politicians. Called **industrial strategy**, the idea is to follow the example of the Japanese and the French by setting up a government planning agency to encourage the particular industries that, in the judgment of the agency, can make the largest contribution to the nation's productivity growth. If it judged that industry C has poor growth prospects while industry D promises the possibility of extraordinary growth, the agency could use means such as tax breaks, loans, and informal pressure to induce a flow of capital and labour out of industry C and into industry D. This, together with some industry-by-industry advice and other attempts to influence business decisions, would, it is hoped, make a major contribution to productivity growth in Canada.

Many economists object that no government agency can do as well as the forces of the market in picking probable future winners and losers. The profit motive already spurs investors to identify the winners and back them with their resources, while withdrawing funds from the likely losers. Private investors do make mistakes. But, in the view of many observers, the mistakes of government agencies are likely to be far more frequent, more serious, and more difficult to reverse, since the individual decision-makers involved do not stand to gain or lose to the same extent as private entrepreneurs.

For this and other reasons, critics of industrial strategy worry that an avowed policy of "picking winners" might degenerate into a habit of "backing losers." This seems to have happened in countries like Britain and Sweden. And recently, some leaders of troubled industries in the United States have proclaimed their support for industrial strategy—interpreting it as a call for trade barriers against imports and for help to sick and dying industries. This is, of course, a perversion of the basic logic of the industrial strategy idea, providing encouragement to the industries with the least promising future rather than to those whose prospects are brightest.

Market Mechanism Industrial Policy

Perhaps more in line with the way economists think is a proposal that might be described as market mechanism industrial policy or "real supply-side economics." This proposal seeks to apply to the economy the approach of our illustrative firm B, which sought to stimulate sales by paying salespersons according to results.

Market mechanism industrial policy would provide reductions in business taxes, but not uniformly for all firms. Rather, firms would be given a rebate based on the rate of increase in their productivity.[7] The faster a firm increases its productivity, all other things being equal, the lower the tax bill it will have to pay at the end of the year. Such a plan would increase the profitability of industries in which it is easy to raise productivity, and reduce the profitability of investment in industries in which it is hard to raise productivity. In this way, the program could induce businesspeople to make the type of decisions that a government agency under an industrial strategy would strive for. But, by avoiding government intervention on an industry-by-industry basis—with its mixture of subsidies, tax breaks, and special stimuli—a market-based approach might achieve the same end at lower economic cost and with less government interference in individual decisions.

The Cost of Productivity Growth

These are but some examples of policies that have been advocated to stimulate productivity growth. What is clear is that there is a large menu of ideas from which to choose. But, if there is to be any hope of making a big improvement in the Canadian rate of productivity growth, small doses of just a few of these remedies will not suffice. As usual, large effects cannot be expected to follow from small measures.

According to some business persons, all that is needed to raise productivity growth significantly is an end to inflation, a sharp reduction in business taxes, and a great decrease in the severity of regulation. It is easy to understand why they advocate such changes. But we can hardly be confident that these changes alone will bring about a great rise in the Canadian productivity growth rate. In this connection, it is suggestive to recall that in the period 1870–1914, when Great Britain lost its lead in productivity, it had no inflation, virtually no business taxes, and virtually no regulation of business.

Effective action to increase productivity growth also cannot be completely painless. At a minimum, it will require an increase in investment relative to GNP, which must entail a painful sacrifice of current consumption, at least in the short run. To use one of the economist's favourite clichés, here, as everywhere, there is no such thing as a free lunch.

[7]This is not the place to discuss how productivity would be measured for this purpose or to examine some other difficulties entailed in carrying out the proposal. It is described here merely to indicate a general approach through which the market mechanism might be enlisted to achieve the goals of an industrial strategy.

Summary

1. Productivity growth is the primary determinant of real income per capita, that is, of standards of living.

2. Over long periods, a small increase in annual productivity growth compounds into an enormous rise in living standards. This is one of our **12 Ideas for Beyond the Final Exam**.

3. In recent decades, Canada has suffered from two different productivity problems: (1) our rate of productivity growth has fallen from about four percent per year to almost zero percent per year; and (2) our rate of annual productivity growth has been less than those of many industrial economies.

4. No one is sure about what has caused productivity growth in Canada (and in other countries) to slow down. Probably, the main causes are a lag in growth of investment in plant and equipment, the rise in energy prices in the 1970s, and some lag in innovation, which may be attributable to the protracted period of simultaneous inflation and unemployment.

5. The decline in Canadian productivity growth from its earlier rates has held back the growth of per capita income, made it harder to finance social programs such as health care and environmental protection, and contributed to inflation.

6. The lag in Canadian productivity growth behind other countries is partly explained by the fact that Canadians save and invest a lower proportion of their incomes than people in some other countries do. In addition, it may be explained in part by a decline in entrepreneurship; by special foreign labour relations practices such as quality circles and lifetime employment (which encourage workers to accept labour-saving innovations); by other countries' government programs to encourage growth; and by the combination of our tariffs and small domestic markets, which keep average costs high.

7. The lag of Canadian productivity growth relative to other countries has reduced relative real wages in Canada and caused heavy adjustment costs by changing the mix of viable Canadian industries. In the long run, however, it will not cause growing Canadian unemployment or loss of all export markets to Canadian industry.

8. Canadian productivity growth can be encouraged by measures such as taxation of real rather than nominal capital gains to encourage investment, by reduced taxation of savings, and by greater government support for basic research.

9. An effective productivity program requires some short-term sacrifices in consumption to make more investment possible, and may entail other costs as well.

10. Supply-side economics is a program to encourage investment and harder work primarily through tax reductions. However, the U.S. program that was tried by President Reagan has been criticized as a tax giveaway, because it did not base the size of an individual's or a firm's tax break to any appreciable degree on what the recipient of the tax advantage has done for productivity growth.

11. Industrial strategy is a proposed program involving a government agency that would select industries whose productivity growth is most promising, and would provide special assistance to those industries. It has been criticized as a source of all the inefficiencies that usually accompany case-by-case government intervention.

Concepts for Review

Compounding of productivity gains	Lifetime employment	Nominal capital gain
Labour productivity	Quality circles	Basic and applied research
Productivity growth	Entrepreneurship	Free-rider problem
Research and Development (R & D)	Capital gain	Supply-side economics
Service industries	Real capital gain	Industrial strategy

Questions for Discussion

1. With a one percent productivity growth rate, productivity will quadruple in about 140 years. With a two percent growth rate it will increase 16 times in about the same period. Can you account for the disproportionate difference?

2. Are there ways to increase income per capita other than raising productivity? Can you give examples? How much can they help a country's living standard in the short run? In the long run? (Hint: Can a country benefit by borrowing from abroad?)

3. Why do you think productivity growth in most industrialized countries fell at about the same time—between the end of the 1960s and the beginning of the 1970s?

4. What do you suspect are the main causes of the slowdown in Canadian productivity growth?

5. What do you think are the main causes of the lag in Canadian productivity growth behind other countries?

6. If Canadian productivity growth continues to lag behind that of other countries for another 50 years, which industries do you think will be hurt most severely? Which industries will benefit? Why? (Hint: Which industries will benefit most from relatively low real wages?)

7. Besides requiring a reduction in consumption, what other sacrifices may be entailed by an increase in productivity growth? (Hint: Do people enjoy working harder? What will be the effects on the environment? May there be any benefits for the environment?)

8. How would you design an effective supply-side program?

9. Discuss the pros and cons of industrial strategy.

10. Suppose that an average annual three percent growth rate of labour productivity is adopted as a target by the Canadian government for the next decade. Discuss what combination of measures offers any hope of achieving such a major increase in productivity growth. (No one is sure of the correct answer to this, or even whether an answer is possible.)

The Free Trade Issue

21

Since attempts to control powerful corporations by direct *regulation* and by competition *laws* have met with only limited success (see *Microeconomics*, Chapters 15 and 16), many economists argue that we should rely instead on the discipline of the *market*. This discipline could be enforced by exposing firms that operate in Canada to more competition with firms already existing elsewhere in the world. This competition is currently limited by a series of import taxes known as tariffs and by import quota regulations. Canada's average tariff rate on industrial products is just under 13 percent, while the comparable figure for the United States is 6 percent; for Japan, 5 percent; and for the European Economic Community, 6.5 percent.

As a result of Canada's tariff barriers, and those imposed by other countries against our manufactured goods, Canadian producers have largely concentrated on the small domestic market. This has meant operating at relatively low volume, with higher unit costs and higher industrial concentration. Tariff cuts by Canada would force our producers to expand operations (to reduce unit costs) and sell a significant part of their output on world markets, or to get out of business.

The *benefits* of this policy are rather obvious: Canadian consumers would be able to buy a host of products at reduced prices, since the increased competition would force producers to more closely approximate the efficiency gains that exist in a perfectly competitive economy. To many people, the *costs* of this policy are equally obvious. They fear that our producers would not be able to compete with those employing "cheap foreign labour." These opponents of tariff cuts think that many business failures and a large increase in unemployment would follow any cut in tariffs. Thus they argue that we simply cannot afford to lower our trade barriers unilaterally. Many economists disagree, and we explain why in this chapter.

To be complete, our investigation into the cost of tariff cuts must take a rather circuitous route. First, we will explain the purposes of foreign trade and the ways in which governments have sought to influence or limit it. Second, we will study the crucial *law of comparative advantage*, which determines what commodities a country finds advantageous to export and what commodities it finds advantageous to import. This principle shows that *even* if there are *no* economies of large-scale production, both trading countries benefit from increased international exchange. Third, we will see how the prices of goods traded between countries are determined by supply and demand. And, finally, we will examine the pros and cons of tariffs and other devices designed to protect a country's industries from foreign competition. By the end of the chapter, we will have exposed the fallacy behind the view that "cheap foreign labour" necessitates tariff barriers.

Issue: The Competition of "Cheap Foreign Labour"

When analysing the issues of international trade, common sense can be extremely valuable; indeed, there is no substitute for it. Yet sometimes conclusions based on common sense without factual confirmation and careful analysis can be very misleading.

One example of a foreign trade issue that has been misunderstood for lack of factual analysis is the argument that buying products made by cheap foreign labour is unfair and destructive to domestic interests. Some Canadian business people and union leaders argue that such purchases take bread out of the mouths of Canadian workers and depress standards of living in this country. According to this view, cheap imports cause job losses and put pressure on Canadian businesses to lower wages.

Yet the facts are not consistent with this scenario. Many of Canada's imports come from Western Europe and Japan. Since the early 1960s, wages have risen far more dramatically in these other countries than here. Yet we keep importing such items as Volkswagens, Volvos, and Datsuns in greater numbers. More important, the rise in these foreign wages, compared with those in Canada, has not brought an increasing strength in the Canadian position in the international marketplace.

In the 1950s, when European and Japanese wages were far below those in Canada, we had no trouble marketing our products abroad. It was far easier then than now to sell the amount of exports needed to pay for the amount of goods that were imported. Then, in the 1960s and 1970s, as wages in Europe and Japan rose closer to—and in some cases surpassed—those in Canada, we ran into serious trouble selling goods abroad. We were, and still are, often unable to export enough to pay for our imports. Clearly, cheap foreign labour does not always serve as a crucial obstacle to Canadian sales abroad, as a "common sense" view of the matter suggests. In this chapter we will see what is wrong with that view.

Why Trade?

The main reason that countries trade with one another rather than try to run completely independent economies is that the earth's resources are not equally distributed across its surface. Canada has an abundant supply of forests and fresh water, resources that are quite scarce in most of the rest of the world. Saudi Arabia has very little land that is suitable for farming, but it sits atop a huge pool of oil. Because of this seemingly whimsical distribution of vital resources, every nation must trade with others to acquire what it lacks. In general, the more varied the endowment of a particular country, the less it will have to depend on others to make up for its deficiencies.

Even if countries had all the resources they needed, other differences in natural endowments—such as climate, terrain, and so on—would lead them to engage in trade. Canadians *could*, with great difficulty, grow their own banana trees and coffee shrubs in hothouses; but these items are much more efficiently grown in such places as Honduras and Brazil, where the climate is appropriate. On the other hand, wheat grows in Canada with little difficulty, while mountainous Switzerland is not good at growing either bananas or wheat.

The skills of a country's labour force also play a role. If New Zealand has a large group of efficient farmers and few workers with industrial experience while the opposite is true in Great Britain, it makes sense for New Zealand to specialize in agriculture and let Great Britain concentrate on manufacturing.

This last point suggests one other important reason why countries trade—the advantage of **specialization**. If one country were to try to produce everything, it would end up with a number of industries whose scale of operation was too small to permit the use of mass-production techniques, specialized training facilities, and other arrangements that give a cost advantage to large-scale operations. Even now, despite the considerable volume of world trade, this problem seems to arise for some countries whose operation of their own international airlines or their own steel mills, for example, seems explainable only in political rather than economic terms. Inevitably, small nations that insist on operating in industries that are economical only when their scale of operation is large find that these enterprises can survive only with the aid of large government subsidies.

Specialization means that a country devotes its energies and resources to only a small proportion of the world's productive activities.

To summarize: International trade is essential for the prosperity of the trading nations for at least three reasons: (1) every country lacks some vital resources that it can get only by trading with others; (2) each country's climate, labour force, and other endowments make it a relatively efficient producer of some goods and an inefficient producer of other goods; and (3) specialization permits larger outputs and can therefore offer economies of large-scale production.

Mutual Gains from Trade

Some of the early writers on international trade implied that one nation could gain from an exchange only at the expense of another. It was pointed out that since nothing is produced by the act of trading, the total collection of goods in the hands of the two parties at the end of an exchange is no greater than before the exchange took place. Therefore, it was argued (fallaciously), if one country gains from a swap, the other country must necessarily lose.

One of the consequences of this mistaken view was a policy prescription calling for each country, in the interests of its citizens, to do its best to act to the disadvantage of its trading partners—in Adam Smith's terms, to "beggar its neighbours." The idea that one nation's gain must be another's loss means that a country can promote its own welfare only by harming others.

Yet, as Adam Smith and others after him emphasized, in any *voluntary exchange*, unless there is misunderstanding of the facts, both parties *must* gain (or at least expect to gain) something from the transaction. Otherwise why would both parties agree to the exchange?

But how can mere exchange, in which no production takes place, actually leave both parties better off? The answer is that while there can be no gain in the *physical quantities* of the products exchanged, the holdings of both parties can end up much better suited to the needs of each. Suppose Brian has four sandwiches and nothing to drink, while David has four cartons of milk and nothing to eat. A trade of two of Brian's sandwiches for two of David's cartons of milk does not increase the total supply of either food or beverages, but it clearly produces a net increase in the welfare of both boys.

Mutual Gains from Voluntary Exchange

Any *voluntary exchange* must promise to make *both* parties better off. Trade can bring about mutual gains by redistributing products in such a way that both participants end up holding a combination of goods that is better adapted to their preferences than the goods they held before. This principle, which is one of our **12 Ideas for Beyond the Final Exam**, applies to nations just as it does to individuals.

International Versus Intranational Trade

The logic of international trade is essentially no different from that underlying trade among different provinces; the basic reasons for trade are equally applicable *within* a country or *among* countries. If we can learn about trade from strictly domestic exchanges why study international trade as a special subject? There are at least three reasons.

First, domestic trade takes place under a single government, while foreign trade must involve at least two governments. At least in theory, the government of a nation is concerned with the welfare of all its citizens. But governments are usually much less deeply concerned with the welfare of citizens of other countries. As we have already seen, a major issue in the economic analysis of international trade is the use and misuse of impediments to free international trade. Later in the chapter such trade barriers will be discussed in greater detail.

Second, all trade within Canadian borders is carried out in a single currency—dollars. But trade across national borders must involve at least two currencies. Rates of exchange between different currencies can and do change. This variability in exchange rates brings with it the host of complications and policy problems that we discussed in Chapter 16.

Third, it is usually much easier for labour and capital to move within a country than to move from one country to another. If there are jobs in Alberta but none in Ontario, workers can move freely to follow the job opportunities. Of course, there are personal costs—not only the dollar cost of moving, but also the psychological cost of giving up friends and familiar surroundings. But such moves are not inhibited by immigration quotas or by laws restricting the employment of foreigners, as are moves from one country to another.

There are also more impediments to the transfer of capital from one country to another than to its movement within a country. The shipment of plant and equipment between countries can be expensive. Such investment abroad is also subject to special risks, such as the danger of outright expropriation if, say, after a political revolution the new government decides to take over all foreign properties without compensation. But even if nothing so extreme occurs, capital invested abroad faces risks from possible variations in exchange rates. An investment in the U.K. yielding a million pounds a year will be worth $2 million to Canadian investors if the pound is worth $2 but only $1 million if the pound should fall to $1.

While labour, capital, and other factors of production do move from country to country when offered an opportunity to increase their earnings abroad, they are less likely to do so than to move from one region of a country to another to gain similar increases.

Comparative Advantage: The Fundamental Principle of Specialization

We have seen that trade can be beneficial to both parties. Some of the reasons are obvious. But now we turn to an important source of mutual benefit that is far from obvious.

We know that coffee can be produced in Colombia using less labour and smaller quantities of other inputs than would be needed to grow it in Canada. And we know that Canada can produce passenger aircraft at a lower resource cost than can Colombia. We say then that Colombia has an **absolute advantage** over Canada in coffee production, and Canada has an absolute advantage over Colombia in aircraft production.

A numerical example will illustrate the idea. According to Table 21-1, one year of labour time in Canada can produce either 50 kilograms of coffee or 1/20 of

One country is said to have an **absolute advantage** over another in the production of a particular good if it can produce that good using smaller quantities of resources than can the other country.

Table 21-1

ALTERNATIVE OUTPUTS FROM ONE YEAR OF LABOUR INPUT

	IN CANADA	IN COLOMBIA
Coffee (kilograms)	50	300
Airplanes	1/20	1/100

an airplane. By contrast, one year of labour time in Colombia can produce 300 kilograms of coffee or 1/100 of an airplane. Thus, six years of labour input would be required to produce 300 kilograms of coffee in Canada, whereas Colombia could do the job with only one year's worth of labour. On the other hand, it would take Colombia 100 years of labour to produce an airplane, a job Canada could do in only 20 years.

Obviously, if Canada wants coffee and Colombia wants airplanes, both can save resources by trading—each exporting to the other the good in which it has an absolute advantage.

Suppose, however, that one country is more efficient than another in producing *every* item. Can they still gain by trading? The surprising answer is *definitely yes*, and a simple parable will help explain why.

The work of a highly-paid business consultant frequently requires computer analysis. Suppose the consultant began her career as a computer operator doing her own data entry, and was extremely good at it. In her current position she may grow impatient with the slow, sloppy work of some of the low-paid support staff who work for her, and at times be tempted to do all the work herself. Good judgment, however, tells her that though she is better *both* at giving business advice *and* at data entry than are her employees, it is foolish to devote any of her valuable time to the low-skilled job. That is because the opportunity cost of an hour devoted to data entry is an hour less devoted to business consulting—a far more lucrative activity.

This is an example of the principle of **comparative advantage** at work. The consultant specializes in business advice despite her absolute advantage in data entry because she has a still greater absolute advantage in her role as a business consultant. She suffers some direct loss by not doing her own data entry. But that loss is more than compensated for by the earnings she makes selling her consulting services to clients.

This example brings out the fundamental principle that underlies the bulk of economic analysis of patterns of specialization and exchange among different nations. This principle is called the *law of comparative advantage*, and it is one of our **12 Ideas for Beyond the Final Exam**. It was discovered by David Ricardo, one of the giants in the history of economic analysis.

One country is said to have a **comparative advantage** over another in the production of a particular good relative to other goods it can produce if it produces that good least inefficiently as compared with the other country.

The Law of Comparative Advantage

Even if one country is at an absolute *disadvantage* relative to another country in the production of *every* good, it is said to have a *comparative advantage* in making the good in whose production it is *least inefficient* in comparison with the other country.

Ricardo's basic finding was that two countries can still gain by trading even if one country is more efficient than another in the production of *every* commodity (that is, it has an absolute advantage in every commodity).

In determining the most efficient patterns of production, what matters is *comparative* advantage, not *absolute* advantage. Thus, one country will often gain by importing a certain good even if that good can be produced at home more efficiently than it can be produced abroad. Such imports will be profitable if the country is even more efficient at producing the goods that it exports in exchange.

The Arithmetic of Comparative Advantage

Let's see precisely how this works using numbers based on Ricardo's own example. Suppose labour is the only input used in producing wine and cloth in two countries, England and Portugal. Suppose further that Portugal has an absolute advantage in both goods, as indicated in Table 21–2. In this example, a week's worth of labour can produce either 12 metres of cloth of 6 barrels of wine in Portugal, but only 10 metres of cloth or 1 barrel of wine in England. So Portugal is the more efficient producer of both goods. None the less, as our multitalented-consultant example suggests, it pays for Portugal to specialize in wine production and get its cloth from England. We will now demonstrate this conclusion.

Table 21–2
ALTERNATIVE OUTPUTS FROM ONE WEEK OF LABOUR INPUT

	IN ENGLAND	IN PORTUGAL
Cloth (metres)	10	12
Wine (barrels)	1	6

The numbers in Table 21–2 indicate that Portugal is 20 percent more efficient than England in producing cloth: It can produce 12 metres with a week's labour, whereas England can produce only 10 metres. However, Portugal is six times as efficient as England in producing wine: It produces 6 barrels per week rather than 1. So we say that Portugal has a *comparative advantage in wine* while England has a *comparative advantage in cloth*. According to Ricardo's law of comparative advantage, both countries can gain if Portugal specializes in producing wine, England specializes in producing cloth, and the two countries trade with one another.

Suppose that Portugal transfers a million weeks of labour out of the textile industry and into winemaking. According to the figures in Table 21–2, its cloth output falls by 12 million metres while its wine output rises by 6 million barrels. (See Table 21–3.) Suppose, at the same time, England transfers 2 million weeks of labour out of winemaking (thereby losing 2 million barrels of wine) and into clothmaking (thereby gaining 20 million metres of cloth). Table 21–3 shows us that these transfers of resources in the two countries increase the world's production of both outputs!

Together, the two countries now have 4 million additional barrels of wine and 8 million additional metres of cloth—surely a nice outcome. But there seems to be some sleight-of-hand here. All that has taken place is an exchange; yet, somehow Portugal and England gain both cloth and wine. How can such gains in physical output be possible?

The explanation is that the trade process we have just described involves more than just a swap of a fixed bundle of commodities. It is also a *change in the production arrangements*, with some of England's wine production taken over by the more efficient producers of Portuguese wine, and with some of Portugal's cloth production taken over by English weavers who are *less in*efficient at producing cloth than English vintners are at producing wine.

Table 21–3
EXAMPLE OF THE GAINS FROM TRADE

	ENGLAND	PORTUGAL	TOTAL
Cloth (millions of metres)	+20	–12	+8
Wine (millions of barrels)	– 2	+ 6	+4

Biographical Note: David Ricardo (1772–1823)

David Ricardo was born four years before publication of Adam Smith's *Wealth of Nations*. Descended from a family of well-to-do stockbrokers of the Jewish faith who migrated to London from Amsterdam and were, in turn, descended from Portuguese Jews, he had about twenty brothers and sisters. At a school in Amsterdam, Ricardo's formal education ended at the age of 13, and so he was largely self-educated. He began his career by working in his father's brokerage firm. At age 21, Ricardo married a Quaker woman and decided to become a Unitarian, a sect then considered "little better than atheist." By Jewish custom, Ricardo's father broke with him, though apparently they remained friendly.

Ricardo then decided to go into the brokerage business on his own and was enormously successful. During the Napoleonic Wars he regularly scored business coups over leading British and foreign financiers, including the Rothschilds. After gaining a huge profit on government securities that he had bought just before the Battle of Waterloo, Ricardo decided to retire from business when he was just over 40 years old.

He purchased a country estate, Gatcomb (now owned by the royal family), where a brilliant group of intellectuals met regularly. Particularly remarkable for the period was the number of women included in the circle, among them Maria Edgeworth, the novelist (who wrote extravagant praise of Ricardo's mind), and Jane Marcet, an author of textbooks, one of which was probably the first text in economics. Ricardo's close friends included the economists T.R. Malthus and James Mill, father of John Stuart Mill, the noted philosopher–economist. Malthus remained a close friend of Ricardo even though they disagreed on many subjects and continued their arguments in personal correspondence and in their published works.

James Mill persuaded Ricardo to go into Parliament. As was then customary, Ricardo purchased his seat by buying a piece of land that entitled its owner to a seat in Parliament. There he proved to be a noteworthy liberal,

strongly supporting many causes that were against his personal interests.

James Mill also helped persuade Ricardo to write his masterpiece, *The Principles of Political Economy and Taxation*, which may have been the first book of pure economic theory. It was noteworthy that Ricardo, the most practical of practical men, had little patience with empirical economics and preferred instead to rest his analysis explicitly and exclusively on theory. His book made considerable contributions to the analysis of pricing, wage determination, and the effects of various types of taxes, among many other subjects. It also gave us the law of comparative advantage. In addition, the book described what has come to be called the Ricardian rent theory—even though Ricardo did not discover the analysis and explicitly denied having done so.

Ricardo died in 1823 at the age of 51. He seems to have been a wholly admirable person—honest, charming, witty, conscientious, brilliant—altogether too good to be true.

When every country does what it can do best, all countries can benefit because more of every commodity can be produced without increasing the given quantity of labour.

If this result still seems a bit mysterious, the concept of *opportunity cost* will help remove the remaining mystery. If the two countries do not trade, Table 21–2 shows that England can acquire a barrel of wine only by giving up 10 metres of cloth. Thus, the opportunity cost of a barrel of wine in England is 10 metres of cloth. But in Portugal the opportunity cost of a barrel of wine is only 2 metres of cloth (again, see Table 21–2). Thus, in terms of real resources forgone, it is cheaper

—for either country—to acquire wine in Portugal. By a similar line of reasoning, it can be shown that the opportunity cost of cloth is higher in Portugal than in England, so it makes sense for both countries to acquire their cloth in England.[1]

The Graphics of Comparative Advantage

The gains from trade can also be displayed graphically, and doing so helps us to understand how these gains arise.

The lines *EF* and *PQ* in Figure 21-1 are the *production possibilities frontiers* of the two countries, drawn on the assumption that each country has 6 million weeks of labour available.[2] For example, with 6 million weeks of labour, Table 21-2 tells us that England can produce 6 million barrels of wine and no cloth (point *E*), 60 million metres of cloth and no wine (point *F*), or any combination in between (the line *EF*). Similar reasoning shows that *PQ* is Portugal's production possibilities frontier.

Note that Portugal's production possibilities frontier lies above England's throughout the diagram. That is because Portugal is the more efficient producer of both commodities. With the same amount of labour, it can obtain more wine and more cloth than England. Thus, the higher position of Portugal's frontier is the graph's way of showing Portugal's *absolute* advantage.

Portugal's comparative advantage in wine production and England's comparative advantage in cloth production are shown in a different way—by the relative *slopes* of the two production possibilities frontiers. Portugal's frontier is not only higher than England's, it is also flatter. What does this mean economically? One way of looking at the difference is to remember that while Portugal can produce six times as much wine as England (compare points *P* and *E*), it can produce only 20 percent more cloth than England (points *Q* and *F*). England is, relatively speaking, much better at cloth production than at wine production. That is what is meant when we say it has a *comparative* advantage in the former.

We may express this difference more directly in terms of the slopes of the two lines. The slope of Portugal's production possibilities frontier is $OQ/OP = 72/36 = 2$. This means that if Portugal reduces its wine production by one barrel it will obtain two metres of cloth. Thus, the *opportunity cost* of a barrel of wine in Portugal is two metres of cloth, as we observed earlier.

In the case of England, the slope of the production possibilities frontier is

[1] As an exercise, provide this line of reasoning.

[2] To review the concept of the production possibilities frontier, see Chapter 3.

Figure 21-1

ABSOLUTE AND COMPARATIVE ADVANTAGE SHOWN BY TWO COUNTRIES' PRODUCTION POSSIBILITIES FRONTIERS

Portugal's absolute advantage is shown by its ability to produce more of every commodity using the same quantity of labour as does England. Therefore, Portugal's production possibilities frontier, *PQ*, is higher than England's *EF*. But Portugal has a comparative advantage in wine production in which it is six times as productive as England. It can produce 36 million barrels (point *P*), compared with England's 6 million barrels (point *E*). On the other hand, Portugal is only 20 percent more productive in cloth production (point *Q*) than England (point *F*). Thus, England is less inefficient in producing cloth, where it consequently has a comparative advantage.

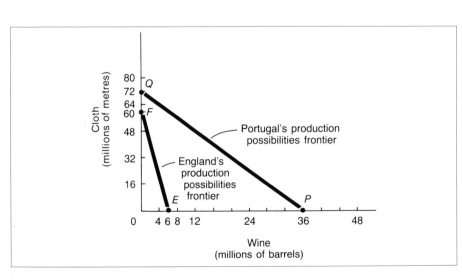

$OF/OE = 60/6 = 10$. That is, if England reduces wine production by one barrel, it gets 10 additional metres of cloth. So in England, the *opportunity cost* of a barrel of wine is 10 metres of cloth.

A country's absolute advantage in production over another country is shown by its having a higher production possibilities frontier. The difference in the comparative advantages of the two countries is shown by the difference in the slopes of their frontiers.

Because opportunity costs differ in the two countries, gains from trade are possible. How these gains are divided between the two countries depends on the prices for wine and cloth that emerge from world trade, which is the subject of the next section. But we already know enough to see that world prices must make a barrel of wine cost less than 10 metres of cloth and more than 2 metres. Why? Because, if a barrel of wine cost more than 10 metres of cloth (its opportunity cost in England), England would be better off producing its own wine rather than trading with Portugal. Similarly, if a barrel of wine fetched less than two metres of cloth (its opportunity cost in Portugal), Portugal would prefer to produce its own cloth rather than trade with England.

We conclude, therefore, that if both countries are to benefit from trade, the rate of exchange between cloth and wine must be somewhere between 10 to 1 and 2 to 1. To illustrate the gains from trade in a concrete example, suppose the world price ratio settles at 4 to 1; that is, one barrel of wine costs 4 metres of cloth. How much, precisely, do England and Portugal gain from world trade?

Figure 21–2 is designed to help us see the answer. Production possibilities

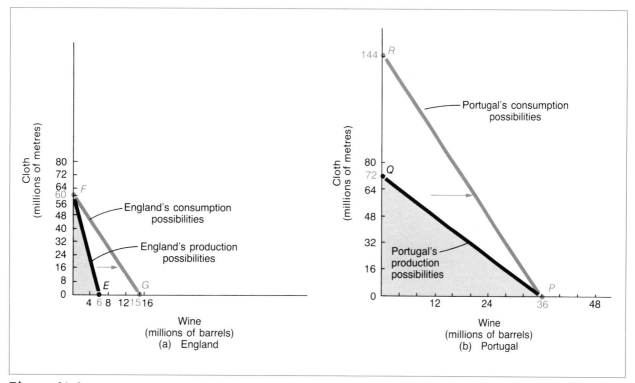

Figure 21-2

THE GAINS FROM TRADE

In this diagram, we suppose that trade opens up between England and Portugal and that the world price of wine is four times the world price of cloth. Now England's consumption possibilities are all the points on line *FG* (which starts at *F* and has a slope of 4), rather than just the points on its own production possibilities frontier, *EF*. Similarly, Portugal can choose any point on line *PR* (which begins at *P* and has a slope of 4), rather than just points on *QP*. Thus both nations gain from trade.

frontiers *EF* in part (a) and *PQ* in part (b) are the same as in Figure 21-1. But England can do better than *EF*. Specifically, with a world price ratio of 4 to 1, England can buy a barrel of wine by giving up only 4 metres of cloth rather than 10 metres (which is the opportunity cost of wine in England). Hence, if England produces only cloth [point *F* in Figure 21-2(a)] and buys its wine from Portugal, England's *consumption possibilities* will be as indicated by the blue line that begins at point *F* and has a slope of 4—indicating that each additional barrel of wine costs England 4 metres of cloth. Since trade allows England to choose a point on *FG* rather than on *FE*, trade opens up consumption possibilities that were simply not available before.

The story is similar for Portugal. If the Portuguese produce only wine [point *P* in Figure 21-2(b)], they can acquire 4 metres of cloth from England for each barrel of wine they give up as they move along the blue line *PR* (whose slope is 4). This is better than they can do on their own, since a sacrifice of one barrel of wine yields only 2 metres of cloth in Portugal. Hence world trade enlarges Portugal's consumption possibilities from *PQ* to *PR*.

Figure 21-2 shows graphically that gains from trade arise to the extent that world prices (4 to 1 in our example) differ from domestic opportunity costs (10 to 1 and 2 to 1 in our example). So it is a matter of some importance to understand how prices in international trade are established. Supply and demand is a natural place to start.

Supply-Demand Equilibrium and Pricing in Foreign Trade

In the context of international trade, the supply-demand model runs into several complications we have not encountered before. First, it involves at least two demand curves: that of the exporting country and that of the importing country. Second, it may also involve two supply curves, since the importing country may produce some part of the amount it uses. The third and final complication is that equilibrium does not take place at the intersection point of *either* pair of supply-demand curves. Why? Because if there is any trade, the exporting country's quantity supplied must be *greater* than its quantity demanded, while the quantity supplied by the importing country must be *less* than its quantity demanded.

These complications are illustrated in Figure 21-3, where we show the supply and demand curves of a country that exports wine, in part (a), and the supply and demand curves of a country that imports wine, in part (b). For simplicity, we assume that these countries do not deal in wine with anyone else.

Where will the two-country wine market reach equilibrium? The equilibrium price in a free market must satisfy two requirements:

1. The price of wine must be the same in both countries.

2. The quantity of wine exported (the excess of the exporting country's quantity supplied over its quantity demanded) must equal the quantity of wine imported (the excess of the importing country's quantity demanded over its quantity supplied).

In Figure 21-3, this happens at a price of $100 per barrel. At that price, the distance *AB* between what the exporting country produces (point *B*) and what it consumes (point *A*) equals the distance *CD* between the quantity demanded of the importing country (point *D*) and its quantity supplied (point *C*). At a price of $100 per barrel, the amount the exporting country has available to sell abroad is exactly equal to the amount the importer wants to buy, and matters are in balance. So $100 per barrel is the market price.

At a price higher than $100, we can expect producers in both countries to

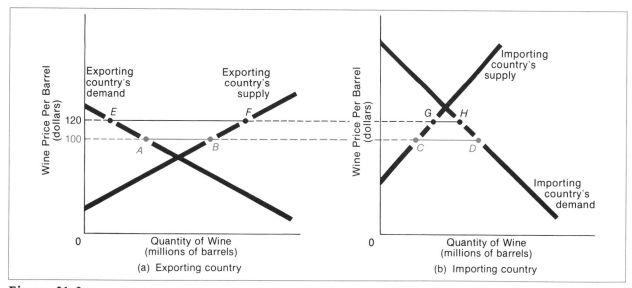

Figure 21-3

SUPPLY-DEMAND EQUILIBRIUM IN THE INTERNATIONAL WINE TRADE

Equilibrium requires that the net exports, *AB* (that is, the exporting country's quantity supplied, *B*, minus the exporter's quantity demanded, *A*), exactly balance imports, *CD*, by the importing country. At $100 per barrel of wine, there is equilibrium. But at a higher price, say $120, there is disequilibrium because net export supply, *EF*, exceeds net import demand, *GH*.

want to sell more and consumers in both countries to want to buy less. For example, if the price rises to $120 per barrel, the exporter's quantity supplied will rise from *B* to *F*, and the exporter's quantity demanded will fall from *A* to *E*, as shown in Figure 21-3(a). As a result, there will be a rise in the amount available for export, from *AB* to *EF*. For exactly the same reason, the price increase will cause higher production and lower sales in the importing country, leading to a shrinkage in the amount the importing country wants to import—from *CD* to *GH* in part (b). This means that the new price, $120 per barrel, cannot be sustained if the international market is free and competitive. With export supply *EF* far greater than import demand *GH*, there must be a downward pressure on price and a move back toward the $100 equilibrium price. Similar reasoning shows that prices below $100 also cannot be sustained.

We can now see the straightforward role of supply-demand equilibrium in international trade:

In international trade, the equilibrium price must be at a level at which the excess of the exporter's quantity supplied over its domestic quantity demanded is exactly equal to the excess of the importer's quantity demanded over its quantity supplied. Equilibrium will occur at a price at which the horizontal distance *AB* in Figure 21-3(a) (the excess of the exporter's quantity supplied over its quantity demanded) is equal to the horizontal distance *CD* in Figure 21-3(b) (the excess of the importer's quantity demanded over its quantity supplied). At this price, the *world's* quantity demanded is equal to the *world's* quantity supplied.

Comparative Advantage and Competition of "Cheap Foreign Labour"

The principle of comparative advantage takes us a good part of the way toward an explanation of the fallacy in the "cheap foreign labour" argument described earlier in the chapter. Given the assumed productive efficiency of Portuguese labour and the inefficiency of British labour in Ricardo's example, we would expect wages to be much higher in Portugal than in England. Indeed, if workers receive all of the nation's output, and wine and cloth are produced in the same proportions in both countries, then this *must* be so, because output per person in Portugal is so much higher.

In these circumstances, one can expect Portuguese workers to be apprehensive about an agreement to permit trade between the countries—"How can we hope to meet the unfair competition of those underpaid British workers?" And British labourers are also likely to be concerned—"How can we hope to meet the competition of those Portuguese, who are so efficient in producing everything?"

The principle of comparative advantage shows us that both fears are unjustified. As we have just seen, when trade is opened up between Portugal and England *workers in both countries will be able to earn higher real wages than before* because of the increased productivity that comes about through specialization.

Figure 21-2 (page 405) shows this fact quite directly. We have seen from our illustration that, with trade, England can end up with more wine and more cloth than it had before, and so the living standards of its workers can rise even though they have been left vulnerable to the competition of the superefficient Portuguese. Portugal also can end up with more wine and with more cloth, so the living standards of its workers can rise even though they have been exposed to the competition of cheap British labour.

The lesson to be learned here is that nothing helps raise standards of living more than does a greater abundance of goods.

Tariffs, Quotas, and Other Interferences with Trade

Despite the mutual gains obtained, international trade has historically been subjected to unrelenting pressure for government interference. In fact, until the rise of a free-trade movement in England at the end of the eighteenth and the beginning of the nineteenth centuries (with such economists as Adam Smith and David Ricardo at its vanguard), it was taken for granted that one of the essential tasks of government was the imposition of regulations to impede trade, presumably in the national interest.

There were many who argued then (and some who still argue today) that a nation's wealth consists of the amount of gold or other monies at its command. Consequently, the proper aim of government policy is to do everything it can to promote exports (in order to increase the amount foreigners owe to it) and to discourage imports (in order to decrease the amount the country owes to foreigners).

Obviously, there are limits to which this policy can be carried out. A country *must* import vital foodstuffs or critical raw materials that it cannot supply for itself; for if it does not, it must suffer a severe fall in living standards. Moreover, it is mathematically impossible for *every* country to sell more than it buys—one country's exports *must* be some other country's imports. If everyone competes in this game and cuts imports to the bone, then obviously exports must go the same way. The result will be that everyone is deprived of the mutual gains that trade can provide.

In more recent times, notably in the United States during the first three decades of the twentieth century, there was a return to an active policy designed to reduce competition from foreign imports. Since then, Western countries have attempted to promote freedom of trade, and barriers have gradually been reduced, though, very recently, there have been moves back the other way.

Three main devices have been used by modern governments to control trade: tariffs, quotas, and export subsidies.

A **tariff** is a tax on imports.
A **tariff** is simply a tax on imports. An importer of wine, for example, may be charged $10 for each barrel of wine he brings into the country. As noted at the

Non-Tariff Barriers to Trade

Many Western countries have committed themselves to tariff reductions by signing the General Agreement on Tariffs and Trade (GATT). By 1987 these commitments will reduce tariffs in the United States and the EEC to less than five percent, and those in Japan and Canada to less than three percent and eight percent, respectively. But non-tariff barriers to trade such as quotas are not covered by GATT regulations, and these have grown noticeably in recent years. The following excerpt from the 1983 Annual Review of the Economic Council of Canada discusses this problem.

Non-tariff barriers ... to trade take a variety of forms: quotas, voluntary export restraints,... administrative delays ... and export subsidies.... Canada has been ... guilty, having used administrative delays in Vancouver to pressure the Japanese into lowering their "voluntary" export quotas....

Except for quotas, in many cases non-tariff barriers are not readily amenable to trade liberalization because they are frequently qualitative aspects of a nation's domestic policy arrangements.... In many respects non-tariff barriers are now a greater threat than tariffs to world trade.... It has been estimated ... that by 1982 ... non-tariff barriers ... covered 34 percent of the market for American manufacturers. In Japan, the comparable figure was 7 percent; in Canada, 10 percent; in West Germany, 20 percent; in France, 32 percent. This does not include ... subsidies.

Non-tariff barriers are now coming under the scrutiny of GATT.... The GATT discussions on non-tariff barriers, which will, to some extent, take negotiators inside the economic decision-making processes of member countries, may raise the whole issue of the legitimacy of "industrial policy"—a generic term covering all kinds of governmental interventions designed to affect the structure of industry. There are considerable ideological differences on this subject, turning on such questions as "picking the winners," "aiding the adjustment of workers and firms out of unviable industries", and "letting the market decide." In some European countries, industrial policy is seen as a crucial part of building a just and equitable society; in Japan, it has been described as a way of unifying the people in a crusade to maximize the nation's economic potential; in Canada, so far, no consensus is in sight about whether industrial policy is even desirable, although a pot-pourri of government aids to industry has been allowed to develop in the pursuit of various ends. Given these diverse attitudes on the subject, the discussion about industrial policy and non-tariff barriers is unlikely to be rapidly concluded.

SOURCE: Economic Council of Canada, *On the Mend*, Annual Review, 1983, pp. 27–29.

---

beginning of this chapter, Canada is a relatively high-tariff country, although there are some countries that rely far more heavily on tariffs to protect their industries. Tariff rates of 100 percent or more are not unheard of. Also, other countries rely more heavily on quotas and export subsidies.

A **quota** is a legal limit on the amount of a good that may be imported. For example, the government might allow no more than 5 million barrels of wine to be imported in a year. In some cases, governments ban the importation of certain goods outright—a quota of zero. In recent years, the combination of high unemployment rates and a deterioration in Canada's competitive position in world trade has led to political pressures for increased use of quotas. One of the more visible quotas in Canada in recent times has been that on Japanese cars.

A **quota** specifies the maximum amount of a good that is permitted into the country from abroad per unit of time.

An **export subsidy** is a payment by the government to an exporter. By reducing the exporter's costs, such subsidies permit exporters to lower their selling prices and compete more effectively in world trade. Export subsidies are used extensively by some foreign governments to assist their industries—a practice that provokes bitter complaints from Canadian manufacturers about "unfair competition."

An **export subsidy** is a payment by the government to exporters to permit them to reduce the selling price of their goods so they can compete more effectively in foreign markets.

How Tariffs and Quotas Work

Both tariffs and quotas restrict supplies coming from abroad and drive up prices. The tariff works by raising prices and hence cutting the demand for imports, while the sequence associated with a quota goes the other way—restriction in supply forces prices up.

Let us use our international trade diagrams (Figure 21-3) to see what a quota does. The supply and demand curves in Figure 21-4 are like those of Figure 21-3. Just as in Figure 21-3, equilibrium in a free international market occurs at a price of $100 per barrel of wine (in both countries). At this price, the exporting country produces 10 million barrels [point B in part (a)] and consumes 5 million barrels (point A), so that exports are 5 million barrels—the distance AB. Similarly, the importing country consumes 8 million barrels [point D in part (b)] and produces only 3 million [point C], so that imports are also 5 million barrels (the distance CD).

Now suppose the government of the importing nation imposes an import quota of (no more than) 3 million barrels. The free-trade equilibrium is no longer possible. Instead, the market must reach equilibrium at a point where both exports and imports are 3 million barrels. As Figure 21-4 indicates, this requires different prices in the two countries.

Imports in part (b) will be 3 million—the distance QT—only when the price of wine in the importing nation is $110 per barrel, because only at this price will quantity demanded exceed quantity supplied by 3 million barrels. Similarly, exports in part (a) will be 3 million barrels—the distance RS only when the price in the exporting country is $95 per barrel. At this price, quantity supplied exceeds quantity demanded by 3 million barrels in the exporting country. Thus, the quota raises the price in the importing country to $110 and lowers the price in the exporting country to $95. In general:

An import quota on a product normally will reduce the volume of that product

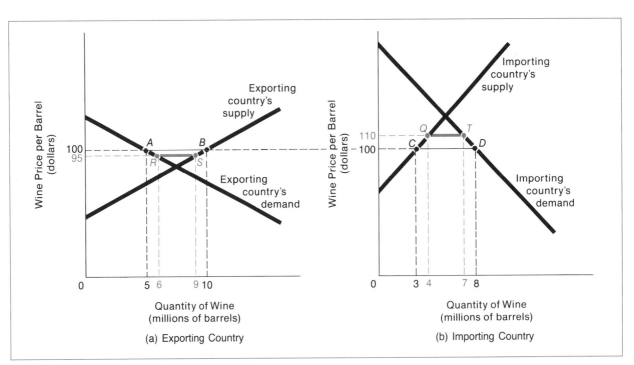

Figure 21-4
QUOTAS AND TARIFFS IN INTERNATIONAL TRADE
Under free trade, the equilibrium price of wine is $100 per barrel. The exporting country, in part (a), sends AB, or 5 million barrels, to the importing country (distance CD). If a quota of 3 million barrels is imposed by the importing country, these two distances must shrink to 3 million barrels. The solution is shown by distance RS for exports and distance QT for imports. Exports and imports are equal, as must be the case, but the quota forces prices to be unequal in the two countries. Wine sells for $110 per barrel in the importing country but only $95 per barrel in the exporting country. A tariff achieves the same result differently. It *requires* that the prices in the two countries be $15 apart. And this, as the graph shows, dictates that exports (= imports) will be equal at 3 million barrels.

traded, raise the price in the importing country, and reduce the price in the exporting country.

The same restriction of trade can be accomplished through a tariff. In the example we have just completed, a quota of 3 million barrels resulted in a price that was $15 higher in the importing country than in the exporting country ($110 – $95). Suppose, then, that instead of a quota the importing nation posts a $15 per barrel tariff. International trade equilibrium then must satisfy the following two requirements:

1. The price that consumers in the importing country pay for wine must exceed the price that suppliers in the exporting country receive by $15 (the amount of the tariff).
2. The quantity of wine exported must equal the quantity of wine imported.

By consulting the graphs in Figure 21–4, you can see exactly where these two requirements are satisfied. If the exporter produces at S and consumes at R, while the importer produces at Q and consumes at T, then exports and imports are equal (at 3 million barrels) and the two domestic prices differ by exactly $15. (They are $110 and $95.) What we have just discovered is a very general result of international trade theory:

Any restriction of international trade (exports and imports) that is accomplished by a quota normally can also be accomplished by a tariff.

In this case, the tariff corresponding to an import quota of 3 million barrels is $15 per barrel.

Tariffs versus Quotas

But while tariffs and quotas can accomplish the same reduction in international trade and lead to the same domestic prices in the two countries, there *are* some important differences between the two types of restrictions.

First, under a quota, profits from the price increases in the importing country usually go into the pockets of the foreign and domestic sellers of the product. Because supplies are limited by quotas, customers in the importing country must pay more for the product. So the suppliers, be they foreign or domestic, receive more for every unit they sell. For example, the Canadian quota on imports of Japanese automobiles raises the profit margins of both Canadian and Japanese automakers.

On the other hand, when trade is restricted by a tariff, the profits go as tax revenues to the *government* of the importing country. In effect, the government increases its tax revenues partly at the expense of its citizens and partly at the expense of foreign exporters, who must accept a reduced price because of the resulting decrease in quantity demanded in the importing country. (Domestic producers again benefit, because they are exempt from the tariff.) In this respect, a tariff is certainly a better proposition than a quota from the viewpoint of the country that enacts it.

Another important distinction between the two measures is the difference in their implications for productive efficiency and long-run prices. A tariff handicaps all exporters equally. It still awards sales to the importers who are most efficient and can therefore supply the goods most cheaply.

A quota, on the other hand, necessarily awards its import licences more or less capriciously—perhaps on a first-come, first-served basis or in proportion to past sales or by some other arbitrary standard or even on some political criteria. There is not the slightest reason to expect the most efficient and least costly suppliers to get the import permits. In the long run, the population of the importing country is likely to end up with significantly higher prices, poorer products, or both.

The Canadian quota on Japanese cars illustrates all of these effects. Japanese automakers responded to the limit on the number of small cars by shipping bigger models equipped with more "optional" equipment, and many more Japanese trucks. And the newer, smaller Japanese automakers—like Subaru—found it difficult to compete in the Canadian market because their quotas were so much smaller than those of Toyota, Datsun, and Honda.

If a country must inhibit imports, there are two important reasons for it to give preference to tariffs over quotas: (1) some of the resulting financial gains from tariffs go to the government of the importing country rather than to foreign and domestic producers; and (2) unlike quotas, tariffs offer no special benefits to inefficient exporters.

Why Inhibit Trade?

To state that tariffs are a better way to inhibit international trade than quotas leaves open a far more basic question: Why limit trade in the first place? There are two primary reasons for adopting measures that restrict trade: First, they may help the importing country get more advantageous prices for its goods, and second, they protect particular industries from foreign competition.

Shifting Prices in Your Favour

How can a tariff make prices more advantageous for the importing country if it raises consumer prices there? The answer is that it forces foreign exporters to sell more cheaply. Because their market is restricted by the tariff, they will be left with unsold goods unless they cut their prices. Suppose, as in Figure 21-4(b), that a $15 tariff on wine raises the price of wine in the importing country from $100 to $110 a barrel. This rise in price drives down imports from an amount represented by the length of the black line CD to the smaller amount represented by the blue line QT. And to the exporting country, this means an equal reduction in exports [see the change from AB to RS in Figure 21-4(a)].

As a result, the price at which the exporting country can sell its wine is driven down (from $100 to $95 in the example) while producers in the importing country—being exempt from the tariff—can charge $110 per barrel. In effect, such a tariff amounts to government intervention to rig prices in favour of domestic producers and to exploit foreign sellers by forcing them to sell more cheaply than they otherwise would.

However, this technique works only as long as foreigners accept tariff exploitation passively. And they rarely do. Instead, they retaliate, usually by imposing tariffs or quotas of their own on their imports from the country that first began the tariff game. This can easily lead to a trade war in which no one gains in terms of more favourable prices and everyone loses in terms of the resulting reductions in overall trade. Something like this happened to the world economy in the 1930s and helped prolong the worldwide depression. At present, it is threatening to happen again. Tariffs or quotas can benefit a country that is able to impose them without fear of retaliation. But when every country uses them, everyone is likely to lose in the long run.

Even if there is no retaliation, the tariff or quota can only rig prices in favour of domestic producers if the country imposing the tariff is a significant part of the world demand for that commodity. This requirement is not satisfied in Canada's case. Indeed, we often represent an insignificant portion of world demand for many of our imports. As a result, Canada is essentially in the same position as an individual firm in a perfectly competitive industry. We are a price taker on the world market for our imports.

With this realistic simplification, our analysis of tariffs can be accomplished without the two-part diagram used above. In Figure 21–5, the demand curve and supply curve of the importing country are shown precisely as they were in Figure 21–4(b). Also, the world supply curve of this commodity (wine) to the small economy is shown as the horizontal line at the price of $100 per barrel. The world supply curve is perfectly elastic at the going world price, since a small country can purchase whatever quantity it desires and have no effect on the world price.

In our example, before any tariff is levied, the country produces 3 million barrels of wine, consumes 8 million barrels and imports 5 million barrels (as indicated by distance CD in Figure 21–5). If world suppliers must pay a $15 per barrel tariff to sell within this economy, the world supply curve shifts up to the $115 point on the price axis. Just as before, equilibrium requires a $15 per barrel gap between the going world price and the price of wine in the country that levies the tariff. However, when the importing country is small, its price rises by the *full amount of the tariff*, and the world price is not forced down at all. This is shown in Figure 21–5, since, after the tariff, domestic production increases to 4.5 million barrels, purchases fall to 6.5 million barrels and imports fall to 2 million barrels (given by distance VW in the diagram). Our analysis simply verifies the common-sense notion that a small country cannot rig world prices in its favour.

We conclude that Canada is too small to shift world prices of imports in her favour. Thus, even without considering retaliation, this is an illegitimate argument for tariffs and quotas in Canada.

Protecting Particular Industries

The second, and probably more frequent, reason why countries restrict trade is to protect particular industries from foreign competition. If foreigners can produce

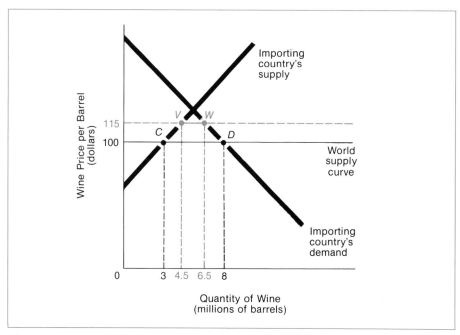

Figure 21–5
QUOTAS AND TARIFFS WHEN THE IMPORTING COUNTRY IS SMALL

Canada is too small to affect the world price of wine, which is $100 per barrel in this example. Under free trade, Canada produces 3 million barrels, consumes 8 million barrels and imports 8 − 3 = 5 million barrels (distance CD). This amount is an insignificant portion of world production. If a tariff of $15 per barrel is imposed in Canada, our price rises by the full amount from $100 to $115 per barrel. Price is unaffected in the rest of the world. Domestic production increases to 4.5 million barrels, consumption falls to 6.5 million barrels, and imports fall to 6.5 − 4.5 = 2 million barrels (distance VW).

steel or watches or shoes more cheaply, domestic businesses and unions in these industries are quick to demand protection; and their government is often reluctant to deny it to them. It is here that the cheap foreign labour argument is most likely to be invoked.

But the fact is that the firms that are unable to compete in the market are the ones whose relative inefficiency does not permit them to beat foreign exporters at their own game. In Ricardo's example of comparative advantage, one can well imagine the complaints from Portuguese clothmakers as the opening of trade led to increased importation of English cloth. At the same time, the English grape growers would, very likely, have expressed equal concern over the flood of imported wine from Portugal. Protective tariffs and quotas are designed to undercut harsh competition coming from abroad; but it is precisely this competition that gives consumers the benefits of international specialization.

Usually, when an industry feels itself threatened by foreign competition, it is argued that some form of protection against imports is needed to prevent loss of jobs. But we know from our discussion of macroeconomics in Part Three that there are better ways to stimulate employment. Yet it must be admitted that any program that limits foreign competition will, in the short run, preserve jobs in the protected industry. It will work, but often at a very considerable cost to consumers, in the form of higher prices, and to the economy, in the form of inefficient use of resources. For example, several recent American studies have estimated that various tariffs and import quotas *cost consumers in the United States about $80,000 for every job they preserve.*

Nevertheless, union complaints over proposals to reduce a tariff or a quota are well justified unless something is done to ease the cost to the individual workers of switching to those lines of production that trade has now made profitable.

The argument for free trade between countries cannot be considered airtight if there is no adequate program to assist the minority of citizens in each country who will be harmed whenever patterns of production change drastically, as would happen, for example, if tariff and quota barriers were suddenly brought down.

Owners of wineries in Britain and of textile mills in Portugal may see heavy investments suddenly rendered unprofitable, as would workers whose investments in acquiring special skills and training are no longer marketable. Nor are the costs to displaced workers only monetary. Often they will have to move to new locations as well as to new industries, uprooting their families, losing old friends and neighbours, and so on. That the *majority* of citizens undoubtedly will gain from free trade will be no consolation to those who are its victims. To help alleviate this problem, it is often argued that Canada should expand its programs to assist workers who have lost jobs because of the changing patterns of world trade. Some **trade adjustment assistance** is provided. For instance, the federal government's Industry and Labour Adjustment Program (ILAP) pays two-thirds of workers' former wages (after unemployment insurance has expired for workers over age 45) if they have been released by declining, low-productivity industries.

Trade adjustment assistance provides special unemployment benefits, loans, retraining programs, or other aid to workers and firms that are harmed by foreign competition.

Other Arguments for Protection

National Defence and Other Non-economic Considerations

There are times when a tariff or some other measure to interfere with trade may be justified on non-economic grounds. If a country considers itself vulnerable to military attack, it may be perfectly rational to keep alive industries whose outputs can be obtained more cheaply abroad but whose supplies might dry up during an emergency. For example, airplane production by small countries makes sense only in such circumstances.

The danger is that every industry, even those with the most peripheral defence relationship, is likely to invoke this argument on its behalf. For instance, the U.S. watch-making industry claimed protection for itself for many years on the grounds that it trained skilled workers whose craftsmanship would be invaluable in wartime. Perhaps so, but a technicians' training program probably could have done the job more cheaply and even more effectively by teaching exactly the skills needed for military purposes.

Non-economic reasons also explain the recent European quotas on seal skins. These quotas may be a competitive boon to the European countries' domestic leather and fur industries, but protection of endangered species rather than protection of industries is their justification.

The Infant-Industry Argument

It is often suggested that temporary protection of a newly established industry can serve the national interest. Until that industry can expand to a point at which it is able to compete unaided with established foreign firms, it may be essential to prevent its strangulation by foreign competition.

The argument, while valid in certain instances, is less defensible than it may at first appear. It makes sense only if the industry's prospective future gains are sufficient to repay the social losses incurred while it is being protected. But if the industry is likely to be so profitable in the future, why doesn't private capital rush in to take advantage of the prospective net profits? The annals of business are full of cases in which a new product or a new firm lost money at first but profited handsomely later. Only where funds are not available to a particular industry for some reason, despite its glowing profit prospects, does the infant-industry argument for protection stand up to scrutiny.

It is hard to think of examples, but even if such a case were found one would have to be careful that the industry not remain in diapers forever. There are too many cases in which new industries were awarded protection when they were being established and, somehow, the time to withdraw the protection never arrived. One must beware of infant industries that never grow up.

Strategic Trade Policy

A new argument for protectionism has become popular in recent years. Advocates of this argument agree that free trade for all is the best system. But they point out that we live in an imperfect world in which some nations refuse to live by the rules of the free-trade game. And they fear that a nation that pursues free trade in a protectionist world is likely to lose out. It therefore makes sense, they argue, to threaten to protect your markets unless other nations agree to open theirs.

This is a hard argument for economists to deal with. While it accepts the superiority of free trade, it argues that threatening protectionism is the best way to establish free trade. Such a strategy might work, but it clearly involves great risks. If threats that Canada will turn protectionist induce other countries to scrap existing protectionist policies, then the gamble will have succeeded. But, if the gamble fails, the world ends up with even more protection than it started with. Probably there would be little effect in other countries from such threats made by Canada, so this is not a compelling argument for Canadian tariffs. For the United States, however, it could be a worthwhile strategy.

The analogy to recent arms negotiations is pretty obvious—and a little frightening. The Americans threaten to install new missiles unless the Russians agree to dismantle some of theirs. If they do, the world is a safer place and everyone is better off. But, if they do not, the arms race accelerates and everyone is worse off. Is the American threat to build new missiles therefore a wise or a foolish policy? There is no agreement on this question, and so we should not expect agreement on the advisability of using protectionist measures in a strategic way.

What Import Price Levels Benefit a Country?

Dumping means selling
goods in a foreign market at
lower prices than those
charged in the home market.

One of the most curious features of the protectionist position is the fear of low prices charged by foreign sellers. Countries that subsidize exports are accused of **dumping**—of getting rid of their goods at unconscionably low prices. For example, in the last few years Japan has frequently been accused of dumping various goods on the Canadian and American markets, and Europe has been accused of dumping its agricultural goods.

A moment's thought should indicate why this fear must be considered curious. As a nation of consumers, we should be indignant when the prices of our imports are *high*, not when they are *low*. That is the common-sense rule that guides every consumer, and the consumers of imported commodities should be no exception. Only from the topsy-turvy viewpoint of an industry seeking protection from competition are high prices seen as being in the public interest.

Ultimately, it is always in the interest of a country to get its imports as cheaply as possible. It would be ideal for Canada if the rest of the world were willing to provide its exports to us free or virtually so. We could then live in luxury at the expense of the rest of the world.

The notion that low import prices are bad for a country is a fitting companion to the idea—so often heard—that it is good for a country to export much more than it imports. True, this means that foreigners will end up owing us a good deal of money. But it also means that we will have given them large quantities of our products and have gotten relatively little in foreign products in return. That surely is not an ideal way for a country to benefit from its foreign transactions.

Our gains from trade do not consist of accumulations of gold or of heavy debts owed us by foreigners. Rather, our gains are composed of the goods and services that others provide minus the goods and services we must provide them in return.

Conclusion

The preceding discussion should indicate the fundamental fallacy in the argument that Canadian workers have to fear "cheap foreign labour." If workers in other countries are willing to supply their products to us with little compensation, this must ultimately *raise* the standard of living of the average Canadian worker. As long as the government's monetary and fiscal policies succeed in maintaining high levels of employment at home, how can we possibly lose by getting the products of the world at little cost to ourselves?

It must be admitted that there are two dangers to this prognosis. First, our employment policy may not be effective. If workers who are displaced by foreign competition cannot find jobs in other industries, then Canadian workers will indeed suffer from international trade. But that is a shortcoming of the government's employment program, not of its international trade policies.

Second, we have noted that an abrupt stiffening of foreign competition resulting from a major innovation in another country, or from a discovery of a new and better source of raw materials, or from a sharp increase in export subsidies by a foreign country, *can* hurt Canadian workers by not giving them an adequate chance to adapt gradually to the new conditions. The more rapid the change, the more painful it will be. If it occurs fairly gradually, workers can retrain and move on to the industries that now require their services. If the change is even more gradual, no one may have to move. People who retire or leave the threatened industry for other reasons simply need not be replaced. But competition that inflicts its damage overnight is certain to impose very real costs upon the affected workers, costs that are no less painful for being temporary.

But these are, after all, minor qualifications to an overwhelming argument. They call for intelligent monetary and fiscal policies and for transitional assistance

Unfair Foreign Competition

Satire and ridicule are often more persuasive than logic and statistics. Exasperated by the spread of protectionism to so many industries under the prevailing Mercantilist philosophy, French economist Frédéric Bastiat decided to take the protectionist argument to its illogical conclusion. The fictitious petition of the French candlemakers to the Chamber of Deputies, written in 1845 and excerpted below, has become a classic in the battle for free trade.

We are subject to the intolerable competition of a foreign rival, who enjoys, it would seem, such superior facilities for the production of light, that he is enabled to *inundate* our *national market* at so exceedingly reduced a price, that, the moment he makes his appearance, he draws off all custom for us; and thus an important branch of French industry, with all its innumerable ramifications, is suddenly reduced to a state of complete stagnation. This rival is no other than the sun.

Our petition is, that it would please your honorable body to pass a law whereby shall be directed the shutting up of all windows, dormers, skylights, shutters, curtains, in a word, all openings, holes, chinks, and fissures through which the light of the sun is used to penetrate our dwellings, to the prejudice of the profitable manufactures which we flatter ourselves we have been enabled to bestow upon the country....

We foresee your objections, gentlemen; but there is not one that you can oppose to us ... which is not equally opposed to your own practice and the principle which guides your policy....

Labor and nature concur in different proportions, according to country and climate, in every article of production.... If a Lisbon orange can be sold at half the price of a Parisian one, it is because a natural and gratuitous heat does for the one what the other only obtains from an artificial and consequently expensive one....

Does it not argue the greatest inconsistency to check as you do the importation of coal, iron, cheese, and goods of foreign manufacture, merely because and even in proportion as their price approaches *zero*, while at the same time you freely admit, and without limitation, the light of the sun, whose price is during the whole day at *zero*?

SOURCE: F. Bastiat, *Economic Sophisms* (New York: G. P. Putnam's Sons, 1922).

to unemployed workers, not for abandonment of free trade and permission for monopoly power to flourish behind protection.

In the long run, labour will be "cheap" only where it is not very productive. Wages will tend to be highest in those countries in which high labour productivity keeps costs down and permits exporters to compete effectively despite high wages.

We note that in this matter it is absolute advantage, not comparative advantage, that counts. The country that is most efficient in every output can pay its workers more in every industry.

We started this chapter by noting that tariff cuts involve both benefits and costs. The benefits are that consumers acquire goods at lower prices, and that the anti-competitive behaviour of firms can be limited without relying on regulations and attempted prosecutions. The costs of tariff cuts are the jobs that many expect would be lost to "cheap foreign labour." This chapter has shown that these costs are very much exaggerated in popular discussion. This is because the principle of comparative advantage is not generally appreciated and because the problems associated with increased competition can be better solved by appropriate monetary, fiscal, and adjustment assistance policies.

Summary

1. Countries trade because differences in their natural resources and other inputs create discrepancies in the efficiency with which they can produce different goods, and because specialization may offer them greater economies of large-scale production.

2. Voluntary trade will generally be advantageous to both parties in an exchange. This is one of our **12 Ideas for Beyond the Final Exam**.

3. International trade is more complicated than trade within a nation because of political factors, different national currencies, and impediments to the movement of labour and capital across national borders.

4. Both countries will gain from trade with one another if each exports goods in whose production it has a comparative advantage. That is, even a country that is generally inefficient will benefit by exporting the goods in whose production it is least inefficient. This is another of the **12 Ideas for Beyond the Final Exam**.

5. When countries specialize and trade, each can enjoy consumption possibilities that exceed its production possibilities.

6. The prices of goods traded between countries are determined by supply and demand, but one must consider explicitly the demand curve and the supply curve of *each* country involved. Thus, in international trade, the equilibrium price must be where the excess of the exporter's quantity supplied over its domestic quantity demanded is equal to the excess of the importer's quantity demanded over its quantity supplied.

7. The "cheap foreign labour" argument ignores the principle of comparative advantage, which shows that real wages can rise in both the importing and exporting countries as a result of specialization and, thus, increased productivity.

8. Tariffs and quotas are designed to protect a country's industries from foreign competition. Such protection may sometimes be advantageous to that country, but not if foreign countries adopt tariffs and quotas of their own as a means of retaliation, and not if the country constitutes a small share of the world market.

9. While the same restriction of trade can be accomplished by either a tariff or a quota, tariffs offer at least two advantages to the country that imposes them: (1) some of the gains go to the government rather than to foreign producers, and (2) there is greater incentive for efficient production.

10. When a nation shifts from protection to free trade, some industries and their workers will lose out. Equity then demands that these people and firms be compensated in some way. The Canadian government has begun experimenting with adjustment assistance to do this.

11. Several arguments for protectionism can, under the right circumstances, have validity. These include the national defence argument, the infant-industry argument, and the use of trade restrictions for strategic purposes. But each of these arguments is frequently abused.

12. Dumping may hurt domestic producers, but it always benefits consumers.

13. Since tariff cuts are beneficial even if domestic industries are competitive (as illustrated by the principle of comparative advantage), they are doubly appealing if domestic industries are non-competitive. Thus, tariff cuts represent a significant element in a country's competition policy.

Concepts for Review

Imports	Comparative advantage	Export subsidy
Exports	"Cheap foreign labour" argument	Trade adjustment assistance
Specialization	Tariff	Infant-industry argument
Mutual gains from trade	Non-tariff barriers	Dumping
Absolute advantage	Quota	

Questions for Discussion

1. You have a dozen eggs worth $1.50 and your neighbour has 500 grams of bacon worth about the same. You decide to swap six eggs for 250 grams of bacon. In financial terms, neither of you gains anything. Explain why you are nevertheless both likely to be better off.

2. In the eighteenth century, some writers argued that one person in a trade could be made better off only by gaining at the expense of the other. Explain the fallacy in the argument.

3. A brilliant chemist is also a master glass blower. In what circumstances does it pay him to hire a glass blower for his lab? When does it make sense for him to do some glass blowing for himself?

4. Country A has lots of hydroelectric power, a cold

climate, and a highly skilled labour force. What sorts of products do you think it is likely to produce? What are the characteristics of countries with which you would expect it to trade?

5. Upon removal of a tariff on shoes, a Canadian shoe-making firm goes bankrupt. Discuss the pros and cons of the tariff removal in the short run and long run.

6. Country A's government believes that it is best always to export more (in money terms) than the value of its imports. As a consequence, it exports more to country B every year than it imports from country B. After 100 years of this arrangement, both countries are destroyed in an earthquake. What were the advantages and disadvantages of the surplus to country A? To country B?

7. The table below describes the number of red socks and white socks that can be produced with an hour of labour in two different cities:

	IN BOSTON	IN CHICAGO
Red socks (pairs)	3	1
White socks (pairs)	3	2

a. If there is no trade, what is the price of white socks relative to red socks in Boston?
b. If there is no trade, what is the price of white socks relative to red socks in Chicago?
c. Suppose each city has 1000 hours of labour available per year. Draw the production possibilities frontier for each city.
d. Which city has an absolute advantage in the production of which good(s)? Which city has a comparative advantage in the production of which good(s)?

e. If the cities start trading with each other, which city will specialize and export which good?
f. What can be said about the price at which trade will take place?

8. Suppose that Canada and Mexico are the only two countries in the world. In Canada a worker can produce 12 bushels of wheat *or* 1 barrel of oil a day. In Mexico, a worker can produce 2 bushels of wheat or 2 barrels of oil.
a. What will be the price ratio between the two commodities (i.e., the price of oil in terms of wheat) in each country if there is no trade?
b. If free trade is allowed and there are no transportation costs, what commodity would Canada import? What about Mexico?
c. In what range will the price ratio have to fall under free trade? Why?
d. Picking one possible post-trade price ratio, show clearly how it is possible for both countries to benefit from free trade.

9. (More difficult.) The table below presents the demand and supply curves for cars in Germany and Canada.
a. Draw the demand and supply curves for Canada on one diagram and those for Germany on another one.
b. If there is no trade between Canada and Germany, what are the equilibrium price and quantity in the car market in Canada? In Germany?
c. Now suppose trade is opened up between the two countries. What will be the equilibrium price of cars in the world market? What has happened to the price of cars in Canada? In Germany?
d. What has happened to the quantity of cars produced, and therefore to employment, in the car industry in Canada? In Germany? Who benefits and who loses *initially* from free trade?

PRICE PER CAR IN BOTH COUNTRIES (thousands of dollars)	QUANTITY DEMANDED IN CANADA (hundreds of cars)	QUANTITY SUPPLIED IN CANADA (hundreds of cars)	QUANTITY DEMANDED IN GERMANY (hundreds of cars)	QUANTITY SUPPLIED IN GERMANY (hundreds of cars)
0	100	0	100	0
1	90	10	90	25
2	80	20	80	50
3	70	30	70	70
4	60	40	60	80
5	50	50	50	90
6	40	60	40	100
7	30	70	30	110
8	20	80	20	120
9	10	90	10	130
10	0	100	0	140

Growth in Developed and Developing Countries

22

The development of capitalist production ... compels [the capitalist] to keep constantly extending his capital ... by means of progressive accumulation.... Fanatically bent on making value expand itself, he ... forces the development of the productive powers of society, and creates those material conditions, which alone can form the real basis of a higher form of society.

KARL MARX

In this chapter we discuss the factors that determine the rate at which an economy grows and examine the desirability of rapid growth. We begin by considering how growth can be measured and go on to examine the effects of population growth on prospects for rising incomes per capita. Next, we examine the views of those who have argued that in wealthier countries economic growth is a mixed blessing that may do more harm than good. Then, in the second part of the chapter, we turn to the special problems of the less developed countries (LDCs) and look at the measures that have been proposed to increase their rate of growth. We show that although in recent years standards of living in the LDCs have begun to rise significantly, their rapid population growth and their vulnerability to such external shocks as the rise in oil prices and other similar perils mean that many problems still threaten their economies. Next, we examine the problems that impede growth in the LDCs, including scarcity of capital, lack of education, and unemployment. While doing this we consider what the LDCs can do to help themselves and what the rest of the world can do to help them.

Growth in General

How to Measure Growth: Total Output or Output per Capita?

Adam Smith, like many of his successors, took it for granted that expansion of productive capacity is inherently desirable. But he also took it for granted, apparently without examining the matter very closely, that growth in the size of population is to be wished for. His reason was that a larger population provides a larger work force, and a larger work force makes a larger national output possible. Few economists since Smith's time have argued in this way. Nowadays we usually measure a nation's prosperity not in terms of its total output but in terms of its output *per person*. India has a GNP more than twice as large as Sweden's. But with a population more than 80 times as large as Sweden's, India remains a poor country while Sweden is highly prosperous. The point is that:

If the objective of growth is the material welfare *of the individuals* who make up a country, then the proper measure of the success of a program of economic development is how much it adds to output per person. The relevant index is not total output. It is total output *divided by total population;* that is, *output per capita.*

From this point of view, the appropriate objective of growth is not, as the old cliché puts it, "the greatest good for the *greatest number*"—it is the greatest good *per person* in the economy. Per-capita figures tell this story well. To make the appropriate comparison of well-being in Sweden and India, we note that per-capita GNP in Sweden is about $14,000 a year; whereas in India, even after a generous adjustment to correct for lower prices in that country, the figure is $260 a year.

Only where the objective of the government is grandeur or military strength may the number of inhabitants alone seem an appropriate part of its goal. A small country like Finland, for instance, cannot hope to overwhelm a giant neighbour like the Soviet Union, even if Finland has a much higher per-capita GNP than that of the Soviet Union.[1] But where the goal of the government is not national power but the elimination of poverty, illiteracy, and inadequate medical care, sheer increase in population becomes a questionable pursuit.

On Growth in Population: Is Less Really More?

In 1798, the Reverend Thomas R. Malthus (who was to become England's first professor of political economy) published *An Essay on the Principle of Population.* This book was to have a profound effect on people's attitudes toward population growth. Malthus argued that sexual drives and other influences induce people to reproduce themselves as rapidly as their means permit. Unfortunately, he said, when the number of humans increases, the production of food and other consumption goods generally cannot keep up.

As the earth becomes more crowded, people must work each piece of farmland more intensively than before, and they must look for new land to farm. But neither of these ways to increase production will help enough to meet the increased need. There are limits to what a given piece of land can produce. Moreover, as people put soil under cultivation, they will naturally tend to pick the best lots first. Thus, as they extend the area that is cultivated, people will be forced to make use of increasingly inferior farmland.

Together, these two phenomena lead to the noted *law of diminishing returns* to additional labour used with a fixed supply of land, a relationship we encounter in *Microeconomics,* Chapter 7. This hypothesis states that if we use more and more labour to cultivate a fixed stock of land we will eventually reach a point at which each additional labourer will contribute less additional output than the previous labourer. Ultimately, as the labour force increases, output per worker will decline.

Malthus and his followers concluded that the tendency of humankind to reproduce itself must constantly exert pressure on the economy to keep living standards from rising. Wages will gravitate toward some minimal subsistence level—the lowest income on which people are willing to marry and raise a family. If wages are above subsistence, the population can and will grow. But, as we have seen, rising population without any rise in available land must reduce output per worker because of the law of diminishing returns. Thus, a wage that is above subsistence will set forces into motion that will drive wages down toward subsistence.

[1]Even where military power is the primary objective, a large but impoverished population may not be a very effective means to that end. China has long had an enormous population, but in the modern era its military presence is certainly quite recent.

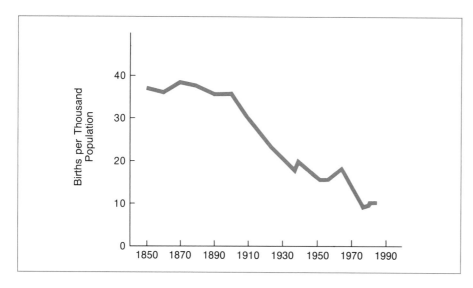

Figure 22-1
GERMAN BIRTHRATES,
1850–1982
This chart shows that birthrates in
Germany have generally been
declining since 1870.
SOURCE: Statistisches Bundesamt,
Statistisches Jahrbuch (Weisbaden,
Germany).

Sometimes, according to Malthus, the population will grow beyond the capability of the economy to support it. Then the number of people will be brought back into line by means that are far more unpleasant than a decrease in wages—by starvation and disease or by wars that produce the required number of casualties.

Later in the nineteenth century and during the first half of the twentieth century, the gloomy Malthusian vision seemed to lose credibility. New technology and improved agricultural practices generally enabled the output of food and other agricultural products to increase faster than the population (at least in the wealthier industrialized nations). In addition, it turned out that as living standards rose, people became less anxious to reproduce, and so the expansion of population slowed substantially. Figure 22-1 illustrates this trend in Germany over a 133-year period. All in all, it began to look as though population growth constituted no significant threat—it was something with which human technological skills and ingenuity could cope.

More recently, however, there has been renewed concern over population. With improvements in medicine—notably improved hygiene in hospitals, the use of such public-health measures as swamp drainage, and the discovery of antibiotics—death rates have plunged in the developing countries, especially for infants. At the same time, birth-control programs in most of these countries have, at least until quite recently, not been very successful. As a result, the populations of developing countries have continued to expand dramatically, eating up a good proportion of any output increases obtained through their governments' economic-development programs.

It has been widely concluded that significant improvement in living standards in the developing areas is impossible without a substantial reduction in their population growth. But the neo-Malthusians, as one dedicated group is sometimes called, go further than this, arguing that a rapid approach to birthrates so low that populations cease expanding—that is, to *zero population growth*—is virtually a matter of life and death even for the most prosperous nations. It is illuminating to consider the logic of their argument.

The Crowded Planet: Exponential Population Growth

In advocating his position, Malthus adopted a line of argument that has caught many imaginations ever since:

Figure 22-2

PROJECTED GROWTH OF
THE WORLD'S POPULATION
IN 175 YEARS AT CURRENT
RATE OF GROWTH

This figure shows the sensational
acceleration of population growth
if population expands
exponentially.

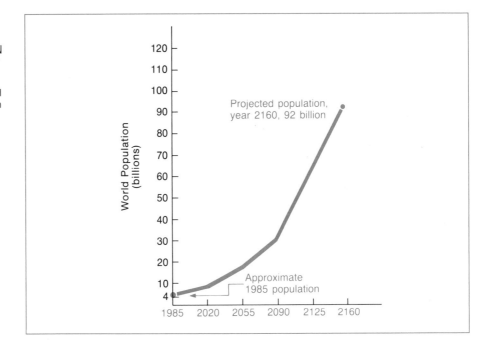

Exponential growth is
growth at a constant
percentage rate.

Population, when unchecked, increases in a geometrical ratio. Subsistence increases only in an arithmetical ratio. A slight acquaintance with numbers will shew the immensity of the first power in comparison of the second.[2]

In modern discussions, such a "geometric" growth pattern is referred to as **exponential growth**, or "compounded growth" or "snowballing." Exponential growth is growth at a constant *percentage* rate. For example, at a 10 percent growth rate, a population of 100 persons will increase by 10 persons a year; but a population of a million persons will increase by 100,000 persons a year. Thus, although the *rate* of growth is the same for large and small populations, the *numbers* are dramatically different. The bigger the population, the more it will add annually. And each year's growth implies still faster growth in the following year. It is like a snowball rolling downhill, accumulating more snow the bigger it gets and so expanding faster and faster all the time.

If the population doubles (grows 100 percent) in 35 years, it will quadruple (grow another 100 percent) in 70 years, increase 8-fold in 105 years, 16-fold in 140 years, and so on indefinitely. The doubling sequence 2, 4, 8, 16, 32, 64 and so on, is the basic pattern of exponential growth. Figure 22-2 shows how astronomical such a growth sequence can be. By projecting the world's population 175 years into the future on the assumption that population will grow exponentially at about its current rate, it shows that by the year 2160 the population will have grown to about 92 billion, with almost 20 times as many inhabitants on the earth as there are today.

It turns out that in his assumptions about exponential growth, Malthus was being conservative. He did not begin to spell out the wonders and the horrors that his premise implied. Consider some calculations by one leading authority on population (who has derived his conclusions simply by carrying through the arithmetic of exponential growth rates):

- *If population were to grow at today's rates for another 600–700 years, every square foot of the surface of the earth would contain a human being;*

[2]Malthus, *An Essay on the Principle of Population* (London, 1798), page 20.

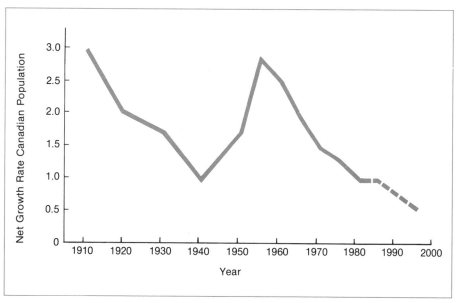

Figure 22-3
ANNUAL PERCENTAGE
GROWTH RATE OF THE
CANADIAN POPULATION
Note how rapidly the rate has
fallen in recent years. It has just
about returned to the low level that
was observed at the end of the
Great Depression.
SOURCE: Canada Year Book.

- *If it were to expand at the same rate for 1200 years, the combined weight of the human population would exceed that of the earth itself;*

- *If that growth rate were to go on for 6000 years (a very short period of time in terms of biological history), the globe would constitute a sphere whose diameter was growing with the speed of light.*[3]

And none of this is conjecture. It is *sure* to come about *if* the present (exponential) rate of growth on the earth's population continues unabated.

Of course, none of this can really happen. Our finite earth just does not have room for that sort of expansion. The fate of humanity is not determined by the rules of arithmetic—it depends on the course of nature and on the behaviour of the human race. It is true that if the number of humans continues to swell until it presses upon the earth's capacity, the process will ultimately be brought to a halt in a Malthusian apocalypse. Disease, famine, and war must finally put a stop to the expansion process.

But there is a better alternative. People can choose to stop raising large families. There is no inevitability about the family of six or ten children. As we have just noted, there has in fact been a decline in the rate of expansion in the wealthier societies—so much so that in North America in the last few years the rate of reproduction has reached what can ultimately give us zero population growth (see Figure 22-3). Even in the developing nations, as we will see later in this chapter, the birthrate has recently been declining.

A more balanced view of the matter recognizes the serious difficulties that rapid population growth can lead to, and suggests that its encouragement will not serve the interests of society. Yet, it does *not* imply that a great catastrophe is necessarily at hand or that the appropriate reaction is panic.

Requirements for Increased Growth

What can be done to increase the growth rate of an economy? Unfortunately, no one has a handy list of sure-fire recipes.

---

[3]Ansley J. Coale, "Man and His Environment," *Science*, vol. 179 (October 9, 1970), pages 132–36. Copyright 1970 by the American Association for the Advancement of Science.

Growth can be attributed to a number of factors that no one knows how to explain: (1) *inventiveness*, which produces the new technology and other innovations that have contributed so much to economic expansion; (2) *entrepreneurship*, the leadership that recognizes no obstacles and undertakes the daring industrial ventures needed to move the economy ahead; and (3) *the work ethic* that leads a work force to high levels of productivity. No one really knows what features of economic organization and social psychology actually lead a community to adopt these goals, as Great Britain is said to have done at the beginning of the nineteenth century, as the United States is reputed to have done in the first half of the twentieth century, and as Japan is apparently doing today. We do know, however, that:

Growth requires two things that people can influence directly:

1. A large expenditure on *capital equipment*: factories, machinery, transportation, and telecommunications equipment.
2. The devotion of considerable effort to research and development from which innovations are derived.

Both these types of expenditures help to increase the economy's ability to *supply* goods, which brings us back to the analyses of Parts Two and Three of this book. There we stressed that the level (and, consequently, the growth) of national income is determined by the interaction of aggregate supply and aggregate demand. It is the need for capital equipment in any growth process that provides a vital link between aggregate demand and aggregate supply, for an economy acquires a larger capital stock by investing. Recall that aggregate demand is the sum of consumption, investment, government spending, and net exports, $Y = C + I + G + X - IM$. But I is the only part of Y that creates more capital for the future.

The *composition* of aggregate demand is a major determinant of the rate of economic growth. If a larger fraction of total spending goes toward investment rather than toward consumption, government purchases, or exports, the capital stock will grow faster and the aggregate-supply schedule will shift more quickly to the right.

Accumulating Capital by Sacrificing Consumption: The Case of the Soviet Union

The importance of the *composition* of demand stands out sharply if we turn away from Canada and consider a *centrally planned* economy, such as that of the Soviet Union.

When the Soviet Union undertook to expand its industrial output very rapidly, it was clear from the earliest stage of planning that a tremendous amount of capital equipment would be required to carry out the expansion. Not only did the Soviets have to build modern factories and acquire sophisticated machinery, they also needed a **social infrastructure**—a transportation network to bring raw materials to the factories and take finished products to the markets, an efficient telecommunications system, and schools in which to train the population sufficiently to be an effective labour force. All this and much more was needed, and all of it required labour, raw material, and fuel for its construction.

Obviously, such a use of resources has its *opportunity cost*. Fuel and steel that are employed to build a train become unavailable for the production of refrigerators and washing machines. The real price of accumulating plant, equipment, and infrastructure is paid in the form of consumer goods that must be given up in order to build that capital equipment. In other words:

Through saving, the public gives up some consumption, which is the price it must pay for the accumulation of plant, equipment, and infrastructure. Without this sacrifice, growth generally cannot occur.

This is the hard lesson that the inhabitants of the Soviet Union have been living with for over half a century. Ever since the Russian Revolution in 1917, the Soviet leadership has been determined to promote rapid economic growth and has imposed on the general public whatever sacrifices of current consumption were deemed necessary for the purpose. Only in the most recent decades has an increase in the supply of consumer goods been assigned any priority. As a result, Soviet living standards have been rising very slowly, particularly because the demands of the military forces have joined those of the growth planners in competing for the resources that might otherwise go into consumption.

The reason for this harsh trade-off is clear enough. If the economy is producing at its full potential—and the Soviet economy generally has been—then real output Y cannot be increased further. Since $Y = C + I + G + X - IM$, and since exports are needed to finance imports, a decision to devote more resources to the production of heavy machinery (which is in I) or armaments (which are in G) is simultaneously a decision to forgo some consumption. Where resources are already fully employed, it is simply not possible to have both more guns and more butter.

The Payoff to Growth: Higher Consumption in the Future

We may seem to be painting a rather grim picture of growth, and indeed, the process has often been harsh in the U.S.S.R. and in other nations that have enforced a high rate of economic growth. But it is also true that if the growth process is successful, the sacrifice of consumption that it requires is only a temporary loss. Consumers give up goods and services now in order to make possible the construction of a productive capacity that will permit them to consume even more goods and services at a later date. After all, from the consumers' point of view, that is what growth is all about. It is not an end in itself, but a means to an end—a standard of living higher than they could have attained without the process of economic expansion.

At least in a consumer-oriented economy, the decision to save in order to promote economic growth is simply an *exchange between present and future consumption*. Consumers sacrifice consumption now in order to be able to increase consumption in the future by more than they gave up in the past.

Of course, the payoff may never come if something goes wrong. An earthquake may destroy factories and roads, or a government with military ambitions may divert the increased productive capacity into the manufacture of armaments. So there is a risk in the decision to give up consumption now for increased consumption later. The growth process is a gamble—it means trading in a relatively sure thing (present consumption) for a risky future return (increased future consumption).

But betting on the future is not necessarily foolhardy. Economies would remain stagnant if people were unwilling to take chances. And some of the risk of investment plans can be reduced if decision-makers understand fully the terms of the trade-off.

Growth Without Sacrificing Consumption: Something for Nothing?

Of course, some growth can be achieved without much sacrifice of present consumption. For at least one of the main engines of growth can be powered with relatively small increases in the nation's stock of factories, equipment, and infrastructure. Research and development can teach society new and more efficient ways of using the nation's productive resources. Thus, *innovation*—the process of putting inventions into operation—can permit an economy to get more output from the same inputs rather than by *expansion* of capital stock.

Everyone knows that this has in fact occurred. From the invention of the steam engine to that of the modern computer, our economy has benefitted from a stream of inventions—some sensational, some more routine—that together have increased enormously the productivity of the nation's resources. Another way of describing this process is to say that while a substantial proportion of growth is *embodied* in increased quantities of plant, equipment, and infrastructure, a very large proportion of the economy's growth is *disembodied*. That is, it is attributable to better ideas—to improved methods of finding and using the same quantities of resources.

Typically, though, growth involves a combination of the two: the new ideas and the commitment of capital to put them into effect. The widespread use of computers could not have happened without the electronic gear from which they are composed and the flow of electricity by which they are operated. Computers are worthwhile because they reduce the quantities of resources necessary to do a given job, but originally some accumulation of resources was required in order to make possible the resulting savings.

For the long run, society has a considerable stake in the relative role of embodied and disembodied growth. Embodied growth has two serious costs that disembodied growth avoids. First, embodied growth necessarily speeds up the use of society's depletable resources: its iron ore, its petroleum supplies, and its stocks of other minerals and fuels. This means that smaller quantities of those resources will be available to future generations.

The second cost of embodied growth is of comparable importance. The resources that are used up in a process of embodied growth must ultimately end up on society's garbage heap. The physical laws of conservation of matter and energy tell us that no raw material can ever disappear. It can be transformed into smoke or solid waste, but unless it is recycled *entirely* (something that is both beyond the capability of our technology and impractical for other reasons), the greater the quantity of resources used in the productive process, the greater the quantity of wastes that must ultimately result.

Economist Kenneth Boulding has likened our planet to a spaceship hurtling through the solar system but constrained by terrestrial littering laws to keep its garbage on board. In spaceship Earth, we can transform waste materials into other forms—as by melting old bottles for reuse or converting them into energy, or by burning combustible garbage for heat—but we cannot simply toss them overboard.

Both of these environmental concerns—resource depletion and waste disposal—lead us to favour disembodied over embodied growth. To the extent that we can succeed in increasing the productivity of our resources, we can reduce both the rate at which they are depleted and the severity of the community's waste-disposal problems.

One final remark on disembodied growth is in order. Economists are fond or pointing out that there is no such thing as a free lunch. Except in rare instances, improvements in technology are not "manna from heaven." They result, instead, from the work of scientists and technicians in government and industrial laboratories, from the labour of inventors in their basements or garages, and from the effort of management specialists studying the organization of factories and assembly lines. This means that labour (along with other resources) is diverted from other activities into the production of knowledge. *In a fully employed economy, the opportunity costs of investing in the discovery of new knowledge are the consumption of and physical investment in goods that would otherwise have been produced.* So even here, we cannot get something for nothing.

Is More Growth Really Better?

A number of writers have raised questions about the desirability of faster economic growth as an end in itself, at least in the wealthier industrialized countries. Yet faster growth does mean more wealth, and to most people the desirability of wealth is beyond question. "I've been rich and I've been poor—and I can tell you, rich is better," a noted stage personality is said to have told an interviewer, and most people seem to have the same attitude about the economy as a whole. To those who hold this belief, a healthy economy is one that is capable of turning out vast quantities of shoes, food, cars, and TV sets. An economy whose capacity to provide all these things is not expanding is said to have succumbed to the disease of *stagnation.*

Economists from Adam Smith to Karl Marx saw great virtue in economic growth. Marx argued that capitalism, at least in its earlier historical stages, was a vital form of economic organization by which society got out of the rut in which the medieval stage of history had trapped it. As we saw in the opening quotation of this chapter, Marx believed that "the development of the productive powers of society... alone can form the real basis of a higher form of society...." Marx went on to tell us that only where such great productive powers have been unleashed can one have "a society in which the full and free development of every individual forms the ruling principle."[4] In other words, only a wealthy economy can afford to give all individuals the opportunity for full personal satisfaction through the use of their special abilities in their jobs and through increased leisure activities.

Yet the desirability of further economic growth for a society that is already wealthy has been questioned on grounds that undoubtedly have a good deal of validity. It is pointed out that the sheer increase in quantity of products has imposed an enormous cost on society in the form of pollution, crowding, proliferation of wastes that need disposal, and debilitating psychological and social effects. It is said that industry has transformed the satisfying and creative tasks of the artisan into the mechanical and dehumanizing routine of the assembly line. It has dotted our roadsides with junkyards, filled our air with smoke, and poisoned our food with dangerous chemicals. The question is whether the outpouring of frozen foods, talking dolls, CB radios, and headache remedies is worth its high cost to society. As one well-known economist put it:

The continued pursuit of economic growth by Western Societies is more likely on balance to reduce rather than increase social welfare....Technological innovations may offer to add to men's material opportunities. But by increasing the risks of their obsolescence it adds also to their anxiety. Swifter means of communications have the paradoxical effect of isolating people; increased mobility has led to more hours commuting; increased automobilization to increased separation; more television to less communication. In consequence, people know less of their neighbors than ever before in history.[5]

Virtually every economist agrees that these concerns are valid, though many question whether economic growth is their major cause. Nevertheless, they all emphasize that pollution of air and water, noise and congestion, and the

---

[4]Marx, *Capital*, vol. I (Chicago: Charles H. Kerr Publishing Co., 1906), page 649.

[5]E. J. Mishan, *The Costs of Economic Growth* (New York: Frederick A. Praeger Publishers, 1967), pages 171, 175.

mechanization of the work process are very real and very serious problems. There is every reason for society to undertake programs that grapple with these problems. (Chapter 19 in *Microeconomics*, which deals with problems of the environment, examines these issues more closely and describes some policies to deal with them.)

Economists agree also that growth in human well-being is measured very poorly by statistics such as GNP, which indicates only the growth rate of the production of *material* goods and services and takes no account of the effects of growth on the quality of life. Two economists at Yale University, William Nordhaus and James Tobin, have attempted to calculate a better set of figures for the purpose. Their index, the *measure of economic welfare* (MEW), attempts to take into account such items as pollution and congestion as well as the more tangible products of the economy.[6] Thus, for example, if the output of goods and services were to go up slightly some year but there was also a huge increase in pollution, the statistics would report that GNP had risen but that MEW, or the quality of life, had decreased. In fact, the calculations show that throughout most of the post-World War II period, both GNP per capita and MEW per capita have been growing but that growth in the latter has been very much slower.

Despite the costs of growth in terms of human and environmental damage, there is strong evidence that if the economy's total output were kept at its present level, the community would pay a high price over and above the loss of additional goods and services.

First, it is not easy to carry out a decision to prevent further economic growth. Mandatory controls are abhorrent to most Canadians. We cannot *order* people to stop inventing means to expand productivity. Nor does it make any sense to order every firm and industry to freeze its output level, since changing tastes and needs require some industries to expand their outputs at the same time that others are contracting. But who is to decide which should grow and which should contract, and how shall such decisions be made? *The achievement of zero economic growth may very well require government intervention on a scale that becomes expensive and even repressive.*

Second, zero economic growth may seriously hamper efforts to eliminate poverty both within our economy and throughout the world. Much of the earth's population today lives in a state of extreme want. And though wealthier nations have been reluctant to provide more than token amounts of help to the underdeveloped countries, less wealth means there would be even less to share. So perhaps the only hope for improved living standards in the impoverished countries of Africa, Asia, and Latin America lies in continued increases in output.

Finally, without continued growth, it will be no easy matter to finance effective programs of environmental protection. To improve the purity of our air and water and to clean up urban neighbourhoods, billions of dollars must be made available every year. Continued growth would enable the required resources to be provided without any reduction in the availability of consumer goods. But without such growth, we may actually be forced to cut back on our programs to protect the environment. Society could thus end up with less goods and a worse environment.

Problems of the Less Developed Countries

While for wealthier countries the desirability of increased growth may not be completely obvious, for the poorer, **less developed countries (LDCs)** there is less question about the matter. In these nations, increasing the level of per-capita income is a top priority.

[6]W. Nordhaus and J. Tobin, "Is Growth Obsolete?" *Fiftieth Anniversary Colloquium*, V, National Bureau of Economic Research (New York: Columbia University Press, 1972).

Living in the LDCs

Three-quarters of the world's population lives in areas whose average per-capita GNP is $750 or less per year, evaluated (as well as it is possible to do) in terms of today's prices in Canada. Table 22–1 shows that there are countries in which annual per-capita income is under $200. Even after adjustment for differences in measurement of GNP in Canada and the poorer countries, this probably comes to an annual income figure under $700.

To us in Canada, residents of an economy that offers an average GNP almost 20 times as high, such a figure is not only likely to seem incredible, it is all but incomprehensible. Few of us can *really* imagine what life would be like it our family income were reduced to, say, $2000 per year. It is even hard to envision survival on such amounts. It must be emphasized that these figures do *not* represent the living standards of a small group of outcasts from their own societies. Rather, they are *typical* of perhaps a majority of those who live in Asia, Africa, and Latin America.

What can life be like in such circumstances? No brief description can really bridge the gulf between our range of experience and theirs. Yet it can offer us a glimpse into a way of life that few of us will want to share.

Inhabitants of many of the less developed countries live with their large families in one-room shanties or apartments, their water supplies are scanty, polluted, and often miles from home, their only source of energy is that of man and beast, and their sparse harvests are wrung from miserable soil in goods years, with starvation threatened perhaps every five years when the rains do not come and the crops fail.[7] With no surplus in production, no good can be put into reserves, and the old, the infirm, and the very young are likely to perish.

The life of a male in an LDC is hard enough, with its low nutritional level, its lack of equipment to help in work, and its frequency of debilitating diseases. But his life is luxurious compared with that of his wife. She is usually married by the

---

[7]It has been estimated that in some famine years in the 1970s, half a million people died as a result in Bangladesh; 200,000 in Ethiopia; 100,000–250,000 in the Sahelian zone of Africa; and more than 800,000 in just three of the states of India (*The New York Times*, October 27, 1976). In 1984, the famine in Ethiopia resulted in another disaster on this same scale.

Table 22–1
PER-CAPITA GNP IN DEVELOPED AND LESS DEVELOPED COUNTRIES, 1982–1983

	(measured in U.S. dollars)
Developed Countries	
United States	13,160
West Germany	12,460
Sweden	14,040
Canada	12,323
Less Developed Countries	
Egypt	690
Bolivia	570
China	310
Haiti	300
Bangladesh	140
Chad	80

SOURCE: Population Reference Bureau.

Table 22–2
INFANT MORTALITY AND LIFE EXPECTANCY IN DEVELOPED AND LESS DEVELOPED COUNTRIES, 1982–1983

	INFANT MORTALITY (deaths per 1000 live births)	LIFE EXPECTANCY AT BIRTH (years)
Developed Countries		
United States	11	74
West Germany	11	73
Sweden	7	76
Canada	13	74
Less Developed Countries		
Egypt	80	56
Bolivia	130	50
China	35	65
Haiti	113	52
Bangladesh	148	47
Chad	147	40

SOURCE: Population Reference Bureau.

age of 14 and bears 8 or 10 children. If (as is true of some 80 percent of the population) she inhabits a rural area, she may have to trudge miles every day to fetch water for the family. She sews all the family's clothes by hand and cooks its meals. There is not enough money for pre-ground flour, so part of the woman's daily work is to pound the grain by hand for food for the family—perhaps an additional two hours of hard labour. She also tends the gardens that produce food for the family, although, except in Moslem countries where women are sequestered, she is also expected to put in a full day in the fields during the six months of the agricultural season.

Another duty of the woman in an LDC is to bring produce, wood, or whatever she has to trade to market a couple of times a week, and she must often walk as many as 10 miles each way with bundles as heavy as she can carry on her back or on her head. She has no respite in the raising of her children, since they are likely not to have a school to attend when they are well or a hospital to go to when they are sick.

Table 22-2 gives the percentage of infant deaths for each 1000 live births and the average life expectancy of a newborn child in some countries ranging from the most underdeveloped to the most affluent. The contrasts are dramatic. In Bolivia, 130 babies die of every 1000 that are born, while the comparable figure in Sweden is only seven. In many countries people survive only until their late 40s, while in Scandinavia they live to be 76. There is little question about the quality of life in less developed lands.

Most of the inhabitants of many LDCs are shockingly poor. Malnutrition and disease are widespread. The sheer process of living and surviving taxes the people to the utmost and makes them old before their time.

Recent Trends

Do recent trends offer hope of improvement? Here there is both good news and bad. The good news is perhaps the most remarkable. In the 1970s, real GNP in the LDCs grew, on average, more than 5 percent a year (see Table 22-3 for examples).

Table 22-1
AVERAGE ANNUAL GROWTH RATES OF REAL GROSS DOMESTIC PRODUCT IN DEVELOPED AND LESS DEVELOPED COUNTRIES, APPROXIMATELY 1960-1979

	APPROXIMATELY 1960-70 (percent)	APPROXIMATELY 1970-79 (percent)
Developed Countries		
United States	4.4	3.2
West Germany	4.4	2.6
Sweden	4.4	2.0
Canada	5.3	3.4
Less Developed Countries		
Columbia	5.1	5.8
Haiti	0.7	4.1
Iran	10.6	8.8
Pakistan	5.2	4.8
Cuba	3.7	2.5
Zimbabwe	6.1	2.3
Zambia	1.8	1.0

SOURCE: United Nations.

Table 22-2
BIRTHRATE MINUS DEATH RATE IN DEVELOPED AND LESS DEVELOPED COUNTRIES, 1983 (ESTIMATED)

	(births minus deaths as percent of population)
Developed Countries	
United States	0.7
West Germany	-0.2
Sweden	0.0
Canada	0.8
Less Developed Countries	
Bolivia	2.7
Burma	2.4
Egypt	2.7
Ethiopia	2.4
Haiti	2.2
India	2.0

SOURCE: Population Reference Bureau.

Even more important, income per capita grew at an annual rate greater than 2½ percent. The world recession of the early 1980s hit some LDCs very hard and enmeshed them in a serious debt burden (see pages 434, 436). Nevertheless, for some LDCs the long-term outlook continues to be promising. This means that:

Despite population increases, some LDCs have succeeded in breaking out of the stagnation trap. If growth continues as it has recently, an average family in an underdeveloped area can look forward to a doubling of its living standards in less than 30 years. Or put another way, standards of living will be increasing faster than they did in Canada in the nineteenth century!

Clearly, the experience of the 1970s offered hope for a major reduction in absolute poverty for many of the LDCs.

Thus, there was good news in the 1970s, though the beginning of the 1980s was not quite so favourable for the LDCs. Aside from their debt problems, which will be discussed a bit later, there are several developments that can be considered either as merely unfortunate or as thoroughly ominous.

First, while the percentage rates of growth of per-capita incomes in the LDCs have been very impressive, the industrialized countries, with their initially high incomes, have not exactly been standing still. Indeed, largely because their population growth has been slower, the percentage growth rate in per-capita incomes has been higher in the developed countries. But even if the *percentage* increases in their per-capita incomes had been very similar, *absolute* incomes would have continued to rise more quickly in the richer lands. Where per-capita income is $100 a year, a 2½ percent growth rate translates into a $2.50 annual improvement; however, where per-capita income is $5000 a year, the same 2½ percent rate of growth adds $125 a year to the income of the average person. As a result:

The purchasing power of the average family in an LDC is falling further behind that of a typical family in a wealthy economy.

Second, many critics emphasize that the 2½ percent growth rate has been accompanied by a worsening distribution of income in some of the LDCs. The rise in population has worsened the living standards of people on marginal lands with inadequate rain (about 40 percent of Indian farmers and a large proportion of Africans). Add the massive explosion of urban unemployment, and one gets several hundred million people who are no better off and possibly worse off.

Third, a continuing problem within the LDCs is the high growth rate of their populations.

While in Canada, the United States, and some countries of Western Europe, net population growth has fallen almost to zero, the population explosion continues in some of the LDCs, particularly in Africa.

Table 22–4 tells the story: For the sample of LDCs shown, the annual growth rate of population continues perhaps ten times as high as it is in the industrialized countries. Clearly, the more closely the growth in population approximates the growth in national income, the more slowly standards of living will rise, since there will be that many more persons among whom the additional product must be divided. If population growth is exactly equal to the growth rate of national income, obviously the average standard of living must be at an absolute standstill. A recent estimate indicates that the rise in population in LDCs is in fact consuming nearly half the increase in their GNP.

Fourth, the relatively high growth rate in per-capita incomes has not been uniform throughout the LDCs. In some countries, such as Sri Lanka, Ghana, Chad, and Cuba, growth rates have been extremely low. Yet in others, notably the Ivory

Coast, Singapore, South Korea, and Taiwan, growth has been so spectacular that some of them are no longer considered LDCs, despite oil shocks, increasing restrictions against their exports, and lack of mineral resources.

Finally, the LDCs have shown themselves highly vulnerable to such events as the oil crisis in 1979 and the high real interest rates of the 1980s. Much as the fall in Iranian oil exports and rise in oil prices affected the industrialized economies, it undoubtedly damaged the LDCs even more, leading to enormous deficits and foreign debts for the countries least able to afford them. (See the boxed insert on page 436). In other words, the new growth trends in the LDCs may be quite fragile, and their continuation cannot simply be taken for granted.

It is ironic that the levelling off of oil prices at the beginning of the 1980s not only left many oil-importing LDCs with their crippling debts, but caused similar problems for some of the oil exporters. As a result, Mexico and Venezuela joined Brazil in the group of countries whose economies are severely constrained by huge indebtedness to the rest of the world.

Before leaving the issue of recent growth in the LDCs, it may be helpful to offer a little perspective on the entire matter. First, it should be recognized that sustained growth is a very recent invention, dating from the Industrial Revolution—the beginning of the eighteenth century. It has been estimated that per-capita income in England in 1800 was no higher than in third-century Rome. Before the Industrial Revolution, real wages in England may have reached their peak in the fifteenth century—the end of the Middle Ages—from which they fell to their lowest level ever reached after the Middle Ages in the reign of Queen Elizabeth, more than a century later.

On the other hand, growth in the LDCs is not an innovation of recent decades. In the three decades before World War I, exports from the tropical countries grew faster than national income in the wealthier countries, and, no doubt, in these LDCs output per capita was also growing. Since income data for that period are not available, we do not know by how much, but we do know that the earlier growth was vulnerable to disruption—World War I, the Great Depression, and other catastrophic events all but ended growth in the LDCs for nearly 40 years. Thus, recent high growth rates cannot just be taken for granted and extrapolated into the future.

Impediments to Development in the LDCs

No one has produced a definitive list of causes of the poverty of the LDCs, just as no one can pretend to have produced a foolproof prescription for its cure. Yet there is general agreement on the main conditions contributing to the economic problems of LDCs. These include lack of physical capital, rapid growth of populations, lack of education, unemployment, and social and political impediments to business activity. Let us examine each of these in turn.

Scarcity of Physical Capital

The LDCs are obviously handicapped by their lack of modern factories and machinery. In addition, they lack infrastructure—good roads, railways, port facilities, and so on. But capital is not easy to acquire. If it is to be provided by the populations of the LDCs themselves they must save the required resources—that is, as we saw earlier in this chapter, they must give up consumption in order to free the resources needed to build plants, equipment, and roads. That is fairly easy in a rich community, where substantial saving still leaves the public well off in terms of current consumption. But in an LDC, where malnutrition is a constant threat, the bulk of the inhabitants cannot save except at enormous sacrifice to their families. Moreover, in many of the LDCs, tradition imputes little virtue to investment in business, so that even the wealthy are not terribly eager to put their savings into productive equipment. Thus:

Because of poverty, which makes saving difficult, if not impossible, and because of traditions that do not encourage investment, the LDCs' growth rates of domestically financed capital are lower than those in the developed countries.

One way to help matters is to obtain the funds for investment from abroad. There is a long tradition of foreign investment in developing countries. For example, throughout much of Canadian history, we drew capital from abroad, to finance such projects as the national railway. In recent decades a considerable share of the resources going to the LDCs from abroad has come from foreign governments as part of their aid programs. While some of the resources provided in this way have been used wastefully, informed observers generally agree that the waste incurred under these programs has not been spectacularly great, and they conclude that these capital transfers from the rich countries to the poor have at least worked in the right direction.

Capital can also be transferred to an LDC when a private firm chooses to invest money in such a country to build a factory or to explore for oil in order to increase its own profits. This too seems to have been helpful to the LDCs. In earlier days, it sometimes gave an unacceptable degree of political influence to the foreign firms, particularly when the LDC was a colony of an industrial country. In recent years this difficulty may have become rarer. Nowadays, it is more often the outside firm that is afraid of the government of the LDC rather than vice versa, with foreign proprietors frequently fearful of rigid control by the government of the LDC in which it invests. Sometimes it even fears outright expropriation—that the government will simply take over its property in the LDC with, or even without, compensation because of the hostile attitudes that residents of many LDCs hold toward large foreign companies.

It is difficult for a resident of an industrialized country like Canada to realize how much hatred and resentment is felt in less developed countries toward the "northern imperialist powers." This resentment is focused in particular on **multinational corporations**—companies like IBM, Royal Dutch Shell, Volkswagen, and Unilever—which have their headquarters in an industrialized country and their operations in a variety of less developed countries. Multinationals may first process their own raw materials in one country, ship them to another to make them into parts, and assemble them in still a third. Some of these corporations, among them the oil companies, specialize in the extraction and/or marketing of raw materials, while others, like IBM and Volkswagen, specialize in manufacturing. Many LDCs regard these and other giant foreign corporations as instruments of imperialist exploitation, not as firms that happen to carry on their activities wherever the dictates of efficiency require, contributing benefits to each of the countries in which they operate.

It is true that foreign firms hope to make more money out of an LDC than they put into it, but that is only natural, since otherwise their investment would not have been expected to be profitable, and the funds would therefore not have been invested in the first place. But there are usually *mutual gains* from trade. Investment will be useful to the LDCs if in the process of earning these profits foreign firms build factories, infrastructure, and provide jobs that leave the community wealthier than it would otherwise have been. The evidence is that this is in fact what foreign private investment has typically accomplished in recent decades.

A problem with foreign business investment that is more serious is the danger that foreign firms will fail to train native personnel in the skills necessary to run the factories built by those companies. Often the foreigner brings with him his own managers, engineers, and technicians, and the work force from the LDCs is kept in menial jobs in which on-the-job training is minimal. In recent years the

The Debt Crisis of the Developing Countries

Although there had been previous isolated cracks in the international debt terrain, it was not until 1982 that the problem erupted in dramatic proportions. In August of that year, Mexico announced that it was unable to meet its debt obligations to foreign creditors, although it was taking steps to rectify the situation. In response, the U.S. Government mounted a rescue operation, involving the creditor banks, the International Monetary Fund (IMF), and other creditor governments. The package included a strict program of adjustment for the Mexican economy and a rescheduling of much of the debt. Nervous banks began to cut back lending to other countries that appeared to be heavily indebted, with Brazil the most obvious target. As long as the banks had been willing to continue lending, the debtor countries had had the foreign exchange necessary to continue servicing their accumulated debt, i.e., making scheduled payments of interest and amortization of principal. As the banks cut back, the debtors found debt-service obligations increasingly difficult to meet. One by one, Brazil, Argentina, and many other debtor countries found it necessary to seek debt relief from their creditors, while implementing programs of economic adjustment monitored by the IMF.

(From the *Economic Report of the President*, February 1984, page 71)

The debt problem threatens to undermine growth in much of Latin America, particularly Mexico, Brazil, Argentina, and African countries such as Nigeria. It was caused by overborrowing and overspending during the 1970s when prosperity and growth seemed easy to sustain; by the high oil prices of the 1970s, which hurt the oil-importing LDCs; by the fall in oil prices in the early 1980s, which hurt the oil-exporting LDCs; and by high interest rates, which hurt them all.

The debt crisis is forcing widespread adoption of austerity policies—reducing already low consumption levels so that less has to be imported and more goods are left over for export. It prevents any ambitious investment programs for the same reason, thus impeding future growth. It is indeed a major problem for the LDCs and, incidentally, for the shareholders of large banks in the industrialized countries to whom the money is owed and who fear the loss of their loans.

LDCs have begun to deal with this problem by restricting immigration of foreign personnel, giving them work permits only for limited periods and requiring at least some minimum employment of native personnel in key positions.

Another danger posed by foreign investment is that it may prevent future financial independence. Profits are a major source of the funds used for investment. If foreign investment takes over the LDCs' most profitable industries, then newly formed capital—new plants and equipment—will also be owned predominantly by foreigners.

Population Growth

Population growth is often described as the primary villain in the LDCs. We have already noted that their populations grow far more rapidly than those in the wealthier countries. And though the growth rate has recently been declining in many of the less developed countries, overall the population of the LDCs is expanding at a rate that will double in less than 30 years, requiring a doubling of housing, schools, hospitals, and so on—a heavy real cost for an LDC.

The growth in population has been stimulated by improvements in medical care, which have reduced death rates spectacularly. Today, in some areas, death rates (ratio of deaths to population) are only one-quarter or one-fifth as high as birthrates. While formerly it was not unusual for half a nation's children to die before the age of 20, today in many countries this is true of only some 4 percent of those populations. This dramatic decline can be attributed primarily to inexpensive public health measures—reduction in stomach diseases through purer water supplies, reduction in the incidence of malaria by the draining of swamps, insecticide spraying of the breeding grounds of infectious mosquitoes, eradication of smallpox by vaccination, and so forth. The more expensive treatment of illness, using modern medical techniques and miracle drugs, seems to have contributed far less.

But not all LDCs suffer from serious population problems. India, Indonesia, and Egypt are frequently cited examples of population pressures. On the other hand, many African countries and parts of Latin America still have populations so small that they are denied economies of large-scale communication and transportation. The economy of a sparsely settled country whose electric power and telecommunication lines must traverse great unpopulated areas is under a costly handicap.

Governments in a number of LDCs have been struggling to find workable ways to cut population growth. Programs set up to distribute contraceptives and propaganda against large families have achieved modest success; but in some countries with particularly severe population problems the governments have been dissatisfied with the results of these voluntary efforts. In India, a program making use of compulsory sterilization aroused the anger of the public and finally led to the downfall of the government.

Ironically enough, it was communist China that, along with Singapore, decided to employ strong financial incentives for the purpose. In China, government support is provided for a first child. For a second, the support is withdrawn and some financial penalties imposed; and for a third child, the penalties are really prohibitive for most people. Because this program has been launched only recently it is impossible to provide clear evidence of its success or failure. However, observers come away impressed with its initial impact. Everywhere in China one meets people who say they are determined to have only one child. If this proves to be reasonably accurate, it may produce one of the most dramatic decreases in birthrates the world has ever seen.

Educational and Technical Training

Everyone knows that educational levels in the LDCs are much lower than they are in the wealthier countries. There are fewer graduates of elementary schools, far fewer graduates of high schools, and enormously fewer university graduates. The percentage of the population that is literate is much lower than in industrialized nations. The issue is how much of a handicap this constitutes for economic growth.

If, by "education," we refer to general learning rather than technical (trade) schooling, the evidence is that it makes considerably less difference for economic growth than is often believed. For example, the number of jobs that clearly require secondary (high school) education rarely seems to exceed 10 percent of the labour force. Various studies that have investigated whether there is a statistical relationship between the economic growth of an economy and its typical educational level have failed to turn up any significant correlation between the two. Other suggestive evidence can easily be cited. For example, in 1840 when Great Britain ruled the markets of the world, only 59 percent of the British adult population was literate, while in the United States, Scandinavia, and Germany, then all relatively undeveloped, the figure was about 80 percent.

All of this is not meant to imply that education is worthless. On the contrary, it obviously offers many benefits in and of itself, which need not be discussed here. But it does suggest that if a government invests in education *purely as a means to stimulate economic growth*, only a very limited outlay is justifiable on these grounds.

Matters are quite different when we turn to technical training. There is clearly a high payoff to the training of electricians, machinists, draftsmen, construction workers, and the like. While the number of persons involved need not be very high in proportion to the population, the role played by such specialists is crucial. However, the LDCs would find it a very heavy drain upon their scarce foreign currency to send young people abroad to learn these skills in the numbers called for by the needs of the economy. One of the main inhibitions to adequate training in these areas is that in many countries such skills are held in low esteem and considered inferior to training in the liberal arts. Consequently, technical education is often handicapped by low budgets, low teacher salaries—which discourage good people from entering the field—and the prejudice of potential students against such fields.

Training in improved farming methods also has a great deal to contribute. In many of the LDCs, agricultural methods produce yields far lower than the best of the known techniques can offer. As one leading observer, Nobel Prize-winner Sir W. Arthur Lewis, has remarked:

If this gap could be closed, the economies of these countries would be unrecognizable. Indeed ... no impact can be made on mass living standards without revolutionizing agricultural performance.[8]

There seem to be no easy ways to provide the necessary education to the farmers who cannot spare the time to attend schools; and training their children also involves a number of critical obstacles. Religious beliefs often lead parents to object to schooling of their children, particularly of girls; in areas where literacy is low (where the problem is generally most serious), truly literate and knowledgeable teachers are almost impossible to find in any substantial numbers; and children who do complete schooling have a tendency to leave the farms and move to the cities.

Programs to provide help to the peasants on their own farms have had only limited success. Indeed, lack of training is only part of the problem. Many other things are needed to make modern farming methods possible—farms larger than the two hectares (or five acres) that are typical in a number of countries are required to permit the use of modern machinery where it is appropriate. Roads and storage facilities must be built. Credit must be made available to farmers. Financial arrangements must be changed so the farmer need no longer give up half his crop to landlords and tax collectors whom he can surely regard as little more than parasites and who undermine his incentives for improved productivity.

Unemployment

One of the most noteworthy features of the growth of the LDCs has been an increase in unemployment as population shifted out of agriculture into the cities. Increased schooling has stimulated the migration out of rural areas, as has unionization, which has often produced a huge gap between urban and rural wages. Government investment policies have also favoured construction of schools, hospitals, and other facilities in the cities, and as a result, large numbers of migrants have entered the cities to swell the ranks of the unemployed. The unemployment rate among young urban workers has been particularly high; indeed, rates as high as 50 percent are not unheard of.

These figures are compounded by the phenomenon of **disguised unemployment**. For example, ten persons may do a job for which only six are needed.

[8]W. A. Lewis, *Development Economics, An Outline* (Morristown, N.J.: General Learning Press, 1974), page 25.

The statistics would show no unemployment among the ten workers, even though four of them really contribute nothing to output. Some observers believe that this is such a widespread problem in rural areas that even a substantial reverse migration of the urban unemployed back to the farms would add very little to production, at least in some of the LDCs.

An important consequence of all this is that in many LDCs unemployment may not be accompanied by any substantial reduction in output, in contrast to the situation in industrialized economies. But this does not mean that unemployment in the LDCs is not a serious problem. What it does mean is that it may sometimes be desirable for those economies to avoid the use of labour-saving equipment, partly because it will result in better use of an abundant resource, and partly because it will contribute to the solution of a serious social problem. Thus, increased output is desirable perhaps primarily because it helps to sop up unemployed labour. This is in contrast to the usual situation in the developed countries in which increased employment is desirable perhaps primarily because it increases income and output.

Social Impediments to Entrepreneurship

As we saw earlier in this chapter, one of the magic ingredients of economic growth is **entrepreneurship**. It is clear that the LDCs need entrepreneurs if their economies are to grow rapidly. But in many of these economies, there are serious inhibitions to entrepreneurship. Traditional social values often accord relatively low status to business activity. Indeed, those traditional values even prevent businesses from seeking ways to attract and please their customers and their work force. In addition, high positions in business in many LDCs are often determined by family connections and inheritance, not by ability.

In the LDCs, growth will be inhibited until customs can be modified to increase the social status of economic activity, to make it respectable for private business people and managers of public enterprises to do their best to attract business and increase productivity, and to assign responsibility on the basis of ability rather than family connections.

Government Inhibition of Business Activity

In addition to social impediments to business, the political situation in the LDCs often is detrimental to business success. Business is not helped by unstable governments or by the uncertainty that accompanies such an environment, especially if there is a high likelihood of revolution. Foreign investment will be discouraged where there is fear of expropriation or of unstable currencies that may fall in value and wipe out hard-earned profits. And native business people may live in fear of nationalization or even imprisonment—possibilities that are not likely to encourage investment.

In addition, in the normal course of events, governments in the LDCs are often inclined to interfere with business activity in a variety of ways that seem relatively innocuous—but whose effects can be deadly. Price controls are often imposed at levels that make the controlled activity totally unprofitable and cause it to wither. Licences and other direct controls are frequently administered by incompetent bureaucrats, who tie up business activity in red tape. As a matter of prestige of the currency, exchange rates are often set so high that exports from the LDC cannot compete on the world market. The governments sometimes expropriate and seek to operate foreign firms before they have trained native personnel to run them. In short:

Poorly conceived economic policies can impede business activity and hence economic growth in the LDCs. But, then, it must be admitted that the LDCs have no monopoly on foolish economic policies!

Help from Industrialized Economies

We have just seen that two of the primary needs of the LDCs are technical skills and capital resources. Happily, these are precisely the things that the more prosperous nations are in a position to offer. We have the trained teachers, classrooms, laboratories, and equipment necessary to provide an education of the highest quality to students from the LDCs.

However, there is a danger here that has received a great deal of attention, the so-called **brain drain**. This refers to the temptation for students from LDCs to try to stay in the countries where they have studied and enjoy the higher living standard, rather than to return home where their abilities are needed so badly.

There are several ways to deal with this. For example, one can require students to return to their homelands for at least some given number of years after completion of the educational program, or offer higher wages for trained persons in the LDCs to make returning more attractive. Yet the problem is there, and the large number of doctors, teachers, and other skilled personnel from LDCs who are seeking jobs in the developed countries suggests that it is not negligible.

A second major contribution that the wealthier countries can make to the LDCs is to offer them trained technicians and technical advice from their own populations. Such counselling and personnel can be very helpful as a temporary measure, but in the long run they can prove detrimental if provision for the training of local personnel for the ultimate replacement of the foreign technicians and advisers is not built into the program.

A third, and very important, type of assistance from the developed to the less developed countries takes the form of money or physical resources provided either as loans made on favourable terms or as outright grants (gifts). In a moment we will consider some of the contributions that the industrial world has recently made in this area.

Fourth, the world can help the LDCs through research. One of the hardest problems for the developing world is what to do in the rural areas that suffer from inadequate rainfall, where several hundred million people live in both Asia and Africa. These people are badly in need of new dry-farming techniques. Until some are discovered, their poverty will increase as their numbers grow. An international research organization devoted to food production in problem areas in the LDCs would have much to contribute.

Finally, and perhaps most important, the developed countries can help by encouraging freedom of trade and investment. This will help those LDCs whose exports are readily expanded but that are now being held back by barriers to trade. Exports of sugar, meat, cotton, and other agricultural products are inhibited by tariffs and other restrictions. There are many discriminatory duties against processed, as distinct from crude, materials. A significant number of LDCs would also benefit substantially from a lifting of quotas and other restrictions upon the export of manufactured goods. Increased freedom of trade will also help those LDCs whose economies offer business prospects sufficiently bright to attract significant quantities of private capital from abroad. All in all, increased freedom of trade is a matter of highest priority for the LDCs.[9]

[9]Not everyone agrees with this conclusion. There are those who have argued that participation of LDCs in international trade is bad for them because it weakens their capacity to develop as self-reliant, mature economies. It is held that new manufacturing industries in the LDCs will not take off without protection from foreign competition. Development of primary product exports creates a rich and politically powerful vested interest that inhibits measures that would favour manufacturing. The extent to which foreign trade and production of exports are in foreign hands inhibits domestic saving and the development of local entrepreneurship.

In this view, LDCs are therefore held back by international trade and they would do better to integrate regionally and develop their own home markets without foreigners, who also bring unsuitable habits, unsuitable tastes, and unsuitable technology, and impart a crippling inferiority complex to the natives.

Loans and Grants to the LDCs

The Canadian International Development Agency (CIDA) is the government department that supervises Canada's aid programs for developing countries. Canada provides assistance to approximately 80 countries, and in 1981–82 this aid amounted to $1.46 billion. Just over one-third of our contributions to developing countries are made directly to the country (bilaterally), and the remainder is made through the U.N., development banks, and other agencies (multilaterally). The bilateral assistance takes the form of grants or low-interest-rate loans. The loans are used to purchase materials or services for industry or agriculture from Canada or to gain access to the Canadian market. Asia receives the largest share of our bilateral aid ($209 million in 1980–81), then Francophone Africa ($137 million), Commonwealth Africa ($110 million), Latin America ($29 million), and the Caribbean ($27 million). The multilateral assistance supports 65 programs, with a major portion going to the World Bank Group and regional development banks.

The World Bank was created after World War II, and has 144 member countries. Each member provides an amount of capital to the bank that is related to the member country's wealth; for instance, the United States has contributed approximately one-third of the total. The Bank makes loans that are financed by bonds that it issues and sells, and has acted as guarantor of repayment to encourage some private lending and has established agencies, that have played major roles in providing funds to the LDCs. The Bank has loaned almost $70 billion to LDCs and to countries that can be considered on the borderline. It has tended to emphasize loans for infrastructure, dams, communications and transportation, and, in addition, has provided technical assistance and planning advice.

The remainder of Canadian aid to the LDCs goes to U.N. programs, relief funds for disaster victims, food aid, business, labour, and academic exchanges, and technical assistance.

In the past few years, expenditures on foreign aid have become less popular politically, and the amounts provided by Canada have consequently gone down from 0.5 percent of GNP in the mid-1970s to 0.4 percent of GNP in 1982. Contributions have fallen more drastically in the U.S., from about half a percent of U.S. GNP in 1965 to well under 0.27 percent of GNP in 1982.

Aid has come from other industrialized countries, notably France, Great Britain, West Germany, and the Soviet Union. While the Soviet funds have obviously been distributed in a way intended to maximize its political advantage, it can hardly be claimed that Western aid programs have been free of political considerations.

Many economists have advocated greater generosity in our assistance to LDCs and have deplored cuts in our aid programs. Aside from any moral responsibility to help the impoverished countries, it is argued that an effective aid program that really helps the growth of LDCs will also serve our own interests. By making those countries more stable economically and politically, we can contribute to our own economic tranquility. By increasing the LDCs' power to buy and sell, we are in effect contributing to the prosperity of the entire world.

The "North–South" Controversy and Commodity Price Stabilization

The conflict of interests between the LDCs and the industrialized countries has come to be called, somewhat inaccurately, the "North–South confrontation," with the "North" referring to the wealthy nations and the "South" denoting the poor countries. The international trade arrangements, which the North considers to constitute a free market for the unhampered exchange of goods for the mutual benefit of all participants, are widely viewed in the South as a thinly disguised instrument of old-fashioned imperialism to be used to exploit the poorer economies.

A major cause of this discontent is the prices of the commodities, such as cocoa and sugar, which the South considers to be unfairly low and distressingly unstable. There has been considerable pressure for international agreements that will take steps to reduce the upswings and downswings of these prices. It has been proposed that a stabilization fund be organized and used to buy such commodities when their prices are falling and to sell them when their prices are rising. That is, by shifting demand outward when prices are relatively low, the fund would raise these prices; and by shifting demand downward when prices are comparatively high, it would force these prices downward.

But negotiations have stalled over at least two issues. First, the industrialized countries want much of the money for the stabilization fund to be supplied by the less developed countries themselves, while the latter want most of the fund to be financed by the industrialized countries who buy these products. So far, a tentative agreement has been reached for the creation of a modest fund with both North and South contributing to it. But the second issue is perhaps more serious. The North intends the stabilization fund to do only what its name implies: to iron out fluctuations in commodity prices, not to raise or lower those prices on the average. But to many southern countries "stabilization" actually is a diplomatic way of referring to their desire to *raise* commodity prices, something the North is predictably reluctant to do.

Can LDCs Break Away from Poverty?

It is easy to jump to the conclusion that the economic problems of the LDCs are staggering and that the prospects of their ever catching up with the industrialized countries are negligible. Certainly, some LDCs are in very bad straits. Yet a number of LDCs and former LDCs have made enormous progress. The African countries Kenya, Cameroon, and the Ivory Coast increased their GNPs during the 1970s at a rate of about 5 percent to 6 percent a year, which is considerably faster than their population growth. In the Americas, Costa Rica's performance has been comparable. Even more striking is the expansion of output in a number of places in the Far East—particularly Hong Kong, Taiwan, South Korea, and Singapore, where prosperity is unprecedented and economic activity is expanding at an astonishing rate. Here per-capita GNPs have been growing at a rate of 6.5 percent a year and more.

But the most impressive case is that of Japan. Many of your professors will remember clearly when North American businesses feared the flood of goods produced by cheap Japanese labour, and when the label "made in Japan" suggested inexpensive and shoddy merchandise. From one of the world's impoverished countries, Japan has risen to one of the world's richest. Its goods are now feared by manufacturers elsewhere not because they are produced and sold so cheaply, but because their quality is so high. Japanese cars and sophisticated electronic equipment find a ready market throughout the world. And as a result, per-capita income in Japan has surpassed that in Great Britain. A less developed country need not lag behind forever.

Summary

1. If growth is evaluated in terms of its effect upon the well-being of individuals, a country's economic growth should be measured in terms of *per-capita* income, not in terms of GNP or some other index of total output of the economy.

2. A rapidly rising population poses a threat to growth of per-capita incomes.

3. On our finite planet, exponential growth (growth at a constant percentage rate) is, in general, impossible except for relatively brief periods.

4. Increases in growth depend heavily on entrepreneurship, accumulation of capital equipment, and research and development.

5. Saving is necessary for the accumulation of resources with which to produce factories, machinery, and other capital equipment. Thus, saving is a critical requisite for growth, particularly in less developed countries.

6. Many observers argue that even if continued growth does not lead to catastrophically rapid depletion of resources (as some have predicted), its desirability is nevertheless questionable because it produces pollution, overcrowding, and many other undesirable consequences.

7. Those who favour growth argue that without it there is no chance of ridding the world of poverty.

8. Standards of living in many LDCs are extremely low; per-capita incomes that are equivalent to $600 a year are not uncommon. Life expectancy is low and daily living is very difficult, particularly for women.

9. GNP and per-capita incomes in many LDCs grew considerably in the 1970s.

10. Nevertheless, the gap between family incomes in the less developed and the industrialized countries has continued to widen.

11. In many LDCs population continues to grow much faster than that in the industrialized countries.

12. Growth in the LDCs is impeded by shortages of capital caused by poverty, traditions that do not encourage investment, rapid population growth, poor education, unemployment, lack of entrepreneurship, and government impediments to business.

13. Industrialized countries can help the LDCs by providing capital through loans and grants, by offering training and education to people from those lands, and by encouraging freedom of trade with the LDCs.

14. In the post-World War II period, many countries have provided money to the LDCs in the form of loans and grants, as does Canada through CIDA.

15. Several international organizations, most notably the World Bank, have been organized to provide economic assistance to the LDCs.

Concepts for Review

Output per capita
Exponential growth
Social infrastructure
Exchange between present and
    future consumption
Embodied growth

Disembodied growth
Less developed countries (LDCs)
Growth rate in GNP vs. per-capita
    income
Multinational corporations
Disguised unemployment

Entrepreneurship
Brain drain
World Bank
CIDA

Questions for Discussion

1. Which do you think has the higher total GNP, Pakistan or Luxembourg? Which has the higher per-capita GNP? In which do you think people are better off economically?

2. Suppose population grows at a constant exponential rate and doubles every 10 years. How many times will it have grown in 30 years? How many years does it require to expand to 16 times its initial level?

3. Can you think of any innovations that permit growth without proportionate increases in use of inputs?

4. Name as many undesirable consequences of growth as you can think of.

5. Are the undesirable consequences of growth more likely to be considered serious in a less developed country or in an industrialized country? Why?

6. To many families living in less developed countries, an income equivalent to $2000 per year is considered a high standard of living. Can you make up a budget for a Canadian family of four earning $2000 a year?

7. Explain how it is possible for the per-capita income of an LDC to grow at a faster rate than that in Canada and yet for the difference between the incomes of

average families in both countries to increase. Can you give a numerical example showing how this happens?

8. Discuss the advantages and disadvantages to an LDC of a Canadian manufacturing company investing in that country.

9. If you were economic adviser to the president of an LDC, what might you suggest that he or she do to encourage increases in saving and investment?

10. No one knows what encourages or discourages the supply of entrepreneurs. Do you have any ideas about policies that may be capable of stimulating entrepreneurship?

11. Name some countries in which entrepreneurship seems to be abundant these days; some countries in which it seems to be scarce.

12. Discuss what you have read in the newspapers and heard from other sources about the Japanese "growth miracle." What does it portend for the future of the Japanese economy? For that of Canada?

Glossary

Page numbers for *Macroeconomics* are shown in regular type, those for *Microeconomics* in **boldface** type.

Numbers in parentheses indicate pages in the text where the terms are discussed.

Ability-to-pay principle The idea that persons with greater ability to pay taxes should pay higher taxes. **(340)**

Absolute advantage Of one country over another in the production of a particular good is said to occur if it can produce that good using smaller quantities of resources than can the other country. (400) **(310)**

Abstraction Ignoring many details in order to focus on the most important factors in a problem. (11) **(11)**

Affirmative action Active efforts to locate and hire members of minority groups. **(462)**

Aggregate demand The total amount that all consumers, business firms, government agencies, and foreigners are willing to spend on final goods and services. (114)

Aggregate-demand curve Graphic presentation of the quantity of national product that is demanded at each possible value of the price level. (75, 150)

Aggregate saving The difference between disposable income and consumer expenditure. (131)

Aggregate supply The total amount that all business firms are willing to produce. (174)

Aggregate-supply curve A graph that shows, for each possible price level, the quantity of goods and services that all the nation's businesses are willing to produce, holding all other determinants of aggregate quantity supplied constant. (75, 174)

Aggregation Combining many individual markets into one overall market. Economic aggregates are the focus of macroeconomics. (74)

Appreciation (of a nation's currency) Is said to occur when exchange rates change so that a unit of its own currency can buy more units of foreign currency. (248)

Arbitration Process in which an outsider is authorized to dictate the terms of a settlement of a labour-management dispute if a voluntary agreement cannot be reached. **(435)**

Asset An item that an individual or a firm owns. (232)

Automatic stabilizer An arrangement that automatically supports aggregate demand when it would otherwise sag and holds down aggregate demand when it would otherwise surge ahead; thus reduces the sensitivity of the economy to shifts in demand. (372)

Autonomous increase in consumption An increase in consumer spending without any increase in incomes. Represented graphically as a shift of the entire consumption function. (167)

Average-cost curve Shows, for each output, the cost per unit, that is, total cost divided by output. **(118)**

Average physcial product (APP) Total physical product (TPP) divided by the quantity of input utilized. **(115)**

Average revenue (AR) Total revenue (TR) divided by quantity. **(147)**

Balance sheet An account statement listing the values of all assets on the left-hand side and of all liabilities and net worth on the right-hand side. (232)

Bank of Canada Canada's central bank. (243)

Bank rate The rate of interest charged by the Bank of Canada when reserves are loaned to the chartered banks (advances from the central bank). It is used as a signal of the direction of monetary policy. (247)

Barter A system of exchange in which people directly trade one good for another, without using money as an intermediate step. (225)

Benefits principle of taxation The idea that people who derive benefits from a service should pay the taxes that finance it. **(341)**

Bilateral monopoly Market situation in which there is both a monopoly on the selling side and a monopsony on the buying side. (742)

Bond A corporation's promise to pay the holder a fixed sum of money at the specified *maturity* date and some other fixed amount of money (the *coupon* or *interest payment*) every year up to the date of maturity. **(170)**

Brain drain Occurs when the educated natives of a less developed country emigrate to wealthier nations. (440)

Budget deficit Amount by which the government's expenditures

exceed its receipts during a specified period of time, usually one year. (318)

Budget line Represents graphically all the possible combinations of two commodities that a household can purchase, given the prices of the commodities and some fixed amount of money at its disposal. **(83)**

Burden of a tax The amount of money an individual would have to be given to make him just as well off with the tax as he was without it. **(341)**

Capital Inventory (stock) of plant equipment, and other productive resources held by a business firm, an individual, or some other organization. **(397)**

Capitalism Method of economic organization in which private individuals own the means of production, either directly or indirectly through corporations. **(470)**

Capital gain An increase in the market value of a piece of property that occurs between the time it is bought and the time it is sold (212, 392) **(336)**

Capital loss A decrease in the market value of a piece of property that occurs between the time it is bought and the time it is sold. (212)

Cartel Group of sellers of a product who have joined together to control its production, sale, and price in the hope of obtaining the advantages of monopoly. **(238)**

Central bank A bank for banks. The central bank of Canada is the Bank of Canada. (243)

Closed shop An arrangement that permits only union members to be hired. **(429)**

Collective bargaining Negotiations between union representatives of an industry's labour force and the employers of those workers. **(434)**

Commodity money An object used as a medium of exchange that also has a substantial value in alternative (non-monetary) uses. (226)

Common stock A piece of paper that gives the holder a share in the ownership of a corporation. **(170)**

Comparative advantage Of one country over another in the production of a particular good relative to other goods it can produce is said to occur if it produces that good least inefficiently compared

GLOSSARY **445**

with the other country. (401) **(311)**

Competition policy Government policy that attempts to control the growth of monopoly and to prevent firms from engaging in "undesirable" practices through the use of legislation and various programs. **(289)**

Complements Two goods are called complements if an increase in the price of one reduces the quantity demanded of the other, all other things remaining constant. **(103)**

Concentration of industry The share of the industry's total output (in money terms) supplied by some given number (usually four) of its largest firms. **(298)**

Concentration ratio Percentage of an industry's output produced by its *four* largest firms. It is intended to measure the degree to which the industry is dominated by large firms, that is, how closely it approximates a monopoly. **(300)**

Conditional grants Transfer payments from the federal government to provincial governments, matching provincial spending in areas specified by the federal government. Discontinued in 1977. **(340)**

Consumer expenditure (consumption) Symbolized by the letter *C*; the total amount spent by consumers on newly produced goods and services (excluding purchases of new homes, which are considered investment goods). (114)

Consumer Price Index The most popular index number for the price level. Its weights are based on the spending patterns of a typical urban household. (109)

Consumer sovereignty Consumer preferences determine what goods shall be produced, and in what amount. **(470)**

Consumption function Relationship between total consumer expenditure and total disposable income in the economy, holding all other determinants of consumer spending constant. (123)

Corporation A firm with the legal status of a fictional individual. It is owned by shareholders and run by elected officers and a board of directors, whose chairman often influences the firm's affairs. **(168)**

Correlation A relationship between two variables such that they tend to go up or down together. Correlation need not imply causation. (14) **(14)**

Cost disease of personal services Tendency of the cost of services such as auto repair and legal counsel to rise faster than the economy's overall inflation rate because it is difficult to increase productivity (output per person hours) in these services. **(258)**

Craft union Represents a particular type of skilled worker regardless of the industry. **(427)**

Cross elasticity of demand For product *X* to a change in the price of another product, *Y*, is the ratio of the percentage change in quantity demanded of product *X* to the percentage change in the price of product *Y* that brings about the change in quantity demanded. **(104)**

Cross subsidization Selling one product at a loss, which is balanced by higher profits on another product. **(275)**

Crowding out Occurs when deficit spending by the government forces private investment spending or exports to contract. (330)

Cyclical unemployment The portion of unemployment that is attributable to a decline in the economy's total production. Cyclical unemployment rises during recessions and falls as prosperity is restored. (92)

Deficit, balance of payments Amount by which the quantity supplied of a country's currency (per year) exceeds the quantity demanded. Such deficits arise when the exchange rate is artificially high. (252)

Deflating (by a price index) Dividing some nominal magnitude by a price index in order to express that magnitude in dollars of constant purchasing power. (110)

Deflation A sustained decrease in the general price level. (80)

Demand, law of States that a lower price generally increases the amount of a commodity that people in a market are willing to buy. Thus, for most goods, demand curves have a negative slope. **(92)**

Demand curve A graph showing how the quantity demanded of some product during a specified period of time will change as the price of that product changes, holding all other determinants of quantity demanded constant. (54) **(54)**

Demand schedule A table showing how the quantity demanded of some product during a specified period of time changes as the price of that product changes, holding all other determinants of quantity demanded constant. (54) **(54)**

Depletability An attribute of private goods, as opposed to public goods. A commodity is depletable if it is used up when someone consumes it. **(256)**

Deposit creation Process by which the banking system turns a dollar of reserves into several dollars of deposits. (233)

Deposit insurance A system that guarantees that depositors will not lose money even if their bank goes

bankrupt. (231)

Depreciation (of capital goods) The value of the portion of the nation's capital equipment that is used up within the year. It indicates how much output is needed just to keep the economy's capital stock intact. (136)

Depreciation (of a nation's currency) Is said to occur when exchange rates change so that a unit of its own currency can buy fewer units of foreign currency. (248)

Depreciation allowances Tax deductions that businesses may claim when they spend money on investment goods. (143)

Devaluation Reduction in the official value of a currency. (249)

Direct taxes Taxes levied directly on the people. **(334)**

Discounting Process of determining the present worth of a quantity of money receivable or payable at some future date. **(398)**

Discouraged worker An unemployed person who gives up looking for work and is therefore no longer counted as part of the labour force. (90)

Discrimination, economic Occurs when equivalent factors of production receive different payments for equal contributions to output. **(451)**

Discrimination, statistical Occurs when the productivity of a particular worker is estimated to be low just because that worker belongs to a particular group. **(453)**

Disguised unemployment Occurs when tasks are carried out by a number of persons larger than the number that can complete them most efficiently. (438)

Disinflation The process of reducing inflation. (83)

Disposable income A measure of income derived by subtracting personal income taxes from personal income. (115, 138)

Diversification An increase in the number and *variety* of stocks, bonds, and other such items in an individual's portfolio of investments. **(172)**

Division of labour Breaking up a task into a number of smaller, more specialized tasks so that each worker can become more adept at his or her particular job. Division of labour creates efficiency and increases productivity. (44) **(44)**

Dual labour market theory Assets that workers generally work in one of two types of jobs—those which offer opportunities for acquisition of skills and promotions, and "dead end jobs" which offer little scope for improvement. **(425)**

Dumping Selling goods in a foreign market at lower prices than those charged in the home market. (416) (326)

Economic model A simplified, small-scale version of some aspect of the economy. Economic models are often expressed in equations, by graphs, or in words. (15) **(15)**

Economic power A buyer or seller is said to have economic power if, by his own actions, he can influence the market price. **(495)**

Economic profit Net earnings minus the firm's opportunity cost of capital. **(194)**

Economic profit, total The total revenue a firm or an industry derives from the sale of its products minus the total cost of its inputs, including the opportunity cost of any inputs supplied by the proprietors. **(146)**

Economic rent Said to be earned whenever a factor of production receives a reward that exceeds the minimum amount necessary to keep the factor in its present employment. **(405)**

Economies of scale Savings acquired through increases in quantities produced. **(132, 275)**

Economies of scope Savings acquired through simultaneous production of many different products. **(275)**

Efficiency The absence of waste, achieved primarily by gains in productivity resulting from specialization, division of labour, and a system of exchange. (43) **(43)**

Efficient allocation of resources One that takes advantage of every opportunity to make some individuals better off in their own estimation while not worsening the lot of anyone else. **(200)**

Elasticity of demand, price Ratio of the *percentage* change in quantity demanded to the *percentage* change in price that brings about the change in quantity demanded. **(97)**

Entrepreneurship The act of starting new firms, introducing new products and technological innovations, and, in general, taking the risks necessary in seeking out business opportunities. **(393)**

Equalization payments *See* Unconditional grants.

Equation of exchange States that the money value of GNP transactions must be equal to the product of the average stock of money times velocity $(M \times V = P \times Y)$. (272)

Equilibrium A situation in which there ar no inherent forces that produce change. Changes away from an equilibrium position occur only as a result of "outside events" that disturb the status quo. (56, 144) **(56)**

Equilibrium level of GNP (on the demand side) Level of GNP which makes aggregate demand equal to production. (145)

Equilibrium price Price at which quantity demanded and quantity supplied are equal. This common quantity is called the equilibrium quantity. (56) **(56)**

Excess burden of a tax The amount by which the burden of the tax exceeds the tax that is paid. **(342)**

Excess capacity theorem Asserts that monopolistic competitive firms will tend to produce outputs lower than those that minimize average costs, that is, that they will tend to produce less than their capacity. **(235)**

Excess reserves Reserves held in excess of the legal minimum. (233)

Exchange A mechanism by which workers can trade the various products resulting from specialization and the division of labour. (44) **(44)**

Exchange controls Laws restricting the exchange of one nation's currency for that of another. (309)

Exchange rate States the price, in terms of one currency, at which another currency can be bought. (67, 177) **(67)**

Exchange rates, fixed Rates set by government decisions and maintained by central bank actions. (252)

Exchange rates, floating or flexible Rates determined in free markets by the law of supply and demand. (249)

Excise tax A tax levied on a particular commodity or service, as a fixed amount of money per unit of product sold or as a fixed percentage of the purchase price. **(93)**

Excludability An attribute of private goods, as opposed to public goods. A commodity is excludable if someone who does not pay for it can be kept from enjoying it. **(256)**

Expansion path The locus of a firm's cost-minimizing input combinations for all relevant output levels. **(141)**

Expected rate of inflation Forecasted rate of price change. Also, the difference between the nominal interest rate and the real interest rate. (101)

Expenditure schedule Illustration of how total spending varies with the level of national income (GNP). (146)

Exponential growth Growth at a constant percentage rate. (424).

Export subsidy Payment by the government to exporters to permit them to reduce the selling price of their goods so they can compete more effectively in foreign markets. (409) **(319)**

Externality, beneficial Result of an activity that causes incidental benefits to others with no corresponding compensation provided to or paid by those who

generate the externality. **(252)**

Externality, detrimental Result of an activity that causes damages to others with no corresponding compensation provided to or paid by those who generate the externality. **(252)**

Fiat money Money decreed as such by the government. It has little value as a commodity, but it maintains its value as a medium of exchange because people have faith that the issuer will stand behind the pieces of printed paper and limit their production. (226)

Final goods and services Those that are purchased by their ultimate users. (78)

Fiscal federalism The system of transfer payments from one level of government to the next. **(339)**

Fiscal policy The government's plan for spending and taxation, designed to steer aggregate demand in some desired direction. (196)

Fixed cost Cost of the indivisible inputs which the firm needs to produce any output at all. The total cost of these inputs does not change when output changes. **(120)**

A 45° line A ray through the origin with a slope of + 1. It marks off points where the variables measured on each axis have equal values, assuming that both variables are measured in the same units. (24) **(24)**

Fractional reserve banking A system under which bankers keep in their vaults as reserves only a fraction of the funds they hold on deposit. (230)

Free-rider problem Arises when provision of a service to one individual or group automatically benefits others (the free riders) whether or not the others contribute to the costs. (393)

Frictional unemployment Unemployment resulting from the normal workings of the labour market. Includes people who are temporarily between jobs because they are moving or changing occupations, or for similar reasons. (90)

Game theory Analyses the behaviour of competing firms mathematically, treating it as analogous to the strategies of rival players in a competitive game. **(241)**

Gold-exchange system (Bretton Woods system) International monetary system that prevailed from 1944 to 1971. Under this system, the United States fixed the value of the dollar in terms of gold, and other countries fixed the values of their currencies in terms of the U.S. dollar. (307)

Gold standard System in which exchange rates are set in terms of gold and pegged by buying or selling gold as necessary. (306)

Government purchases Symbolized by the letter *G*, all the goods and services purchased by all levels of government. Transfer payments to individuals (such as welfare benefits) and payments from one level of government to another are not included. (114)

Gross national product (GNP) The sum of the money values of all final goods and services produced by the economy during a specified period, usually one year. (76, 133)

Gross national product, nominal Calculated by valuing all outputs at current prices. (77)

Gross national product, real The sum of the real values of all final goods and services produced by the economy during a specified period, using the prices that prevailed in some agreed-upon year (1971 at the time of writing). (77)

Gross national product deflator Price index obtained by dividing nominal GNP by real GNP. (110)

Growth, disembodied Refers to increases in an economy's output which can occur without being accompanied by (embodied in) additional capital stock. (428).

Growth, embodied Refers to increases in an economy's output which are made possible by increased or improved plant, equipment, or other forms of capital. (428)

High-employment budget Hypothetical budget Canada *would have* if the economy were operating near full employment. (324)

Horizontal equity The notion that equally situated persons should be taxed equally. **(340)**

Human capital theory Interprets education as an investment in a human being's earning power, just as an improvement in a factory is an investment in the factory's earning capacity. **(423)**

Incidence of a tax An allocation of the burden of the tax to specific individuals or groups. **(343)**

Income effect A portion of the change in quantity of a good demanded when its price changes. A rise in price cuts the consumer's purchasing power (real income), which leads to a change in the quantity demanded of that commodity. That change is the income effect. **(79)**

Income-expenditure diagram (45° line diagram) A plotting of total real expenditure (on the vertical axis) against real income (on the horizontal axis). The 45° line marks off points where income and expenditure are equal. (149)

Incomes policy Variety of measures

to curb inflation *without* reducing aggregate demand. (363)

Incomes policy, tax-based Uses the tax system to provide incentives favouring non-inflationary behaviour. (368)

Increasing costs, principle of As the production of one good expands, the opportunity cost of producing another such unit generally increases. (39) **(39)**

Indexing Provisions in a law or contract whereby monetary payments are automatically adjusted whenever a specified price index changes; sometimes called *escalator clauses*. (368)

Index number A number indicating the percentage change in some variable (such as the price level) between the base period and some other period. Typically, the value of the index number in the base period is arbitrarily set to 100. (108)

Indicative planning Government guidance rather than direct control of economic activity. **(477)**

Indifference curve Line connecting all combinations of commodities that are equally desirable to the consumer. **(85)**

Indirect taxes Taxes levied on specific economic activities. **(334)**

Induced increase in consumption An increase in consumer spending that stems from an increase in consumer incomes. Represented graphically as a movement along a fixed consumption function. (167)

Induced investment Investment that rises when GNP rises and falls when GNP falls. (146)

Industrial union Represents all types of workers in a single industry. **(428)**

Inferior good A commodity whose quantity demanded falls when the purchaser's real income rises, all other things remaining equal. **(79)**

Inflation A sustained increase in the general price level. (76)

Inflation, creeping Inflation that proceeds for a long time at a moderate and fairly steady pace. (105)

Inflation, galloping Inflation that proceeds at an exceptionally high rate, perhaps for only a relatively brief period. This type of inflation is generally characterized by accelerating inflation rates, so that the inflation rate is higher this month than last month. (105)

Inflation accounting Adjusting standard accounting procedures for the fact that inflation lowers the purchasing power of money. (321)

Inflationary gap The amount by which equilibrium real GNP exceeds the full-employment level of GNP. (153)

Innovation The act of putting a new

idea into practical use. **(409)**

Interest Payment for the use of funds employed in the production of capital; measured as a percent per year of the value of the funds tied up in the capital. **(398)**

Intermediate good One that is bought for resale or for use in producing another good. (78)

International Monetary Fund (IMF) International organization set up originally to police and manage the gold-exchange system. (307)

Invention The act of generating a new idea. **(409)**

Investment Flow of resources into the production of new capital. **(397)**

Investment, gross private domestic Sum of business investment expenditures on plant and equipment, residential construction expenditures, and inventory change. (134)

Investment good An item that is used to produce other goods and services in the future rather than being consumed today. (42) **(42)**

Investment schedule Table or curve showing how investment spending depends on GNP. (157–58)

Investment spending Symbolized by the letter *I*, the sum of the expenditures of business firms on new plant and equipment, and inventories, plus the expenditures of households on new homes. Financial "investments" and resales of existing physical assets are not included. (114)

Jawboning Informal pressures on firms and unions to slow down the rates at which prices and wages are rising. (363)

Labour force The number of people employed or seeking employment. (88)

Labour productivity A measure of total output divided by the amount of labour used to produce it. It is a measure of output per unit of labour employed. (382)

Laissez faire A program of minimal interference with the workings of the market system. **(202)**

Less developed countries (LDCs) Countries whose share of output composed of agricultural products, mining, and the like is relatively high, which engage in relatively little industrial high-technology activity, and whose per capita incomes are generally comparatively low. (430)

Liability An item that an individual or a firm owes; collectively, liabilities are known as *debts*. (232)

Liability, limited Legal obligation of a firm's owners to pay back company debts only with the money they have already invested in the firm. **(168)**

Liability, unlimited Legal obligation of a firm's owners to repay company debts with whatever resources they own. **(166)**

Libertarianism School of thought that emphasizes the importance of individual freedom. **(492)**

Liquidity, of an asset The ease with which it can be converted into cash. (229)

Long run Period of time long enough for all the firm's commitments to come to an end. **(123)**

Lorenz curve Graph depicting the distribution of income. **(448)**

M1 The narrowly defined money supply, which is the sum of all coins and paper money in circulation, plus pure chequing deposits at chartered banks. (228)

M2 The broadly defined money supply which is the sum of currency in public hands, plus chequing and all savings deposits at chartered banks. (229)

Macroeconomics The study of the behaviour of entire economics. (74)

Marginal cost, long-run *Addition* to the supplier's total cost resulting from the supply of the output *including whatever additional plant and equipment* is needed in the long run to provide that output. Inclusion of this marginal capital cost (of the necessary additions to plant and equipment) is the crucial distinction between *long-run* and *short-run* marginal cost. **(280)**

Marginal-cost curve Shows, for each output, the increase in the firm's total cost required if it increases its output by an additional unit. **(118)**

Marginal land Land that is just on the borderline of being used. **(404)**

Marginal physical product (MPP) Increase in total output that results from a one-unit increase in an input, holding the amounts of all other inputs constant. **(116, 394)**

Marginal propensity to consume (MPC) Ratio of the change in consumption to the change in disposable income that produces the change in consumption. On a graph, it appears as the slope of the consumption function. (123)

Marginal propensity to save (MPS) Graphically, the slope of the saving function, which indicates how much more consumers will save if disposable income rises by one unit. (132)

Marginal returns, law of diminishing Asserts that if the quantities of all other inputs are held constant, the employment of additional quantities of any one input by a firm or an industry will eventually yield smaller and smaller (marginal) increases in output. **(116)**

Marginal revenue (MR) The *addition* to total revenue resulting from the addition of one unit to total output. Geometrically, marginal revenue is the *slope* of the total revenue curve. **(147)**

Marginal revenue product (MRP) Additional revenue earned as a result of increased sales when an additional unit of an input is used. **(126, 394)**

Marginal social cost (MSC) The sum of *marginal private cost (MPC)*, which is the share of marginal cost caused by an activity that is paid for by the persons who carry out the activity, and *incidental cost*, which is the share borne by others. **(253)**

Marginal utility, law of diminishing Asserts that additional units of a commodity are worth less and less to a consumer in money terms. As the individual's consumption increases, the marginal utility of each additional unit declines. **(75)**

Market The set of all sale and purchase transactions that affect the price of some commodity. **(182)**

Market-demand curve Shows how the total quantity demanded of some product during a specified period of time changes as the price of the product changes, other things being constant. **(92)**

Market power The ability of a firm to raise its price significantly above the competitive price level and to maintain this high price profitably for a considerable period. **(304)**

Maximin criterion Selecting the strategy that yields the maximum payoff, on the assumption that your opponent does as much damage to you as he can. **(242)**

Mediation Process in which an outsider is brought into a labour–management negotiation in the hope that this person can lead the two sides to a voluntary agreement through persuasion. **(435)**

Merger The combining of two previously independent firms under a single owner or group of owners. A **horizontal merger** involves two firms producing similar products. A **vertical merger** involves two firms, one of which supplies an ingredient of the other's product. A **conglomerate merger** is the union of two unrelated firms. **(291-92)**

Microeconomics The study of the behaviour of individual decision-making units, such as farmers or consumers. (73)

Minimum-wage law Requires all employees (with some specified exceptions) to be paid at least some fixed given dollar amount per hour. **(418)**

Monetarism Mode of analysis that uses the equation of exchange to organize macroeconomic data. (275)

Monetary policy Actions that the Bank of Canada takes to change the equilibrium of the money market; that is, to alter the money supply, move the exchange rate, or both. (257)

Monetizing the deficit The effect of the central bank's purchasing the bonds that the government issues. (328)

Money Medium of exchange; that is, the standard object used in exchanging goods and services. (225)

Money fixed asset Asset with a face value fixed in terms of dollars, such as money, government bonds, and corporate bonds. (126)

Monopolistic competition Competition among firms, each of which has products that are somewhat different from those of its rivals. **(232)**

Monopoly, pure Industry in which there is only one supplier of a product for which there are no close substitutes, and in which it is difficult or impossible for another firm to coexist. **(218)**

Monopsony Market situation in which there is only one buyer. **(434)**

Moral hazard Tendency of insurance to discourage policy-holders from protecting themselves from risk. **(263)**

Multinational corporations Corporations whose production activities occur in a number of different countries. (435)

The multiplier The ratio of the change in equilibrium GNP (Y) divided by the original change in spending that causes the change in GNP. (161)

National debt The federal government's total indebtedness, which has resulted from previous deficits. (318)

National income The sum of the incomes of all individuals in the economy earned in the forms of wages, interest, rents, and profits. It excludes transfer payments and is calculated before any deductions are taken for income taxes. (115)

National income accounting Bookkeeping and measurement system for national economic data. (133)

Nationalization Government ownership and operation of a business firm. **(287)**

National product The total production of a nation's economy. (74)

Natural monopoly Industry in which advantages of large-scale production make it possible for a single firm to produce the entire output of the market at lower average cost than a number of firms each producing a smaller quantity. **(219)**

Natural rate of unemployment Also referred to as the "full-employment" unemployment rate.

The specific rate of unemployment toward which the economy's self-correcting mechanism tends to push the unemployment rate. (345)

Near moneys Liquid assets that are close substitutes for money. (229)

Negative income tax (NIT) Transfer program under which families with incomes below a certain threshold (the "breakeven level") would receive cash benefits from the government; these benefits would decline as income rose. **(458)**

Net exports Symbolized by $X - IM$, the excess of foreign expenditures on our products over our purchases of their goods (Canadian exports minus Canadian imports). (114)

Net national product (NNP) Gross national product minus depreciation. (136)

Net worth The value of all assets minus the value of all liabilities. (232)

Oligopoly Market dominated by a few sellers, at least several of which are large enough relative to the total market to be able to influence the market price. **(236)**

Open-market operations The Bank of Canada's purchase or sale of government securities through transactions in the open market. (245)

Opportunity cost The forgone value of the next best alternative that is not chosen. (37) **(37)**

Origin The lower left-hand corner of a graph where the two axes meet. In two-variable diagrams, both variables equal zero at the origin. (20) **(20)**

Paradox of thrift The fact that an effort by a nation to save more may simply reduce national income and fail to raise total saving. (169)

Partnership A firm whose ownership is shared by a fixed number of proprietors. **(167)**

Patent A temporary grant of monopoly rights over an innovation. **(302)**

Perfectly contestable market One in which entry and exit are costless and unimpeded. **(246)**

Personal income A measure of income derived by subtracting corporate profits, retained earnings, and payroll taxes from national income, then adding in transfer payments. Personal income measures the income that actually accrues to individuals. (138)

Phillips curve Graph depicting the rate of unemployment on the horizontal axis and either the rate of inflation or the rate of change of money wages on the vertical axis; normally downward sloping, indicating that higher inflation rates are associated with lower unemployment rates. (341)

Phillips curve, vertical (long run)

Shows the menu of inflation/unemployment choices available to society in the long run; a vertical straight line at the natural rate of unemployment. (345)

Potential gross national product The real GNP the economy would produce if its labour and other resources were fully employed. (95)

Poverty line Amount of income below which a family is considered "poor." **(444)**

Predatory pricing Price cuts that take place only to keep other firms from entering the industry. **(294)**

Price ceiling Legal maximum price that can be charged. (64) **(64)**

Price discrimination Charging different prices, relative to costs, to different buyers of the same product. **(293)**

Price floor Legal minimum price that can be charged. (66) **(66)**

Price leadership One firm sets the price for the industry and the others follow. **(239)**

Private good Commodity or service whose benefits are depleted by an additional user and for which people are excluded from its benefits. **(256)**

Production function The *maximum* amount of product that can be obtained from any specified *combination* of inputs, given the current state of knowledge. **(127)**

Production-indifference curve (sometimes called an *isoquant*) A curve in a graph showing quantities of *inputs* on its axes. Each indifference curve indicates *all* combinations of input quantities capable of producing a *given* quantity of output. **(138)**

Production possibilities frontier A graphical presentation of the different combinations of various goods that a producer can turn out, given the available resources and existing technology. (38) **(38)**

Productivity The amount of output produced by a unit of input. (177)

Productivity of labour The amount of output produced per hour of labour input. (216)

Progressive tax One in which the average tax rate paid by an individual rises as his income rises. **(334)**

Property tax Tax on assessed value of real property. **(338)**

Proportional tax One in which the average tax rate is the same at all income levels. **(334)**

Proprietorship Business firm owned by a single person. **(166)**

Public good Commodity or service whose benefits are *not depleted* by an additional user and for which it is generally difficult or *impossible to exclude* people from its benefits, even

if they are unwilling to pay for them. **(256)**

Purchasing power The purchasing power of a given sum of money is the volume of goods and services it will buy. (97)

Purchasing-power parity theory (of exchange rates) Theory that the exchange rate between any two national currencies adjusts to reflect differences in the price levels of the two nations. (299)

Quantity theory of money A simple theory of aggregate demand based on the idea that velocity is constant, so that nominal GNP is proportional to the money stock. (271)

Quota Specifies the maximum amount of a good that is permitted into the country from abroad per unit of time. (409) **(319)**

Random walk The time path of a variable, such as the price of a stock, when its magnitude in one period equals its value in the preceding period plus a completely random number. **(177)**

Rate of interest, nominal The percentage by which the money the borrower pays back exceeds the money that he borrowed, making no adjustment for any fall in the purchasing power of this money that results from inflation. (101)

Rate of interest, real The percentage increase in purchasing power that the borrower pays to the lender for the privilege of borrowing. It indicates the increased ability to purchase goods and services that the lender earns. (101)

Rational decision A decision that best serves the objective of the decision-maker, whatever the objective may be. The term "rational" connotes neither approval nor disapproval of the objective. (37) **(37)**

Rational expectations Forecasts that, while not necessarily correct, are the best that can be made given the available data. If expectations are rational, forecasting errors are pure random numbers. (352)

Ray through the origin (or ray) A straight line emanating from the origin, or zero point on a graph. (24) **(24)**

Recession A period during which the total output of the economy declines. (76)

Recessionary gap The amount by which the equilibrium level of real GNP falls short of potential GNP. (151)

Regressive tax One in which the average tax rate falls as income rises. **(334)**

Relative price The price of an item in terms of some other item rather than in terms of dollars. (98)

Rent seeking Unproductive activity in the pursuit of economic profit. **(263)**

Required reserves The minimum amount of reserves (in cash or the equivalent) required by law. Required reserves are usually proportional to the volume of deposits. (231)

Resale price maintenance Forcing retailers to keep the price of a product at or above that specified by the wholesaler. **(294)**

Research, basic Research conducted to increase knowledge, with no particular practical use in mind. (393)

Retained earnings (ploughback) The portion of a corporation's profits that management decides to keep and reinvest in the firm's operations rather than pay out directly to shareholders in the form of dividends. **(169)**

Revaluation Increase in the official value of a currency. (249)

Run on a bank An event that occurs when many depositors withdraw cash from their accounts simultaneously. (224)

Sales maximizing firm One whose objective is to sell as much of its outputs as possible (measured in terms of the revenue they bring in) rather than to maximize the company's profits. **(239)**

Saving function The schedule relating total consumer saving to disposable income in the economy, holding other determinants of saving constant. (132)

Saving schedule Table or curve showing how saving depends on GNP. (158)

Scatter diagram Graph showing the relationship between two variables. Each year is represented by a point in the diagram. The co-ordinates of each year's point show the value of the two variables in that year. (120)

Self-correcting mechanism The economy's way of curing inflationary or recessionary gaps automatically via inflation or deflation. (186)

Service industry One that does not turn out physical products. (385)

Shortage An excess of quantity demanded over quantity supplied. When a shortage exists, buyers cannot purchase the quantities they desire. (56) **(56)**

Short run A shorter period of time than the long run so that some, but not all, of the firm's commitments will have ended. **(123)**

Slope of a budget line Amount of one commodity the market requires an individual to give up in order to obtain one additional unit of another commodity without any change in the amount of money spent. **(86)**

Slope of a curved line At any particular point, the slope of the straight line that is tangent to the curved line at that point. (23) **(23)**

Slope of an indifference curve Referred to as the marginal rate of substitution between the commodities involved, represents that maximum amount of one commodity the consumer is willing to give up in exchange for one more unit of another commodity. **(86)**

Slope of a straight line The ratio of the vertical change to the corresponding horizontal change as we move to the right along the line. The ratio of the "rise" over the "run." (21) **(21)**

Socialism Method of economic organization in which the state owns the means of production. **(470)**

Specialization The process whereby a country devotes its energies and resources to only a small proportion of the world's productive activities. (399) **(309)**

Speculation Investment in risky assets in the hope of obtaining a profit from expected changes in the prices of these assets. **(176)**

Stabilization policy The name given to government programs designed to prevent or shorten recessions and to counteract inflation (that is, to *stablize* prices). (83)

Stagflation Inflation that occurs while the economy is growing slowly ("stagnating") or having a recession. (83)

Store of value An item used to store wealth from one point in time to another. (226)

Structural unemployment Refers to workers who have lost their jobs because they have been displaced by automation, because their skills are no longer in demand, or for similar reasons. (92)

Substitutes Two goods are called substitutes if an increase in the price of one raises the quantity demanded of the other, all other things remaining constant. **(103)**

Substitution effect Change in quantity demanded of a good resulting from a change in its relative price, exclusive of whatever change in quantity demanded may be attributable to the associated change in real income. **(79)**

Supply curve A graph showing how the quantity supplied of some product during a specified period of time will change as the price of that product changes, holding all other determinants of quantity supplied constant. (56) **(56)**

Supply–demand diagram Diagram showing both a supply curve and a demand curve. (56) **(56)**

Supply schedule A table showing how the quantity supplied of some product during a specified period of time changes as the price of that

product changes, holding all other determinants of quantity supplied constant. (55) **(55)**

Surplus An excess of quantity supplied over quantity demanded. When there is a surplus, sellers cannot sell the quantities they desire to supply. (56) **(56)**

Surplus, balance of payments Amount by which the quantity demanded of a country's currency (per year) exceeds the quantity supplied. Such surpluses arise when the exchange rate is artificially low. (253)

Tariff Tax on imports. (207, 408) **(318)**

Tax rate, average Ratio of taxes to income. **(334)**

Tax rate, marginal Fraction of each *additional* dollar of income that is paid in taxes. **(334)**

Tax shelter A special provision in the Income Tax Act that reduces or defers taxation if certain conditions are met. **(336)**

Tax shifting Occurs when the economic reactions to a tax cause prices and outputs in the economy to change, thereby shifting part of the burden of the tax onto others. **(343)**

Technostructure Professionals who, according to Galbraith, run most of the important economic institutions, including corporations, government bureaus, and large unions. **(497)**

Theory A deliberate simplification of factual relationships whose purpose is to explain how those relationships work. (14) **(14)**

Time-series graph A type of two-variable diagram that depicts the change in a variable over time. The horizontal axis always represents time. (26) **(26)**

Total-cost curve Shows, for each possible quantity of output, the total amount which the firm must spend for its inputs to produce that amount of output plus any opportunity cost incurred in the process. **(118)**

Trade adjustment assistance Provides special unemployment benefits, loans, retraining programs, and other aid to workers and firms that are harmed by foreign competition. (414) **(324)**

Transfer payments Sums of money that certain individuals receive as grants from the government rather than as payments for services rendered to employers. (116)

Unconditional grants Transfer payments from the federal government to the provinces, with "no strings attached," paid to provinces that would have to levy very high taxes in order to raise per capita revenues equal to the national average. Also known as "equalization payments." **(340, 461)**

Unemployment insurance

Government program under which some, but not all, unemployed workers receive transfer payments. (93)

Unemployment rate The number of unemployed people, expressed as a percentage of the labour force. (88)

Union shop An arrangement under which non-union workers may be hired but then must join the union within a specified period of time. **(429)**

Unit of account The standard unit for quoting prices. (226)

Utility, marginal Of a commodity to a consumer (measured in money terms), is the maximum amount of money he or she is willing to pay for *one more unit of it*. **(74)**

Utility, total Of a quantity of goods to a consumer (measured in money terms), is the maximum amount of money he or she is willing to give in exchange for it. **(74)**

Value added The value added by a company is its revenue from selling a product minus the amounts paid for goods and services purchased from other firms. (136)

Variable cost Any cost that is not a fixed cost. **(120)**

Velocity Number of times per year that an "average dollar" is spent on goods and services; the ratio of nominal GNP to the number of dollars in the money stock. (271)

Vertical equity The notion that differently situated persons should be taxed differently in a way that society deems fair. **(340)**

Wage-price controls Legal restrictions on the ability of industry and labour to raise wages and prices. (364)

Wage-price freeze An outright ban on wage or price increases. (366)

Wage-price guidelines Numerical standards for permissible wage and price increases. (364)

Welfare state A variety of government programs aimed at assisting the poor and protecting individuals from the rigours of the marketplace. **(475)**

Workers' management System under which employees of an enterprise make most of the decisions normally reserved for management. **(479)**

Index

Page numbers for *Macroeconomics* are shown in regular type, those for *Microeconomics* in **boldface** type.

Pigou, A. C., **353, 359**
Planning
  in China, **486**
  vs. free markets, **470-73**
  in Galbraithean model, **496-97**
  indicative, **477-78**
  production, **202, 203, 215-16**
  in Soviet Union, **484-86**
Ploughback, **169**
Policy lags. *See* Lags
Pollution, **353-71**
  as detrimental externality, **358-59, 361**
  by government, **358**
  monopoly and, **217-18, 226-28**
Pollution taxes, 17, **17, 363-64, 365-67**
Population growth
  effect on demand curve, 59, **59**
  exponential, 423-25
  in less developed countries, 436-37
  in Ricardian distribution model, **414-16**
  zero, 423
Portfolio, investment, 172-74
Potential GNP, 95-96
Poverty, **443-64**
  in less developed countries, 442
  policies to combat, **457-58**
Poverty line, **444-45**
Predatory pricing, under Combines
  Investigation Act, **294**
Prejudice, economic discrimination and, **453-54**
Present value, **412-14**
Price ceilings, 53, 64-66, **53, 64-66**
  vs. price floors, **270**
Price changes
  demand curve and, **88-89**
  effect on budget line, **86-87**
  effect on total expenditure, **101**
  quantity demanded and, **79-81**
Price controls, 52, **52**
  for depletable resources, **380-81**
  in Galbraithean model, **496**
  shortages in, **380-81, 381-82**
  see also Price ceilings
Price determination, under monopolistic
  competition, **221-22, 233-35**
Price discrimination, under Combines
  Investigation Act, **293, 303-04**
Price effect, **101**
Price elasticity of demand. *See* Elasticity of
  demand
Price elasticity of supply, **103**
Price floors, 6, 66-67, **6, 66-67**
  marginal vs. full cost, **279-80**
  price ceilings, vs. **270**
Price increases, public interest and, **206-08**
Price indexes, deflating by, 110
Price leadership, in oligopolies, **239**
Price level
  consumer spending and, 126
  equilibrium and, 149-51
  money and, 267-71
Price mechanism, 6-7, **6-7, 212**
Price supports, 66-67, **66-67**
Price system, **199-216**
  critical role of, **209-210**
Prices
  effects of deregulation on, **285**
  effects on aggregate supply curve, 61-63,
    61-63
  effects on demand curve, 60, **60**
  effects on supply curve, 62-63, **62-63**
  equilibrium, 56, **56**
  income distribution and, **211-12**
  inflation and, 182-84
  input, **141-42**
  marginal revenue and, in monopoly, **221-22**
  quantity demanded, 52-54, **52-54, 78-81,**
    103-04, 395-96
  regulation and, **278-79**
  relative, 98-99, **79**

of resources in the twentieth century, **378-81**
  in Soviet economy, **481-82**
  sticky, **232**
  substitutions and, **384**
  see also Pricing
Prices and Incomes Commission, 364
Prices of related goods, quantity demanded
  and, **103-04**
Pricing
  of depletable resources, **374-84**
  efficiency and, **207**
  environmental damage and, **359**
  in international trade, 406-07, **316-17**
  marginal cost, **280-81**
  peak, off-peak, **211-12**
  predatory, **294**
  under Combines Investigation Act, **293-94**
  under perfect competition, **183-84**
  Ramsey rule, **281-82**
Principle of increasing costs, 39-40, 55, **39-40,**
  55
Principle of marginal productivity, **394-95**
The Principles of Political Economy and
  Taxation (Ricardo), 403, **313**
Private goods, **256-57**
Production, 44, **44**
  factors of, **393, 410-11**
  GNP as measure of, 136
Production, ownership of means of, **470**
Production function, **127-30**
Production-indifference curves, **138-39**
  characteristics of, **139**
  see also Indifference curves
Production planning
  as co-ordination task, **202, 203**
  invisible hand and, **215-16**
Production possibilities frontier, 38-41, **38-41**
  efficient resource allocation and, **200-01,**
    250-52
Productive efficiency
  in market economy, **470-72**
  in planned economy, **471-72**
Productivity, 5, **5**
  effects on aggregate-supply curve, 177
  inflation and, in Canada, 389
  measuring, 382
  supply-side economics and, **393-94**
  see also Productivity growth gap
Productivity growth gap, 382-89
  causes of, 386-89
  consequences of, 389-90
  costs of, 395
  reasons for slowdown, 384-85
  remedies for, 392-95
  savings and, 386, 392-93
Productivity problems, 381-96
Profit, **407-10**
  economic, **146, 194-95**
  effects on deregulation, **285**
  excess, **274-75, 278**
  marginal, **150-51**
  maximization, **145-46, 148-51**
  monopoly, **408**
  public opinion on, **409**
  regulation of, **274-75, 278**
  total, **146-48**
  zero economic, **194-95**
Profit maximization, **145-46**
  fixed cost and, **152-54**
  in Galbraithean model, **496**
  graphical interpretation, **148-51**
  marginal analysis and, **150**
Profit-maximizing output, **222-23**
Profit motive, allocation of resources and,
  260
Profit rates, inflation and, 103
Profit taxation, **410**
Progressive taxes, **334, 335, 337**
Proof of double intent, Combines
  Investigation Act and, **292-93**

Property taxes, **334-337**
Proportional taxes, **334**
Proprietorships, **166-67**
Protectionism, 413-15, **323-25**
Public good, **332**
Public goods, **256-57**
Public interest
  environmental damage and, **359**
  government intervention and, **263**
  price increases and, **206-08**
Public policy, libertarianism and, **494-95**
Public schools, property taxes and, **338**
Public-sector bargaining, **435-36**
Public utilities
  deregulation of, 103
  as monopolies, **220**
  regulation of, 103, **274-77**
Public welfare
  monopolistic competition and, **244-46**
Purchasing power, 4, 97, **4**
  inflation and, 98-99
Purchasing power parity theory of exchange-
  rate determination, **299-301**
Pure monopoly, **182, 218**

Q
al-Qaddafi, Muammar, **381**
Quality circles, 387
Quantity demanded, **91-92, 92-93**
  demand and, 52-55, **52-55**
  equilibrium, 56-57, **56-57**
  income change and, **103**
  price and, 53-54, **53-54, 78-81, 103-04, 395-**
    96
  variables in, **103-04**
  see also Demand
Quantity effect, **101**
Quantity of output, price and, **150-51**
Quantity supplied, supply and, 55-56, **55-56**
Quantity theory of money, 265, 271-73
Quotas, 409-10, **319-20**
  vs. tariffs, 411-12, **321-22**

R
Radical economics, **491, 499-506**
Radicalism, 47-48, **47-48**
Ramsey, Frank, **281-282**
Ramsey pricing rule, **281-282**
Rand Formula, **429**
Random walks, stock prices as, **177-79**
Rasminsky, Louis, 244
Rate of return, deregulation and, **284**
Rate regulation, **277-78**
  marginal vs. fully distributed cost in, **279-90**
Rational behaviour, 15-16, **15-16**
Rational choice, true economic costs and, 7-8,
  7-8
Rational decisions, 36, **36**
Rational expectations, 352-54
Rays through origin, in graphs, 24, **24**
Reagan, Ronald, 83, 185, 195, 214, 215, 216,
  218, 363, 374
Real capital gain, 392
Real GNP, 77
  Keynesian model and, 268, 270, 276
Real rate of interest, 101, 321
Recession, 76, 77
  budget deficits and, 331-33
  fiscal policy and, 354-56
  monetary policy and, 354-56
  national debt and, 319
Recessionary gap, 151-53, 179-80, 184-85
  elimination of, 344
  fiscal policy and, 209
Recycling, **356-58**
Reforming Regulation (Economic Council of
  Canada), **271**
Regional transfer payments, **461**
Regressive taxes, **334, 337**
Regulation, **269-88**
  efficiency of operation and, **282-87**

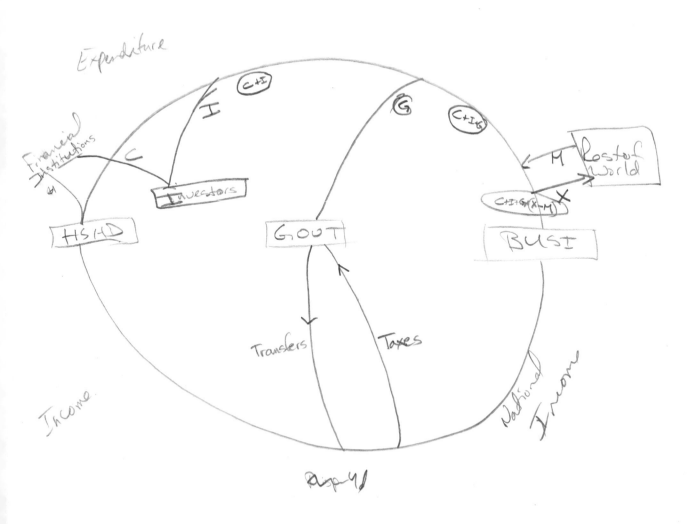